■ The Slippery Slope to Gen

The Slippery Slope to Genocide

Reducing Identity Conflicts and
Preventing Mass Murder

EDITED BY
I. William Zartman
Mark Anstey
Paul Meerts

OXFORD
UNIVERSITY PRESS

OXFORD
UNIVERSITY PRESS

Oxford University Press, Inc., publishes works that further
Oxford University's objective of excellence in research,
scholarship, and education.

Oxford   New York
Auckland   Cape Town   Dar es Salaam   Hong Kong   Karachi
Kuala Lumpur   Madrid   Melbourne   Mexico City   Nairobi
New Delhi   Shanghai   Taipei   Toronto

With offices in
Argentina   Austria   Brazil   Chile   Czech Republic   France   Greece
Guatemala   Hungary   Italy   Japan   Poland   Portugal   Singapore
South Korea   Switzerland   Thailand   Turkey   Ukraine   Vietnam

Published by Oxford University Press, Inc.
198 Madison Avenue, New York, New York 10016
www.oup.com

Library of Congress Cataloging-in-Publication Data
The slippery slope to genocide : reducing identity conflicts and preventing mass murder /
edited by I. William Zartman, Mark Anstey, and Paul Meerts.
    p. cm.
Includes bibliographical references and index.
ISBN 978-0-19-979174-3 (hbk.) 1. Genocide—Prevention. 2. Ethnic conflict.
3. Ethnic groups. I. Zartman, I. William. II. Anstey, Mark. III. Meerts, Paul. IV. Title.
HV6322.7.S59 2011
364.15'1—dc22   2011003541

9 8 7 6 5 4 3 2 1

Printed in the United States of America on acid-free paper

To Francis Deng,

Traditional Brother, Modern Scholar,
Skillful Diplomat, Tireless Conciliator

■ FOREWORD

▨ THE CHALLENGE OF MANAGING IDENTITY CONFLICTS

This book is in many ways a product of intellectual and moral courage. Conventional wisdom, supported by a preponderance of scholarly opinion, has it that identity conflicts are rarely amenable to negotiations, far less resolution. Some even argue that such identity factors as race, ethnicity, or "tribe" are fictional constructs that are manipulated by political entrepreneurs in their quest for power, wealth, or other tangibles. However, the fact that these political entrepreneurs are able to manipulate identity groups, on whatever bases these groups are defined, is evidence of their empirical existence. The tendency toward denial of identity in conflicts is the result of misperception or misrepresentation of the role identity plays in conflicts. What generates conflict is not the mere differences but the implications of those differences in terms of participation in the political, economic, and social processes and, in particular, the gross inequalities associated with those differences.

This became quite evident to me over nearly three decades of carrying out the responsibilities of two highly sensitive United Nations mandates that are closely related to the consequences of identity-based conflicts: first as Representative of the Secretary-General on Internally Displaced Persons, from 1992 to 2004, and since 2007, as Special Adviser of the Secretary-General on the Prevention of Genocide.

It must be noted at the outset that the UN, itself not so united, is an organization of divided nations, many of which suffer from acute crises of national identity. These crises manifest themselves in discriminating cleavages among various identity groups, some of whom enjoy the rights of citizenship, while others are denied those rights, discriminated against, dispossessed, and even persecuted. Deprived of national protection, they turn to the international community for protection and assistance. But when they do, the state invokes national sovereignty as a barricade against outside involvement. This means that there is clearly a gap between the idealism or aspirations that the UN symbolizes and the realities on the ground.

Oftentimes, international actors, intimidated by the government's prohibitive assertion of sovereignty, cave in and refrain from advocating the cause of the vulnerable populations. They must avoid confrontation with governments, as that would adversely affect and even disrupt their work in the country. As I see it, the alternative is to negotiate with the government constructively on the basis of "sovereignty as responsibility," a concept that we at the Brookings Institution's Africa Project developed in response to post–Cold War conflicts in Africa. This concept has since evolved into the emerging concept of "the responsibility to protect," enshrined in the 2005 outcome document of the World Summit of Heads of State and Government.

Let me now elaborate on my experiences with the mandates on both internal displacement and the prevention of genocide. The circumstances of my appointment under the two mandates were very similar. Secretary-General Boutros Boutros Ghali surprised me with a phone call to tell me that my name had been proposed and that he was pleased to offer me the position. I said I was honored, but could he have his people give me more information on what the position would entail before giving him my final response? He reacted by saying, "Francis, I know you very well and how much you care about this problem." He and I had been State Ministers of Foreign Affairs of our respective countries, Egypt and Sudan, and had worked closely together. "This is not only a global crisis, but one that affects our continent of Africa the most and, in Africa, it is your country, the Sudan, that is the worst hit, and, in the Sudan, it is your people in the South who are the primary victims. I cannot see how you can say 'No.' I will therefore tell them that you have accepted and if, later, you still are undecided, we can discuss it further."

My appointment by Secretary-General Ban Ki-moon also came as a surprise. I received an email telling me that the Secretary-General was about to appoint a Special Adviser on the Prevention of Genocide, that my name was on the list, perhaps on top of the list, and that he wanted to know whether I would consider accepting the position if it were offered to me. I said that the information came as a total surprise to me, but that if I were asked to take the position, I would consider it a call of duty and a service to humanity that I could not take lightly. I met the Secretary-General two days later, and my appointment was announced about four days after our meeting.

At the time of my appointment as Representative of the Secretary-General on internally displaced persons (IDPs), there were some 25 to 30 million displaced people in over 50 countries throughout the world. These were people who had been forced to flee their homes or areas of normal residence by armed conflicts, internal strife, and systematic violations of human rights but who had remained within their national borders. Had they crossed international borders, they would have been considered refugees for whom the international system has a legal and institutional framework for their protection and assistance. Because IDPs remain within their countries, they have no legal or institutional bases for receiving protection and assistance from the international community.

For the same reason, internal displacement raises sensitive issues of sovereignty, which is why the establishment of the mandate of the Representative of the Secretary-General on IDPs was highly sensitive and controversial. From the beginning, I had to factor this into my approach to the mandate. If the mandate were seen by governments as a threat to national sovereignty, doors would be closed and I would not have access for dialogue with the national authorities no the displaced populations whose cause I was mandated to advocate.

I applied the concept of sovereignty as responsibility as the normative basis of my engagement with governments. As I have often said, the first five minutes with the president or the minister concerned were crucial to getting the message across that I realized the problem was by definition internal and fell under state sovereignty, that I was respectful of state sovereignty, but that I saw sovereignty positively as a concept of state responsibility for protecting and providing assistance to its needy populations, and, if necessary, requesting assistance from the international community. I then added politely, but affirmatively, that if the state failed to discharge that responsibility, with the consequence that the population concerned was threatened with suffering and death, the international community would not watch and do nothing; it would find one way or another to get involved. The best way to protect sovereignty was therefore to discharge the responsibility of sovereignty.

Working with a team of international lawyers, we developed the Guiding Principles on Internal Displacement, building on human rights law, humanitarian law, and analogous refugee law as a normative framework for protecting and assisting IDPs, primarily by the state concerned but with international cooperation where needed. The Guiding Principles have since become widely accepted by governments, have provided a basis for national legislation, and were used by the African Union in drafting its Convention on Internal Displacement.

On the whole, the approach of engaging governments on the basis of sovereignty as responsibility was quite successful and made internal displacement a legitimate concern for state cooperation with the international community. However, on my missions, I often found representatives of international organizations to be so reluctant to engage the national authorities on internal displacement that, even as I successfully pleaded with the authorities to respond to the needs of their internally displaced populations, they remained skeptical and cautious. Toward the end of my mission, they would acknowledge the change in government policy and begin to respond positively to follow-up on the results of the mission.

Even more than internal displacement, genocide is a particularly sensitive issue. Although it is acknowledged as one of the most heinous crimes on which humanity is expected to unite to prevent, stop, and punish, for the same reason it evokes emotionalism and denial from both the perpetrators and those who would be called upon to intervene to stop it. This is why genocide is generally recognized after the fact, when the perpetrators are gone or are defeated and the determination of the crime becomes a judgment of the victor over the vanquished. Early prevention before the crisis escalates to genocidal levels and denial sets in becomes the most constructive way to go.

Early prevention means working closely with governments on the basis of the three pillars of responsibility in the normative framework of sovereignty as responsibility and the responsibility to protect. These pillars are the responsibility of the state for its people; the responsibility of the international community to assist the state to discharge its national responsibility; and the responsibility of the international community to step in should the state be manifestly failing to discharge its responsibility. This last pillar has been misconstrued to make the responsibility to protect be perceived as a potential tool for intervention by the powerful states of the global North in the weaker countries of the South, which is why the concept has become so controversial.

In order to facilitate constructive dialogue with governments and other key stakeholders, I am striving to shift genocide from being viewed as too sensitive an issue for comfortable discussion to a situation that can be prevented or halted by being better understood as an extreme form of identity-related conflicts. As noted at the outset, these conflicts do no emanate from mere differences, but from gross inequalities generally reflected in egregious human rights violations, discrimination, marginalization, exclusion, dehumanization, and denial of fundamental rights.

In virtually all genocidal situations, society is acutely divided between in-groups, who enjoy the rights and dignity of citizenship, and out-groups, who are excluded from enjoying fundamental rights and freedoms. It is often the out-group's reaction to these gross inequalities, and the counterreaction by the dominant group, that provokes insurgencies and genocidal counterinsurgencies. The challenge then becomes one of constructive management of diversity to promote equitable distribution of power and resources and ensure respect for human rights.

Diversity is a global phenomenon. Hardly any country in the world today can claim to be homogeneous. Even Somalia, which was considered one of the most homogeneous countries in the world, is torn apart by clan conflicts. Since problems of diversity and disparity are global, the potential for genocidal conflicts is equally global, although some regions and countries are more vulnerable than others. Furthermore, not all countries perform equally well in their management of diversity. Some manage well, others not so well, and still others fail dismally.

South Africa is, for instance, an intriguing case of a potentially genocidal situation that was averted. The powerful white minority, faced with the existential threat of armed resistance by the black and colored majority, could have inflicted a genocidal onslaught on the majority. It did not happen. Was this outcome structural, or was it the wisdom of the leadership, or was it the intervening role of the international community? Or was it perhaps all three and more?

Kenya, and the way the international community helped to stop the 2007–2008 postelection violence, is often discussed as a case of the responsibility to protect. However it is labeled, it is obvious that the world did not want to see another Rwanda, and Kofi Annan, having been at the helm of the UN Department of Peacekeeping Operations at the time of the Rwandan genocide, was particularly motivated to prevent history from repeating itself. And he proved to be very successful.

Given the variation in the success or failure of states to manage their diversity constructively, it is important to conduct case studies to identify practices that make for success and should be emulated, and those that account for failure and should be avoided. Ultimately, the challenge of managing diversity constructively to avoid genocidal conflicts is the responsibility of the state. It is also one that calls for a global partnership between the states concerned and the international community. If we see prevention in the broad structural sense I have tried to outline, then there should be a role for virtually all UN and non-UN actors.

It is worth noting that intergroup relations and conflicts are dynamic, not static. In virtually all the countries affected by conflict-induced internal displacement that I visited, I found two versions of historical memory. One version maintained that the relations between the concerned groups had always been cooperative and conciliatory: "We shared our happy and sad occasions. We intermarried. We do not know where this conflict came from." The other version saw the conflict as endemic, entailing a chain of recurrent episodes. In a sense, both versions are valid. When groups live next to one another, they must inevitably come into conflict. But by the same token, they also find ways of managing their differences constructively to promote cooperation in their mutual interest. When conflict erupts, groups tend to recall past conflicts and emphasize the history of differences; and when they succeed in negotiating a peaceful resolution to their conflicts, they tend to emphasize the cooperative and conciliatory version of their history.

Another theme I observed in identity-related conflicts is that the divisive elements are rarely clear-cut. Often, identify factors overlap. But paradoxically, the more the groups have in common, the more they emphasize what divides them. Identity conflicts become a way of asserting exaggerated differences to remove the ambiguities. In my visits to countries undergoing identity conflicts, it was never easy to distinguish between the groups in conflict. This was the case, for example, in the former Yugoslavia with the Serbs, the Croats, and the Bosnian Muslims. In the Darfur region of Sudan, one would be hard pressed to identify who is an Arab and who is a black African. In Burundi and Rwanda, I could identify some as Tutsis and some as Hutu, as they have been stereotyped, with many whom I could not classify. I asked the Foreign Minister of Burundi whether one could always tell Tutsis from Hutu. With a sense of humor, he answered, "Yes, but with a margin of error of thirty-five percent."

The case of people with much in common exaggerating their differences is illustrated by the Sudanese crisis of national identity, which takes two forms of distortion. The first is that a minority that has dominated the country, though a hybrid both racially and culturally, misperceives itself as homogeneously Arab. The second distortion is that this distorted self-perception is projected as the identity framework for the nation, with the Sudan described as an Arab country with Islam as an integral component, although the overwhelming majority in both the South and the North are Africans. This distorted characterization inevitably discriminates against non-Arabs and non-Muslims. This national identity crisis has been at the core of the conflicts that have devastated the country since its independence.

A good example of exaggerated differentiation is evident among the Baggara "Arabs," who exhibit a great deal of racial and cultural affinity with their Dinka neighbors to the South with whom they have intermarried. It is well known that in tribal wars between them, it is the descendants of Dinka mothers or grandmothers who demonstrate greatest valour at the front line of the battles with the Dinka to affirm their "Arabness."

Social scientists maintain that the pivotal factor in determining identity is self-perception, not objective factors. This is understandable where what is involved is innocuous self-perception with no adverse consequences for other groups. Where erroneous self-perception has an adverse effect on others, the gap between myths and realities of identity needs to be exposed and corrected. In the Sudan, this is what the vision of the New Sudan, with which the late leader of the Sudan People's Liberation Movement/Army, Dr. John Garang, challenged the country, is all about.

Managing diversity constructively requires prescribing normative principles that address the problem of conflict-ridden inequalities. We have developed an Analysis Framework, in close consultation with UN colleagues and international experts, that guides us in assessing the risk of genocide in a given situation. Where there is cause for concern, my office conducts an in-depth analysis based on eight sets of factors that document the risk of genocidal violence. These factors are:

Intergroup relations and a record of discrimination
Circumstances that affect the capacity to prevent genocide
Presence of illegal arms and armed elements
Motivation and acts that encourage divisions between groups
Circumstances that facilitate the perpetration of genocide
Acts that could be elements of genocide
Evidence of intent to destroy in whole or in part
Triggering factors

When fully developed and operationalized, the Framework can be a tool with which states can look at themselves in the mirror, assess their own performance, identify where they are doing well, where they need improvement, and what preventive measures need to be taken.

In assessing the risk of genocide, popular perceptions may be more important than the legal determination of the crime. It is true that the word *genocide* is often used loosely and at variance with the legal definition of the crime. But it is also true that from the perceptive of prevention, once the crime is legally determined, it is too late, while popular allegations of the crime represent alarm bells that have a preventive utility.

This was vividly demonstrated to me in the Democratic Republic of the Congo (DRC). In preparing for my mission there, I was advised to refrain from referring to ethnicity and genocide, since they were considered very sensitive. Many commentators even dismissed ethnicity as a factor in the conflicts in the DRC, viewing the root causes as competition over resources and ethnicity as an element that was being exploited by politicians for personal reasons, the stereotypical explanation. Contrary to what I had been told, I found that all the groups in conflict not only identified themselves in ethnic terms, but claimed to have been victims of past and ongoing genocidal violence. While these claims would not be legally justified, the emotionalism associated with the perceptions was a serious source of concern about the gravity of the situation and the perpetuation of identity-based violence.

To end with the point with which I began, what I try to do in discharging my mandate is to bridge between idealism and realism, to uphold the normative principles of universal values and aspirations, but also to negotiate sovereignty as responsibility to protect and assist those in whose name national sovereignty is asserted. While we must continue to aspire to the vision of an ideal world, we must also live with the realities on the ground and engage with governments constructively in the interest of those who need help. The point that needs to be reemphasized, and that this book so amply makes, is that it is not the identity differences per se that generate genocidal conflicts or mass atrocities, but how identity relations are managed in the competitive quest for resources, development opportunities, public services, and other distributional issues. The critical fault line is gross inequality based on identity differences. Seen in that light, the solution must be to strive toward inclusive human dignity defined as the broadest shaping and sharing of all values, without discrimination based on any identity differences. This is an aspiration that is not achievable in absolute terms, but it is one that must be pursued within the ranges of the possible. That is the challenge for both bilateral negotiations and third-party mediation of identity-related conflicts.

Francis M. Deng

■ PREFACE

▦ ABOUT THE PROCESSES OF INTERNATIONAL NEGOTIATION (PIN) PROGRAM

Since 1988, PIN has been conducted by an international Steering Committee of scholars and practitioners, which meets three times a year to develop and propagate new knowledge about the processes of negotiation. The Committee, for 22 years based at (IIASA) in Laxenburg, Austria, but now located at Clingendael, the Netherlands, conducts a book workshop every year devoted to the current collective publication project and involving analysts and diplomats from a wide spectrum of countries, in order to tap a broad range of international expertise and to improve the understanding and practice of negotiation. It also offers mini-conferences (road shows) on international negotiation in order to disseminate and encourage research on the subject. Such road shows have been held at the Argentine Council for International Relations, Buenos Aires; Beijing University; the Center for Conflict Resolution, Haifa; the Center for the Study of Contemporary Japanese Culture, Kyoto; the Geneva Center for Strategy and Policy; the Swedish Institute of International Affairs, Stockholm; the University of Cairo; University Hassan II, Casablanca; the University of Helsinki; the School of International Relations, Tehran; Nanjing–Johns Hopkins Universities; Harvard University; Carleton University; the University of Warsaw; and the UN University for Peace, San Jose, Costa Rica. The PIN Program publishes semiannual newsletter *PIN Points* and sponsors a network of over 4,000 researchers and practitioners in negotiation. The Program has been supported by the William and Flora Hewlett Foundation, the Smith-Richardson Foundation, and the U.S. Institute of Peace.

Members of the PIN Steering Committee include Rudolf Avenhaus, The German Armed Forces University at Munich; Mark Anstey, Michigan State University in Dubai; Franz Cede, University of Budapest/Austrian Foreign Ministry; Guy Olivier Faure, University of Paris V-Sorbonne; Fen Osler Hampson, Carleton University; Paul Meerts, the Netherlands Institute of Relations-Clingendael; Valerie Rosoux, Catholic University at Louvain; Rudolf Schüssler, University of Bayreuth; Gunnar Sjöstedt, the Swedish Institute of International Affairs; Mikhail Troitskiy, (MGIMO) in Moscow; I. William Zartman, Johns Hopkins University; and Ariel Macaspac Penetrante, University of Vienna, administrator (2008–2010) and Wilbur Perlot, Netherlands Institute of International Relations, administrator (2011 to present). www.pin-negotiation.org

▦ SELECTED PUBLICATIONS OF THE PIN PROGRAM

Unfinished Business: Saving International Negotiations from Failure, Franz Cede and Guy-Olivier Faure, editors. 2011. University of Georgia Press, Athens, GA.

The Slippery Slope to Genocide: Reducing Identity Conflicts and Preventing Mass Murder, Mark Anstey, Paul Meerts, and I William Zartman, editors. 2011. Oxford University Press, New York.

Negotiating with Terrorists? G. O. Faure and I. W. Zartman, editors. 2010. Routledge,

Engaging Extremists: Trade-Offs, Timing and Diplomacy, I. W. Zartman and G. O. Faure, editors. 2010. United States Institute of Peace Press, Washington, DC.

Negotiated Risks: International Talks on Hazardous Issues, R. Avenhaus and G. Sjöstedt, editors. 2009. Springer, Heidelberg, Germany.

Escalation and Negotiation, I. W. Zartman and G. O. Faure, editors. 2005. Cambridge University Press, Cambridge, UK.

Peace versus Justice: Negotiating Backward-and Forward-Looking Outcomes, I. W. Zartman and V. Kremenyuk, editors. 2005. Rowman & Littlefield Publishers, Inc., Lanham, MD.

Negotiating European Union, P. W. Meerts and F. Cede, editors. 2004. Palgrave Macmillan, Basingstoke, UK.

Getting It Done: Post-Agreement Negotiations and International Regimes, B. I. Spector and I. W. Zartman, editors. 2003. United States Institute of Peace Press, Washington, DC.

How People Negotiate: Resolving Disputes in Different Cultures, G. O. Faure, editor. 2003. Kluwer Academic Publishers, Dordrecht.

Professional Cultures in International Negotiation: Bridge or Rift? G. Sjöstedt, editor. 2003. Lexington Books, Lanham, MD.

Containing the Atom: International Negotiations on Nuclear Security and Safety, R. Avenhaus, V. A. Kremenyuk, and G. Sjöstedt, editors. 2002. Lexington Books, Lanham, MD.

International Negotiation: Analysis, Approaches, Issues, 2nd edition, V. A. Kremenyuk, editor. 2002. Jossey-Bass Inc. Publishers, San Francisco.

Preventive Negotiation: Avoiding Conflict Escalation, I. W. Zartman, editor. 2001. Rowman & Littlefield Publishers, Inc., Lanham, MD.

Power and Negotiation, I. W. Zartman and J. Z. Rubin, editors. 2000. University of Michigan Press, Ann Arbor.

International Economic Negotiation: Models versus Reality, V. A. Kremenyuk and G. Sjöstedt, editors. 2000. Edward Elgar Publishing Limited, Cheltenham, UK.

Negotiating International Regimes: Lessons Learned from the United Nations Conference on Environment and Development (UNCED), B. I. Spector, G. Sjöstedt, and I. W. Zartman, editors. 1994. Graham & Trotman Limited, London.

International Multilateral Negotiation: Approaches to the Management of Complexity, I. W. Zartman, editor. 1994. Jossey-Bass Inc. Publishers, San Francisco.

International Environmental Negotiation, G. Sjöstedt, editor. 1993. Sage Publications, Inc., Newbury Park, CA.

Culture and Negotiation: The Resolution of Water Disputes, G. O. Faure and J. Z. Rubin, editors. 1993. Sage Publications, Inc., Newbury Park, CA.

Processes of International Negotiations, F. Mautner-Markhof, editor. 1989. Westview Press Inc., Boulder, CO.

◼ ACKNOWLEDGMENTS

We are grateful for the support of the Smith Richardson Foundation for this project of the Processes of International Negotiation (PIN) Program and to the Office of the Under-Secretary General, Special Advisor of the UN Secretary General on the Prevention of Genocide. We are also grateful to Isabelle Talpain-Long for carefully monitoring the manuscript.

CONTENTS

◼ CONTRIBUTORS

Mark Anstey
Emeritus Professor
Labor Relations and Human
    Resources Unit
Nelson Mandela Metropolitan
    University
Port Elizabeth, South Africa

Franz Cede
Department of Diplomacy
Andrassy-University in Budapest
Budapest, Hungary

Tassos Coulaloglou
National Democratic Institute for
    International Affairs
Washington, DC

Moty Cristal
NEST Consulting
Ramat Hasharon, Israel

David Cunningham
Department of Government and Politics
University of Maryland
College Park, MD

William Donohue
Department of Communication
Michigan State University
East Lansing, Michigan

Fen Osler Hampson
The Norman Paterson School
    of International Affairs
Carleton University
Ottawa, Ontario, Canada

Jannie Lilja
Department of Peace and
    Conflict Research
Uppsala University
Uppsala, Sweden

Ariel Macaspac Penetrante
Institute for Infrastructure and
    Resources Management
University of Leipzig
Germany

Fedor Meerts
Ministry of Security and Justice,
    The Netherlands

Paul Meerts
The Processes of
    International Negotiation
    Program
The Netherlands Institute of
    International Relations
Clingendael, The Netherlands

Erik Melander
Department of Peace and
    Conflict Research
Uppsala University
Uppsala, Sweden

Frida Möller
Research Assistant
Policy, Research and
    Development (PRD)
Folke Bernadotte Academy
Stockholm, Sweden

Frank Pfetsch
Heidelberg Institute for International
  Conflict Research
Department of Political Science
University of Heidelberg
Heidelberg, Germany

Jesús Romero-Trillo
Department of English Studies
Universidad Autónoma de Madrid
Madrid, Spain

Jay Rothman
President,
The ARIA Group

Joshua Lerner Smilovitz
International Crisis Group
New York, New York

Ervin Staub
Department of Psychology
University of Massachusetts
Amherst, Massachusetts

Peter Wallensteen
Department of Peace and
  Conflict Research
Uppsala University
Uppsala, Sweden

Marie-Joëlle Zahar
Department of Political
  Science
University of Montreal
Montreal, Quebec,
  Canada

I. William Zartman
The Paul H. Nitze School of
  Advanced International
  Studies
Johns Hopkins University
Washington, DC

PART ONE

Introduction

1 The Problem

Preventing Identity Conflicts and Genocide

■ I. WILLIAM ZARTMAN AND MARK ANSTEY

"Give me your identity," he said hesitantly, the
words hurting his parched throat. "I shall just
look at it and return it to you."
His neighbor did not seem to understand.
"I mean your card," he urged, extending his hand
with a trace of impatience. "Your identity card."

Azzam (1974, p. 20)

Genocide does not burst out unannounced; it is preceded and prepared by identity conflict that escalates from social friction to contentious politics, from politics to violence, and eventually to targeted mass killing.[1] The United Nations in 1946 defined genocide as "a denial of the right of existence of entire human groups" and redefined it in 1948 as "acts committed with intent to destroy in whole or in part a national, ethnical, racial or religious group" (Chalk & Jonassohn, 1990, p.23). It can be carried out by rebel movements but more frequently is the work of the sovereign state, making external peacemaking efforts difficult. More strikingly, it is generally not an aggressive but a defensive reaction, pathologically defensive, against a perceived existential threat (Fein, 1990, p. 56). Instigators of identity conflict feel themselves targeted, ultimately for extinction, by another identity group whom they feel must be defeated and ultimately exterminated, and so, in a security dilemma, they themselves target the perceived threateners for extinction (Straub, 2001). Expressed in these terms, the message makes it easy for political entrepreneurs to rally support for their designs. Whether this fear is realistic or not is irrelevant; often it is not, usually it has some grain of evidence taken out of proportion, and sometimes it is at least ostensibly accurate. But the point, which will serve as the entry point of analysis, is that political entrepreneurs sell this fear to their client public to gain their support. Peacemakers have the challenge of removing the tinder before the arsonist gets to throw a match at it.

Solutions of removing political entrepreneurs from the public present dilemmas in free societies, even as they use the space provided by democratic rights of free association and speech to mobilize overtly or covertly around identity markers. The necessity is to separate the public from the political entrepreneurs' appeals by reducing the fears of identity groups and protecting identity diversity. This means a return to (or toward) the ideal condition of *normal politics*, where government responds to the fears, needs, and demands of all of its citizens and the citizens regularly review the record of the government in adequately providing this response. However, such fears are often deep-rooted, and trust in constitutional arrangements and agents of authority is shallow. Alternative action to create social, economic, and political conditions that reduce the need and opportunity to mobilize around identity markers are expensive and may alienate other parts of society. If the motivating fears cannot be exorcized, then measures must disarm those who hold them and render them incapable of causing damage. This is a necessarily intrusive challenge, especially when the political entrepreneur is a government. The conflicting parties are most unlikely to take preventive measures by themselves (or, put differently, if they do, the situation is no longer of policy interest, except for its provision of lessons from which to learn). Let it be understood that *conflict* does not necessarily mean "violent conflict"; the violent stage is an escalation from the initial, political stage of incompatible demands and cannot be understood in isolation from it (Hocker & Wilmot, 2000). The violent stage of demonized parties, in turn, is the predecessor of genocide itself.

Obviously, not all identity conflicts end in genocide, so it becomes important to understand the mechanism by which some do (Straus 2007). Most identity conflicts go through the usual conflict evolutions to victory, stalemate, or fatigue (Cronin, 2008 Zartman, 1995, 2010, Zartman & Faure, 2005, 2011). One side wins, the conflict reaches an impasse and turns to negotiation, or the protesting rebels weary of their efforts and go home. But some go on, ever escalating the images of the Other until they reach the ultimate confrontation, confirming the fears of their opponents. Entrapment is the motor of the mechanism (Fearon & Laitin, 2000; Jesse & Williams, 2011; Lake & Rothchild, 1998; Meerts, 2005). Leaders become entrapped vis-à-vis their public; they have identified the scapegoat, and now they must do something about it. Leaders become entrapped vis-à-vis each other; they enter into spirals of outbidding that force them into action. Leaders and followers alike become entrapped vis-à-vis the Other; they must increase their defenses against fear and threats and so enter into the security dilemma and a "spiral of vengeance." Followers become entrapped vis-à-vis each other; they must follow the mass paroxysm of their neighbors or become its victims. The following chapters examine aspects of this mechanism and then look for ways to break it.

What can negotiation do in such a situation, and what can external parties do to foster negotiation of the measures that are necessary to prevent conflict escalation on the slippery slope toward mass killing and genocide? Blocking that slide means listening for the frequent early warnings and taking early action. Operational (precrisis) prevention measures include dialog, ripening, and preemptive accountability to forestall identity conflict escalation. International organizations, notably the UN Security Council, have a role in providing their own measures, such as peacekeeping forces, mediation, and sanctions. Postcrisis intervention ("lest it happen again") includes monitoring and reconstruction, followed by reconciliation and remediation, once the violence has been brought under control.

Dealing with identity conflicts carries special challenges. On the policy side, these challenges pose the crucial question of acceptable outcomes. To identity extremists and the *needs* school and identity extremists, the only acceptable outcome is full national self-determination and self-realization by control of the state, either through secession or through dominance. This merely shifts the dispute to a definition of *self*, begging the question over doctrines of state and national self-determination and ignoring claims between overlapping selves. To governments and the *state legitimacy* school, the only acceptable solution is a return to the established national order. This ignores grievances of misgovernance, discrimination, and the breakdown of normal politics. In between, split-the-difference, half-a-loaf, and compromise solutions are salient but satisfactory to neither side. In such situations, the design of systems to service and then manage grievances becomes critical. What should be a coordination problem for negotiation or Chicken Dilemma is a collaboration problem of violence and escalation or Prisoners' Dilemma, perpetuated in a bloody, protracted conflict. As such, identity conflicts elude any characteristic of ripeness, containing neither a mutually hurting stalemate nor a single salient way out; instead, they turn into an S^5 situation—a soft, stable self-serving stalemate—from which nether party has any incentive to move, the hallmark of intractable conflict (Zartman, 2005c). The role of a mediator becomes singularly unattractive for a third party, no matter how strong its interest in ending the conflict.

On the analytical side, identity conflict poses a major challenge to the current understanding of negotiation. The literature is essentially based on the assumption of defined (even if pluralistic) parties arriving at a single, mutually satisfactory outcome. In internal identity conflicts, on the other hand, there are as many parties as one chooses to make, and the process of negotiating and mediating can well produce—intentionally or unintentionally—even more. Indeed, the conflict may turn internal to one or both sides over the very issue of negotiation. Experience suggests that this is the time when the Hitlers, Lenins, and Mussolinis step up—but arguably also the Gandhis, Mandelas and de Klerks, Ataturks, and Titos. All of these persons offered new identities, suggesting that those who created national supra or unifying identities, not just those who pushed identities into violent conflict, deserve attention. Things change when the creative leaders are gone and spoilers and outbidders push back into traditional identity groupings. The challenge then is not merely to analyze multiparty negotiations but to take into account the fact that sides are not constituted, corporate parties with leaders and organizations, ready and prepared for negotiations. Thus, the first task in any such negotiations and mediations is to identify and crystallize viable partners while clarifying issues (which may cause partners to disintegrate at the same time).

On both sides—analysis and policy—the basic problem is that identity does not easily lend itself to negotiation. Who one is can be a major intangible, indivisible, undefinable absolute, little amenable to the concessions, compensations, or constructions that lie at the basis of negotiation. Yet it can also be malleable and lend itself to accommodation, the form of which is negotiable. If the issue and outcome of identity are malleable, then the question becomes at what times, under what circumstances, by whom, for what ends? Identity may reflect differing levels of adherence among members in a society, be harder or softer under differing conditions, and be more or less negotiable in different contexts. Not naturally a matter of conflict, identity becomes its source when it becomes zero-sum, when one party's identity can only be realized at the expense of another's, giving rise to perceptions of threat and fear. Turning such a conflict into a positive-sum outcome, which is the essence of negotiation, demands special types of efforts. Once one moves past fundamentalists and extremists, accommodation might be found for *hard identity* groups, and more permeable identities might be developed for *soft identity* groups. "Peace involves a profound crisis of identity. The boundaries of self and other, friend and foe, must be redrawn."

The focus of this project is on the dynamics of the threatened/threatening identity groups and the role of the external mediator in this situation, based on the assumption that the parties are unable to break the stalemate by themselves. How does an external party bring parties in an internal identity-based conflict to negotiation and bring the conflict to an end before it escalates into violence and then into genocide? And in more precise terms: How is identity manipulated to project fear? Who can work to prevent identity conflict, and how do particular tasks line up with particular agents? What is the role of nongovernmental organizations (NGOs), states alone or in concert, and international organizations? Are different types of negotiations particular to different agents? What are the limiting and enabling standards that affect conflict prevention in the case of identity disputes and genocide? What legal and practical constraints limit intervention? And then, when can negotiations occur in conflict life cycles? What turns identity conflicts into violence and violent identity conflicts into genocide? What parties should be included and excluded? How can internecine conflicts (conflicts within conflicts) be handled? How can identity be negotiated, how are identity conflicts overcome, and how is legitimacy established in identity conflicts? When is autonomy a sufficient substitute for secession, a stable end stage rather than a step to secession? How can S^5 situations be prevented and mediated? How can ethnic cleansing be prevented and arrested? What pressures and techniques are best suited? Since there are several correct answers to all of these questions, these issues must be analyzed as "Which, when, why?" matters.

■ IDENTITY

The first challenge posed by internal identity conflicts and their negotiation is the matter of identity itself. It is commonly argued that identity cannot be negotiated, yet it also seems that identity is multitiered and quite malleable under certain circumstances. Identity conflicts are concerned with matters of civilization, culture, race, religion, language, and other such markers, Their expression and resolution usually have an economic or territorial or coordination or system redesign character. Their intensity may vary with the presence or demise of particular leaders. If identity has a degree of malleability, and if the resolution of identity conflicts, or the regulation of their expression, can be negotiated, then the key is to understand the conditions that give rise to identity as a component of a conflict and the utility it has for groups under such circumstances. This requires attention not only to the process dimensions of conflict moments but also to the structural variables that maintain them. Bringing about a cease-fire in Gaza in no way addresses the wider structural conditions that inform the long-term Israeli–Palestinian conflict. It may have knocked down (rather than out) a radical party on the Palestinian side and offered the Israelis and more moderate Palestinian groups an opportunity to negotiate a deal, but it has probably also hardened attitudes and generated enemies at wider levels. In addition, it did not in any way respond to the issues of occupation, violence, and statehood that are so central to the conflict.

Identity theory is concerned with how individuals and groups give themselves identity, are ascribed identity by other groups, and ascribe others identity. Social psychologists propose that social identity comprises three key elements (Tajfel & Turner, 1986): *categorization* (in which people place themselves and others into categories, thereby framing expectations of each other's behavior), *identification* (in which people define themselves and are defined by others as belonging to a particular group), and *social comparison* (in which people evaluate their worth in relation to other groups). A closely related concept is that of *culture* as a reference to the patterns of thinking, feeling, and acting learned by individuals within their social environments. Hofstede and Hofstede (2005, p. 4) see culture as a form of collective mental programming (or "software of the mind") that distinguishes one group from another. Groups are defined by shared patterns of dressing, greeting, eating, emotional expression, gender relations, hygiene habits, child-rearing practices, treatment of the elderly, belief systems, and rituals of worship inter alia. Members of cultural groups share *symbols* (which often only they understand), *heroes* (who embody important identifying characteristics), *rituals* (in greetings, forms of recognition, or worship), and *values* (preferred ways of believing and acting). These define a cultural identity and who is in or out of a group. Processes of categorizing, identifying and comparing, or defining in- or out-groups are seldom passive. They translate into systems of discrimination, access to opportunity, and the distribution of wealth and power, and these turn dynamic in conflict when one group bumps up against another. Negotiators of identity conflicts therefore need to be concerned with the utility of identity: What uses does it have for the individuals and groups involved?

The Utility of Identity

Definitions of the Other are not biological but social and political constructs (Barbujani, 1996; Modiano, 1996). In his *Clash of Civilizations*, Huntington (1998, p. 21) has proposed an overarching concept of *civilizations* within which similar cultures cluster, with religions being central to their identity. He sees these identity categories as rather immutable and suggests that "we know who we are, only when we know who we are not, and often only when we know whom we are against." Similar primordialist sentiments are reflected in the African sayings: "The son of a snake is always a snake" (Guest, 2004, p. 109) and "Even in a hundred years a log can never become a crocodile." Alongside this view of culture as relatively fixed is another, couched in more flexible terms, arguing that people make choices about their identities, and that history reveals identity to be subject to manipulation—with dangerous consequences (Hanf, 1989; Laitin, 2006).

A history of religion and social movements over the last century suggests that identity is malleable (Burleigh, 2006). The Communists under Lenin and then Stalin sought to destroy Orthodox Christianity, closing down its sources of revenue and influence and attacking and ridiculing its symbols, rituals, and leaders. In its stead they deified the state, offering an alternative belief system with new heroes, symbols, songs, rituals, and mass gatherings. This practice was driven by tactics intended to create fear (ruthless violence) amongst nonbelievers, resisters, and "wreckers," but a sense of hope, meaning, and belonging for those committed to the new movement. Salvation was offered through a new identity. Hitler and Franco used different strategies in relation to the churches, but they used similar mobilization tactics in building mass movements in Germany and Italy. Conditions were helpful; they mobilized in the context of periods of national despair, collapsed economies, crises of national identity and pride, and weak states with vacillating governments. Internal solidarity was strengthened through identification of problem groups (the Other)—Jews, Communists, foreigners, capitalists, landowners—who somehow threatened national well-being. In more recent times, the fingering of Tutsis by the Hutu majority in Rwanda in 1994, white farmers by the Zimbabwe African National Union-Patriotic Front (ZANU-PF) in Zimbabwe, and mutual blame between Palestinians and Israelis, Tamils and Buddhists, and Indians and Pakistanis in recent years reflects the same dynamic.

Most people have several levels of identity, the salience of any one of them being defined by the situation. Thus people may share a national identity; be differentiated at another level by regional, ethnic, or religious differences; and be distinguished at still other levels by gender, generation, social class linked with education and profession, or affiliation with a work organization or trade union. These levels are not always in harmony, especially within societies undergoing rapid development and change. Modernization brings more levels of identity to individuals and prevents polarization to the extent to which they crosscut; that is, membership in group A is not coincident with membership in group B and group C. Polarization, so that he who is not with me in my group is against me, comes with the alignment of identities into fewer groups. "Radicalisation can be defined as this process of losing identities. . . . [T]he identities I am building up through relations around me are categorized into those who resist with me and those who[m] I have to resist against. Each identity I lose or subordinate to the identity of friend or foe is one step further on the road to [the] radicalization ladder" (Goerzig, 2010, p. 12).

Identity with particular groups offers individuals important means of meeting basic human needs for *protection, participation, power, privilege,* and *purpose.* At its most basic, it might have utility as a defensive tactic in the face of an external threat. Once a group declares its own identity boundaries, it pushes others into identity groups (especially if they feel threatened), reinforcing the first group's mobilization tactics as they do so, creating a security dilemma (Posner, 1993). Then identity offers belonging and *participation,* a sense of belonging but also often access to *privilege* and *power,* giving an inflated sense of self to the adherent. Participation translates into pressures for conformity; membership in a group requires adherence to its core beliefs and behavioral norms. Those needing affirmation or social esteem must succeed within a society's dominant group and measure their worth by their status within it. At another level, belonging to a particular group may offer *purpose,* a sense of meaning through dedication to an important cause beyond oneself. Such experiences are reported in Solzenhitzyn (1974), in Burleigh (2006, p. 77), and in Sereny's (1996) study of Albert Speer, Hitler's architect.

The powerful need to belong and thence to conform translates into obedience, under certain circumstances, even when the acts required would usually be seen as unacceptable. Victims of genocide are dehumanized and deindividuated for the greater good, to preserve the struggle, the Party, or the Faith. Solzenhytzin (1974, pp. 173–174) wrote that "to do evil a man must first of all believe that what he is doing is good, or else that it's a well considered act in conformity with natural law. . . . Ideology—that is what gives evildoing its long-sought-for justification and gives the evildoer the necessary steadfastness and determination." The conviction of a cause and the fear of the Other were what empowered the agents of the Inquisition, colonialists, the Nazis, the Jacobins, the Communists, and Islamic fundamentalists, among others. In periods of heightened conflict, these tendencies are more salient. Positions polarize and become increasingly rigid; hawkish leaders outbid and replace those looking for negotiated solutions; "with us or against us" sentiments close down the middle ground; and pressures to conform and use violence to punish anyone betraying the cause increase (Anstey, 2006; Pruitt & Kim, 2004).

Once atrocities have been committed, people need to explain their behavior. Rationalization maintains psychological balance, deepens stereotyping, and hardens resolve. These tendencies are very powerful but not primordial. People make choices within situations—and then, under changed circumstances, seek to distance themselves from them. Despite the strength of conviction that bound the Nazis or the apartheid Nationalists, within a short period of the demise of their causes, few would confess easily to have been one of their supporters or a member of their security apparatus.

Protection, participation, power, privilege, and *purpose* are proposed here as core drivers of identity choices. The fact that they are malleable and choice-based does not imply the absence of rigidity. The problem is that once converted, convinced, and conforming, people seek to convert, convince, and confirm their identities by expanding membership in their groups to include those who are eligible, often by overt exclusion and persecution of Others. Identity issues present special problems for these reasons. A Middle East peace in effect would require parties on each side to begin to trust the other more than the radical elements on their own side. It would demand a realignment of weight and energies on each side from confrontation to a deal acceptable to both—in effect, a more moderate position, which in the context would represent a radical shift by both at the same time. If such a deal were to be democratically achieved and sustained, the majority of citizens on each side would have to back it. The negotiating authorities would have to accept the charge by some that their deal did not go far enough and by others as betrayal, either for reasons of ideology or simply because their lives would be so threatened. In short, a peace deal would imply internal dissension within each side, and conservative and radical spoilers would have to be managed. Parties to a peace would have to be more radically committed to it than those opposed to it (always a difficult mix). They would have to survive internal dissension, referendums, and elections; they would have to trust that they could prevail in any internal conflict over a deal; and their leaders might risk assassination (as in the cases of Anwar Sadat and Yitzhak Rabin). The rhetoric used over the years to identify the Other as an enemy would have to be transformed into one in which the Other is identified as a new partner or at least a trustworthy opponent. The negotiating parties run the risk of breaking up old identity coalitions that have sustained them and the conflict to this point, and then they must face the task of bringing to heel elements on their own side that they previously used to perpetrate war with the Other. They may risk the loss of support of important secondary actors who may have alternative agendas to a peace at a particular moment. They have to find ways to break through the spin of their own stereotyping over the years. This is why locating a peace is often far less comfortable than perpetuating a conflict in which identity serves a purpose and may have become a major force against a resolution.

In short, people mobilize around ethnic differences because it has utility. The result is that *identity conflicts* are often expressed in other terms—economic, territorial, or the design of electoral or political systems. These, in turn, may be expressed in identity terms as ethnic entrepreneurs exploit racial, cultural, or religious differences to mobilize in pursuit of economic or territorial objectives. In countries such as Zimbabwe, South Africa, and Malaysia, ethnic tensions may be less over differing customs, rituals, or values and more over how these are translated into access to or distribution of economic resources such as land, business ownership, or jobs. In Kosovo as in other colonized areas, ethnic conflict has been translated into a sovereignty issue, covering the issue of access to economic, cultural, and political expression in the populations' own land. In Kenya, ethnic tensions have been translated into a debate over distribution of power between presidential privilege and legislative power. Van Eck (2008) recently argued that tensions in the eastern DRC would not be resolved unless attention was given to the ethnic divides (Hutu/Tutsi) that informed them. In a powerful riposte, Sezibera (2008) countered that ethnicity was not the problem and that continued focus on ethnicity would only entrench such divisions. The source of the tensions was the long-term consequence of colonial tactics of divide and rule that self-serving elites had perpetuated in their own interests. But in fact, the groups, tactics, and elites all refer to ethnicity as the targeting factor.

Identity Conflicts

Social groups—whether defined by ethnicity, religion, class, or political affiliation—have different interests, needs, and values, and they have unequal access to power and resources. These circumstances necessarily generate competition and conflict (Nathan, 1996, p. 4). Identity conflicts, it is commonly suggested, are more difficult to settle than those of a simply economic nature, evoking zero-sum positioning, greater emotion, and more complex dynamics. Huntington (1998) suggests that the possibility of resolving such conflicts by neutral third parties is bleak, not simply because of the depth of the division between the parties but also because it is impossible to locate an acceptable mediator. Hanf (1989, p. 104) too recognizes that "the prospects of reaching . . . solutions . . . without first experiencing the futility of violence are bad. People and societies have a habit of learning not from the history of others but only from their own bloody experience." Beyond this, it seems that some are unable to learn even from their own experience!

Despite their apparent clarity, identity conflicts are in fact quite hard to define. They may be recognized as an element in intractable conflicts, but analysts are divided over their nature, what makes them intractable, and thus how they might best be approached. Primordialists argue that culture, tribes, and clans are immutable in conflict scenarios. Marxists counter that culture is a false consciousness— the basic issues are class and poverty. Others agree with the false consciousness analysis of the Marxists but from a different angle. Nativists, for instance, suggest that ethnic tensions in Africa are the consequence of colonialism.

Divided analyses create more than simply academic dilemmas. They make it more difficult to support and coordinate external interventions to resolve an internal conflict. Thus, some have argued that mediation in the Zimbabwe crisis should focus less on the internal protagonists and more on Britain, which is seen as having played a major part in the collapse of the economy by withholding financial aid it had promised for land redistribution purposes. This played out in larger forums. Britain's prime minister, Gordon Brown, refused to attend the 2008 European Union–Africa summit if Robert Mugabe was included. The African Union, declining to be told who to include on its team, refused to exclude him. Little progress was made on issues of trade, immigration, governance, human rights, or international security at the "Brownless" summit, but the editor of *African Business*, Versi (2008, pp. 14–15), declared it a victory for Africa in which a Europe in disarray was forced to yield ground. He argued that Africa's conflicts were largely the consequence of foreign intervention and that its worst leaders were inserted and maintained by foreign interests. In deciding whether to proceed with the summit, Europe, faced with a threat of alternative investment from the East, had chosen Mugabe over Brown. Africa had supported Mugabe because he had returned its land to its people despite British failure to fund land redistribution. Mugabe was reported as being jubilant with his "victory" over the British. In the case of Zimbabwe, conflicting analyses have, of course, not only scuppered a summit, they have left ordinary Zimbabweans in a miserable no-man's land as African nations rally to Mugabe's support against Western "interventionism," as he portrays the nation's collapse as the consequence of neocolonialism. In short, competing analyses of the source of the problem have played out in policy positions and have effectively undermined a coordinated international response to the Zimbabwean crisis.

Another problem is that identity conflicts are not easily isolated or categorized as such. Was the Northern Ireland conflict one of religion or nationalism? Is the Israeli–Palestinian conflict one of religion or territory? Is the Zimbabwe situation one of race or land/economics? The definition of the conflict matters a good deal in determining the nature of the required solution. The knee-jerk response is to classify any conflict in which there is evidence of ethnic or tribal or religious mobilization as a conflict of identity. Yet there is evidence suggesting that people very seldom engage in violent conflicts simply over their cultural differences. True, small groups of zealots may be prepared to kill and die for their causes, but for the most part, people do not attack one another simply over cultural differences, and most states do not condone religious intolerance. Following an extensive quantitative analysis, Laitin (2006) concluded that ethnic differences, internal ethnic fragmentation, or even situations of ethnic hatred very seldom generate violent conflict. Indeed, he concluded that only about 5 of every 10,000 potential ethnic conflicts in Africa become violent; for the most part, people get along.

The question, then, is why some situations deteriorate into bloody ethnic, cultural, or religious confrontation—what utility is there for mobilizing under ethnic or other identity markers? It is now well established (Collier, 2003) that a situation of a small number of ethnic or other identity groups, rather than just one or a large number, is the most conflict prone, as one group seeks to dominate the other(s) and deprive them of their just participation and power for fear of being dominated if they do not. Collier's proposition, then, is that people mobilize under ethnic markers to compete for scarce resources. In less developed economies, Hanf (1989) suggests that ethnic markers are the most visible and easy to rally around. Class mobilization is a more sophisticated conceptual process and is harder to achieve.

Along the contours of societal cleavages and stratification, the greatest threat to stability occurs not in cases of extremely unequal incorporation, but in cases where the contest is tight and cultural and class divides have become synonymous. In such situations, the leaders of a dominant group mobilize those most threat-ened by change—those on the lower rungs of a patronage system. They are coun-tered by aspirant leaders of lower classes who have experienced periods of economic improvement but expect more—the J-curve relative deprivation thesis (Davies, 1964; Gurr, 1970.). In scarce-resource, multicommunal economies, people mobilize more readily around communal rather than class identity markers because it requires a less advanced consciousness and because communal identi-ties are physically and culturally closer (Hanf, 1989). It might be added that class consciousness also requires a society with classes—that is, a level of economic development. Notably, tensions within the African National Congress (ANC) in South Africa reflect a mobilization across communal lines that are different from those in Kenya or the DRC, although there is still evidence of ethnic mobilization in South Africa's wider politics. Also, ethnic or communal conflicts generally reflect a situation in which certain groups feel despised or excluded on account of their religion, ethnicity, or other identity. In short, identity translates into economic or symbolic deprivation. Communal conflicts may in fact deepen class conflicts while concealing them.

Laitin (2006) and Collier et al. (2003) suggest that the core conflict generator in identity conflicts is the weak state, although this factor is only a contributor or an indicator of proneness rather than a cause. There can be little doubt that weak states unable to collect revenues or deliver education, health, security, or services to their people are a key element in generating violent ethnic tensions. They are weak, however, because in most instances they are poor. In the tough world of politics, governing parties tend to distribute access to power and privilege first within their family, clan, and tribal systems, thus entrenching communal markers as those that matter. The cause of identity conflicts, then, is that the state-holders are greedy rather than weak; the greed factor does exist as a cause of revolt, but in the hands of the state, not of the rebellion (Arnson & Zartman, 2005).

It is also clear that identity groups concentrate in an identifiable territory, and the resulting conflict is especially heightened when that territory has formerly known independence and has religious associations (Laitin, 2006) suggests that conflict is more likely to arise when groups are poorly integrated and live in separate clusters. Bloomfield et al. (1998), however, point out that conflicts can arise from separation in which antagonisms based on assumptions and stereotypes are allowed to prosper through lack of contact, but also from proximity in which day-to-day contact fuels a sense of difference (among Malays, Chinese, and Indians in Malaysia; among indigenous Fijians and Indo-Fijians in Fiji). In short, tensions over identity play out and are often managed or regulated through the *design* of economic policies and political and electoral systems (Rothchild, 2009; Vasquez & Valeriano, 2009). Does a third party assisting the protagonists then seek to negotiate an end to hostilities by helping them design such systems, or is the focus on the attitudes of parties—breaking down stereotypes, building new, more positive perceptions of each other, building trust, helping parties discover their common humanity? A holistic approach must tackle both. This thinking suggests that interventions involve demobilization, cultural reprogramming, and social reengineering. This has serious implications for third parties. It shifts their work beyond simply keeping warring parties apart or brokering quick deals to resolve presenting issues in a dispute. Intelligence agencies might have been happy to venture into "hearts and minds" campaigns, but many mediators like to think that they are not actors in this arena!

This brings the work of external interventionists into sharper focus. The holistic approach, mooted here, is essentially focused on *structure* and *attitude change,* but what are the boundaries of such interventions? At one level, mediators must attend to the regulation of the expression of conflict (its symptoms). At another level, they must focus on how and why groups mobilize under identity markers; the conditions that facilitate such mobilization; the needs, fears, and interests of people that prompt tightening of ethnic or religious identity boundaries; and the types of leader–follower interactions that characterize the development of mass movements and identity conflicts.

This difficult path then leads to some basic conclusions. Differences in identity alone are seldom the cause of violent conflict; people generally do not go to war simply over differences in culture or religion. Fundamentalist identity groups do, of course, exist who undertake violent struggles and who, in a high-technology world, now have the means for massive destruction (Faure & Zartman, 2010; Zartman & Faure, 2011). These must be placed, in the first instance, in a category of their own. They are very dangerous in their own right, but their real danger lies in their capacity to polarize the wider society along identity lines. Terror has been well used as a mobilization vehicle for identity conflicts (Burleigh, 2006). Arguably, the real objective of a radical act is to evoke a wider response setting off a much larger and self-reinforcing conflict escalation process along identity lines.

Why, how, and under what conditions are people mobilized around identity markers? The indications are that such mobilization is contingent. Thus, some Islamic groups may demand the right to wear religious symbols where they are a minority in a secular society (e.g., the right to symbolize their beliefs in France) or where they feel a need to return to roots threatened by secularization as a majority (e.g., in secular Turkey), while others push for secularization of symbols in Roman

Catholic Italy, where crucifixes adorn the walls of public buildings (the desire to curb the expression of dominant Others). People make choices about where their best prospects lie and redefine themselves within this reality. Identity—the definition of self, in-groups, or "us" and out-groups or the Other—is subject to choice and to manipulation. These choices locate people in a society, offering access to power and privilege, serving to attenuate or increase discrimination, and, in extreme situations, determining the chances of survival. Not being a Jew in Europe during the 1940s and not being a Tutsi in Rwanda in 1994 offered better prospects of survival. The lot of South Africa's Coloured population illustrates the choices to be made in a changing society. Before 1994, some sought to pass as white, after 1994 as black. It is not uncommon to hear the comment "Under apartheid we were too black; now we are too white." While malleability of identity is clear, it is equally clear that core values (belief systems, religious affiliation) are more resistant to change than practices (modes of dress, consumption patterns, sports, and leisure activities).

Identity is seldom actually negotiated. In the process of a current violent exchange, negotiators' attention is focused first on achieving a cease-fire and then usually on the terms of a deal that would allow peace. This latter area is one in which structural issues of economic distribution, opportunity, or political design are evident—in other words, how identity groups might accommodate one another's interests. Negotiations might attend to other structural conditions that underpin such conflicts—poverty or structural imbalances or entrenched attitudes—and around which mobilization along identity lines had utility. Wider and deeper negotiations dealing with conflict resolution, beyond structure or management, would face the challenge of changing attitudes. In short, the game is seldom one of negotiating identity per se; it is really one of reducing fear, threat, and the need for groups to mobilize around identity markers (addressing the conditions that give rise to such a need) and then, when conflicts informed by identity mobilization do emerge, of seeking ways to regulate their expression in nonviolent ways.

■ PREVENTION

To begin with, one has to step outside the problem and consider the legitimacy of becoming involved.[2] What gives the right to intervene to prevent identity conflict before it leads to genocide? How, and how early, can and should this right or duty be exercised? What can be done to preempt the need for physical/military intervention before it becomes the remaining resort? The object of the intervention—the danger to be prevented—is the element that confers legitimacy on the intervener, but there is no agreed-upon threshold of seriousness or moment of effectiveness that compels intervention. There is a growing feeling that under some circumstances still to be consensually defined, the egregious exercise of targeted oppression justifies intrusive foreign action. The mandate concerns preventive intervention, that is, diplomatic rather than military interference in internal affairs and also external pressures and inducements affecting state policies and policymaking (Ban, 2009). The concern in the present work is intervention through direct negotiation or third-party mediation—hence, intervention when the conflict is brewing but before the full force of repression and revolt has occurred.

Still, there is no consensus on the degree of conflict required to justify prevention: How bad does it have to be? And how intrusive can the intervention be—merely friendly advice or irresistible compulsion? Friendly warnings and predictions from other sovereign states and strident broadcasts from NGOs are certainly justified by actions clearly leading to genocide. But when they are not heeded, do they justify threats and promises, constraints and sanctions? And even if legitimized, do they justify the intervening agency's expenditure of public or private treasure and attention, and even lives? And if the ultimate measures are beyond acceptability, should the initial effort be made at all?

Rules of the game for preventers and interveners are still unclear, and measures for successful preventers' behavior are absent. Even if standards of societal health were available and the threshold of unhealthiness was clearly discernible, the canons of remedy would remain uncertain. The main limitation on action is proportionality or "no net harm," taken from the laws of war; that is, the cure should not be more costly or damaging than the illness (Evans & Sahnoun, 2001, I, p. xi). There is also a general consensus that collective action, with collective responsibility, is preferable to individual action, even if sanctioned by a UN agency, although there are plenty of situations in which (nonmilitary) prevention is best done by a single state. Efforts by a coalition of actors serve to heighten the effectiveness and soften the risk of one party's being left with the cost and responsibility for prevention. Another relevant principle is *subsidiarity*, which requires that responsibility be borne at the lowest level, beginning with the state itself, next assumed by the neighbors in the region and then by global organizations. In part, but only in part, this is a matter of capability, another element involved in the mandate; often, multiple interveners are needed to amass the required capability to prevent the expected damage. Mediating problems include questions of mediators' interest, of free riding or leaving the job up to someone else, and of uncertainty about the evidence of the need for intervention (Avenhaus & Sjöstedt, 2009; Olson, 1965; Zartman, 2005b). These problems too have no clear answer, but it is necessary to consider them.

Negotiation and Mediation

Negotiation and mediation are needed to prevent identity conflict escalation and genocide when the conflict moves to the point where the parties are unable to turn from violence on their own and need help to resolve their conflict. *Negotiation* is an encounter between parties attempting to resolve the incompatibilities—that is, the conflict—between their positions on given issues. *Mediation* is third-party involvement in conflict management and resolution to help the parties accomplish the negotiation that they are not able to conduct by themselves (Anstey, 1993; Bercovitch, 2007;, Smock & Smith 2008; Touval & Zartman 2007). Both negotiation and mediation carry the implication that there is a perceived legitimate grievance, that the parties have legitimate interests to be protected, that none of them is seeking self-destruction, and that the interests of all parties need to be considered in ending the violence and restoring a functioning political system. Since the present volume is primarily concerned with third-party assistance to conflicting parties in resolving their identity conflict, the terms *mediation* and *negotiation* will be used interchangeably, but *mediation* more frequently, in addressing the third-party role. The work of the High Commissioner on National Minorities (HCNM) of the Organization for Security and Cooperation in Europe (OSCE), examined in a later chapter, is a prime institutional embodiment of this role.

Third-party attention to an internal conflict is generally resisted by governments, since it implies that a government cannot handle its own problems; that the rebellious or repressed groups deserve recognition and equal standing before the mediator; and, in the end, that the only resolving outcome will be a revised political system that accords these identity groups a legitimate place in politics. The mediator's challenge is to appeal to the actors' desire for settlement while assuaging their fears. It was under these assumptions that Sant'Egidio (backed by the United States, Russia, Portugal, Italy, Zimbabwe, Kenya, and Zambia) mediated between rebels and the government—RENAMO and FRELIMO, respectively—in Rome in 1990–1992 and Portugal; that the United States and the UN mediated between UNITA and MPLA in Estoril in 1992, in Lusaka in 1994, and in Luanda in 2001–2002 to overcome conflicts of grievance gradually becoming ethnic in Mozambique and in Angola, respectively; that the Quint mediated in Kosovo between the Kosovo Liberation Army (KLA) and the Serb government in 1998–2008; that the OSCE HCNM has mediated in Estonia, Romania, and Ukraine since the mid-1990s, as laid out in the chapter by Meerts and Coulaloglou; and that the United States and the rest of the Quartet continue to press for a solution to the Israel–Palestine conflict—all identity conflicts in various forms with mass killings in their course.

Negotiation has been defined as the process combining conflicting positions to produce a common outcome under a decision rule of unanimity. The focus is on the issue and the divergent positions held on its substance; the assumption is that the common outcome will be found somewhere between the conflicting positions through concessions and compensations or by the parties' overcoming their incompatibilities through construction or reframing. The parties are viewed as the bearers of the incompatible positions. For mediation and negotiation to work, valid spokesmen for the various parties are required. If the parties are many or the spokesmen are not clearly authorized, the mediator may first have to form coalitions and to designate spokesmen for mediation purposes, necessitating deeper involvement in internal politics and seriously complicating the task. The United States at Dayton arranged for Serbian President Slobodan Milosevic to speak for the Bosnian Serbs and Croatian President Franjo Tudjman to speak for the Bosnian Croats, but not without complications for the process and the subsequent implementation. The United States and Nigeria in Abuja in 2007 unwisely picked and pressed some of the rebels, to the exclusion of others, in an attempt to craft an agreement to end the genocide in Darfur, but the excluded rebels continued the fight.

Mediation is exceptionally difficult when identity takes an ideological form, when the violence has escalated to terrorism, and where the rebels have an independent source of funding that allows them to enjoy their Sherwood Forest existence. For example, it has been hard to find an appropriate mediator in the Colombian, Somali, or Sierra Leonean conflicts. In Colombia, ideology and the drug trade have made the Revolutionary Armed Forces (FARC) and the National Liberation Army (ELN) uninterested in seeking a solution through talks with the government, despite the state's varied attempts to find a basis for discussion, and various would-be mediators have found little purchase on the situation (Civico, 2010). In Sierra Leone, the Revolutionary United Front (RUF) proved unworthy of mediation and broke the Abidjan (1996), Conakry (1997), and Lome (1999) Agreements made by West African mediators (Mutwol, 2009). In such cases, it is only when the spoilers are worn out and have become fully isolated from a population alienated by their own tactics that they become amenable to a return to civil politics and the conflict becomes susceptible to mediation. Otherwise, they must be defeated. Mediation as a means of preventing identity conflict and genocide is not merely a matter of making peace; it must be a means of reforming and restoring the political fabric of the state in order to render it a functioning entity again.

But in many cases of identity (and other) conflict, the parties are not evident. Conflicting positions of the various sides are indeed present but disembodied, not fully represented by any actor but awaiting their formulator and spokesman. A number of parties are the grist of the conflict, but they are not fully aware of what they are fighting for; they are only aware of whom (in the plural) they are fighting against. Often, the ideational conflict concerns notions of identity and its implications, things done to and by people identified in ascriptive terms, yet with no consensual representative and spokesman for the aggrieved and/or the aggriever. Aggrieved groups await saviors who offer an identity in periods of social disintegration, to whom identity give purpose and prospect. After a while, the problem becomes that the party cannot change positions without losing its identity.

Under these conditions, a different approach to negotiation may be required. Negotiation in these cases is a process of selecting an appropriate partner and constructing a joint pact. The focus in this approach is on the parties, who become the vehicles, representatives, and articulators of positions but whose selection for treating these matters and for the establishment of a pact is the subject of the negotiation; it is the pact, not the settlement of the issue, that is their outcome. Negotiating selection is indicated by ripeness theory as well. In addition to the two substantive elements of ripeness—a mutually hurting stalemate and a way out—the need for a third, procedural element has often been emphasized: the presence of a valid spokesman (Zartman, 1989). Although necessary, the first two elements are insufficient if there is no representative and authoritative party to speak for its side, to feel the existence of the other two subjective elements, and to undertake to negotiate a pact as a result. The pact is an agreement to cooperate in the establishment of future relations and the handling (management or resolution) of the conflict. It sets out the terms of that management or resolution, but it also engages the parties to cooperate together in a new political relationship. As such it includes, and also excludes, two major decisions. The pact recognizes and legitimizes the parties involved, each acknowledging the other's status as representative of its side.

It also codifies a decision in regard to spoilers, whether they should be included at the cost of substantive difficulty in reaching agreement or excluded at the cost of procedural difficulty in delivering that agreement. Finally, the pact codifies substantive decisions on the content of the agreement and the issues of the conflict it covers and excludes.

References to well-known identity conflicts (if not genocide) illustrate these questions. A most interesting case is the 2005 Comprehensive Peace Agreement in Sudan. The natural and accepted representative of the South was the Sudanese Peoples Liberation Movement/Army (SPLM/A), agreed to by the North over other breakaway Southern factions, but representation of the North was less obvious. It could have been either the government or the governing party (Sudanese National Congress Party [NCP]) that held power militarily in the North, or the opposition parties that most observers agree represent—and have historically represented—the majority of the Northern population, or both. A pact with the opposition parties had already been tried, in the Koka Dam agreement of 1995, which had no major impact on the conflict. So it was the government, to the exclusion of the majoritarian parties, that made the pact with the SPLM/A, letting the latter into a joint government, excluding the other parties, and strengthening the NCP for the upcoming elections. At Oslo in 1993, the Israeli government chose to recognize and make a pact with the Palestine Liberation Organization (PLO), to the exclusion of and against Hamas; the Oslo Agreement gave birth to the Palestine Authority (PA) governing an autonomous Palestinian area. After the 2006 election that brought Hamas to power, some movement was begun to renegotiate a new and fuller pact between the PLO/PA and Israel, again to the exclusion of Hamas.

Negotiations in South Africa in the early 1990s were dominated as much by the question of who was making the transitional pact out of apartheid as by the contents of the pact itself (Sisk, 1995; Zartman, 1997). Although the Conference for a Democratic South Africa (CODESA) and its successor, the Multi-Party Conference, were ostensibly multilateral meetings of all political parties, they were in fact bilateral pacting sessions between the African National Congress (ANC) and the National Party (NP), operating under but not involving the NP-dominated government; to come to fruition at the end, this bilateral pact was opened slightly to include the Inkatha Freedom Party (IFP), otherwise poised for spoiling. In Rwanda in 1993, the overarching question in the negotiations between the Rwandan Patriotic Front (RPF), the Rwandan National Movement for Development (MRND), and the opposition parties was whether the racist and ultimately *génocidaire* Coalition for the Defense of the Revolution (CDR) would be included or not; the final pact between the first three groups of parties was not wholeheartedly accepted by any of them and was destroyed by the excluded spoilers, who would doubtless have made any agreement impossible if included. In each of these cases, and many others, negotiations were dominated by a choice of pacting partner and an exclusion of others, with the choice of parties to the pact determining its substantive contents. It would be silly to discount the intricate negotiations that went on over the substance of the emerging agreement, but what was negotiated was determined by who negotiated it.

Thus, it is not merely that the guest list characterizes the signatories of the pact; it also determines its formula for agreement. In Sudan, the inclusion of the SPLM/A meant that a secular state with religious freedom in at least the South would be the outcome, but the selection of the NCP as the partner meant that the SPLM/A would be brought *into* a government where the NCP held critical elements of power, including control of the election process in the North. The basis of the Oslo Agreement was the mutual recognition of Israel and the PLO, one as a state and the other as the movement representative of its people, an unequal status that was reflected in all the provisions of the agreement. In South Africa, the two leading parties were recognized as the parties sharing power in the transitional government that would institute free and fair elections and majority rule. In Rwanda, the selection of the parties, even without the CDR, determined an agreement that none could live with and where the MRND's adherence was never fully confirmed. In all these cases, the inclusion of the parties to the pact determined its basic formula rather than the reverse. In Kashmir and Nagorno-Karabakh, inclusion of the disputed territories representative in a three-party negotiation makes a world of difference in the shape of the outcome; "any attempt to strike a deal between two without the association of the third will fail to yield a credible settlement" (Fai, 2010,).

Thus, in this view, it is the process of selecting the parties that is the major focus of the negotiations. These negotiations, procedural in nature, are different from the substantive give-and-take of the negotiations over the contents of the agreement, as usually analyzed. To begin with, *selection* is the wrong word, since neither side is able to reach into the other and pick a partner. To do so would usually delegitimize the party selected and destroy its representativeness. Yet the party representative on each side does seek to influence that selection, so the process is located on a scale somewhere between total neutrality and absolute selection. Facing that processual spectrum is an array of parties on each side. On the government side the choice is generally quite limited, although the group of official representatives can contain its own spectrum of opinions and authorities; in addition, rebels can reach out to opposition parties in the hope that they may come to power, sometimes strengthened by a claim that they can deal with the rebels.

On the rebel side, the spectrum is larger and often not a spectrum at all but a gaggle of groups with unclear positions and unclear authority to represent the referent group. In fact, these group are often not constituted but are inchoate organizations, unfocused on their needs and demands and unformed in their internal organization. In addition, similar to but characteristically worse than the government's condition, the factions on the rebel side can be expected to be engaged in a serious struggle of outbidding and position politics, as analyzed in the subsequent chapter by Jannie Lilja. They vie among themselves to be the negotiating spokesman and also not to be the negotiating spokesman for their side, and they use this contest to weaken and delegitimize competing factions. Even when a well-established rebellion begins to take on the institutionalized nature of a protostate, governing its territory and institutionalizing its services, it is vulnerable to splits and internecine contests, as the history of many identity movements—SPLM/A in

Sudan, FARC in Colombia, LTTE in Sri Lanka, MFDC in Casamance, GAM in Aceh—testify. Some factions focus on their institutionalized interests, as explored by Marie-Joëlle Zahar in a later chapter, and others on the hard-line demands of their identity conflict, as analyzed by Jannie Lilja in her chapter on outbidding.

There is also a temporal element in this contest. In the course of the rebellion, when the petition phase fails, it is followed by a consolidation phase in the conflict (Zartman, 1995). Within the rebel side, factions evolve and turn to a contest among themselves for leadership and representation of their reference group. This contest tends to be more violent than the conflict with the government itself, and its outcome determines the strategy and tactics that the rebels will adopt when they do turn their guns on the government. Although this contest determines who will eventually negotiate for the rebel cause and with the government, it puts those negotiations on hold until leadership is decided. Even afterward, it can continue to pose problems for substantive negotiations in the form of spoilers and single shooters if the selection process for leadership is not conclusive or if the tactic represented by the winning leadership faction flags (Zartman & Alfredson, 2010). As negotiations proceed, the possibility of payoffs for participation provides an incentive for proliferation of parties. Breakaway groups adopt a single-shooting strategy, hoping to gather the goodies of an agreement for themselves, or else a buy-in strategy in which they seek to share some of the collective benefits. Left out, they become spoilers—*tactical spoilers*, in Stedman's (2000) term—holding out until they can eek out the last drop of power from their position (Shapley & Shubik, 1954).

How, then, is selection accomplished? Within the rebellion, factional leadership will be negotiated by two criteria: the physical strength of the various factions and the proposed tactics' appeal to their referent group. The first indicates that the contest for leadership will be an active political, and soon violent, outbidding conflict among the factions, as noted. Intimidation, group battles, and, often, individual assassinations are characteristic. The second is less direct. Putative leaders have to prove that they accurately represent the tenor of opinion among the group they propose to represent; this is indeed the material of any political campaign, but there is no scheduled election to confirm the decision: It is a campaign without a formal ending. On the government side, there are similarities but a big difference: The campaign is generally ended by a formal selection of government spokesmen. However, interagency and intraleadership conflicts may well continue after formal selection has been accomplished.

In this entire process of selection by negotiation, the relation between the procedural (selection) and substantive negotiations has to be kept in mind by the participants as well as the analysts. Selection negotiations determine the scope of substantive negotiations, and the intended Zone of Possible Agreement (ZOPA) of substantive negotiations determines the range of selectable parties. However, at the same time, the internal dynamics within each side also influence the range of selectable parties and the ultimate selection process. The first prize for pacting purposes goes to deals with core identity groups; the second prize, however, goes to the same with meaningful breakaway or softer identity groups. The first option may produce a meaningful peace; the second weakens the opposition in terms of backing but runs the risk of hardening it and pushing it to more radical action. This may, of course, suit those who seek to vilify the opponent as evil. At best, it may produce a fragile peace subject to ongoing attacks and also raise the question of who defines the spoilers. Spoilers for radical elements are those who enter pacts and erode group solidarity; for the peacemakers they are the ideological recalcitrants. At some point, the soft-liners might have to become tougher than the hard-liners in the interests of the larger whole.

There are many examples of identity conflicts (again, verging on genocide) to illustrate this process. Consolidation is the normal process in any revolt, as illustrated by the internecine battles among the Algerian nationalists in the 1950s, the Angolan nationalists in the 1960s that lasted out the century, the Eritrean nationalists in the 1960s, the Tamil nationalists in the 1970s, and the Sahrawi nationalists in the 1970s, putting off negotiations until the movement had achieved a dominant voice. Preparation and maturation for negotiations was a major problem for RENAMO in Mozambique throughout the 1980s, for the RUF in Sierra Leone in the 1980s and 1990s, and for the ELN in Colombia, further delaying substantive negotiations until the rebel organizations were consolidated and then trained to negotiate, not always with success. Proliferation bedeviled the rebel movements in Liberia in the 1990s, the Burundian rebels in the 2000s, the Southern Sudanese rebels in the early 2000s, and the Congolese rebels during the War of the Zairean Succession in the 1990s, among others. The Darfur rebels in the 2000s never did consolidate, and their negotiations were plagued by maturation and proliferation problems throughout the early 2000s. In Colombia, in the mid-1980s when the government offered a normalization process for FARC, the movement underwent a "soft split," the moderates forming the Patriotic Union (UP) with the skeptical assent of the radical wing. Success of the opening was cut short by the assassination of most of its leaders by right-wing paramilitaries. In the PLO, the attempted opening in the 1970s met a similarly violent end but from the radical core of the organization, which assassinated moderate leaders open to contacts with Israel.

More developed negotiation processes of selection occurred in other conflicts. In 1998, U.S. mediators made contacts with various factions in the KLA in an effort to seize the moment when negotiations with Serbia appeared possible. The attempts ended up in the constitution of a heterogeneous delegation to formal negotiations at Rambouillet, although earlier chances of productive contacts that might have foreclosed a Serbian offensive were missed (Daalder & O'Hanlon, 2000; O'Brien, 2005; Zartman, 2005a). In the Oslo talks, the two sides actually negotiated appropriate representatives from either side. Preceding the talks, Israel sought informal contacts with the PLO in the shadow of the stalled Madrid/Washington talks. The Oslo talks themselves began with discussions between private Israelis and authorized PLO officials after Israel had tested the official status of the Palestinians by requiring them to produce a procedural change in the behavior of the Jordanian-Palestinian delegation to the Washington talks. After five rounds of talks, the PLO delegation told the private Israelis that they would continue no further until they could talk with Israeli officials, which produced the arrival of Uri Savir and then Joel Singer as official representatives. More recently,

Israel and the PA (Fatah) have actually been negotiating with each other over the appropriate spokesman for the Palestianians, including the role of Hamas and the selection of a leader to succeed Mahmoud Abbas, including quintuple-life-sentenced Mohammed Barghouti.

In Northern Ireland, the British held secret talks with Sinn Fein/Irish Republican Army (IRA) representatives as the Belfast process began to take shape, gradually bringing in appropriate Republican spokesmen, a process that continued all the way to the Good Friday Agreement, when Sinn Fein was excluded on two occasions as punishment for infringing the Mitchell Principles and then let back in to continue the talks. In South Africa, businessmen and even official representatives of the government began contacts with ANC leaders as early as the mid-1980s, finally shaping the terms of a formula—nonviolence in exchange for legality—that was the basis for the release of Nelson Mandela, the unbanning of the ANC, and the beginning of the negotiations (Zartman, 1995). These are just some salient and condensed examples of the long and delicate process of negotiation over spokesmen that precedes and determines the subsequent substantive negotiation process, overshadowing it in importance. The South Africa lesson was the number of levels on which pacting took place up, down and across society, to stabilize the political deal-making process and create a groundswell of momentum for the final outcome, breaking down rigid stereotypes at all levels in society, not just a simple reliance on political deal-making.

In sum, in order to analyze negotiations in the internal identity conflicts so characteristic of the current era, an approach is needed that takes into account the selection of parties for the negotiation process, focusing not only on the substantive determination of outcomes, but also on negotiations to select negotiating parties from the conflicting sides in order to provide an appropriate settlement of the conflict and a durable pact between the sides before the conflict slides further toward genocide and mass killings. Once that selection is negotiated, within but also between the sides, the outlines of the subsequent agreement have already been designed, opening up the process for a final agreement as a pact between parties in the name of sides. Yet the selection negotiations are always open to upsets and are never fully completed until the final pact is signed. This approach will guide the analysis of this work.

Negotiated Measures

It cannot be restated too often that early warnings abound. The problem is the absence of early awareness and early action, that is, the ability to listen, hear, and act on the early warnings. Academic analyses and government files are filled with indications of ethnic conflict and impending genocide, even if the exact dates of the crash are not predictable. Yet, curiously, discussions of prevention continually return to the need for early warning systems when the real problem remains: the analytical inability to distinguish the storm warnings that precede hurricanes from those that do not (the *tropical storm problem*) and to act upon them (Zartman, 2005, 2010). Faulty perception is worsened when bureaucratic inertia blocks action (the *three-monkeys' problem*), when current crises overshadow future danger signs (the *smoke-and-fire problem*), and when repeated false warnings wear out credibility (the *cry-wolf problem*), among other impediments to policymakers' hearing and responding to the many visible signs of impending conflict (Ivanov & Nyheim, 2004; Zartman & Faure, 2005).[3] Surprises in this business are rare, but deafness is widespread. Many of these problems require a conscious decision to give attention and credit to proactive efforts at prevention instead of simply providing reactive crisis management after the fact. As the debate over the Iraqi and Afghan interventions clearly showed, it is easier to be eloquent about what needs to be prevented than about how to prevent it. Since identity conflict and genocide are a joined continuum, there are innumerable cases of states that began the slippery slide and caught themselves in time, early or late, by their own efforts or with the help of external friends. It is the ones that get through the net of advisable and acceptable practices that pose the problem. Otherwise the Curse of Kosovo, referred to as the world's most early-warned conflict, will become endemic (Ivanov & Nyheim 2004, p. 165).

Negotiation and mediation can foster prevention, at various points between the appearance of an identity conflict not yet violent and the outbreak of genocidal violence, through a number of measures. These include *dialogue, ripening, separation*, and *coercive accountability*. While they are discussed discretely here to bring out their characteristics, these measures often overlap (see also Rothchild, 1986).

Dialogue for a constructive consideration of the elements of the conflict offers an occasion to deal coolly with them before they sharpen into violence and ethnic cleansing. The targeted identity group and its targeter—usually the government—may not easily agree to sit down together, so a firm and helpful conciliator is often needed. Both sides have become deeply committed to their publics by this point, as noted, making it hard to retreat from established perceptions and positions. Any external intervention is bound to be seen by the government as an indication that it cannot correctly handle its own affairs. Such an effort is also particularly difficult because it is not a brief one-shot activity; it needs sustained attention to overcome the hardened perceptions and reverse the sharpened policies, and that requires repeated, not far-spaced, meetings, a suspension of actions that might be interpreted as hostile, and an effort to use external events positively, as an occasion to meet, explain, and work out common responses. Measures to be used include a cooling-off period, a disengagement of forces, and a hard look at grievances and images. Since the political entrepreneur or agent provocateur behind the identity conflict is likely to lose his job in the process and others are busy profiting from the conflict, there is certain to be resistance.

Each step poses challenges for the third party in the process. The first is to achieve welcome entry into the impending conflict. International organizations, friendly states, and NGOs need to develop the parties' awareness that the current policy is heading toward a costly deadlock, that problems and perceptions are better handled positively, and that the mediators are useful in this direction. This is a circular effort since external parties need to use entry to gain entry, as Special Representative of the Secretary-General (SRSG) Alvaro de Soto did in El Salvador in 1990–1992. The second challenge is to combine an appropriate amount of pressure with attractive incentives (including the lifting of pressure). Early discussions need organization rather than pressure; dialogue deeper into the conflict may require more stringent pressures. Third parties arranging a confrontation to head off violence cannot be limited to good counsel; they need to provide incentives as well as constraints against defection from the path of reconciliation. Too little pressure leaves the course of conflict costless, but too much pressure arouses a defensive reaction and closes the door to external attentions. As in any adolescent behavior, the best kind of pressure is peer pressure. A third challenge is to find appropriate ways—"Golden Bridges"—for the parties to back down (Ury, 1991). The aggressing party—usually the government—must find ways to explain to its public that it is sitting down with and then assuaging the very parties that it claimed were posing an existential threat.

The biggest challenge, however, concerns spoilers, those entrepreneurs who are set on ethnic cleansing as the path to power and are uninterested in any reconciliation or attenuation of their fears, as discussed by Marie-Joëlle Zahar in a later chapter. The initial challenge for precrisis prevention is to wean weaker spoilers away from the hard core and involve them in the dynamics of the confrontation process. But dealing with the spoilers who remain requires a different kind of tactic, involving isolation and neutralization until they become powerless to undermine or block the ongoing reconciliation. Thus, dialogue as a precrisis strategy has a positive and a negative face, and the two are indissociable: The conflicting parties must be brought to see that their mutual fears are unwarranted, but they must also be made to see that the alternative to reconciliation is costly and that their extreme elements must be rendered incapable of upsetting the developing reconciliation.

These concerns can be illustrated in both success and failure. SRSG Ahmedou ould Abdallah sprang into action, alerting and consulting interested parties in 1994 in Burundi to head off an imitative reaction to events in Rwanda when the shooting down of the president's plane triggered the genocide. World diplomatic and economic pressure against the apartheid regime in South Africa brought the government to engage its opponent, the ANC, in dialogue and then, through negotiation, to shape a new political system in South Africa before widespread violence broke out. In Zimbabwe in 2008, repeated attempts by President Thabo Mbeki to get President Robert Mugabe to sit down and defuse a conflict that was at least in part ethnic failed due to Mugabe's stubborn and vicious insistence on holding power and physically destroying the opposition; failure came because the efforts were weak and unaccompanied by clear condemnation and penalties for noncompliance. Between the Israelis and Palestinians, a low-level campaign to create dialogue groups grew gradually during the 1980s and early 1990s, culminating in the Oslo contacts and agreement, but were unsupported by vigorous official efforts after Oslo and then were undercut during the Benjamin Netanyahu and *intifada* period of the mid-1990s. In Jos in Nigeria, interfaith and interethnic dialogue groups were set up after identity riots in 2001, but an incident in 2008 swept aside their efforts and provoked deadly riots over the next two years.

Ripening is required if the parties are to feel themselves caught in a mutually hurting stalemate that pushes them to begin lowering tensions. Conflicting parties do not look for a way out of a conflict if they think they can win and if the conflict is not hurting them. Therefore, to open their minds to precrisis prevention, whether before the conflict has turned violent or after, they must be made aware both of the impossibility of winning and of the cost of attempting to do so; in other words, the conflict must be ripened for prevention in their perceptions. This is a primary challenge for external parties. The perception of stalemate is enhanced by measures to show that victory is not allowed, either not possible or not legitimate even if achieved—for example, that coveted territory cannot be seized and even if it is, the conquest will not be recognized, or that cleansing an ethnic group will be prevented and even if it is not, the resulting government will not be recognized (Zartman & deSoto, 2010). The perception of cost is enhanced by measures to make the parties realize that identity conflicts entail penalties larger than expected benefits, either at the hands of the repressed identity group or by the international community. For example, the third party must convince the repressor that repressed groups can offer a more costly resistance than expected and that continued ethnic conflict and cleansing will be met by sanctions and withheld recognition. This is a job for the NGOs and nonstate actors as well as friendly officials and intergovernmental organizations (IGOs).

There are more cases to cite where ripening succeeded in preventing identity conflicts from continuing once violence had occurred than from turning violent in the first place; the former is easier, albeit costlier, because the objective evidence for the hurting stalemate is present, not merely prospective, and the latter is harder to prove since violence has not (yet) taken place. In El Salvador in 1990 the conflict, in part involving the repression of native American populations, between the Farabundo Marti National Liberation Front (FMLF) and the Salvadoran government, opened itself to UN mediation when, after a FMLF offensive with no prospect of further success, the mediator helped the parties see that neither side could win but both were sustaining unbearable losses. In the Israeli–Palestinian conflict in 2008 over Gaza, an imperfect cease-fire was arrived at between Israel and Hamas when both sides saw that they could not prevail but costs were mounting, a realization of ripeness sharpened by Egyptian mediation. Backed up by examples of political conflicts turning dirty, a series of international mediators, ending with former UN Secretary-General Kofi Annan, were able to convince the presidential candidates in Kenya in 2008 to negotiate a power-sharing agreement rather than plunge the country into ethnic violence. In sum, negotiators seeking to ripen identity conflicts for prevention need to muster enormous skills of persuasion, but they may also need to affect objective facts on the ground to enhance the subjective perception of ripeness.

Separation and *power sharing* are formulas for overcoming identity conflicts through preventive negotiation, providing space and time for fears to dissipate and more harmonious relations to develop. They can be used in various ways in precrisis periods as well as during a crisis. Separation pulls the conflicting parties apart, giving them space to breathe and room to reflect; power sharing pulls them together and induces cooperation under controlled conditions. Pulling the identity groups apart reduces the danger of a security dilemma, in which intermingled groups take measures to improve their security and in so doing threaten the security of other groups, and so on. Separation may take the form of a pause or delay in impending precrisis developments, a truce, a cease-fire, a safe haven, buffer zones, disengagement in the midst of a conflict that threatens to escalate, or withdrawal and cantonments as conflict ends. It can be carried out by the original instigators of the conflict who have come to their senses, or by a moderate faction that has taken over and leads the conflicting party—rebellious group or government—in a more constructive direction. External parties dealing with the conflict can encourage moderate factions to develop and contest radical leadership in identity conflicts.

Separation is particularly useful as a longer-term solution in identity conflicts, either before or after a crisis, in the form of autonomy or some other form of regional self-government or, less frequently, through consociational power sharing (Lijphart, 1972). When identity conflicts move from substantive (grievance) to procedural (governance) issues, where the minority no longer believes that it can trust the government with its fate, self-determination can be implemented short of secession by allowing the identity group to handle its own affairs or to have a distinct role in government. The Iraqi Kurds, Southern Sudanese, Tatars, Sud Tyroleans, Catalans, Zanzibaris, and Acehnese were given autonomous self-government (under whatever name) to end their identity conflict, and the first two also enjoyed a share in central government power. Separation must be accomplished by negotiation, with the agreement of the parties; forced separation of intermingled populations, particularly under harsh conditions, is ethnic cleansing, a form of identity conflict itself and a low-level form of genocide, depending on the number of deaths the forced migration brings. Although some may see "gentle" ethnic cleansing as a way to resolve and avoid identity conflicts, it is merely a sanitized way of achieving ethnic conflict results (Kaufmann 1996). It has sometimes been objected that autonomy merely leads to secession, but the record shows that it is annulled autonomy that leads to secession, as in Eritrea, Sudan, Nigeria, and Kosovo.

Peacekeeping forces (PKFs) can be used preventively to separate the parties, either before, during, or after violent conflict. "Early late" prevention can help defuse a situation nearing violence by introducing a trip wire, removing the excuse from either party that it is merely responding to the other's provocation. Less well recognized, there is often a moment within violent conflict when the parties pause, temporarily exhausted, leaving an opportunity for the introduction of separating PKFs before they can regroup, rearm, and pick up the offensive. After hostilities, PKFs monitor and, with a proper mandate, enforce the cease-fire.

Policing properly conducted, with evenhanded authority, is a minimal function of government that can obviate the need for separation by military forces; it is often all that is needed to keep hotheads and public passion from bursting into flame. Since riots are frequently the initial step in identity conflict and violence, escalation can often be checked simply by effective policing, assuming that the government is not the agent of the identity conflict; when the government is the agency, external pressures for it to assume its responsibilities or more invasive measures may be needed. Outbursts of civil violence usually involve a determined core of agitators (the political entrepreneurs referred to earlier) and an inflammable mob—the arsonists and the tinder—and the police's job is to separate the two, sending the first group to jail and the second home. Even when government is not the instigator or the tacit cover of identity violence, the police often remain passive for fear of facing the inflamed crowds with insufficient forces. Thus adequate police forces dedicated to law and order constitute a basic element of prevention, to be provided by external intervention if not by the state.

Special forms of separation have been put to timely use in recent identity conflicts. Secessionist conflict was averted in Russia in 1994 when Tatarstan representatives agreed to be a state "united with" but not within the Russian Federation; conflict was ended in Indonesia in 2007 when Aceh representatives, wary of "autonomy" that had proven inadequate, accepted the status of "self-government." Albanian representatives in Macedonia in 2001 drew back from secessionist demands in exchange for greater recognition in the political and social system. PKFs provided an unusual example of precrisis interposition in Macedonia in 1992–1998 as the UN Preventive Deployment (UNPREDEP). A crucial occasion for a PKF in a mid-conflict calm in intergroup/interpartisan conflict in Congo-Brazzaville in 1997 was turned down by the UN Security Council, which ordered a study of African conflicts instead!

Police forces were present in the early 2000s in Anbar province in Iraq, where they dampened interethnic violence, among many other unpublicized places where demonstrations were carefully kept peaceful. They were absent in Abidjan in the same period, where ethnic violent was promoted by the Ivoirian government and its supporting militia and civilians were harassed for DWM ("driving while Muslim") reasons. Nigerian police forces were ineffective in 2008 in Jos, where they favored one group, and in 1994 in Rwanda, where they melted before or joined the *génocidaires*; in Chechnya, they acted as an arm of government repression. After Jean-Bertrand Aristide's return in 1994, the international community created a new police force in Haiti, free of the corruption and excesses of the military regime's police; unfortunately, it soon was forced into the same habits under Aristide, showing the difficulty for the international community of keeping the police neutral and helpful to the population when the government wants to use it for its own repressive and partisan purposes, but it was restored in the post-Aristide era and provided useful service in restoring order in the 2010 earthquakes.

Sharing power, on the other hand, brings the parties together as separate groups, assuring them a role in government. Power sharing is actually a form of separation in that it freezes the identity group divisions in society and accords them participation in governance only through their representatives, precluding the possibility of gradually erasing the salience of separate identities in politics. Indeed, it can lead to renewed conflict when the separated groups do not receive the distribution of power and benefits that they feel is rightfully theirs, as in Zimbabwe. Perhaps for that reason, power sharing is less utilized than recommended in extensive academic discussions. Power can be shared legislatively or executively. The first takes the form of separate reserved seats, quotas, and assigned roles in legislative bodies, preselected or not decided by systemwide processes such as general elections. The second makes the executive a coalition of identity-group representatives in a consociational form of government. Preventive power sharing among identity groups brought decades of peace to Lebanon before it fell apart due to demographic and generational changes among the groups; it is in use in Iraq, trying to stave off more violent conflict. It was the key to a special regional settlement negotiated in South Tyrol/Alto Adige in Italy in 1969 that has lasted, and a federalized system in Belgium after 1970 that is gradually falling apart. Power sharing between identity groups is also the core of the negotiated Good Friday Agreement of 1998 in Northern Ireland, which has gradually been put into place despite criticisms for perpetuating identity groups and politics. To work effectively, power sharing has to be complemented by an overarching sense of loyalty to the greater system, adaptability to changing power balances, cross-cutting (horizontal) cleavages to counteract identity (vertical) divisions, and a culture of compromise and mutual understanding.

Preemptive accountability is necessary in order to prevent a culture of impunity from taking hold to legitimize identity conflict. The national heroic status accorded to the political entrepreneur in identity conflicts, whether victorious or—curiously—defeated, tends to encourage emulation and, if necessary, another try. International judicial enforcement of the ban on genocide serves as a threat to counter this tendency. Like any threat, it works best when not used often, but it must be used on occasion to make the threat credible. On the other hand, judicial accountability can operate as a strong impediment to peaceful negotiation of identity conflict, since leaders who know they will be tried are unlikely to find the prospect of a peace agreement inviting. As a result, indictments should be issued only once the subject is already captured.

Preemptive accountability needs to be considered in the extreme case where ethnic repression and genocide can be unambiguously traced to the long rule of an egregious dictator. He operates on a shrinking ethnic power base of his own in a hard, brittle state, alienating ever larger numbers of citizens but destroying the organized opposition and creating a vacuum around himself. Preventing genocide depends on removing the ruler: Hopes of reforming him are vain, and mere power sharing only prolongs the pain. Rulers are sacred objects in international relations, and although genocidal rulers have been removed, the onus and the action have lain on individual states, acting individually and discreetly applauded by the international community. Jean Bedel Bokassa, Idi Amin Dada, and Saddam Hussein were deposed, arresting targeted ethnic violence in the Central African Republic and Uganda in 1979 and Iraq in 2003, respectively. Since there were other cases for other reasons, some more criticized than others, preemptive account-ability is very much of a last-resort action. The single currently acceptable vehicle is judicial: the International Criminal Court (ICC) and its local affiliates or univer-sal jurisdiction exercised by individual states, but it is only a legitimizer, not an operative agent.

In any case, no action to enforce accountability on a sitting ruler should be undertaken in the absence of a mechanism to provide a legitimate successor, for the vacuum created will inevitably create even more deadly ethnic conflict. There are three nonmilitary ways of removing an egregious ruler—vote him out, talk him out, or buy him out (or a combination of them); the alternative is to take him out. Removal by election has the strong advantage of providing a successor and thereby limiting the dangers of a political vacuum, but it too often needs active intervention by external patrons to take effect. It was present in the deposition of Ferdinand Marcos in the Philippines in 1986, of Raoul Cedras—and arguably of Jean-Claude Duvallier—in Haiti in 1994 and 1986, and it could have been used against Samuel Doe in Liberia in 1985 or Robert Mugabe in 2008 (Zartman, 2005a). If elections are to be regarded as a valued means of stability and succession, there should be no hesitation over forceful negotiation to enforce them when necessary; a few crucial enforcements work to reduce the need for similar actions in subsequent instances.

It is difficult to assess the judicial use of preventive accountability, since it is hard to find instances where the threat of indictment kept an identity conflict from escalating. Cases of failure are clear enough: The threat of indictment by the ICC in 2008 did not prevent Sudanese President Omar al-Bashir from pursuing a policy of involving wide-spread killing of Sudanese citizens in Darfur or Joseph Kony of the Lord's Resistance Army from similar operations in northern Uganda (and then in Congo and Southern Sudan as well), and it made them more resistant. Neither the ICC nor the UNSC had the wisdom to indict President Robert Mugabe of Zimbabwe on charges of crimes against humanity, authorizing his removal before the black hole he created would suck in neighboring regions and countries. In an instance of popular (nonjudicial) accountability, the violent overthrow of Nicolas Ceaucescu at the end of 1989, reported on CNN, moved Beninois dictator Matthieu Kerekou to give way to the Sovereign National Conference in 1993.

Analyses

The following chapters use these ideas to pursue this analysis of crucial aspects in the negotiation of identity conflict prevention. The study is advanced in two parts, introduced by an analysis of the roots and prevention of genocide and related mass violence by Ervin Staub. He develops an account of the ways in which identity conflicts emerge, evolve, and escalate, and the corresponding ways in which that escalation can be arrested by appropriate, early personal and societal interactions, including engagement by bystanders.

Part Two then examines the internal dynamics of the parties and the way in which they affect the strategies arrayed to prevent identity conflict and its escalation. William Donohue presents the Identity Trap, a sort of security dilemma, into which competing identity groups fall and so tighten their own identity needs and fixations. Early awareness of vulnerable situations and action are needed to hold back the fears that start the cycle moving. Jesús Romero-Trillo continues to discuss the use of language in portraying identity, with the goal of establishing *otherization* to rally support for one's own identity and thus set in motion the security dilemma of fear that Donohue identifies. With this background, he identifies as the preventive target the self-justifying way in which language is used. Identity is also affected by the way groups are treated by the government; it can be constructed out of inchoate elements and heightened by repression, in a self-sustaining cycle of prejudices and violence, as analyzed by Ariel Macaspac Penetrante. But left to themselves by weak state capabilities, awaked groups can handle their own welfare and security rather then escalating the formative violence. These characteristics are dynamic, however, and they change in their effect on the shape of an agreement as the conflict proceeds. So do diasporas, the overseas elements of identity groups. Fen Osler Hampson shows how such separated segments have their own dynamics, which can both exacerbate conflict and be helpful in the reconciliation process, as their own attitudes change within constant identities.

Thus, in seeking the development of an interparty pact, the mediator will have to face intraparty divisions. The tendency of internal dynamics will be to engage in outbidding, as leadership challenges escalate both up to and during negotiations. Jannie Lilja examines the characteristics of outbidding, in both deed and discourse, and its effect on the search for agreements that prevent the further escalation of conflict. This requires an active mediation initiative, bringing the mediator into the very dynamics of the leadership conflict. Active mediation to help the parties develop a more coherent internal position and enable them to convey a fuller understanding of their grievance to the opponent in the identity conflict is further pursued by Jay Rothman, who turns the party focus of the negotiation analysis around and brings out the need for the mediator to engage the parties in internal examinations of grievances before attempting to bring the two sides together to handle their conflict. The parties who make up a side need to come to agreement on their own positions, the reasons why they feel wounded by the other in the past, and the nature of their disagreement with their opponent in order then to reconcile with the Other in agreements on future relations. A key to the development of a coherent position and an ability to negotiate is the degree of institutionalization and sensitivity to risk, as discussed by Marie-Joëlle Zahar. Changes in the structure of the parties as the conflict evolves are likely to bring about changes in their attitudes, producing distinctions between responsible representatives and spoilers and opening the way to more effective tactics of prevention. On the other hand, a key to the development of resistance to negotiation and the escalation of the conflict is the tendency to intraparty leadership rivalry and outbidding.

Part Three then turns to the conditions of third-party intervention and mediation, introduced by a chapter by Joshua Smilovitz that turns the previous discussion around and lays out the nature of the identity issues and the requirements and capacities of an effective mediator. Thereafter, steps in the process are described, including understanding the conflict, finding appropriate parties, developing strategies and then tactics, and implementation and verification. The mediator needs to recognize the parties as they appear and find the most appropriate partner to deal with in negotiating a future pact for overcoming identity conflict, as laid out by Moty Cristal in the concept of *partnerism*. Successful prevention of escalation depends on working with representative, legitimate, capable, accountable, responsible spokespersons, despite the wishes of the mediator or the opposing party for a more agreeable partner. Frank Pfetsch examines the conditions for internal compared to external conflict management, finding that mediation is more practiced and more successful in the latter than in identity cases. However, the mediator matters, David Cunningham shows. By examining who gets what in mediated identity conflicts, he shows that mediators have a greater effect on the outcome than does battlefield strength, and that parties' evaluation of outcomes continues after the agreement to settle the conflict, with important implications for its stability. Franz Cede lays out the evolving dispositions of international law that govern the possibilities and responsibilities of intervention and protection. The advent of humanitarian intervention, and then of the responsibility to protect, weakens the walls of sovereignty and enlarges the possibilities of external assistance in the case of identity-based conflict, but the thresholds, conditions, and limitations of such action are still under vigorous debate.

Peter Wallensteen, Erik Melander, and Frida Möller examine more closely the role of international organizations, concentrating on peacekeeping, preventive diplomacy, and sanctions. These measures, like others that are available, have been effective on occasion and are most effective when coordinated. A specific agency that works on identity conflicts is the Organization for Security and Cooperation in Europe's (OSCE) High Commissioner on National Minorities (HCNM). As presented by Fedor Meerts and Tassos Coulaloglou, the HCNM is a model intervener in identity conflict, seeking entry early, pursuing delicate mediation whenever possible and direct negotiation when the aggrieved party is in a weak position. Reconciliation is the Commissioner's goal, and his effectiveness shows the real possibility of meaningful preventive intervention that leaves all sides in a better position afterward. The difficult challenges of mediating in identity conflicts can also be attenuated by mediators' attention to related aspects of relations, such as economic, territorial, or structural ones, as well as by a range of approaches to identity groups' status—subjection, cooperation, or separation and their subforms. Mark Anstey discusses pacting on the basis of experience in Africa.

In Part Four, the book ends with lessons for theory and for practice, drawn by the editors. The management of fear and repression and the selection of appropriate partners are two crucial elements in reducing identity conflict, either as prevention or as a path to resolution. Measures to bring attitudinal change and measures to bring structural change are explored as ways of both preventing movement down the slippery slope to genocide and restoring societies that have had a close brush with it. The same theme is joined in lessons for practice. Identity groups do not have to lose their identities but rather to seek new methods of expressing them in a way that accommodates the identity needs of others and does not threaten them. It is not a matter of resolving identity differences in themselves as much as designing social and political systems that reduce perceptions of threat or injustice and, over time, transform relations from destructive competition to more collaborative forms. This requires that all identity groups achieve a sense of legitimacy and respect, becoming partners in a new order of mutual accommodation.

Notes

1. For a discussion of the difference between genocide and mass killings see Semelin (2002).

2. This section draws on I. William Zartman, *Preventing Identity Conflicts Leading to Genocide and Mass Killing* (New York: International Peace Institute, 2010).

3. For the reasons for lack of early action, see Zartman and Faure (2005, chap. 1).

References

Anstey, M. (1993). *Practical peace-making: a mediator's handbook*. Cape Town, South Africa: Juta.

Anstey, M. (2006). *Managing Change, Negotiating Conflict*. Cape Town: Juta.

Arnson, C., & Zartman, I. W., (Eds.). (2005). *Rethinking the economics of war: The intersection of need, creed and greed*. Washington: Woodrow Wilson Center Press; Baltimore: Johns Hopkins University Press.

Avenhaus, R., & Sjöstedt, G. (Eds.). (2009). *Negotiating risk*. Berlin: Springer.

Azzam, S. (1974). Palestinian. *New Outlook*, (pp. 20–26).

BanKi-Moon (2009). Implementing the responsibilty to protect, Report of the Secretary-General. UN General Assembly A/63/677 of 12 January 2009.

Barbujani, G. (1996). Genetic Variation Within and Among Human Beings. In Bekker, S. and Carlton, D. (Eds.) *Racism, Xenophobia and Ethnic Conflict*. Durban, Indicator Press. (pp. 119–138).

Bercovitch, J. (2007). Mediation. In I. W. Zartman (Ed.), *Peacemaking in international conflict* (pp. 163–194). USIP.

Bloomfield, D. (1998). Northern Ireland. In Harris, P. and Reilly, B. (Eds.), *Democracy and Deep-rooted Conflict: options for negotiators*. Stockholm: International Institute for Democracy and Electoral Assistance.

Burleigh, M. (2006). *Sacred causes: Religion and politics from the European dictators to al Qaeda*. London: Harper Perennial.

Carment, D., & Schnable, A. (Eds.). (2004). *Conflict prevention from rhetoric to reality*. Lanham MD: Lexington.

Chalk, F., & Jonassohn, K. (1990). *The history and sociology of genocide*. New Haven, CT, and London: Yale University Press.

Civico, A. (2010). Eluding peace? Negotiating with the ELN. In. I. W. Zartman & G. O. Faure (Eds.), *Engaging extremists* (pp. 254–272). Washington DC: USIP.

Collier, P. et al. (2003). *The conflict trap*. Washington:World Bank; Baltimore: Johns Hopkins University Press.

Cortright, D., (Ed.). (1997). *The price of peace*. Lanham, MD: Rowman & Littlefield.

Cronin, A. (2008). *How terrorism ends*. Princeton: Princeton University Press.

Daalder, I., & O'Hanlon, M. (2000). *Winning ugly: NATO's war to save Kosovo*. Washington, DC: Brookings Institution.

Davies, J. (1962). Toward a theory of revolution. *American Sociological Review*, 27(1): 5–18.

Evans, G., & Sahnoun, M. (Eds.) (2001). *The responsibility to protect*. Ottawa: International Commission of Intercention and State Sovereignty.

Fai, D. (2010). *Solution of Kashmir lies in a peaceful and negotiated settlement*. Retrieved 10 January 2010, from, kacouncil@kashmiri.com

Faure, G. O. & Zartman, I. W. (Eds.) (2010). *Negotiating with Terrorists: Strategy, Tactics and Politics*. London: Routledge.

Fein, H. (1990). Genocide: A sociological perspective. *Current Sociology*, 38(1), 56–78.

Goerzig, C. (2010). *Mediating identity conflicts*. Berghof Occasional Paper No. 30. Berlin: Berghof Conflict Research.

Guest, R. (2004). *The Shackled Continent*. London: Macmillan.

Gurr, T. (1970). *Why men rebel*. Princeton, NJ: Princeton University Press.

Hanf, T. (1989). The prospects of accommodation in communal conflicts. In H. Giliomee & L. Schlemmer (Eds.), *Negotiating South Africa's future* (pp. 89–113). Johannesburg: Southern Book Publishers.

Harf, B. (2003). No lessons learned from the Holocaust? Assessing risks of genocide and political mass murder since 1955. *American Political Science Review, 97*(1), 57–73.

Hocker, J., & Wilmot, W., (2000). *Interpersonal conflict* (6th ed.). New York: McGraw-Hill.

Hofstede, G., & Hofstede, G. (2005). *Cultures and organizations: software of the mind.* New York: McGraw Hill.

Huntington, S. (1998). *Clash of civilizations and the remaking of world order.* New York: Simon & Schuster.

Ivanov, A., & Nyheim, D., (2004). Generating the means to an end. In D. Carment & A. Schnable (Eds.), *Conflict prevention from rhetoric to reality* (pp. 163–176). Lanham MD: Lexington.

Kaufmann, C. (1996). Possible and impossible solutions to ethnic civil wars. *International Security, 20*(4): 136–175.

Laitin, D. D. (2006). *Nations, states and violence.* Oxford: Oxford University Press.

Lake, David & Rothchild, Donald (Eds.) (1998). *The International Spread of Ethnic Conflict.* Princeton NJ: Princeton University Press.

Lijphart, A. (1972). *Democracy in plural societies.* (New Haven: Yale university Press).

Meerts, Paul (2005). Entrapment in international negotiation. In I. W. Zartman & G. O. Faure (Eds.), *Escalation and Negotiation in International Conflicts.* Cambridge: Cambridge University Press.

Modiano, G. (1996). The Old and the New Concept of Race. In Bekker, S. and Carlton, D. (eds) *Racism, Xenophobia and Ethnic Conflict.* Durban: Indicator Press. (pp. 139–157).

Mutwol, J. (2009). *Peace agreements and civil wars in Africa.* Amherst: Cambria.

Nathan, L. (1996). Analyse, Empower, Accommodate. *Track Two,* September 4–6.

O'Brien, J. (2005). The Dayton agreement in Bosnia. In I. W. Zartman & V. Kremenyuk (Eds.), *Peace vs. justice* (pp. 89–112). Lanham, MD: Rowman & Littlefield.

Olson, M. (1965). *The logic of collective action.* New York: Schocken Books.

Posner, B. (1993). The security dilemma and ethnic conflict. In Michael Brown (Ed.), *Ethnic Conflict and International Security.* Princeton: Princeton University Press.

Pruitt, D. G., & Kim, S. H. (2004). *Social conflict.* New York: McGraw-Hill.

Kennedy, G. (Eds.), *Ethnic preference and pubic policy in developing states.* Boulder, Co: Lynne Rienner.

Rothchild, D. (2009). Ethnicity, negotiation, and conflict management. In J. Bercovitch, V. Kremenyuk, & I. W. Zartman (Eds.), *The SAGE handbook of conflict resolution* (pp. 246–263). Sage.

Sacks, J. (2003). *The dignity of difference.* London: Continuum.

Sémelin, J., (2002). *Analyser le massacre: Réflexions comparatives.* Questions de recherche no. 7 Paris: CÉRI.

Sereny, G. (1996). Albert Speer: his battle with truth. Knopf.

Sezibera, R. (2007, December 2). The problem isn't ethnic. Sunday Times, SA.

Shapley, L. S. & Shubik, M. (1954). A method for evaluating the distribution of power in a committee system. *American Political Science Review, 48*(3): 787–792.

Sisk, T. (1995). *Democratization in South Africa: The elusive social contract.* Princeton: Princeton University Press.

Smock, D. & Smith, A. (2008). *Managing a mediation process.* Washington: USIP.

Solzenhitzyn, A. (1974). The Gulag Archipelago. Glasgow, Collins.

Staub, E., (1989). *The roots of evil: The origins of genocide and other group violence.* Cambridge: Cambridge University Press.

Stedman, S. J. (2000). Spoiler problems in peace processes. In Paul Stern & Daniel Druckman (Eds.) *International Conflict Resolution after the Cold War* (pp. 178–224). Washington: National Academy Press.

Straus, S. (2007). Second-generation comparative research on genocide. *World Politics*, 59(3): 476–501.

Straus, S. (2001). Contested meanings and conflicting imperatives: A conceptual analysis of genocide. *Journal of Genocide Research*, 3(3): 349–375.

Tajfel, H., & Turner, J.C. (1986). The social identity theory of inter-group behavior. In Worchel, S. and Austin, L.W. (Eds.). *Psychology of Intergroup Relations*. Chicago: Nelson Hall.

Touval, S., & Zartman, I. W. (Eds.). (1985). *International mediation in theory and practice*. Boulder, CO: Westview Press.

Touval, S., & Zartman, I. W. (2007). International mediation after the cold war. In C. Crocker, F. Hamson, & P. Aall (Eds.), *Leashing the dogs of war* (pp. 437–454). Washington, DC: United States Institute of Peace Press.

Ury, W. (1991). *Getting past no*. New York: Bantam Books.

Vasquez, J., & Valeriano, B. (2009). Territory as a source of conflict and a road to peace. In J. Bercovitch, V. Kremenyuk, & I. W. Zartman (Eds.), *The SAGE handbook of conflict resolution* (pp. 193–209) Sage.

Van Eck, J. (2008, November 18). Ignoring the ethnic cancer in the Congo precludes true peace. Sunday Times, SA. Retrieved from www.timeslive.co.za/sundaytimes/article88132.ece

Versi, A. (2008). The Lisbon EU–Africa summit: Africa stands firm. *African Business*, *338*, 12–18.

Zartman, I. W. (1989). *Ripe for resolution*. New York: Oxford University Press.

Zartman, I. W. (Ed.) (1995). *Elusive peace: Negotiating to end civil wars*. Washington, DC: Brookings Institution.

Zartman, I. W. (Ed.) (1997). *Governance as conflict management*. Washington: Brookings.

Zartman, I. W. (2005a). *Cowardly lions: Missed opportunities to prevent deadly conflict and state collapse*. Boulder, CO: Lynne Rienner.

Zartman, I. W. (2005b). Analyzing intractability. In C. Crocker, F. O. Hampson, & P. Aall (Eds.), *Grasping the nettle* (pp. 47–64). Washington, DC: United States Institute of Peace Press.

Zartman, I. W. (2010). *Preventing identity conflicts leading to genocide and mass killings*. New York: International Peace Institute.

Zartman, I. W., & deSoto, A. (2010). *Timing mediation initiatives*. Washington DC: USIP

Zartman, I. W., & Faure, G. O. (Eds.). (2005). *The dynamics of escalation and negotiation*. Cambridge: Cambridge University Press.

Zartman, I. W. & Faure, G. O. (Eds.) (2011). *Engaging extremists: Trade-offs, timing and diplomacy*. Washington: USIP.

Zartman, I. W., & Alfredson, T. (2010). Negotiating with terrorists and the tactical question. In R. Reuveny & W. Thompson (Eds.) *New views on terrorism* (pp. 247–286). Syracuse, NY: Syracuse University Press.

2 The Roots and Prevention of Genocide and Related Mass Violence

■ ERVIN STAUB

What are the motivations of perpetrators of genocide and mass killing? How do those motivations evolve, and how do inhibitions against killing whole groups of people decline? What are the instigating conditions, the characteristics of cultures and societies, and the psychology of perpetrators and bystanders that contribute? How can violence be prevented or, after violence has occurred, how can reconciliation be promoted so that new violence does not arise?

The influences leading to mass killing and genocide greatly overlap. The United Nations (UN) genocide convention defines genocides as "acts committed with intent to destroy in whole or in part, a national, ethnical, racial or religious group." The genocide convention does not appropriately clarify the meaning of "in part," that is, when killing *some* members of a group is genocide and when it is not, nor does it include the killing of political groups as genocide.

Among the many definitions of genocide that have been offered since the publication of the UN genocide convention, mine comes closest to that of Helen Fein (1993b, p. 24), who defined genocide as "sustained, purposeful action by a perpetrator to physically destroy a collectivity directly or indirectly, through interdiction of the biological and social reproduction of group members, sustained regardless of the surrender or lack of threat offered by the victim." In my definition, "a government or some group acts to eliminate a whole group of people, whether by directly killing them or by creating conditions that lead to their death or inability to reproduce" (Staub, 2011, p. 100). In contrast to genocide, I see mass killing as "killing (or in other ways destroying) members of a group without the intention to eliminate the whole group, or killing large numbers of people" without a focus necessarily on group membership (Staub, 1989, p. 8).

Violence and its psychological and social bases evolve progressively. When the conditions that lead to mass violence are present and an evolution is in progress, one cannot predict which of these kinds of violence might be the outcome (Staub, 2011). Moreover, mass killing, which makes later genocide more likely (Harff, 2003), can be a way station to genocide. Therefore, prevention must focus on preventing increasing violence between groups, not specifically genocide. In actuality, a focus on genocide has become a problem. While the international community usually remains passive even in the face of genocide, it feels even less obligated to act in the face of mass killing or intense mutual violence. Arguing about definitions, nations and the UN tend to resist calling a genocide what it is in order to avoid the obligation to act.

Genocide is the result of a combination of influences. These include the conditions in a society, the characteristics of its culture, their psychological effects and the social processes they give rise to, the political system, the evolution of increasing violence and its psychological and social bases, and the passivity or complicity of internal and external bystanders. The more of these influences are present and the fewer of those that can inhibit the evolution, the more likely that genocide will take place. Halting genocide once it begins and preventing mass violence when predictors suggest that it is about to begin are essential tasks. However, early prevention is less costly in both human and material terms (Lund, 2009; Staub, 2011). It has rarely been used but would certainly be more effective by inhibiting or even transforming the influences that lead to mass violence. It must become the aim of the international community.[1]

■ INSTIGATORS OR STARTING POINTS AND THEIR PSYCHOLOGICAL AND SOCIAL EFFECTS

Difficult life conditions include severe economic problems, great political disorganization within a society, or great, rapid social changes and their combinations. Harff (2003) notes that poverty is not associated with genocide. However, case studies show that a *deterioration* of economic conditions can be a starting point for group violence (Davies, 1962; Gurr, 1970; Staub, 1989). Moreover, inequality between groups, of which poverty is an important aspect, can give rise to social processes that lead to violence.

Difficult life conditions have an intense psychological impact on people. They frustrate basic, universal psychological needs for security, positive identity, feelings of effectiveness and control, a positive connection to people, autonomy and comprehension of reality (Staub, 1989, 2003, 2011). Difficult life conditions and the frustration of basic needs are starting points that can give rise to further psychological and social/group processes that satisfy these psychological needs to various extents, but they don't address the actual societal problems and begin an evolution toward group violence.

In response to the difficulties of life, individuals tend to turn to groups for identity, security, and belonging. They tend to elevate their group by devaluing other groups, and over time by acting to diminish others. They scapegoat another group as a way of protecting their self-image or identity, and maintaining their understanding of the world in the face of the helplessness created by intense life problems. Ideologies are developed that offer hope and a vision of a better life (nationalism, communism, Nazism, Hutu power in Rwanda, and so on), but they are destructive in that they identify enemies who must be "dealt with" (which often means, in the end, that they must be destroyed) in order to fulfill the ideology. Scapegoating and destructive ideologies turn the group against others. People can respond to the frustration of basic needs in positive ways—for example, by joining together with a constructive vision for a better future. But to address the real difficulties of life is challenging and requires time and persistence. Instead, especially in the presence of certain cultural characteristics, people at times join in groups or turn to leaders who move them toward the destructive satisfaction of these needs through scapegoating and destructive ideologies. These initiate a group process that becomes a starting point for an evolution that can lead to mass violence (see Faure, 2008; Staub, 1989, 2003, 2011).

Most aspects of difficult life conditions have joined in well-known cases of mass violence. There had been significant economic deterioration in Germany before the Nazis came to power, in Rwanda, in the former Yugoslavia, and even in the Darfur region of the Sudan. There was political confusion and political and social changes in these countries before mass violence began.

Conflict between groups, especially identity groups, is another instigating condition or starting point. The study of group conflict and genocide have been separate disciplines, partly perhaps because it was the Holocaust, the genocide of the Jews, that was the early and most studied case of genocide. There was no actual conflict between Germans and Jews preceding the Holocaust, except in the minds of the Nazis. However, group conflict, especially as it becomes persistent, intractable and violent, is often the instigating condition or starting point for genocide (Staub, 2011).

Conflict can involve vital material interests, such as the need for territory as living space or for water as a resource. A material conflict of a different kind, between a dominant and a subordinate group in a society, has been a source of mass violence in many instances since 1945 (Fein, 1993a). However, even when conflicts have objective material elements, they usually also have psychological elements, such as devaluation of the other group and mistrust and fear of the other. Moreover, over time, if conflict persists, and becomes violent and intractable (not yielding to resolution), these psychological elements develop further and become more intense. The conflict frustrates basic needs. The other group comes to be seen as responsible for the conflict, as at fault, and as immoral, while one's own cause is seen as just and one's group as moral (Bar-Tal, 2000; Crocker, Hampson, & Aall 2004, 2005; Kelman & Fisher, 2003). These psychological elements, present in both groups and mirror images of each other, make the conflict especially difficult to resolve.

Frequently, issues of identity are present or increasingly enter. Groups with less power, access, privilege, and wealth often differ in ethnicity, race, or religion from those with more of these attributes. Differences in language and culture—values, beliefs, standards of conduct, perception and interpretation of events, how much focus there is on particular basic needs such as connection, identity or autonomy—can be further bases of differentiation. Demands by a less privileged group for greater rights, for the use of language or other aspects of identity, or for greater participation in society tend to be resisted by the more powerful. In the course of this resistance, elements of either group may initiate violence.

Here also, ideologies enter. The protection by the more powerful of their rights and privilege is usually supported by ways of seeing the world that justify their greater rights or privilege—by their intelligence, diligence, past accomplishments, or inherent superiority. Thus, dominant groups protect not only their rights and privilege but also their identity, their place in the world, and their comprehension of reality. Researchers have explored legitimizing ideologies, such as a social dominance orientation that justifies the dominance of those with power and privilege

(Sidanius & Pratto, 1999), and system justification, which justifies whatever social arrangements exist (Jost, Banaji, & Nosek, 2004), and found that they have wide-ranging influence.

Conquest was common in earlier times, and mass killing was associated with it (Kiernen, 2007), driven by material interest or the desire of nations and their leaders to elevate themselves. In modern times, superior groups have engaged in practices, whether direct violence or creating conditions that destroy a group's environment and what that group needs to sustain its life, to exploit land for its natural resources or for other uses. Indigenous groups have suffered greatly, and have sometimes been extinguished, through development practices in areas where they lived (Totten, Parsons, & Charny, 1997). In such conflicts, driven by self-interest, difficult life conditions are not necessary as an instigator. However, devaluation of a group and other influences that contribute to mass violence are invariably present.

Genocides often take place in the context of war. Sometimes genocide is directed against the opponent in the war, as in the civil war in Rwanda (where, at the time the genocide began, there was a cease-fire). At other times, the victim is a party not involved in the war, as in the Holocaust. War represents significant evolution of violence, which makes further violence easier. In addition, war can be a cover under which it is easier to turn against a group toward which intense hostility has already evolved, and/or which has been identified as an ideological enemy.

Group conflict and difficult life conditions often join as instigators. Difficult life conditions can intensify the dissatisfaction of less privileged groups. However, it is not necessary for both conditions to be present. Before the Holocaust there was no actual conflict between Germans and Jews, the latter a peaceful minority in Germany, except in the mind of the Nazis. In contrast, there was a long history of conflict between Hutus and Tutsis in Rwanda. The difference between Hutus and Tutsis is a combination of historical difference in wealth and power and, to an unclear degree, ethnicity (des Forges, 1999; Mamdani, 2001; Staub, 2011). The clear difference is that of identity. Before 1959 the Tutsis were dominant, their dominance enhanced, and the Hutus oppressed under Belgian overrule. After a revolution in 1959, the Hutus in power devalued, discriminated against, and occasionally engaged in mass killing of Tutsis. Before the genocide in 1994 there were severe economic problems, political chaos, and a civil war.

■ THE EVOLUTION OF DESTRUCTIVENESS

Intense violence does not just spring up; hostility and violence evolve and intensify. This evolution is avoided or halted if all subgroups of a society work together to address difficult conditions of life or if groups are committed to resolve conflict through negotiation and mutual concessions. Such constructive modes of fulfilling needs and addressing differences often are not used. Instead, groups engage in scapegoating, create destructive ideologies, blame each other for their conflict, and begin to harm each other. This can start a psychological and behavioral evolution. Individuals and whole groups "learn by doing." As they harm others, perpetrators and the whole society they are part of begin to change. This evolution can be one-sided or, in the case of violent conflict, mutual.

People who harm others have to justify their actions. They devalue those they have harmed; they get accustomed to or habituate to discrimination and violence against them. Both perpetrators and passive bystanders, who know what is happening but take no action against it, tend to do this. They engage in *just-world* thinking—believing that the world is a just place and that those who suffer must somehow deserve their suffering (Lerner, 1980). Increasing devaluation leads to *moral exclusion*, the exclusion of the victimized group from the moral realm, that is, from the realm of people to whom moral values and standards apply (Fein, 1979; Opotow, 1990; Staub, 1989, 2011). Perpetrators of violence may also replace moral values that protect people's welfare and life with other values, such as obedience to authority or loyalty to the group. As a final step, there may be a *reversal of morality*: killing members of the designated enemy group becomes the right thing to do. As the evolution progresses, individuals change and the norms of social behavior change. New laws and new institutions may be created to support actions against the victims, such as special offices to deal with them and paramilitary groups (Staub, 1989, 2011).

In some cases, one can see a continuous progression of this kind. But often there are breaks, periods of time when there is no further evolution. However, the elements that have developed remain part of the deep structure of the culture, and as conditions change, the evolution can restart. For example, in the Holocaust, the Nazis used both devaluative propaganda against Jews and symbols, such as the yellow star they were forced to wear, that were used in much earlier historical periods. In Turkey there was a mass killing of Armenians in 1894–1896, followed by the genocide in 1915–1916. In Rwanda there was repeated mass killing of Tutsis before the genocide. Earlier mass killing is especially dangerous, since it makes mass killing and genocide conceivable and psychologically accessible (Staub, 2011; see also Harff, 2003).

■ CULTURAL CHARACTERISTICS THAT MAKE DESTRUCTIVE MODES OF NEED FULFILLMENT MORE LIKELY

Certain characteristics of a culture make it more likely that in a difficult time, or in the face of group conflict, the psychological reactions and events that have been described will take place.

"Us and them" thinking, cultural devaluation, and ideologies of antagonism are core influences in mass violence. The devaluation can be less intense (the other is lazy, less intelligent, and so on) or increasingly intense (the other is manipulative, morally bad, dangerous, an enemy that intends to destroy one's own group). Laboratory research shows that even when people are not a threat, just hearing them derogated can lead to more harmful actions against them (Bandura, Underwood, & Fromson, 1975). Cases studies of genocides suggest that groups that are seen as morally bad or a threat, especially if they nonetheless do relatively well in a society—such as the Jews in Germany, the Tutsis in Rwanda, and the Armenians in Turkey—are especially likely to become victims (Staub, 1989).

The tendency to categorize people into "us" and "them" is strong. It can have trivial bases. Identities can be formed around small differences. Sometimes hostility against those who differ only slightly from one's own group is especially intense. Anti-Semitism may have developed out of the need of early Christians to create a separate identity. The Bolsheviks hated the Mensheviks, who differed from them only in limited ways, and heretics have been intensely persecuted.

Sometimes two groups develop intense mutual hostility. They see the other as their enemy and themselves as an enemy of the other. Being an enemy of the other becomes part of their identity. This makes intense violence easier and more likely. An *ideology of antagonism* can develop as part of an evolution of violence, or it can be a relatively stable aspect of groups' orientation to each other that has developed over an earlier historical period (Staub, 1989, 2011).

Overly strong respect for authority in a society makes it difficult for people to deal with instigating conditions. Accustomed to being led, they are more likely to turn to leaders and ideological groups. They are unlikely to offer opposition when their group increasingly harms another group. They are also more likely to follow direct orders to engage in violence. Nazi Germany, Rwanda, and most other countries in which genocide or mass killing were perpetrated were countries where the culture, child-rearing practices, and hierarchical social organizations fostered and maintained strong respect for authority.

A monolithic (versus a pluralistic) culture and autocratic political systems facilitate destructive responses to difficult life conditions or group conflict. The more varied are the values in a society and the more freedom there is to express them, the less likely is a genocidal process to evolve; people will be more likely to oppose the evolution toward genocide. This is one aspect of pluralism. Another is that members of all groups in a society have the right and the possibility to participate in the public domain(Staub, 2011); that they have a voice, access to the media, can participate in business life and political processes. Pluralism and authority orientation are a matter of both culture and the system of government. Mass killing—violence against large numbers of people who may be members of various identity groups but who are regarded as political opponents or enemies, as well as mass violence of other kinds—is more likely in autocratic political systems and can be pursued under such systems as government policy (Fein, 2007; Rummell, 1994). Democracies are unlikely to engage in genocide; this is especially true of mature democracies, with civic institutions that have deepened democracy. However, the U.S. and other democracies have supported repressive dictatorships that engage in violence against their people. They also at times engage in violence or war, especially against nondemocratic countries (Staub, 2011).

Unhealed wounds from past victimization or suffering have severe psychologically effects. Groups often focus on past trauma, which becomes a lens through which they see the world (Volkan, 1997, 1998). When a group has been victimized in the past, healing is important to prevent further violence. Without healing, the group will continue to feel diminished and vulnerable and see the world as a dangerous place. At times of difficulty or in the face of new conflict, such groups may feel an intense need to protect themselves. They may engage in what they think of as necessary self-defense, which, instead, could be the perpetration of violence against others (Staub, 1998, 2011).

A history of aggression in a society as a means of resolving conflict makes violence accessible as a way of responding to new conflict or to the hostility that evolves from difficult life conditions. Both statistical analysis of a large number of cases (Harff, 2003) and case studies (Staub, 1989; 2011) indicate that past violence in a society makes renewed violence more likely.

■ WITNESSES' OR BYSTANDERS' ROLES IN WORSENING IDENTITY CONFLICTS

The passivity of bystanders, of witnesses who are in a position to know (but often close their eyes to) what is happening and are in a position to take some kind of action, greatly encourages perpetrators. It helps them believe that what they are doing is right. Unfortunately, bystanders are often passive. By continuing with business as usual, both internal and external bystanders often become complicit in the violence.

Internal bystanders participate in the discriminatory system set up against victims. Like perpetrators, they tend to justify their passivity by devaluation, just world thinking, and other methods. They also undergo an evolution and contribute to the evolution toward violence in their group or society. These bystanders, who are members of the same society as the perpetrators, have also internalized the cultural devaluation of the victim group and the respect for authority. In addition, it is difficult to oppose one's group, especially at a time of severe life problems or group conflict. To reduce their empathy, which makes them suffer, and their feeling of guilt, bystanders often distance themselves from victims (Staub, 1989, 2011). As they change, some bystanders become perpetrators (Lifton, 1986).

External bystanders, outside groups and other nations, also tend to remain passive, continue with business as usual, or even support the perpetrators. For example, U.S. corporations and those of other countries continued to do business in Germany during the 1930s in spite of the increasing persecution of Jews and the brutality of the Nazi regime against all those it saw as enemies. France supported the Rwandan government during the civil war militarily, in spite of the tremendous hate propaganda against the Tutsis and the occasional killing of large numbers of Tutsi civilians, and continued to support the government during the genocide (Malvern, 2004). France also helped the perpetrators escape when the genocide was brought to an end by a Tutsi-led rebel group, and allowed them to take their arms with them, including heavy equipment. The perpetrators' subsequent attacks on Rwanda were an important reason for the war in neighboring Zaire, renamed the Democratic Republic of the Congo, which has continued for many years, by 2011 resulting in close to 6 million deaths. Nations have traditionally not seen themselves as moral agents. They have used national interest—defined as wealth, power, and influence—as their guiding value. Sometimes old ties to a country and to a particular group within it lead some nations to support the perpetrators—as in the case of French support for the Rwandan government—rather than the people who are being harmed (Staub, 2011).

Leaders and elites have important roles in shaping and influencing societal conditions. To a large extent, it is the inclinations of populations, the result of conditions in the society, group conflict, and the characteristics of culture, that create the possibility and likelihood of mass killing or genocide. People select or turn to leaders who respond to their inclinations and fulfill their needs at the time. On the other hand, leaders already in power, or newly arising leaders, including leaders of ideological movements, are both themselves affected by existing conditions and use these conditions for their own purposes.

These leaders can attempt to deal with problems in a society and the causes of conflicts between groups using peaceful, constructive means. Or they can look for enemies and engage in actions that instigate violence. They can scapegoat and offer destructive ideologies, using propaganda to intensify negative images and create or strengthen hostility toward potential victims. They can create hate media, paramilitary groups, and other institutions to promote hostility and serve violence. Often leaders are seen as doing these things purely to gain support or enhance their power. For prevention, it is important to see them as members of their society, impacted by life conditions and group conflict and, at least in part, acting to satisfy their own and the population's basic psychological needs. However, there can be truly destructive leaders as well. Both leaders and other perpetrators can be—*sleepers* (Steiner, 1980), people who act in normal ways in normal times but have an inclination to hostility and violence that can emergence at times of social chaos and disorganization (see also Zartman, 1989).

■ PREVENTION OF INTENSE VIOLENCE BETWEEN GROUPS

Halting Violence and Late Prevention

When there has already been significant violence or when the predictors described above are present at a significant level, so that large-scale violence can be expected, decisive action is essential. With regard to such late prevention, as well as early prevention, important questions are what is to be accomplished, how it is to be done, and who is to do it.

In responding to a crisis and halting already occurring mass violence, actions that aim at prevention include threats to leaders/countries, sanctions and boycotts, and, as a last resort, military intervention. Often none of this is done, or it is done too late or ineffectively. For example, nothing was done in Rwanda—except for many countries sending military personnel and aircraft to evacuate their own citizens, thereby telling the perpetrators that they could do as they wished to their own citizens (Hatzfeld, 2003; Malvern, 2004).

Sanctions and boycotts often do not work because some countries do not participate in them or abide by them. Also, while they can create great suffering in the population, as the boycott of Iraq under Saddam Hussein did (Richardson, 2006), leaders often don't care enough about the population and are themselves not sufficiently affected to change their policy. A newer approach to sanctions and boycotts is to focus on the leaders: their finances, bank accounts, and ability to travel. Broad-based sanctions may be more effective in countries that have a substantial industrial/business class whose interests are affected, and who can exert influence on the leaders and the political system, as was the case in South Africa. In addition, in South Africa, there were internal actors fighting the apartheid system, which has been found to be important for the effectiveness of sanctions.

At times, military intervention is essential. As the Task Force on the Prevention of Genocide, chaired by Madeleine Albright and William Cohen, indicated (Albright & Cohen, 2008), military intervention is a not an either/or matter. Military exercises in a neighboring country can discourage leaders and perpetrators. The presence of a sufficiently large peacekeeping force can do the same. In Macedonia in 2001, after fighting between the Albanian minority and the government forces, peacekeepers were helpful in creating time and space to address the issues between the parties. However, they may also have been effective because a number of early intervention processes were ongoing. These included efforts to overcome hostile attitudes in the population through newspaper articles showing the similarity in the lives of the members of the different ethnic groups in the country, as well as activities that prepared the ground for the government to create new laws addressing the grievances and enhancing the rights of the Albanian minority (Burg, 1997; Staub, 2011).

Often, to be effective, peacekeepers must have UN permission, training, and equipment to fight. But fighting has usually been contrary to UN rules and practice. Peacekeepers have been sent to inhibit violence by their presence or to keep peace already agreed to, at least on paper. When violence flared up, they were not to act and often could not even defend themselves. It has become increasingly clear that peacekeepers—perhaps paradoxically, given their name, but essential, given their intended function—need to be able to fight to keep the peace. Moreover, for military intervention, as the action of last resort, a ready rapid strike force ought to be created. This needs to be a standing force under UN control, since nations are often reluctant to contribute their own soldiers even in an extreme crisis. While there is international resistance to creating such a military unit, it is essential.

Varied forms of preparedness are necessary to halt ongoing violence or to respond to crises. The Task Force Report indicates that there is no agency in the U.S. government to address crises of genocide or mass atrocities and no plans of action that could be drawn on in emergencies. This is certainly also true of other countries.

While threats, sanctions and boycotts, peacekeeping, and military intervention may at times all be necessary, even at a late point, human interaction, engagement, dialogue, negotiation, and mediation need to be attempted. In cases of late prevention, for preventive diplomacy to be effective, high-level actors must be involved. In Kenya in 2008, following disputed election results, as violence between groups began, the involvement of the former Secretary-General of the UN, Kofi Annan, foreign ministers of various countries including the United States, and presidents of neighboring countries led to a speedy agreement on power sharing (Carson, 2008). Although this agreement did not solve long-standing problems, it brought the violence to an end. Such conflict management is essential as a prelude to conflict resolution. Very-high-level leaders, such as the U.S. president, are usually reluctant to get involved this way, presumably concerned that failure to resolve a crisis or halt violence will reflect badly on them. But their involvement can make a huge difference.

UN officials ignored the entreaties of General Romeo Dallaire, the head of the UN peacekeeping force who was warned about plans for the genocide in Rwanda, to be allowed to search for and destroy the machetes that were the intended means and eventually became the primary means of genocide. What might have happened if, at that time, under the auspices of the UN or of several individual nations, influential external leaders had engaged Rwandan leaders? And what might have happened if they had engaged France, the unconditional supporter of the Rwandan government (Malvern, 2004)? Or if President Bill Clinton had brought together leaders of powerful countries, as well as those of neighboring states, and Serb, Croat, and Bosnian leaders, when violence in the former Yugoslavia began (Staub, 2011)? Powerful leaders, especially if they are also respected and trusted, can have substantial influence in many cases.

Early Prevention

Early prevention can be initiated and fostered by external bystanders, but internal actors are crucial. Early prevention has to address the population, the leaders, and those in the society, such as the media, that can have both upward and downward influence (Lederach, 1997; Staub, 2011). One aim of early prevention is the creation of structures that will make violence less likely. These include structures in which people work together to achieve shared goals or democratic institutions that promote the participation of everyone in society and their fair treatment. However, even though, to some degree, institutions have a life of their own, it is people who create, maintain, and change institutions. The motivation to shape or create institutions that can prevent violence and promote peace requires psychological changes in people.

Early responses to difficult life conditions can limit their instigating power. The policies developed by the Roosevelt administration after the Great Depression limited its economic impact on people. By providing people with jobs, these policies also increased the sense of a shared community, with people facing their difficulties together and feeling that the country cared about them. Poor countries need financial help to address deteriorating economic conditions. However, their governments can still do a great deal to give people a sense of shared community and help to satisfy psychological needs for identity and connection, and through that to create a feeling of security.

Practices to create more positive attitudes toward the "other" are crucial for the prevention of violence. This is the case when there is "progress" in the evolution of violence against a potential victim group, such as increasing public devaluation and discrimination, as well as when there is increasing conflict between identity or interest groups.

One method for creating a more positive attitude is to promote *contact* between members of groups. A great deal of research in social psychology, and practical projects bringing members of hostile or prejudiced groups together, show that significant, deep contact creates more positive attitudes (for overviews, see Pettigrew & Tropp, 2006; Staub, 2011). Having people work together to bring about outcomes beneficial to both groups, through joint projects in the service of goals superordinate to their separate goals, is especially useful. The more conditions are created for such contact to occur naturally, the better. Hindus and Muslims working together in institutions, and having developed good working relations, have acted together in potentially explosive situations to prevent violence (Varshney, 2002). In schools that introduce cooperative learning, the deep engagement by majority and minority students with each other in the course of working together on tasks create positive attitudes and interactions (Aronson, Stephan, Sikes, Blaney, & Snapp, 1978). Anstey and Zartman (this volume) note, however, that contact between members of different groups living next to each other can also develop hostility. There are many reasons that people devalue each other, including differences in physical characteristics, culture, values and ways of life, or one group exploiting another and justifying their relationship by devaluation (Staub, 1996). People belonging to different groups often have very superficial contact (Deutsch, 1973); living next to each other without deep engagement, people can respond to differences and devalue each other more easily. Humanizing others by what we say about them, and deep contact are both essential to overcome devaluation.

Dialogue is an important form of contact. One aspect of dialogue is addressing practical issues between groups—for example, in problem-solving projects and workshops (Kelman, 2008). But a crucial aspect is to increase mutual understanding and trust, which then increases the ability of groups to resolve practical issues and abide by agreements.

Humanizing the other is extremely important in changing attitudes. Leaders can do this by the way they talk about the other group and the way they engage with its leaders. Schools can do it by treating children from all groups with respect, insisting that the children treat each other with respect, and by what they teach about each group. In Macedonia, one of the constructive preventive actions was having journalists from different ethnic groups come together, write about the lives of people in each of the groups, which were quite similar, and then publishing their articles in the newspapers of each ethnic group. Their articles humanized all the groups, and their contact with each other affected their later writing about group relations (Bug, 1997).

Healing the wounds of past victimization and certain collective memories make unnecessary violence by victims and renewed violence by perpetrators less likely. After group violence, healing is best approached through group activities, since violence and the experiences of victimization are group based, and often the societies are communal (Rosoux, 2001; Staub & Pearlman, 2006). The practices of healing can include testimonies by people of what has happened and shared commemoration in which all members of society participate. Too intense a focus on the painful past can be harmful, contributing to the development of a "chosen trauma"; in addition to grieving about the past, looking to a better future is valuable. Acknowledging the role of rescuers, members of the perpetrator group who have attempted to save lives at times of violence, can contribute to healing by both survivors and members of the perpetrator group. So can justice processes and understanding the roots of violence.

Even in cases of violence by one group against the other, the perpetrators tend to blame their victims. In the case of mutual violence, usually each group blames the other. They may emphasize different events in the past and differ especially in their interpretation of events. Coming to some form of shared view of history is an aspect of the resolution of conflict and makes new violence less likely (Rousoux, 2001; Staub, 2011; Zartman & Kremenyuk, 2005). This requires, in part, changes in a group's collective memory. Healing from past trauma makes this easier. The work of historians can be important. In Israel, the original collective memory held that Palestinians left during the war of 1948 to escape the violence or were encouraged by their leaders to leave for the duration of what they believed would be a short war. A group of new historians showed that this was partly true but also that many Palestinians were expelled (Morris, 2004). This new history slowly spread throughout Israeli society. In the wake of group conflict, commissions can be created to explore actual history and collective memory and to negotiate a shared history— which can require compromises (Staub, 2011).

Understanding the origins or influences leading to, and avenues for the prevention of, genocide, and of group violence based on identity and/or interests, can be a significant contributor to effective prevention. In work in Rwanda, in its first phase, my associates and I conducted workshops/trainings with varied groups (facilitators who work with community groups, national leaders, community leaders, and journalists). Two important elements of these trainings were promoting understanding of the influences that lead to group violence, along the lines described in this chapter, and describing its traumatic impact on people. Further elements were considering avenues to prevention as well as reconciliation, which can be both an aspect of prevention between hostile groups and an avenue to the prevention of renewed violence.

In trainings with mixed Tutsi/Hutu groups, participants heard lectures and extensively discussed ideas, which they intensely engaged with as they applied them to the genocide in Rwanda. We used examples from other settings, but they themselves explored the extent to which the influences we have discussed as leading to mass violence were present in Rwanda. This process seemed to lead to a deep *experiential understanding* of the influences leading to mass violence (Staub, 2006, 2011; Staub & Pearlman, 2006; Staub et al., 2005; Wolpe, 2005; Zartman & Kremenyuk, 2005). The nature of this training, discussing events of the past in relation to concepts, rather than focusing on who did what, creates positive engagement between members of hostile groups and limits the intensity of feelings. It could serve as a valuable preparation for conflict resolution practices, dialogue, and negotiation.

As an extension of these trainings, in collaboration with La Benevolencija, a Dutch nongovernmental organization (NGO), we developed educational radio programs, using the same conceptual material and approach, first in Rwanda and later in Burundi and the Congo as well (Staub, 2008, 2011; Staub, Pearlman, Weiss, & Hoek, unpublished). There have been several types of radio programs in each of these countries, including informational programs and programs about justice.

But a major type was radio drama, with educational content embedded in the story. In Rwanda, the program "Musekeweya" ("New Dawn") centered on a conflict between two villages, with all the elements of origins, and then, progressively, with elements of prevention and reconciliation infused in the story. Evaluation of the effects of the original training (Staub et al., 2005) and of the radio drama in Rwanda (Paluck, 2009; Staub, 2011; Staub & Pearlman, 2009; Staub, Pearlman & Bilali, 2010) showed changes in attitudes, such as a more positive orientation toward and more empathy with members of the other group, reduced trauma symptoms, and *conditional forgiveness,* as well as changes in behavior, such as more independence of authority and more willingness to speak out and engage in public discussion.

The way the press writes about events, and educational programs on radio and television, can inform people and make them aware of their potential influence as active bystanders. They can make it more likely that people will not passively stand by, but engage early, before destructive ideologies become extreme and violence evolves, and before action becomes highly dangerous. While each person has limited capacity to change the direction of a group, and while it was once difficult for people to exchange information and organize themselves, the Internet has made this easier—both for harmful actions, such as terrorism, and for positive action.

Constructive ideologies are an important means of prevention. The power of ideas is great, especially affect-laden ideas. Positive visions of social arrangements and human relations can give people hope in difficult times and in the midst of conflict. Constructive visions that embrace all groups and allow everyone to participate in their fulfillment can inhibit/overcome the power of destructive ones. Such a constructive vision for Israelis and Palestinians can be an economic community that improves people's lives materially and also creates peace (Peres, 1995; Staub, 2011).

In Rwanda, the current leaders have offered a seemingly constructive but problematic vision: We are all Rwandans; there are no Hutus and Tutsis. They have strongly discouraged the use of the latter designations and public discussion of issues between the groups. However, identity groups tend to be deeply committed to their identity, and a common groups membership may be best promoted by also allowing subidentities as members of different ethnic groups (Dovidio, Gaertner, & Saguy, 2009; Staub, 2011). Thus, a more effective, constructive vision would be to advocate a future in which people consider themselves and each other Rwandans, but allow and encourage pluralism and the discussion of past differences and current issues. In such a framework, hate speech, which was a strong contributor to and background for the genocide, could still be prohibited. This may be a useful framework but it is not an easy task, especially for a minority group in power that is deeply wounded by a recent genocide against it, and which itself has engaged in mass killing of members of the other group after the genocide (particularly of Hutu refugees in the Congo) and feels defensive about this, and with perhaps substantial elements of the majority still hostile.

Constructive groups provide positive means to satisfy basic needs, and an alternative to identity groups focused on conflict and to destructive ideological movements. In difficult times, people turn to groups—their ethnic group or another established identity group, or to ideological groups—that are all too often destructive. Membership in such groups and the ideology they develop help fulfill needs for security, connection, and identity, as well as promote effectiveness as people engage in the fulfillment of ideologically prescribed goals. Constructive groups that are inclusive in membership and have positive goals, whether small and limited or large-scale social goals, would provide important alternatives in difficult times. There are many such possible groups: those working together on economic projects, on social change projects, and others. Stable groups of this kind in a society, or groups created in response to life problems, make it less likely that people will turn to destructive ideological movements (Staub, 2011).

Training about the roots, the psychological impact, and the prevention of violence is important to provide for leaders. In Rwanda, we provided such training in workshops with leaders. We then had them engage in exercises, in particular to evaluate whether policies the government had just introduced or was planning to introduce would make violence more or less likely. The government ministers, heads of national commissions, advisors to the president, members of the Supreme Court, and others who participated deeply engaged with these trainings (Staub, 2011; Staub & Pearlman, 2006). Howard Wolpe of the Woodrow Wilson Center and his associates had Tutsi and Hutu leaders in Burundi engage with each other, begin to know and develop some trust in each other, and learn skills of effective interaction (Wolpe, 2005; Wolpe & McDonald, 2008). Such trainings can bring about changes in leaders' policies and practices, their attitudes toward the other group, and their ability to engage in dialogue and resolve practical issues. If such trainings became regular, normal activities for leaders, they could make an important contribution to prevention of violence.

Development practices and democratization are widely seen as means of prevention. But it is important for them to be equitable and to diminish rather than increase the difference between more and less powerful groups (Hamburg, 2007). Democracy promotes pluralism and moderates respect for authority. But it is mature democracies in which internal violence is especially unlikely. Mature democracies require effective civic institutions and broad public participation. For these to be created—for example, a justice system that treats people equally—requires some of the psychological changes, for example, in attitude toward the other, that I have discussed.

■ THE WHO OF GENOCIDE PREVENTION

In addition to the genocide convention, and other conventions and principles that the UN has developed to protect human lives and rights, in 2005 the Principle of Responsibility to Protect was approved by the UN General Assembly, as discussed in Franz Cede's chapter. This makes it the responsibility of nations to protect their citizens. If they do not, other countries become responsible to engage and intervene. Unfortunately, when and how the principle is activated, and mechanisms for action, are still lacking. The UN Secretary-General has appointed Francis Deng as Under-Secretary-General for the Prevention of Genocide, with an active mandate.

If the danger of genocide and mass killings, and the identity group conflicts that can lead to them, is to be reduced and then eliminated, the UN and its member states must be important actors in preventive efforts. The effectiveness of the UN depends to a large extent on the behavior of its member states. Other international NGOs, as well as many national NGOs, can contribute to early prevention. But how can they be engaged? Albright and Cohen's (2008) Task Force suggests for the United States a complex high-level government interagency group to coordinate the U.S. response. However, there ought to be very-high-level officials in the U.S. government and those of other countries who are directly responsible for gathering information and initiating preventive actions. High-level Central Office(s) for the Prevention of Mass Violence ought to be created in foreign ministries (Staub, 2010). Only if it is the primary or sole responsibility of officials with sufficient power is it likely that they will be concerned enough about problems in faraway countries, have the determination to generate the political will for action, and develop ways to initiate effective action.

The Task Force, whose members have been high-level government officials or members of Congress, suggested that an interagency group is essential for effective cooperation among government agencies in responding to events. They are highly experienced people, and what they suggest is likely to be right. But they may not appreciate the psychological shifts in people, the rearrangements of values and goals, when their primary responsibility is to some other work and to colleagues and officials who do other work, and the prevention of genocide and mass atrocities is at most a secondary responsibility. This consideration suggests that, as I suggest above (and for a more extensive discussion, see Staub, 2011), there should also be an independent separate office, as well as an interagency group that includes members of this office. Effective prevention is more likely if responsible officials in different countries work in coordination with each other, the UN, relevant NGOs, and other agencies in their governments.

The Holocaust Museum, United States Institute for Peace (USIP), and other institutions currently train varied professionals and help develop knowledge in this area. International Centers for the Prevention of Genocide, proposed by David Hamburg (2007), are other institutions where knowledge can be further developed and where extensive training of leaders/government officials and practitioners in genocide prevention can take place.

For a system that effectively promotes preventive actions to be created, and for governments to respond to events in faraway places, citizen action is important. The large citizen movement in response to the violence in Darfur was likely to have had a role in the International Criminal Court's indictment of the president of Sudan for crimes against humanity in February 2009. While there were immediate negative actions by the Sudanese government in response, contrary to what was feared, by late in 2009 the violence in Darfur nearly came to a halt. Unfortunately, in 2011, there is new violence by Sudan, for example, in the Nuba Mountains in the state of Southern Kordafan. Clearly, in a constantly changing world, an indictment by itself is not enough.

Through public education and constructive groups, citizens can come to see both the importance of preventing mass violence and their role in bringing this about. When citizens demand it, leaders will create the institutions that can move them, the leaders and their countries, to action in response to crises and bring about early prevention as a systematic, ongoing enterprise.

Note

1. The following analysis draws extensively on Staub (1989) and especially Staub (2011); both of these books, and the current chapter, in turn, are informed by the work of others. I refer to a variety of instances, but I use the Rwandan genocide, and the Holocaust—the genocide of the Jews— as primary examples.

References

Albright, M., & Cohen, W. (2008). *Preventing genocide: A blueprint for U.S. policy makers. Task Force Report*. Washington, DC: U.S. Holocaust Museum.

Aronson, E., Stephan, C., Sikes, J., Blaney, N., & Snapp, M. (1978). *The jigsaw classroom*. Beverly Hills, CA: Sage.

Bandura, A., Underwood, B., & Fromson, M. E. (1975). Disinhibition of aggression through diffusion of responsibility and dehumanization of victims. *Journal of Research in Personality, 9*, 253–269.

Bar-Tal, D. (2000). *Shared beliefs in a society: Social psychological analysis*. Thousand Oaks, CA: Sage.

Burg, S. L. (1997). *Preventing ethnic conflict: Macedonia and the pluralist paradigm*. Presented at the Woodrow Wilson Center, February 19. Retrieved June, 21, 2009 from http://www.wilsoncenter.org/index.cfm?fuseaction=topics.print_pub&doc_id=18947&group_id=7427&topic_id=1422&stoplayout=true

Carson, J. (2008). Ambassador Carson speaking on the panel "What Went Right, What Went Wrong in Kenya" at the Conference on the Prevention of Genocide, organized by the State Department, Washington, DC, October 30.

Crocker, C., Hampson, F. O., & Aall, P. (2004). *Taming intractable conflicts*. Washington DC: United States Institute for Peace.

Crocker, C., Hampson, F. O., & Aall, P. (Eds.). (2005). *Grasping the nettle*. Washington DC: United States Institute for Peace.

Davies, J. (1962). Towards a theory of revolution. *American Sociological Review, 27*(1), 5–18.

Des Forges, A. (1999). *Leave none to tell the story: Genocide in Rwanda*. New York: Human Rights Watch.

Deutsch, M. (1973). *The resolution of conflict: Constructive and destructive processes*. New Haven, CT: Yale University Press.

Dovidio, J. F., Gaertner, S. L., & Saguy, T. (2009). Commonality and the complexity of "we": Social attitudes and social change. *Personality and Social Psychology Review, 12*(1), 3–20.

Faure, G. O. (2008). Demonizing. *PINPoints, 30*.

Fein, H. (1979). *Accounting for genocide: Victims and survivors of the Holocaust*. New York: Free Press.

Fein, H. (1993a). Accounting for genocide after 1945: Theories and some findings. *International Journal of Group Rights, 1*(1), 79–106.

Fein, H. (1993b). *Genocide: A sociological perspective*. London: Sage.

Fein, H. (2007). *Human rights and wrongs: Slavery, terror, genocide*. Boulder, CO: Paradigm.

Gurr, T. (1970). *Why men rebel*. Princeton, NJ: Princeton University Press.

Hamburg, D. (2007). *Preventing genocide: Practical steps toward early detection and effective action*. Boulder, CO: Paradigm.

Harff, B. (2003). No lessons learned from the Holocaust? Assessing risks of genocide and political mass murder since 1955. *American Political Science Review, 97*(1), 57–73.

Hatzfeld, J. (2003). *Machete season*. New York: Farrar, Straus and Giroux.

Jost, J. T., Banaji, M. R., & Nosek, B. A. (2004). A decade of system justification theory: Accumulated evidence of conscious and unconscious bolstering of the status quo. *Political Psychology, 25*, 881–920.

Kelman, H. C. (2008). Reconciliation from a social-psychological perspective. In A. Nadler, T. E. Malloy, & J. D. Fisher (Eds.), *The social psychology of intergroup reconciliation* (pp. 15–32). Oxford and New York: Oxford University Press.

Kelman, H. C., & Fisher, R. J. (2003). Conflict analysis and resolution. In D. Sears, L. Huddy, & R. Jervis (Eds.), *Political psychology* (pp. 315–357). Oxford: Oxford University Press.

Kiernen, B. (2007). *Blood and soil: A world history of genocide and extermination from Sparta to Darfur*. New Haven, CT: Yale University Press.

Lederach, J. P. (1997). *Building peace: Sustainable reconciliation in divided societies*. Washington, DC: United States Institute of Peace Press.

Lerner, M. (1980). *The belief in a just world: A fundamental delusion*. New York: Plenum Press.

Lifton, R. J. (1986). *The Nazi doctors: Medical killing and the psychology of genocide*. New York: Basic Books.

Lund, M. S. (2009). Conflict prevention: Theory in pursuit of policy and practice. In I. W. Zartman, V. Kremenyck, & J. Bercovitch (Eds.), *Handbook of conflict resolution* (pp. 285–321). Thousand Oaks, CA: Sage.

Malvern, L. (2004). *Conspiracy to murder: The Rwanda genocide*. London: Verso.

Mamdani, M. (2001). *When victims become killers: Colonialism, nativism, and the genocide in Rwanda*. Princeton, NJ: Princeton University Press.

Morris, B. (2004). *The birth of the Palestinian refugee problem revisited*. Cambridge: Cambridge University Press.

Opotow, S. (1990). Moral exclusion and injustice. *Journal of Social Issues, 46*(1), 1–20.

Paluck, E. L. (2009). Reducing intergroup prejudice and conflict using the media: A field experiment in Rwanda. *Journal of Personality and Social Psychology, 96*(4), 574–587.

Peres, S. (1995). *Battling for peace*. New York: Random House.

Pettigrew, T., &, Tropp, L. (2006). A meta-analytic test of intergroup contact theory. *Journal of Personality and Social Psychology, 90*(4), 751–783.

Richardson, L. (2006). *What terrorists want: Understanding the enemy*. New York: Random House.

Rosoux, V. (2001). *Les usages de la mémoire dans les relations internationals*. Brussels: Bruylant.

Rummel, R. J. (1994). *Death by government*. New Brunswick, NJ: Transaction.

Sidanius, J., & Pratto, F. (1999). *Social dominance: An intergroup theory of social hierarchy and oppression*. New York: Cambridge University Press.

Staub, E. (1989). *The roots of evil: The origins of genocide and other group violence*. New York: Cambridge University Press.

Staub, E. (1996). The cultural-societal roots of violence: The examples of genocidal violence and of contemporary youth violence in the United States. *American Psychologist, 51*(1), 117–132.

Staub, E. (1998). Breaking the cycle of genocidal violence: Healing and reconciliation. In J. Harvey (Ed.), *Perspectives on loss* (pp. 231–241). Washington, DC: Taylor & Francis.

Staub, E. (2003). *The psychology of good and evil: Why children, adults and groups help and harm others.* New York: Cambridge University Press.

Staub, E. (2006). Reconciliation after genocide, mass killing or intractable conflict: Understanding the roots of violence, psychological recovery and steps toward a general theory. *Political Psychology, 27*(6), 865–895.

Staub, E. (2008). Promoting reconciliation after genocide and mass killing in Rwanda—and other post-conflict settings. In A. Nadler, T. Malloy, & J. D. Fisher (Eds.), *Social psychology of intergroup reconciliation* (pp. 395–423). New York: Oxford University Press.

Staub, E. (2011). *Overcoming evil: Genocide, violent conflict and terrorism.* New York: Oxford University Press.

Staub, E., & Pearlman, L. A. (2006). Advancing healing and reconciliation. In L. Barbanel & R. Sternberg (Eds.), *Psychological interventions in times of crisis* (pp. 213–245). New York: Springer-Verlag.

Staub, E., & Pearlman, L. A. (2009). Reducing intergroup prejudice and conflict: A commentary. *Journal of Personality and Social Psychology, 96*(4), 588–594.

Staub, E., Pearlman, L. A., & Bilali, R. (2010). Understanding the roots and impact of violence and psychological recovery as avenues to reconciliation after mass violence and intractable conflict: Applications to national leaders, journalists, community groups, public education through radio, and children. In G. Salomon & E. Cairns (Eds.), *Handbook of peace education* (pp. 269–287). New York: Psychology Press.

Staub, E., Pearlman, L. A., Gubin, A., & Hagengimana, A. (2005). Healing, reconciliation, forgiving and the prevention of violence after genocide or mass killing: An intervention and its experimental evaluation in Rwanda. *Journal of Social and Clinical Psychology, 24*(3), 297–334.

Staub, E., Pearlman, L. A., Weiss, G., & Hoek, A. Public education through radio to prevent violence, promote trauma healing and reconciliation, and build peace in Rwanda and the Congo. Available at, www.ervinstaub.com

Steiner, J. M. (1980). The SS yesterday and today: A socio–psychological view. In J. Dimsdale (Ed.), *Survivors, victims and perpetrators: Essays on the Nazi Holocaust* (pp. 405–457). New York: Hemisphere.

Totten, S., Parsons, W. S., & Charny, I. W (Eds.). (1997). *Century of genocide: Eyewitness accounts and critical views.* New York: Garland.

Varshney, A. (2002). *Ethnic conflict and civic life: Hindus and Muslims in India.* New Haven, CT: Yale University Press.

Volkan, V. D. (1997). *Blood lines: From ethnic pride to ethnic terrorism.* New York: Farrar, Straus and Giroux.

Volkan, V. D. (1998). Tree model: Psychopolitical dialogues and the promotion of coexistence. In E. Weiner (Ed.), *The handbook of interethnic coexistence.* New York: Continuum.

Wolpe, H. (Ed.). (2005). *Leadership and building state capacity.* Washington, DC: Woodrow Wilson International Center.

Wolpe, H., & McDonald, S. (2008). Democracy and peace building: Rethinking the conventional wisdom. *The Round Table 97, 394,* 137–145.

Zartman, I. W. (1989). *Ripe for resolution: Conflict and intervention in Africa.* New York: Oxford University Press.

Zartman, I. W., & Kremenyuk, V. (Eds.). (2005). *Peace vs. justice: Negotiating forward-and backward-looking outcomes.* Lanham, MD: Rowman & Littlefield.

PART TWO

Internal Dynamics

The Parties

3 The Identity Trap

Managing Paradox in Crisis Bargaining

■ WILLIAM A. DONOHUE

The hate speech inciting the 1994 Rwandan genocide is well documented by Simon (2006). Hutu media outlets produced a tidal wave of hate speech advocating the ethnic cleansing of the Tutsi minority. One radio station even identified targets for Hutu militias, and executives of this government-backed station were later convicted for their role in the genocide. While the airing of these messages alone did not cause the genocide, it is clear that these repeated communications played a role. This series of events leading to the genocidal events in Rwanda illustrates the relationship between the climate created by public rhetoric and genocide.

In his article asking whether the Rwandan genocide could have been prevented, Stanton (2004) argues that prevention means understanding the social climate change within any given state and how that climate devolves into one group seeking to exterminate another. He identifies eight stages of social change, each yielding markers that, if recognized, can serve as early warning systems signaling the need for intervention. The first three stages are Classification ("us versus them"), Symbolization (groups are given names or symbols of their second-class citizenship such as ID cards), and Dehumanization (groups are given names of bad things such as cockroaches or cancer) that essentially marks the death spiral toward genocide. Stanton argues that intervening in the social climate at the early stages provides a greater chance of success than waiting until extermination begins and then trying to stop that process.

These three early stages are important because they place the greatest potential for prevention on first understanding how the public rhetoric displayed through the media and other outlets is classifying, symbolizing, and dehumanizing groups within that society. Based on that understanding, interventions can then be crafted to turn that rhetoric in a different direction. Nevertheless, the stages suggest that crafting an intervention and negotiation strategy means first focusing on the language themes established by the rhetoric that sets the social context within the society at risk for genocide. The purpose of this chapter is to create a framework for thinking about how language themes start to degenerate into the reification of a culture that tolerates and even encourages classification and dehumanization. Understanding these language themes becomes an early warning system that begins to signal the beginning of a genocidal spiral. This framework will be termed the *Identity Trap*, and its development begins by better understanding how rhetoric establishes social contexts in the course of ethnic disputes.

■ RHETORIC AND SOCIAL CLIMATE

In a recent paper focusing on Israeli–Palestinian rhetoric leading up to the Oslo accords, Donohue and, Druckman (2009) sought to understand how leaders from both groups framed their public rhetoric to create the larger social context surrounding the secret negotiations. Selecting a series of speeches and interviews in the six months leading up to the Oslo I accords, these authors coded the extent to which the messages were displaying power/affiliation, trust/mistrust, and forward/backward-looking relational message frames. The study found that the Palestinian rhetoric was consistently more power-oriented, was more focused on justice themes, and displayed less trust. The primary explanation for this "tougher"-looking rhetoric centered on the notion of *outbidding*, which is a strategy that nonstate actors often adopt to appear tougher to their constituents. In contrast, the Israeli rhetoric was both tough and affiliative, while also appearing more forward-looking and trusting. This vacillation reflected more of a front-stage orientation that is typical of state actors who must moderate their rhetorical positions to appeal to broader political audiences.

The Donohue et al. (2009) study also explored the intersection of these three kinds of frames. When speakers' issues focused on the past (looking backward, with an emphasis on justice concerns), these issues were more likely to be accompanied by messages of high power and mistrust. However, when they focused on the future and the formulation of peace issues, speakers were more likely to infuse their rhetoric with trust and affiliation messages. In short, the data suggest that these constructs are highly interdependent; the use of more collaborative or competitive relational messages appears to be a function of whether individuals adopt a justice or a peace frame in their communication. These results build on and extend the forward-backward, peace vs. justice theme explored in Zartman and Kremenyuk (2005) by adding relational features to their substantive distinction.

This finding is relevant to the issue of genocide because it reveals a rhetorical profile that typifies the "classification" rhetoric described by Stanton (2004) and by Romero-Trillo in this volume. When individuals explore themes in their rhetoric that threaten tribal identity, such as justice themes about decayed status and welfare, they do so from a perspective of high power (seeking to impose a solution, secure compensation, right injustices, etc.), and low affiliation (little liking, respect, and trust). The argument in this chapter is that this looking-backward talk forms an Identity Trap in the sense that it creates a paradoxical state that pulls enemies closer together in a struggle to push each other apart. This paradox is difficult both to recognize and to escape without some kind of guided introspection or political reconciliation process (Moon, 2008). For example, when one party publicly attacks a group's tribal identity by referencing past atrocities in an attempt to seek justice, it lures the attacked tribe into a trap by requiring that offended parties defend their identity. Over time, these exchanges promote a culture of classification and can move quickly toward symbolization and ultimately dehumanization. To unpack this process and then ultimately point toward ways of locating Identity Traps in public rhetoric that might signal genocidal intentions, it is important to begin sorting out the respective constructs. We will begin by describing the relational paradox.

■ CONFLICT AND PARADOX

To begin, it might be useful to review the kinds of relational frames participants bring to a conflict in the course of managing their material issues. In an earlier essay, Donohue, Kaufmann, Smith, and Ramesh (1991) make a distinction between crisis and normative communication. The idea is that during the course of a conflict, individuals place various weights on either relationship/expressive or substantive/material issues as they move forward. In the early stages of conflict, or in intractable conflict exchanges, parties often focus on relational issues about power, role, trust, and status (identity) as they seek to asset their demands and/or grievances. As these identity issues are addressed and in some sense become less salient, disputants place more weight on substantive issues to focus on the material issues dividing them. In the course of any conflict, disputants shift back and forth between an emphasis on expressive and material concerns. But as conflicts escalate, they can be characterized by more emphasis on expressive identity concerns.

Hammer and Rogan (1997) make a similar distinction in their communication-based negotiation model between instrumental, relational, and identity concerns in a negotiation. These issues are all intertwined, but as they become more balanced, individuals can concentrate on moving toward a negotiated settlement. Situations that stay in crisis have little chance of productive movement since relational and identity concerns dominate. In fact, most of the recommendations that appear in the Rogan, Hammer, and Van Zandt (1997) volume concentrate on how to achieve this transition from a crisis to a normative communication mode. This chapter will focus on how crisis communication creates a competitive paradox that is largely identity driven, that traps interaction into a spiraling escalation of relational attacks and begins an escalating march toward cultural classification. To better understand the theoretical foundations of this devolution, it is important to address two key issues. First, what is identity and what drives it? Second, what are paradoxical relational states, and how do identity issues create a paradoxical relational state that essentially forms an Identity Trap that is responsible for the spiraling escalation of classification rhetoric?

Identity and Its Foundations

Based on Schutz's (1958) FIRO (Fundamental Interpersonal Relationship Orientation) theory, each individual must resolve three fundamental issues in belonging to a social unit: inclusion (boundaries, roles, alliances, membership, position), control (ability to have an impact or change the environment to satisfy needs), and integration (the sense of trust and fellowship resulting from having successfully negotiated inclusion and control; Haberman & Danes, 2007). To resolve these issues and become accepted by some social order or group (e.g., a family, a sports team, or even a terrorist group), the individual must form an identity, or set of beliefs about the self, that allows him or her to be seen as a competent role player in that group. As individuals manage their work, social, and family lives, they move quickly among often very different roles. Stryker's (1987) Identity Theory claims that individuals create multiple senses of self (beliefs about the self) that are necessary to play these various roles. The more salient these roles are, the higher they emerge on the individual's hierarchy and thus drive their behavior.

These two issues of control and integration are very important in explaining the difference between crisis and normative communication. Normative communication is characterized by each party viewing the other as a competent role player who does not threaten his or her identity. Normative communication typically appears as information exchange, proposals, counterproposals, concessions, and agreements. The relational focus is more about integration since parties have demonstrated that they can work with one another in a trusting manner. By contrast, crisis communication is essentially a rejection of the other's ability to perform competently, and thus as a threat to the need for inclusion, control, and integration. Crisis communication is more about control issues related to power, demands, accusations, fears, and trust violations. Once that threat to the fundamental needs for inclusion, control, and integration occurs, the person being attacked must move away from a focus on the material, substantive issues and instead focus on recovering his or her need to be seen as competent. Research on politeness terms this move *face restoration* (Brown & Levinson, 1978). The individual must protect the need to be included and in control by performing competently in that role.

This perspective suggests that during any sustained interaction between adversaries, individuals frequently slip in and out of normative and crisis communication modes, as the research by Donohue et al. (2009) demonstrated. The question is, how does this relationally focused Identity Trap become paradoxical and, in so doing, create an escalatory cycle toward classification and ultimately genocide? This chapter now turns to a discussion of Relational Order Theory and the notion of paradox in negotiation.

Relational Order Theory and Paradox

In a set of papers, Donohue and colleagues (Donohue, 1998; Donohue & Hoobler, 2002; Donohue, Kaufmann, Smith, & Ramesh, 1991; Donohue, Ramesh, & Borchgrevink, 1991) outlined a theory to account for the dynamic evolution of relationships in conflict. Based on Strauss's (1978) Negotiated Order Theory, Relational Order Theory contends that interactants continuously create and tacitly negotiate relational limits that serve to constrain their ability to discuss or raise issues about material differences. That is, underneath every exchange lies a set of relational parameters that locates each party's assumption about what kind of relationship is in place during that exchange. For example, the rhetoric from one source might send more cooperative messages, while the rhetoric from the other side rebuffs those cues by responding with more competitive attacks.

The two main relational parameters or limits that communicators negotiate while they interact are *affiliation* and *interdependence*. These two parameters serve as the key issues individuals orient to in the context of developing and defining their relationship with one another (Brown & Levinson, 1978; Burgoon & Hale, 1987). Interdependence focuses on the extent to which parties can influence or exert behavioral control over one another in the context of the relationship between them. As parties become more interdependent through increased contact, trade, cultural exchanges, and so on (on a macro level), or by being more personally disclosing or more direct (less ambiguous) about their needs or opinions (on a micro level), they work to expand their right to demand more and incur more obligations to comply with others' demands. When the interdependence is reward-ing, parties acquiesce to one another's demands, and they focus more on their obligations to, and their investment in, the relationship. When the interdependence is punishing, parties focus more on their individual right to demand more autonomy and escape the toils of togetherness.

The relational cluster contributing most to whether parties emphasize rights or obligations in the context of their interdependence is termed *affiliation* and focuses on affective expressions of attraction (see Winter, 1991, for a review). Affiliation is defined as the extent to which individuals communicate attraction, liking, depth, acceptance, and trust. Parties can exchange these messages of affiliation directly through overt performance, or they can frame their messages indirectly with expressions of approval, liking, and trust. Relational Order Theory positions interdependence and affiliation in relation to one another to define four relational conditions, or contextual orientations, that negotiators create as they continually define and redefine the limits of affiliation and interdependence: collaboration, cooperation, coexistence, and conflict. To understand paradox, it is important to define the frames that are formed by the intersection of interdependence and affiliation.

Collaboration

When parties communicate using expressions of high affiliation and high interdependence, they are proposing to become more involved with one another in a collaborative manner. In the Duel Concern Model (Rhodes & Carnevale, 1999), the concept of collaboration is one in which parties seek to facilitate another's goals and strive to create a relational context that honors role obligations over individual rights. In other words, individuals are more concerned about how they can best implement their role requirements and less concerned about their right to pursue autonomous activities. Because the parties are focused on their role obligations, their needs for inclusion, control, and integration are not being challenged and thus are removed from the focus of the interaction. This frees the parties to concentrate on open information exchange in the spirit of looking forward to building mutually constructive enterprises.

Coexistence

However, when parties inject their rhetoric with low levels of both affiliation and interdependence, they send messages of separation and isolation. Parties seek to simply coexist by reducing their ties and isolating themselves from the relationship. This is a state of coexistence in the sense that parties are not fighting, but they are not moving forward productively with their substantive agenda. Perhaps they might need time to recover from some incident with the other party. Or they might need to isolate themselves for a while to restore identity in order to appear more competent in the performance of their roles. Interaction in this condition might consist of less frequent and superficial information exchanges simply to keep up the appearance of adhering to old role prescriptions. Or parties might try to distribute messages supporting their own face to maintain their credibility while they are trying to withdraw from the relationship. Collaborative relational exchanges emphasize constructive processes and movement on material issues, whereas coexistence exchanges emphasize relational withdrawal.

Neither of these two relational conditions is paradoxical for communicators. When parties interact within a collaborative frame, they balance their cues of high interdependence with expressions of increased affiliation. When they establish a coexistence frame, a similar match occurs in the opposite direction; that is, parties seek to separate by decreasing both their interdependence and their affiliation. There are no mixed messages guiding the rhetoric.

Cooperation

In this condition of low interdependence and high affiliation, parties exchange messages that work to retain their role autonomy yet demonstrate approval and positive affect for one another. They assert few rights because they are not sufficiently interdependent to demand much. Yet, they remain friendly and polite, generally in an attempt to adhere to socially acceptable norms of interaction. This frame defines the relational condition of cooperation because the parties are typically testing one another to decide whether to expand their interdependence and role obligations. Parties may be aware of one another's goals, but they are more focused on achieving their own than on being committed to achieving goal attainment for both parties. For example, after a long freeze in formal diplomatic relations, parties might begin sending public messages showing some affiliation or willingness to talk as a feeler signaling an interest in a broader cooperative relationship. But this commitment to increased liking and trust is not unconditional, as it is in a collaborative relationship in which parties make a commitment to encumber their role obligations frame by virtue of their highly interdependent relationship. A rhetorical bid to be cooperative, as in a diplomatic feeler, is conditional; the party has a right to expect that the other will also respond with a cooperative feeler before further interdependence can go forward.

As a result of these mixed messages, cooperation can be labeled the *cooperative paradox* because parties must manage an approach-avoidance frame. On the one hand, parties express trust and openness while at the same time remaining timid about increasing interdependence. This paradox is cooperative in the sense that it sets the stage for becoming more interdependent but falls short of a total commitment to a comprehensive working relationship. On the other hand, this condition provides some tension about the direction of the relationship.

Competition

In this final condition, parties send unaffiliative and disapproving messages challenging their needs for inclusion, control, or integration in the context of high codependence. The focus moves away from group or dyadic priorities toward parties asserting their rights aimed at achieving their own goals while also resisting their group or alliance obligations. Because the emphasis is on asserting rights and resisting obligations, the communication carries almost a moral imperative and authority with it. Parties must resist with all their resources because key, central, and defining rights have been violated and, thus, their identity has been attacked. This is the kind of communication Winter (1991) observed during the first few exchanges between leaders dealing with the Cuban missile crisis of 1962. The United States certainly asserted its right to enforce the Monroe Doctrine, which seeks to prevent non–Western Hemisphere powers from establishing military dominance in the Western Hemisphere. Yet, as the letters from Khrushchev became more conciliatory, the United States shifted its focus from rights to specific substantive issues. The parties moved away from aggression temporarily by agreeing to reduce their interdependence.

This condition can be labeled the *competitive paradox* because parties must manage their avoidance-approach conflict. To defeat their rival, parties must increase interdependence to pull their opponent closer in order to initiate/intensify communication or aggression while also pushing the opponent away through a show of negative affiliation by being unfriendly and untrusting. When parties are in this condition, they communicate directly while showing signs of negative affect (Donohue & Roberto, 1993).

This competitive paradox results in the spiraling Identity Trap that is difficult for parties to escape. Parties publish rhetoric that works to pull them closer together psychologically, and often physically, in order to push each other away or defeat each other over fundamental identity challenges. Attacks, signs of mistrust or disrespect, and other confrontational displays challenge the needs for inclusion, control, and integration. The rhetorical exchange forms a trap because each party is seeking to restore its identity needs by simply fighting back. But, more importantly, this condition represents a trap because it is difficult to see and reflect upon. The more the trap is sprung, the more interdependent parties become to restore their identity by fighting back. Only when they learn to manage the competitive paradox can they begin to escape the Identity Trap. How, then, is this accomplished?

▪ MANAGING THE PARADOXES

To answer this question, it is probably useful to begin with the cooperative paradox. The challenge of the cooperative paradox is to remain affiliative but cautious. Achieving this relational goal demands strategic ambiguity (Eisenberg, 1984; Leitch & Davenport, 2002). Parties politely share background information about the issues dividing them, but they remain cautious about being too direct or detailed about specific positions. This ambiguity results from assuming a role relationship that would allow the parties to make demands on one another.

These relational messages are common in opening remarks in hostage negotiations, for example (Donohue & Diez, 1985). The hostage negotiators remain positive (or at least nonthreatening), and even polite, by avoiding tasks that might create controversy and decrease affiliation.

Ambiguity works in a very different manner in attempts to mitigate the effects of communicating within a competitive paradox. As parties exchange rhetoric that moves them deeper into a competitive paradox, affiliation drops and interdependence intensifies. When they violate affiliation parameters by challenging one another's fundamental interpersonal needs, they are more direct with one another as they assert their rights and seek redress for past grievances, placing greater emphasis on the fulfillment of obligations. They may restate positions and even use threats as a way of fighting back. Fighting back is essentially a move to assert rights while demanding obligations from the other. More demands often result in more resistance, thereby perpetuating the paradox and making it difficult to escape the Identity Trap. Relational Order Theory predicts that ultimately parties will find a means of escaping this competition and learn to coexist, which provides some respite from this paradox (Donohue & Roberto, 1993; Donohue & Taylor, 2006).

What kinds of expressions, performances, or messages do parties exchange to increase or decrease affiliation or interdependence in order to escape the paradox of the Identity Trap? In a recent paper, Taylor and Thomas (2005) examined the linguistic style of hostage takers and hostage negotiators along three dimensions: structural features of language (word count, articles, negations, tense, propositions), social affect (negative and positive emotion, relational references), and cognitive contributions (causation, insight, discrepancy, certainty, and exclusivity). The hostage takers in these transcripts ranged from criminals caught in the act to actors in domestic disputes to mentally impaired individuals. The authors found that the hostage negotiator and hostage taker in the successful (a negotiated outcome) condition were synchronous on all but 4 of the 18 categories across these language choices. In the unsuccessful condition (the situation was resolved tactically), the parties were synchronous on only two parameters. Further, when the data were analyzed on a turn-by-turn basis, it was found that the hostage negotiator in the negotiation condition drove the frame choices, whereas in the tactical condition, the hostage taker drove the frame choices. In other words, successful negotiations were characterized by more frame coordination and the use of more collaborative frames with fewer transitions between frames (Donohue & Taylor, 2006). In comparison to unsuccessful negotiations, the dialogue of successful negotiations involved greater coordination of turn taking, reciprocation of positive affect, a focus on the present rather than the past, and a focus on alternatives rather than competition. These interactions avoided identity challenges by not threatening interpersonal needs.

This research on hostage negotiation using Relational Order Theory suggests that parties lost within the Identity Trap have greater difficulty moving toward collaborative exchange. Are there other lines of research that might provide more insight into the idea of relational paradoxes that plunge individuals into more of a crisis bargaining mode? This chapter now turns to the issue of more specific kinds of relational paradoxes that influence hostage negotiation outcomes.

■ EXTORTIONATE RHETORIC

In a classic book on policing, Muir (1977) describes the kinds of coercive relationships that often emerge in the course of police work. Coercive relationships, or controlling others through threats to harm, precipitate extortionate communication in which parties seek their ends through the use of threats, which, in police work, may take the form of hostages and ransoms. Coercion is a classic case of needs violation because it works to threaten both inclusion and control.

Muir argues that extortionate transactions are organized around a series of paradoxes and that reconstructing these transactions requires managing the paradoxes. Of most interest here is the Paradox of Face. This paradox focuses on the broad issue of identity and often, in a classification rhetoric preceding genocide, on the narrower issue of threat. Parties vacillate between communicating both toughness and reasonableness and often must do so simultaneously. For example, the professional police role identity is rooted in a desire to be both firm and tough, while being tempered with an ability to be understanding and fair. The hostage taker's role identity is rooted in being perceived as a credible threat to secure a desired outcome, although not so much of a threat that the police are likely to take tactical action (force) to preserve the lives of the hostages. The hostage taker must strike a balance between being tough and reasonable so that negotiation appears more viable as a strategy than tactical action (force). The hostage's face can shift from being a helpless victim to being a hostage taker supporter or even an overt detractor.

Of particular interest in managing this paradox is interpreting threats. In a classic work on threats, Shelling (1956) indicates that for threats to be credible, they must be specific and perceived as within the willingness and capability of the threatener. This threat then binds it to the identity of the threatener and becomes part of the threatener's face. In an empirical test of coercive power and concession making in bilateral negotiation, deDreu (1995) found that balanced power produced fewer threats and demands than unequal power. This result suggests that the role of the police is to manage this paradox by seeking to balance identity issues in such a way as to make threats less necessary so that the parties can shift to a more normative bargaining context and resolve the situation appropriately.

Clearly, any set of rhetorical exchanges can devolve into an extortionate abyss thrusting the parties into crisis as they try to overwhelm one another with coercive force to fight back and restore their identity. That's what genocide is all about. The declaration to commit genocide, as in the Rwandan case, is an admission that the ability to restore identity through continued communication and coexistence has failed. Only wiping out the other tribe will restore identity. Interestingly, these declarations adopt a central hate message. One kind of message form that assumes this structure is the rhetorical trope, which this chapter now explores.

■ RHETORICAL TROPES AND PARADOX IN CLASSIFICATION RHETORIC

Another approach to understanding the concept of paradox in the context of classification rhetoric leading to genocide is found in the work on dialectical tensions by Rawlins (1989) and Baxter (1990). The basic idea of this work is that, in any relationship, people struggle to resolve three fundamental dialectal tensions or paradoxes: openness/closedness, autonomy/connection, and novelty/predictability. Parties use communication to determine how much information to share or reveal, how much they should be free to express themselves as individuals or be constrained by the corporate relational structure, or how predictable they should be when deciding how to act.

An interesting line of research evolving from this perspective is the work of Putnam (2004), who examines the concept of rhetorical tropes (the use of metaphors, irony, metonymy, and synecdoche) to understand how individuals reference and manage relational tensions. She focuses specifically on the use of metonymy (a figure of speech in which a word stands for its constituent parts, like using the word *culture* to stand for an organization's values, rituals, and myths) and synecdoche (a figure of speech in which the part stands for or symbolizes the whole, like substituting the word *crown* for the role of the king or queen). In other words, how are people using words rhetorically to conceptualize complex relational dialectics that define the nature of the parties' interdependencies?

In her research, Putnam (2004) focuses on how tropes are used to negotiate autonomy and interdependence in a teacher bargaining context. She found that the term *language* referred to the creation and discussion of policy issues and the term *money* referred to any budget-related item. The bargaining often revolved around who owned the money and the ability to craft the language that would ultimately guide the negotiation. Thus, these concepts were used to negotiate the dialectical tensions of autonomy and interdependence between the parties.

In classification rhetoric, similar kinds of tropes might emerge that serve to build Identity Traps. The rhetoric can become fixated on specific issues, such as *injustice*, and use that word to introduce examples of how the other tribe has become oppressive or unwilling to integrate and adopt majority values. For example, a member of one tribe in an interview might say, "So, you'd better stop the injustice" in reference to fulfilling a demand for some kind of behavior, like learning the majority tribe's language. In response, speakers from the other side might try to reframe this concept by focusing on how they have complied with different demands. What these parties are doing is managing their relational dialectics by focusing on a specific synecdoche that begins to take on a life of its own and embody a much larger and more important negotiation.

In another study, Jameson (2004) examined how parties negotiated autonomy and connection through politeness in a medical context. She discovered that indirectness and ambiguity are the most common ways of negotiating the autonomy-connection paradox. Ambiguous communication can often take the form of small talk and humor rather than genuinely self-disclosing true feelings. Jameson examined face-saving identity restoration strategies as a means of negotiating autonomy and connection. She found that in negotiating treatment options, medical professionals often emphasized respect for and acknowledgment of each other's competence while also emphasizing solidarity and providing explanations as a means of simultaneously saving face and supporting face. These face strategies acknowledge the other's right to autonomy while carefully framing how the parties ought to be connected. In the initial stages of a hostage negotiation, the police want to concentrate on relational development and have as a specific goal not threatening the autonomy of the hostage taker or creating the impression of "boxing in" the hostage taker. Many exchanges during these early phases are devoted to the use of small talk and humor, in addition to expressions of support as a means of supporting the hostage taker's face and avoiding identity challenges. The goal is to find a balance between autonomy and connection in the development of the relationship that will allow for the transition from a crisis to a normative bargaining mode.

▪ INTEGRATING THE PARADOXICAL PERSPECTIVES

At this point, it is useful to understand how these various approaches to the study of paradox work together to help us understand how hostage negotiators can avoid the Identity Trap and ultimately transform the negotiation into a more productive form. To summarize the issue of paradox in the context of crisis communication, it appears that parties create and manage relationships by negotiating their identity as they exchange information. As they become more interdependent (pulling each other closer and being more direct) and less affiliative (pushing each other away through expressions of mistrust and dislike), they find themselves immersed in an Identity Trap.

As the Identity Trap deepens and conflict escalates, the interaction might result in a mutually hurting stalemate that Zartman (2000) argues leads to *ripeness*, or a willingness to move out of the identity-focused conflict trap and into a more constructive frame. This movement, or ripening, requires that parties focus quickly on two separate issues before they can begin dealing with the substantive or material concerns in the dispute: their relationship to each other and the context that has emerged in the course of the dispute. The challenge with the first issue is building a consensus about the fundamental parameters of their relationship simply as communicators. Regarding affiliation, how are they prepared to manage the issues of trust/mistrust, openness/closedness, and public/private? And how can they also manage their interdependence issues focusing on connection/autonomy or control/yielding? They might engage in a variety of face-saving and face-maintaining strategies all aimed at finding new levels of affiliation and interdependence that will free them from the trap and allow them either to communicate again more constructively or disengage for some period to cool off.

For example, in response to a mutually hurting stalemate fed by one identity-riddled crisis after another, one side may choose to renegotiate affiliation by being more open and revealing some sensitive information to show that it is being more trusting. Or one side might yield control over some critical negotiation procedure that it used to stonewall the other. The parties might also agree to work with a third party that was previously not acceptable. The key here is that once parties feel the trap and see themselves imprisoned by it, the conflict is ripe for renegotiation.

The second issue that the parties must confront deals with how they are going to read the context and determine how best to renegotiate the affiliation and interdependence parameters. Are they going to do a major shift or pick more cautiously at the margins? According to Muir (1977), parties in a crisis situation might respond by being more or less dispossessed, detached, nasty, or irrational. For example, a hostage taker might say, "You better start cooperating because I'm gonna strangle her and she's gonna die right here on the floor and then I'm gonna go to the electric chair. So, you better get a gun if you want to save her life" (Holmes, 1990). As the hostage taker seeks to detach from both the life of the hostage and his own life, he is also negotiating parameters associated with autonomy and control. In addition, he is using the trope "cooperating" as a means of renegotiating these parameters.

This example illustrates that multiple paradoxes are in play at any given point, and the job of those seeking to mitigate or redirect the crisis communication is to identify those parameters that seem most important to address at the moment. In this example, the detachment issue is clearly apparent, but the control and autonomy issues also bear strategic attention. However, the issue of detachment probably ought to take priority as a means of persuading the hostage taker to value something, hopefully his own life, to gain leverage in the negotiations. Of course, in this example, the hostage taker is also threatening the hostage negotiator's identity and need for control, which might distract the negotiator from focusing on the hostage taker and the issues of detachment and value. Negotiators should be aware of these kinds of negotiations to avoid losing the crucial focus on the most important paradox.

■ MANAGING THE IDENTITY TRAP: PALESTINIAN/ISRAELI RHETORIC

To explore how parties set Identity Traps through their rhetoric, it is helpful to consider the use of rhetoric prior to the Oslo negotiations, as referenced in the work of Donohue et al. (2009). The first example is an interview with Faruq Qaddumi conducted on the radio program "Voice of the Arabs in Cairo" on January 22, 1993. At the time, Qaddumi was head of the Palestine Liberation Organization's Political Department in Tunis. The interviewer was Shihatah Abu al-Majd who also hosts the radio program The "Dialogue from Afar" from Cairo, Egypt. During the interview, Qaddumi was asked to comment on the Israeli policy regarding the deportation of Palestinians:

> We must examine the essence of Israeli policy and the behavior of the Israeli government and Israeli officials. The reports we read about certain developments do not indicate a clear change in the expansionist Israeli mentality that seeks to build more settlements and accommodate more immigrants and refuses to recognize the Palestinian people's legitimate rights. Israel's behavior and policies remain the obstacle to peace. This was clearly seen in the autonomy plans it offered. These mean that Israel wants the Palestinians to be mere employees while retaining primary authority over the occupied territories. It means it would retain sovereignty. There is no contradiction in Israeli policy. This is the essence of Israeli policy whether Likud or Labour has power. Yitzhaq Rabin is known as the iron-fisted man who threatened to break the bones of the Palestinians when the blessed intifadah began. His government policy statement included a number of threats to the Palestinians if they did not accept his plans, which are designed to abolish the Palestinian cause.

This excerpt provides several examples of classification rhetoric. Israelis are "expansionists" and make the Palestinians "mere employees." The goal of this out-bidding rhetoric is to classify the Israelis as unreasonable, unjust, and oppressive. The expansionist label, like so many used by both groups, serves as a rhetorical trope to capture the essence of Israeli intentions from the Palestinian perspective.

It is also interesting to see how paradoxes are interwoven within this rhetoric. The excerpt references two key paradoxes about Palestinian life inside and outside of Israel. Notice first that Qaddumi references Palestinian rights in the second sentence, then goes on to reference Rabin's threat to break Palestinian bones later in the statement. These references clearly suggest low affiliation with and trust for the Israelis. Yet, there are also references to high interdependence associated with Israel's proposing sovereignty over the occupied territories and continued involvement in Palestinian affairs. Thus, the rhetoric continues to trap the Palestinians within an Identity Trap by using the classification rhetoric.

The Israeli rhetoric is similarly laced with classification rhetoric. Here is an excerpt from an interview with Prime Minister Yitzhak Rabin by Gadi Sukenik on Israel Broadcasting Authority TV in Jerusalem on March 30, 1993 (emphasis added):

> I wish to address you, the Israeli citizen. I understand the pain, the worry and the rage. We are indeed experiencing a difficult period of rising *Palestinian* terrorism. Last month, fifteen Israelis were murdered in Judaea, Samaria, Gaza and the territory of the sovereign State of Israel. Terror has accompanied the lives, and unfortunately the deaths, of many of us for a long time. Terror has never beaten us and never will. I would like to extend my condolences to the families that lost their dear ones and wish that the wounded may get well. The question is: What are we required to do? Firstly, we must wage war on terrorism with all our might. Secondly, we have to strengthen our spirit, face the test and win it, so that our enemies do not believe that we have weakened. Thirdly, not to lose the faith, the hope that we will attain peace and solve the Arab–Israeli conflict, including the *Palestinian*–Israeli one.

In this excerpt, Rabin labels the Palestinians as terrorists and enemies, and states that the solution is to wage war on the Palestinians in addition to strengthening the national spirit and continuing to work toward peace. These classifications, which also serve as rhetorical tropes, certainly reference reduced affiliation for the Palestinians, yet they also reference Israeli interdependence with them since they must continue to work with them to gain peace. Once the classification process begins in earnest, as shown by both the Palestinian and Israeli rhetoric, the paradox of the Identity Trap is sprung, making it very difficult to escape the intractable conflict.

▪ LESSONS LEARNED FOR AVOIDING THE IDENTITY TRAP

The key to avoiding Identity Traps is first to recognize that one is present or looming in the rhetoric and then, once caught in a trap, to figure out a way of transforming the culture from a crisis communication to a more normative rhetorical display. To achieve this goal, it might be useful to summarize some lessons learned about recognizing Identity Traps. The first lesson is that traps start to emerge from fears when interpersonal needs are being challenged. Often, these displays can be very subtle. Showing disrespect by dismissing a point, demonstrating a lack of interest in listening to the other, or labeling the other as unjust or a terrorist challenge needs for inclusion and control. These displays work to compromise affiliation. Repeated over time with more intense language or reference to sensitive topics, they can further erode affiliation and escalate the classification into symbolization.

Another aspect of the Identity Trap that emerges is a fixation on a rhetorical trope. Tropes represent frames for shaping the negotiations. They often serve as windows for disclosing paradoxes. Words such as *expansionist* or *terrorist* are not only used to classify all the individuals who identify with the other side, but also serve as a rhetorical tool to justify actions. For example, the Israeli fixation on referring to all Palestinians as *terrorists* represents a classic Identity Trap. The Israelis use this term in their rhetoric to express their fears and press their demands with the Americans and other supporters while also using it to resist demands and assert rights. The Palestinians use their terms, like *expansionist*, to serve exactly the same objectives. Thus, whatever trope either side uses represents a bid for autonomy, role, and identity while also signaling the entrance into the Identity Trap. The Palestinians and the Israelis have argued for years about complying with various United Nations resolutions. The fight was not about the resolutions but the lack of trust and affiliation; the resolutions kept them lost in their respective Identity Traps that such language continues to set for themselves and one another.

Once caught in a trap, which is often very difficult to avoid, it is important to understand how the interaction can be transformed to escape the trap. The most obvious strategy is to recognize first that the other party is setting a trap with some kind of identity attack. Reciprocating the attack closes the trap. Avoiding the attack by reestablishing another topic or focusing on the substantive issue begins to circumvent the trap. Another strategy for avoiding the trap is to simply decrease interdependence. Sometimes it is useful to separate for a while and not continue to interact. Or one can bring in a mediator to create and enforce interaction rules.

Another way of avoiding a trap is to focus on issues presented by the other side that do not create traps. Khrushchev's letters to Kennedy described above in Winter's (1991) research are telling here. Rather than responding to Khrushchev's attacks, Kennedy choses to pick up on and respond to issues that were not filled with traps. And more collaborative language ensued. In the Rabin interview above, the last line references the hope for peace with the Palestinians and the suggestion that peace is possible. This attempt to avoid an Identity Trap is rather implicit. If Rabin had said something like "And we recognize that the Palestinians will be a full partner in the peace process," he would have avoided the trap. Of course, this rhetoric emerged after the Oslo I accords were signed, but at this point the Identity Traps were being sprung continuously.

■ ESTABLISHING AN EARLY WARNING SYSTEM FOR GENOCIDE AVOIDANCE

If classification rhetoric signals the slippery slope toward genocide because it springs an Identity Trap, then what kinds of systems ought to be in place to detect such rhetoric and then to mitigate its effects? Creating a rhetorical early warning system would be the easy part of the process. One could imagine a system in which a computer program could analyze the language coming from various media broadcasts or computer Web sites and then look for trends over time to determine the appropriateness and timing of intervention. If the output from that system were fed into a central site that monitors such rhetoric, it would be possible for those analyzing the information to create a list of countries/areas on a genocide "watch list" of some kind. As the rhetoric intensified, the more vulnerable places would be targeted for some kind of action.

What action would be appropriate to mitigate classification rhetoric? Aside from military intervention, there are various aid programs that seek rhetorical moderation through economic development. Factions from different groups could learn to work together and benefit from job creation and increased prosperity. Underlying these efforts could also be attempts to create dialogue groups that would allow individuals from different sides to simply become more comfortable with one another. The Oslo I accords happened only because of a relational transformation among the two sides. And, as we know from our earlier work, public rhetoric often set the tone for progress in private talks. The point of this chapter is that language is real—rhetoric is real, and it matters. The more we come to grips with that reality, the more quickly and effectively we can create interventions to detect and avoid genocide.

References

Baxter, L. A. (1990). Dialectical contradictions in relationship development. *Journal of Social and Personal Relationships, 7,* 69–88.

Brown, P., & Levinson, S. (1978). Universals in language usage: Politeness phenomena. In E. Goody (Ed.), *Questions and politeness: Strategies in social interaction* (pp. 56–289). Cambridge, MA: Cambridge University Press.

Burgoon, J. K., & Hale, J. L. (1987). The fundamental topoi of relational communication. *Communication Monographs, 51,* 193–214.

De Dreu, C. K. (1995). Coercive power and concession making in bilateral negotiation. *Journal of Conflict Resolution, 39,* 646–670.

Donohue, W. A. (1998). Managing equivocality and relational paradox in the Oslo peace negotiations. *Journal of Language and Social Psychology, 17,* 72–96.

Donohue, W. A., & Diez, M. E. (1985). Directive use in negotiation interaction. *Communication Monographs, 52,* 305–318.

Donohue, W. A., & Druckman, D. (2009). Message framing surrounding the Oslo I accords. *Journal of Conflict Resolution, 53,* 119–145.

Donohue, W. A., & Hoobler, G. D. (2002). Relational frames and their ethical implications in international negotiation: An analysis based on the Oslo II negotiations. *International Negotiation, 6,* 143–167.

Donohue, W. A., Kaufmann, G., Smith, R., & Ramesh, C. (1991). Crisis bargaining: A framework for understanding intense conflict. *International Journal of Group Tensions, 21,* 133–154.

Donohue, W. A., & Roberto, A. J. (1993). Relational development as negotiated order in hostage negotiation. *Human Communication Research, 20,* 175–198.

Donohue, W. A., & Roberto, A. J. (1996). An empirical examination of three models of integrative and distributive bargaining. *International Journal of Conflict Management, 7,* 209–229.

Donohue, W. A., & Taylor, P. J. 2006. *Testing Relational Order Theory in hostage negotiation*. Presented at the meeting of the International Association for Conflict Management.

Eisenberg, E. (1984). Ambiguity as strategy in organizational communication. *Communication Monographs, 51*, 227–242.

Haberman, H., & Danes, S. M. (2007). Father-daughter and father-son family business management transfer comparison: Family FIRO model application. *Family Business Review, 20*, 163–184.

Hammer, M. R., & Rogan, R. G. (1997). Negotiation models in crisis situations: The value of a communication-based approach. In R. Rogan, M. Hammer, & C. Van Zandt (Eds.), *Dynamic processes of crisis negotiation* (pp. 9–23). Westport, CT: Praeger.

Holmes, M. E. (1990). *Hostage negotiations and the extortionate transaction*. Unpublished manuscript, University of Minnesota.

Jameson, J. K. (2004). Negotiating autonomy and connection through politeness: A dialectical approach to organizational conflict management, *Western Journal of Communication, 68*, 257–277.

Leitch, S., & Davenport, S. (2002). Strategic ambiguity in communicating public sector change. *Journal of Communication Management, 7*, 129–139.

Moon, C. (2008). *Narrating political reconciliation: South Africa's Truth and Reconciliation Commission*. London: Centre for the Study of Human Rights.

Muir, W. K. (1977). *Police: Streetcorner politicians*. Chicago: University of Chicago Press.

Putnam, L. L. (2004). Dialectical tensions and rhetorical tropes in negotiations. *Organization Studies, 25*, 35–53.

Rawlins, W. K. (1989). A dialectical analysis of the tensions, functions and strategic challenges of communication in young adult friendships. In J. A. Anderson (Ed.), *Communication yearbook 12* (pp. 157–189). Newbury Park, CA: Sage.

Rhoades, J. A., & Carnevale, P. J. (1999). The behavioral context of strategic choice in negotiation: A test of the dual concern model. *Journal of Applied Social Psychology, 29*, 1777–1802.

Rogan, R. G. (1997). Emotion and emotional expression in crisis negotiation. In R. Rogan, M. R. Hammer, & C. Van Zandt (Eds.), *Dynamic processes of crisis negotiation* (pp. 25–44). Westport, CT: Praeger.

Rogan, R. G., Hammer, M. R. & Van Zandt, C. R. (Eds.). (1997). *Dynamic processes of crisis negotiation*. Westport, CT: Praeger.

Schelling, T. C. (1956). An essay on bargaining. *The American Economic Review, 36*, 281–306.

Schutz, W. C. (1958). *A three-dimensional theory of interpersonal behavior*. Oxford, England: Rinehart.

Simon, J. (2006). Of hate and genocide. *Columbia Journalism Review, 44*, 9.

Stanton, G. H. (2004). Could the Rwandan genocide have been prevented? *Journal of Genocide Research, 6*, 211–228.

Strauss, A. (1978). *Negotiations: Varieties, contexts, processes, and social order*. San Francisco: Jossey-Bass.

Stryker, S. (1987). Identity theory: Developments and extensions. In Y. Krysia & T. Honess (Eds.). *Self and identity: Psychological perspectives* (pp. 89–103). Oxford, England: John Wiley & Sons.

Taylor, P. J., & Thomas, S. (2005). *Linguistic style matching and negotiation outcome*. Presented at the annual meeting of the International Association for Conflict Management, Seville, Spain.

Winter, D. G. (1991). Measuring personality at a distance: Development of an integrated system for scoring motives in running text. In A. J. Stewart, J. M. Healy, Jr., & D. J. Ozer

(Eds.), *Perspectives in personality: Approached to understanding lives* (pp. 59–89). London: Jessica Kingsley.

Zartman, I. W. (2000). Ripeness: The hurting stalemate and beyond. In P. Stern & D. Druckman (Eds.), *Conflict resolution after the cold war* (pp. 225–250). Washington, DC: National Research Council.

Zartman, I., & Kremenyuk, V. (2005). *Peace versus justice. Negotiating forward and backward-looking outcomes.* Lanham, MD: Rowman & Littlefield.

4 The Identity Narratives

■ JESÚS ROMERO-TRILLO[1]

Possibly our world had never realized the importance of the media in the ignition of a conflict until April 1994, when the *Radio Mille Colline* blasted out its message of hatred in Rwanda, calling for a genocide that eventually killed about 800,000 people of that small country in approximately 100 days. The phenomenon was not new, as it can be recalled in the work of the ministries of propaganda during the Second World War. However, linguistics started to pay detailed attention to the role of language in the manipulation of the beliefs and, consequently, of the will of a population only in the early 1990s.

The dramatic deaths suffered by Rwandans have occurred in more recent times in other civil populations—those of the Democratic Republic of Congo, Sri Lanka, and the Balkans, among others—and the public has witnessed with dismay how the media have provided ancillary support to the political interests of the parties in conflict. For instance, in the last days of December 2008, the world observed with impotence the mutual escalation of tension between India and Pakistan that started, symbolically, on the first anniversary of Benazir Bhutto's assassination and as an aftermath of the recent hotel sieges and massacres in Mumbai exactly one month before. For five days (December 27–31) the tension escalated militarily, and verbally in the media.

This chapter will discuss the function of language and power in several facets of identity conflict, within different linguistic traditions, and will illustrate its tenets with an analysis of the language of newspapers during the days of the preconflict between India and Pakistan mentioned above, based on an analysis of the information that appeared on the front pages of four of the most popular English-language newspapers in India and Pakistan. The aim of this analysis is to assess the construction of the cognitive scenario of the conflict and its function as a key element in conflict escalation. For Pakistan the *Daily Times, The Nation, Pakistan Observer,* and *World Tribune Pakistan* were selected, and for India *The Telegraph, The Hindu, Greater Kashmir,* and *Times of India.*

■ LANGUAGE AND POWER

In the course of history, language and power have had an inextricable relationship that has enabled the ideological domination of some people/s over others. Sociolinguistics has been the discipline that has studied the unequal relationships between speakers in several domains: the analysis of standard versus nonstandard dialects, the appraisal of educated versus uneducated varieties, and the description of the social influence—and power—of some dialects as a characteristic of cultural dominance (Fasold, 1984; Ferguson, 1959; Fishman, 1968). Another field of linguistic interest has been the effect of power on conversation through the study of turn-taking (Sacks et al., 1974) as a means to describe how social conventions interact with daily communicative activities on the basis of casual interaction (Jefferson, 1988). In all, the studies carried out by these scholars, classified under the tradition of ethnomethodology, have tried to identify who has the power to start or finish a conversation, who can interrupt, who can participate, and so on, and what linguistic mechanisms are used to carry out these conversational activities through lexis, intonation, or even gestures. This research has extended its applications to sociological inquiry: the creation and solution of conflict in adults (Grimshaw, 1990) and in children (Maynard, 1985), the dialogue of negotiation (Jefferson & Schenkein, 1977), the strategies of blaming (Pomerantz, 1978), and, to finish this enumeration, the use of mechanisms such as laughter to minimize conflict, (Jefferson, 1984; Zartman 1999).

The question of conflict has always puzzled linguists as it characterizes discourse features that make language emphatic: use of intonation, repetition of ideas and structures, lack of respect for turn-taking, use of impolite terms, overlapping, and others. With these features in mind, two approaches to the description of conflict and its solution in speech can be identified. The first approach has favored the detailed analysis of the interaction from a linguistic perspective: verbal processes, prosody, language functions, and so on, and it has shown an inclination to the study of discourse markers as prototypical elements of the cognitive representation of reality (Romero-Trillo, 2006).

The second approach has tried to elucidate the socioideological implications of the use of certain lexical and grammatical structures to illustrate the ideology of a certain piece of discourse via the linguistic discipline termed *Critical Discourse Analysis* (CDA). This tradition, consolidated in the seminal work of Fairclough (1989), has tried to reconcile politics and language as the two faces of a coin whose aim is to buy the will of a population by putting more weight on one or the other side, depending on the historical moment. In recent years, scholars have pursued this path and have applied CDA to the analysis of political speeches (e.g., Van Dijk, 1993).

However, most linguists have tried to apply traditional linguistic concepts, such as metaphor, to analyze the discourse of power and war (Lakoff, 1991). A more recent development has been the study of English *stricto sensu* as a lingua franca in diplomacy, constituting a productive path to pursue in the analysis of the language of conflict and peace, with the basis of real data from the media and from transcripts of peace/conflict talks.

■ CONFLICT AND IDEOLOGY

Conflict management is an essential skill for political/military leaders, who know that their power to escalate tension has to be parallel to the influence and support of the media. Similarly, the deescalation of a conflict can be achieved mainly through the use of language in the press. The ambivalent role of power in public life is well described by Diamond (1996, p. 13): "power is not just the ability to coerce someone or to get them to do something against their will, but rather, it is the ability to interpret events and reality and have this interpretation accepted by others." In other words, the aim of a leader in the escalation of a conflict is not to make citizens start with a violent attitude toward the *Other,* the enemy, but to make his or her population accept the facts and words presented in the argumentation to initiate a conflict without challenge (Brubaker, 2002).

In fact, the most important achievement of a leader in an identity conflict is to arrive at the *otherization* of the enemy in what linguists call *membership categorization analysis*: the clear-cut definition of the line between Us and Them. Otherization is a transversal phenomenon that affects all lexical and grammatical categories and primarily aims at the defeat of the enemy in the discourse. The main objective of otherization is to destroy any possibility for the Other to pose his or her arguments verbally. Cognitively speaking, otherization presents the denial of a dialogic solution of a conflict for the sake of truth and the correction of lies. Often, leaders resort to the media to publicize their intentions by dramatizing examples of the cruelty of their enemies, of the Other's abject intentions, and of the enemy's insidious and wicked linguistic strategies to deceive not only the other side's people but also its own. These examples often carry the implicit or explicit duty to liberate the Others from their *caudillo* (Atawneh, 2009), leading to Donohue's Identity Trap, described in this book.

Escalating conflict through language is a multifaceted phenomenon that unites ideology and language, especially with the help of metaphors, as they are tropes that combine clarity and ambiguity in the discourse of those who want to seem objective and impartial in the defense of an ideal. Metaphors are useful tools in persuasive political/propagandistic discourse, as they navigate between cognition and emotion (Bhatia, 2009). In fact, it is well known that to create conflict and mobilize a population, the mere presentation of facts, however heinous they might be, is not enough; there is always the need for an emotional hook that descends into the subconscious to engage the individual's basic ideals. This emotional stirring is often linked to the defense of identity, race, religion, human rights, the weak, the poor, the minorities, and so on. Thus, metaphors cause a "semantic tension"—to use Charteris-Black's (2004) terminology—that makes discourse uncomfortable for readers and impels them to react emotionally and cognitively.

Obviously, deescalating the negative image of the other is a complex task that can only be achieved through language. The actors in peace talks in any conflict must bear this in mind and must try to use neutral terms of address, careful adjectivization, and accurate politeness techniques to elaborate a discourse of confidence building. This is crucial after the use of language that has often been employed in explosive speeches linked with military attacks.

■ THE SEARCH FOR A COMMON LINGUA FRANCA

A further difficulty lies in the use of English as a lingua franca in mediation processes. Often, English is the working language in peace talks between belligerent parties in a conflict. In other cases, English is the mother tongue or second language of the mediators, who are assisted by interpreters due to the lack of enough knowledge of English of the representatives or the insufficient knowledge of the language of the parties of the mediators. This fact increases the possibility of misunderstanding in communication, as the use of emotions in language translates badly in a second language. In these cases, essential linguistic elements, such as prosody, rhythm, discourse markers, and others that definitely contribute to the transmission of interactional knowledge, are overridden by stilted translations of facts and ideas without the generous wrapping of the features that convey linguistic nuances in speech.

As a result, peace initiatives must be assisted by linguists who can study the interactions of the participants attentively to assess their pragmatic behavior. This analysis can contribute to the translation of intentions, ideas, and attitudes and avoid what has been defined as "pragmatic fossilization" (Romero-Trillo, 2002), which can mar any attempt at peace building in a conversation between nonnative speakers of a language. A careful analysis of the discourse of the participants, especially in the suprasegmental and paralinguistic domains, will help negotiators to understand the linguistic schemata of the interlocutors and, then, their opinions, declarations, and speech acts in order to build a common discourse of solutions to a conflict.

Finally, there is another important step that conflict managers will eventually have to tackle: how to transmit the deescalation news after some progress in peace talks has been made. This step is a true quandary for participants in conflict resolution dialogue, as it involves reframing the image of the Other, and also of the self, vis-à-vis some expectations that do not need to be always true and, in many cases, vis-à-vis some information that cannot be unveiled to the general public—perhaps metaphorically—but can be better understood with a scalar presentation of information geared to the target audience.

This chapter seeks to contribute to the understanding of the role of language in peace/conflict building. Specifically, it will describe the language of menace and bellicose argumentation from the perspective of Pragmatics and corpus linguistics (Romero-Trillo, 2008). *Pragmatics* can be described as "the study of those relations between language and context that are *grammaticalised* [italics in the original], or encoded in the structure of a language" (Levinson, 1983, p. 9). In other words, it is the branch of linguistics that attempts to interpret the semantics of a proposition/utterance in its context, with the resulting consequences in the real world (i.e., the performative function; Austin, 1962). As a result, pragmatics offers a dynamic and addressee-oriented analysis to real language, as opposed to more traditional semantic approaches. To complement this approach, corpus linguistics bases its analysis on the capacity to compile principled large databases of real language (spoken and written) in order to describe language in use.

■ ANALYSIS OF DATA

The corpus under analysis consists of two subcorpora of four Pakistani and four Indian newspapers in English, collected from December 27 to 31, 2008, at the inception of the mutual escalation of military threats (Tables 4.1 and 4.2). The Indian subcorpus has 8,491 words and the Pakistani 6,854, according to the following distribution:

TABLE 4.1. *Indian Newspapers*

Times of India	1,819
The Telegraph	2,495
The Hindu	2,110
Greater Kashmir	2,067
TOTAL WORDS	**8,491**

TABLE 4.2. *Pakistani Newspapers*

Daily Times	935
The Nation	2,896
Pakistan Observer	2,069
World Tribune Pakistan	954
TOTAL WORDS	**6,854**

The linguistic richness of each subcorpus—measured in terms of the type/token ratio, that is, the number of different lemmas divided by the total number of words—is 20.60 for the Indian sample and 23.75 for the Pakistani sample. This means that the level of linguistic lexical complexity, although slightly higher in the Pakistani newspapers, is approximately the same in both subcorpora; therefore, we may assume that the audience for both samples has the same level of education. In terms of the average length of sentences, which indicates the complexity of subordinate clauses, the Indian papers have a higher mean length, 34.92 words, compared to 29.76 in the Pakistani papers. In sum, the result of the structure of clauses is nonsignificant at the surface level.

The following quantitative analysis of *lexical frequency* to evaluate lexical implications will focus on the most frequent lexical items that appear within the 147th position in both subcorpora. The term *Pakistan* is the seventh most frequently used term in both repertoires, occurring 120 times (1.75%; but *Pakistani* only 31 times [0.45%]) in the Pakistani press and 126 (1.48%) and 29 (0.34%) times, respectively, in the Indian papers. This shows that, in both samples, Pakistan appears as the more important actor—as offender or innocent, depending on the perspective—while the word *India* occurs 110 times (1.60%) and *Indian* appears 49 times (0.71%) in the Pakistani press (ninth position), and only 79 times (0.93%) and 33 times (0.39%), respectively, in the Indian newspapers. These figures indicate that the Pakistani press is assigning more weight to the innocence of its country and presents both countries as actors/recipients in the conflict in a discussion of national responsibility.

Indian newspapers highlight the word *Mumbai* (the 18th most frequently used word and the 3rd lexical one after *Pakistan* and *India*) 52 times (0.61%) in the corpus. By contrast, *Mumbai* appears in the Pakistani press only in 36th position, occurring 31 times (0.39%). Obviously, the fact that the Indian press places the name of this city in third position indicates its intention to make its readers relate the present situation to the recent massacre and avoid mention of India's active responsibility. In the Pakistani press, however, *Mumbai* appears after other significant words that support Pakistan's cause, such as *troops*, in 29th position, and *tension,* in 31st position. Therefore, the Pakistani press tries to avoid any significant weight of the concept *Mumbai* in the mental scenario of its readers.

Regarding the key words *war* and *peace, war* appears in 36th position in Indian newspapers (33 times; 0.39%), while in the Pakistani press it does not appear within the 147 words; therefore, its use is marginal. By contrast, the term *peace* in the Pakistani press appears in the 57th position (17 times; 0.25%), but in the Indian press it appears in the 79th position (16 times, 0.19%). This finding is very illuminating, as it shows the aggressive attitude of the Indian media, with the term *war* in key conceptual locations and its complete absence—transformed into the term *peace*—in the Pakistani press.

Another interesting example is the use of *terror* and *terrorist.* In the Indian press, the term *terror* appears in the 64th position (19 times; 0.22%), while in the Pakistani press the term *terrorist* occurs in the 75th position (13 times; 0.19%). Both frequencies are very similar statistically, but the use of the terms follows the same ideological stance shown previously: India avoids acceptance of any responsibility for the present situation and avers its opposition to the notion of terror. In contrast, the Pakistani press always uses the term *terrorist* as a disclaimer vis-à-vis that accusation.

Next, the analysis focuses on the linguistic imagery used by the media regarding the possibily of solving the conflict. It is important to mention the use of the term *dialogue,* which appears in the Indian press in the 106th position (12 times; 0.14%) and in 95th position in the Pakistani corpus (10 times; 0.15%). As shown, in both corpora, dialogue has a marginal presence with almost equal percentages, which indicates the small importance that the press gives to the solution of the conflict. As the data indicate, both countries relegate the question of dialogue to a secondary sphere and concentrate mainly on the accusations and disclaimers toward the escalation of reciprocal menace.

To finish the analysis of lexical frequency, it is very revealing to mention that there are no references to the terms *religion, Hindu,* or *Muslim* and their related derivations. This indicates that, according to the media, there is a complete absence of religious connotations at the source of this conflict and, more importantly, that both sides seem to have no intention of to creating such ideas in the minds of their readers and limit all these events to the political sphere.

Lexical Concordances

Beyond the frequency of words lies their *lexical concordances,* showing the cognitive scenario ascribed to them by the media. The importance of concordances in lexical studies derives mainly from the seminal work of Sinclair (1991), who demonstrated how words seem to be selected in pairs and groups, and who showed that many uses of words and phrases attract other words in strong collocations, as seen in the terms *hard work, hard luck,* and *hard facts,* and, by so doing, they create a mental lexicon consisting of a string of words that are inextricably linked in their grammatical and conceptual presentation.

In Indian newspapers, with the lexemes *India/n,* the most recurrent concordance relates to the moves of the Pakistani army toward the border of its country. The following examples show the preposition at the beginning of the concordance that indicates movement or coverage:

- To the Indian border
- Along the Indian frontier

In this respect, it is also interesting to mention that India is the affected country in most cases, as in the sentence "Pakistan moves troops towards Indian border" (*The Hindu,* December 27, 2008), except in the quotations from external institutions or countries specifying that the border is shared by both countries, such as "The United States has urged India and Pakistan to avoid an escalation of tensions after Islamabad redeployed troops to their common border" (*Greater Kashmir,* December 28, 2008).

Regarding the words *Pakistan/i,* it is very interesting to note that the country usually appears as the indirect object in a ditransitive construction with a "to-infinitive" (Quirk et al., 1985, pp. 1215–1216). Some examples follow:

- International pressure on Pakistan to accept that
- Expected Pakistan to accept immediate
- To persuade Pakistan to act against.
- Waiting for Pakistan to act as it
- Pressing Pakistan to crack down

This construction shows the possibility of the country's becoming an actor in the solution of the conflict. Another recurrent concordance is "Pakistan(i)-occupied Kashmir," which also gives a flavor of the ideology behind the argumentation of Indian newspapers.

As indicated in a previous section, the word *Mumbai* deserves more attention because it appears 52 times in the subcorpus and the concordance "Mumbai (terror) attack(s)" appears 31 times (59.6%). Other collocations are "Mumbai terror strikes," "Mumbai carnage," and "Mumbai mission."

The lexeme *peace* is primarily linked not to the direct solution of the conflict in this particular case, but to the abstract interest of the situation in general: "in the interest of peace and security," "China wants peace in the region," "peace and stability in the region," and the more anecdotic "we need development, peace and tourism." Its opposite, the term *war* correlates mainly with the collocation "war hysteria" attributed to the Pakistani side (7 cases out of 33) and the classic "war on terror," which appears side by side with the more dramatic "war or vengeance."

The term *dialogue,* as mentioned above, offers few examples, and they concentrate mainly in the collocations that indicate positive intentions: "engage in dialogue," "cooperation and dialogue," "resumption of a dialogue," "peace dialogue," "comprehensive dialogue" and the more curious use of *investigative* as a premodifier of the term: "we are having a very active diplomatic and investigative dialogue with India" (*The Times,* December 27, 2008), in a report quoting Pakistani authorities.

As far as the concept *terror/ist* is concerned, in Indian newspapers, apart from the examples above, we find collocations such as: "terror/ist camps," "terrorist groups," and "terrorist activities." These are the most frequent uses of this lexical entry.

In Pakistani newspapers, the use of *India* undergoes an interesting transformation compared to its use in the Indian press, as it tends to appear in close connection to *Pakistan* (even hyphenated in some cases):

- Pak–India situation
- Between Pakistan and India
- Pak–India tension
- Good Pak–India relations
- Cordial Pakistan–India ties
- Pakistan and India as neighbors
- Existing Pak–India standoff

These examples confirm the tendency to neutralize the negative situation and appraise the historical ties as positively as possible. We also find the mirror example of Indian-controlled Kashmir, as in the case of Pakistani newspapers, which indicates the crucial role of this territory for the stability in the region.

The word *Pakistan* appears in some examples of the subcorpus as the recipient of aggression, as for example:

- Indian attacks inside Pakistan
- Approach against Pakistan
- Military confrontation with Pakistan
- Launching an attack on Pakistan
- Give ultimatum to Pakistan
- "Surgical" strike inside Pakistan
- Instructions for attack on Pakistan
- An opportunity to attack Pakistan
- Diplomatic offensive against Pakistan
- Land aggression against Pakistan
- Military action against Pakistan
- Plan to attack Pakistan
- Through air strikes in Pakistan

This language of aggression against the country, which appears in an object/affected position in syntactic terms, contrasts with the overall number of concordances of the adjective *Pakistani* (31) that present the following neighboring elements:

- Pakistani (military) officials: nine instances (29%)
- Pakistani leaders: three instances (9.6%)
- Pakistani Army: three instances (9.6%)

It is clear that these references are neutral and defend an intense sense of statehood to eliminate any mental reference to absence of control in its territory or to localized belligerent wishes against India by terrorist groups.

The unavoidable reference to Mumbai enjoys more lenient, and fewer, collocations (27 hits). There are only two references to terror, "Mumbai terror/ist attacks," while the rest are divided in frequency between "Mumbai attacks" and other, more neutral language such as "Mumbai incidents" (four examples), "Mumbai tragedy," and "Mumbai assault."

The concept of *war* appears only 16 times in the subcorpus—perhaps as an attempt to eliminate this possibility from the mental script of the readers. It appearance is related to a menace in the region: "The war clouds are hovering over South Asia" (*World Tribune Pakistan*, December 27, 2008); to an attack on the population: "People realize war would be more costly in its impact" (*The Nation*, December 29, 2008); or to the unavoidable aftermath of India's aggression, as in the headline "Pakistan does not want war, but will defend itself if attacked' (*World Tribune Pakistan*, December 28, 2008).

Regarding the concept of peace, it is very interesting to note that Pakistani newspapers use collocations that indicate their longing for it: "Desiring peace in the region" or "we are the torch-bearers of peace and remain committed to our desire for peace" (*Pakistan Observer*, December 27, 2008). Other concordances insist on the concepts "peace and stability in/of the region" in an attempt to include the neighbouring countries in the problem (as mentioned above).

The concept of *dialogue* is much appreciated, as in sentences and phrases such as "Cooperation and dialogue was the only way forward," "Dialogue is the key to resolving," and "importance of dialogue." It is also significant to find the metaphorical headline "Dialogue Is Our Biggest Arsenal" (*The Nation*, December 28, 2008).

With reference to the concept of *terror/terrorist*, excluding the examples above, we find significantly fewer references in the Pakistani press than in the Indian newspapers. There are no examples of the collocation "terrorist activities," and there is only one reference to the phrase "terrorist training camps" and one to "terrorist groups."

■ DISCUSSION

The analysis of the data shows how "language war" (Lakoff, 2000) permeates the hypothetically objective presentation of facts by newspapers. The crucial factor in the creation of an atmosphere of prewar through language is the phenomenon of otherization. Otherization is a subtle linguistic and cognitive tool that fosters maintenance of the distance between one group and the other group on the basis of ethnic, religious, language, or other affiliations. This is perhaps why this phenomenon has been exploited in recent times by politicians and, subsequently, by the media in an attempt to leave countries and international institutions unscathed and to blame certain groups that are perceived to have a blurred organization. In this sense, the notion of a "war on terror" is possibly the epitome of a loaded and an empty notion that might include or exclude, depending on the moment, citizens and (dis)organized groups that can be present anywhere, with no formal ties to a defined territory. The examples presented above show how the idea of terrorism underlies the threats and appeals to dialogue scattered throughout the texts.

The phenomenon of international terrorism has obvious sociopolitical implications worldwide, but especially for Western societies. The terrorist attacks suffered by New York, Madrid, and London, to mention only a few paradigmatic cases of Western cities in which the perpetrators were ordinary and, in some cases, well-respected citizens, have unleashed the process of otherization of individuals who belong to certain groups. This phenomenon has been masterfully portrayed in fiction, as for instance in the novels *The Reluctant Fundamentalist* by Mohsin Hamid (2007) and *Terrorist* by John Updike (2006), where, from different viewpoints, readers can follow the development of self-otherization in the minds of young citizens with different levels of social integration in their communities. Terrorism does not only intend to subvert a certain political status quo; its primary aim is to "modify the behavior of a target audience" (Weinberg & Davis, 1989, p. 6), and its practice can be attributed both to governments and to groups, depending on the perspective of the speaker. In fact, in the international sphere, the concept of a double standard applied to states that exert armed power over groups or regions is a common accusation that the international community seems to avoid clarifying.

The problem is how to identify the notions that configure otherization in the mental scenario of individuals and groups. For this purpose, I will use the categories that personify the representations of terrorism and must be the target of conflict prevention activists by extension. The cognitive categories used to differentiate my (group) behavior from the Other's are (Bhatia, 2009) good versus evil, law versus lawlessness, civilization versus barbarism, and freedom versus tyranny. Although it is obvious that these categories pertain to the moral/ethical domain and cannot be always objectified in facts or behaviors, this is precisely why they are subject to manipulation—in the neutral sense—by the media and can also be used to deescalate a conflict. My intention in this chapter is to propose the negative elements in these dyads as the key stages of otherization: evil > lawlessness > barbarism > tyranny.

Evil has in recent times been popularly equated with President George W. Bush's famous enumeration of the countries belonging to the "axis of evil" after the September 11, 2001, attacks and, as a coextension, with the redefinition of nuclear weapons as "weapons of mass destruction." Demonization or "evilification" (Lazar & Lazar, 2004, p. 236) is a phenomenon by which the Other acquires some negative moral features that automatically allow us to take action for self-defense. As a result, I may become an accomplice of evil if I do not act immediately. This identification of evil in the media, and the position that readers have to adopt in front of it, are issues to tackle in conflict prevention. As Bhatia (2009) says, evilification of the Other implies the assumption of the continuation of this behavior on the basis of previous experience—that is, there is no room for peace negotiations—and the certainty that this experience is primarily based on universal common sense—that is, not on objective and observable facts necessarily.

The questions of lawlessness and barbarism also try to delineate the moral standards of the in-group versus the out-group. International community regulations, United Nations (UN) resolutions, and other documents attempt to impose norms and sanctions that not all actors seem to abide by, especially when the actors do not have a recognized entity (terrorist groups, guerrillas, army factions, etc.). In this sense, the implication is that the violation of certain laws by certain groups and countries leads to the notion of barbarism in opposition to civilization. By contrast, violations of certain international regulations and UN sanctions by other actors, mainly countries in this case, are considered violations of the laws, usually with the excuse of self-defense. This dual understanding is reflected in the press and serves to deepen otherization, as the notion of barbarism conveys the image of danger for the collective thought. Conflict mediation needs to take these facts into consideration and has to make belligerent parties agree on certain norms that are respected equally. For this purpose, negotiation rules obviously need to follow what the international community dictates but must also avoid intrusion from the media. They must be supplemented by ad hoc norms that enable the parties in the conflict to guarantee their will to find a peaceful solution at the negotiation table, beyond all stereotypes.

To finish the process, the fourth representation of otherization is tyranny. Tyranny is the opposite of freedom and raises great concern in collective imagery. The examples of tyrannies are legion in past and recent history, and they represent the last stage in the unfortunate down-the-hill cline of the four proposed phases of otherization: evil leads to lawlessness, lawlessness to barbarism, and barbarism to tyranny via its institutionalization. The identification of tyrannical behavior by parties in a conflict is one of the preferred excuses by the media and their support of one side or the other. Atrocities and violations of civil rights by the military, or by armed groups, constitute justifications for opponents and are, therefore, facts that are aired worldwide in the media. Often, these violations are attributed to dictatorial regimes that practice tyranny in its varied political and physical fashions. Experts in conflict management must be aware of these facts and should aim at determining what acts can clearly be defined as tyranny—as the consequence of previous stages—or can be attributed to propaganda as a means to achieve international acquiescence to certain causes. It can be said that the tyrant is the extreme example of otherization, as the concept embodies all the most heinous features that any human being can imagine. Tyranny is therefore the last stage in the process, and there is usually universal agreement on its political annulment.

■ **CONCLUSIONS**

This chapter has shown the essential role of language in the management of conflict, both in its escalating and in its deescalating phase. Language is not neutral or objective in daily life; it always carries the ideological load of the speaker or writer. This load is especially crucial when language intersects with bellicose situations in which leaders try to mobilize a population against a common enemy. For this purpose, leaders usually resort to the media to create a derogatory image of the opponent through language tools that explain the past, present, or future atrocities of the enemy.

Careful study of the language of conflict will help conflict managers understand the imagery of the parties in dispute, and it can be a useful tool to start negotiations that might prevent or solve a conflict. Also, detailed linguistic analysis of actual peace talks can indicate possible linguistic paths to engage in fruitful conversations that confront the fears and expectations of negotiators through linguistic techniques. As an example, this chapter has illustrated the position of the media in the escalation of a conflict from the perspectives of two nations: India and Pakistan. Although the facts in any conflict are theoretically objective, it seems clear that the propaganda machines of India and Pakistan in this case did their best to both hide and unveil what was more relevant to their interests.

Through the analysis of lexical choices, this chapter has revealed the intricate cognitive patterns that the hypothetical readers of each set of newspapers are prone to accept without challenge. This embrace between intention and acceptance in dialogic discourse—the linguistic "given-new" of the interpersonal metafunction (Halliday, 1994)—serves as a baseline for the ideological scaffold of language in the media. CDA makes use of linguistics to shed light on the subconscious responses of readers/recipients to any language embedded in a given context. In this sense, this chapter shows the role of Indian and Pakistani newspapers in hinting at the division of attackers and attacked, belligerents and peace lovers, from each point of view.

To sum up, the purpose of this chapter has been to draw the attention of readers, politicians, and journalists to the essential role of language in the escalation or deflection of a conflict toward a peaceful solution.

Note

1. I am grateful to the Spanish Ministerio de Ciencia e Innovación for its support (Project FF12009–08395).

References

Atawneh, A. M. (2009). The discourse of war in the Middle East: Analysis of media reporting. *Journal of Pragmatics*, *31*, 263–278.

Austin, J. L. (1962). *How to do things with words*. Oxford: Oxford University Press.

Bhatia, A. (2009). The discourses of terrorism. *Journal of Pragmatics*, *31*, 279–289.

Brubaker, R. (2002). *Ethnicity without groups*. University of California Press.

Charteris-Black, J. (2004). *Corpus approaches to critical metaphor analysis*. Hampshire, UK: Palgrave Macmillan.

Diamond, J. (1996). *Status and power in verbal interaction*. Amsterdam and Philadelphia: John Benjamins.

Fairclough, N. (1989). *Language and power*. Essex, UK: Longman.

Fasold, R. (1984). *The sociolinguistics of language*. Oxford: Blackwell.

Ferguson, C. (1959). Diglossia. *Word*, *15*, 325–340.

Fishman, J., (Ed.). (1968). *Readings in the sociology of language*. The Hague: Mouton.

Grimshaw, A. D. (Ed) (1990). *Conflict talk*. Cambridge: Cambridge University Press.

Halliday, M. A. K. (1994). *An introduction to functional grammar* (2nd ed.). London: Edward Arnold.

Hamid, M. (2007). *The reluctant fundamentalist*. Bloomsbury: Hamish Hamilton

Jefferson, G. (1984). On the organization of laughter in talk about troubles. In J. M. Atkinson & J. Heritage (Eds.), *Structures of social action* (pp. 346–369).

Jefferson, G. (1988). On the sequential organization of troubles—talk in ordinary conversation. *Social Problems*, *35*, 418–441.

Jefferson, G., & Schenkein, J. (1977). Some sequential negotiations in conversation: Unexpanded and expanded versions of projected action sequences. *Sociology*, *11*, 87–103.

Lakoff, G. (1991). The metaphor system used to justify war in the Gulf. *Peace Research, 23*, 25–32.

Lakoff, R. T. (2000). *Taking power: The politics of language in our lives*. New York: Basic Books.

Lazar, A., & Lazar, M. M. (2004). The discourse of the new word order: "Out-casting" the double face of threat. *Discourse and Society, 15*, 223–242.

Levinson, S. C. (1983). *Pragmatics*. Cambridge: Cambridge University Press.

Maynard, D. W. (1985). How children start arguments. *Language in Society, 14*, 1–30.

Pomerantz, A. M. (1978). Attributions of responsibility: Blamings. *Sociology, 12*(1), 15–21.

Quirk, R., Greenbaum, S., Leech, G., & Svartvik, J. (1985). *A comprehensive grammar of the English language*. London: Longman.

Romero-Trillo, J. (2002). The pragmatic fossilization of discourse markers in non-native speakers of English. *Journal of Pragmatics, 34*, 769–784

Romero-Trillo, J. (2006). Discourse markers. In K. Brown (Ed.), *Encyclopedia of language and linguistics* (pp. 639–642). Oxford: Elsevier.

Romero-Trillo, J. (Ed.). (2008). *Pragmatics and corpus linguistics: A mutualistic entente*. Berlin and New York: Mouton de Gruyter.

Sacks, H., Schegloff, E. A., & Jefferson, G. (1974). A simplest systematics for the organization of turn-taking in conversation. *Language, 50*, 696–735.

Sinclair, J. (1991). *Corpus, concordance, collocation*. Oxford: Oxford University Press.

Updike, J. (2006). *Terrorist*. New York: Penguin Books.

Van Dijk, T. A. (1993). Principles of Critical Discourse Analysis. *Discourse & Society, 4*, 249–283.

Weinberg, L., & Davis, P. (1989). *Introduction to political terrorism*. New York: McGraw-Hill.

Zartman, I. W. (Ed.). (1999). *Traditional cures for modern conflicts; African conflict "medicine."* Boulder, CO: Lynne Riener.

5 Negotiating Memories and Justice in the Philippines

■ ARIEL MACASPAC PENETRANTE

The Southern Philippines provides an interesting example of how violence contributes to the development and maintenance of identity in a self-sustaining conflict cycle. It reflects a conflict whose complexity has been reduced simplistically to one of a Muslim minority in contest with the state. An intervention based on superficial analysis may, however, not simply fail to resolve the conflict and end the violence, but fuel new conflicts. This chapter proposes a disaggregation of the levels of conflict and the design of interventions appropriate to each to raise the prospects of success. Particular attention is given the role of civil society and nongovernmental organizations (NGOs) in peace processes.

Identity defines the very existence of a collective group, both in terms of how it sees itself and how it is perceived by others. It provides a frame of reference for the group's *rationality system* defining the motivations and actions of both individual members and the collective. Identity has important organizational functions within groups, serving as the guiding framework (value system) for the codification of sanctions and rewards. The definition of social norms through which identity groups regulate uncertainty is key to understanding their systems of inclusion and exclusion. Identities constructed through primordial ties and kinship connections reflect categories resulting from the givens of birth such as "blood," language, religion, territory, and culture. However, Huntington's (1996) assumption that you only know who you are when you know who you are against as implied by his identification of culture and religion as the primary source of future conflicts is seen as incorrect. Identities built through primordial ties and kinship connections are, of course, exclusionary, but tolerance of nonmembers is likely in most cases because these identities are not constructed primarily as a defense mechanism against threats. Intolerance arises in reaction to threats.

The construction of identities of minorities can arise as a consequence of nonaccommodation of subgroup value systems and social norms in an existing society at large. Identity is shaped through memories and experiences of violence and injustice specific individuals have experienced. These memories and experiences lead to the internal process of evaluating one's status, and when the political elite "name it" or give it a specific term, a *social contract* evolves from the suggestion and a *group* is constructed. On the other side, the minority group faces ascription of features from the society at large that are accommodated in the group's identity-building process. This notion implies that the group's own definition of itself is in reference to the ascription given by the society at large. Compared to identities established through primordial ties and kinship connections, identities that are initiated by an outside actor through marginalizing ascription are largely shaped by a sense of existential threat.

■ METHODOLOGY

This chapter begins by making use of hierarchy and misrecognition theories to analyze the identity conflict in the Southern Philippines. Effective strategies of conflict resolution are best drawn from real conflicts. Analysis of actual conflicts facilitates understanding of their complexities, allows identification of recursive dynamics, and weaves together factors that lend themselves to particular forms of intervention. Hierarchy theory borrowed from ecology is concerned with the significance of different levels of analysis in filtering information when observing phenomena (Ahl & Allen 1996). Although a continuous association between the different scales is relevant in analyzing internal identity conflicts, an attempt is made first to disassociate them from each other to more deeply understand their internal dynamics and then, afterward, to reassociate them with the other levels. This process allows scholars and practitioners to recognize different sets of priorities in formulating strategies of intervention within each level.

Secondly, the analysis concerns itself with the dynamics of *misrecognition* (defined as status subordination) where state policy formulation is dominated by a specific group to the exclusion of minorities considered a threat and their political and economic marginalization. This is also known as a situation of *structural imbalance*. This analysis of the Southern Philippines conflict draws on these theories to identify and explain the dynamics of mobilization around *identity markers* leading to the construction of identity. Identity is inter alia the means whereby individuals and groups acquire security and well-being (see the chapter by Zartman and Anstey and the chapter by Staub in this book), and can be constructed through marginalization, mass violence, and exclusion.

Finally, attention is given to the design of grassroots negotiation interventions in the Southern Philippine conflict in which there is armed struggle for recognition and the need for empowerment of isolated communities in conflict-affected areas. Armed groups such as the Moro National Liberation Front (MNLF) and the Moro Islamic Liberation Front (MILF) are (still) regarded as being incapable of pursuing grassroots empowerment. In some instances, NGOs are assuming mediation roles between communities, undermining elements propagating mass violence. Because NGOs provide welfare functions for people, they have greater legitimacy than armed groups striving to mobilize popular support for violence as a means of change. In this case, civil society has had some success in containing potential violence through its intervention in the process. This bottom-up approach is to be classified as an external intervention, because the main source of violence is the "first track" (government vs. rebels). The question is raised: If the MILF had the capacity to provide welfare functions, would it have to be reduced simply to an identity as a mere agent of violence? In short if it became an empowered civil society group, it and the wider society might make different choices about its identity.

■ CONFLICT AND THE CRYSTALLIZATION
OF BANGSAMORO IDENTITY

A short historical analysis of the Philippine conflict is necessary to explain the dynamics leading to the construction of identity and mobilization around identity markers. The discontent of the Muslim population can be classified into two categories. The first category of discontent refers to misrecognition, which refers to the inability to participate as social peers in societal interactions (Fraser, 2003). The marginalization of the Muslims was initiated during the American colonial period and continued during the state-building period after the independence from the United States. Muslim and other peripheral ethnolinguistic groups fell victims to the social engineering by the Philippine state when mass migration to the South was promoted. Mindanao's original Muslim inhabitants were reduced from as much as 76% of the population in 1903 to 18% in 2000 (Santos, 2000, p. 208). (See Figure 5.1.)

The second category of discontent refers to the experience of violence from the society at large. Identity "entrepreneurs" sell inclusion to members in exchange for loyalty and participation in organized competition against the "occupying" Philippine state. The use of violence makes the claim for recognition a security issue, legitimizing policies of further repression and exclusion in the society. The security dilemma is a "protracting" factor facilitating deterioration of relations and violent ethnic, cultural, or religious confrontation. The Philippine case illustrates how the experience of recursive violence facilitates the construction of identity.

The identity of the Bangsamoro as a political collectivity, however, was crystallized and codified only in the 1960s. Prior to that time, the members of the ten ethnolinguistic groups with Islam as their religion primarily identified themselves as members of these ethnolinguistic groups. However, when members of the Armed Forces of the Philippines massacred more than 28 Moro Muslim recruits[1] on March 18, 1968, on the Philippine island of Corregidor (called the *Jabidah massacre*), the sentiments of the Muslims in the Philippines led to the mobilization of the Muslim population, subsequently leading to the formation of the MNLF, led by the University of the Philippines professor Nur Misuari, that was able to challenge the Philippine state in terms of arms. The armed struggle of the Muslims was seen as a threat not only by the Christian settlers now facing the prospect of having to leave the land they considered home but also by the Philippine government. The government was planning to annex Sabah from Malaysia following the formation of the Federation of Malaya in 1963; previously Sabah, had merely been leased to Britain through the Sulu Sultanate in Mindanao. The Muslim population was trapped in the middle of the armed confrontation between the Philippine military and the MNLF, and Muslims also faced a series of violent attacks by citizen militias supported by the military, partisan armed groups, private armies, and Christian vigilante groups. These attacks on the Muslim population were reactions by Christian settlers to the perceived upcoming threat of Muslim separatism, which was not conspicuous prior to the escalation in the 1960s.

Furthermore, it should be noted that aside from Muslim ethnolingustic groups in Mindanao, 18 indigenous groups such as the T'boli, B'laan, Ata, Bagobo, and

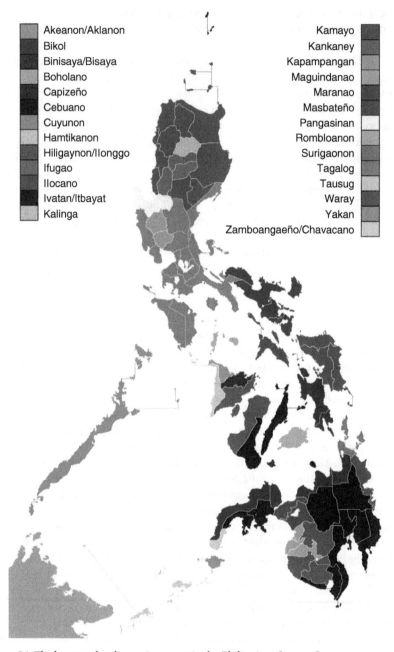

Akeanon/Aklanon
Bikol
Binisaya/Bisaya
Boholano
Capizeño
Cebuano
Cuyunon
Hamtikanon
Hiligaynon/Ilonggo
Ifugao
Ilocano
Ivatan/Itbayat
Kalinga

Kamayo
Kankaney
Kapampangan
Maguindanao
Maranao
Masbateño
Pangasinan
Rombloanon
Surigaonon
Tagalog
Tausug
Waray
Yakan
Zamboangaeño/Chavacano

Figure 5.1 The largest ethnolingustic groups in the Philippines *Source*: Commons Wikimedia 2010.

Manobo, collectively called *Lumads*, had inhabitated Mindanao before the other groups arrived from Malaysia and Indonesia. More than 95% of the Lumads still maintain their animistic religion. Both the Muslim ethnolinguistic groups and indigenous people experienced marginalization following the state-sponsored mass migration initiated by the American colonial administration, which will be described later in this chapter. However, the Muslim groups, unlike the indigenous people, had been politically organized since before the Spanish colonization and could easily mobilize. In addition, the Muslim ethnolinguistic groups, unlike the indigenous groups, were able to use their religion as an identity marker, not only making mobilization easier, but also enabling the resistance movement to attract significant support from Muslim countries such as Malaysia, Indonesia, Iran, and Libya, allowing the Muslims to provide credible resistance to the Philippine state.

In short, the experience of being victims of mass violence served to crystallize an identity that already existed in looser form. Prior to the series of violent attacks, religion was largely politically unexpressed. When Muslim and other peripheral groups came under attack, their members retreated to religion as the main primordial tie to seek protection. Identity boundaries hardened. They were further hardened by the majority Christians' reaction to the group's claims for identity recognition as distorted and dysfunctional. In turn, the majority group's attitude hardened further when claims for recognition were later complemented by the use of violence and threat. A self-sustaining cycle of prejudice and violence was established. The conflict became more complex. Policies with good intentions could easily be counterproductive. For instance, giving back land to Muslims to bring justice leads to injustice to Christian settlers who have been living in Mindanao for half a decade. Furthermore, indigenous groups claim the same lands claimed by the Muslims, arguing that they are the original inhabitants. This issue was the reason why the peace process fell into a stalemate in 2009 following the intervention of the Philippine Supreme Court, which nullified the Memorandum of Agreement on Ancestral Domain (MOA-AD).

The establishment of the Autonomous Region of Muslim Mindanao (ARMM) in August 1989 and its expansion in 2001 consolidated Muslims' individual rights and gave recognition to the collectivity. However, it minoritized Christian settlers in the region and strengthened Christian paramilitaries, which, assisted by state-sponsored migration programs, expelled the Moros to the most isolated areas in Mindanao. The narratives of atrocities and animosity of the Christians toward the Moros legitimized and consolidated their struggle for recognition.

The year 2009 started with a major setback in the prospects for a negotiated political settlement in the Southern Philippines. The MOA-AD between the government of the Philippines under the administration of President Gloria Macapagal-Arroyo and the MILF was declared unconstitutional by the Philippine Supreme Court in October 2008, triggering attacks by rogue MILF commanders on several villages in North Cotobato, Sarangani, and Lanao del Norte. The Philippine military retaliated, and the cease-fire agreement reached in 2003 was terminated.

The MOA-AD, with its provisions for the creation of the Bangsamoro Juridical Entity (BJE), would, among others things, have given the separatist group the power to enter into treaties and have their own courts and police force. The consequence has been an estimated 600,000 internally displaced persons staying in improvised evacuation centers and several hundred people killed, adding to the estimated deaths of 100,000 to 150,000 since 1971 (Ploughshare, 2008). Furthermore, Malaysia, Libya, Brunei, and Japan dissolved the international peace monitoring team following the collapse of the peace negotiations, leading to more insecurity for both Christians and Muslims. Although both the government and the MILF expressed willingness to restart negotiations, both also expressed concerns and demands: security issues (surrendering the rogue and lawless elements of the MILF that were pillaging remote communities and engaging in kidnapping for ransom as a profitable cottage industry[2]); the role of Malaysia as the third-party mediator, which is seen by several stakeholders, such as local leaders in Mindanao and nationalists, as ineffective and as pursuing its own interests related to the territorial disputes with the Philippines (some nationalists are demanding the replacement Malaysia through Indonesia); and the guarantee that future agreements will not be blocked again by the Supreme Court and that the MOA-AD will be revived. Sidney Jones of the International Crisis Group stated, "in Mindanao, you've got far more problems and far more spoilers" (Gomez, 2009).

■ COMPLEXITIES OF UNRAVELING A MULTIDIMENSIONAL IDENTITY CONFLICT

The goal set by Former Filipina Muslim Senator Santanina Rasul (1999), "We must continue to destroy the prejudices of the past and begin to remake the history of the Filipino people without the social barriers that tend to divide us," is more complex than it seems. The conflict defies easy classification as an ethnic conflict. The so-called Bangsamoro identity was constructed during the height of mass violence in the 1970s, and the identity-building process has continued up to the present time. In this regard, identity became both a means to an end and an end in itself (Giannakos, 2002). On the one hand, the construction of identity represents the institutionalization of the struggle for inclusion and/or recognition that can be understood in its utility. Identity building becomes a defense mechanism, expressed as a societal structure perceived to provide a greater degree of security. Identity is therefore, in this context, to be understood as a "community of destiny" (*Schicksalsgemeinschaft*; Bauer, 1907). Common experiences function particularly for the Bangsamoro as basis for a "national consciousness" (*National-bewusstsein*; Bauer, 1907).

On the other hand, the construction of identity as an end involves the invention of *primordial attachments* based on given independent variables such as kin connection or membership in a religious or language community (Geertz, 1963). However, in the case of the Muslims in Mindanao, it can be argued that religion as a primordial attachment rather represents the second layer of identity building, with language and tribal membership as the main primordial attachments. The reason for this can be the rather late conversion of groups to Islam in the fifteenth century. Another reason can be that a more secular version of Islam reached Southeast Asia through Muslim traders following the opening of trade in that area.

The evolution involves the invention of a specific cultural community that prerequired the elevation of the ten ethnolinguistic groups to a single identity group called the Bangsamoro, with religion serving as the "glue" of the collectivity. This Bangsamoro identity, rather than ethnolinguistic membership, later becomes the identity to be defended. In short, the Bangsamoro identity has developed as a means of ensuring security (preservation) and in response to the need for group belonging (participation). However, outside the security domain, Muslims still regularly return to their ethnolinguistic groups, which sometimes impedes coherence within the Bangsamoro group. For instance, currently different armed groups, such as the MNLF, the MILF, and even the Abu Sayaff,[3] are seen to represent the different Muslim ethnolinguistic groups. The Bangsamoro identity is still in the process of inventing itself. There are current movements within the group competing over the definition of this identity (e.g., secular or Islamist) and legitimizing it in the eyes of its members.

▪ CULTURAL TRAUMA AND COLLECTIVE MEMORY: THE CRYSTALLIZATION OF IDENTITY

Categorization of peoples by religion and ethnicity is not in itself conflictual; it is the politicization of these differences that makes it so. Identities harden in contexts of structural imbalance. They become the structural markers of conflict when they harden following the establishment of discriminatory policies during state-building processes in which a dominant group defines structures of governance, rationality, and value systems, leaving some groups feeling excluded. The subordination of the state to meet the interests a particular group often serves to legitimize the use of violence for struggle groups who feel that there is no other means of influence. The politicization of differences elevates identity as a tool for the power interests of the majority group; it has utility. When this happens, identity develops utility for those who are marginalized, offering group membership and meaning in a struggle either for secession (separateness) or participation with greater influence.

The logic is transferred to the cultural level. The culture of the Others is perceived as undermining the integrity of a dominant group's own collective culture and the foundation of a common weal on its own terms (Meyer, 2002). Differences become seen as dangerous, and the *securitization of diversity* follows. Peaceful diversity depends very much on the choices of a dominant group in the way it defines the threshold of tolerable differences. For some, a minor difference such as an accent or a dialect is enough to exclude or legitimize claims for uniformity through assimilation.

Ethnicity, then, seems to a larger extent to be initially defined by the dominant group and not primarily by minority group members themselves. On the one hand, identities constructed through primordial ties and kinship connections involve making members themselves responsible for shaping group perceptions and actions. On the other hand, identities constructed through experiences of marginalization are largely imposed and suggest reduced responsibility of members for determining their own group's perceptions and actions.

It is worth asking if the crystallization or hardening of identity leading to mobilization of members was and is, ironically, a critical factor that might have fostered the prevention of genocide in the Philippines. The mobilization of the Bangsamoro enabled it to pose a legitimate and efficient defense to violent attack. Genocides such as those in Armenia and Rwanda were carried out primarily because of the lack of an armed opposition able to resist the coercive force of the perpetrators. Although identity has consequences for the lives of the members at the individual level, it is not an individual property, but rather a social process of balancing between contesting expectations (Meyer, 2002). The shaping and expression of all identities involved reflect a process of social bargaining within and between groups. Group members are likely to demand security and welfare from the elite and other ethnic entrepreneurs in exchange for legitimacy and a sense of belonging. Identity is an open power-driven bargaining process between self-perception and the image defined by the social partner (e.g., society at large). However, in asymmetrical conditions, the image provided by the dominant partner dictates the self-perception of the weaker party. Differences become obvious when they are reflected in an unfair distribution of socioeconomic resources.

Ethnicity or group membership is a construct; the definition of ethnic front lines must follow subjective indicators. However, a group's subjective reality is the objective reality of a conflict. This is where a mediator or a negotiator interested in responding to the reality of the Other starts.

■ THE BANGSAMORO IDENTITY

The hypothetical identity narratives of the Bangsamor[4] (Moslem People) in the Southern Philippines can be summarized as follows:

"I am a member of the Bangsamoro, deprived of our rights in our own homelands by the occupying Philippine state."

This self-representation offers a personal ("I am") narrative about the contemporary experience of marginalization ("deprived of our rights"); the demand for recognition of the group; modalities of self-awareness ("own homelands") implying the perceived dissociation from the society at large; and the historical event representing the cultural trauma ("occupying Philippine state") that delegitimizes the current status quo based on either imagined or real injustice and atrocities committed in the past.[5] Collective memory plays an important role in the manner in which the relationship to the soil is conceptualized ("own homelands"; Rouometof, 2006). The consciousness of the group identity is in cognitive terms maintained by cultural trauma (Alexander, 2004).

Cultural trauma occurs when members of a collectivity feel that they have been subjected to a horrendous event that leaves indelible marks on their group consciousness, marking their memories forever and changing their future identity in fundamental and irrevocable ways (Alexander, 2004, p. 1). Trauma is not simply the result of a collectivity experiencing pain, but rather the result of a profound sense of threat to its existence as an identity group. The collectivity decides or is led to represent social pain as a fundamental threat to its sense of who it is, where it came from, and where it wants to go (Alexander, 2004, pp. 10, 24). Trauma can be understood as a sociopsychological process that defines a painful injury to the collectivity, establishes the victim, attributes responsibility, and distributes the ideal and material consequences. In this process, history is crucial; it is what permits the justification of forms of resistance to the society at large.

Philippine civil society has responded to two dimensions of the peace process in Mindanao: the larger peace process between the government and the MILF and interventions into the microdynamics (this will be discussed later) within conflict-affected communities. A 2002 study by the Asia Foundation suggests not only that violence was based on Muslim–Christian discord, but also that the most dominant form was violence "between families, clans and tribes [that] often center[ed] on faction fights, family disputes or personal reasons. The second common reason was related to environmental, resources, or agricultural issues. Muslim–Christian conflicts also take place because of personal disputes but discrimination and inequality are also mentioned" (Dayag-Laylo, 2004, p. 5).

Muslim separatist movements in the Philippines seek to justify their armed struggle more by reference to the past than by religion (but they organize and therefore have an identity by a religious marker). Muslims tend to refer to present and past injustices following patterns of state construction and transformation as legitimacy for the pursuit of independence rather than claiming the struggle as a "religious duty" every Muslim should perform, as implied by the almost non-existence of suicide bombers. Past and present injustices are then combined with nostalgia for an embryonic state reflective of a golden age, catalyzing popular support (Gilquin, 2005, p. 63). The romanticism of the ancient sultanates of Sulu and Maguindanao serves as a point of reference for the recognition struggle of the Muslim population. The question of whether past pain was inflicted on the basis of religion as an identity marker is an interesting one in the analysis of the conflict. Religious practices were not forbidden, although they were not guaranteed and protected by the state as individual rights.

Figure 5.2 illustrates the process of identity crystallization through collective trauma. Subgroups A, B, and n were forcibly incorporated (but not assimilated) into the society at large during the state-building process, which is regarded as a cultural trauma. Historical memory has provided for the production and repro-duction of newly formed identities suggesting the political use of history (Lowenthal. 1985). However, it is not the reconstruction of the past in the present that matters as much as the consequences of the past (real or imagined) for the lives of contemporary individuals, such as poverty due to a history of deprived access to resources and state welfare (Schudson, 1997, pp. 3–17).

Collective trauma alone is not sufficient to instigate an armed identity-based conflict. Collective memory is sustained only in specific social circumstances. Hence, as Victor Roudometof (2006, p. 7) argues, the memory of events is closely connected to collective representations produced by contemporary policies. Group identities harden when members feel collectively marginalized by virtue of their membership in a group.

The internal dynamics illustrated reflect a subgroup in opposition to the society at large. The identity politics of subordination and superordination

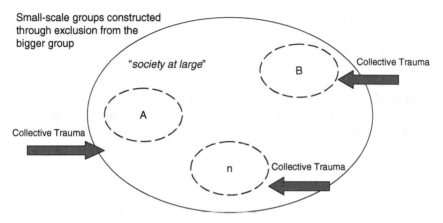

Figure 5.2 Collective trauma and construction of identity.

(recognition) are incompatible. Incompatibility of identity politics is further defined by contestation over imagined and/or real narratives (histories) and over contemporary issues. David Lowenthal (1985, p. 7) proposes that the relationship between memory and history is selective: A group chooses from the pool of past experiences for specific reasons, including the legitimization of strategic measures. For reasons of nationalism and dominance, the wider society tends not to acknowledge the marginalization of members of a subgroup as negative. Policies and institutional structures are so formulated that any deviation from a uniform value system is perceived as a threat to national sovereignty and the integrity of the state. Just as a subgroup has imagined and/or real narratives, so does the society at large. For Christians, Muslims in the Philippines are perceived as "aggressive rebels" and "terrorists" threatening the integrity and sovereignty of the state. Muslims, on the other hand, hold to the narrative that they were once part of an independent sultanate that was forcibly incorporated in the Philippine state. In general, Figure 5.2 illustrates the confrontation between identities, national labels, national narratives, and political mobilization. Narratives allow little room for mutual accommodation: The "truth" can be bargained for only in all-or-nothing (absolute) terms, leaving no room for possible concessions and compromises. Aggravating the competition between groups is the "territorialization of identity" in which cultural representation is connected to a nation's soil (Malki, 1992). The development of the sense of belonging associated with a specific homeland generates further tensions, especially when homelands between groups overlap.

In summary, the construction of identity is proposed here to occur when people symbolize their closeness to each other through common experiences or "destiny." Closeness is established through a "collective fear of the future," serving as the source of political mobilization (Lemarchard, 1994, p. 27). Identity has utility in ensuring protection and safety from the other group, and is kept alive by memories of marginalization and mass violence.

■ IDENTITY POLITICS AND CONFLICT DYNAMICS

Overt conflict does not emerge in every heterogeneous society. It requires a complex of factors to be present. Louis Kriesberg (1998, p. 31) suggests four specific conditions that must be minimally satisfied for conflicts to emerge. First, the parties must have developed a sense of themselves as entities separate from one another. This indicates that the state-building process has not effectively integrated all ethnic and national labels. Second, one or more of the parties must have a grievance. Figures 5.1 and 5.2 illustrate the development of identity groups' sense of themselves as entities in which narratives (memories) and contemporary issues (grievances) are connected with each other in a group-building dynamic, shaping mutual policies of exclusion. Third, one or more of the parties must develop goals to change the other party or parties in order to reduce the grievance. Fourth, the aggrieved party must believe that it can be successful in changing the other party. The aggrieved party calculates strategically which measures (engaging in armed struggle, inviting international intervention, or both) will be most effective. Conflict arises when the society at large is unable or unwilling to accommodate this claim for self-determination and recognition and when the subgroup is perceived as a competitor or a threat to national sovereignty or even group dominance, manifested by assimilative policies and claims for subordination (e.g., of the value system, beliefs, and religion of the subgroup), justifying the use of coercive means to reach these goals. In addition, members of the society at large understand that the goals and claims of the subgroup are not only different from but also incompatible with or in opposition to their own goals and claims (Coy & Woehrle, 2000, p. 2).

■ MISRECOGNITION CONTEXTS OF STRUCTURAL IMBALANCE

Group identity is at the core of the recognition paradigm (Hobson & Lindholm, 1997, p. 475), with the denial of social recognition serving as the motor of social movements in which feelings of injustice, unfairness, and inequality become sources of political motivation (Honneth, 1995, p. 139). The very framing of injustices as grievances shapes a group's cognitive processes, bonding its members in a common understanding of their plight as members of a devalued and disadvantaged group (Hobson & Lindholm, 1997). Recognition politics involve claimers (actors) seizing political opportunities, refashioning public discourses, and reconfiguring the politics of redistribution (Hobson, 2003, p. 6).

The Muslim minorities in the Philippines are not primarily depreciated in the quality of their religious life. Religious and traditional practices are not prohibited and not limited to the private sphere. Depreciation occurs through social subordination in the sense of being impeded from participating as a peer in social life. Claims for redistribution and for the introduction of "fair" and "just" game rules are resisted by mainstream society, particularly by nationalists, who refuse to recognize the Muslim minorities as peers because they are perceived as threats both as individual citizens and as a group. The perception of the Muslims as a threat is derived from religion as an identity marker. However, I argue that religion is not really the source of threat but is merely used for labeling when referring to the collectivity. In this sense, it becomes a category of a religious conflict. It is not that religion produces conflict, as Samuel Huntington argues, but that religion serves as an identity marker. This differentiation is significant when formulating policies. Falsely referring to the conflict in Mindanao as a "clash of civilization," as Huntington does, leads to counterproductive policies. For instance, it can be observed that Muslims in Mindanao are undergoing a process of fundamentaliza-tion of Islam due to the influx of Saudi Arabian foundations importing a stricter version of Islam.

Breakthroughs in identity conflicts are difficult because members of the major-ity group instrumentalize their idea of citizenship through resistance to the recog-nition struggles of the minority group. The only route to recognition is assimilation to majority norms in the name of secularism, universalism or republicanism, group enclaving (isolation), or even ethnic cleansing (Fraser, 2003, p. 22). The society is shaped in a manner that denies the legitimacy of the organizing markers of the Muslim group. Minorities are seen as those with distorted identities that cannot be accommodated by the society at large because they are defined by values considered unacceptable (e.g., claims by the majority that Islam is not compatible with democracy and good governance).

Misrecognition is a process of institutionalized social subordination in which some groups are denied the status of a full partner and peer in social, political, and economic interaction on the terms of identity they want or need as a group. It is perpetuated through institutionalized patterns of cultural values, the workings of social institutions that regulate interaction according to parity-impeding cultural norms (profiling and stigmatizing groups) and that define some groups as norma-tive and others as deficient or inferior (Muslims are violent, aggressive, cheaters). Misrecognition is also institutionalized informally—in associational patterns, long-standing customs, and sedimented social practices in civil society (latent anti-Muslim bias as seen in the media, in narrative stories, and in individual relationships with Muslims—for instance, in granting bank loans or contracts; Fraser, 2003, p. 27).

■ THE DYNAMICS OF MISRECOGNITION IN THE PHILIPPINES

The Southern Philippines has over 100 ethnic groups, including the Tagalog, Cebuano, Ilocano, Illongo, and Waray, who identify themselves through parental lineages and language distinctions (primordial ties). The so-called Moros com-prise various ethnolinguistic groups in Mindanao whose ancestry is similar to that of to other ethnic groups but whose religion is Islam. The conflict, it is argued here, however, is neither cultural nor religious. Other ethnic groups (even animist ethnic minorities in the Northern Philippines and elsewhere) aside from the Muslim ethnic groups also experience marginalization, as manifested by poverty, isolation, and political exclusion. It is not primarily a religious conflict because there was no contestation in the sense of one religious group seeking dominance by prohibiting the practices of the other religious group. The conflict in the Southern Philippines

(Mindanao), then, is less a cultural or religious matter than a political phenomenon, although the salient identity groups have defined themselves around religious markers. While many groups are marginalized, only the Muslim group offers organized opposition with coercive resources, and this allows its expression as an identity conflict. Hence, ethnicity in the Philippines operates within contemporary political contexts and imagined and/or real memories.

In this multidimensional, multilevel conflict, the *scale of range method* enables a more strategic understanding of the conflict. While religion does play a role in political mobilization, the root causes of the conflict are diverse, depending on the scale of the picture. Socioeconomic differences, socioeconomic marginalization, political patronage, ethnic rivalry, competition for concessions from foreign mining companies, four decades of militarization, and conflicting land claims define what is currently perceived by the Filipinos as a conflict between Muslims and Christians (Bück, 2007, p. 101). On each scale, there are different stakeholders, different temporal dynamics, and different sets of issues and claims, as well as specific strategies and measures to achieve resolution of the conflict. The complexity of the conflict demands both systemic and reductionist approaches for analytic purposes. From a reductionist perspective, there are observable vertical and horizontal conflicts in evidence, not simply of levels but also of types (ethnic, power, resource). There seems to be a tendency to put all these apples and pears in one analytical basket; the basket is then regarded as the conflict itself, leading to further confusion. Using a systemic approach enables identification of existing interdependencies and linkages between different factors that are to be understood above the simple cause–effect relation. Combining both perspectives can support policymakers and decision makers in identifying targeted measures complementing the strategic measures implemented in other scales (Table 5.1).

■ HAS THE MOBILIZATION OF THE BANGSAMORO SERVED TO MITIGATE A POSSIBLE GENOCIDE?

This section analyzes the dynamics in which cycles of violence, including mass killing, mass deportation, and genocide are legitimized by notions of security and the right to survival. It is a paradox that perpetrators often claim that it is actually they who are the victims, showing the role of fear in instigating genocide (Fein, 1990, p. 3). For instance, the Armenians were viewed as a secessionist threat by Turkey. In 1915 the onset of World War I brought the prospect that the Armenians would side with Turkey's enemies, leading to their deportation to Syria and Mesopotamia.

Muslims in the Philippines are viewed as separatists, terrorists, and troublemakers. The Muslim insurgency in the country described in the first part of this chapter started when more than 28 Moro Muslim soldiers refused an order by President Ferdinand Marcos to infiltrate Sabah in his quest to occupy the Malaysian territory claimed by the Philippines. They were massacred (the Jabidah massacre) on the night of March 18, 1968. This event is regarded as having been the catalyst of the modern Moro insurgencies in the Southern Philippines.

TABLE 5.1. *Range of Scales on the Mindanao Conflict*

	Scale 1	Scale 2	Scale 3	Scale 4
Negotiating conflict parties	Government of the Philippines vs. MNLF, MILF	Center vs. periphery (urban Manila vs. rural Mindanao)	Ethnic, religious, and social communities, clans, warlords, and political dynasties vs. each other	Interpersonal relationships (Mario vs. Pedro/Anita vs. Gloria)
Claims	National sovereignty vs. self-determination (independence or autonomy) (Lingga, 2008, p. 61)	Centralization vs. decentralization/ resource sharing and empowerment of rural areas/ political representation	Clan A vs. clan B on local hegemony/ empowerment of isolated communities Security	Individual rights and liberties Empowerment Security
Issues	• Recognition of MILF/MNLF as negotiation partners; demobilization of MILF, MNLF; withdrawal of government troops in Mindanao (military) • Banning terrorism as a coercive strategy by the MILF (political) • National control of local resources in Mindanao and economic aid to ARMM (economic) • Autonomy in the educational system (cultural) • Adoption of *sharia* as law order (legal) • Inclusion of ancestral domains now dominated by Christians in the (ARMM) (territorial/ ancestral domains)	• Distribution of income from concessions from foreign mining companies • Allocation of development funds and international aid • Solidarity funds • Investment in infrastructure • New forms of governance structures	• Control of the local government units • The right to build mosques in Christian-dominated communities • Access to roads and other infrastructure • Access to water • "Cleaning" of the demonized image of the Muslims and inferior images of other ethnic groups	• Access to health services • Access to education • Employment • Personal security • Enough food for the family • Adequate income

Mass violence in the Philippines did not follow a script. There was no state ideology or intention to get rid of Moro Muslims as a group, but there was none as well to prevent their marginalization, their reduction to minority status in a region, and the elimination of their claims in the larger political system. There were no measures to preserve the homelands of the Muslims, who had no concepts of land titles because land was regarded as God's property and therefore was not to be owned by humans. Only in the course of escalation did the conflict gain an ethnoreligious flavor when the Bangsamoro identity was introduced by the Moro Muslim elite, confirming the role of leadership in mobilizing support and legitimacy. The label *Bangsamoro* is part of the mobilization process. Mass violence creates conditions conducive to further violence. Sporadic violence involving individual cases, such as petty crimes and homicides, is elevated to collective violence because of the lack of a clear distinction between violence aimed at members of the collective due to their group membership and violence aimed at individuals regardless of group membership. Mass violence, such as mass killing and mass deportation, creates social situations and the social structures and processes that could lead to genocide (Chalk & Jonassohn, 1990, p. 30).

The number of deaths (100,000–150,000) over the 40 years of this violent struggle in the Philippines does not classify it as a genocide under Mark Levene's (1994, p. 11; Straus, 2001, p. 366) concise definition: "when a state, perceiving the integrity of its agenda to be threatened by an aggregate population—defined by the state as an organic collectivity, or series of collectivities—seeks to remedy the situation by the systemic, en masse physical elimination of that aggregate, in toto, or until it is no longer perceived to represent a threat." The killings fall short of systemic physical elimination of a group by the state. However, the dynamic of continued marginalization, though not specifically organized by state agencies, is likely to lead to continued violence. The experiences of mass violence remain constantly fresh in the memory of all generations, and because almost all group members experience it, it seems irrelevant whether the violence occurred 40 years ago or this year. The key question, then, is not whether this is a formal genocide but how to stop mass killings in a context that seems to perpetuate it.

In summary, the mass violence in the Southern Philippines could have become a genocide, but past and present societal elements and ongoing multitrack negotiations have mitigated escalation. As in Rwanda, elements such as vigilante Christian groups claiming to represent the state have started several waves of violence. Fortunately, these claims were not supported by the mass Christian population in Mindanao, partly because of the active role of NGOs. Furthermore, the abrogation of the central state in this area in terms of security and welfare has consolidated the role of local elite groups who seem to have less interest in conducting genocide. Agents of violence have not been successful in using state institutions such as the media to propagate violence because of their near-absence in the area. The central state, instead, has created informal partnerships with local elite groups to provide services such as welfare and security.

The original political conflict with an ethnic flavor has been transformed. The militarization of Mindanao has established a unique security environment in which communities recognize that the Philippine state has abrogated its responsibility to provide security in the area. Groups then are forced to rely on private security forces. The inclusion of private security providers (private armies or partisan groups) adds to the number of actors in the conflict and contributes to a recursive "economy of violence." Over and above this, there are few breaks in a continuing (and therefore permanent) low-intensity war. People have little memory of life in a period of peace; war has become normative. Adaptation to the condition follows. Mitigation is neglected. It seems then that the identity conflict has transformed itself into a societal reality—a way of being.

■ HOW SHOULD NEGOTIATION BE USED IN IDENTITY-BASED CONFLICTS?

The negotiation process in identity-based conflicts should address the challenge of reconciliation through restorative justice in which historical animosities are confronted. Interventions should be carefully designed, bearing in mind the risks and opportunities. Negotiating restorative justice requires a deep understanding of what is to be restored, by whom, and how. Designing the intervention process should focus on the inclusion of justice and reconciliation as outcomes (surely justice would be a means to reconciliation and an outcome), accommodating divergent justice issues present at the different scales. The negotiation process in identity-based conflicts should not merely involve negotiations between the government and a specific rebel group. A multilevel, multidimensional approach would demand an inclusive approach—a "concert" of multiple actors at multiple levels. This affords the process political legitimacy. In particular, the Muslim groups in the Philippines have achieved political legitimacy through negotiation. In this regard, negotiation can be seen as a process in which rebel groups representing collectivities are transformed from mere agents of violence into legitimate political parties. The MNLF, for instance, gained political legitimacy when it achieved observer status (the only observer representing a national Muslim community) at the Organization of the Islamic Conference (OIC) in 1977 after it agreed to negotiate with the Philippine government, leading to the legitimacy of the MNLF in the international community. When this legitimacy was not further contested, the political capital for additional negotiations was increased, and in 1996 a peace agreement was signed by the stakeholders. The OIC member states, particularly Malaysia and Libya, have been active in establishing communication between the conflicting parties (both the MNLF and MILF with the Philippine government) and enabling the establishment of negotiations. The first-track negotiation, however, fell short of addressing societal reconciliation. The 1996 peace agreement was not enough to bring sustainable peace. NGOs could be successful in bridging the gap. The following section outlines how this shortcoming is being addressed in the Philippines.

The prenegotiations between the Philippine government and the MNLF in the 1970s, with the intervention of Libya and the OIC, settled the issue of independence. The Philippine government would not start negotiating until the MNLF dropped its claim for independence. The OIC, with the leadership of Libya, was successful in setting the negotiation formula that eliminated independence as the desired outcome. The Tripoli Peace Agreement of 1976 served as the framework for the following agreements and memorandums, not only for the negotiations with the MNLF but also for those with the MILF.

■ DESIGNING THE INTERVENTION PROCESS: NEGOTIATING FAIRNESS AND JUSTICE

Peace (the elimination of violence) requires the introduction and maintenance of social and political systems that are felt to be fair. How justice issues are handled in a political negotiation process affects the prospects for a subsequent consolidation of peace. However, not all justice issues can be addressed in a formal (track 1) negotiation. Returning to Table 5.1 (see page 154), each scale has its own justice issues. In scale 4, the primary justice issue is fair access to welfare and resources for individual citizens, regardless of their group membership.

In scale 1, the primary justice issue is *procedural justice*, in which the government and the rebel group need to find a fair process for enabling meaningful peace talks. It includes shouldering the expenses of trips and meetings, finding an appropriate place for the negotiation, securing the safety of the negotiators from both sides, and guaranteeing the immunity of negotiators from persecution. A significant discussion is whether actors guilty of violent acts will be forgiven if they come to negotiate peace at least in the initial stage of negotiations. This is an important issue; it seems logical that these actors will not engage in negotiations without a guarantee that they will not be persecuted when they arrive at the negotiation table. Furthermore, because the situation has created a "space of violence" (*Gewalträume*), it is questionable whether violent acts occurring inside this space can be considered crimes because of the dissolution of any legal system in this particular area. In addition, these actors will question the jurisdiction of the legal system of the society at large, particularly when they are already able to establish a de facto state.

In designing the intervention, the distinction between *forward-looking* and *backward-looking* principles of justice should be made (Zartman & Kremenyuk, 2005). Forward-looking notions of justice seek the establishment of new cooperative relations based on mutual interests between parties. They refer to *transitional justice* in which norms and instruments on the basis of which a society or a new government, in transition from armed conflict and/or authoritarian rule, are established to prevent further atrocities and marginalization and secure justice in the future, for example, through a new justice system (Call, 2004). They aim for the creation of mechanisms that would reconcile conflicting rationalities. They include the establishment of new power-sharing schemes based on the newly established reconciling mechanisms of fairness and justice, such as quota systems and formal reservation of a certain number of government seats for minorities.

However, addressing transitional justice in the negotiation process is not enough to bring a consolidated peace. This requires restorative justice, which implies backward-looking notions of justice. Backward-looking notions are zero-sum and seek justice restropectively for past wrongdoings, rights and entitlements—for example, issues of accountability, compensation, reparations, and punishment. One challenge of restorative justice is addressing the appropriate party that was the victim. In several cases of mass violence, there might be no clear distinction between perpetrators and victims, particularly in situations of escalation. Furthermore, apologizing to a collectivity does not ensure that the needs of individuals are confronted. Unofficial dialogues and problem-solving workshops with people outside the government are discussed extensively in the literature as a necessary and effective means to address various deep-rooted needs (Albin, 2009, p. 583). Backward-looking notions of justice involve measures for reconciliation between groups, communities, and individuals. They involve the reintroduction of trust and social capital between groups and individuals.

■ THE NEGOTIATION PROCESS IN THE PHILIPPINES: THE ROLE OF THE CREATIVE CIVIL SOCIETY

The specific functions of NGOs in conflict resolution are often overlooked (Call, 2004). The NGOs are seen as being outside the negotiation process because they lack the capacity, legitimacy, and recognition to engage directly in negotiation. They lack the capacity to influence parties' behavior or decision-making processes in conflicts (Griffiths, 2005). Their legitimacy deficits include problems brought about by unequal distribution of resources among NGOs and by their need to compete for resources, so that they may be subject to pressures from donors pursuing their own interests. Furthermore, some see increased involvement of NGOs in decision-making processes as undermining democracy since they are not democratically elected actors.

Despite these deficits, NGOs can respond to the vacuum left by states unable or unwilling to provide the services necessary to engage all actors in a conflict in a constructive peace process (Bartoli, 1999). Arguably, because they are not dependent on periodical democratic elections, they are free to act on principle rather than populism. The NGOs can (equally, may not) add legitimacy through inclusion of all actors in the political process while not being bound by the constraints of the political system Governments recognize that the involvement of NGOs provides an opportunity to explore options not always possible within formal political structures. Governments can develop politically sensitive and unpopular measures through their support of specific NGOs, thus expanding alternatives in the bargaining process. However, government support can increase the risk of accusations of bias on the part of an NGO, reducing its credibility across interest groups. Furthermore, NGOs may be freed to follow longer-term strategies as opposed to the short-term strategies of official actors with shorter operation timetables (Matthews, 2001). In addition, NGOs can generate a political process through the representation of people's interests, memories, and needs that are not properly represented in the official channels of negotiation. In this regard, a communication chain between actors—for instance, in a situation of escalation—can be provided by NGOs. The lack of coercive capacity is perceived by conflicting parties as positive, paving the way for a stronger process of bargaining through the increased mobilization of political capital that would have been impossible in the absence of NGOs (Bartoli, 2009; Hume, 1994). Surely the principle is a simple one: NGOs cannot act as political parties or pretend to represent groups in conflict, but they can work to enable effective engagement of such parties and to deescalate conflicts. The key is to have a clearly understood role.

The conflict resolution advocacy and work of NGOs in Mindanao have given impetus to peace talks, interreligious dialogue, peace zones, cease-fire monitoring, and empowerment of isolated communities in the conflict areas. Civil society groups, particularly NGOs, pinpoint the failure to address interpersonal issues of the conflict in past interventions (Bück, 2007). Civil society groups in the Philippines have been successfully integrated into the Philippine political structure, in which NGOs and other civic society groups, such as cooperatives and other organizations funded by government officials and other politicians, can be elected as representatives in the Philippine Congress through the *party-list* system. According to Bück, the Philippines is famous for its strong civil society.

Unlike in many other countries, NGOs in the Philippines are regarded as a form of opposition to the state in the political landscape due to their long history of resistance against the military regime of former President Ferdinand E. Marcos. The Securities and Exchange Commission (SEC) has a register of about 30,000 NGOs and 35,000 cooperatives for the Philippines. Werning and Reese furthermore explain that this figure could even be as high as 249,000 if other NGO-like organizations such as cooperatives are considered (Werning & Niklaus, 2006, p. 237). The broadest regional NGO network in Mindanao, MinCODE, hosts 539 member organizations, such as cooperatives focusing on the economic improvement of local residents and addressing the contemporary issue of economic grievances, indirectly contributing to conflict resolution in Mindanao. However, civic society groups can also represent armed groups or be affiliated with a political group. Such groups are regularly used by political actors to legitimate the outcomes of their actions while pretending that they have a mass base of support (Cagoco-Guiam, 1999).

Philippine civil society has been particularly active in promoting peace talks. The Philippine government has responded to civil society advocacy and lobbying on several occasions. Civil society groups such as the Gaston Z. Ortigas Peace Institute sponsor a community of peace advocates—nongovernmental and people's organizations, academic institutions, and civil society networks—that contributes to institutionalizing peace work in the Philippines, asserting the role of the citizens in the peace process, engaging youth in several creative demonstrations for peace, and participating in joint meetings with other NGOs, policymakers, and representatives from the Muslim Moro community. Raising public awareness of the urgency of a cease-fire and continuation of the peace talks serves as a counterstrategy to the current indifference of the public due to accustomization. The majority of the public was born before the conflict in Mindanao escalated. They do not know how it is to live without the conflict. Civil society groups also call for representation as third-party negotiators during formal peace talks in order to ensure political solutions that can be shared by all stakeholders in Mindanao rather than simply the MILF and the national government. It seems that NGOs obtain multiple roles as partially accredited negotiating partners in scale 1 and as mediators for reconciliation in scales 3 and 4. They also act as independent watchdogs, monitoring the implementation of any formal peace agreement signed by the parties in conflict (*Mindanao Times,* 2005). In 2001 many civil society groups in Mindanao convened the Bantay Cease-fire (Cease-fire Watch), which serves as an independent monitoring agency. The agency is facilitated by the secretariat of the Mindanao People's Caucus (MPC) and Initiatives for International Dialogue (IID). The cease-fire watchdog group consists of a broad network of grassroots monitors who join investigative missions in case of cease-fire violations. Bantay Cease-fire publishes its report and has successfully lobbied for the introduction of the international monitoring team led by Malaysia.

Civil society groups such as the Immaculate Conception Parish (ICP) encourage interreligious dialogue through group trauma therapy, common festivities, and the experience of solidarity with members of the groups with grievances (Bück, 2007, p. 124). Furthermore, civil society groups have successfully convinced conflicting parties not to engage in armed confrontation in several *peace zone areas* that serve as buffer zones between adversaries, and offer sanctuary for local residents of all religious and ethnic affiliations. Since the Final Peace Agreement of 1996 between the MNLF and the government, peace zones have become a prominent form of community-based peace building (Rood, 2004).

To sum up, multiparty and multilevel negotiation in the Philippines increased political capital for the peace process. The MNLF and the MILF gained political legitimacy by engaging in negotiations. Negotiation reduced hierarchies and asymmetries in relations between actors, increased their political capital, and made the negotiation channel more attractive than coercive means. Negotiation served to improve international recognition of the MNLF. Furthermore, multiparty and multilevel negotiations established a more and more consolidated and acceptable political framework. For instance, NGOs as external parties in the first-track negotiations assumed the roles of monitors of peace agreements complementing the international monitoring teams led by Malaysia. NGOs have continuously increased the stakes of the government and the rebel groups to engage in negotiations, particularly in situations of escalation by establishing mechanisms of naming and blaming.

■ CONCLUSION: LESSONS AND CHALLENGES FOR THEORY AND PRACTICE

Negotiation is the intervention of choice in resolving identity conflicts. Several lessons for theory and practice can be drawn from the Philippine case. From a theoretical and practical perspective, identity-based conflicts should be treated as multidimensional and multilevel phenomena. Through the identification of internal dynamics in each scale, various strategic intervention measures may be formulated. Third parties can intervene at a variety of levels according to where they are located. For instance, because reconciliation requires both forward-looking and backward-looking attention to justice issues, intervention implies a more complicated and complex bargaining or trading-off process. In the Philippine case, forward-looking reconciliation is negotiated at the first level between the government and the Muslim rebel groups. It involves negotiation focusing on the restructuring of the political system to guarantee political representation of Muslim minorities. Backward-looking reconciliation involves negotiation at the community level, catering to the needs of those who were personally affected by the conflict. As indicated, reconciliatory talks between communities, as mediated by NGOs, are necessary activities in identity-based conflicts.

In addition, community empowerment accompanies reconciliation due to the spillover effects of increased interaction between members of communities as group memberships expand and overlap, and as political and social capital increases through the weakening of contestation lines (as shown in Figure 5.2). Identifying the political logic behind the construction of identities enables the strategic formulation of intervention measures such as organizing public debates and dialogues on how to change the perception of the society at large to the minorities as threats. Changing this perception can change positions and, ultimately, policies. Establishing structural conditions for forward-looking and backward-looking approaches to justice issues, and eventually reconciliation, is a requirement for a durable peace.

One lesson for theory is that occidental concepts such as *statehood* or *state sovereignty*, expected by scholars to provide absolute peace, are not fully applicable in all cases. Historical processes are determined not only by specific political, cultural, social, and economic conditions that differ from region to region and country to country, but also by strata upon strata of contextual distinctiveness developed through experiences and real and/or imagined memories. Muslim Moros in the Philippines have a different understanding of the term *state-building process*. In their case, it involves an understanding of repression, animosities, and subordination as manifested in their personal experiences and narratives. Working with real or imagined grievances enables a clearer vision of how the wider society should work so that their minority status does not impede their participation as peers. The lesson for practice here is that objectives of state consolidation can result in (at least short-term) violence due to contesting value systems, narrative histories, and current interests within a society. Refusing to recognize that a state can be strong within the framework of diversity is a main feature of identity conflicts.

While some argue that it is violence that focuses the minds of negotiators and keeps power realities present, it is clear that if the prospects for negotiation are to be enhanced, violence should be minimized. At the micro level, the negotiation process can be promoted through the identification of the truth behind the violence, recognizing the faults and acts of others and one's own groups (backward-looking). Violence can be the result of provocation and of accidents, and may not be particularly aimed at specific groups as collectivities. The recognition of the truth and the wider context of violence can contribute to the reconciliation process allowing diffusion of bad memories. In addition, the Philippine case illustrates that even though some preconditions for genocide exist, a vigilant civic society engaging in community-level reconciliatory negotiations can prevent the outburst of mass killing or genocide.

An important lesson for practice revealed in the Philippine case is that a negotiation process does not end with the signing of a peace agreement. It is a starting point for the peace process, and interveners such as civil society bodies should be involved in its implementation. The peace agreement between the government of the Philippines and the MNLF in 1996 did not end the identity conflict, not simply because of the unsuccessful transformation of the MNLF from a rebel group into a political actor with administrative skills, but also because the internal dynamics of the conflict at the micro level were not addressed by the first-track negotiators. Paradoxically, the agreement of the MOA-AD in 2008 did not bring the conditions necessary for peace but rather escalation, mass violence, and stalemate.

Probably the biggest challenge in the Philippine case is to prevent intervention itself from aggravating the conflict. Intervention can be counterproductive if the wrong formula is introduced. It requires a thorough understanding of the conflict. For instance, the conflict in the South is regarded as mainly religious in nature. This chapter argues that it is instead a political conflict with ethnic and religious overlays. It is a matter of the relationship between dominant and weaker agents. The Muslims are mainly marginalized not because they are Muslims, but because they are regarded as threats to security. Islam is demonized not because of the substance of the religion, but because it is the religion of the collective minority challenging the existing hierarchical system. The conflict lies less in the contesting values of the religions and more in the interactions between the actors, with the majority subordinating the minority. Islam is one identity marker under which a larger number of repressed groups have organized themselves.

Understanding the dynamics of a conflict is necessary for designing interventions. For instance, several Philippine NGOs and scholars argue that economic development should not be limited to the Muslims, but should also benefit other groups. Development projects exclusively for Muslims would consolidate inequalities in the region. Poverty is not a problem reserved for the Muslims in the Philippines; it also affects other ethnic minorities in the region. It is a problem of the whole of Mindanao. Development programs of the Philippine government, and aid from international donors, should address the empowerment of the whole region, not only of the Muslims, to prevent another conflict that might arise from the perceived injustice. For instance, Muslims are themselves regarded by the Lumads, the indigenous population of Mindanao, as settlers. Granting the Muslims absolute control over the area, with redistribution to the Muslims of lands also claimed by the Lumads as their ancestral homelands, and minoritization of the indigenous people would mean a possible new conflict. Giving preference to Muslim Moros instead of to all people of Mindanao creates other issues of injustice. Hence, the negotiation process on all tracks should anticipate future sources of mass violence. Anticipation within the context of uncertainties is a complex challenge for both theorists and practitioners. However, strategic thinking in the intervention process could provide the knowledge needed in confronting uncertainties through structuring. Another challenge is to find an adequate concept of resource sharing or control over the natural resources involving forward-looking mechanisms to address basic justice issues. The negotiation process aims to establish a new fair and just social contract.

Notes

1. There is no exact number of Moro casualties. Estimates range from 28 to 60, according to the Philippine government, and to over 200, according to the MNLF.
2. *Cottage industry* is another term for *kidnap for ransom*. Instead of ransom, "board and lodging fees" are demanded from hostages.
3. The Abu Sayaff has been described as "Muslim bandits," "outlaws with an agenda" (Frake, 1998), or "a dirty trick division" of the the MNLF or MILF. Abu Sayaff is not included in the analysis of this chapter because of the lack of legitimacy of the group among the Muslim population as well as the absence of political demands from the group. To date, the group has not participated in any negotiation with the Philippine government.
4. The name *Bangsamoro* was actually first used by the Muslim leaders to differentiate themselves from the Christian Filipinos and denote the citizens of the "new" nation.
5. Though the Bangsamoro are generally Muslims, there are Christian Bangsamoro as well as Christian armed members of the MNLF, or Muslim paramilitary forces affiliated with the Armed Forces of the Philippines (AFP). Interview with Rexall Kaalim, Initiatives for International Dialogue (IID), February 14, 2006, quoted in Bück (2007, p. 101).

References

Ahl, V., & Allen, T. F. H. (1996). *Hierarchy theory: A vision, vocabulary, and epistemology.* New York: Columbia University Press.
Albin, C. (2009). Peace vs. justice–and beyond. In J. Bercovitch, V. Kremenyuk, & I. W. Zartman (Eds.), *The Sage handbook of conflict resolution* (pp. 580–594). Los Angeles and London: Sage.
Alexander, J. C. (2004). Toward a Theory of Cultural Trauma. In J. Alexander, R. Eyerman, B. Giesen, N. J. Smelser, & P. Sztompkar (Eds.). *Cultural trauma and collective identity* (pp. 1–30). Berkeley, California: University of California Press.
Bartoli, A. (1999). Mediating peace in Mozambique: The role of the community in Sant'Egidio. In C. A. Crocker, F. O., Hampson, & P. Aall (Eds.), *Multiparty mediation in a complex world* (pp. 245–274). Washington, DC: United States Institute of Peace Press.
Bartoli, A. (2009). NGOs and conflict resolution. In J. Bercovitch, V. Kremenyuk, & I.W. Zartman (Eds.), *The Sage handbook of conflict resolution* (pp. 392–412). Los Angeles and London: Sage.
Bauer, O. (1907). *Die Nationalitätenfrage und die Sozialdemokratie.* Vienna: Verlag der Wiener Volksbuchhandlung Ignaz Brand.
Bück, P. (2007). Civil society and conflict in Mindanao. In P. Kreuzer & R. Werning (Eds.), *Voices from Moro land: Perspectives from stakeholders and observers on the conflict in the Southern Philippines* (pp. 99–124). Petaling Jaya, Malaysia: Strategic Information and Research Development Center, Vinlin Press Sdn. Bhd.
Cagoco-Guiam, R. (1999). A critical partnership: Civil society and the peace process. In *Accord: An international review of peace initiatives.* London: Conciliation Resources, Retrieved June 21, 2011, from http://www.c-r.org/our-work/accord/philippines-mindanao/critical-partnership.php
Call, C. (2004). Is transitional justice really just? *Brown Journal of World Affairs, 11*(1), 101–113.
Chalk, F., & Jonassohn, K. (1990). *The history and sociology of genocide.* New Haven, CT, and London: Yale University Press.

Commons Wikimedia. (2010). *Philippine ethnic groups per province.* Retrieved June 21, 2011, from http://commons.wikimedia.org/wiki/File:Philippine_ethnic_groups_per_province. PNG

Coy, P. G., & Woehrle, L. M. (Eds.). (2000). *Social conflicts and collective identities.* Lanham, MD, Boulder, CO, New York, and Oxford: Rowman & Littlefield.

Dayag-Laylo, C. C. (2004). *Exploring conflict management in the ARMM.* Presented at the 4th Asian Regional Conference of the World Association for Public Opinion Research, Asian Institute of Management Conference Center, February 23–24.

Fein, H. (1990). Genocide: A sociological perspective. *Current Sociology, 38*(1), 1–126.

Frake, C. (1998). Abu Sayaff: Displays of violence and the proliferation of contested identities among Philippine Muslims. *American Anthropologist, 100*(1), 41–54.

Fraser, N. (2003). Rethinking recognition: Overcoming displacement and reification in cultural politics. In B. Hobson (Ed.), *Recognition struggles and social movements: Contested identities, agency and power* (pp 21–34). Cambridge: Cambridge University Press.

Geertz, C. (1963). *The integrative revolution: Primordial sentiments and civil politics in the new states.* Glencoe: Free Press.

Giannakos, S. A. (Ed.). (2002). *Ethnic conflict: Religion, identity, and politics.* Athens: Ohio University Press.

Gilquin, M. (2005). *The Muslims of Thailand.* Chiang Mai: Silkworm Books.

Griffiths, M. (2005). *Talking of peace in a time of terror: United Nations mediation and collective security.* Center for Humanitarian Dialogue. Geneva.

Gomez, J. (2009, September 11). *Moro rebel talks have many spoilers. Philippine Daily Inquirer.* Retrieved June 21, 2011, from http://www.inquirer.net/specialfeatures/mindanaopeaceprocess/view.php?db=1&article=20090119-184

Groups meet to talk about MNLF lessons. (2005, December 9). *Mindanao Times,* p. 1.

Hobson, B. (Ed.). (2003). *Recognition struggles and social movements: Contested identities, agency and power.* Cambridge: Cambridge University Press.

Hobson, B. & Lindholm, M. (1997). Collective identities, women's power resources, and the making of welfare states, *Theory and Society,* Volume 26, Number 4, August, pp. 475–508.

Honneth, A. (1995). *The struggle for recognition: The moral grammar of social conflicts.* Cambridge: Polity Press.

Hume, C. R. (1994). *Ending Mozambique's war: The role of mediation and good offices.* Washington, DC: United States Institute of Peace Press.

Huntington, S. P. (1996). *The clash of civilizations and the remaking of world order.* New York: Simon & Schuster.

Kriesberg, L. (1998). *Constructive conflicts: From escalation to resolution.* Lanham, MD: Rowman & Littlefield.

Lemarchand, R. (1994). *Burundi: Ethnocide as discourse and rractice.* Cambridge: Cambridge University Press.

Levene, M. (1994). Is the Holocaust simply another example of genocide?" *Patterns of Prejudice, 28*(2), 11, pp. 3–26.

Lingga, A. S. M. (2008). Negotiating peace in Mindanao. In I. Narongraksakhet, I. A. Kaba, & Y. Talek (Eds.), *Peace building from various experiences* (pp. 61–75). Pattani, Thailand: Saudara Press.

Lowenthal, D. (1985). *The past is a foreign country.* Cambridge: Cambridge University Press.

Malki, L. (1992). National geographies: The rooting of peoples and the territorialization of national identities among scholars and refugees. *Cultural Anthropology, 7*(1), 24–44.

Matthews, D. (2001). *War prevention works: 50 stories of people resolving conflict*. Oxford: Oxford Research Group.

Meyer, T. (2002). *Identitätspolitik. Vom Missbrauch kultureller Unterschiede*. Frankfurt am Main: Suhrkamp Verlag.

Ploughshare. (2008). *Armed Conflicts Report: Philippines–Mindanao (1971– first combat deaths)*. Retrieved October 15, 2010, from http://www.ploughshares.ca/libraries/ACRText/ACR-PhilippinesM.html#Deaths

Rasul, S. (1999, February 12). *The legacy of Islam in the Philippines*. Speech delivered by Former Senator Santanina T. Rasul during the "Sister of Peace Ceremony, Women Breaking Barriers for Peace" sponsored by the Women's Federation for World Peace at the Manila Hotel. Retrieved June 21, 2011, from http://www.witness-pioneer.org/vil/Articles/politics/legacy_of_islam_in_the_philippines.htm

Rood, S. (2004). *Civil society and conflict management*. Third Study Group Meeting, February 27 to March 3. Washington, DC: The Asia Foundation.

Roudometof, V. (2006). *Collective memory, national identity, and ethnic conflict: Greece, Bulgaria, and the Macedonian question*. Westport, CT: Praeger.

Santos, S., Jr. (2000). *The Moro Islamic challenge: Constitutional rethinking for the Mindanao peace process*. Quezon City: University of the Philippines Press.

Schudson, M. (1997). Lives, laws, and language: Commemorative versus non-commemorative forms of effective public memory. *The Communication Review, 2*, 3–17.

Straus, S. (2001). Contested meanings and conflicting imperatives: A conceptual analysis of genocide. *Journal of Genocide Research, 3*(3), 349–375.

Werning, R., & Reese, N. (Eds.), (2006). *Handbuch Philippinen*. Bad Honnef: Horlemann Verlag.

Zartman, I. W., & Kremenyuk, V. (Eds.) (2005). *Peace vs. justice: Negotiating forward- and backward-looking outcomes*. Lanham, MD: Rowman & Littlefield.

6 Diasporas and the Politics of Identity in International Negotiations

■ FEN OSLER HAMPSON[1]

Diasporas, immigrants, ethnic minorities, and groups living outside of their homeland are the subject of increased scrutiny by students of conflict management. The impact of such groups on conflict dynamics and peace processes, in particular, is the focus of a number of important studies, which have found that such groups, when mobilized, not only contribute to the intensification and protracted nature of violence in identity-based conflicts, but their presence also greatly heightens the recidivist potential of violence after a formal peace treaty has been signed. The impact of such groups on conflict dynamics, however, is not entirely negative. Other studies have found that diasporas and displaced groups have the potential to enhance the prospects for peace when they mobilize in support of a peace process and serve as a positive force for development and reconstruction in their home country by offering financial support through various kinds of human and social capital investments. This chapter explores the impact and special role that diasporas and refugee communities can play in the negotiation processes leading up to a peace settlement as well as during the ongoing negotiation processes that generally take place during the settlement's implementation and postconflict reconstruction efforts.

The term *diaspora* refers to those groups and communities that have been forced to leave their homelands because of ethnic cleansing, genocide, racism, famine, slavery, or war. As Soysal (2000, p. 2) explains: "Diaspora is the location where . . . background finds meaning. Diaspora is a past invented for the present, and perpetually labored into shapes and meanings consistent with the present. As such, it exists not as a lived reality but as part of a broader scheme to insert continuity and coherence into life stories that are presumably broken under the conditions of migrancy and exile. It is the reification of categorical homelands, traditions, collective memories and formidable longings."

Originally, *diaspora* was used to describe the plight of Jews who were exiled from the lands of Judea and Sumeria, first by the Babylonians in the sixth century BC and then by the Romans in the first century AD. In addition to the Jewish diaspora (which refers to those Jews living outside of the state of Israel), other diaspora groups now include the African diaspora (those Africans and their descendants who were forcibly removed from the African continent as a result of slavery, as well as those displaced by the brutal civil wars the continent experienced in the twentieth century), the Irish diaspora (the Irish who left Ireland during the great potato famine and as a result of political repression by the British), the French Canadian diaspora (Quebecois who migrated to the United States for economic reasons), the Tamil diaspora (the Tamils who went to Canada and Norway looking for opportunities they had lost in Sri Lanka), the Somali diaspora (the Somalians who fled the chaos of their country and then returned to contribute to it), the Armenian diaspora (the Armenians who fled the Ottoman Empire in the late nineteenth and early twentieth centuries), and various ethnic groups in the former Soviet Union who were forcibly resettled under Stalinist rule.

Other ethnic groups who have suffered persecution and/or have been displaced by war or shifting national boundaries and who have come to share the diaspora label include the Gypsies, the many refugees of the wars in Southeast Asia, overseas Chinese, Palestinians who fled Palestine during the first Arab–Israeli war in 1948, Afghans, Chechens who fled Chechnya during the insurgency against Russia in the 1990s, and the Tutsis of Rwanda who were chased out of their country in successive waves of internal repression and eventually launched the war against the French-supported Kigali regime in 1990 that helped to trigger the 1994 genocide (Kuperman, 2002).

▪ DIASPORAS AND THE POLITICS OF IDENTITY

Diaspora groups clearly play an important role in the formation and maintenance of ethnic and religious identities. The social and political identities of many groups do not stop at the boundaries of the nation-state. Many diasporas have spawned social, cultural, economic, and political networks that tend to reinforce group-based affiliations and loyalties across space and time (Stanfield, 1996).

Some diaspora groups, however, are more active in international relations and the politics of identity, irredentism, conflict, and intervention than others. They also display the capacity for "independent and assertive political action" (Shain, 2002, p. 116). Among the key factors affecting the salience and efficacy of diasporic activity are the degree to which the groups are motivated to influence events in their homeland, the nature of the political regime in their "host" country (democratic regimes are generally most hospitable to groups that wish to organize themselves for political purposes), and the nature of their homeland (in addition to democracies, there are so-called weak states, which are more permeable to diasporic activity than strong or authoritarian states, which can fend off outside interventions; Shain & Barth, 2003).

The political motivation for diaspora groups to mobilize, however, is also affected by the degree to which the population of the diaspora is concentrated geographically and whether it has the requisite critical mass and leadership to rally its members. As Tarrow (2005) argues more generally, activists rooted in their domestic society and polity are more likely to be effective than those that are "detached" from their local base. (Diaspora populations that are widely dispersed and loosely affiliated, e.g., Gypsies, are likely to experience greater difficulty mobilizing their constituents.) The beliefs and value systems of a diaspora group and the intensity with which they are shared are also key factors affecting a diaspora group's level of political engagement. Organized religion plays a critical role in strengthening the bonds of a diasporic community by creating a shared sense of identity and fostering group cohesion. Diaspora groups who have been victims of political repression, ethnic cleansing, and/or genocide also tend to share a much stronger set of communal affiliations than groups who have been displaced by natural disasters or forced to leave their homeland because of changing economic fortunes or circumstance. Jews, for example, who have been regular victims of political repression, discrimination, and genocide throughout history, especially during the twentieth century, have forged strong diasporic bonds with the state of Israel. In contrast, the so-called French Canadian diaspora in the United States is a diaspora in name only. Although there are millions of Americans who can trace their ancestral roots to Quebecois who left Canada in the late nineteenth and early twentieth centuries in search of greater economic opportunities, which were denied to them because of the overpopulation of rural areas and the land tenure system in Quebec, they are almost completely assimilated and have few real ties to their country of origin.

Some argue that the onset of globalization has strengthened the role of diaspora groups in international relations and the sense of kinship and identity felt within different diasporic groups (Dirlik, 2004). Modern forms of communication, along with greater levels of financial, capital, and labor mobility, have also led to an upsurge in the level of activity and support that diaspora groups and exiles have provided in their countries of origin. Diasporas have been called "regressive globalizers" because they generally tend to favor "nation-state thinking" due to their support for nationalist (or secessionist) struggles in their homeland (Østergaard-Nielsen, 2006).

There is a large and burgeoning literature on the conditions under which diasporas are created. The case of the former Yugoslavia provides an excellent illustration of the different pressures and factors that are involved. For example, the Croat-Canadian community that left during Communist leader Josep Tito's reign was strongly nationalistic and anti-Serb (largely because Slobodan Milosevic and Serbia were identified as Communist); thus, Gojko Šušak, the millionaire "pizza man" from Toronto, became one of the most important figures in Croatia's efforts to rearm and eventually became Croatia's defense minister (Andreas, 2004). The Serbian community that left Belgrade and other large cities in the 1990s, however, was of a very different nature (Gagnon, 1994–1995). It was largely middle-class and professional, and many of its members came to Canada. They were not mobilized in favor of Serbian policies and did not play a proactive role in the conflict. Their absence from Serbia, however, was an important factor in Serbia's radicalization, and they were not there to block Milosevic's turn to the right and his alliance with Vojislav Šešelj and others. Finally, the Kosovar diaspora in Europe played a key role in the Kosovo Liberation Army's (KLA) rise to power in the late 1990s, especially through an organization called "Homeland Calling" (Judah, 2002). The group raised an enormous amount of funds, both legally and otherwise, and bankrolled the insurgency that changed the balance of power in 1998 and led to the decline of the peaceful Kosovar policy of nonviolent protest associated with Ibrahim Rugova and the Democratic League of Kosovo (LDK). The former Yugoslavia thus offers a good all-in-one example of the multiple roles played by diasporas—a role that very much depends on the timing and circumstances of their departure from their homeland.

Much of the prevailing literature, including several major empirical studies, views diaspora groups as peace immobilizers in identity-based conflicts. That is to say, diaspora groups are generally viewed as an impediment to peace and as supporting violent conflict because of their amplified sense of attachment to their place of origin and/or their solidarity with groups in the homeland and their "spoiler" role in peace processes in their homeland. As Baser and Swan (2008, pp. 80-810) note, "To many, diaspora groups are obstacles to conflict resolution and peacebuilding. They do not hesitate to describe diaspora as an extremist, long distance nationalist community that pursues radical agendas taking advantage of freedom and economic upliftment that the host land provides them." In addition to serving as sources of funding (remittances), recruits, and arms for those who are involved in secessionist or other kinds of struggles (Fagen & Bump, 2006), however, diasporas can also exert a negative influence on the policies of external state actors who are actual (or potential) interveners in the conflict by threatening the coherence of foreign policy initiatives (including peacemaking efforts by third parties), influencing or skewing electoral results, and/or interfering in the security policies of their home state (Shain & Bristman, 2002); Sheffer, 1994).

Contributing to Intractability

There is strong empirical evidence that the presence of diasporas contributes to the risk of ongoing civil war and the outbreak of renewed violence after a peace settlement is signed. Collier (2007, p. 202) notes that "[i]f a country has an unusually large American diaspora, its chances of [experiencing a renewed outbreak of] conflict are 36 percent. If it has an unusually small diaspora, its chances of conflict are only 6 percent." Other studies point to the importance of diasporas in sustaining civil insurgencies (Byman, Chalf, Hoffman, Rosenau, & Brannan, 2001). Diasporas can also alter the balance of power between rebels and government forces: Rebel groups that receive financial support from diasporas are generally more likely to defeat government forces than those that do not (Collier & Hoeffler, 2001, 2004). The key reason why diasporas may be so important to rebel movements and the continuation of violence in ethnic-based civil wars is that they lower the opportunity costs of rebellion (via the transfer of wealth and arms to insurgent groups) versus political alternatives such negotiating a peace settlement (Fearon & Laitin, 2000). For example, the Free Khalistan movement was financed and supported by members of the Sikh community in Canada and Europe, especially after the Indian army attacked the Golden Temple in Amritsar in 1984 and killed the extremist Sikh leader Jarnial Singh Bhindranwali and many of his followers. The bombing of Air India flight 182 in 1985 was widely viewed as an act of revenge by Canadian Sikh extremists who wanted to retaliate for the massacre of thousands of Sikhs in India after Indira Gandhi was assassinated by two of her Sikh guards (*Canadian Encyclopedia*, 2010; Fair, 2005).

Hardening Identities

The expected utility calculations of the economic costs/benefits of rebellion may also be reinforced by perceptions of political grievance, which are sustained and nurtured by the diaspora via institutionalized memories that strengthen kinship mythologies and a shared sense of ethnic grievance or injustice that hardens over time (Lyons, 2007; Sambanis, 2001). To the extent that diaspora groups define their particular identity in specific geographic terms, that is, in the form of strong, immutable bonds and attachments to a homeland, this may serve "as a focal point of diaspora political action and debate" (Lyons, 2004, p. 5). Furthermore, "[a]s the intrinsic value of territory diminishes . . . the homeland's symbolic importance may grow . . . laden with symbolic meaning for those [who] identify with it from afar. As a consequence, diaspora groups are less likely to support compromise or a bargain that tradeoffs [sic] some portion of the sacred homeland for some other instrumental end" (ibid.). Shain (2002, p. 127) notes that "Armenians in the United States and France . . . [have been] responsible for instilling into the current Armenian–Azeri conflict an echo of the Armenian genocide . . . [which has] also become the central 'chosen trauma' of the Armenian state."

Diasporas as Third-Party Spoilers

The term *spoiler* is now firmly entrenched in the lexicon of peace and conflict management studies, developed in the chapter by Zahar. There are a number of important articles on the subject (Kydd & Walter, 2002; Stedman, 1997; Werner, 1999) that discuss the issue of spoilers and spoiler management strategies in considerable depth. Spoilers are characterized as extremist elements or groups in a conflict who have been radicalized and are more prone than the other parties to the conflict to resort to violence to pursue their demands (demands that, it is important to note, may be nonnegotiable). Spoilers are therefore not interested in compromise. If some sort of compromise has been reached by some of the parties to the conflict, spoilers will generally do their best to create the conditions that will destroy or upset the compromise. Much of the literature on external actors in conflict processes focuses on the activities and impact of *greedy spoilers*, that is, those who are war profiteers or external actors whose rent-seeking activities are dependent on a continuation of violence (Berdal & Malone, 2001; Collier, 2007; Collier & Hoeffler, 2001, 2004; Collier, Hoeffler, & Soderbom, 2001). These actors do not necessarily resort to direct violence to secure their interests, but their activities may nonetheless contribute to a highly stable conflict equilibrium and can thus directly or indirect thwart the prospects of negotiating a successful peace settlement.

Diaspora groups represent a special kind of external spoiler who can compromise peacemaking efforts. They do not necessarily profit directly from violence when they export partisan loyalties from their homelands and are prepared to lend their political and financial support to those struggles. Instead, the "rewards" they secure may be largely symbolic and identity based. They may succeed as spoilers because they "raise new questions within a peace process, divert attention, provide marginalized actors with a voice, delay or postpone progress in a future round of talks, prevent implementation of agreements, or illustrate the need to include other actors in discussions" (Newman & Richmond, 2006, p. 109). Diasporas are thus not simply a domestic constituency in their home state, but are also "independent actors" who "appear to have made peace negotiations into a three-level game" (Shain, 2002, p. 120). As Lisher (2005) also argues, displaced persons, who may also be members of a diaspora community, can also be transformed into "refugee warriors" and return to fight for independence and liberation movements in their former homeland, as in the case of some of the Sudanese refugees who fled Darfur across the border into neighboring Chad in 2003 or Somali youth, well established in the United States, who returned to their contry of origin to engage in warlord and Islamicist rebellions in the 1990s and 2000s.

Reinforcing Commitment Problems

By lending various kinds of support (political, financial, etc.) to warring parties, diasporas can alter the bargaining strategies of disputants and reinforce commitment problems in negotiating a political settlement. The problem of credible commitment, as discussed by Zartman (1989, 2008) and Fearon (2004), focuses on the incentives structure of the parties to conclude a lasting political settlement. Parties always have some incentive to agree to a settlement that will satisfy their demand for political autonomy or some degree of independence in secessionist struggles. But when rebel groups are certain that that they have strong external sponsors or backers, they are more likely to escalate their demands and seek major concessions from the other side as opposed to those situations where rebel sources of external support are limited or weak and the presence of a mutually hurting stalemate forces them to look for a political way out of the conflict. As Fearon explains, "when rebels do better day-to-day in a civil war (due to contraband or outside support, for instance) they need to be given more in a regional autonomy deal to be willing to accept it. But the more the government has to give away, the more tempted it will be to renege when it is again in a strong position, which makes it harder to construct a credible negotiated settlement" (pp. 295–96). Some settlements may be altogether elusive because of the incurable covenant risks that are associated with an agreement, that is, the fear that a negotiating partner is not going to live up to his or her obligations after an agreement is signed because this party has strong external allies in the diaspora who will allow him or her to exploit the terms of an agreement after it is signed and/or lower the costs of defection (Hampson, 2006).

A good illustration of the commitment problem in interethnic bargaining is the conflict in southern Sudan. Reviewing the course of negotiated efforts to end this country's ongoing civil war in the late 1980s, Lesch (1993, pp. 130–131) observes that aside from the problems posed by factional struggles and high levels of mistrust between the parties, there were religious belief systems and complex diasporic and religious interests, which raised the costs of negotiated concessions and made it difficult to discuss any kind of settlement in spite of the escalating economic and political costs of the conflict to the Sudanese government and other parties. The goal of the Sudanese People's Liberation Movement (SPLM), which had emerged in the south, was to establish a "nonreligious, non-ethnic government in which all the diverse peoples of Sudan would have an equal share". However, this was not the goal of the central elites in Khartoum, who felt that the rebellion in the south could be contained by only minor concessions.

A similar dynamic was in play in successive rounds of peace negotiations between the Singhalese-led government and the Liberation Tigers of Tamil Eelam (LTTE) in Sri Lanka. The Tamil diaspora, which is based in Western countries but predominantly in Canada, Australia, the United Kingdom, and the United States, has been an enthusiastic supporter of the LTTE and the establishment of Eelam, a separate Tamil state in Sri Lanka (Fair, 2005). Over the years, the LTTE success-fully pushed more moderate Tamil parties to the periphery of Tamil politics while escalating its own demands for an independent Tamil state. In successive rounds of externally sponsored negotiations with the Tamils, the Singhalese-led govern-ment generally tended to assume that it could defeat the LTTE militarily or weaken it "to the point where it would settle for something much less than the separate state for which it has fought so long" (de Silva, 2001 p. 460). As a consequence, efforts to draft a new constitution for the country that would devolve power to the provinces under a quasi-federal set of arrangements failed and a durable foundation for the peace talks that would resolve the Sri Lankan conflict eluded the parties. And eventually, the government did defeat the Tamil insurgency in counteroffensive operations in 2009.

Another interesting case is that Turkey's Kurdish community. The Kurdistan Workers' Party (PKK) is supported in large part by Kurdish diaspora communities in Germany and other European countries. Their activities, along with those of the Armenian diaspora, have greatly complicated Turkey's entry into the European Union (EU). The PKK's rise to prominence among the Kurds has been significantly influenced by the activities and support of the Kurdish diaspora (Marcus, 2007).

Thwarting the Formation of Viable Coalitions

Diasporas can also make interethnic bargaining more difficult and thwart the formation of viable political coalitions that are required to simplify bargaining processes in complex multiethnic and religious wars where there are many differ-ent factions jockeying for power and influence even as they allegedly share a common goal, which is to defeat the government in power, press for indepen-dence, or seek major political reforms. For example, the Ethiopean diaspora has played a key role in supporting political leaders of different militant factions. As Lyons (2007, pp. 539–540) points out: "When the opposition Southern Coalition entertained the idea of engaging the EPRDF Ethiopian People's Revolutionary Democratic Front regime and competing in the 1995 elections, the diaspora was sharply critical and labeled Beyene Petros, the coalition's leaders, as a traitor. Unable to ignore this pressure, the Southern Coalition ultimately boycotted the elections. . . . When splits within the core EPRDF group known as the Tigray People's Liberation Front erupted in March 2001, both factions immediately sent high-level delegations to the United States to shape how the diaspora understood the intraparty conflict and to build support for their respective factions. Many of the more vigorous and dedicated supporters of the Oromo self-determination and the OLF Oromo Liberation Front are in the diaspora."

Reducing the Supply of Mediators

The pressure of diasporas on the foreign policy choices and bargaining strategies of external third parties may also reduce the potential supply of mediators, especially from democratically elected Western governments. The Israeli–Palestinian conflict is rife with three-level negotiation games involving not just the key parties to the conflict but also mobilized constituencies within different diaspora communities in the United States and other Western democracies. The historic role of the United States as the mediator in this conflict highlights the many complex issues related to diaspora pressures and their impact on U.S. foreign policy coherence and priorities. Recent administrations have found themselves increasingly torn by crosscutting domestic and foreign policy pressures. And in the case of other conflicts—Cyprus, Nagorno-Karabakh, Northern Ireland, and Sudan—administrations have been very conscious of the impact of their intermediary efforts on relations with particular diaspora groups and communities.

In some instances, mediation ventures may be derailed by the conflicting pressures of diaspora communities who are reluctant to see any variation from the status quo. This appears to be the fate of the Minsk group (comprised of representatives from a dozen countries and cochaired by France, Russia, and the United States), which was set up to mediate a resolution to the conflict over Nagorno-Karabakh between Azerbaijan and Armenia. As Thomas de Waal (2010, p. 160), a close observer of this conflict, writes, "Although the Minsk Process has appeared poised to deliver success on several occasions, it seems stuck in a perpetual cycle of frustration and disappointment." Part of the reason is the presence of powerful Armenian diaspora communities in France, Russia, and the United States that are keen to see Armenia maintain its control over the Nagorno-Karabakh region and don't want to jeopardize relations with Yerevan.

Although some small countries, like Norway, do not have large immigrant populations or diaspora communities and are thus able to play intermediary roles in different conflict zones, other Western democracies, like Canada, have deliberately chosen to shy away from such roles—even the track II variety—for fear of antagonizing local diaspora communities. Prior to the peace talks that began under Norwegian mediation in 2000, the Sri Lankan government had approached Canada, one of the country's largest donors, to mediate the dispute. Although Canada's top diplomatic envoy to Sri Lanka recommended that Canada respond favorably to the invitation and take the lead in the peace process, when it was reviewed by the Canadian cabinet it was rejected because of the concern that such a highly visible role would adversely affect the government's relations with the Tamil community in Toronto—an important constituency for the Liberal Party, which was in power at the time. The Canadian government also dropped its support for the Canadian Fund for Dialogue and Development between the Israelis and Palestinians in the late 1990s not only because of the worsening situation in the region, but also out of fear that the dialogue might generate a political backlash among Jewish and Muslim groups at home.

Shifting Attitudes

Over time, members of a diaspora community may choose to mobilize against the conflict's status quo and become champions of a peace process and/or efforts to seek some sort of political accommodation between rival communities in their homeland (Brinkerhoff, 2005, 2006; Lyons, 2004, 2007; Østergaard-Nielsen, 2006; Smith & Stares, 2007). This turnabout in attitudes underscores the fact that diasporic identities are not immutable (Nagel & Staeheli, 2005). Many have commented on the important political influence exercised by the so-called Jewish lobby in shaping U.S. policy in the Middle East since Israel's victory in the 1967 war and the development of a "special relationship" between the two countries. Since the 1980s, however, the diaspora has not been monolithic. American Jews were deeply split over Yitzhak Rabin's overtures to the Palestinians in the Oslo peace process; many supported Oslo, although a vocal and increasingly strident minority were deeply opposed (Shain, 2002, p. 123). With Oslo's collapse, these differences appear to have widened. As Mearsheimer and Walt (2006, p. 2) observe: "Many of the key organizations . . . such as the American-Israeli Public Affairs Committee (AIPAC) and the Conference of Presidents of Major Jewish Organizations, are run by hardliners who generally support the Likud Party's expansionist policies, including its hostility to the Oslo peace process. The bulk of U.S. Jewry, meanwhile, is more inclined to make concessions to the Palestinians, and a few groups—such as Jewish Voice for Peace—strongly advocate such steps." The creation of J-Street—"pro-Israel, pro-peace"—in Washington in the 2000s signals an important split in the diaspora.

The most remarkable turnabout in diasporic attitudes in recent years is the change in attitude of Irish Americans toward the conflict in Northern Ireland. During the 1960s and 1970s, many Irish Americans directly or indirectly lent their support to the Irish Republican Army (IRA) in Northern Ireland. This support came in many forms: "There were Irish Americans who waved the Irish flag once a year on St. Patrick's Day and admired the IRA's cause but felt queasy about the methods. There were Irish Americans who collected money for Catholic charities in Northern Ireland without condoning the IRA at all. There were Irish Americans who, while claiming to be 'aiding the families of political prisoners,' were in fact helping to arm IRA terrorists" (Appelbaum, 2005, p. A19). Successive U.S. administrations generally tended to turn a blind eye to these activities, at least until Ronald Reagan was asked by British Prime Minister Margaret Thatcher to clamp down on IRA funding. Key groups like the Irish Northern Aid Committee (NORAID) and the Irish National Caucus (INC) were constant critics of British government policy, lobbying Congress and the White House to support the republican cause. "Despite being a relatively small group, NORAID activists were gifted publicists and managed to generate sufficient media interest, especially during times of political crisis in Northern Ireland. NORAID managed to help internationalize the political conflict in Northern Ireland and provided the Provisional IRA with vital international support for their claim that their 'armed struggle' was a war of national liberation rather than domestic criminality" (Cochrane, 2007, p. 26).

However, the attitudes of many Irish Americans shifted in the late 1980s and early 1990s, as did U.S. policy. The March 1988 bombing in Enniskillen, which killed 11 Protestants, horrified not only the Unionist community in Northern Ireland but also many republican sympathizers, including many Irish Americans. There was growing support for negotiation efforts, which began with the dialogue between John Hume, leader of the moderate nationalist Social Democratic and Labor Party (SDLP), and Gerry Adams, leader of Sinn Féin, the political wing of the IRA. In the United States, a new group, Americans for a New Irish Agenda (ANIA), emerged. ANIA lobbied the incoming president, Bill Clinton, to actively support the peacemaking efforts of the British and Irish governments—a process that eventually culminated in the Good Friday Agreement of April 10, 1998. The most dramatic indication of this turnabout was the decision by the Clinton administration in February 1994 to allow Gerry Adams to visit the United States to attend a conference organized by the National Committee on Foreign Policy in New York. "Subsequent visas, the privilege of raising funds in the United States, invitations to the White House and Capitol Hill, and the continued support of the Clinton Administration reinforced the call to Sinn Féin to engage in the process of political dialogue" (Arthur, 1999, p. 485).

The reasons underlying major shifts in diasporic attitudes are a fascinating topic for further study. In the case of Northern Ireland, the change was precipitated not just by the emergence of a new peace lobby group, the ANIA, but also by a fundamental change in the perceived moral dimensions of the conflict. Irish Americans could no longer turn a blind eye to the activities in Northern Ireland, which were prolonging—if not escalating—the violence and killing innocent civilians. Stopping illicit financial and arms transfers, which sustained the conflict, was morally seen as the right thing to do. The growing support Irish Americans and key U.S. leaders, like President Clinton and Senator Edward Kennedy, lent to the peace process was also based on the perception that the conflict had gone on too long and was a festering sore in the conscience of all Americans.

By contrast, the moral dimension of the Israeli–Palestinian conflict is far more ambiguous because of continuing fears about the long-term survival of a key U.S. ally, which rubs up against broader U.S. strategic and security interests in the Middle East (Shain & Bristman, 2002). The situation is further complicated by the long-standing tug of war between conflicting political interests (and values) in the Israeli homeland and within the Jewish diaspora itself, which, in the eyes of one observer, have tended to feed off one another: "Reform Jews in the United States . . . promoted a Palestinian–Israeli rapprochement in part because they viewed the Israeli occupation of the West Bank and Gaza as belying the liberal political principles that underlay their identity as Jewish-Americans and which, they argued, were the foundation of Israel's natural and close alliance with the United States. By contrast, religious Zionists in the United States, whose identity as an ethnic group in American society is much less important to them than their religious identity, opposed the peace accords because they required Israel to relinquish land which the religious community considered part of the biblical patrimony and a necessary vehicle to fulfill Israel's redemptive function" (Shain, 2002, pp. 136–137).

In some diaspora communities, traditional communal identities may be transformed or simply wane as members of the group find different forms and outlets to express their identity, and as beliefs and values change with the passage of time and prolonged exposure to the values of a liberal, open society. Stanfield (1996, p. 11) observes that "[p]eople who are ethnically different and integrate tightly around similar goals and tasks tend to discard stereotypes over time and use other criteria for bonding and conflict. This is especially the case when it comes to those networks rooted in primary group locations such as families, neighborhoods, religious and other community civic organizations as well as in secondary institutions and sectors with explicit social integration norms and incentives (such as the U.S. military institutions and corporations and academic institutions with senior administrators who are clearly committed to ethnic diversity and who reward middle managers [who] follow their leads)." This process may help explain why surveys show that slightly more than one-third of American Jews say they have little if any emotional attachment to the state of Israel (Mearsheimer & Walt, 2006, p. 8).

Members of a community living outside the zone of conflict are also more likely to be exposed to contradictory sources of information and evidence that challenge preexisting belief systems and biases. Stein (2001, p. 197) notes that "[i]mages can also change incrementally over time. As people consider information about an adversary inconsistent with their previous knowledge, they incorporate into their belief the conditions under which the image does not hold. This kind of process permits gradual change and adjustment." Bertrand (2004, p. 108), for example, finds that attitudes within the sizable populations of Greek and Turkish Cypriots living in the United Kingdom have become increasingly complex and differentiated over the years. Some have decided to abandon their traditional Cypriot identity altogether and have "chosen their British one, or at least remain silent. Others 'voice' against the status quo in the island and against nationalism. Others express their 'loyalty' to the 'communal leaders' . . . and advocate the separation of the communities, if not the legalization of the partition."

Direct Agents of Political Change

Individual members of diasporas can also play direct role in peacemaking and peacebuilding processes by returning to their homeland to become influential members of the local political community and by assuming leadership positions in a newly formed government: supporting the formation of political parties that have progressive, liberal agendas and even directly supporting mediation efforts. As Baser and Swain (2008, p. 16) observe, many cabinet members of Hamid Karzai's government in Afghanistan were drawn from the Afghan diaspora, just as members of the post-Mobutu government in Congo came from the Zairean dispora.

Through conflict resolution training workshops, the establishment of intercommunal contact groups, and other initiatives that bring together individuals who are influential members of the diaspora community, third parties can also help bring about a change in core attitudes and beliefs, thus reinforcing the turnabout and waning effects. There are some striking examples of facilitation efforts directed at receptive diaspora communities, which have explored possibilities for recognizing new options in seemingly intractable conflicts in the homeland (Baser & Swain, 2008; Fisher, 1990; Loizos, 2006; Lyons, 2004, 2007). There is also evidence that positive intergroup contacts among different diaspora groups, especially when they are unplanned and serendipitous, can lead to more tolerant values and critical reflection even if the conflict is experiencing an escalation in the general level of violence (Coleman & Lowe, 2007).

Host State Policies

Policies that directly target diaspora groups who are considered to be national security threats may also lessen their influence and ability to engage in clandestine activities in support of conflicts in their country of origin, thus reinforcing the waning effect. Antiterrorism laws in Europe following the 9/11 terrorist attacks on the United States have severely curtailed the political activities and fund-raising efforts of the PKK in Europe (Østergaard-Nielsen, 2006, p. 8). The post 9/11 environment in the United States has had the effect of further reducing Irish American tolerance for groups associated with terrorism, including former NORAID activists, who found themselves more vulnerable to arrest and deportation by the Department of Homeland Security under post-9/11 legislation such as the Patriot Act (Cochrane, 2007, p. 226). In 2006, Canada and the EU finally took steps to outlaw the LTTE by formally labeling them a terrorist organization. Although the LTTE waged an intensive campaign that targeted the expatriate Tamil population, politicians, and the general public, their sources of funding and support eroded as local authorities clamped down on their acitivities. Tamil activists were allegedly frustrated by the "insufficient activities" of their branches in Canada and the United Kingdom (*National Post*, May 27; 2007a *National Post*, November 6, 2007b). However, there are obvious limits to how far a government can go to curtail the activities of such groups. Such interventions, especially if they are directed at religiously based groups or ethnic minorities, may be seen as discriminatory in liberal democratic states.

■ CONCLUSION

This chapter has argued that diasporas allow parties to a conflict to expand their resource base and levers of influence through the politics of identity. Diasporas may adversely affect interethnic bargaining processes by undermining the commitment of parties to a political settlement. They can also thwart the formation of viable political coalitions and otherwise act as spoilers. But diasporas also have the potential to serve as "helpful fixers" in a peace process. History shows that identities are not immutable and that diaspora communities can experience a turnabout in their basic attitudes and values toward a conflict. This turnabout can be nurtured by external actors who are interested in conflict resolution, but it also springs from deeper social and political transformations that take place within the diaspora community itself. In recent years, various kinds of legislative and regulatory initiatives have also targeted the activities of diaspora groups, thereby reducing their sources of influence.

The policies and level of tolerance exhibited toward diaspora communities in the host country are obviously critical to their survival. Liberal democratic societies provide much of the oxygen diasporas require to survive. But the romanticized attachment such groups feel to their homeland or place of origin may well diminish with the passage of time as traditional cultural and political loyalties are challenged by the crosscutting allegiances and values of an open society.

Note

1. I am most grateful to detailed comments and suggestions on this chapter provided by James Ron.

References

Andreas, P. (2004). The clandestine political economy of war and peace in Bosnia. *International Studies Quarterly, 48*(1), 29–52.

Applebaum, A. (2005, August 3). The discreet charm of the terrorist cause. *Washington Post,* p. A19.

Arthur, P. (1999). Multiparty mediation in Northern Ireland. In C. A. Crocker, F. O. Hampson, & P. Aall (Eds.), *Herding cats: Multiparty mediation in a complex world* (pp. 469–502). Washington, DC: United States Institute of Peace Press.

Baser, B., & Swain, A. (2008). Diasporas as peacemakers: Third party mediation in homeland conflicts. *International Journal on World Peace, 25*(3), 7–28.

Berdal, M., & Malone, D. M. (Eds.). (2001). *Greed and grievance: Economic agendas in civil wars.* Boulder, CO: Lynne Rienner.

Bertrand, G. (2004). Cypriots in Britain: Diaspora(s) committed to peace? *Turkish Studies, 5*(12), 93–110.

Brinkerhoff, J. M. (2005). Digital diasporas and governance in semi-authoritarian states: The case of the Egyptian Copts. *Public Administration and Development, 25,* 193–204.

Brinkerhoff, J. M. (2006). Digital diasporas and conflict prevention: The case of Somalinet.com. *Review of International Studies, 32*(1), 25–47.

Byman, D., Chalk, P., Hoffman, B., Rosenau, W., & David Brannan, D. (RAND Report). (2001). *Trends in outside support for insurgent movements.* Santa Monica, CA: RAND Corporation.

Canadian Encyclopedia. (2010). *Sikhism in Canada.* Historica-Dominion Institute. Available at: http://www.thecanadianencyclopedia.com/index.cfm?PgNm=TCE&Params=A1ARTA0007391

Cochrane, F. (2007a). Irish-America, the end of the IRA's armed struggle and the utility of "soft power." *Journal of Peace Research, 34*(2), 215–231.

Cochrane, F. (2007b). Civil society beyond the state: The impact of diaspora communities on peace building. *Global Media Journal: Mediterranean Edition, 2*(2), 19–29.

Cohen, S. (2005). Intractability and the Israeli–Palestinian conflict. In C. A. Crocker, F. O. Hampson, & P. Aall (Eds.), *Grasping the nettle: Analyzing cases of intractable* conflict (pp. 343–356). Washington, DC: United States Institute of Peace Press.

Coleman, P. T., & Lowe, J. K. (2007). Conflict, identity, and resilience: Negotiating collective identities within the Israeli and Palestinian diasporas. *Conflict Resolution Quarterly, 24*(4), 377–412.

Collier, P. (2007). Economic causes of civil conflict and their implications for policy. In C. A. Crocker, F. O. Hampson, & P. Aall (Eds.), *Leashing the dogs of war: Conflict management in a divided world* (pp. 197–218). Washington, DC: United States Institute of Peace Press.

Collier, P., & Hoeffler, A. (2001). *Greed and grievance in civil war.* Policy Research Working Paper, 235. Washington, DC: The World Bank.

Collier, P., & Hoeffler, A. (2004). *Greed and grievance in civil war.* Oxford Economic Papers, 56. Oxford: 563–595.

Collier, P., Hoeffler, A., & Söderbom, M. (2001). *On the duration of civil wars.* Presented to the World Bank Development Research Group. Washington, DC: The World Bank. Available at: http://siteresources.worldbank.org/DEC/Resources/duration_of_civil_war.pdf

de Silva, K. M. (2001). Sri Lanka's prolonged ethnic conflict: Negotiating a settlement. *International Negotiation, 6,* 437–469.

de Waal, T. (2010). Remaking the Nagarno–Karabakh peace process. *Survival, 52*(4), 159–176.

Dirlik, A. (2004). Intimate others: [Private] nations and diasporas in an age of globalization. *Inter-Asia Cultural Studies, 3,* 491–502.

Fagan, P. W., & Bump, M, (2006, February). *Remittances in conflict and crises: How remittances sustain livelihoods in war, crises, and transitions to peace.* Policy Paper. International Peace Academy. New York.

Fair, C. C. (2005). Diaspora involvement in insurgencies: Insights from the Khalistan and Tamil Eelam movements. *Nationalism and Ethnic Politics, 11,* 125–156.

Fearon, J. D. (2004). Why do some civil wars last so much longer than others? *Journal of Peace Research, 41*(3), 275–301.

Fearon, J. D., & Laitin, D. (2000). Violence and the social construction of ethnic identity. *International Organization, 54*(4), 845–877.

Fisher, R. J. (1990). *The social psychology of intergroup conflict and international conflict resolution.* New York: Springer-Verlag.

Gagnon, V. P. (1994–1995). Ethnic nationalism and international conflict: The case of Serbia. *International Security, 19*(3), 130–166.

Hampson, F. O. (2006). The risks of peace: Implications for international mediation. *Negotiation Journal, 22*(1), 13–30.

Harbom, L., & Wallenstein, P. (2005). Armed conflict and its international dimensions, 1946–2004. *Journal of Peace Research, 42*(5), 623–635.

Judah, T. (2002). *Kosovo: War and revenge.* New Haven, CT: Yale University Press.

Kuperman, A. J. (2002). *The limits of humanitarian intervention: Genocide in Rwanda.* Washington, DC: The Brookings Institution.

Kydd, A., & Walter, B. F. (2002). Sabotaging the peace: The politics of extremist violence. *International Organization, 56*(2), 263–296.

Lesch, A. M. (1993). Negotiations in Sudan. In D. R. Smock (Ed.), *Making war and waging peace: Foreign intervention in sub-Saharan Africa* (pp. 107–131). Washington, DC: United States Institute of Peace Press.

Lischer, S. K. (2005). *Dangerous sanctuaries: Refugee camps, civil war, and the dilemmas of humanitarian aid.* Ithaca, NY: Cornell University Press.

Loizos, P. (2006). Bicommunal initiatives and their contribution to improved relations between Turkish and Greek Cypriots. *South European Society and Politics, 11*(1), 179–194.

Lyons, T. (2004, April). *Engaging diasporas to promote conflict resolution: Transforming hawks into doves.* Fairfax, VA: Institute for Conflict Analysis and Resolution, George Mason University.

Lyons, T. (2007). Conflict-generated diasporas and transnational politics. *Ethics and Development, 6*(4), 529–549.

Marcus, A. (2007). *Blood and belief: The PKK and the Kurdish fight for independence.* New York: New York University Press.

Mearsheimer, J., & Walt, S. (2006). The Israeli lobby. *London Review of Books, 28,* 6 (March 23). Available at: http://www.lrb.co.uk/v28/n06/john-mearsheimer/the-israel-lobby

Nagel, C. R., & Staeheil, L. A. (2005). "We're just like the Irish": Narratives of assimilation, belonging and citizenship amongst Arab-American activists. *Citizenship Studies, 9*(4), 485–498.

National Post. (2007a). Tamil leader frustrated with fundraising. May 27.

National Post. (2007b). Tamil Tigers trying to influence politics. CSIS report. November 6.

Newman, E., & Richmond, O. (2006). Peacebuilding and spoilers. *Conflict, Security and Development, 6*(1), 100–110.

Østergarrd-Nielsen, E. (2006, March). *Diasporas and conflict resolution: Part of the problem or part of the solution?* DIIS brief. Copenhagen: Danish Institute for International Studies.

Sambanis, N. (2001). Do ethnic and nonethnic civil wars have the same causes? *Journal of Conflict Resolution, 45*(3), 259–282.

Shain, Y. (2002). The role of diasporas in conflict perpetuation or resolution." *SAIS Review, 22*(2), 115–144.

Shain, Y., & Barth, A. (2003). Diasporas and international relations theory. *International Organization, 57*(3), 449–479.

Shain, Y., & Bristman, B. (2002). The Jewish security dilemma. *Orbis, 46*(1), 47–71.

Shain, Y., & Sherman, M. (2001). Diasporic transnational flows and their impact on national identity. *Nationalism and Ethnic Politics, 7*(4), 1–36.

Sheffer, G. (1994). Ethno-national diasporas and security. *Survival, 36*(1), 60–79.

Smith, H., & Stares, P. (Eds.). (2007). *Diasporas in conflict: Peacemakers or peace wreckers?* Tokyo: United Nations University Press.

Soysal, Y. N. (2000). Citizenship and identity: Living in diasporas in post-war Europe? *Ethnic and Racial Studies, 23*(1), 1–15.

Stanfield, J. H., II. (1996). Multiethnic societies and regions. *American Behavioral Scientist, 40*(1), 8–17.

Stedman, S. J. (1997). Spoiler problems in peace processes. *International Security, 22*(2), 5–53.

Stein, J. G. (2001). Image, identity, and the resolution of violent conflict. In C. A. Crocker, F. O. Hampson, & P. Aall (Eds.), *Turbulent peace: The challenges of managing international conflict* (pp. 189–208). Washington, DC: United States Institute of Peace Press.

Tarrow, S. (2005). *The new transnational activism.* New York: Cambridge University Press.

Van Hear, N. (2003, June 1). *Refugee diasporas, remittances, development, and conflict.* Migration Information Source. Available at: http://www.migrationinformation.org/feature/print.cfm?ID=125

Werner, S. (1999). The precarious nature of peace: Resolving the issues, enforcing the settlement, and renegotiating terms. *American Journal of Political Science, 48*(3), 912–934.

Zartman, I. W. (1989). *Ripe for resolution.* New York: Oxford University Press.

Zartman, I. W. (2008). Ripeness revisited: The push and pull of conflict management. In I. W. Zartman, *Negotiation and conflict management: Essays on theory and practice* (pp. 232–244). London: Routledge.

7 Outbidding and the Decision to Negotiate

■ JANNIE LILJA

Everyone who comes has an agenda. If those agendas are a barrier to the main agenda—Tamil Eelam or self determination . . . then that agenda has to be removed.

Tamil Tiger leader Vellupillai Prabhakaran on competing Tamil parties and the struggle for a separate Tamil Eelam state.

The literature on negotiation has little to say about the internal dynamics on the nonstate side when it comes to getting to peace through negotiated agreement. However, leadership of the nonstate party can be problematic in internal armed conflicts that take on a pronounced identity, or ethnic, dimension (Pearlman, 2008). During an ongoing conflict, who decides whether or not to negotiate, and who represents the nonstate side in negotiations, are rarely obvious. The logic of escalation predicts that the most extreme faction in the nonstate camp will prevail. Outbidding, a form of escalation, means that an actor uses nonconciliatory deed and discourse to establish representation and leadership of the identity group. Political extremism and violence are used to signal resolve and commitment to the group's cause. The result is that the moderates will give way to the hard-liners (cf. KYDD & Walter, 2006). Hence, even though a rebel group may want to work for peace via negotiation, outbidding could make it impossible. The questions is thus how it is possible at all for a nonstate party to initiate negotiations and reach an agreement, and what external interventions—both diplomatic and nongovernmental organization (NGO)—could assist this process.

The aim of this chapter is to explore what outbidding strategies the rebel negotiator in an ethno-separatist conflict uses to get to an negotiated agreement and, on the basis of these findings, to identify opportunities for external support for preventive negotiations. Negotiation success is the result of a confluence of factors. Conventional explanations center on the strategic interaction between the government and the rebel group (Zartman, 1995a, 1995b). This study shifts the focus from the negotiation between the main protagonists to the internal dynamics on the nonstate side, exploring the interaction between factions within one negotiating camp, inspired by the work of Robert Putnam (1988; Putnam, Evans, & Jacobsen 1993). Although the state has been examined in this light, little theoretical work has furthered a comparable understanding of the nonstate party. Given that most current conflicts are internal and protracted in nature, exploring this issue is essential from an empirical standpoint. This chapter explores three intertwined questions: What outbidding strategies are used by rebel negotiators on the way to the table to conclude an agreement? What outbidding strategies are associated with what types of negotiation outcomes? How could external diplomatic intervention facilitate negotiation processes involving a nonstate party?

This chapter seeks to make four main contributions. The first is to develop the concept of outbidding in relation to nonstate actors' involvement in negotiations aimed at ending civil war. The chapter begins by distinguishing the horizontal and vertical dimensions of outbidding. On this basis, expected outbidding strategies are formulated and explored in relation to actual strategies used by rebel negotiators in three comparable identity conflicts: Sri Lankan Tamil Eelam, Indonesian Aceh, and Senegalese Casamance. The rebel groups are strongly dominated by one respective ethnic identity—Tamil, Acehnese, and Jola. Identity involves ethnicity in the sense of a common language closely linked to territory and to notions of shared history, values, and interests. This territorially based identity has translated into separatist claims for all groups. The second contribution comes from new primary interview data on actual outbidding strategies, while the third one comes from exploring associations between particular outbidding strategies and negotiation outcomes. The fourth contribution is to distill important policy implications for external diplomatic intervention.

■ OUTBIDDING: DEED AND DISCOURSE

Outbidding needs to be disentangled into a horizontal and a vertical dimension. In a situation of identity conflict, factions within the nonstate camp use nonconciliatory deed and discourse to convince constituents that they have greater resolve than other factions and therefore are worthy of support (cf. Horowitz, 1985; Rabushka & Shepsle, 2009; Sartori, 1966).[1] The government is portrayed as the aggressor, nonstate actors calling for compromise are branded as traitors, and moderates are sidestepped, silenced, threatened, or even killed (Byman, 2002). Deed thus often takes a violent form. Violence is used for at least three purposes: first, to signal resolve and commitment to the group cause; second, to intimidate constituents; and third, to provoke government attacks on constituents to make them rally around the faction advocating armed struggle rather than negotiation (Kydd & Walter, 2002). The expected end result is that the most hard-line and violent faction will prevail, and their opponents will be killed, intimidated, or deprived of their constituency. Hence, outbidding occurs when there is competition for leadership and when the population is uncertain about who best represents their interests (Bloom, 2004). Outbidding is thus about aspiring leaders' wish to enhance their identity group credentials and their commitment to the group's cause (Duffy-Toft, 2007; Snyder, 2000).

Outbidding can thus be seen as a way for leaders to earn public recognition without elections or alongside elections. Many times leaders on the nonstate side are unelected, as electoral participation may risk legitimizing a prevailing political order considered to be unjust. The meaning of popular recognition in the context of protracted conflict is not always clear. Competing claims about legitimacy and the right to represent the identity group may thus be made on the basis of, for example, military, political, ethical, religious, or customary authority.[2]

(Since everyone within the identity group, by definition, is expected to have the same identity, identity appeals per se cannot serve as a source of authority.)

The Logic of Horizontal Outbidding: Eliminating Competitors

Since there may be significant rivalry among unelected leaders in a nonstate camp, there may be significant internal rivalry about representing the identity group, and negotiations entail significant risk taking. Horizontal outbidding means that different rebel entrepreneurs compete for exclusive leadership and seek to eliminate each other (Kydd & Walter, 2006, pp. 58–59). Outbidding could be viewed as characteristic of the "consolidation" phase in the conflict, when negotiation with the government is a distraction (Zartman, 2005, 2008). Once consolidation takes place, the emergent nonstate leader can turn back to confrontation with the government through armed struggle or negotiation. Prolonged in-camp confrontation, however, magnifies the tactical question of whether to fight or negotiate. There is no necessary linear progression. Factionalism can throw the conflict back into consolidation and move the conflict back into a phase where negotiation is not on the agenda.[3]

The presence of rival nonstate groups in an identity conflict means that both the participation in negotiations and the compromises made during negotiations are risky. Concessions pertaining to separate statehood are particularly sensitive. The level of risk depends on competing factions' ability to coordinate against, or otherwise punish, the negotiator. This hinges on negotiators' ability to control information, discern threats, and protect themselves against them (Weeks, 2008). Extremists within the nonstate camp may make counteroffers to dissuade negotiating moderates from making concessions or use violence against them (Bueno de Mesquita, 2005).

The Logic of Vertical Outbidding: Securing Constituents

Whereas outbidding is largely aimed at defeating competing rebel factions, the battle is aimed at leadership of the identity group. However, the question is how much freedom the "rebel constituency" has when it comes to supporting leaders' decisions on negotiation.[4] It is not evident that rebels need the explicit buy-in from constituents for negotiation purposes. In this regard, rebels' resource dependency on the population could sensitize them to constituents' preference in regard to negotiations and the Tactical question (Bloom, 2003, p 55; Zartman & Alfredson, 2009). During war, rebels may lack both the motive and the opportunity to hold popular consultations or public referenda. Rebels' "popular" support for negotiation could thus consist of the population's passive acceptance or of lack of violent resistance. Support thus has to do with the population's confidence in the rebel group's ability to represent the group's interest.

Thus, rebels risk incurring constituent audience costs when going for negotiations. In fact, rebels' violent capacity could be what gives them popular legitimacy, although violence may also be used against constituents (Kalyvas, 2006). Factions use violence, including acts of terrorism, to radicalize constituents by pitting them against more moderate competing factions. Through fighting, rebels convince constituents that their faction has greater resolve than their rivals. As violent acts become a source of honor, factions make competing claims of responsibility to, for example, enhance recruitment. Violent outbidding thus applies when violence resonates positively with the civilian population.[5] As violence increases, support becomes more necessary for the militants and more risky for the population. Given the uncertainty among constituents about what faction best represents their interests, tangible losses incurred by rebels signal commitment and trust-worthiness. Support for militants could also stem from a desire to be represented by a hard-liner in negotiations rather than a soft dove. Otherwise, the nonstate side may get a peace deal reflecting a worse outcome than what could have been possible with continued armed struggle.[6] Should the rebel leadership attain political office, a demonstrated commitment to the cause also reduces the concern that it will become corrupt.

A nonstate negotiator thus, first, risks having to pay an audience cost of treason. The negotiator may be seen by constituents as betraying the cause. If armed strug-gle and violence function as a commitment signal, the audience cost is incurred even if negotiation is chosen only as a temporary tactical option. Furthermore, if concessions made during negotiations are made public, there is a further risk of losing the support of critical population segments, such as sponsors whose resource contributions enable the militants to increase violence in the case of negotiation failure (Bueno de Mesquita, 2005, p. 172; Weeks, 2008). This challenge is particu-larly severe when it comes to concessions regarding separate statehood. A second cost of credibility is that rebels' own propaganda may turn against them as they opt to negotiate. Rebels may have portrayed the state as an existential threat to the identity group, radicalizing rebel constituents to support aggressive antistate measures (Maoz & McCauley, 2008). Constituents may therefore require a new "de-mobilization" discourse, making it difficult to revert to a harder line without considerable credibility loss should negotiations collapse. The milder faction then becomes entrapped in its moderation, playing into the hands of the state.

Violent vertical outbidding strategies result in genuine attitudinal support by con-stituents, who view rebels' use of violence as evidence of their commitment. Violence against rival groups is unlikely to generate popular support in itself; it needs to be combined with the notion that it is carried out selflessly on behalf of the identity group. Alternatively, vertical violence strategies mean that constituents are intimi-dated to support a particular faction to maximize their own survival odds. Civilians may thus cooperate with rebels but still not elect them if left free to choose.

▨ EXPECTED OUTBIDDING STRATEGIES

Now that I have outlined the outbidding concept on the basis of existing literature and divided it into a horizontal and a vertical dimension, it is possible to formulate outbidding strategies of deed and discourse that a rebel negotiator would be expected to use to initiate negotiations and get to agreement.

Being the only nonstate representative in town would be positively associated with the decision to negotiate and reach an agreement. If only the most extreme nonstate group is left to negotiate peace, no other faction can seriously spoil the peace process. Prior to negotiation, a rebel group would hence use three horizontal deed strategies to eliminate competition. The first is a strategy of violence against rival factions and faction leaders. Short of violence, a second strategy would be the silencing, threatening, or sidestepping of moderates. (This refers to Zartman's [2005] argument on phasing, meaning that a faction needs to eliminate competition before it can expose itself to the risks that negotiations entail.) A third, nonviolent, horizontal prenegotiation strategy is to build the capacity to control information to discern threats against one's own faction. A prenegotiation vertical strategy to signal resolve before constituents would be the use of spectacular acts of violence, including terrorism.

Once negotiations are underway, outbidding strategies can be expected to shift from deed to discourse. However, as the choice to negotiate may put the faction's entire existence at risk, a horizontal strategy of violence will be used parallel to talks (Höglund, 2004; Hoglund & Zartman, 2006). During the talks, a vertical outbidding strategy would be to push the government for tangible deliverables.

Before negotiations, an outbidding logic would result in open claims of responsibility for violent acts committed (and those not committed) and an aggressive discourse leveled against the government. Discourse-based outbidding strategies would increase in importance during talks. For negotiations aimed at a peace agreement, a vertical demobilization discourse would have to be pursued with respect to critical constituency segments. Being the only nonstate representative facilitates this type of discourse. Aside from using the demobilization discourse, rebels need to continuously assert their commitment to the group's cause (Weinberg & Pedahzur, 2003). Rebels may also introduce superordinate goals, such as defeating a common enemy, to reduce factional differences and attain constituent buy-in (Pruitt & Kim, 2004).

Deed-based outbidding strategies are largely expected to be associated with negotiation failure. Violent strategies in particular risk undermining the government's trust in the rebel negotiator and make it more difficult to "sell" the negotiation option to government constituents. A mainly discourse-based outbidding strategy is likely to be more conducive to negotiation success.

■ OUTBIDDING IN THREE IDENTITY CONFLICTS: SRI LANKA, INDONESIA, AND SENEGAL

These ideas can be tested by an explorative and comparative case study approach. Outbidding strategies are inductively identified across cases. There are three types of negotiation outcomes: breakdown of talks (failure), a cease-fire agreement (partial success), or a peace agreement (success). Acknowledging that negotiation outcomes depend on a confluence of factors, notably the strategic interaction with government, negotiation failure may not necessarily be the direct result of rebels' outbidding strategies.

Rebel groups from three identity conflicts have been selected for structured comparative exploration: the Liberation Tigers of Tamil Eelam (LTTE) in Sri Lanka, Geracan Aceh Merdeka (GAM) in Aceh-Indonesia, and Mouvement des Forces Démocratiques de la Casamance (MFDC) in Senegal. The three cases, representing a subsample of identity conflicts, are comparable across a number of dimensions. They are all identity based, separatist, protracted (all of them started in the early 1980s), and marked by intense competition for group leadership. In all cases, identity is closely linked to territory, which translates into stated separatist objectives for all groups. Although the respective groups are strongly dominated by one ethnicity—here Tamil, Acehnese, and Jola—identity encompasses ethnicity, a common language, a shared history, and shared cultural values and interests.

Comparative cases are used to create richness and variation in outbidding strategies and outcomes. GAM and MFDC have attained negotiation success, whereas the LTTE talks ended up in failure. Varying outcomes allow for a reconstruction of similarities and differences in outbidding strategies through a method of difference. The empirical data consist largely of personal interviews with individuals involved in the negotiation processes in the respective conflicts, about 70 in all. These novel primary sources are complemented with secondary ones, including published documentary and archival material, and reports.

LTTE and the Tamils in Sri Lanka: Outbidding Strategies Used

The Sri Lankan conflict has witnessed five peace negotiation processes since its inception in large-scale violent form in 1983 (Shanmugaratnam, 2008). The conflict was between the Sri Lankan government, dominated by an ethnic Sinhalese majority, and the ethnic Tamil minority. The first negotiation, the Thimpu talks in 1985, ended in failure; the second peace negotiation, between the governments of Sri Lanka and India, resulted in the 1987 Indo-Lankan accord. The third talks in 1990 between the Sri Lankan president and the LTTE concerned the departure of the Indian Peacekeeping Force (IPKF), mandated to oversee the implementation of the Indo-Lankan accord. From this moment on, the LTTE acted as the Tamil negotiation representative. A fourth set of negotiations in 1994 between the LTTE and the government resulted in breakdown. The fifth peace process in 2001 produced a cease-fire agreement, but this broke down in 2003.

In the Thimpu talks in 1985 between the Sri Lankan government and a coalition of the main Tamil armed groups, including the LTTE, the coalition put forward a declaration of principles, notably the need to recognize a Tamil homeland for which self-determination would be a stated right.[7] After the collapse of the Thimpu talks, Tamil infighting began because the LTTE wanted to establish itself as the sole Tamil representative. India, as a financial backer of all of the Tamil groups, was against separate statehood. Whereas the non-LTTE groups were willing to compromise on this point, the LTTE was not and considered the others as traitors.[8] The LTTE has since been described as a maximalist hard-liner constantly pushing for the creation of a separate Tamil Eelam state[9] The LTTE went on to violently eliminate competing Tamil groups through large-scale attacks, killing hundreds of persons (Lilja and Hultman 2011). After these events in 1986, there was a qualitative shift in the Tamil community: "Then there was fear. People dared not challenge [the LTTE] the way they had done before. We just couldn't believe it. It really shook us" (anonymous). Rival Tamil militant groups sought protection from the state, and the LTTE ended up as the only Tamil organization fighting against it.

In the 1987 Indo-Lankan talks the LTTE, not being an official negotiation party, appears to have been forced not to spoil the agreement. The charismatic LTTE leader, Velupillai Prabakharan, was reportedly forced by the Indian prime minister to accept the settlement within a unitary Sri Lankan state, although declining a personal offer of a ministerial post. With the deployment of the Indian IPKF in 1987, new dynamics appeared. All Tamil groups and the Sri Lankan government joined forces to throw the IPKF out of Sri Lanka. Different Tamil groups coordinated attacks to compete for Tamil public support, and the most successful attacks attracted new recruits. The LTTE, however, proved militarily superior.[10]

With the IPKF departure in 1990, the LTTE could start claiming the role as the main Tamil representative based on its de facto control over territory and people in Sri Lanka's northern and eastern regions (Perera, 2006, pp. 232–233). In addition, the Tigers demanded that the government not hold talks with the other Tamil groups (Jayatilleke, 2006, p. 160). The ensuing talks between the LTTE and Sri Lankan president Ranasinghe Premadasa were described more as discussions to seek common interests. The LTTE presence and recruitment in government-controlled areas in 1991 suggested the conclusion of an informal LTTE–government deal.[11]

However, in the course of the Premadasa talks, the horizontal outbidding shifted from occurring between competing Tamil groups to within the Tiger organization instead. Whereas Mahattaya, the deputy head of the LTTE, having spearheaded the anti-IPKF military campaign, wanted to explore the possibility of a peace settlement, Prabakharan was concerned about slackening the momentum of the war effort and wanted talks to be called off. Mahattaya posed a challenge to Prabakharan's leadership based on his own military credentials and personal popularity. Accused of being an Indian intelligence collaborator, Mahattaya was tortured and assassinated on Prabakharan's orders (Swamy, 2005).[12]

The 1994 negotiations with the new president Chandrika Kumaratunga, served a horizontal outbidding function, allowing the LTTE to reassert its status as the sole Tamil representative. However, the process also revealed LTTE's coercion of Tamil constituents in Tiger-controlled areas. The government used a multiethnic negotiation team composed of Tamil delegates competing for the support of the same Tamil constituency, interestingly suggesting vertical outbidding between the LTTE and the government. The October 1994 talks exposed the unabated enthusiasm for negotiation on the part of Jaffna residents, who gave a tumultuous welcome to the government delegation. When the government negotiators revisited Jaffna in January 1995, people were conspicuously absent from the streets. The Tigers had sensed that people were being "seduced," as the government had signaled that peace talks would help separate the Tamil people from the LTTE, and thus "advised" people to stay home.[13] Following the negotiation breakdown, Prabakharan was concerned about the disillusionment among LTTE fighters who had felt that the talks had disproportionately benefited the government.[14]

In November 2000 Prabakharan announced that the LTTE would hold unconditional talks,[15] indicating its readiness to absorb all associated audience costs. Prabakharan unilaterally declared a cease-fire in December 2000. However, late 2001 saw LTTE military advances. The cease-fire agreement that came into effect in February 2002 was relatively easy to negotiate from an outbidding perspective: horizontally, in officially acknowledging the LTTE's de facto land holdings by demarcating lines of territorial control, and vertically, on the pretext of giving the population a respite from the war.[16] At this point, the Tigers claimed another reason for serving as the Tamil representative: administrative structures. In the words of the late LTTE political ideologue Anton Balasingham, "You are not dealing with a political party. We have a judicial system, various structures where civilians are participating. So you have to take us seriously, that is what we say, just don't ignore us."[17]

The substance of the following peace talks in 2002–2003 made the LTTE extremely vulnerable to outbidding. Balasingham declared that the LTTE was open to explore a federal solution,[18] a statement reiterated by Prabakharan in November 2002.[19] For the first time, the LTTE had deviated from its hard-line stand on separate statehood. Although qualified in terms of internal self-determination, the proposal did represent a major shift. The Tamil community did not openly contest the position, but it is likely to have caused significant repercussions within the military wing, which was feeling uncertain about its implications.[20] The future Tamil state plays a key role in the recruitment and training of cadres who have to pledge their lives to Tamil Eelam.[21] During the cease-fire cadres were still in combat mode, carrying out "graduation work" types of incidents.[22] Fighters were again reportedly demotivated by the "negotiation show."[23]

The peace negotiations also created a new split at the LTTE leadership level. The negotiations gave Prabakharan's deputy and the only military representative on the LTTE negotiation team, Karuna, the opportunity to interact with the government, to which Karuna defected in the spring of 2004.[24] However, by then, the LTTE had formally abandoned the peace process on the pretext of exclusion from a major peace-building donor conference held in Washington. D.C. However, the underlying reason is believed to be Balasingham's stated willingness to explore a federal solution. Whereas this position was sanctioned by Prabakharan at that point in the peace talks, it is not evident that the LTTE leader foresaw the fundamentally disruptive impact the position threatened to have internally.[25] The Tigers also perceived that the government had tried to corrupt individual negotiators.[26] The talks broke down on both sides, and the ensuing government offensive crushed the LTTE, killing Prabhakaran.

GAM and the Acehnese in Aceh Indonesia: Outbidding Strategies Used

The separatist conflict in Aceh has witnessed three sets of negotiations since its inception in 1982. Geracan Aceh Merdeka represented the Acehnese community in all of these negotiations with the Indonesian government. The first one, in 2000, resulted in a cease-fire agreement, the "humanitarian pause." The second negotiation, in 2002, produced another cease-fire, the Cessation of Hostilities Agreement (COHA), followed by peace talks that broke down in 2003. The third peace process, starting in early 2005, resulted in a substantive peace treaty, the Memorandum of Understanding (MOU), the same year.

Upon the lifting of the military emergency rule (the Daerah Operasi Militer, DOM) in August 1998, enhanced mobility and freedom of expression increased activity in the Acehnese camp. However, GAM, established in 1976 by Hasan di Tiro, was the only functional militant group struggling for independence and the only one with an infrastructure that covered the entire Aceh.[27] Geracan Aceh Merdeka had taken the risks and borne the costs of importing weapons during the intense security force repression in the DOM period.[28] Short of acquiring territory, GAM had managed to assume control over local government administration through persuasion, replacements, and abduction of lower-level officials.[29]

The first real outbidding dynamic that could be witnessed in 1997–1998 was thus internal and horizontal, linked to leadership succession rather than to positional differences on negotiation (Int 41). Di Tiro suffered a major stroke in 1997, causing a rift between his former chief of staff, Huseini Hasan, and the circle of the people closest to di Tiro, including Abdullah Zaini, the foreign minister in the GAM shadow government, over his succession.[30]

Yet, it was the invitation by an external facilitator, the Geneva-based Centre Henri Dunant (or Center for Humanitarian Dialogue CHD), to cease-fire talks in 1999, that is, the prelude to the humanitarian pause, that caused the real split within the GAM leadership. Huseini had formed a faction called MP-GAM Eropa, announcing its willingness to start negotiations with the government at any time (Miller, 2006). Despite a united stand for independence by the original GAM, the di Tiro faction was reportedly not keen to negotiate. Huseini was considered soft and too much in favor of a negotiated solution, which earlier had induced di Tiro to remove him from the inner leadership circle.[31] The CHD had invited both original GAM and MP-GAM for a first meeting. Zaini reportedly stated that "We said that CHD either negotiate with us or them [MP-GAM]."[32] The CHD realized that Huseini lacked the di Tiro faction's close contact with field commanders and was unable to command troops.[33] The MP-GAM members were isolated and publicly denounced by di Tiro, and one of them was shot dead in Kuala Lumpur.[34] For the second meeting, only the di Tiro faction was invited[35] and its participation in the talks seemed to strengthen its leadership[36] Another horizontal and vertical dimension of intraorganizational outbidding connected to the humanitarian pause was the relationship between the exiled political leadership and the military field commanders. The di Tiro leadership's more than two-decade-long exile in Stockholm reportedly forced them to play their cards hard, convincing their military counterparts in Aceh of their commitment.[37] The military was arguably more pragmatic and less interested in the symbolic issue of independence, merely wanting an end to the bloodshed (Int 40).

By 1999 new nonstate groupings emerged in Aceh. Among these was SIRA (Sentral Informasi Referendum Aceh), a student-led referendum movement. Initially, SIRA had no links to GAM, actually opposing GAM in offering people a choice on independence through referendum.[38] The SIRA leader reportedly asked GAM for permission to hold demonstrations and also received logistical assistance from GAM to mobilize and transport protesters to Banda Aceh.[39]

From mid-2000 on, GAM did not need to engage much in horizontal outbidding with Acehnese political activists, as the security forces failed to distinguish them from GAM—beating and arresting SIRA members on the pretext of being "GAM without guns." Because of these actions, coupled with the seemingly indiscriminate government attacks on civilians, Acehnese previously advocating a negotiated settlement became increasingly hard-line and supportive of GAM's taking the lead as the Achenese representative.[40]

In mid-2001, the government unsuccessfully tried to drive a wedge between the Stockholm leadership and the GAM field commanders by calling for talks directly with the commander-in-chief, Abdullah Syafi'ie. Syafi'ie declined, referring "political" decision making to Stockholm.[41] After the arrest of GAM negotiators in Banda Aceh, negotiations broke down.[42] The fact that GAM military leaders continuously asserted loyalty to di Tiro made intraorganizational outbidding easier—both horizontally, in relation to higher GAM military commanders, and vertically, in relation to cadres. However, it could be seen as the result of successful internal outbidding strategies, as will be demonstrated below.

Resumption of talks in 2002 resulted in the COHA cease-fire agreement in 2003, but during the ensuing peace talks, the government issued an ultimatum that GAM had to abandon its independence demand and disarm completely. As GAM was not prepared to surrender, negotiations broke down.[43] The Indonesian military relaunched a full-scale operation in Aceh.[44]

The cohesion between GAM's political and military wings, which made intraorganizational horizontal outbidding a nonissue after the initial fractionalization in 1999, could be explained by two outbidding strategies.[45] The first was the direct personal bonding between di Tiro and the military officers in 1986–1989 in Libya, where all officers underwent the same military and political history training provided by di Tiro himself.[46] In the words of one participant, "between di Tiro and the men there developed a sort of an emotional bond . . . almost like love."[47] In fact, every field commander was nominated by the Stockholm leadership.[48] The sustained loyalty 20 years after Libya, however, suggests the use of a second strategy built on controlled internal communication and information flows. The Di Tiro leadership issued military directives from Stockholm, keeping abreast of troop movements and communicating daily with field commanders.[49] Malik Mahmud had been formally nominated as di Tiro's deputy at a GAM meeting in Norway in 2000.[50] While based in Malasyia and Singapore, Malik was considered part of the Stockholm leadership. Malik thus served an important bridging function to field commanders,[51] compensating for di Tiro's absence.

The security force crackdown after the negotiation failure in 2003 once again decreased the need for horizontal outbidding. Members of SIRA were killed and others were now forced to seek GAM protection.[52] The situation also highlighted the opportunistic aspect of letting the Stockholm leadership negotiate on behalf of the Acehnese. After all, the exile leadership was able to act and voice opinions, whereas Aceh-based representatives were not.[53]

Although the official GAM position was independence,[54] the di Tiro leadership agreed to start negotiations in January 2005 in spite of the precondition posed by the mediator, former Finnish president Martti Ahtisaari, that any future agreement would be "within the Indonesian constitution."[55] Internal discussions within the GAM political leadership on solutions short of independence had started in

2004. Malik had informally showed an interest in favor of this outcome.[56] The decision of GAM to negotiate despite Ahtisaari's preconditions suggests that intraorganizational outbidding had taken place before.

During the talks, it appears that GAM formally abandoned its position on separate Achenese statehood some time after the second round. After the third round, the concept of self-government was dropped (Enia, 2006).[57] Changes must have taken place internally, as the explicit abandonment reportedly did not create significant tensions within GAM.[58] The notion that the timing of the tsunami disaster was not the determinant causal factor behind this decision is shared by GAM as well as non-GAM personnel. The tsunami, claiming an estimated 130,000 Acehnese lives, was considered to have accelerated the process, not determined it.[59] The tsunami kept Acehnese civil society and the military part of GAM preoccupied, which reduced GAM's need for outbidding.

The intraorganizational outbidding strategies used by the GAM negotiators during the 2005 peace talks are noteworthy. A peculiar feature was that decisions were taken only in the presence of all five core team negotiators to prevent one-on-one deals. Strategic decisions were taken by the highest leader[60] Communication between the GAM negotiators in Helsinki and the military leadership in Aceh was continuous during the negotiations, although reports differ on whether negotiators merely informed military commanders of positions taken or whether the latter influenced actual negotiating positions.[61] With the GAM intelligence chief, Irwandi Yusuf, joining the third round of talks in Helsinki, telephone conferences with all military district commanders in Aceh could take place in real time.[62] One observer noted that Malik was very apprehensive in talking to field commanders, saying nothing that they would not accept.[63]

The carefully monitored information flow from the talks helped vertical outbidding.[64] Also important were the three face-to-face consultative meetings held by GAM. A restricted set of 15 participants, SIRA members and a few trusted others, attended the first meeting in Stockholm. A second meeting, with 25 participants, also included some GAM critics. A third session with a wider set of participants—around 150 in all—took place in Kuala Lumpur shortly before the signing of the agreement.[65] The main purpose was to outline GAM's negotiation positions on independence and self-government. Opinions were incorporated whenever possible, but decisions taken by the GAM negotiators could not be overruled. Meeting participants disseminated the information directly upon their return to Aceh[66] The big mosque in Banda-Aceh was used to make announcements on GAM's advances in the negotiations.[67] In addition, GAM used its own network to convey information.[68] A substantial treaty on "special autonomy" for Aceh was concluded between GAM and the Indonesian government in August 2005.

MFDC and the Casamancais in Senegal: Outbidding Strategies Used

The low-intensity conflict—3,000 to 5,000 deaths by 1998—between Senegal and the MFDC has witnessed numerous negotiations since the Ziguinchor manifestations of December 1982. These negotiations were informal in character and ended in a large number of cease-fire agreements, for example in 1991, 1993, and 2001, along with a peace framework agreement of 2004.[69]

The MFDC political leader, the Catholic priest Augustin Diamacoune, has been the signatory to most of these agreements, alone or together with representatives of the MFDC military wing. Diamacoune was the first to publicly call for a separate Casamance state in a letter to the Senegalese president in the 1970s.[70] Faced with popular protests in the early 1980s, the Senegalese government imprisoned Diamacoune, inadvertently turning him into an MFDC martyr and the leader of the nonstate camp partly against his will:[71] "The government wants to make me the leader of MFDC. They have made me responsible . . . but I accept it."[72]

There has been no named organized horizontal competition to the MFDC to represent the Casamance cause. A complicating factor is, however, that the MFDC can be viewed as a collection of separate organizations.[73] From the time of the first split in its military wing in 1991, different factions have demonstrated patterns of localized resource dependence and external ties while maintaining a common MFDC banner for apparent (vertical) legitimacy purposes.[74]

The MFDC outbidding has thus been intraorganizational and has played out mainly within the military wing, Atika, established in 1985 by Sidy Badji while Diamacoune was still imprisoned.[75] Although Badji and his deputy, Léopold Sagna, distinguished themselves as military leaders through other fighting experiences, they did not challenge Diamacoune's position as political leader.[76]

Both Diamacoune and Badji accepted the cease-fire negotiations in 1991 resulting in the Cacheu accord signed by Badji.[77] No one protested Badji's representation of the MFDC in the cease-fire negotiations; he communicated MFDC negotiation positions on the radio and held consultations in a relatively transparent manner.[78]

After the 1991 cease-fire agreement, and despite Diamacoune's release from prison as a result of it, military wing members of the MFDC accused Badji of having renounced independence and of taking government bribes.[79] Badji challenged Diamacoune's leadership and denounced armed struggle on the pretext that Diamacoune had failed to prove his claim of having negotiated a deal with former president Léopold Senghor that would grant Casamance independence.[80] Badji transferred some of his combatants to northern Casamance and provided them with new equipment.[81] As a result, Badji was put under house arrest by his own military wing members.[82]

Outbidding over the leadership of the MFDC's military wing commenced. A young hard-line commander, Salif Sadio, argued that the new leader should be chosen on the basis of military merit.[83] To assist Sadio and sideline Sagna, the natural successor to the commander-in-chief position, a campaign was spearheaded by a handful of MFDC political wing members.[84] They announced that Sadio was the new commander-in-chief and helped him acquire combatant name lists. Diamacoune agreed to divide the commander-in-chief function into three, waiting for the military wing to elect their leader. However, Sadio was granted operational responsibility and control over MFDC weapons stocks, which put him in an advantageous position.[85] In April 1992, the military wing formally split as Badji escaped and formed Front Nord (FN).[86] Hostilities resumed between the remaining faction, Front Sud (FS), and Senegal, while FN chose to adhere to the 1991 ceasefire.

Threatened by arrest, Diamacoune escaped from Ziguinchor in August 1992 to join FS in the bush. Despite the leadership competition between Sagna and Sadio, Diamacoune did nothing to assume control over the maquis during his stay with them.[87] A second cease-fire accord, facilitated by Guinea Bissauan president João Bernardo Vieira, was achieved in July 1993 in Guinea Bissau.[88] This agreement was reportedly signed by Diamacoune and Sagna. After the 1993 cease-fire Sagna met the Senegalese president in Dakar. As photos of the meeting were leaked to FS, it was now Sagna's turn to be accused of government corruption by his own militants.[89]

Intraorganizational horizontal outbidding between competing MFDC military leaders intensified. Sadio placed Sagna under house arrest on treason and corruption charges and proclaimed himself the FS leader.[90] Sagna was tortured and kept in a bunker, dying from physical weakness in 1996. Interestingly, the reason for not killing Sagna outright could have been the wish not to upset the MFDC spiritual guides.[91]

Faced with the military wing's outbidding for the commander-in-chief position, Diamacoune took a passive let-things-play-themselves-out approach, continuously asking the military to select their own leader, whom Diamacoune would then recognize. Diamacoune clearly lacked the ability or the will to control the MFDC military wing.[92] "Abbé was the commander of the maquis, but he did not give orders to Sadio."[93] As Sadio had taken power by force, Diamacoune could not recognize him.[94] At the same time, Diamacoune never openly protested against Sadio even as the latter started to systematically kill off Sagna's closest men.[95] "Diamacoune left things to resolve themselves . . . awaiting for consensus to emerge."[96]

When Diamacoune returned to Ziguinchor in 1993 the government put him under house arrest, implying that he could only have indirect contact with military faction leaders and with the head of the MFDC's external political wing, Nkroumah Sané, in Paris. Despite this, Diamacoune's role as the principal MFDC leader was never challenged. Yet, the military wing considered Diamacoune as being under constant government pressure: "He has not betrayed [the cause]—he is constrained to do it."[97] "Abbé had to say certain things but we know that these are not his true words. We gathered intelligence to this end, to find out what was going on," one of Sadio's commanders explained.[98] In 1999 a faction opposing Sadio's brutal methods broke off from FS, "Kassolol," under César Badiat, resulting in violent infighting from late 2000 on. Kassolol established an alliance with FN against Sadio.[99] All military faction leaders, however, claimed adherence to Diamacoune.[100]

In the context of the intensified military wing infighting, Diamacoune was invited for cease-fire negotiations by newly elected president Abdoulaye Wade in 2000. From the start of talks, the government also assisted Diamacoune in intraorganizational outbidding by providing deliverables, for example, through a reduction in arrests of MFDC members. The Senegalese president, having campaigned on a platform of peace, was keen to demonstrate progress. The cease-fire treaty of 2001 established conditions to launch future peace negotiations, which commenced in 2002 and resulted in the 2004 agreement.[101]

Diamacoune hardly consulted with the military wing on the substance of the 2004 peace framework agreement.[102] He sent envoys to all military factions concerning the need to negotiate and to inform them of whom he was meeting,[103] possibly to stifle corruption allegations. In July 2004, Diamacoune invited the combatants to join the MFDC negotiation team.[104] The offer was declined by all military factions on the pretext that the Senegalese state could not guarantee their security if the meetings took place in Senegal.[105] Sadio, in addition, feared reprisals from rival factions and exposure to corruption charges if he were to be involved in negotiations.[106] Substituting for the militants' participation in consultations, the state instead helped the MFDC political wing to organize consultations with the Casamancais population. The government reportedly wanted the civil society to take on a decision-making function.[107]

In December 2004, Diamacoune signed the peace process agreement, stipulating that the MFDC would renounce armed struggle and that final negotiations on the political and economic future of Casamance would take place. Up to the day of signing the MFDC negotiating position had been hard-line, calling for separate Casamance statehood.[108] On that very day, Diamacoune was picked up by the police and separated from his MFDC negotiation team. However, two reportedly government-friendly MFDC representatives were allowed to accompany the MFDC leader as he signed the agreement drafted by the government.[109] No third party was involved. Diamacoune reportedly found it difficult to refuse to sign the agreement, faced with the pressure of a scheduled high-profile ceremony and out of fear of being scapegoated for not wanting peace,[110] but it is suggested that he distorted his own signature in an effort to signal defiance.[111]

There was a remarkable lack of outbidding by the MFDC military wing connected to the 2004 agreement. One reason was the lack of opportunity to physically attack Diamacoune, who was under constant security force surveillance. Another reason was that Diamacoune was considered to have been forced to sign by the government. A third reason may be that the violent intramilitary outbidding made military wing leaders dependent on Diamacoune, considered to be the only MFDC leader acceptable to all. Reasons of organizational survival and the need to uphold the image of the MFDC as one movement rather than many may have entered into the calculation. The infighting kept the militants preoccupied and could have facilitated Diamacoune's participation in the negotiations and his ability to sign the agreement. Badji's subsequent death induced his faction to support the accord to achieve the spoils of peace.[112] Front Sud adopted a wait-and-see approach. Although Sadio was against the 2004 agreement, he did not openly contest Diamacoune's decision. Sadio announced in general terms his unconditional loyalty to Diamacoune, as he had made enemies throughout the movement and otherwise risked complete dissociation from it.[113] However, there is also a fundamental cleavage between the political and military wings of the MFDC to be noted. Some view the MFDC as a social movement with open recruitment rather than as a proper rebel group.[114] The opposite view is that the politico-military cleavage is a strategic choice on how to structure the organization: "That is how MFDC is built up . . . combatants wage war and abbé negotiates."[115] An FS commander explains: "There are different sorts of men—men of politics and combatants. 'It is not us who make the ceasefires.' When they say ceasefire they do so because they want to negotiate." "We have supported abbé's negotiation efforts and we are always with him, but a ceasefire negotiation is a political thing."[116]

In sum, it is clear that nonstate negotiators have used both deed and discourse strategies but to different degrees. The LTTE's outbidding strategies of deed predominated over those of discourse. The MFDC negotiator took the opposite approach by mainly using discourse-based outbidding strategies. Violent outbidding was used within the MFDC military wing but, interestingly, not primarily in connection with negotiations. Negotiations instead signified instances of interaction with government in a closed-door setting, triggering the suspicion of government attempts to corrupt MFDC negotiators, which explains why military leaders have been exposed to outbidding after negotiations. Geracan Aceh Merdeka was in between, employing a mixture of largely nonviolent deed and discourse strategies.

■ PATTERNS IN OUTBIDDING STRATEGIES AND THEIR LINKS TO NEGOTIATION OUTCOMES

It is possible to discern three patterns of outbidding strategies. The first striking finding is the salience of intraorganizational outbidding, particularly that of a horizontal nature. These struggles for internal leadership have not received much attention in the existing literature, which deals mostly with outbidding between competing factions (Pearlman, 2008). It turns out that second-tier leaders within a rebel group are particularly prone to deed-based outbidding by the highest leader, who needs to take strategic decisions on negotiation. The buy-in of key military commanders is also necessary. Vertical intraorganizational outbidding strategies take on increasing salience during negotiation, specifically when it comes to foot soldiers' fighting morale.

The second main finding is that although outbidding is linked to the general jockeying for leadership of the identity group, the negotiation situation as such implies close interaction with the government, making individual negotiators' trustworthiness and group commitment absolutely critical. Suspected corruption of LTTE negotiators was one alleged reason for the Tigers' withdrawal from talks. In the MFDC case, these corruption charges were aggravated in the absence of a third party. Geracan Aceh Merdeka managed these challenges by taking decisions only in the presence of all negotiators.

The third finding of importance for external interveners is that discourse-based strategies are key during negotiations. This was clearly highlighted in the case of GAM. Two factors seem relevant. The first is the presence of a communication and information infrastructure both internally, within the rebel organization, and externally, in relation to competing groups and to the population at large. The LTTE and MFDC faced internal communication challenges partly due to the physical isolation of their respective leaderships. The second factor is that the substance of communication should be concrete and specify the meaning of separate statehood rather than being framed in abstract peace and justice terms.

The findings underscore that the essence of outbidding is the signaling of trustworthiness. Current literature may have associated outbidding and its manifestations too much with terrorist violence and political extremism at the expense of more subtle nonviolent strategies. This conclusion resonates with a more comprehensive notion of trustworthiness signals as divided into three categories: present performance or deed, reputation and the record of past deeds, and visible appearance (Sztompka, 1999). Signals of trustworthiness may differ across cultural contexts, and prevailing societal practices may be incorporated by rebel leaders and rebel negotiators in their strategies for gaining legitimacy aimed at vertical segments. For instance, for the MFDC, cultural aspects, such as someone's supposed possession of mystical powers, is considered to have generally reduced the use of violence for outbidding purposes. The potential perpetrator feared "spiritual punishment."[117]

Deed-Based Outbidding Strategies

It is surprising to see that violent outbidding strategies are complemented, or even dominated, by deed strategies of nonviolence. A number of strategies seem related more to being trusted as a nonstate leader than about the mandate to negotiate peace. These strategies may have not been previously understood in their function as trustworthiness signals.

This said, some outbidding strategies do conform with the theoretical expectations. First has been the elimination of horizontal competitors, both external and internal. The LTTE is the group that comes closest to the conventional expectations of launching violent attacks on rival Tamil groups since the mid-1980s. The LTTE is also the group that conforms most closely to the predicted use of spectacularly violent acts and keeping a finger on the trigger. The Tigers maintained constant military readiness by escalating their violence before the 2001 talks and using it parallel to negotiations to selectively attack allegedly pro-government targets. (GAM reportedly also used the cease-fires to enhance its military capacity.) However, GAM and MFDC did not face similar levels of external horizontal competition. Interestingly, for all groups, the main source of competition came instead from within their own organizations, and the second-tier leadership in particular. As second-tier leaders wanted to negotiate or proceed with negotiations, such as Mahattaya in the LTTE, these decisions needed the buy-in of the highest leadership. When this was not achieved, the pro-negotiation proponents were viewed as internal traitors, and were assassinated, tortured, sidelined, denounced, or silenced in all three groups. Within the MFDC, horizontal outbidding manifested itself through a virtual "culture of detention."

Second, both the LTTE and GAM established control over administrative structures in line with the expected strategy of building up their capacity to control information to discern threats. It was partly for this reason that the LTTE also created an extensive intelligence wing (Lilja, 2009). The MFDC is also claimed to have a vast network of intelligence, although it appears to be significantly less developed and systematic. A third expected vertical strategy of pushing the government for tangible deliverables was used by the LTTE and MFDC. During the 2002–2003 talks LTTE pushed for humanitarian and development assistance (Gooneratne, 2007).

However, the rebel negotiators also used outbidding measures beyond the predicted deed-based strategies. One set of nonviolent outbidding measures had to do more directly with the initiation and disruption of peace talks. Both the

LTTE and GAM demanded sole representation at the negotiation table to secure leadership over the identity group. Linked to this was the *repeat negotiator* phenomenon, implying that once a rebel group had served as the nonstate negotiator one time, outbidding became less of an issue for future negotiations. Another measure was to break off talks, which the LTTE seemed to do mainly for intraorganizational purposes to uphold the morale of fighters and diaspora contributors.

Another unpredicted outbidding strategy used by GAM was the maintenance of direct and continuous intraorganizational communication with horizontal segments, notably military field commanders. The GAM leadership thus went beyond controlling one-way information flows to identify threats against it. The internal information and communication strategy was manifested through daily phone communications and meetings in Malaysia, Singapore, and Stockholm. During the 2005 talks, commanders were continuously updated on, and giving feedback to, GAM negotiating positions.[118] By contrast, MP-GAM lacked these communication channels, instead desperately using external means of communication such as the internet. In addition, GAM seemed able to control external information flows through their influence on the local Acehnese government administration, which gave the group an edge over external competitor factions and helped to convey negotiating positions to the population during negotiations. These findings led to the discourse strategies used by the three groups.

Discourse-Based Outbidding Strategies

Discourse-based strategies were important both before and during negotiations. Contrary to expectations, it is not evident that the number of claims for violent acts committed increased or that messages to the government turned particularly aggressive prior to negotiations. The government was rather absent from the groups' discourse.

Discourse outbidding strategies appear to have been pursued mainly for vertical outbidding purposes. One such vertical strategy, used particularly before talks, was to point to the sacrifice and risk taking on the part of the charismatic individual leader and the rebel group as a collective. This could entail military achievements and heroic violent acts, as for the LTTE leader, Prabakharan, who, since the IPKF war, held the status of a feared demigod, embracing suffering and the risk of death (Swamy, 2005). Having fought since his youth and reportedly having declined lucrative personal offers, Prabakharan was portrayed as sincere and not driven by self-interest, although his commitment is also described in terms of fanaticism.[119] In fact, the Tigers' discourse on martyrs could be understood in line with this commitment logic. Di Tiro and Diamacoune were similarly portrayed as brave front-runners for their respective independence struggles, although neither of them had military credentials. The image of di Tiro as selflessly having abandoned the comfortable life of a diplomat and family man to serve the Acehnese people was important.[120] A mythological dimension was added, making di Tiro a semireligious larger-than-life figure of resistance.[121] In Casamance, Diamacoune was the first person to publicly call for a separate state, and repeated arrests turned him into an MFDC martyr. His only potential competitor as MFDC leader, the head of the external wing, Nkroumah Sané, in Paris, did not pose a threat, as Sané was considered not to have sacrificed enough personally for the cause. Moreover, the leaders of LTTE, GAM, and MFDC were kept distant or inaccessible to the public, which enabled myth making.[122] Collective risk taking and sacrifice for the cause by members of the respective rebel groups were also used as an argument to represent the nonstate side in negotiations. An accumulated loss of lives gave rise to a sense of entitlement. The deaths of group members were depicted as investments rather than sunk costs, the LTTE being a case in point. The sheer number of fallen LTTE members was seen as a signal of commitment to the Tamil cause among some Tamil civilians, who perceived it as a moral duty to support the LTTE.[123] Collective level risk taking did not need to entail violent sacrifice. For instance, SIRA's staging of the nonviolent mass demonstrations in Banda Aceh despite the risk of heavy military reprisals impressed many.[124]

All three rebel negotiators experienced vertical outbidding challenges during the peace talks. Within the respective groups, it was the motivation of fighters, financial contributors, and political activists that was at stake. The vertical discourse strategy used by the MFDC negotiator during the 2004 peace talks was threefold. First was the use of abstract rhetoric in line with the logic of a demobilization discourse. Diamacoune talked in vague terms about peace, reconciliation, and the general need to negotiate. In contrast to GAM, there was intentional ambiguity as to the actual content of independence or separate statehood. Second was Diamacoune's use of dual communication. While preaching peace in public, the MFDC leader in private encouraged fighters not to give up the armed struggle.[125] The third discourse strategy was one of silence. This meant that Diamacoune never in public contradicted allegations made by the military wing of him negotiating or taking particular negotiating positions due to government pressure. This left room for the interpretation that Diamacoune was in fact forced by the government to state certain things.[126] It is not clear what discourse the LTTE leadership used with respect to fighters during the 2002–2003 peace talks. There might even have been silence and a potential absence of a discourse strategy due to the challenge of explaining why the LTTE would suddenly consider a political solution short of separate statehood, given the fundamental role played by the Tamil Eelam state in mobilization.

The most effective vertical demobilization discourse proved not to be abstract rhetoric about peace and reconciliation. Geracan Aceh Merdeka tackled the most critical issue of separate statehood head on. It received outside assistance to help unpack and concretize the concept of statehood and formulate creative solutions to attain its desired ends in internal discussions. The close interaction between GAM's political leadership and the military commanders allowed the former to steer the negotiation process. A staged consultation procedure was used whereby meetings were held initially with representatives of key competitor groups as a horizontal outbidding strategy of inclusion. The circle was broadened in a second step to also include GAM's critics. Finally, GAM turned to the population to pursue a broader vertical demobilization discourse to sell in the position on independence already taken. Geracan Aceh Merdeka's external communication infrastructure in the form of influence over local administration and community leaders was used. The tsunami, while keeping the Acehnese civil society preoccupied, also served an external enemy function in GAM's discourse, framing the peace settlement as an end to the overall suffering of the Acehnese people. It is not clear that the LTTE used the same strategy, although Tamil-populated areas in Sri Lanka were also hardly struck by the tsunami.

Linking Outbidding Strategies to Negotiation Outcomes

All groups used both deed and discourse outbidding strategies, although to different degrees. The LTTE's outbidding strategies of deed predominated over those of discourse. The opposite approach was taken by the MFDC negotiator, who mainly used discourse-based strategies. GAM negotiators employed a mixture of nonviolent deed- and discourse-centered strategies.

Violence and coercive deed strategies aimed at horizontal competitors seemed sufficient to make it to the negotiation table and to attain a cease-fire agreement, that is, partial success. The LTTE's extensive use of violent strategies, for instance, did not pose a problem for the conclusion of the cease-fire agreement of 2001. This agreement worked as a horizontal outbidding measure in itself by cementing the LTTE's land holdings. However, violent strategies fall short of achieving a final peace settlement and are also associated with negotiation breakdown. For the LTTE, the failure to attain a peace agreement seemed tied to in-group outbidding: vertical, through a perceived need to handle fighter and diaspora morale, and horizontal, in the form of fears of the government corrupting individual LTTE negotiators. Balasingham's stated openness to discuss federal alternatives to Tamil Eelam may thus have been deemed too sensitive and induced the LTTE leader to break off talks in 2003.

Nonstate negotiators use a plethora of nonviolent deed strategies. The buildup of an internal communication structure allowing for two-way communication, as opposed to mere control over information flows, improved the likelihood of negotiation success for GAM. The communication infrastructure was used to carry out effective discourse strategies during talks. There was direct communication between negotiators and field commanders, which was important for internal horizontal outbidding and with possible knock-on effects on GAM fighters relevant for internal vertical outbidding. The substance of the successful discourse strategy was *precise*, implying that the most critical issue, here statehood, was unpacked into concrete components and first discussed internally between political and military wing leaders. In a second step, external actors—competing (horizontal) groups and broader constituent (vertical) segments—were invited to contribute. Less successful were *dual* or *absent* discourse strategies, which may represent a safe bet for a rebel negotiator not wanting to antagonize military wing or diaspora hard-liners. However, dual messages or silence risked undermining negotiations, as seen in the MFDC and LTTE cases. Discourse outbidding of high abstraction, ambiguity, and double communication used by the MFDC negotiator resulted in the production of treaties, although the peace framework of 2004 did not represent a final political settlement. Lack of transparency and a peculiar division of labor between the political and military wings assisted the

MFDC negotiator in this endeavour, but resulted in a schizophrenic disconnect whereby MFDC military hard-liners could dissociate themselves from the agreements at their own convenience. The negotiation success achieved by GAM was helped by a mixture of nonviolent deed and discourse outbidding strategies.

■ IMPLICATIONS FOR EXTERNAL DIPLOMATIC INTERVENTION

The findings on actual outbidding strategies used within the nonstate party and their connection to different negotiation outcomes suggest both opportunities and constraints for external diplomatic intervention through mediation or facilitation. This section addresses external intervention against the backdrop of outbidding by discussing a first set of *who* issues such as the identity of the external party and who should become the interlocutors on the nonstate side. A second set of *when* issues relate to the timing and length of negotiations. The last set of *what* issues have to do with the substance of external intervention.

WHO? Get Involved as an External Party and Sequence Inclusion

The first step is to get involved as a facilitator or mediator. The conditions are obviously that the government and the nonstate side are willing to accept the intervention of a third party, and that the third party, in turn, agrees to take on this role (Betts, 1999; Crocker, Hampson & Aall 2004). The mere presence of an external party could enhance transparency and reduce the risk of corruption charges as nonstate negotiators closely interact with the government in connection with talks (Ross & LaCroix, 1996). A third party of high status may enhance the relative standing of the rebel negotiator in the nonstate camp, thus reducing the horizontal outbidding dilemma, as shown in the GAM and LTTE cases. The risk of having the state serving as the external party is that it is perceived by the rebels as internal meddling by the government to bolster its own negotiation position. When the Senegalese government helped the MFDC organize consultations with the Casamance civil society, rebels interpreted it as the government's desire to exclude certain MFDC members from the peace process while trying to invest non-MFDC with decision-making powers, which contributed to a sense of alienation from the negotiations by MFDC politicos and militants alike.[127] The findings also caution against the use of an external party with an identity connection to the nonstate side, as this could turn into a new outbidding dilemma in which the intervener becomes a competitor instead. The Indian intervention in Sri Lanka was perceived by the LTTE as challenging the loyalty of its Tamil constituency.

As to interlocutors on the nonstate side, the findings suggest the unfruitfulness of sidestepping the rebels' highest leadership, as this can play a key role in getting to a substantive peace settlement.[128] This said, a sequenced inclusion of new sets of nonstate actors could be made. The Acehnese example shows that whereas initially only the rebels were approached, in a second step the consultations also included representatives from a select number of horizontal competitor groups. This set of people was later broadened to include harder critics as well. In a final step, consultations were widened to also include vertical segments. Different external parties could serve complementary roles in this process. In the Aceh case the mediator was assisted by an NGO, the Olof Palme International Center, which helped to organize consultations with different actors in different locations.

WHEN? Triggering Change by Issuing Invitations to Formal Talks and Keeping Them Short

Instead of waiting for an opportune moment, issuing invitations to peace negotiations could serve as a catalyst for change by sparking an internal process concerning who will actually represent the nonstate side and develop a negotiation position (Cronin, 2006, p. 25). Obviously, this may trigger unintended internal dynamics of coercion on the nonstate side, which will be beyond the control of the external party. It is not clear that an external party will be able to forestall the delaying effects of outbidding. One may, however, assume that early on in the conflict cycle—in the situation where nonstate actors have started engaging in violence— an external party can get engaged and attempt to influence the government to open a dialogue or negotiation as opposed to propagating a "law and order only" approach. In the Aceh case the facilitator, the Henry Dunant Centre, pitted MP-GAM against the original GAM. When MP-GAM declared its willingness to negotiate, this pressured the di Tiro faction to develop a political strategy and commence negotiations. In terms of outbidding, it meant the acceleration of critical decision making by the leadership.

There is also another concern when it comes to timing. Conventional wisdom holds that the rebels have time on their side. However, this may not be the case when it comes to the actual duration of formal peace negotiations. Again, the reason is linked to intraorganizational outbidding. For instance, up to the time of the 2002 peace talks, the LTTE leadership perceived that negotiations could not drag on beyond 100 days, as it feared a weakening of motivation among fighters and diaspora contributors.[129]

WHAT? Enhance Transparency, Facilitate Communication, and Control Information

The salience of intraorganizational discourse-based outbidding during negotiations is relevant for external diplomatic intervention in a number of ways. The findings, first, suggest that external information flows from negotiations should be restricted when critical issues such as statehood or autonomy are still being explored.

Second, attempts could be made to assist rebels' internal communication to the greatest extent possible when talks are going on. This communication would need to flow across functional parts of the rebel organization, that is, the military and political wings, and across the organizational hierarchy. Even if military commanders are not physically present at the talks, attempts could be made to link them up for purposes of information sharing and consultation. Terrorist proscriptions may obviously complicate this communication.

Third—and crucially important—is the need to deal with the uncertainty and insecurity of nonstate actors who are not present at the table, which may well include the highest rebel leadership. Decision-making procedures should be made transparent to circumvent suspicions of one-on-one deals and different sorts of corruption by nonstate negotiators. The fragmentation of the negotiation team or the isolation of individual negotiators may not be advisable, as it may generate suspicions and fears, which are likely to increase if effective communication cannot be sustained between the negotiators and relevant leaders of the organization.

Security guarantees for the nonstate side, and the military factions in particular, is another measure to consider. This highlights the relevance of the location of talks. In Senegal, militants declined participation in the peace talks on the pretext that their security could not be guaranteed. In Aceh, GAM military commanders could not attend negotiations for fear of arrest. Interestingly, political wing leaders may also need security guarantees from their fellow militants. In Senegal, the MFDC leader Diamacoune was threatened by his own militants and required protection guarantees from Guinea Bissau to meet with the MFDC armed factions.[130] It may also be wise to refrain from "procedually cornering" the nonstate negotiator. A planned high-profile ceremony made it difficult for Diamacoune to refuse signing, although he reportedly did this in defiance.

When it comes to positions on substance taken by the external party in relation to the government, it may—contrary to conventional policy practice—not be advisable to require the nonstate negotiator to fully disarm and demobilize. This could spur deed-based outbidding within the nonstate camp. Second, the external party could attempt to influence the government to provide deliverables to the nonstate negotiator to enhance its position relative to horizontal competitors. The Senegalese government assisted Diamacoune in providing deliverables, for example, by reducing the number of arrests of MFDC members. Third, an external party may also want to caution the government to refrain from deliberately dividing groups and isolating individuals as part of the negotiation process.

Notes

1. Cf Rabushka and Shepsle (2009), who define outbidding as the "politics of ethnic extremism" and the "demise of moderation" (p. 151). The authors, however, largely focus on outbidding between different identity groups: "when politics takes on a distributive quality [—] ethnic affiliations . . . become important symbols of political alignment, symbols which ambitious politicians attempt to manipulate" (p. 82). After a while, "outbidding becomes the rule of the game. Somebody is always prepared to offer more for less, and the bluff cannot be seen" (p. 82). Beyond certain limits, the "politics of over-promising" and outbidding is the very negation of competitive politics," writes Sartori (1966, p. 158). Horowitz (1985, pp. 269–270), in a similar fashion, largely views divisions within the non-state camp as coinciding with ethnic differences.

2. Darby (2001, p. 119) states that a peace process should include all actors who represent a significant portion of their community, as well as all actors who have the ability to destroy an agreement, adding that the two groups are often coterminus.

3. Zartman (2005, pp. 267–268) divides identity conflict into three phases: 1. petition (spokespersons from the aggrieved group request redress for discrimination by authorities), 2. consolidation (political entrepreneurs compete for exclusive leadership), 3. confrontation (confronting the government with arms with the support of the identity group).

4. However, when internal legitimacy clashes with a lack of perceived legitimacy on the part of international actors, nonstate leaders may still not be allowed to represent the nonstate party, Hamas in the Israeli–Palestinian conflict being a case in point.

5. See Bloom (2004, pp. 71–74, 85). Bloom even suggests that in the absence of a monopoly of force, competing groups outbid each other through more spectacular bombing operations for which they claim responsibility to the point where "violence has become the source of honour among Palestinians" (p. 74). See also Bueno de Mesquita and Dickson (2007).

6. Kydd and Walter (2006, pp. 76–78; Bloom (2004, p. 71).

7. Apart from the LTTE, there were also the Tamil Eelam Liberation Organisation (TELO), the Eelam Revolutionary Organisation of Students (EROS), and the Eelam Peoples Revolutionary Front (EPRLF)—together forming the Eelam National Liberation Front (ENLF).

8. Interview 31.

9. Compare Bloom (2003, p. 35, pp. 76–77).

10. Interview 13.

11. Interview 19.

12. Interview 11. Jayatilleke (2006, p. 162).

13. Rajanayagam (2006, 170–174, 184); Perera (2006, p. 228).

14. Swamy (2005, p. 254).

15. Uyangoda (2006, p. 246); Interview 33.

16. Sivaram (2006, pp. 175–177); Interview 31; 32; 33; 26.

17. Rajanayagam (2006, p. 219); cf. Kingsbury (2006); Sivaram (2006, p. 178).

18. Interview 50.

19. TamilNet. (2002, November 27). *LTTE leader calls for autonomy and self-government for Tamil homeland.* Retrieved November 27, 2002, from http://www.tamilnet.com/art. html?catid=13&artid=7902

20. Interview 31, 32.

21. Interview 32.

22. Interview 34.

23. Interview 31.

24. Interview 31.

25. Interview 50.

26. Interview 34.

27. Human Rights Watch (1990).

28. Interview 42, 43.

29. Human Rights Watch (2003, p. 9; 2001, p. 10).

30. Interview 43.

31. Interview 40.

32. Interview 41.

33. Interview 43.

34. Interview 36; 41.

35. Interview 41.

36. Aspinall and Crouch (2003, pp. 10–12).

37. Interview 40.

38. Human Rights Watch (2001, pp. 7–8, 19).
39. Interview 43; 56.
40. Human Rights Watch (2001); Interview 37.
41. Aspinall and Crouch (2003, pp. 10–12, 27).
42. Human Rights Watch (2001, p. 2).
43. Aspinall and Crouch (2003, pp. 44, 54); Morfit (2007, p. 115); Interview 38.
44. Aspinall and Crouch (2003, p. 43); Human Rights Watch (2003, p. 10).
45. Morfit (2007, p. 122).
46. Interview 43.
47. Interview 43.
48. Interview 40.
49. Interview 37; cf. Aspinall and Crouch (2003, p. 48);
50. Interview 41.
51. Interview 40; 53.
52. Interview 36.
53. Interview 40.
54. Interview 38.
55. Morfit (2007, pp. 119, 132–133).
56. Interview 40.
57. Enia (2006); Interview 41; 42.
58. Interview 42; 38.
59. Interview 52; 54; 55.
60. Interview 41.
61. Kingsbury (2006, p. 27); Interview 42.
62. Interview 51.
63. Interview 40.
64. Morfit (2007, pp. 116, 138); Interview 42.
65. Kingsbury (2006, pp. 27, 92–95, 100); Interview 52.
66. Interview 38.
67. Interview 42.
68. Interview 38.
69. In the Casamance context, slight confusion persists as to what constitutes a *negotiated treaty*. At times, joint MFDC–government communiqués are also referred to as *accords*. This section describes the conditions surrounding the cease-fire agreements of May 31, 1991; July 8, 1993, and March 16, 2001, and the peace framework accord of December 30, 2004.
70. Interview Senegal (SE) 19; SE8.
71. Interview SE26; SE23.
72. Interview SE26.
73. Exemplified by comments made by MFDC civilian wing members on the financing of one of the MFDC militant factions: "We don't know how Sadio finances himself. The state or the Gambian state may give money to the maquis" (SE23). "Sadio listened more to Ansoummanah Mané, who armed him than to Diamacoune" (SE11A).
74. Interview SE29. The MFDC does not have a significant financial base (SE9).
75. Hall (1999, p. 5); SE5; SE19.
76. Interview SE9; SE26.
77. Interview SE8; SE5; SE11B.
78. Interview SE9; compare SE20.
79. Interview SE11A; SE23.
80. Interview SE26.

81. Interview SE5; SE11B; SE23; SE4.

82. Interview SE4; SE23; SE5.

83. Interview SE20.

84. Interview SE5.

85. Interview SE23; cf. SE11AED.

86. Interview SE20.

87. Interview SE20.

88. Interview SE11YD.

89. Interview SE11AED.

90. Interview SE13; SE11; SE7; SE23.

91. Interview SE13. *"MFDC maquis don't kill traitors"* (SE11B).

92. Interview SE23; SE8; SE13; SE20; SE24.

93. Interview SE30.

94. Interview SE23.

95. Interview SE8; SE11YD.

96. Interview SE24.

97. Interview SE7: César Badiat, FS military commander.

98. Interview SE30: FS–Sadio military commander.

99. Interview SE13; SE23; SE20.

100. Interview SE27A.

101. Interview SE8; SE16; SE11A.

102. Interview SE23; SE24; SE20.

103. Interview SE19; SE24.

104. Interview SE15.

105. Interview SE20.

106. Interview SE23; SE8.

107. Interview SE23.

108. Interview SE8.

109. Interview SE15; SE22. In the words of a combatant, "It is not MFDC who have chosen him [MFDC Secretary General Ansoummanah Badji, who accompanied Diamacoune to the signing] as leader, it is the Senegalese state" (SE20A).

110. Interview SE22.

111. Interview SE15.

112. Interview SE20.

113. Interview SE26; SE8; SE27.

114 Interview SE26; SE20.

115. Interview SE16.

116. Interview SE7.

117. SE14; SE23; SE20.

118. Interview 42; 51; 53.

119. Swamy (2005, pp. xvi, 267); Interview 21; 2.

120. Interview 42; 43.

121. Interview 36; 37; 38; 41; 42.

122. Interview 11.

123. Interview 21; 3; 6; cf. Swamy (2005, p. 253).

124. Interview 37.

125. Interview SE8; SE11; SE7.

126. Interview SE24.

127. SE23.

128. See Cronin (2006, pp. 25–26) for a slightly contrasting view.

129. Interview 50.
130. Interview SE27A.

References

Aspinall, E., & Crouch, H. (2003). *The Aceh peace process: Why it failed*. Policy Studies (vol. 1). Washington, DC: East-West Center.

Betts, W. (1999). Third party mediation: An obstacle to peace in Nagorno Karabach. *SAIS Review*, 19(2), 161–183.

Bloom, M. (2003). Ethnic conflict, state terror and suicide bombing in Sri Lanka. *Civil Wars*, 6(1), 54–84.

Bloom, M. (2004). Palestinian suicide bombing: Public support, market share and outbidding. *Political Science Quarterly*, 119(1), 61–88.

Bueno de Mesquita, E. (2005). Conciliation, counterterrorism and patterns of violence. *International Organization*, 59(1), 145–176.

Bueno de Mesquita, E., & Dickson, E. S. (2007). The propaganda of the deed: Terrorism, counterterrorism, and mobilization. *American Journal of Political Science*, 51(2), 364–381.

Byman, D. L. (2002). *Keeping the peace: Lasting solutions to ethnic conflicts* (pp. 36–38). Baltimore: Johns Hopkins University Press.

Crocker, C., Hampson, F. O., & Aall, P. (Eds). (2004). *Taming intractable conflict: Mediation in the hardest cases*. Washington, DC: United States Institute for Peace Press.

Cronin, A. K. (2006). How al-Qaida Ends: The Decline and Demise of Terrorist Groups. *International Security*, 31(1), 7–48.

Darby, J. (2001). *The effects of violence on peace processes*. Washington, DC: United States Institute of Peace Press.

Enia, J. (2006). *Peace in its wake: The 2004 tsunami and internal conflict in Indonesia and Sri Lanka*. Working paper http://www.princeton.edu/jpia/past-issues-1/2008/1.pdf

Gooneratne, J. (2007). *Negotiating with the Tigers (LTTE) 2002–2005: A view from the second row*. Pannipitya, Sri Lanka: Stamford Lake Publication.

Hall, M. (1999). *The Casamance conflict 1982–1999*. Research and Analytical Papers. London: African Research Group, Foreign and Commonwealth Office. August, 1999. Retrieved from http://www.fco.gov.uk/resources/en/pdf/pdf4/fco_pdf_casamance

Höglund, K. (2004). *Violence in the midst of peace negotiations: Cases from Guatemala, Northern Ireland, South Africa and Sri Lanka*. Report No. 69. Uppsala: Department of Peace and Conflict Research, Uppsala University.

Horowitz, D. L. (1985). *Ethnic groups in conflict*. Berkeley: University of California Press.

Human Rights Watch. (1990, December). Indonesia: Human rights abuses in Aceh. *News from Asia Watch*, December 27, 1–4.

Human Rights Watch. (2001, August). Indonesia: The war in Aceh. 13(4C).

Human Rights Watch. (2003, December). Aceh under martial law: Inside the secret war. 15(10).

Jayatilleke, D. (2006). The year 1989–90: The Premadasa–LTTE talks: Why they failed and what really happened. In K. Rupesinghe (Ed.), *Negotiating peace in Sri Lanka: Efforts, failures and lessons* (vol. 1, 2nd ed., pp. 149–163). Columbo: Foundation for Co-Existence.

Kalyvas, S. (2006). *The logic of violence in civil war*. Cambridge: Cambridge University Press.

Kingsbury, D. (2006). *Peace in Aceh: A personal account of the Helsinki peace process*. Jakarta: Equinox.

Kydd, A., & Walter, B. F. (2002). Sabotaging the peace: The politics of extremist violence. *International Organization, 56*(2), 263–296.

Kydd, A. H., & Walter, B. F. (2006). The strategies of terrorism. *International Security, 21*(1), 49–80.

Lilja, J. (2009). Trapping constituents or winning hearts and minds? Rebel strategies to attain constituent support in Sri Lanka. *Terrorism and Political Violence, 21*(2), 306–326.

Lilja, J. & Hultman, L. (2011) Intraethnic Dominance and Control: Violence against Co-Ethnics in the Early Sri Lankan Civil War. *Security Studies, 20*(2): 171–197.

Maoz, I., & McCauley, C. (2008). Threat, dehumanization and support for retaliatory aggressive policies in asymmetric conflict. *Journal of Conflict Resolution, 52*(1), 93–116.

Miller, M. A. (2006). *Reformism and rebellion: Jakarta's security and autonomy policies in Aceh—May 1998–May 2003.* Doctoral thesis, Charles Darwin University.

Morfil, M. (2007). The road to Helsinki: The Aceh agreement and Indonesia's democratic development. *International Negotiations, 12*, 111–143.

Pearlman, W. (2008). Spoiling inside and out: Internal political contestation and the Middle East peace process. International Security, *33*(3), 79–109.

Perera, J. (2006). An analysis of the breakdown of negotiations in the Sri Lankan ethnic conflict. In K. Rupesinghe (Ed.), *Negotiating peace in Sri Lanka: Efforts, failures and lessons* (vol. 2, 2nd ed., pp. 223–238). Columbo: Foundation for Co-Existence.

Putnam, R. D. (1988). Diplomacy and domestic politics: The logic of two-level games. *International Organization, 32*(3), 427–460.

Putnam, R. D., Evans, P. B., & Jacobson, H. K. (Eds.) (1993). *Double-edged diplomacy: International bargaining and domestic politics.* Los Angeles: University of California Press.

Rabuschka, A., & Shepsle, K. A. (2009). *Politics in plural societies: A theory of democratic instability.* Upper Saddle River, NJ: Longman.

Rajanayagam, P. (2006). Government–LTTE negotiations 1994–5: Another lost opportunity. In K. Rupesinghe (Ed.), *Negotiating peace in Sri Lanka: Efforts, failures and lessons* (vol. 1, 2nd ed., pp. 165–222). Columbo: Foundation for Co-Existence.

Ross, W., & LaCroix, J. (1996). Multiple meanings of trust in negotiation theory and research: A literature review and integrative model. *The International Journal of Conflict Management, 7*(4), 314–360.

Sartori, G. (1966). European political parties: The case of polarized pluralism. In J. LaPolombara & M. Weiner (Eds.), *Political parties and political development* (pp. 137–176). Princeton, N.J.: Princeton University Press.

Shanmugaratnam, N. (Ed.). (2008). *Between war and peace in Sudan and Sri Lanka.* Oxford: James Currey.

Sivaram, D. (2006). The Tamil perspective. In K. Rupesinghe (Ed.), *Negotiating peace in Sri Lanka: Efforts, failures and lessons* (vol. 2, 2nd ed., pp. 159–191). Columbo: Foundation for Co-Existence.

Snyder, J. (2000). *From voting to violence: Democratization and nationalist conflict.* New York: W. W. Norton.

Swamy, N. M. R. 2 (2005). *Inside an elusive mind: The first profile of the world's most ruthless guerrilla leader* (3rd ed.). Colombo: Vijitha Yapa Publications.

Sztompka, P. (1999). *Trust: A sociological theory.* Cambridge: Cambridge University Press.

Toft, M. D. (2007). Getting religion: The puzzling case of Islam and civil war. *International Security, 31*(4), 97–131.

Uyangoda, J. (2006). Government–LTTE negotiation attempt of 2000 through Norwegian facilitation: Context, complexities and lessons. In K. Rupesinghe (Ed.), *Negotiating peace in Sri Lanka: Efforts, failures and lessons* (vol. 1, 2nd ed., pp. 239–267). Columbo: Foundation for Co-Existence.

Weeks, J. (2008). Autocratic audience costs: Regime type and signaling resolve. *International Organization, 63*(1), 35–64.

Weinberg, L., & Pedahzur, A. (2003). *Political parties and terrorist groups.* London: Routledge.

Zartman, I. W. (Ed.), (1995a). *Elusive peace: Negotiating to end civil wars.* Washington, DC: The Brookings Institution.

Zartman, I. W. (1995b). *Collapsed states.* Boulder, CO: Lynne Rienner.

Zartman, I. W. (2005). Need, creed, and greed in intrastate conflict. In C. Arnson & I. W. Zartman (Eds.), *Rethinking the economics of war: The intersection of need, creed, and greed in intrastate conflict* (pp. 256–284). Washington DC: Woodrow Wilson Center Press.

Zartman, I. W. (2008). Ripeness revisited: The push and pull of conflict management. In I. W. Zartman, *Negotiation and conflict management: Essays on theory and practice* (pp. 232–244). London: Routledge.

Zartman, I. W., & Alfredson, T. (2009). Negotiating with terrorists and the tactical question. In R. Reuveny & W. Thompson, *Coping with Terrorism Origins, Escalation, Counterstrategies, and Responses.* Albany, NY: State University of New York Press.

8 The Insides of Identity and Intragroup Conflict

■ JAY ROTHMAN

A major reason why negotiations over identity-based conflicts fail is that inadequate attention is given to the process of intragroup prenegotiation. Identity-based conflicts, both within countries and transcending borders, present a fundamental challenge to a more peaceful world order (Gurr, 2000). They are similar to all conflicts in that they include struggles over resources or, politically stated, struggles over who gets what, when, and how (Lasswell, 1935; Zartman, 1964). Moreover, like most conflicts, they are about clashing and competing goals and priorities (Wilmot & Hocker, 2000). However, identity-based conflicts are also a unique class of conflicts that require special handling because, unlike goal or resource conflicts, they are deeply rooted in historical fears and frustrations of groups' existential needs and values (Rothman, 1997). Too often such conflicts go from bad to worse when the parties meet prematurely and try to solve problems or negotiate solutions before sufficient intragroup agreement has occurred. Characteristic of many identity-based conflicts is that the deeper they run and the longer they last, the more internal schisms within each side become part of the Gordian knot of the conflict. Then as moderate groups within each side begin to lean toward one another, the hard-liners within each side lean out and the likelihood of intergroup agreement further diminishes. Intragroup prenegotiation focusing first on the internal dynamics of disagreement and consensus building *within* the groups could enhance the chances of successful negotiation *between* them by disabling this tendency before it takes root. This chapter will set an agenda for promoting intragroup prenegotiation as one method of improving intergroup negotiations in identity-based conflicts.

In such conflicts, where people's individual and collective senses of purpose, safety, and relatedness are at stake, and often at risk, having sides focus on their own differences and solidarity (or common ground) can help build a trajectory for the same kind of analytical process to occur constructively between the sides. When groups are internally divided and splinter into opposing camps, reaching agreement with an outgroup becomes even more difficult. This is the common cyclical dynamic in intransigent conflicts: (1) Internal dynamics lead at least to differences over agenda and tactics, if not over essential strategies—the Tactical Question (Zartman & Alfredson, 2010). (2) The sides become convinced, or are coerced to believe, that negotiation is somehow useful at this point (or less harmful than not engaging in it). (3) Parties begin negotiation without sufficient internal agreement. (4) Then such internal dynamics play themselves out vociferously when the sides meet. Such dynamics include projections of each side's failings as a way in part to avoid, or even heal, continuing rifts within one's "own family"; attributions about the perfidity of the other side's nature; and polarization between the good Us and the bad Them, as identified in the Identity Trap by William Donohue in this book (see also Rothman, 1997).

Thus, to make progress in what are variously called "protracted social conflicts" (Azar, 1990), "identity-based conflicts" (Rothman, 1997), "intractable conflicts" (Coleman, 2000 & 2011; Crocker, Hampson, & Aall, 2005), or "intransigent conflict" (Ross & Rothman, 1999; Rothman, 1992), something has to break this internal external conflict escalation cycle. What is needed is a two step process of goals-to-grievances that each side engages in, first within each side and then again between the sides. The first step is to gather key representatives of central, often opposing positions within each side toward the other and to reach agreement on their shared goals for the future. The second step is for participants in this intragroup prenegotiation process to reach agreement on their grievances with the other side, framed in terms of barriers the other side has constructed in the past through its attitudes and actions to achieving this future. These two steps are then repeated when the sides meet, however, in reverse order. First, groups surface and engage in dialogue about their respective grievances. When the sides feel that their concerns are adequately aired and on the table, then and only then do they move from the identity-based grievances about the past to cooperative and goal-oriented negotiation for a new future, as will be illustrated below (Gorman, 1999).

One of the key problems this sequencing addresses is the inability of parties to develop an adequate or authentic future orientation due to these lurking but unsurfaced grievances about the past when they come in normal interest-based negotiation to the table with deep grievances that are not systematically aired. Making explicit those grievances, making them discussable, can go a long way to creating the psychological space necessary for parties to develop the necessary perspective that allows them to see the past for what it is—important, often painful, and not to be forgotten. It opens the possibility that a future can be forged based on future goals, and lessons from the past can be learned and not subconsciously, or aggressively, repeated.

In addition to reducing the likelihood of intergroup explosion and enhancing the possibility of mutually acceptable outcomes, the internal negotiation process may usefully serve as a form of intragroup *conditioning*. For instance, when groups that have historically had deep internal rifts discover that through sufficient and disciplined preparation they can reach agreement over a shared agenda for discussions with the other side (i.e., shared goals and defined grievances), they begin to see the value of such a process and may be willing to use it to encourage and facilitate constructive engagement with the other side.

Henry A. Kissinger, U.S. secretary of state from 1973 to 1977, is famous for saying that he never began a negotiation until the agreement was already in hand (Sheehan, 1976). A bit more modestly, I suggest that in identity-based conflicts, negotiations should be launched after each side separately, often with the assistance of third parties, works on its own "house" in ways that also set an agenda for meeting with the other side. Once successful outcomes are in sight during negotiations, each side must again strategize, both separately and in a coordinated way, about how best to communicate with—and often persuade—its own hard-liners that agreement with the other side is not abdication or dangerous concession but, instead, fuller expression and protection of its own identity needs.

■ A CONTINGENCY APPROACH

It is important to distinguish operationally between identity conflict and more routine conflict. A good place to start is with a cogent definition. The editors of this volume provide one: Identity is "conflictual when two identities are negatively interdependent, in a zero-sum or threatening relationship. When my being me depends on you not being you, or when your being you threatens my being me, there is an identity conflict." It is useful to distinguish operationally identity-based conflicts from other, more routine conflicts such as those over goals and resources (Rothman, 1999). This can be done by metaphorically picturing conflict as an iceberg, with identity conflicts at the murky bottom. Goal conflicts rise above identity-based conflicts and reside translucently just beneath the water's surface. Resource conflicts are above the water in plain sight; they are empirical and the most tangible of the three (Figure 8.1).

Identity conflicts, as in the metaphor, are far beneath the surface; they cannot be understood or seen empirically. Rather, they are deep and murky. The bottom of the iceberg is what sank the *Titanic*; identity issues are what cause many negotiations to fail and wars to begin. In short, identity-based conflicts are about existential needs and values that are threatened, frustrated, or pursued in conflict between groups.[1] They are commonly mired in fear and deeply rooted in emotional issues that make straightforward solution seeking extremely difficult at best.

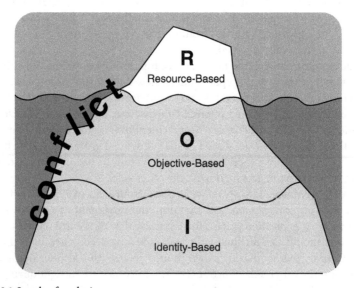

Figure 8.1 Levels of analysis.

Continuing with the metaphor, going up the iceberg toward the surface but still just below it, conflicts are commonly about mismatched goals. Goals, in their most elemental form, are those things we seek to accomplish or attain. Problems or conflicts, most essentially, are those things that keep us from fulfilling our goals. In a widely quoted operational definition of conflict, Hocker and Wilmot (1985) suggest that "conflict is the interaction of interdependent people who perceive incompatible goals and interference from each other in achieving those goals" (see also Folger, Poole, & Stutman, 2005). Like the iceberg beneath the water, conflicts are opaque. One can't quite see the goals of the other side, and even one's own goals are often ill-defined or too complex to articulate simply. However, unlike identity-based conflicts, when one is engaged proactively and in an environment of good listening, problem solving, and effective communication, goal-based conflicts need not be too troubling or difficult to manage successfully. Rather, without a great deal of emotional content, goal-based conflicts can often be dispassionately and fairly rationally managed by disputants with or without third-party assistance. Finally, above the water, conflicts occur frequently over competition for scarce resources—who will get them, when, and how. With effective and timely negotiation and problem solving, resource conflicts also can commonly be settled and mutual gains achieved for all parties.

This levels-of-analysis approach also visually suggests an important feature of identity-based conflicts that distinguishes them from the other two. Identity-based conflict contains within itself the other two levels of conflict as well. A conflict— for example, over *home* and one's access to and control over it (the root of many international identity-based conflicts)—will also be about goals (e.g., goals to achieve sovereignty and territorial integrity) and resources (e.g., ways to protect and promote economic resources). On the other hand, goal conflicts will be primarily about goals and resources (e.g., to establish an independent state in order to be able to gain and control economic and military resources). And resource conflicts, while also containing seeds of goal disputes and even identity issues if poorly handled, are fundamentally about tangible resources and who controls them, when, and how (e.g., gaining access and control).

Another way of differentiating these conflict levels of analysis is to think about identity-based conflicts as the ultimate set of "whys": Why do we care so deeply? Why are we feeling threatened, frustrated, and fearful? Goal conflicts are about "what for": What are we seeking? What are our goals and priorities that are at stake? Resource conflicts are simply the "what" of conflict: What are we seeking to get or preserve?

With such a levels-of-analysis approach, the next step before focusing on seeking a solution—through negotiation or some other problem-solving process to foster collaboration and coordination between conflict parties and to reduce destruction and violence—is determining the right approach for each level of conflict. In their classic article, Sander and Goldberg (1994) describe the importance of "fitting the forum to the muss." Fisher and Keashley (1991) describe the need for and outlines of a contingency approach to conflict analysis and resolution that is at the cutting edge of the dispute resolution field.

Anyone who has dealt with identity-based conflicts, whether at home or abroad, knows they are deeply emotional and require a special type of handling. Applying conventional interests-based models to them can make them worse. Why? Because they are rooted in the deep past and the indignities, physical suffering, and psychic wounding that has occurred to stimulate them in the first place. They fester and worsen if not addressed. When the antagonism of the past is engaged, all the hurts and emotions of that past break forth and are volatile. However, bringing identity conflicts to the surface is essential if they are not to fester and explode, and this process can be very therapeutic (Rothman, 1997, 1992). On the other hand, if a premature focus is placed on solution seeking, or on common interests beneath conflicting positions (Fisher & Ury, 1981), such conflicts can deepen and worsen for the "treatment."

When identity conflicts are identified and can be evaluated carefully and revealed safely (first within groups and then between them), they can be rationalized and viewed as also including contending goals and resource competition. Then identity conflict can begin to be moved "upward" (as in the iceberg model) toward more negotiable goal or resource conflicts where conflict management and interest-based bargaining may become possible. For indeed, while deep conflicts are about identity, and by no means easily negotiable (though definitely not static), they are also about goals, which may be coordinated when well articulated, and about resources, which indeed are often, or should often be, the focus of bargaining.

Having safely allowed antagonism to surface—which is commonly done in a process of interactive and narrative articulation of core needs and values that each side fears has been threatened or frustrated by the conflict with the other side (Kaufman & Davies, 2002; Kelman, 1987; Rothman, 1998)—it is now time for parties to engage in some form of coordinated goal-setting process. Finally, once the parties have articulated their goals and to some degree engaged in integrative bargaining such as log-rolling and other forms of goal trade-offs, only then can these parties who were locked in identity conflict engage in a more formal bargaining process over resources.

The bulk of this chapter will now delve into the whys and hows of safely revealing identity-based conflicts, initially through intragroup processes, to make them ready for conflict management, problem solving, and negotiation over goals and resources. I will describe a process I have been using and lay out my own agenda for launching this process within each side locked in identity group conflicts prior to intergroup encounter.

Identities and Goals: Past or Future Orientation

The main difference between goal-based and identity-based conflicts is their respectively past or future orientation. The former looks toward some new future. Differences in goals arise over definitions, interests, and priorities. Such goals are mired in a *conflict goal field* in which contending goals compete with one another for primacy (Klein, 1989; Klein & Rothman, 2008; Zartman & Kremenyuk, 2005). Often, as will be discussed in some depth below, a major reason for goal conflicts between groups is that there are ill-defined and unresolved goal conflicts *within* each group that then spill over into goal conflicts between the sides.

Identity-based conflicts look back at some set of "chosen traumas" from the past and the ways in which they continue to influence and cloud the present. In ethnic conflicts, parties select certain historical traumas they have suffered and hold fast to them as ways of defining their distinctive identity (Volkan, 1988). These traumas are often symbolized in specific historical events and sometimes with artifacts. An example of the latter is a key commonly found among Palestinian refugees representing their exile from their homes (Havrelock, 2010). A narrative example of an identity conflict came in an encounter with an old Cypriot man Broom (2005),[2] In response to Broom's question about the hurts of his past, the old man waved his hand forward past his right ear, saying, "right before my eyes." Broom inquired, "Don't you mean your past is behind you?" (waving his hand backward past his left ear). "No," the old man responded, continuing to wave his hand forward, "my past is before my eyes like it were today, my future" (now joining Broom in waving his hand behind him) "is very unclear." Indeed, identity-based conflicts are often those with high emotional content that live on in memory, and deeply, often negatively, influencing the way life is experienced in an ongoing basis.

Another classic example is the story of Palestinians with a key to the family home from which parents or grandparents were exiled. "When my grandfather was on his deathbed," began Khwala, a Palestinian-Israeli student,[3] "he took the key from the house from which he was exiled in 1948 and went for a last visit. The Jewish woman in the house was alarmed when we knocked on the door and asked us to leave." The student told the story with burning anger in her eyes. I asked her why this story was so important to her. This kind of "why" question is delicate; often inquiries about identity can sound controversial or deeply caring (Friedman, Withers, & Rothman, 2006). She answered quietly with a tear in her voice, "because my grandfather died a month later and never saw the inside of his home again. Because my family is scattered. We don't live in our home. We are exiles here in Israel."

In the field of conflict resolution, a common distinction is made between positions and interests (Fisher & Ury, 1981; Rothman & Olson, 2001).[4] The former are those unbridgeable attitudes and beliefs about a conflict that divide parties from each other. The latter are understood as underlying concerns that often overlap in interdependent ways that can be dealt with through cooperative and functional solutions. Distinctions between identities and goals are more complex and therefore should be more precise. This is partly the case because all identities contain goals and resources. In fact, some would say that identities are constituted of specific goal configurations in which, as an example, someone could have intraspsychic conflicts within his or her various internal goal fields (e.g., as a hard-working professional and a devoted parent and the competing time demands and constraints on each role), just as groups could have internally and externally contending goals (Jones & Brinkert, 2008, chap. 4).

This complexity is what commonly leads people to believe that all conflicts are identity based. But this is an important mistake that leads to imprecision in conflict analysis and intervention design, part of which a good contingency model could help correct. It is important to understand that while all identity conflicts do contain goal and resources issues, the reverse is not necessarily the case, as the "iceberg" discussion above indicates. That is, sometimes a cigar is just a cigar and sometimes goals are not deeply rooted in existential issues; they are, for example, just about "getting it done." But higher-level conflicts can fairly easily move downward. For example, when resource issues are not addressed, there is a reverse trajectory that commonly occurs and contending goals begin to emerge. Moreover, when goal conflicts are not proactively or effectively addressed, threats and fears commonly emerge and identity conflicts follow. Thus, getting the analysis as right as possible and in a timely matter on a contingency basis (if we have a conflict at this level, we should use this type of intervention) is important.

A more nuanced and differentiated way of viewing resources, goals, and identities could be a key in preparing for effective intergroup negotiation on identity-based conflicts. A major problem in intergroup negotiation where identity issues are key is that parties, while ostensibly bargaining over how best to meet overlapping or competing goals, are actually engaging indirectly in deeper disputes regarding their historically threatened or frustrated identities. If so, it is important to keep the two bargaining disputes conceptually and practically distinguished. This would help prepare the ground for constructive intergroup negotiation. The following process has been experimented with over the past few years:

1. *Intragroup goal setting:* Each side in a prenegotiation process begins with a clear articulation of its respective goals and values in general, which may be furthered in a negotiation with an adversary (particularly in a substantive stalemate where the desired outcomes are currently blocked, or perceived to be blocked, by that adversary). Where there are internal differences about these goals or about how best to achieve them with particular reference in to the other side, these differences should be bridged as much as possible before an intergroup meeting, or at least clarified where bridging is not possible, in part so that these internal dynamics will not unnecessarily spill over into intergroup work.

2. *Intergroup encounter (i):* After viewing and discussing each other's goals interactively, it is determined whether the groups can move to a future-oriented dialogue or negotiation about their conflicting and shared goals or if, beneath the goals, there are deeper identity conflicts that must be brought to the surface and engaged first. As an example of the former, in a workshop for educators from Greek and Turkish communities on the island of Cyprus, a cooperative project was launched to create youth exchanges and educational tools for mutual understanding (Rothman, 1999). On the other hand, in an intervention between Israelis and Palestinians conducted in 2009, the Israeli goals were primarily operational in nature, whereas the Palestinian goals were more fundamental and reflected a less negotiable set of requirements and expectations; the parties were not ready to continue the intergroup dialogue.

3. *Intragroup conflict framing:* In this latter case of identity-based conflicts emerging in the goal discussion between the sides, each side goes back to continue its own work separately and confront the procedural stalemate.

Each discusses the kinds of identity-based grievances it feels toward the other side (e.g., "their goals are too general and conditional," "their goals are too narrow") and that it believes need to be at least brought to the surface and made discussable, even if not resolved, to establish room for progress in goal-based negotiations.

4. *Intergroup encounter (ii)*: The sides are then ready to meet again to discuss their respective antagonisms and are guided by the facilitator through the difficult process of airing these grievances. Having them heard, and eventually reaching agreement that a focus on the future is both necessary and possible and that further focus on the grievances of the past will be unconstructive, is necessary to the process, as announced by both Mahmoud Abbas (1995) and Uri Savir (1998, p. 15) in the Oslo negotiations. Moreover, at this point in the dialogue, parties commonly are fed up with the ongoing and generally fruitless recitation of blame and counterblame (necessary though it has been) and agree that they want assistance from a fairly directive third party to help them move to this future and goal-oriented focus despite what might be a natural tendency to move back to grievances about the past (see Rothman, 1992, 1996).

5. *Preparing for intergroup negotiation*: When groups that historically have had deep internal rifts discover during intragroup discussions that they can talk about those issues effectively and reach for agreement over a shared agenda for discussions with the other side, they begin to see the value of such a process. This fosters a kind of negotiation conditioning in which aspects of this same process can be usefully repeated in the intergroup phase:

   i. Reaching goal agreements for the intergroup dialogue or negotiation.
   ii. Dealing effectively with disagreements en route to reaching goal agreement without trying to solve them, but rather making them discussable and recognizing each other's voice and the legitimacy of each other's perceptions (Bush & Folger 1995; Rothman, 1996).[5]
   iii. Analytically rearticulating previously emotionally volatile grievances and reframing them from practically unbridgeable and emotionally laden identity issues to potentially bridgeable goals and resources for the future.

■ CASE STUDIES

Israelis and Palestinians: Talking about the Same Things in the Same Way for the Same Reason

In the following case study, Israeli and Palestinian peace activists begin with goal setting but, as in the model described above, find that they are stuck in antagonisms about the past. Thus, they reveal their differences separately and discuss them. Then they talk about underlying concerns and values and finally move on to planning for future cooperation.

One of the most important things about this approach to dealing with deep conflict effectively is that it helps disputants *talk about relatively the same things in mostly the same ways for essentially the same reasons.* While the sides often think they are talking about the same things, when they dig into each other's assumptions and priorities, they often discover that they are missing each other entirely. In this case of a two-day workshop for Israeli and Palestinian peace activists who were beginning to work together on a joint project to develop and train others in a new methodology for dialogue and development (called KUMI), we began by asking the two groups to come up with internal agreement about their goals for their work together as a coalition. When they listed their separate goals, two goals appeared to me to overlap and provide direction for collaboration. I was quite wrong.

The Palestinians said their goal was to "End the Occupation."

The Israelis said theirs was to "Transform the Conflict and End the Occupation as a Short-Term Goal."

When I suggested to the two sides that these goals appeared to greatly overlap and provide a frame for cooperative goal setting, the Israelis said yes but the Palestinians emphatically said no. Said one Palestinian participant, "The question of ending the occupation should take precedence over any question of basic needs." The Palestinians said that they viewed the Israeli goals as "conditioned responses." Another Palestinian participant added, "While it seems that you, the Israelis, see ending the occupation as a means to an end, we see it as an essential purpose in and of itself. At this point, ending the occupation is core to our expression of our identity at this time in our history." Thus, while the Israelis were ready to move on to future-oriented dialogue and planning, the Palestinians were not. They felt unheard and largely misunderstood.

As suggested in the levels-of-analysis iceberg model, the Israelis were working on goals for their future, in which ending the occupation would lead to fulfilling their shared ideal of a two-state solution. The past, they felt, could and should be put behind them and a new future clearly and cooperatively pursued. The Palestinians, on the other hand, said, "For us, ending the occupation is a statement of identity; occupation is the prime example of the way the past and your oppression dominate our present and make us uninterested in talking about the future, at least to start with."

Thus, with agreement from the Israelis to move backward before a hoped-for future orientation might follow, each group reconvened and made its own list of things that it "blamed the other for" regarding their respective and different goals (Zartman & Kremenyuk, 2005). Their respective lists are presented in Table 8.1.

For the some of the Israelis, this was a painful experience that several of them felt would be counterproductive. "Why do we need to blame them?" they asked, but eventually they joined their group in bringing their complaints to the surface. After making their respective lists, the groups reconvened and asked questions of clarification about the points on the other side's list. This antagonistic discourse went on for a couple of hours, sometimes quite vociferously, with some necessary breaks and even some tears. When the participants were asked if they felt progress was being made, some said it was crucial to raise these issues, but they mostly, and with almost one voice, said that they were eager and ready to move beyond this blaming dynamic. After all, that's why they were seeking to work with each other. Said one participant, "It is difficult to go through such an experience, but I'm glad

TABLE 8.1 *Antagonism*

Israeli complaints	Palestinian complaints
• You speak as representatives of Palestinian, not as unique individuals. • If Ending Occupation is the primary goal (Contradiction) and we only work on structure, conflict will not be transformed and violence will continue. • By forcing/imposing on us to accept Ending Occupation as our primary goal, you're hampering our efforts to influence the conflict within Israeli society and between Israelis and Palestinians. • Concerned that conflict transformation is not seen by you as an overall goal. • Want you to take some responsibility for the situation • We won't have legitimacy within our constituency without partnership with you on the "big picture" (e.g., just peace)	• Ending Occupation is conditioned with a process that may take a long time and may not be applicable. • Lack of direct action on the ground as peace believers (peace camp). • Peace camp confused regarding 1948 Palestinians and their status. • Peace believers have many internal conflicts, confusions that are reflected in their lack of power in the Israeli community and lead to an undefinable mainstream

that we have. I've been wondering when these issues would come up. I had thought that maybe we all had such similar opinions that no disagreements would come up, which I didn't believe. We are all going to be working [together] as trainers, and it is important that we will have at least examined these issues even if we don't come to agreements about all of them. So overall I'm feeling a bit spent, but looking forward to the next steps in the process."

When asked if they wanted to move on to a different type of discourse and analysis, everyone but one Palestinian woman, whom we will call "Raida," was emphatic in saying that they had had enough. She, on the other hand, said that she hadn't expressed the full depth of her hurt and anger. I invited her to say more. She did. Then the group as a whole was asked if they were ready to move on to a discussion of their respective *resonance* (or the whys of their antagonism: when you point your finger at someone, note that the other three fingers point back at yourself. Thus, instead of talking further about what you blame them for, talk about why your anger and concerns are so important to you. Share in narrative form the reasons why these complaints about them are so deeply rooted and important for you in your life experience). (For more information the "power of why" process and theory, see Friedman, V., Rothman, J., & Withers, B, (2006). Again the group said yes, and very eagerly, as they were weary and wary about further antagonism, but Raida stood her ground. "No," she said, "I am not really finished. However, to not block the group, I am willing to try to move in the direction you recommend." Asked if she was sure, she nodded, but with some continued reticence.

After a break, as the participants shared in narrative form their deeper concerns and inquired of each other about their respective stories, Raida continued to frame her narrative in terms of what the Israelis had done to her instead of why it so deeply mattered to her, as most of the others had done. Asked if they needed to respond in kind, the Israelis said they did not. We took another break, and Raida was asked privately if she felt finished with the blaming phase now and was ready to move on to a more internal narrative discourse that could set a stage for a future-oriented discussion. She said yes firmly, and when we reconvened, she was fully in step with the rest of the group.

At this point, the group moved fairly quickly to resetting their goals in a two-step sequence in which ending the occupation as a statement of principle would be followed with on-the-ground planning and efforts to foster trust and cooperation between the two sides to build conditions for transforming the conflict in practical and concrete ways.

To move toward resonance in their discourse (i.e., speaking in the first person but in relation to the other side and the dilemmas they share), the participants were told, "At this point, it is about going beyond feeling good or badly toward each other and moving toward a change in the way we think, that is, toward analytical empathy. 'I don't necessarily agree with you, but I deeply understand that for you it is reality.' Each participant is now invited to share his or her narrative."

Palestinian woman: "Sometimes I think, why do this work with the Israelis (accusations at home, difficulties in moving over risky roads to Beit Jala, can work in my own society, etc.)? I so far find answers about personal interest (skills, etc.) or commitment to my workplace. I wanted to share these doubts with you. You (pointing to an Israeli male) were not online when the Israeli army was in Gaza. I was asking myself, is he in Gaza in reserve duty? I didn't ask him. I was fearful that the answer is that he was there."

Moderator: "What do you tell your family about all this?"

Same Palestinian: "My sister works with the Israelis. With her it is easier. But in the family, others tease me—this is normalization; why do you work with the Israelis? Also, at work, two colleagues refuse totally to attend. I try to talk about changing public opinion in Israel; Israel is the powerful side. It will not change until Israeli minds and society will change. This is how the director of my organization explained to me the need—we should know more of Israelis; support our friends in the Israeli peace camp."

Israeli woman: "[After working for many years for peace and] just before the war in Gaza I said, 'I cannot continue with this any longer.' I decided to enter a bubble in Tel Aviv. I wrote an email to a Palestinian friend, 'I am here but I cannot do it anymore.' He answered, 'What do you want me to say to my colleagues: that the only friends we had on the other side no longer want to work with us? And what will you tell your children?' This brought me back. I think we are really interdependent. My daughter still says, 'It is not about dialogue, it is about politics.' What I know very clearly is that we need you—Palestinians—there. I understand antinormalization and its reasons, and at the same time see that this killed the peace camp."

Palestinian man: "Almost from the first word that was uttered, I was having flashbacks of 'conflict groups,' 'people to people work,' the very processes which lead us nowhere. Now more than ever we know that if it took us months for us to agree to be part of the project, then we need to make sure that the Kumi process will be something different. I'm not referring simply to hope, which the Palestinians gave up on long ago. To start any process, our condition is to end occupation. What we are doing right now seems to be moving toward connecting on the human level, but that is not the issue. We know each other and agree upon most things. The difficulty is that we will have to go back to our societies. If I go back and tell them that I took part in a dialogue that sounds remotely like the things that have gone on until now, I will simply be told that they do not want to see me anymore. It is crucial that we bring these questions to the fore if we are going to avoid repeating the projects that have failed."

Moderator: "*Why does ending the occupation mean all those things to you which you mentioned—honor, dignity, etc.?*"

Palestinian man: "*Freedom is a very basic thing—it means that it shouldn't be conditioned. The conditions thing is about identity and about freedom. We all know that ending the occupation does not necessarily mean living in peace. When I say Palestinians mean it when they say that ending the occupation should not be simply a stage in the process. After 20 years in the process, talk about hope, trust doesn't mean anything. We are talking about a very primary level. Even though ending the occupation sounds huge, it has to be understood that this is very primary, it is the least we can ask.*"

This conversation proceeded for a couple of hours and then shifted to an option-generating mode for cooperation that was quite creative and future oriented. Joining in mixed groups, Israelis and Palestinians came up with several action ideals:

- Develop new conflict engagement methodology, tools, and skills; train others in it and spread it far and wide; establish joint think/do tanks to work separately and together.
- Develop Web-based networking tool for people who have participated.
- Improve the capacity of grassroots movements to access the community to influence decision makers; integrate extremists to limit future violence.
- Develop support system for reentry of participants in their home communities after these conflict engagement workshops end.
- Inform our families and others in our communities that there are Israelis and Palestinians who are committed to working with each other for peace.
- Develop a reality show about efforts to build bridges between Israelis and Palestinians.

As is so often the case with this process, it is truly about going slow to go fast. First, the antagonism about the past is safely framed (i.e., through intragroup problem listing) and revealed (i.e., through joint inquiry and carefully facilitated statements of hurt, disappointment, and anger). This is often a long and quite difficult experience. The participants who understandably express reservations about replaying the conflict dynamic "out there" in the room are reminded that it is a kind of artistic intensification of reality that will in the scheme of things be short and will make room for something new. However, it is often the case that it is fairly easy to move quickly at this point in to a future-oriented goal setting and action-planning process that is deeply owned by everyone and sustained by them.

Cincinnati Police–Community Relations Collaborative: A Broad-Based Process

In this case study of a citywide goal-oriented but conflict-initiated vision process, a focus on goal setting enabled a city to move away from confrontation politics (including a riot) and confrontational policymaking (through a federal court) toward a deeply collaborative agenda-setting and policymaking process. While its origins lay in accusations of racial profiling, a riot in response to a police shooting of an unarmed African American male, it kept a future-oriented focus on police–community relations, beginning with goals and objectives including a good deal of narrative about values and identities, and projected into a future-oriented resource and policy-oriented process of new police practices and problem-solving-oriented community policing and partnerships with the community itself in fighting crime and disorder and building a new sense of partnership and trust.

The Cincinnati Collaborative for Improving Police–Community Relations following race riots in 2001 was order by a federal judge. It involved data gathering from 3,500 stakeholders and meetings between 900 of them to form goals and action plans to shape the future of police–community relations. Through an online questionnaire and data analysis Web system (supplemented by interviews and paper-and-pencil questionnaires when useful), citizens were invited to answer a simple what, why, how questionnaire (see Box 8.1):

- *What* are your goals for future police–community relations in Cincinnati?
- *Why* are those goals important to you and what experiences, values, beliefs, and feelings influence your goals?
- *How* do you think your goals can best be achieved?

After only a month of a "getting out the voice" campaign, the first of 8 four-hour feedback sessions was held at a local church with religious and social service leaders, who specifically requested the opportunity to kick off the process. Following this first session, at the rate of one or two a month for the next six months, each stakeholder group was invited to participate in feedback sessions with other members of their own group (e.g., intragroup meetings) to discuss and reach a consensus on a platform of principles. Participants in each feedback session selected representatives to work together with representatives from the other seven groups (e.g., intergroup meetings) to develop a platform of goals for improving police–community relations. This intergroup platform then guided the negotiators, consisting of the lawyers for the parties (who had all year served on the Mediator's Advisory Group), as they worked to craft a settlement agreement forged out of the

---

BOX 8.1 ■ Vision of the Future: A Collaborative Platform

1. Police officers and community members will become proactive partners in community problem solving.
2. Relationships of respect, cooperation, and trust will be built within and between police and communities.
3. Education, oversight, monitoring, hiring practices, and accountability of the Cincinnati Police Department will be improved.
4. Equitable, courteous, and fair treatment for all will be ensured.
5. Methods to establish the public's understanding of police policies and procedures and recognition of exceptional service in an effort to foster support for the police will be created.

BOX 8.2 ■ Participants' Voices

The following examples illustrate the types of "whys" (resonance) that emerged from the process:

- "I would really like to see people respect each other's values and beliefs, even when they are different. I want all cultures to be treated with respect and fairness . . . in order for us and our children to feel safe. Everyone must be treated fairly; it is the only way."
- "For once in my life, I'd like to feel safe. I fear for safety, especially for young people."
- "Police are afraid of doing their job . . . we need to understand their side too."

"Vision of the Future" given to them by the representatives of the 3,500 participants (see Box 8.2).

While the result of the process was ratified in a federal court Agreement signed in August 2002 mandating court oversight during a five-year implementation process for which $5 million was set aside by the city, the lasting power of the process was much more internally derived. That is, people's hearts and hopes shaped this agreement. When they shared their "why" responses, first on the questionnaire and afterward in small groups during the feedback sessions, they established the value basis of the entire effort. People's "why" stories captured concerns about fairness and respecting differences, the need for safety, and expressions of support for the police. These discussions were tremendously powerful. They enabled the citizens of Cincinnati to experience resonance with one another—to find commonalities between their own and others' fears, hurts, hopes, and dreams. Many found this outlet to express themselves critical. Up to that point, they felt that they were not being listened to and their concerns were not being heard. As a young African American woman said, "When we felt pain, no one from the city came to listen to us. We needed someone to comfort and listen to us."

Healing began as the city leaders finally heard people's ideas. The inclusive and participatory process has helped citizens to feel a sense of ownership for the agreement, and it has helped them to move from fear and mistrust to cooperation and joint problem solving. The ability and willingness to truly listen and hear others will continue to be critical as Cincinnati's citizens and public officials begin to implement the changes outlined in the settlement agreement.

Intergroup negotiations, whether in the form of tough bargaining or interest-based win-win processes, are normally future oriented. In interest-based bargaining, for example—an analytical process of interactively uncovering and communicating each side's needs and interests, including those frustrated in the past—the focus is upon what could be done to foster mutual goals or positive-sum outcomes for each side's future. I believe this is one major reason identity-based conflicts are often unresponsive to such processes and are declared to be intractable.

Given how past-oriented such conflicts are, a future-oriented process misses the main issues and may even cause further frustration among those who commonly feel that their main concerns and grievances are often overlooked or even willfully disregarded. Too often they hear the common reframe, "Just get over it already and move on." A major need expressed by parties locked in identity-based conflicts is that their narratives must be heard and their grievances recognized as valid and important (Rothman, 1992). Indeed, a major part of engaging identity-based conflicts is about making possible a rich telling of and deep listening to each side's hurts, grievances, fears, and frustrations (Northrup, 1989). When an exchange of this description and recognition does occur in such conflicts regarding historical narratives, a psychological space otherwise clouded and narrow may be somewhat opened up. This may then make room for the kind of future-oriented goal negotiations so lacking and ultimately necessary for deeply rooted identity-based conflicts to become less destructive and more responsive to negotiation.

■ **FOCUSING WITHIN: A RESEARCH AND PRACTICE PROPOSAL**

To repeat the main hypothesis of this chapter: A major reason negotiations over identity-based conflicts fail is that inadequate attention is given to intragroup prenegotiation. Too often conflicts go from bad to worse when opponents in ethnic and identity-based conflicts meet prematurely and try to solve problems or negotiate solutions before sufficient intragroup agreement and conditioning have occurred. Instead, intragroup prenegotiation, focusing first on the internal dynamics of disagreement and consensus building *within the conflict parties,* could enhance the chances of successful negotiation *between them.*

Insufficient focus on each side's internal conflicts fundamentally prevents sufficient—much less sustainable—change in the hearts and minds of participants in these encounters. Without this focus, conflicts with the other side become a source of deeper division *within* each side, that is, within one's own group. Then the agenda for an encounter with the other side, including negotiation, reverts to a more aggressive win-lose dynamic that characterizes deep conflict. Finally, conflicts within groups become projected onto the conflict with the other side, and intractability follows.

Moreover, if intergroup encounters and negotiations are somewhat successful, with parties bridging differences and reaching agreements, it is not uncommon for their respective hard-liners to "blow up" (sometimes quite literally) agreements reached in the negotiation room. Even if this does not happen, the fear that it will often keeps each side closed and wary of taking risks and building bridges. Thus, another benefit of adequate prenegotiation is a process of postnegotiation in which both sides work separately, and as useful in a coordinated way, to package private agreements for at-home public "consumption."

Most broadly characterized, prenegotiation is the effort by groups on all sides of a divide to quietly, out of the public eye and in nonbinding, exploratory ways, set an agenda for eventual negotiation (Rothman, 1991). More specifically, prenegotiation has the double goal of helping to establish a will to negotiate as well as a momentum that carries negotiations to a successful conclusion. If, as defined in this volume, "negotiation is the process of identifying an appropriate partner and constructing a joint pact," then prenegotiation is the process of helping parties define issues around which a joint pact becomes possible and helps adversaries find avenues toward partnership.

The conventional wisdom about negotiation is that it should forge some type of compromise between adversaries in which each side attempts to gain as many concessions as possible and to make as few concessions as necessary. Most often, negatively interacting and mutually enforcing exclusive positions limit the individuals engaged in negotiations because they are typically interested in winning the battle of public opinion and shoring up their positions. However, in identity-based conflict, the purpose and the process of negotiation require considerable reformulation. Because conflicts are about identity, the normal concession-convergence model may be counterproductive. If issues of identity (control over destiny, safety, dignity, etc.) are at the heart of the conflict, then compromise over such "nonnegotiable" needs and values may well be impossible. Indeed, such negotiations might even cause the conflict to escalate if they fail, as in the second intifada following the failed U.S.-brokered negotiations in 2000 between the Israelis and Palestinians. Instead, if, before getting to the table, negotiators reenvision negotiation as a mutually beneficial and joint problem-solving process that helps each side to address its respective and overlapping identity needs, instead of as a different type of win-lose game or as war by other means, sustainable and positive outcomes for all sides may be more readily achieved during negotiation.

In identity-based conflicts, a coordinated prenegotiation phase in which each side examines and resolves its internal differences may be essential for successful intergroup negotiation. In this way, each side may prevent its members from externally playing out internal divisions at the negotiation table. More specifically, unless each side bridges its internal differences during a coordinated prenegotiation phase, each side runs the risk that its internal hard-liners, who hold and espouse attributional analyses of the other side, may wreak havoc before or during the actual negotiations. For example, internal spoilers might keep parties from arriving at the negotiation table in the first place. Or they might successfully push through an adversarial agenda by antagonistically framing issues and viewing negotiation as a win-lose battle, thereby making their attributions of the other side self-fulfilling prophecies. Moreover, if the spoilers do not achieve their maximalist positions, they might later wreck the negotiation process.

As an example, after a recent negotiation, powerful outside stakeholders rejected a deal that negotiators from their *own* side had reached with the other side. After these powerful stakeholders/hard-liners replaced the initial negotiators, they quickly marginalized some members of the new team when these members sought to accommodate the other side during the subsequent negotiation. As a result, because the maximalist agenda prevailed, the two sides ultimately failed to reach an agreement. If, in contrast, the group had invested time in dealing with its own internal divisions by finding some "golden mean" between them by clarifying their goals and values before settling on opposing strategies, it could have most likely and fairly easily reached an agreement with the other side.

The central message is that if each side builds necessary and sufficient internal agreement about its underlying needs and values and the ways to achieve them through negotiation with the other side during a coordinated prenegotiation process, both sides are more likely to negotiate and to create mutual positive outcomes during negotiation. Furthermore, if each side forges agreement across its own internal divisions, then *both* sides may mirror this dynamic during eventual negotiation *between* the sides and, for that reason, create a problem-solving instead of a win-lose orientation.

In identity-based conflicts, where the main issues are often threatened or frustrated needs and values, deep internal consensus may be forged around such needs and values. Thus, an intragroup negotiation process could be designed to be most responsive to such an agenda once it is articulated separately and coordinated interactively (perhaps with the help of "internal" mediators who have helped guide the intragroup prenegotiations).

Both in theory and in practice, international conflict resolution tends to neglect the area of intragroup relations and internal prenegotiation. Therefore, if meaningful and sustainable progress is to be made in creatively and constructively handling identity-based conflicts between groups, this neglect must be corrected. Otherwise, attributions rule, projections continue, and, predictably, failures flourish. While intragroup prenegotiation is not a panacea, it is the place where preventive negotiation on identity conflict begins.

Notes

1. The needs approach to identity-based conflicts suggests that the main cause of such conflicts and the reason they are often unresponsive to conventional negotiation, and even to interest-based bargaining, is that they are rooted in the threat and frustration of basic human needs and their fulfillment. Such needs are variously defined by different negotiation, peace and conflict theorists. John Burton (1979, 1990) described them as irreducible collective human needs for security, predictability, recognition, distributive justice, meaning, and control. Negotiation theorists Dean Pruitt and Jeffrey Rubin (1986) defined them as needs for security, identity, social approval, happiness, clarity about one's world, and physical well-being. Peace studies pioneer Johan Galtung (2004) articulated them as needs for security, freedom, welfare and identity. Anstey and Zartman, in this volume, define them as needs for protection, participation, power, privilege, and purpose. Legal expert on minority affairs Yousef Jabarin (2008) summarized needs in one main category: "participatory equality."

2. Personal communication.

3. Personal communication during attendance at a Fulbright Fellowship at Jezreel Valley College in Israel in 2006; shared with permission.

4. In many of my previous writings, I have suggested the distinction between interests and identities. I believe the distinction between goals and identities is more useful and precise. See in particular Rothman and Olsen (2001).

5. An important new approach to conflict resolution has emerged with the publication of a book called *The Promise of Mediation* (1995), by Baruch Bush and Joseph Folger which suggests that a major purpose of mediation is voice and empowerment (or

recognition) of the sides in a conflict, not necessarily the end or resolution of the conflict itself.

References

Abbas, M. (1995). *Through secret channels.* Reading: UK, Garnet Publishing.

Azar, E. (1990). *The management of protracted social conflict: Ten propositions: Theory and cases.* UK: Dartmouth. Aldershot,

Broome, B. (2005). Building Bridges Across the Greenline: A Guide to Intercultural Communiction in Cyprus. Nicosia, Cyprus. The United Nations Development Programme.

Burton, J. (1979). *Deviance, terrorism and war.* Suffolk: UK, Martin Robertson.

Burton, J. (Ed.). (1990). *Conflict: Human needs theory.* New York: St. Martins Press.

Bush, B., & Folger, J. (1995). *The promise of mediation: Responding to conflict through empowerment and recognition.* San Francisco: Jossey-Bass.

Coleman, P. (2000). Intractable conflict. In M. Deutsch & P. Coleman (Eds.), *The handbook of conflict resolution: Theory and practice* (pp. 131–143). San Francisco: Jossey-Bass.

Coleman, P. (2011). The Five Percent: Finding Solutions to Seemingly Impossible Conflicts. New York: Public Affairs.

Davies, J., & Kaufman, E. (2002). *Second track/citizens diplomacy.* Lanham, MD: Rowman & Littlefield.

Fisher, R., & Keashly, L. (1991). The potential complementarity of mediation and consultation within a contingency model of third party consultation. *Journal of Peace Research, 38*(1), 29–42.

Fisher, R., & Ury, W. (1981). *Getting to yes: Negotiating agreement without giving in.* Boston: Houghton Mifflin.

Folger, J., Poole, M., & Stutman, R. (2005). *Working through conflict* (5th ed.). Boston: Allyn & Bacon.

Friedman, V., Rothman, J., & Withers, B, (2006). The power of why: Engaging the goal paradox in program evaluation. *American Journal of Evaluation, 27*(2), 1–18.

Galtung, J. (2004). *An introduction to conflict work (peace by peaceful means).* London: Pluto Press.

Gorman, D. (1999). Moving towards peace in Jerusalem. In *Theory and practice in ethnic conflict management: Theorizing success and failure* (pp. 161–174). London: Macmillan.

Gurr, T. (2000). *Peoples versus states: Minorities at risk in the new century.* Washington, DC: United States Institute for Peace Press.

Havrelock, R. (2010). Pioneers and refugees: Arabs and Jews in the Jordan River Valley. In I. W. Zartman (Ed.), *Understanding life in the borderlands: Boundaries in depth and motion* (pp. 189–216). University of Georgia Press.

Hocker, J., & Wilmot, W. (2000). *Interpersonal conflict* (6th ed.). New York: McGraw-Hill.

Jabareen, Y. (2008). Toward participatory equality: Protecting minority rights under international law. *Israel Law Review, 41*(3), 635–676.

Jones, T., & Brinkert, R. (2008). *Conflict coaching: Conflict management strategies and skills for the individual.* Thousand Oaks, CA: Sage.

Kelman, H. The political psychology of the Israeli–Palestinian conflict: How can we overcome the barriers to a negotiated solution? *Political Psychology, 8*(3), 347–363.

Klein, G. (2010). *Streetlights and shadows: Searching for the keys to adaptive decision making.* Cambridge, MA: MIT Press.

Klein, G., & Rothman, J. (2008, November–December). Staying the course when your destination keeps changing. *Conference Board Review,* 24–27.

172 ■ The Slippery Slope to Genocide

Lasswell, H. (1935). *Politics: Who gets what, when, how.* New York: McGraw-Hill.

Northrup, T. (1989). The dynamic of identity in personal and social conflict. In L. Kriesberg, T. A. Northrup, & S. J. Thorson (Eds.), *Intractable conflicts and their transformation* (pp. 55–82). Syracuse, NY: Syracuse University Press.

Pruit, D.G. & Rubin, J.Z., (1986). *Social Conflict.* McGraw Hill.

Rothman, J. (Ed.). (1991). Special Issue on Pre-Negotiation. *The Jerusalem Journal of International Relations, 13*(1).

Rothman, J. (1992). *From confrontation to cooperation: Resolving ethnic and regional conflict.* Thousand Oaks, CA: Sage.

Rothman, J. (1996). Reflexive dialogue as transformation. *Mediation Quarterly, 13*(4), 345–352.

Rothman, J. (1997). *Resolving identity-based conflict in nations, organizations and communities.* San Francisco: Jossey-Bass.

Rothman, J. (1998). Dialogue in conflict: Past and future. In E. Weiner (Ed.), *The handbook of interethnic Coexistence* (pp. 217–235). New York: Continuum Press.

Rothman, J. (1999). Conflict management training: Opening the window to new ideas. *Strategic Management Group Business Review, 16*, 9–11.

Rothman, J., & Olson, M. (2001). From interests to identities: Towards a new emphasis on interactive conflict resolution. *Journal of Peace Research, 38*(3), 289–305.

Sander, F., & Goldberg, S. (1994). Fitting the forum to the fuss: A user-friendly guide to selecting an ADR procedure. *Negotiation Journal, 10*(1), 49–68.

Savir, U. (1998). *The process.* New York: Random House.

Sheehan, E. (1976). "How Kissinger did it: Step by step in the Middle East. *Foreign Policy, 22*, 3–70.

Volkan, V. (1988). *The need for enemies and allies: From clinical practice to international relationships.* Northvale, NJ: Aronson.

Zartman, I. W. & Alfredson, T. (2010). Negotiating with terrorists and the Tactical Question. In R. Reuveny & W. R. Thompson (Eds.), *Coping with Terrorism: Origins, Escalation, Counterstrategies, and Responses* (pp. 247–286). Albany, NY: SUNY Press.

Zartman, I. W. & Kremenyuk, V. (Eds.). (2005). *Peace vs. justice.* Lanham, MD: Rowman & Littlefield.

Zartman, I. W. (1964). Problems of New Power: *Morocco.* New York: Atherton Press.

9 Handling Spoilers and the Prospect of Violence

■ MARIE-JOËLLE ZAHAR

History, Stephen said, is a nightmare from which I am trying to awake.
James Joyce, *Ulysses*

Identity conflicts are among the hardest to mediate. Chaim Kaufman (1996, p. 137) makes the point with reference to ethnic wars: "both hypernationalist mobilization rhetoric and real atrocities harden ethnic identities to the point that cross-ethnic appeals are unlikely to be made and even less likely to be heard." Identity conflicts can also be among the deadliest. Most if not all genocides and mass killings in history involve the demonization of one group by another. As Zartman and Faure (2005) argue, the demonization process can result in an escalation of the image of the counterpart that results in suspension of the normal considerations of human behavior and respect. The context of civil war can shroud massacres in confusion; the fog of war obfuscates the need for urgent outside intervention to save lives (Power, 2001). In such instances, mediators—though handed an unenviable job—are crucial. Without their intervention, little can be done to break stalemates and create conditions for ripeness; little can prevent conflicts from becoming massacres and massacres from becoming full-fledged genocides.

Although most massacres and genocides are perpetrated by states, these are often aided and abetted by nonstate armed groups (NSAGs) such as the Interahamwe in Rwanda or the Janjaweed in the Sudan. These NSAGs are seldom studied by scholars and/or engaged by mediators as political actors in their own right. Likewise, policymakers tend to deal directly with the governments or political actors considered to be the master puppeteers. A feature of Cold War politics, in which many actors—governments and NSAGs alike—were denied agency and cast as either Soviet or American puppets,[1] this tendency continues to be strongly in evidence in present-day international mediation. In the wake of the UN experiences in Bosnia and Somalia, debates raged over the appropriateness of reaching agreements with NSAGs for access to, and protection of, civilians (Chesterman, 2001; Zahar, 2001). Critics argued that international aid and the deployment of peacekeepers allowed combatants to sidestep their responsibilities toward civilians, often prolonging conflicts (Anderson, 1999). Researchers, when they study NSAGs, tend to focus on such issues as individual psychological motivations for joining, rewards obtained from participation in massacres, and the like (Mueller, 2000; Zahar, 2009). While recent research has made strides in moving away from purely psychological explanations (Humphreys & Weinstein, 2008; Kalyvas, 2003; Tanner, 2007), there are still many open questions and unresolved debates about the conditions under which such groups may be willing to negotiate a peace settlement and put down their weapons.

Unlike states, NSAGs are not easily held to commitments under international humanitarian law, reflecting a lesser sensitivity to considerations of risk and cost (Bruderlein, 2000; Hoffman, 2006; Munoz-Rojas, 2003). Where they are mobilized around identity, they are also likely to hold very strong preferences over outcomes. In other words, such actors are candidates for the label *total spoilers*, actors who believe that peace "threatens their power, worldview, and interests, and use violence to undermine attempts to achieve it" (Stedman, 1997, p. 5). When such NSAGs perceive peace efforts as existential threats, they are likely to use violence to derail any settlement. These are actors who, according to Stedman (1997, 2003), must be subjugated and/or eliminated by force if sustainable and lasting peace is to prevail. If this is true, then handling such *identity spoilers*, indeed preventing them from thwarting mediation's course by any means necessary, becomes a, if not the, critical issue in determining the success or failure of mediation efforts and in preventing transition violence from escalating to the level of massacres, ethnic cleansing, or genocide.

This chapter focuses on identity-based NSAG violence and the conditions under which mediators can successfully devise winning strategies to bring identity conflicts to an end. It first develops a two-pronged argument to specify if, and when, ethnic NSAGs can be described as total spoilers. Identity, though important, does not constitute the only determinant of their decision making. There are conditions under which context provides a set of constraints on the ability of identity-based NSAGs to resort to violence. This makes it possible to develop a typology of identity-based NSAGs and to identify the specific strategies most likely to bring such groups to the negotiating table and to ensure their commitment to peace. In a second stage, the Bosnian civil war is used as an example with which to probe the expectations of the model. An internationalized civil war where regional state actors were closely associated with NSAGs, the war in Bosnia and Herzegovina saw widespread ethnic cleansing culminating with the July 1995 massacre at Srebrenica. The Bosnian conflict also saw intense international mediation efforts, the most important of which were the Vance-Owen Peace Plan of 1993, the Contact Group Plan of 1994, and the Dayton Peace Agreement (DPA) of 1995 (Touval, 2002; Zartman, 2005). This case will be used not so much to prove as to illustrate the potential of the proposed explanatory framework.

■ BRINGING ETHNIC NSAGS TO THE NEGOTIATING TABLE: THE DOMINANT VIEW

Identity conflicts are notoriously intractable (Crocker, Hampson, & Aall, 2004, 2005). Governments and NSAGs involved in these wars are said to be particularly resistant to compromise as total spoilers. Because of their preferences for outcomes and their commitment to the achievement of specific goals, these actors are likely to use violence to spoil any peace process that does not meet their exacting requirements. In the lead-up to Rwanda's genocide, Hutu frustration with the requirement of the 1993 Arusha Peace Agreement that Hutus share power with Tutsis has been identified as an important turning point in the radicalization of the ruling Mouvement Révolutionnaire National pour le Développement (Kakwenzire & Kamjura, 1999).

The total goals of identity extremists leave little if any room for compromise. When in power, they are not willing to share. When in opposition, they seek as much autonomy as they can get, often demanding secession—either to form their own country, as was the case in Kosovo,[2] or to join kin states, as was the stated objective of the Bosnian Serbs—or seeking asymmetrical federal arrangements of the sort that Iraqi Kurds and Southern Sudanese were able to wrest away in recent years. Herein lays the complication for identity-based NSAGs. Both of their preferred solutions are unacceptable to the state. Secession goes against the very notions of territorial sovereignty and integrity that are deeply embedded in the contemporary international system. Nowhere was this made clearer than in Serbia's inability to come to terms with the demands of Kosovar Albanians and the subsequent unilateral declaration of Kosovo's independence. And a wide margin of autonomy is often seen as the prelude to sovereignty in the near future. This problem has been raised in connection with transitional arrangements in the Sudan, where former ethnic NSAGs have become partners in highly asymmetrical arrangements that grant them extensive powers over the conduct of their own affairs, including the right to hold referenda on secession.

Identity extremists, governments and NSAGs alike, are also highly committed to the achievement of their goals (Zartman, 1995). This commitment can take multiple forms. Governments often refuse to entertain the possibility that NSAGs have any legitimacy, casting them as greedy rebels or, worse, as terrorists, as Russia and China have done in dealing with Chechen and Uighur unrest, respectively.[3] Identity-based NSAGs may be more willing than most to initiate violence against a much stronger enemy, as is, for example, the case with the Hamas movement and Israel (Fearon, 1998). Not only are they likely to be more risk-prone, they are also likely to be less cost-sensitive. David Laitin and James Fearon (2003) have rightly identified the existence of a capability gap separating governments from insurgents. The weaker NSAGs are, the less they have to lose and the less sensitive they are to costs. Their preferences over outcomes and their commitment to achieving their objectives suggest that identity-based NSAGs will be less vulnerable than most other civil war protagonists to the impact of stalemates and precipices. Occasions for ripeness may thus go either unrecognized or unexploited (Zartman, 1989). The history of the Sri Lanka conflict illustrates many, if not most, of these dynamics (Wriggins, 1995). The Sri Lankan government's unwillingness to compromise and its policy of treating the Liberation Tigers of Tamil Eelam (LTTE) as mere terrorists were mirrored by Tiger intransigence and insensitivity to costs, even as it became increasingly clear that they could not really mount a successful defense against a much stronger enemy.

Extrapolating from this discussion, one could come away with a very bleak prognosis for the prospects of mediation in identity conflicts. To the extent that identity actors, especially NSAGs, are likely to behave like total spoilers, they should not be included in negotiations. Following Stedman's advice, custodians of peace ought to devise military ways of managing them and preventing them from hurting the implementation of peace. If included in peace processes, identity extremists are to be expected to negotiate in bad faith. At most, their participation in mediation efforts and peace processes would be a strategic ploy to gain time in order to rest and regroup (Horowitz, 1985).

■ BRINGING NSAGS TO THE NEGOTIATING TABLE: AN ALTERNATIVE VIEW

The traditional view presented in the preceding section can be challenged on empirical and conceptual grounds. Empirically, one cannot systematically link the exclusion of identity-based NSAGs to the success of negotiations, nor can their inclusion be linked to failure. Exactly the reverse was the fate of the 1993 Arusha Agreement in Rwanda. The Israeli–Palestinian conflict, though not an instance of civil war, is also telling in this regard. The inclusion of Yasser Arafat—considered a total spoiler until the early 1990s—was a linchpin of the Oslo accords.[4] The exclusion of the Hamas leadership—considered since the early 1990s but especially after September 11, 2001, as identity extremists in comparison with Arafat's Palestinian Liberation Organization (PLO)—did not bring peace either. Similar examples abound: The exclusion of the Bosnian Serbs and Croats from the Dayton Peace Agreement did not secure the smooth implementation of its provisions, nor did the inclusion of the Irish Republican Army (IRA) in the Good Friday Agreement spell the death of peace in Northern Ireland; to the contrary.

Conceptually, the association of identity extremists with total spoilers is flawed. I have argued elsewhere that this conflates a negotiating position opposed to peace with the instrument of that rejection, the use of violence (Zahar, 2005, 2006). Those who reject peace need not use violence to derail negotiations, nor do those who use violence necessarily reject peace (Walter, 1997). Even if we accept that identity extremists hold very strong, indeed unchanging, preferences for certain outcomes—something that will be challenged below—it does not automatically follow that they will pursue these preferences at all costs, nor does it follow that violence is the only way to pursue them. The argument here then proceeds to question the two assumptions that underpin the dominant view in the field, notably that identity-based NSAGs have very strong (and thus hard-to-change) preferences over outcomes and that these groups also have little sensitivity to risks and costs.

The category *identity-based NSAGs* is in dire need of disaggregation, which can be done by building on factors whose importance has already been established in the relevant literature: their order of preferences and their sensitivity to risk. Both depend in large part on the development stage at which these groups find themselves (Zahar, 2000). The more institutionalized NSAGs are, the more likely it is that their preference ordering will not be fixed and their sensitivity to risk will increase. Institutionalized NSAGs are those groups that have developed complex organizational structures, norms, and routinized patterns of interaction with other societal actors, particularly populations living in their zones of control. This broadens the scope of action of the NSAGs as they move beyond the strict military realm into the political and socioeconomic spheres. In the process, considerations other than the pursuit of their identity objectives enter into their calculations and affect their preference ordering. Identity-based NSAGs become concerned with potential losses rather than simply the pursuit of identity gains, an element also discussed in a later chapter by Cunningham. Institutionalization also affects an NSAG's ability to incur costs and its subsequent sensitivity to risks. The more groups have to lose, the more their actual or potential losses become a factor in their decision making. For both sets of reasons, institutionalized NSAGs are less likely to behave as total spoilers, at least not under all circumstances.

Amid the destruction and chaos that accompany civil wars, there is creation and order, though of a different kind. Insurgents often create their own parallel structures of government and control. The institutions that structure everyday life in the insurgents' zone of control affect the choices of insurgent leaders. At the outset of conflict, nonstate actors are usually weak relative to the governments they are fighting (Zartman, 1995). This "fundamental fact about insurgency" means that the rebels have two options to survive: either continuously hide from government forces or increase their strength (Fearon & Laitin, 2000, p. 7). Empirically, rebel strategies include a mix of both: Most insurgencies seek hide-outs in remote areas outside the reach of government forces; most also engage in activities to increase their manpower and weaponry. Much as they provided the building blocks for state formation in Europe, efforts to secure recruits and arms are at the origin of the process of NSAG institutionalization (Tilly, 1985, 2007). Without weapons and recruits, and the institutions that secure a relatively steady supply of both, insurgents would fail to pose a sustained challenge to the government. The longer they hold out, the greater the need to institutionalize.

Insurgencies that secure military and manpower increase their chances of successfully challenging government forces. In Ethiopia, the Eritrean People's Liberation Front (EPLF)—one of the most successful identity insurgencies ever—established "a reciprocal process: in order to move freely through the rural areas, the population of the latter was necessary for support of the armed bands, and as a source of recruits, sustenance for armed guerrillas and intelligence" (Pool, 1998, p. 30). The military successes scored by insurgents produce arrangements that can deliver resources for nonmilitary as well as military purposes. In medieval Europe, war provided the fundamentals of state making: territorial consolidation, centralization, differentiation of the instruments of government, and monopolization of the means of coercion (Tilly, 1975). Likewise, insurgents embroiled in domestic conflict often gain control over territorial enclaves that they organize and run like fiefdoms. During Latin America's insurgencies in the 1960s, guerrilla movements often provided a full array of social contract services to the local populations. A Venezuelan peasant summarized this situation by distinguishing "the guerrillas' *gobierno de arriba*, or government up in the hills, from the normal government down in the towns, or *gobierno de abajo*" (Wickham-Crowley, 1991, p. 39). In the Ethiopian Sahel region, one nomadic clan leader referred to the EPLF in 1977 as a *hukuma*, the Arabic word for government (Clapham, 1998). In Republika Srpska, the provision of collective goods was a centerpiece of relations between the Serb Democratic Party (SDS) and the population. The Bosnian Serbs put in place *war municipalities* that provided, among others, relocation and gainful employment to

Serb refugees. The expansion of a group's scope of activities necessitates the development of a complex organizational framework.

While the argument is not specific to identity-based NSAGs, they are particularly likely to tread such a path to institutional development (Zahar, 2001). Whether they want to secede or to renegotiate the role of their community in the future polity, identity actors typically seek to displace governments as the locus of legitimacy in the hearts and minds of their kin. To do so, they need to become the provider of order and services to the community. Often facing authoritarian regimes, they also want to attract international attention to their predicament. But since we live in a world of states where legitimacy goes hand in hand with statehood, NSAGs face particular challenges as they attempt to be "heard, perceived, and recognized by nation-states and international organizations" (Selim, 1991, p. 198). The more successful they become, the more likely NSAGs are to be portrayed as mavericks threatening international security. For both sets of reasons, identity-based NSAGs have particular reason to develop the structures of governments-in-waiting. They appropriate the forms and procedures of states to achieve the ultimate objective of gaining legitimacy and recognition in their community and in the international community (Bahcheli, Bartmann, & Srebrnik, 2004).

Before we turn to the impact of institutionalization on the behavior of identity-based NSAGs, one more issue needs to be addressed. It has been convincingly argued that an important factor in inducing local populations not to denounce the active rebels is local knowledge, private information at the village level that allows the rebels to credibly threaten sanctions for denunciation and opposition to their rule (Kalyvas, 2006). The NSAGs are likely to adopt such methods. However, rule by terror does not negate the possibility of institutionalization. No one would contest, for example, that the Mafia—a particularly violent organization—established rules and procedures that allowed it to control economic activity in its areas of operation. Likewise, European barons performed important social functions in spite of their abuse of power and at times unattractive behavior (Mackinlay, 2000, p. 49). Rule by terror can coexist with, if not create, its own institutionalized methods of social control, as is the case in authoritarian states. In other words, even groups using reprehensible tactics can and often do organize.

The institutionalization of NSAGs has an impact on their preference ordering and their sensitivity to risk. It creates new preferences that compete with their stated objectives and can even displace them as the primary consideration in deciding whether to continue to fight or give peace a chance. It also affects their vulnerability to losses on the battlefield, thus increasing their sensitivity to losses and risks.

Institutions create opportunities for new preferences to emerge alongside and eventually compete for primacy with the NSAG's stated political objectives. The more organized an identity-based NSAG is, the more capable it will be to take advantage of economic opportunities associated with the conflict. The literature on war economies identifies several such opportunities in civil war settings including revolutionary taxation, control over scarce resources, and the taxation of international aid. Nowhere is the impact of resources on rebel behavior better discussed than in the debate over greed and grievance (Arnson & Zartman, 2005;

Berdal & Keen, 1997; Collier, 2000; Naylor, 1993; Ross, 2004). The emergence and later consolidation of financial stakes create opportunities for internal strife over the management of resources and the distribution of spoils.

As NSAGs transform into large, complex organizations, bureaucratic politics and interservice rivalries become more prevalent. A new class of leaders competes for access to and control of the "commanding heights" of NSAG leadership. Being at the helm provides individuals with the means to achieve their vision of a just settlement, pursue power for power's sake, or dispose of the group's assets for personal purposes. The larger and more successful the insurgent group, the more acute such infighting and outbidding are expected to be, as Jannie Lilja discusses in her chapter. The Bosnian Serb case provides ample illustration of this dynamic. Radovan Karadžić's momentous decision to mend fences with Belgrade in 1995 had little to do with the Serb reversal in fortunes in Bosnia and, as will be detailed below, more to do with the internal struggle between Karadžić and army commander, Ratko Mladić.

While institutionalization increases the absolute level of NSAG capabilities, institutions can be a source of political and military vulnerability. The NSAGs are politically vulnerable when the fight over allocations of resources or bureaucratic politics creates internal power struggles. In such instances, leaders are primarily interested in survival, defined broadly as retaining power, and the demands of personal survival may clash with the demands of cause or organizational survival. Indeed, it matters little if a leader is "ideological" or merely "instrumental." To reach his or her ultimate objectives, the leader needs to remain at the helm (Ames, 1987; Mayhew, 1974; Saidman, 1998). Infighting can create the conditions for ripeness by forcing leaders to go to the negotiating table in an attempt to consolidate their leadership, as in the 1979 Lancaster House negotiations over Zimbabwe (Stedman, 1991). Of course, it may also make it more difficult for leaders to commit to negotiations, as the chapter by Lilja explains.

Institutions increase the number of fixed material assets and thus the visibility of NSAGs. They become easier targets.[5] Herein lies one of the paradoxes of insurgency. Insurgents are so weak relative to governments that they need to hide out and to remedy their weakness if they want a fighting chance; however, too much of the remedy can kill the patient. The trajectory of the PLO is a telling example. Its transformation from a guerrilla movement into a government-in-exile for Palestinian refugee populations involved tremendous infrastructural development. The 1982 invasion of Lebanon underscored the vulnerability of this infrastructure. Israel "sought out and physically destroyed $400 million worth of PLO infrastructure and assets in the form of factories, offices, commercial real estate, hospitals and schools, as well as seizing bank records that might have permitted them to trace financial assets around the world" (Naylor, 1993, p. 43). Some might argue that this denotes not so much a net increase in vulnerability as a change in the kind of vulnerability. It is not. A division of labor and an increasing reliance on technology for the conduct of warfare accompany the growth of institutions. While often central to improving the odds of a military victory, this professionalization may paradoxically lead to large losses of military hardware. In the early stages of a civil war, insurgents who suffer a military reversal of fortune have the option of withdrawing to the bush, regrouping, and resuming the fight. Institutionalized groups face more difficulties in overcoming military reversals. The unraveling of their military and social institutions deprives these groups of what, in the meantime, has become their organizing framework. Going back to the PLO example, the organization, which managed to regroup its forces after severe setbacks in the late 1960s and 1970s, could not reconstitute its fighting potential as easily in the wake of the Lebanon defeat. The next military challenge to Israel did not emanate from PLO camps outside Israel but from a popular insurgency in the West Bank and the Gaza Strip.

As seen, the preference ordering and sensitivity to risk of identity actors change with their degree of institutionalization. Both kinds of vulnerability—the one emanating from infighting, the other from "outfighting" (the balance of forces in the overarching conflict)—affect an identity actor's attitude toward mediation efforts. Infighting raises the prospect that an identity actor may be forcibly removed from power by internal competitors. In such conditions, and regardless of his or her beliefs, the identity actor may be more likely to compromise to stay in power. Severe reversals in military fortunes can, likewise, threaten the survival of an institutionalized identity-based NSAG and thus create conditions for ripeness. Institutional development thus induces pragmatism in groups that are otherwise described and expected to behave as ideological extremists.

> Proposition 1: Noninstitutionalized NSAGs are more likely to be total spoilers than their institutionalized counterparts.
> Proposition 2: Identity-based NSAGs are more likely to compromise if their survival is at stake (see Table 9.1).

■ DEVELOPING APPROPRIATE MEDIATION STRATEGIES

Mediators must not only understand the actors that they are dealing with but also the context in which they carry out their mediation efforts. Thus far, I have argued that NSAGs facing a threat to survival are most likely to compromise, although the urgency of this compromise will be greater the more institutionalized the actor. This already suggests that would-be mediators need to engage selectively with identity-based NSAGs. Identifying those actors most likely to accept the principle of mediation is the first step to success.

How does one identify threats to survival? And how serious are these threats? In the same way as the category identity-based NSAG was disaggregated, mediators need to unpack the notion of *threat to survival* if they are to properly assess the

TABLE 9.1. *Identity-Based NSAGs and Likelihood of Compromise*

	Low institutionalization	High institutionalization
No threat to survival	Least likely to compromise (total spoiler)	Not likely to compromise
Threat to survival	Less likely to compromise	Most likely to compromise

starting chances of their mediation efforts. Some conflict environments create acute threats to survival akin to Zartman's (1989) notion of precipices, while other such threats, though real, can be managed by identity-based NSAGs. The more acute the threat, the more favorable the context to a mediation attempt.

The conflict environment shapes the ability of NSAGs to sustain military strategies. In situations where such groups are faced with a threat to survival, the conflict environment influences their assessment of the acuteness of the threat. Some conflict environments are more favorable to violence than others (Zahar, 2005).[6] In attempting to use force in order to address a threat to survival, NSAGs must be able to sustain a return to fighting. To this effect, they need a minimal amount of military resources. These resources can still be obtained where actors have access to (1) valuable tradable commodities and a regional underground network to produce, ship, and trade these commodities and/or (2) foreign patrons with a stake in regional destabilization and a willingness to provide the groups with resources to this effect.

Where actors have access to regionally based war economies, they can use such financial resources to buy weapons, disrupt cease-fires, and derail mediation efforts. Regional economic linkages often predate the conflict, and even when used for activities that belong to the gray economy, they tend to possess functional aspects (Pugh & Cooper, 2004). When war erupts, warlords either seek to control or simply utilize those linkages to finance their military activities.[7] Outside actors, mediators, peacekeepers, and custodians of peace alike, often fail to grasp the historical and functional dimensions of these linkages. Their strategies are narrowly based on a conception of "national" territories that does not take into account the vital economic connection and the complementarities of national and regional networks.[8] For this reason, they leave open loopholes that facilitate the return to violence by NSAGs and other protagonists. Experience in Afghanistan, the Balkans, and elsewhere shows that these regional complexes are key in providing NSAGs with the means to finance a return to violence.

Alternatively, where actors can depend on outside patrons for weapons, recourse to violence remains a viable option. External forces with a stake in the outcome of a civil conflict can become complicating factors at the negotiating table. "Sometimes such a regional power . . . may see its interests best served by the prolonging of a stalemate until the situation forces a settlement it can accept, rather than commit itself wholeheartedly to the course of conflict resolution" (De Silva & Samarasinghe, 1993, p. 14). Regional actors have often attempted to dictate hard or soft stances to their clients out of self-interest.[9] One need only remind oneself of the relations between Bosnian Serbs and Belgrade, or of the ties between the Christian Lebanese Forces and Israel, to make the point. The interests and calculations of outside patrons need not necessarily coincide with the best interests of the war-torn country or the designs of international mediators. The regional ambitions or long-term political goals of external actors, when not addressed in the course of a specific mediation effort, provide these actors with incentives to continue to interfere in the politics of the country. When the incentives of outside patrons and the needs of identity-based NSAGs coincide, the patrons can step in and provide these groups with the military and financial resources necessary to resume the violence.

In brief, two factors, a regional economic complex and foreign patrons, combine to create particularly unstable conflict environments. In such environments, reversals of military fortune do not necessarily create a plateau or a precipice for NSAGs. Threats to survival are easier to weather when groups are confident that they still possess the means to fight another day.

> Proposition 3: The more volatile the conflict environment, the less sensitive NSAGs will be to risk.
>
> Proposition 4: The less sensitive NSAGs are to risk, the higher the chances that they will use violence to derail mediation efforts.
>
> Proposition 5: Institutionalized NSAGs will be more sensitive to risk than their noninstitutionalized counterparts (see Table 9.2).

Potential mediators therefore need to calibrate their strategies to maximize their chances of success. They must be capable of recognizing situations in which NSAGs are facing acute threats to survival and to differentiate them from more moderate threats. This point has already been made by Zartman (1989, esp. pp. 255–288) in his elaboration of the concept of ripeness for resolution. In the current elaboration of his argument, ripeness is not only a function of the military balance of forces but also a function of the sensitivity of identity-based NSAGs to risk, a sensitivity heightened by the process of institutionalization.

Mediators do not only react and adjust their strategies to conflict environments; they can help shape these environments. As they intervene in a civil war setting, mediators attempt to influence protagonists' assessments of costs and benefits so as to edge them away from violence. The contents of peace proposals are but one aspect of this effort; other elements include sanctions, weapon embargoes, threats of force, economic and other incentives, and the like. Mediators need to develop context-sensitive strategies. Where the risks of violence are high, third parties will either have to refrain from mediating a conflict or accept that any successful mediation will require the backbone of a military deterrent. Outsiders will need not only to commit sufficient troops but also to be willing to use them and eventually incur casualties to see the process through. A study of 16 peace agreements (Stedman 2002, p. 664) makes a similar point with reference to peace implementation strategies:

> In certain limited situations, strategies that derive from traditional peacekeeping (with its underlying emphasis on confidence-building) can be effective. In more challenging situations, however, when predation coexists with fear, confidence-building will prove

TABLE 9.2. *Conflict Environments and Sensitivity to Risk*

	Regional war economy	No regional war economy
Outside Patrons	Extremely volatile conflict environment Little sensitivity to risk	Volatile conflict environment Medium sensitivity to risk
No Outside Patrons	Volatile conflict environment Medium sensitivity to risk	Stable conflict environment High sensitivity to risk

inadequate, and implementers will need to compel and deter to ensure compliance with a peace agreement.

This raises the issue of *incentive compatibility*, or the fact that the chances of engagement in a mediation process are proportional to the perceived self-interest of critical actors. It also underlines the fact that volatile conflict environments are difficult environments for both mediation and implementation purposes. They require more resources, greater involvement, and more coercive strategies. Often, these are not forthcoming "because no major or regional power perceives peace in a given country to be in its own vital strategic interest."[10] Where major or regional powers have defined peace as a vital strategic interest—as the North Atlantic Treaty Organization (NATO) did in Bosnia—third-party commitment has acted as a barrier against the use of spoiling tactics by identity extremists. This commitment and the adoption of appropriate strategies work to increase the sensitivity of identity-based NSAGs to risk.

> Proposition 6: Mediation efforts will be more successful if the strategies adopted are appropriate to the specific conflict environment.
> Proposition 7: Mediation efforts will be more successful if the strategies adopted increase NSAGs' sensitivity to risk.

In brief, the argument has been made that identity-based NSAGs are not necessarily total spoilers. Rather, the institutionalization of these groups triggers internal dynamics that increase the groups' sensitivity to risk. The sensitivity of NSAGs to risk will be increasingly affected by the conflict environment as they institutionalize. Not only are institutionalized NSAGs more sensitive to changes in the military balance of power, changes in the conflict environment can and often do affect their preference ordering. Groups that face acute threats to survival may choose to privilege their continued existence as groups over the achievement of their stated ideological objectives. That is all the more so if the groups have, in the meantime, developed other interests. Mediators must appreciate these internal developments if they are to develop appropriate strategies and ultimately successful mediation efforts.

■ A PRELIMINARY PROBE: NSAGS AND MEDIATION EFFORTS IN BOSNIA AND HERZEGOVINA

Bosnia and Herzegovina (BiH) provides a perfect case to probe the propositions developed in the theoretical section of this chapter. The war in BiH not only pitted groups mobilized along ethnic lines,[11] these groups also engaged in violence against each other on a level unseen in Europe since World War II. The Bosnian conflict was an internationalized civil war with local Serb and Croat nonstate armed groups tightly connected to Belgrade and Zagreb, respectively. In an effort to end the bloodshed, multiple mediation attempts were launched with variable success. Where the Vance-Owen, Vance-Stoltenberg, and Contact Group efforts failed, the Dayton Peace Agreement (DPA) succeeded in ending the war.

This preliminary probe focuses on the relationship between mediators and the Bosnian Serbs at the time of the DPA. This focus is prompted by a number of considerations. Following the 1991 decision of the Bosnian parliament to declare independence from the then-crumbling Federation of Yugoslav Republics and the March 1992 referendum that confirmed this choice, Bosnian Serbs sought to secede and join their ethnic kin in Serbia. In the process, they engaged in extensive ethnic cleansing. Bosnian Serbs were also held responsible for the failure of a number of earlier attempts to bring the war to an end. In 1993 and 1994, Slobodan Milošević reached agreements with the international community (the Vance-Owen Peace Plan and the Contact Group Plan) that were rejected by the Bosnian Serb parliament and leadership. Twice, the Bosnian Serb leadership let Milošević down at the last minute, not only causing him to lose face but also causing a tightening of international sanctions against Serbia. In July 1995, Bosnian Serb forces under the command of General Ratko Mladić massacred upwards of 8,000 men and boys in the safe area of Šrebrenica. In other words, the behavior of the Bosnian Serbs seems to fit the dominant pessimistic view of identity-based NSAGs as spoilers and of the limited ability of mediators to bring them to the negotiating table.

In 1995, the world credited NATO bombings for bringing the Serbs to the negotiating table. According to this view, the August 30–October 5 strikes tipped the equation in favor of the Muslims and Croats (Holbrooke, 1998). Although the Bosnian Serb political leadership in Pale signaled its willingness to negotiate shortly before the NATO bombings, in his account of events leading to the DPA, America's chief negotiator, Richard Holbrooke, recounts the three overtures, only to conclude that they had rightly been rejected in light of events that followed. By then, the Bosnian Serbs had become pariahs. American negotiators refused to deal with Radovan Karadžić and his aides directly; they insisted that Bosnian Serbs be represented by Belgrade.

A closer look at developments within Republika Srpska suggests that Karadžić's overtures may have been more serious than the record of Bosnian Serb attitudes toward international mediation would have led one to believe. Accounts of the events leading to the DPA report that Karadžić signed an agreement with President Milošević on August 30, before the NATO air strikes even began. The Patriarch Paper, as it came to be known, created a joint Yugoslav–Bosnian Serb delegation led by Milošević that would represent the Bosnian Serbs in all future peace talks. In the event of a tie vote, the head of the delegation would prevail. By signing this document, Karadžić gave up the one thing he and his acolytes had staunchly tried to maintain throughout the war: autonomous decision making. The Patriarch Paper put the fate of the Bosnian Serbs in the hands of Slobodan Milošević. This, the most significant indication of Karadžić's willingness to compromise, is either dismissed as another ploy or simply left unexplained. The following section traces Karadžić's decision to sign the Patriarch Paper to developments within Republika Srpska, notably infighting between Karadžić and Mladić over the control and purpose of the institutions of Republika Srpska. These developments created a ripe moment for negotiations. For the first time since the outset of the conflict, internal developments within Republika Srpska and military developments on the ground converged to acutely threaten the hold of Radovan

Karadžić on power. This provided a tipping point for a mediated outcome to the war.

Unlike most NSAGs, the Bosnian Serbs did not start in a position of relative weakness vis-à-vis the Bosnian Muslim (Bošniak) government forces. Two factors account for the strength of the Serbs: support from Belgrade and local institutional development. In 1992, the Serb Democratic Party (SDS, led by Karadžić) broke ranks with the Parliament of Bosnia and Herzegovina and established the Serb Republic of Bosnia-Herzegovina (later renamed Republika Srpska). In theory, state and party were separate. In practice, power was exerted through the party line.[12] Authority was highly centralized in a small group of SDS high-ranking officials who controlled the crisis committees, the Bosnian Serb Assembly, and the police apparatus.[13] In their effort to organize the Serbs, these officials took advantage of the institutional structures left behind by the defunct Yugoslav federation. They also established institutions of their own.[14]

The most valuable institution that the Bosnian Serbs inherited was the Vojska Republike Srpske (VRS), or the Bosnian Serb Army. When the Yugoslav National Army (JNA) withdrew from Bosnia in May 1992, it established the foundations of the VRS, comprised of "about 90,000 'regulars,' consisting of ex-JNA personnel, volunteers and conscripts, and 20,000 irregulars, presumably meaning semi-independent armed groups such as the Tigers, Chetniks, Panthers, and White Eagles" (O'Balance, 1995, p. 127). The VRS maintained strong links to the JNA; Bosnian Serb officers remained on the JNA payroll throughout the war and used their strong personal connections in the Yugoslav army to get supplies for their troops. Local institutions were initially set up to assist implementation of the SDS's policy of ethnic cleansing. The Bureaus for Population Exchange consisted of a system that terrorized Muslims into giving up their material property in return for the right to leave Republika Srpska (Silber & Little, 1995). Real property was awarded to the "war municipality" or "crisis committee" of the particular town. The Serbian National Assembly regulated this arrangement through legislation on "abandoned property" and "temporary occupancy." Last, but not least, SDS top officials developed a highly sophisticated black market to bust sanctions and finance their war effort. The organization and control of the black market was made possible by SDS control of state institutions such as customs offices and key ministries such as the interior and resource ministries. "Illicit traffic was institutionalized during the war between all warring sides. Many people lined up their pockets but some of the money also went to organizing the RS" (Silber & Little, 1995, p. 246).

At the outset of the conflict, Bosnian Serb institutions were more developed than the institutional structure of most NSAGs. However, that did not prevent, and might even have sped up, their demise. Indeed, institutions created the conditions for infighting and outbidding in the top ranks of the Republika Srpska leadership. This would have consequences not only for unity within the ranks but also for the ability of the VRS to conduct successful military operations.

Disagreement among members of the Bosnian Serb leadership can be traced back to the emergence of SDS financial interests tied to the black market. While SDS politicians developed financial stakes in the war, the army was more ideological. It perceived itself as the guardian of the Bosnian Serbs entrusted with the liberation of their historic lands in preparation for the establishment of a Greater Serbia. As of 1993, voices within the army started criticizing the party's association with war profiteering and questioning the political leadership's reluctance to negotiate a settlement at a time when military supremacy had been achieved (Judah, 1997, p. 252).[15] The SDS attempted to influence the army by putting its own people in decision-making positions.[16] However, the army's autonomous sources of financing prevented its takeover by the SDS clique. Tensions between party and army soared when Belgrade imposed sanctions on Pale for rejecting the Contact Group plan in the summer of 1994. The embargo provided an excellent opportunity for enrichment of the black market barons.[17] The sale of general consumption goods to the Bosnian Serb population became an additional source of financial gain. Core SDS officials traded general consumption goods tax free in return for contributions to their bosses in the state structure. They then sold the goods at inflated prices to the Bosnian Serb population. While the party officials were getting rich off the sanctions regime, the army bore the brunt of the sanctions.

Bosnia specialists generally agree that the Bosnian Serb Army's superiority was due less to the prowess of individual fighters than to the technological advantage that Yugoslav support afforded the VRS. Belgrade's decision to impose sanctions exposed the vulnerability of the VRS. Although the blockade was not airtight, the VRS lacked supplies, ammunitions, fuel, and sometimes food. In spite of the growing tension between army and party, troops became increasingly dependent on SDS-controlled municipalities for logistical support.[18] The army became at risk for political machinations aimed at weakening its support base. "At the beginning of 1995, lots of troops from the Eastern RS [loyal to the SDS] started being allocated to the area of the northwest [the army's stronghold] and they could often be recalled on overnight notice."[19] The army claimed that such practices prevented it from performing its functions properly.[20] In August 1995, members of Parliament exchanged accusations with the generals, the former blaming the latter for the loss of territory, while the generals blamed their first military setbacks in three years of war on the diversion of gasoline to the black market.

The latent conflict between army and party erupted on August 4, 1995. Radovan Karadžić relieved General Mladić of his functions as VRS commander, citing the loss of two strongholds, Bosanski Grahovo and Glamoč. In fact, analysts argue that Karadžić was motivated by his fear of Mladić's popularity, ties to Belgrade, and position on war profiteering (Block, 1995). While these intra-Republika Srpska tensions were being played out, the neighboring Republika Srpska Krajina, the Serb stronghold in Croatia, was swiftly overrun by the Croat army. Given the deteriorating military situation and the increasing vulnerability of the Bosnian Serb Army, Karadžić was worried that a serious internal split would lead to the destruction of Republika Srpska (Mociboh, 1996). After a weeklong standoff, Karadžić went back on his decision. "Instead of shoring up his own power, [Karadžić] turned General Mladić into the de facto leader of the Bosnian Serbs. . . . [T]here was talk among the Serbs about a military takeover of Bosnia in which [Karadžić] would be ousted" (Block, 1995).

In summer 1995, the vulnerability of the Bosnian Serb political leadership reached critical levels. Sensing a threat to his position at the helm, Radovan Karadžić sought to change the balance of internal forces to safeguard his incumbency; his attempt to remove Ratko Mladić from power backfired. In a deteriorating military context, Karadžić had to weigh his ideological against his personal objectives.

The NATO campaign "challenged the Bosnian Serb command structure and altered the ability of Serbs to hold on to territory."[21] In conjunction with NATO's offensive, Croat and Bosnian Muslim forces gained over-the-horizon capacity and the ability to react quickly. The increasing military vulnerability of the Bosnian Serbs helped tip the balance further in favor of the Croat-Muslim camp. By the end of September, the shift in the front lines had reduced Serb-controlled territories from 70% to about half. However, it is not clear that the military campaign alone would have brought the Bosnian Serb leadership to the negotiating table. The army leadership's defiant attitude in the face of a deteriorating balance of power seems to corroborate this assertion. Two weeks into the NATO air strikes, General Mladić was still refusing to withdraw his heavy weapons from around Sarajevo. In a meeting with United Nations Protection Force UNPROFOR Commander Bernard Janvier, Mladić threatened to attack the remaining "safe areas" and refused to negotiate until the bombing had ended. In spite of substantial territorial losses, the Serbs started to push the Bosnian 5th Corps back around Bosanska Krupa by the end of September. According to one observer, "There were already signs that the Serb withdrawal had not been as costly as some had imagined, nor their fighting potential so reduced as some had predicted. The new confrontation line appeared to be defensible by the Bosnian Serbs" (Owen, 1995, p. 339).

The confrontation between Karadžić and Mladić was decidedly turning to the advantage of the latter. On August 30, Radovan Karadžić signed the Patriarch Paper mending fences with Belgrade. In light of events within Republika Srpska, this decision can be interpreted as "killing two birds with one stone." Not only would the move spare Republika Srpska the fate of all-out military defeat and potential eradication, as happened with the Serb Krajina in Croatia, it would also allow Karadžić to restore the internal balance of power between himself and Mladić. Indeed, though he was dismissed from his position as leader of the Republika Srpska, Karadžić managed to retain "complete control over the Serb entity and its still thriving black market and smuggling operations," at least until 1997, when his informal hold on power was challenged by then-Republika Srpska president, Biljana Plavšić (Weschler, 1997, p. 31).

■ CONCLUSION: BRINGING IDENTITY-BASED NSAGS TO THE NEGOTIATING TABLE

What conclusions can researchers draw from the probe into Bosnian Serb reasons for accepting the DPA? The argument developed in this chapter is limited to one case study. It provides an alternative account of the way to Dayton. More research on this and other mediation attempts needs to be carried out to test the applicability of the argument. There are, however, a number of important lessons that one can take from the Bosnian case. First, identity-based NSAGs are not spoilers by definition. They can and do accept agreements that do not meet their stated objectives. In this, Bosnia's Serbs are not alone. Examples of compromise include, but are not limited to, groups involved in long and protracted conflicts such as the PLO and the IRA. Whereas the standard lesson of Bosnia seems to be that Bosnian Serb acceptance of the DPA was wrestled by force, it took internal dynamics to outbid the spoilers. Military defeat is not always required for NSAGs to accept mediated outcomes. Second, identity-based NSAGs, particularly leaders, hold multiple and often competing preferences. Mediators can play on these preferences in such ways as to offer the groups both carrots and sticks (Chinchilla, 2008; Stedman, 2000). In the Bosnian Serb case, the unintended consequence of international sanctions was the rise of a profitable black market controlled by the SDS and the concomitant increase in SDS–VRS conflict. Indeed, the impact on Serb politics of international sanctions provided the real tipping point for Karadžić. These consequences seem not to have been appreciated by American negotiators at the time. Mediators must therefore gain a better understanding of the manner in which preferences create strains within NSAGs, as well as the manner in which they can shape those preferences to sort out moderates, extremists, and opportunists among spoilers as negotiation partners and pact members and, in the process, increase the chances of success of mediation efforts.

Notes

1. In Angola, Zartman (1989, p. 256) suggests that the inability of the United States to treat Angola's MPLA regime as more than a Soviet puppet was to blame for the failure of negotiations in the 1977 Shaba crisis.

2. Though some would object to the fact that the KLA were identity extremists, I would forcefully argue that this was a case where both protagonists were identity extremists, though the reasons for their extremism might have differed.

3. In both instances, the NSAGs were Muslim groups, a fact that facilitated their demonization in a post-9/11 environment.

4. One could also argue that their implementation failure, though pinned on Arafat, was due to a larger set of factors.

5. Naylor (1993) draws a parallel between warring groups and criminals. "For successful criminals are precisely those most desirous of a public front of respectability which simultaneously provides them with a means for disguising the origins of their income and wealth. By contrast, successful guerrillas seek notoriety in terms of public confrontation with the authorities, in which case identifiable assets are susceptible to counter attack by the state."

6. In making decisions about the potential use of violence, identity actors assess the costs and benefits of each course of action. Though information is at best partial and incomplete and the rationality of such a cost-benefit calculus is naturally bounded, there are standard categories of costs and benefits that they consider. For a detailed discussion of these costs and benefits see Zahar (2003, 2005).

7. This is an important corrective to the literature on war economies not least of all because it also demonstrates that greed and grievance are not polar opposites but often parallel, if not overlapping, tracks.

8. I am indebted to Susan Woodward for this observation.

9. In the Third World, "the 'Big Powers' and the superpowers' intervention in civil conflicts have added to their severity and cost and introduced protractedness . . . to what otherwise could have been a less salient set of conflictive interactions" (Azar et al, p. 47).

10. Ibid.

11. Although groups were mobilized along ethnic lines, many excellent analyses contest that the war in BiH was an ethnic war. See Gagnon (2004).

12. Author's interview with David Stewart-Howitt, European Community Humanitarian Organization (ECHO) Officer, Banja Luka, and former aide to UNPROFOR Commander General Sir Michael Rose, September 2, 1998.

13. Author's interview with Vladimir Milin, Advisor in the Economic Department, Office of the High Representative, Banja Luka, and former JNA officer (subsequently VRS liaison with the international community), September 5, 1998.

14. For more detail on the organization of Republika Srpska, see Zahar (2004).

15. Author's interview with David Stewart-Howitt, September 2, 1998.

16. Author's interview with Branko Perić, Editor-in-Chief, Alternative Information Network [Alternativna Informativna Mreza], Banja Luka, September 5, 1998.

17. Author's interview with Branko Perić, September 5, 1998.

18. Author's interview with Vladimir Milin, September 5, 1998; see also Judah (1997, p. 223).

19. Author's interview with Vladimir Milin, September 5, 1998.

20. Author's interview with Vladimir Milin, September 5, 1998.

21. Author's interview with David Stewart-Howitt, September 2, 1998.

References

Ames, B. (1987). *Political survival: Politicians and public policy in Latin America.* Berkeley and Los Angeles: University of California Press.

Anderson, M. B. (1999). *Do no harm: How aid can support peace or war.* Boulder, CO: Lynne Rienner.

Arnson, C., & Zartman, I. W. (Eds.). (2005). *Rethinking the economics of war: The intersection of need, creed, and greed.* Washington, DC: Woodrow Wilson Center Press; Baltimore: Johns Hopkins University Press.

Bahcheli, T., Bartmann, B., & Srebnik, H. (2004). *De facto states: The quest for sovereignty.* London: Routledge.

Berdal, M. & Keen, D (1997). Violence and economic agenda in civil war: Some policy implications. *Millennium: Journal of International Studies, 26,* 795–818.

Block, R. (1995, October). The madness of General Mladic. *The New York Review of Books, 37*(15).

Bruderlein, C. (2000). *The role of non-state actors in building human security: The case of armed groups in intra-state wars.* Geneva: Centre for Humanitarian Dialogue.

Chesterman, S. (Ed.) (2001). *Civilians in war.* Boulder, CO: Lynne Rienner.

Chinchilla, F. (2008). *Paix soutenable: Rapports de forces et affaiblissement des extrémismes dans des contextes de guerre civile.* Doctoral dissertation, Université de Montréal.

Clapham, C. (Ed.). (1998). *African guerrillas.* Oxford: James Currey; Bloomington: Indiana University Press.

Collier, P. (2000). Rebellion as a quasi-criminal activity. *The Journal of Conflict Resolution, 34*(6), 839–853.

Crocker, C. A., Hampson, F. O., & Aall, P. (Eds.). (2004). *Taming intractable conflicts: Mediation in the hardest cases.* Washington, DC: United States Institute of Peace Press.

Crocker, C. A., Hampson, F. O., & Aall, P. (Eds.). (2005). *Grasping the nettle: Analyzing cases of intractable conflict*. Washington, DC: United States Institute of Peace Press.

De Silva, K. M., & Samarasinghe, S. W. R. (1993). Introduction. In K. M. De Silva & S. W. R. Samarasinghe (Eds.), *Peace accords and ethnic conflict*. London and New York: Pinter.

Fearon, J. (1998). Commitment problems and the spread of ethnic conflict. In D. Lake & D. Rothchild (Eds.), *The international spread of ethnic conflict: Fear, diffusion, and escalation* (pp. 107–126). Princeton, NJ: Princeton University Press.

Fearon, J., & Laitin, D. (2000). Weak states, rough terrain, and large-scale ethnic violence since 1945. Presented at the annual meeting of the American Political Science Association, Washington DC, August 31–September 3.

Gagnon, V. P., Jr. (2004). *The myth of ethnic war: Serbia and Croatia in the 1990s*. Ithaca, NY: Cornell University Press.

Hofmann, C. (2006). Engaging non-state armed groups in humanitarian action. *International Peacekeeping, 13*(3), 396–409.

Holbrooke, R. (1998). *To end a war*. New York: Random House.

Horowitz, D. (1985). *Ethnic groups in conflict*. Berkeley: University of California Press.

Humphreys, M., & Weinstein, J. L. (2008). Who fights? The determinants of participation in civil war. *American Journal of Political Science, 52*(2), 436–455.

Judah, T. (1997). *The Serbs: History, myth, and the destruction of Yugoslavia*. New Haven, CT: Yale University Press.

Kakwenzire, J., & Kamjura, D. (1999). The development and consolidation of extremist forces in Rwanda 1990–1994. In H. Adelman & A. Suhrke (Eds.), *The path of a genocide: The Rwanda crisis from Uganda to Zaire* (pp. 61–91). New Brunswick, NJ: Transaction Books.

Kalyvas, S. N. (2003). The ontology of "political violence": Action and identity in civil wars. *Perspectives on Politics, 1*(1), 475–494

Kalyvas, S. N. (2006). *The logic of violence in civil war*. Cambridge: Cambridge University Press.

Kaufman, C. (1996). Possible and impossible solutions to ethnic civil wars. *International Security, 20*(4), 136–175.

Laitin, D., & Fearon, J. (2003). Ethnicity, insurgency and civil war. *American Political Science Review, 97*(1), 75–90.

Mackinlay, J. (2000). Defining warlords. *International Peacekeeping, 6*(1), 48–62.

Mayhew, D. R. (1974). *Congress: The electoral connection*. New Haven, CT: Yale University Press.

Mocibob, D. (1996, November 13). *The ongoing changes in VRS: Analysis and assessment*. Media analysis, Office of the Commander (COMARRC), Allied Command Europe Rapid Reaction Corps, NATO.

Mueller, J. (2000). The banality of "ethnic war." *International Security, 25*(1), 42–70.

Munoz-Rojas, D. (2003). *Violations of international humanitarian law: Their psycho-sociological causes and prevention*. Presented at "Curbing Human Rights Violations by Non-State Armed Groups," a conference organized by the Armed Groups Project, Centre of International Relations/Liu Institute for Global Issues, University of British Columbia, Vancouver, November 14–15.

Naylor, R. T. (1993). The insurgent economy: Black market operations of guerrilla organizations. *Crime, Law and Social Change, 20*(1), 13–51.

O'Ballance, E. (1995). *Civil war in Bosnia, 1992–94*. Houndmills, UK: Macmillan; New York: St. Martin's Press.

Owen, D. (1995). *Balkan odyssey*, New York: Harcourt Brace; London: Victor Gollancz.

Pool, D. (1998). "The Eritrean People's Liberation Front." In Clapham, C. (Ed.). (1998). *African guerrillas* (pp. 19–35). Oxford: James Currey; Bloomington: Indiana University Press.

Power, S. (2001, September). Bystanders to genocide: Why the United States let the Rwandan tragedy happen. *The Atlantic Monthly*, 84–108.

Pugh, M., & Cooper, N., with Goodhand, J. (2004). *War economies in regional context: The challenges of transformation*. A Project of the International Peace Academy. Boulder, CO: Lynne Rienner.

Ross, M. (2004). How do natural resources influence civil war? Evidence from thirteen cases. *International Organization, 58*(1), 35–67.

Saideman, S. M. (1998). Is Pandora's box half empty or half full? The limited virulence of secessionism and the domestic sources of disintegration. In D. Lake & D. Rothchild (Eds.), *The international spread of ethnic conflict: Fear, diffusion, and escalation* (pp. 127–150). Princeton, NJ: Princeton University Press.

Selim, M. (1991). The survival of a non-state actor: The foreign policy of the Palestine Liberation Organization. In B. Korany & A. H. Dessouki (Eds.), *The foreign policy of Arab states: The challenge of change* (2nd ed., pp. 197–240.). Boulder, CO: Westview Press.

Silber, L., & Little, A. (1995). *Yugoslavia: Death of a nation*. London: Penguin Books.

Stedman, S. J. (1995). *Peacemaking in civil war: International mediation in Zimbabwe 1974–1980*. Boulder: Lynne Rienner.

Stedman, S. J. (1997). Spoiler problems in peace processes. *International Security, 22*(2), 5–53.

Stedman, S. J. (2002). Policy implications. In S. Stedman, D. Rothchild, & E. Cousens (Eds.), *Ending civil wars: The implementation of peace agreements* (pp. 663–672). Boulder, CO: Lynne Rienner.

Stedman, S. J. (2003). Peace processes and the challenge of violence. In J. Darby & R. M. Ginty (Eds.), *Contemporary peacemaking* (pp. 103–113). Houndmills, Basingstoke: Palgrave.

Tanner, S. (2007). Saisir la violence de masse: le nettoyage ethnique en Bosnie et l'apport d'une perspective locale et d'une approche de réseau. *Déviance & Société, 31*(3), 235–256.

Tilly, C. (Ed.). (1975). *The formation of national states in Western Europe*. Princeton, NJ: Princeton University Press.

Tilly, C. (1985). War making and state making as organized crime. In P. Evans, D. Rueschemeyer, & T. Skocpol (Eds.), *Bringing the state back in* (pp. 170–187). Cambridge: Cambridge University Press.

Tilly, C. (2007). *Coercion, capital and European states: AD 990–1992*. New York: Wiley.

Touval, S. (2002). *Mediation in the Yugoslav wars: The critical years 1990–95*. London: Palgrave-Macmillan.

Walter, B. (1997). The critical barrier to civil war settlement. *International Organization, 51*(3), pp. 335–364.

Weschler, L. 19 (1997, August 18). Letter from the Republika Srpska: High noon at Twin Peaks. *The New Yorker*.

Wickham-Crowley, T. (1991). *Exploring revolution: Essays on Latin American insurgency and revolutionary theory*. New York: M. E. Sharpe.

Wriggins, H. (1995). Negotiating in Sri Lanka. In I. W. Zartman (Ed.), *Elusive peace: Negotiating an end to civil wars* (pp. 35–58). Washington, DC: Brookings Institution Press.

Zahar, M.-J. (2000). *Fanatics, brigands, mercenaries and politicians: Militia decision-making and civil conflict resolution*. Doctoral dissertation, McGill University.

Zahar, M.-J. (2001). Protégés, clients, cannon fodder: Civilians in the calculus of militias. *International Peacekeeping, 7*(4), 107–128.

Zahar, M.-J. (2003). Reframing the spoiler debate in the peace process. In J. Darby & R. M. Ginty (Eds.), *Contemporary peacemaking* (pp. 114–124). London: Palgrave.

Zahar, M.-J. (2004). Republika Srspka. In T. Bahcheli, B. Bartmann, & H. Srebrnik (Eds.), *De facto states: The quest for sovereignty* (pp. 32–51). London: Routledge.

Zahar, M.-J. (2005). Political violence in peace processes: Voice, exit and loyalty in the post-accord period. In J. Darby (Ed.), *Violence and reconstruction* (pp. 33–51). South Bend, IL: Notre Dame University Press.

Zahar, M.-J. (2006). Understanding the violence of insiders: Loyalty, custodians of peace, and the sustainability of conflict settlement. In E. Newman & O. Richmond (Eds.), *Challenges to peacebuilding: Managing spoilers during conflict resolution* (pp. 40–58). Tokyo: United Nations University Press.

Zahar, M.-J. (2009). Fieldwork, objectivity and the academic enterprise. In C. L. Sriram, J. C. King, J. A. Mertus, O. Martin-Ortega and J. Herman. (Eds.), *Surviving field research: Working in violent and difficult situations* (pp. 191–212). London: Routledge.

Zartman, I. W. (1989). *Ripe for resolution: Conflict and intervention in Africa.* New York: Oxford University Press.

Zartman, I. W. (Ed.). (1995). *Elusive peace: Negotiating an end to civil wars.* Washington, DC: Brookings Institution Press.

Zartman, I. W. (2005). *Cowardly lions: Missed opportunities to prevent deadly conflict and state collapse.* Boulder, CO: Lynne Rienner.

Zartman, I. W., & Faure, G. O. (Eds.). (2005). *Escalation and negotiation in international conflicts.* Cambridge: Cambridge University Press.

PART THREE

Intervention Dynamics
The Mediator

10 Mediation and Identity Conflicts[1]

■ JOSHUA LERNER SMILOVITZ[2]

Identity is a concept that is both malleable and permanent. It is determined by context and can change over time. As a socially and personally constructed concept, identity can instigate, cause, and contribute to many internal conflicts. Identity conflicts are by nature both intangible and tangible. They usually involve land connected with a combination of specific historical, religious, or ethnic characteristics, but they also involve abstract values, dislikes, rivalries, and demoneries. Parties to identity conflicts usually need help to overcome their contestations and enmities. The purpose of this chapter is to develop a conceptual analysis that lays out the steps necessary to effectively mediate internal identity conflicts. It is important to understand how to help the parties cut through the fog of fears and threats in order to be able to construct a satisfactory abatement of their conflict. *Mediation* is a rather formal term, but it will be used here, for economy of language, to refer to any type of third-party intervention or involvement in an identity-based conflict to reduce its intensity and inhibit its escalation. To this end, three prevailing areas are of interest: the mediation process, the context of the dispute, and the tangible and intangible characteristics of the disputants and the greater conflict. As expected, the process of mediating internal identity conflicts involves a wide range of actors and issues.

▓ THEORIES OF MEDIATION

To grasp the unique characteristics of mediating identity conflicts, certain theoretical lenses can be applied. The rationalist, contingency, structuralist, and social-psychological approaches are discussed. These theories dominate the debate concerning the study of international mediation.

As a way of investigating a decision-making process involving two or more actors, when a payoff is dependent on each actor's actions, theoretical models allow for the study of mediation to incorporate expectations and beliefs about what a particular actor will do in the future. Of these, *rational choice* models provide constructive knowledge about the contours of conflict and efficiency (Nicholson, 1991), as well as a common assumption of rationality (Crawford, 2000). When studying war, Fearon (1995, p. 379) argues "that even rational leaders who consider the risks and costs of war may end up fighting nonetheless." This leads to the observation that the inseparability of the issues being negotiated "can provide a coherent rationalist explanation for war" (Fearon, 1995, p. 390). Contextual rationality puts forward the understanding that motivations have a communal character because they represent a familiar point of reference for a community's values (Lloyd Jones, 2000). While rational choice models provide unique insight into the motivations and actions of actors within a given mediation effort, by largely focusing on individual actions they can miss the potential role of the greater community and are restricted to the exceptional characteristics of a particular conflict.

If mediation has many context- and process-related factors that occur within a distinct circumstance, then it must follow a particular process. This understanding of mediation is the *contingency* approach since it accounts for numerous input variables, explains how a mediator is viewed as an active participant in the mediation process, and relates how the nature of the dispute influences strategy. Additionally, in a contingency approach, mediators strive to recognize and analyze the various dispute-related difficulties and alter their behavior correspondingly (Carnevale, Lim, & McLaughlin 1989). Though extremely valid to the study of mediation within a particular internal identity conflict, the contingency approach does not clarify what particular actions, features, or standards are exclusively necessary for the mediation of internal identity conflicts.

Where the contingency approach leaves off, the *structuralist* perspective provides useful insight. This approach posits mediation as caused by objective factors (Celik & Rumelili, 2006; Crocker, Hampson, & Aall, 2002). Consequently, the issues under consideration can be effectively resolved. The structuralist paradigm posits a direct and significant importance to such issues as ripeness and the mutually hurting stalemate (Touval & Zartman 1985; Zartman, 2000, 2003), as well as symmetry (Cunningham, this volume; Zartman & Rubin, 2003) and other contextual features of conflict. By relying on the importance of timing, this approach accounts for the fact that the parties being mediated must be ready to be mediated. In internal identity conflicts this is usually not so. This type of conflict rarely reaches ripeness or a mutually hurting stalemate, so a potential mediator can be disinclined to intervene. Structuralism also accounts for the degree of side payments a mediator can proffer, whether or not certain "carrots and sticks" are applied by the mediator or other outside actors, as well as how the potential prerequisites for progress influence the mediation effort. The structuralist approach identifies the tangible features to mediation, but minimizes the intangible aspects to identity conflict and the communication processes exhibited within a mediation effort.

In juxtaposition to the structuralist approach, the *social-psychological* point of view presents the causes of the conflict as subjective (Celik & Rumelili, 2006). Since *identity* is a concept that by necessity excludes some people and includes others, it is at the apex of personal and individual relations and communications. Through the development of "a forum to explore options and develop solutions, often outside the highly charged arena of a formal negotiating structure" (Crocker et al., 2002, p. 234), the social-psychological approach hopes to alter the disputants' outlook. By relying on changing the perspectives and viewpoints of the disputants by creating an opportunity for dialogue and discussion, mediation can succeed in "identifying the underlying needs" (ibid.) of the parties and, in so doing, has the potential to alter their opinions. By acknowledging the possibility that mediators can work to create "new norms" (Bush & Folger, 1994), there is the potential to generate new identities. Which actors can be involved in this process, as well as when and why this transformation occurs, are the critical questions that must be tackled. This involves addressing a host of constituency-related issues concerning individual attitudes, collective action, and elite leadership. The social-psychological approach hopes to transform identity from a cause of conflict to a catalyst for resolution.

The rationalist, contingency, structuralist, and social-psychological approaches all offer different ways of viewing international mediation. None of these theories alone provides a full explanation for the requirements of mediating internal identity-based conflicts. While all of these approaches provide useful insights, none of them efficiently explains the requirements and necessities for an effective approach to this type of mediation effort. Rational choice models offer useful information regarding the structure of the conflict and the actions of actors. But, by focusing on individual actions, they can overlook the bigger role of identity relations between the in-group and the out-group, as well as the intermixing of tangible and intangible components. Perhaps the social-psychological model comes closest by preparing the mediator for the necessity of altering the perspectives of the parties, yet it does not prime the mediator for how best to deal with the wide range of process- and context-related variables at play in the conflict, aside from those related to perception, understanding, and feeling. While the structuralist approach demonstrates how important the objective aspects to the conflict are, it does not deal with the underlying identity of the disputants, which work to form and shape particular perspectives. The contingency approach tries to match "the type of third party intervention to certain characteristics of the conflict in question" (Keashly & Fisher, 1996, p. 239). However, it does not provide an apparent and universal framework for how best to engage and mitigate the particular issues surrounding identity conflict since mediation is understood as a distinctive process in each individual circumstance. While all of these theories provide useful insights to the mediation of internal identity-based conflicts, none of them efficiently explains the requirements and necessities for an effective approach to this type of mediation effort.

▪ IDENTIFYING IDENTITY

Now that we have discussed some of the dominant strains of thought regarding the way to approach third-party efforts to reduce conflict, the concept of identity must be examined. Identity is constructed from three primary elements: existential, psychological, and cultural (Rothman, 1997). The existential occurs under conditions of life and death, while the psychological is concerned with emotional or rational issues. *Culture* is particularly important, but it is difficult to study since it is considered a "fuzzy" term that is problematic to evaluate (Bercovitch & Elgstrom, 2001; Faure & Rubin, 1993). Without a doubt, cultural, existential, and psychological factors are critical to any identity conflict.

Identity is a term of reference that has many different meanings, connotations, and explanations. The theory of *constructivism* in political science assumes that identity is a collectively created idea. Simply put, this means that people have multiple identities based on how they view themselves in comparison to others and on where they are situated within society. The result is that identity achieves three clear purposes for an individual. It informs the individual who he or she is, it informs others who the individual is, and it informs the individual who other people are (Hopf, 1998). By explaining who a person is or who a group of people are, identity necessitates a series of concerns or partialities as related to a preferred course of action and/or with specific regard to certain individuals. How durable or fluid a particular identity is can influence its ability to be used as a mobilizing or catalyzing factor within a population (Druckman, 2001). Furthermore, because identity is constructed from social systems, interests must be consistent with the customs, traditions, and structure of the identity (Hopf, 1998).

In understanding the distinction between different identity associations, three categories are useful: the personal self, the relational self, and the collective self (Brewer & Gardner, 1996). These representations of the individual provide a format for understanding the relevance of identity. For instance, the *personal self* is the distinguishing of the individual concept of the self, while the *relational self* is developed from human dealings centered on associations and roles with others. The *collective self* is social identity, which arguably plays the most notable and prominent role in the mediation of identity conflicts. Since identities "are sets of meanings that an actor attributes to itself while taking the perspective of others" (Wendt, 1994, p. 385), social identity inevitably has internal and external components that work with and against one another, both simultaneously and conjunctively. This means that every modern individual has multiple identities. Arguably, the more cosmopolitan and connected an individual is to the modern world, the more likely that individual will have numerous identities. In contrast, the more traditional an individual, the more likely that individual will have fewer identities, most likely making his or her existing smaller range of identities stronger and more powerful. Quite possibly, if an individual or group of individuals have a predominant recognition factor, instead of many factors, that dominating identity characteristic is more salient. Consequently, for individuals in traditional or modern societies, there can be a corresponding variance in the importance and relevance of their identity to the mediation effort.

Identity has multiple social and individual structures working together or at cross-purposes. Identity is a "cognitive schema" that permits individuals to know who they are within a particular situation, as well as their position "in a social role structure of shared understandings and expectations" (Wendt, 1994, p. 385). For an individual, social relationships are built around common identities and bonds (Brewer & Gardner 1996). According to the model offered by Caporael and Brewer (1995), four societal configurations are apparent: dyads (a 2-person group), teams (3–7 people within a family or working group), demes (a community of roughly 30–50 people who engage in face-to-face interactions), and tribes (a large grouping of demes with shared identity and "informational interdependence without continual face-to-face interaction" [p. 33]). All of these forms of identity intersect and build upon one another to form certain groupings within society that act to distinguish one person from another.

One result of identity in general, heightened in ethnic and religious identity, can be in-group and out-group distinction. In-group preference does not automatically correlate with enmity directed at an out-group (Allport, 1954). However, the demonstration of in-group preference within an internal conflict is not an exceptional occurrence. Internal conflict, understood as conflict that occurs within the borders of a nation-state, usually pits the state and its supporters against a grouping of people that are in one way, shape, or form challenging the authority, security, or hegemony of the state. On the other hand, in-group preference could also manifest itself between two groupings within the state, allowing the state to act as a potential mediator. At the nation-state level, the in-group and out-group distinction is a major identity factor. In-groups act as indicators for an individual performing self-evaluation and at the interpersonal level for the "selection of significant others" (Brewer & Gardner, 1996, p. 85). Resulting from this interpretation, members of an in-group are more likely to be liked than individuals from an out-group when no knowledge is present about the individual characteristics of a person. In identity conflicts, the push to differentiate between them and us is paramount since identity is built around certain defining parameters that make you you and me me. In order to transform this sharp them-versus-us conflict into something positive, the mediator must be perceived positively.

By no means is it easy to resolve conflicts occurring within a state that are focused on issues of religious identity. When of a forceful and select nature, religious identification can produce dramatic cleavages within society. Through certain symbols, actions, buildings, or actors, religion is a prominent form of identification that is often observable and recognizable. Given that people with intense religious beliefs are predisposed to suppose that their religion is preferential to another person's religion, this is an intrinsic obstacle that must be overcome for effective mediation of religious conflicts. In many religious interpretations there are "depictions of divine wars in which Good battles Evil" (Treverton, Gregg, Gibran, & Yost, 2005, p. 4). This notion of cosmic war works to "explain why things are as they are . . . [and] provides the foundation for doing something" (ibid.). In essence, "cosmic war" works to relate individual issues to and within an expansive community.

While religion can influence conflict, few conflicts are of a strictly religious nature. In Northern Ireland, Protestants and Catholics, both of the Christian persuasion, were fighting for political control and incorporation within a particular nation, Great Britain or Ireland. In the Punjab, India battled Sikhs who sought political separation through religious fanaticism. If religion is such a salient identity factor and if it impacts conflict within a broader society, when does religion become the root of conflict? The answer can be simply put: always and never. While there is no conflict of a strictly religious nature, there are also very few conflicts devoid of a religious dimension or influence (Arnson & Zartman, 2005; Gopin, 2001).

Ethnic conflicts are a bit different from religious conflicts since they are related to "a sense of collective and separate identity, common ancestry, a shared culture and history, and an attachment to a specific piece of territory"

(Bercovitch & Derouen, 2004, p. 148). A range of factors contribute to ethnicity, including the following:

> The group must have a name for itself . . . the people in the group must believe in a common ancestry . . . the members of the group must share historical memories . . . the group must have a shared culture . . . the group must feel an attachment to a specific piece of territory . . . [and] the people in the group have to think of themselves as a group in order to constitute an ethnic community. (Brown, 1993, pp. 4–5)

Since ethnicity is "about myths and beliefs in common origins" (Welsh, 1993, p. 29), it is difficult to mediate between ethnic rivalries and divisions if such beliefs turn conflictual.

Ethnic conflicts are likely to arise when a certain ethnic group views the structure of government as being unable to represent their requirements (Bercovitch & Derouen, 2004). Miall (in Rothman and Olson, 2001) defined ethnic conflicts as associated with the rights, recognition, and status of ethnic groups. The result is that ethnic conflicts are related to a "perceived need deprivation" or discrimination (Arnson & Zartman, 2005; Bercovitch & Derouen, 2004, p. 148). Mediation can be a medium for altering access to rights associated with an ethnic identity and provide for recognition and status by changing the perspectives of the disputants toward the governing body and/or the ethnic group that threatens a particular governing structure.

To alter ethnic or religious conflict, dialogue is a critical tool. Dialogue can change an individual's point of view by altering the distinction between in-group and out-group. The distinct possibility that an affirmative in-group appraisal will lead to viewing the out-group negatively must be overcome. To put it another way, there is an inherent preference toward someone or something that is identified as being similar to a person, and there is a simultaneous prejudice against someone or something that is viewed as different. This in-group preference and out-group bias is an important factor for a mediator to identify and engage. Since "[i]mprovements for the in-group do not necessarily translate into better relations between groups" (Leach & Williams, 1999, p. 891), a mediator must recognize how in-group and out-group distinctions factor into the decision-making and negotiating processes of the relevant parties. In-group and out-group attitudes can also be attenuated by cooperative structures, common projects, and exchanges of contacts and information, since distinctions thrive on separation.

■ WHO, HOW, AND WHEN

This brings us to the question of who can actually navigate the mediation effort. The range of possible mediators for internal identity conflicts is immense and diverse. Mediators can be states, official institutions/organizations, nongovernment organizations (NGOs), or individuals (Bercovitch & Schneider, 2000). The choice of a mediator in internal identity conflicts is affected by the mediator's identity in relation to the conflict. In the framework of Wehr and Lederach (1991), mediators can fall within distinct categories: insider-partial, insider-neutral, outsider-neutral, outsider-partial, and external, among other variants.

For identity-based conflicts, it would seem that outsider or external mediators would be more likely to foster resolution since, by definition (unless there is religious, ethnic, ideological, or some other form of identity overlap), they do not figure in the identity conflict of the disputants. Nevertheless, an insider mediator who demonstrates partiality or nonneutrality toward one of the parties or shares identity with one of them—such as Cardinal Obando y Bravo in Nicaragua, the Vatican in the Beagle Channel Dispute, Roger Cardinal Etchegaray in the Mozambique mediation by Sant'Egidio, or U.S. Secretary of State Henry Kissinger in the Middle East dispute—can be a valuable mediator in identity-related conflicts if his actions are credible and he delivers the party to which he is partial (Touval & Zartman, 2007; Wehr & Lederach, 1991). Diasporas complicate the picture further, as Hampson explains in his chapter, since they can pressure governments, thereby influencing policy decisions that can result in limiting the number of potential mediators.

Mediator neutrality, partiality, and bias are significant in determining how a mediator is perceived by the disputants. For disputants in identity conflicts, the choice of whether to opt for an openly neutral or nonneutral mediator is of immense consequence to how conflicting parties strategize, undertake, and perceive the mediation effort. Neutrality is not equated with fairness, so both neutral and nonneutral mediators can benefit the disputants by providing in-process guidance about what matters to the mediation effort and what is probable, both from a structural and a process perspective.

Partiality "describes a condition internal to the mediator" (Cobb & Rifkin, 1991, p. 43). This "condition" is not automatically destructive because mediators must "allow themselves some latitude in their degree of partiality . . . to express their preference" (Touval & Zartman, 2001, pp. 433–434). For disputants, the decisive factor should be the mediator's ability to "provide an acceptable outcome," not his/her level of impartiality. Bias is consequential to both mediator neutrality and partiality because it functions concurrently on both content (the behavior of the mediator) and source dimensions (the mediator's relationship with the disputants; Carnevale & Arad, 1996, p. 45). As Cunningham showed in his chapter, in civil war conflicts a mediator biased toward the government will tend not to favor rebels' integration into the military, while a mediator biased toward the rebels will favor integration. No matter how neutrality, partiality, or bias is perceived by the disputant, without a doubt the mediator's behavior will be viewed through the prism of disputant identity. And, since "no third party is an altruist" (Salacuse, 2004, p. 258), to one degree or another, no matter when the mediator intervenes, he/she will have certain opinions and beliefs that will influence the mediation effort.

With particular reference to identity, how can mediator acceptability be understood? One example is what occurred in Burundi in the 1990s. In 1996, when the ruling Hutu government was overthrown by Tutsi Army Major Pierre Buyoya, the Organization of African Unity (OAU), the UN, and regional leaders allowed former Tanzanian President Mwalimu Nyerere to be their principal mediator. However, Buyoya viewed Nyerere as anti-Tutsi. Though sanctions were imposed directly after the coup, which definitely hurt the Buyoya-led government, and although the situation was arguably ripe for mediation, the imposition of a mediator who was perceived as being in opposition to the identity of Buyoya dramatically harmed the mediation effort. The lesson to be learned from this example is that while the conflict might seem to be ready for mediation, the imposition of a mediator who is viewed as being hostile to the identity of one party can hinder the mediation effort. This shows the crucial significance of mediator identity within the mediation process.

Alongside the question of who is mediating a particular conflict is the matter of when that mediator is called upon, the particular context of the conflict, and the disputants' perception of the mediator. There is much debate over how and at what time the mediator should spring into action. Maundi, Zartman, Khadiagala & Nuamah. (2005) identify 16 key lessons for understanding the mediator's entry into a conflict, including the creation of order, self-interest, and other interests. Prior to entry into a conflict, certain variables act to identify the mediator, such as leverage and status (Kleiboer, 1996), as well as power and ideology (Bercovitch & Schneider, 2000). Hence, the strategies and tactics a mediator chooses when engaging the parties are particularly relevant to how those parties view the mediator and the resolution of the conflict. Whether the mediator approaches the conflict with a conflict resolution or a conflict management mindset is an important distinction. Additionally, how the mediator acts toward the parties is relevant to how those parties perceive the mediator and a potential settlement.

Given that mediation is a consent-oriented activity, when should a mediator intervene in a conflict? A conflict is described as ripe for mediation when a mutually hurting stalemate exists (Zartman, 2006). This means that the conflict has become "a situation uncomfortable to both sides that appears to become very costly" (Touval & Zartman, 1985, p. 16). But the mediators' job does not wait for ripeness to fall into their laps; the primary challenge to mediators is to ripen, to make sure that the parties realize that their unilateral efforts to prevail are stalemated, that the stalemate is painful to them, and that the other party is willing and able to join them in seeking a joint solution to the problem. This preliminary effort, before any direct mediation toward an agreement, requires major persistence and repeated efforts on the part of the mediator (Zartman & de Soto, 2010). This is a major challenge, more daunting than the ripening process in interstate conflicts. Then repressed or rebel movements are usually fighting an existential conflict, buoyed by deep commitment to ethnic, religious, or ideological visions, and can wait a long time to achieve their goals. The state is also animated by deep fears, justified or not; if the repressed group's rebellion is doing well, the fears seem justified, and if they are not, the repression is costless. Neither side wants to hear that it is in a stalemate or that the pain it feels as a result is anything but further justification of its efforts. Ripening is a long process.

If mediation is understood as ranging from ripening to resolving, how are mediators likely to engage in identity conflicts? What strategies are they more inclined to adopt (Bercovitch & Gartner, 2006)? Communication-facilitative strategies are needed from the beginning to ripen relations in internal identity conflicts where the parties are unable to even talk or sit together at the same table. This strategy can help reach agreements when it is "psychologically or procedurally impossible" (Touval & Zartman, 1985, p. 12) for a party to concede directly to another party. The potential benefit of this strategy should not be underestimated. Methods used include conveying messages or communications from one party to another, sustaining compromises, and establishing the initial contacts between the parties.

Communication-facilitative strategies occupy a needed role. They allow for the understanding that the flow of information between parties does little to exercise prescribed control over the development and substance of the mediation effort. This strategy can be advantageous when parties have limited understanding of one another based upon lack of communication. If mediators are merely go-betweens, then the resolution of an identity conflict is not likely to occur. To resolve identity conflicts, perception and understanding of the other party must be altered.

In identity conflicts, the ARIA (antagonism, resonance, invention, and action) approach offered by Rothman (1997) is applicable. This approach blends the social-psychological (attitudinal) with the structural. In the first stage, it allows disputants to let their anger surface so they can study and examine it. Next, disputants express their particular beliefs based on common characteristics, which then leads the parties to jointly formulate innovative answers to move toward a resolution. Finally, disputants take certain actions that will actually achieve the resolution. The ARIA approach provides a detailed process containing an inherent strategic approach to combating identity conflicts that is centered on creating analytical sympathy with the other disputants.

Mediators can use individual contacts before proceeding to joint brainstorming to construct creative ideas, offer new interpretations, and provide imaginative ways to move the mediation process forward (Fisher & Shapiro, 2005). To effectively change the perspectives of the parties, mediators may need to employ directive-oriented strategies to shape the subject matter and issues related to the mediation process (Gartner & Bercovitch, 2006; Rothman, 1997). A mediator may be required to develop rules of fairness concerning the condition and process of the mediation effort. A mediator will "determine such factors as the mediation environment, the number and type of meetings with the adversaries, the agendas covered in those meetings, the control of constituency influences, and the distribution of information and resources to the parties" (Gartner & Bercovitch, 2006, p. 832). The Mitchell Principles gave a strict form to the Northern Ireland discussions in 1998, but before the parties got to such a formal process, a loose set of contacts was required to prepare for these procedural rules (Clancy, 2010; Irwin, 2002). Finnish President Martti Ahtisaari, mediating the Aceh conflict in 2005, established the procedural rule that "nothing is agreed until everything is agreed." The 1991 peace accord in South Africa was an elaborate code of conduct for interracial relations parallel to the formal negotiations to end the long-standing identity conflict (Anstey, 1993).

Formulator-oriented strategies relying on a mediator to use "[s]ympathetic, accurate, straightforward prodding and suggestion" (Touval & Zartman, 1985, p. 12) are inclined to alter the viewpoints of the parties toward the conflict and, hopefully, toward one another (Capelos & Smilovitz, 2008). This approach can be used in either a passive or active way in the hope of fundamentally changing the perception, though not the nature, of the conflict. Since formulator strategies are focused on the identification of issues and the suggestion of particular responses, their value might be limited in internal identity conflicts where the recipe for agreement is not entirely centered on the tangible aspects of the conflict.

In general, identity conflict is only partly a resource conflict allowing the stakes to be divided and allocated. Allocation is bound to be important; hence, compensation and construction are required to keep the process from being zero-sum. Zero-sum situations are the essence of fear; mediation is needed to open the sums of the outcome. The strategies that a mediator applies within the mediation process are definitely influenced by the context of the dispute. Since tangible issues, such as land, resources, and various forms of wealth, can be divided, even if not easily, whereas identity-related issues such as values, needs, and beliefs cannot, a mediator must be able to differentiate between the underlying issues at stake so as to know whether or not identity is a key aspect of the conflict. The result is that manipulator strategies, where leverage in the form of carrots and sticks principally related to tangible elements is used, should not be the mediator's primary strategy. Browbeating or offering to provide certain (dis)incentives would seem to work more effectively in a tangible conflict than in an intangible one.

The mediator, as a third party intervening in an existing conflict, is uniquely situated to alter the perspectives of the disputants. This can include how the disputants perceive each other, how the disputants perceive the conflict, what conflict-related factors the disputants consider relevant to their identity, and how disputant identity is recognized as contributing to the continuation of the conflict. Whether the mediator is seeking to alter viewpoints or reach strategic-oriented goals is important. Identity, as related to a person, is dependent on perception. Conflict, as an ongoing relationship of sorts, whether violent, semiviolent, or nonviolent in manner, can be altered through the creation of new sensitivities about the reality that constructs the conflict environment. Identity is created through historical connections and interactions; thus, new interactions and histories can be created through the mediation process.

■ TANGIBLE AND INTANGIBLE CONTEXTS

In any mediation effort there are three contextual factors: preexisting, concurrent, and background (Bercovitch & Houston, 1996). The *preexisting* context is related to the conflict's specific circumstance, as well as the particular internal and external characteristics of the parties. This context also includes the issues under mediation and the potency of the conflict. For the *concurrent* context, the mediator's rank, identity, and relationship with the disputant, the environment where the mediation occurs, and the instigation and phasing of the mediation are recognized as the salient features. Lastly, the *background* context includes previous mediation attempts and their direction, outcome, and efficacy, plus the mediator's prior experience with mediation. For identity, the preexisting context is dominant since it works to define the specific contours of the conflict and the unique identity aspects of the disputants. How the mediator proceeds to interact with the parties will have consequences for the concurrent contextual elements. In view of the fact that identity conflicts are of a somewhat intractable nature, involving an intangible issue, most likely there will have been some form(s) of official, unofficial, formal, or informal mediation attempt.

Prior to, during, and after any mediation effort, there is always a mix of tangible and intangible factors in play. For the mediation of identity conflicts, this is particularly true. Many mediators will misidentify the primary issues at stake as principally involving only the tangible sphere. Tangible issues are "concrete elements" (Zubek, Pruitt, Mcgillicuddy, & Syna, 1992, p. 550), while intangible issues concern the "nonsubstantive" (ibid.) as well as "face, reputation, status, and appearance of strength" (Weiss-Wik, 1983, p. 719). To further clarify this distinction, Vasquez (1983, p. 181) identifies tangible issues as those that can be "photographable," while intangible issues are those that "cannot be seen directly." Since an issue "define[s] the subject of the conflict" (Diehl, 1992, p. 334), addressing identity is critical to the mediation effort. However, identity cannot be engaged by a mediator in a fashion similar to that of conflicts that are strictly focused on tangible elements. There is a reason that certain internal conflicts have been mediated unsuccessfully for a prolonged period (e.g., Cyprus, Israel–Palestine, Kosovo, Nagorno-Karabakh, Transniestra, Lebanon, Sudan, and the former Yugoslavia). Throughout the conflict resolution literature, the argument has been posited that tangible issues "are more amenable to successful conflict management than intangible issues involving beliefs, principles, ideologies, legitimacy and images" (Bercovitch & Jackson, 2001, p. 69). The significance of this revelation for the mediation of internal identity-related conflicts cannot be understated or underestimated.[3]

Territory can be distinguished by its intrinsic value, which means that it is "recognized as valuable regardless of whose perspective is considered," or by its relational value, which means that territory has "different degrees of significance for different states" (Goertz & Diehl, 1992, p. 14). When relational territory issues are at stake, a situation referred to as *territoriality*, a key defining aspect is that their relevance "does not have to be the same for each side" (Diehl, 1992, p. 338; Vasquez, 1995). So, territorial issues can be laden with intangible aspects that cannot be easily quantified, given up, or separated from identity.

While the disputants' identity might consist of multiple levels of association and recognition of the self, there is no way that a mediator can divide the individual disputants from their personal perception of their identity. A similar situation is in play at the societal level, where religious and ethnic identities create a certain group cohesion that is reflected in a joint identity, such as Christian, Muslim, Jewish, or Irish, British, Armenian, Azeri, and so on. As a predominant, intangible element that all humans have to one degree or another, with one level of intensity or another, identity is always a relevant feature in mediation. However, whether the conflict is *centered* on identity or not is the crucial question. If a conflict, such as the Nagorno–Karabakh dispute, is viewed as merely involving land, this simplifies the dispute and minimizes its historical identity-related aspects. The implications of identity are readily displayed in the name of the area. *Nagorno* is a Russian word meaning "mountainous," while *Karabakh* has a Persian and Turkish heredity meaning "black garden." Ethnic Armenians, who are largely Christian, are competing for control with ethnic Azeris, who are principally Muslim. Though both ethnic-religious groupings seek control over a particular piece of land, this dispute is also centered on the intangible aspect of identity rather than just on tangible control over a specific piece of land. The land is a vehicle through which the identity conflict manifests itself.

As demonstrated in the Nagorno–Karabakh dispute, a mediator must be able to recognize the source(s) of an identity-related conflict. The implication is that a mediator needs exceptional analytical skills. A mediator might perceive the conflict to be based on tangible elements when in actuality the intangible element, identity, is the main factor. It is essential for a mediator not to misidentify an identity conflict as a resource one. This is much more easily said than done since many conflicts have multiple elements and actors in play at any one point in time. It is necessary for the mediator to understand the fundamental roots of the conflict, as well as the qualities and needs of the disputants.

The traditional methods of mediation, such as a focus on tangible resources, are not sufficient in identity-related conflicts within a nation-state (Rothman, 1997). As Pfetsch in his chapter demonstrates, mediation is more commonly used in international conflicts involving tangible issues rather than identity issues. What is effective is to have the parties relate creatively to one another, thus transforming the conflict from one where a disputant is solely focused on *its* concerns, needs, and desires to one where the disputant focuses on *our* concerns, needs, and desires. This shift in perception is critical. Without it, there is little chance of a settlement surviving the work of the inevitable spoilers. The Northern Ireland case aptly demonstrates this point. A power-sharing government, after many years (over a decade) of fits and starts, has finally shown some progress. Over time, the rigid distinction between Protestant defeat and Catholic victory, and vice versa, has been transformed into a mutual desire to create a government that reflects the religious and ethnic diversity of Northern Ireland's population and accounts for the various needs of the parties and people. One may ask, how has this change occurred? One possible answer is that the passage of time has healed wounds and changed perspectives. Another is that a new perception of the conflict situation has been induced in which violence has been shown to be incapable of achieving its goals and cooperation has been seen to be possible and jointly productive. Mediator-assisted changes in attitudes permitted mediator-assisted changes in structure, which allowed further attitudinal changes, ever so gradually.

In any mediation effort, a range of tangible and intangible issues will be at stake. For identity conflicts, the tangible is arguably subordinate to the intangible. However, this does not mean that one set of issues can be negated at the expense of the other. When engaging these various issues there are two possible venues, the substantive and the procedural. In a substantive stance, tangible issues such as land or resources can be divided and parceled out between the disputants. But certain tangible issues, like territory, can take on intangible features, such as when land becomes sacred to a particular ethnic or religious group (Norlen, 2003). When this happens, it is necessary for the mediator to engage the disputants procedurally so as to transform their perspective on the land. This is no easy task.

■ A CONCEPTUAL PROCESS FOR MEDIATING INTERNAL IDENTITY CONFLICTS

Identity conflict needs to be approached by mediators differently than other types of conflict. In this section, a generic step-by-step process is offered that identifies different ways of approaching and understanding how best to mediate internal identity conflicts. By no means conclusive, this process should be extended and amended by future scholars and practitioners.

The first step to be addressed is *discovering an acceptable mediator*. In some ways, this is decided by the disputants through their consent to be mediated; in other ways, it is determined by the context of the dispute and by what third party is available or willing to mediate. Whether an impartial, neutral, or biased mediator is preferable depends on many factors. Whatever the case may be, the determination of who mediates should be party contingent. When identity is at issue, it is necessary for both parties to feel a degree of satisfaction with the mediator, whether from an identity, security, monetary or other perspective.

When the mediation is in the ripening phase, multiple mediators are likely and helpful. When actual three-party talks begin, however, a single mediator is necessary; multiple mediators are an invitation to outbidding by the conflicting parties and consequent failure of the intervention. Anytime there are multiple mediators, notably in the first phase, coordination and a single leader are imperative. Identifying who can be an effective mediator from the perspective of both parties and engaging the participation of that individual is a difficult but necessary initial step. In Northern Ireland in the late 1990s this was George Mitchell, a perfect blend of status, experience, and a desire to mediate, who was viewed by the concerned parties as an acceptable mediator. Mitchell was acceptable for two specific reasons: his provenance as a United States senator and his personal characteristics. Further research is needed to determine some general guidelines for who is an acceptable mediator in an identity conflict. It would help disputants to have an existing set of rules and features with which to review a mediator, instead of just going by instinct or hoping for the luck of the draw. The difficulty is identifying a framework for selecting a mediator that would lead to continued success.

The second step is *recognizing the problem*. This involves the mediator's assessing and analyzing what the actual concerns of the parties are and how they are interconnected to both tangible and intangible issues. Without this basic recognition of what is at stake, both from a tangible, intangible and mutually tangible and intangible perspective, the mediator will almost certainly overlook important factors. Identity-related territory cannot be dealt with in a compensatory manner, while resources can. Beyond this aspect, mediators must also examine intragroup as well as intergroup factors (Rothman, this volume). The substantive distinction between tangible and intangible, as well as the one between intragroup and intergroup factors, will help lay the groundwork for how the mediator actually engages the parties in the process of mediation.

The third step is *ripening the conflict*. The mediator(s) and, indeed, as much of the international community as possible must make sure that the parties are ready to join in a search for a shared solution to their conflict. This sense comes from a realization that they are both stalemated in their efforts to reach a unilateral solution and that the stalemate is painful to them, their supporters, their efforts, and their goals. Trying to engage in three-party talks is pointless unless the sense of a mutually hurting stalemate is present; if it is not, would-be mediators must focus their efforts on making it so. This involves changes in the parties' perception of their situation—the subjective factor—but it may also go so far as to involve changing the objective situation. In the end, it is the subjective perception that matters, and the mediator's primary method is persuasion.

The fourth step is *identifying the appropriate actors*. After recognizing the range of substantive factors that have influenced the conflict, the mediator must decide whom to engage and how to actually engage the parties. The crucial questions at this stage are: Whom does the mediator feel can constructively speak for each party? Will and should every party be represented? How and how much does a mediator influence who is going to represent a specific side? Within a particular side, is mediation attempted with the whole range of actors representing that side or just some of them? Perhaps utilizing informal actors who have close connections to decision makers would be best to begin with, as demonstrated during the Oslo peace process between the Israelis and Palestinians. However, at some point, in some way, engaging the top-level decision makers is necessary, as was done in the aftermath of the ethnic violence following the December 2007 Kenyan presidential election. Should the mediator encourage all relevant actors to participate or only those deemed able to bring about an agreement, isolating potential spoilers? These and other critical questions related to who actually takes part in the mediation process must be addressed in detail.

Mediators are often able to bring groups (or subgroups) into the process that can reinforce moderates and provide constructive partners (Anstey and Zartman: this volume). It is not necessary for one side to accept the other side, for the other side to have legitimacy and relevance and be the right match for the mediation effort (Cristal: this volume). Whatever the case may be, the mediator needs to decide who is going to be represented at the table without actually dictating to the parties the specific representatives. Who is present is a controversial issue in many respects. As much as possible, the mediator must help to ensure that productive participants represent all sides.

The fifth step is *planning the mediation strategy*. Once the mediator has been engaged, understands the context of the conflict, and establishes the parties to the mediation process, this and the next step are intimately linked: *planning the strategy* and *choosing the tactics*. The mediator needs to determine what methods, strategies, and tactics can be used to move the conflict from a state of turmoil to a state of peace. *Strategically*, a mediator should know whether the conflict is ripe or needs ripening and whether the mediation is attempting to resolve the conflict or just to manage it (Zartman, 2007. This crucial distinction between resolution of the conflict issues and management of the means to pursue the conflict will influence the strategic efforts of the mediator.

One issue of particular relevance is the mediator's position within the mediation process. Rothman (1997, p. 152) contends that facilitators need "to work with both driving and restraining forces." This understanding posits a high degree of control and influence for the mediator. However, this is not always the case. So, when is it better for the mediator to sit back and let the parties direct the process, and when is it not? An answer to this question involves assessing the particular requirements of different mediator positions. For instance, if the parties are unable to even engage one another at the table, it is necessary for the mediator to be actively involved and assume a take-charge role or to be satisfied with shuttling between the parties involved in the talks to craft an agreement. If, on the other hand, the parties can acknowledge one another's presence, the mediator must assess when it is best to direct the effort, or to encourage dialogue to create a space for learning (Saunders, 2003), or to have limited involvement and let the parties' interaction take its natural course.

One way that a mediator can change the perspective of the disputants is to get them to focus on the future instead of the past (Zartman & Kremenyuk, 2005). Past grievances, wrongs committed, hatreds bred, myths propagated, and so on can contribute to feelings of retribution and vengeance that must be exacted (Rosoux, 2008). For a mediator to get the parties to look to the future, so as to be able to build sustainable and profitable economies for both of them, is key. Role reversal using a reflexive or integrative strategy can help the disputants focus on their mutual dilemmas and concerns (Rothman, 1997).

Another strategy for engaging the parties to a conflict is *convocation*, which is "practiced when there is a need to provide new leadership and fill the vacuum" (Zartman, 2005, p. 216). Convocation can be seen as a type of controlling mediation offered at a ripe moment; in other words, the mediator has provided "an invitation that cannot be refused at a moment when it is welcome" (ibid., p. 220). For example, the November 2007 Annapolis summit between the Israelis, Palestinians, and others, convened by the United States, roughly fits this model, although this step was never pursued by the parties or the mediator (see the next step below). With convocation and other forms of mediation where the mediator is actively involved in resolving the conflict, all types of strategies are in play.

Thus, the sixth step (concomitant with the fifth) involves *choosing the tactics*. Besides using different strategies, mediators can choose from an assortment of distinct tactics. *Tactically,* a range from creative to conventional actions (Fogg, 1985) designed to achieve a particular goal are available to a mediator. Five general categories of tactics have been identified (Posthuma, Dworkin, & Swift, 2002), although others are possible. The first is *pressure*, which corresponds to the expression of irritation by a mediator who is powerful. Next are *procedural* tactics, which focus on context and the agenda. *Friendliness* tactics have an underlying humorous disposition, while the fourth tactic, *avoiding negative emotions*, is centered on reducing antagonism and guiding the disputants away from personal attacks. Finally, *discussing alternatives* subsumes a range of substantive tactics and can include the mediator's talking about specific settlement options.

At the beginning of the mediation effort, mediators might utilize communicator-related tactics to familiarize the parties with one another's stances. Simultaneously, or even before these tactics are employed, formulator-oriented tactics can be helpful by giving the parties the opportunity, through the mediator, to invent new options for dealing with the conflict. In this initial stage, it can be helpful for the mediator to give the parties the opportunity to express their emotions and feelings about the conflict, a process otherwise known as *venting*.

Once the mediation process is underway, disputants may vent toward one another or the mediator. With venting, the possibility for catharsis is great, but so is the possibility to harm the mediation effort. A distinction in venting between a problem-solving and a conflict-resolving process should be examined in further research. Clearly, venting can be a turning point in the mediation effort, though whether this turn is for the worse or the better depends a great deal on the skill, competence, and experience of the mediator. "Venting often causes more harm than good," and if an individual vents "to the person who angered us [it] can be disastrous" (Fisher & Shapiro, 2005, p. 157). The mediator must be ready to end the venting stage and turn to a constructive search for answers to the vented injuries. A striking example occurred at the 1993 Oslo peace talks, where both parties initially spent time making it clear to each other how much they were injured and how much they believed it was the other party that was responsible. At one point someone said, "If we keep up like this, we will never reach any improvement of the situation," and the talk then turned positive. The remarkable fact is that both the Palestinian participant and the Israeli claimed that it was *he* who made the turning statement, a remarkable instance of negotiation ownership (Abbas, 1997; Savir, 1999). Since identity is an emotionally laden concept, it is important for the mediator to give the disputants the chance to express their personal and collective sentiments before or during the discussion of specific issues. However, the mediator must be careful not to let this process turn into a runaway train. It is necessary for the mediator to monitor and steer the discussion into useful emotional expression that reveals the salience and importance of a particular issue to the other side.

The mediator should not focus on a compromise at the beginning of the process. This can produce problems instead of helping to foster a solution, since the core of the conflict is related to the existential requirements of the parties; in other words, the price of cooperation might be less than the gain from nonresolution (Rothman, 1997). The mediator must address mutual grievances, perceptions about the origins of the conflict, security desires, and other nontangible identity-related factors that are not directly related to the tangible elements that probably led to the mediation of the conflict, such as resources, territory, or deaths, and let compromises and specific measures emerge from the process.

After each side has thought about the conflict in different ways, and has engaged at an emotional and a substantive level, the parties can hopefully move forward. This could involve the disputants expressing their desires and needs concerning both tangible and intangible issues. At this point, it may be helpful for the mediator to divide the conflict into manageable pieces, switch from a political solution to a technical or even a social one, induce incremental change, or implement a single-text negotiation (Fogg, 1985), among other possibilities. Most important is for the mediator to be able to convert intangible objectives into tangible goals. This is difficult, but it can be accomplished by various forms of inducement and modification that alter viewpoints and aims while maintaining overall aspirations.

It is necessary for both sides to develop their thinking so as to be able to put on the table what they actually hope to achieve and how the conflict, from their perspective, can be resolved through the mediation effort. After this articulation, the mediator must allow some space for each side to contemplate what the other side has said. Then the mediator, in conjunction with each side, must formulate some strategies and options that address each side's particular security, territory, resource, and other needs while always bearing in mind the significant relation to the community's identity factors. This stage is predicated on compromise—concession, compensation, and construction between the conflicting parties that seek to reach a joint outcome by reframing the conflict in new, mutually satisfying terms. Without some give, there can be no take. How that give is structured is important, and how that take is received is key. New and innovative ways of separating territory, one of the most significant aspects of identity conflict, need to be created. Autonomy, sovereignty, division, separation, incorporation, dual-ness, tri-ness, and many other inventive ways of dividing and reformulating common perceptions of national dominion can be constructed. A mediator is able to play a critical role here by reframing and offering new and different viewpoints.

A mediator can also help to or offer to impose a higher authority over the disputants. For instance, arguably, the Catalonian and Basque independence movements in Spain have been weakened by the existence of a strong European Union (EU). The EU presence has had the effect of diluting nationalist tendencies by creating a safe place for the expression of cultural and identity- related factors. The creation of a supranational entity or cross-border institution that influences "the expression of multiple group identities" or the "pooling of sovereignty" (Jesse & Williams, 2005, p. 113) can mitigate conflict while enhancing and recognizing the importance of identity. If mediators strive to create international institutions that "play an important role in promoting overlapping identities" (ibid., p. 125), then perhaps identity-based conflict can be mitigated. While not applicable to all conflicts, in the right context a supranational entity can offer hope by working to both contain old identities and create new ones.

A mediator can and should offer creative ideas and solutions, but ultimately the parties need to feel that they prevailed in the settlement, that the resolution came from them and for them. Regardless of the tactics employed by the mediator, it is vital that a sense of ownership is created between each disputant and the resolution. Outside actors can offer rewards or constraints to disputants. They can help make a party with a similar identity not forget that it is part of the "family," so to speak, and is representing "our" identity. In many ways, whether outside actors are productive to the mediation effort is party contingent. In reaching an agreement, the disputants must not feel that an outside actor is imposing a settlement on them, but rather that they, the conflicting parties, have created a genuine and workable arrangement beneficial to all sides.

After an agreement has been reached, the decisive phase of realization of the resolution is entered. This final step is called: *implementation and verification*. It involves the actual actions the parties need to take to execute the agreed-upon settlement. Should the mediator be involved at this stage or not? It is critical that some outside party be involved to ascertain independently, and if necessary

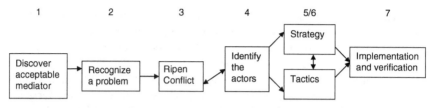

Figure 10.1 A step-by-step process to mediating internal identity conflict.

enforce, each party's implementation of its commitments within the agreement. Whether this is the mediator or not should be up to the parties and the particular settlement. But since the mediator has already been intimately involved in crafting a resolution that acknowledges the various intangible and tangible aspects of the conflict, the mediator is well situated to serve in this capacity (see Figure 10.1).

The step-by-step process offered here seeks to address some of the many issues and stages related to successful mediation of internal identity conflicts. This process can have a long horizon, potentially lasting for years or even decades, and can involve multiple mediation efforts. This conceptual effort has focused on understanding and explaining how mediation can be used in internal identity conflicts, not to put forward and examine specific hypotheses. Empirical evidence needs to be used to test this model. As a first step, this chapter provides future researchers with a generic process that is ready to be tested by practitioners and academics to ascertain the extent of its contribution to our knowledge and understanding. This model, deductively constructed, utilizes critical discourse, analytical synthesis, and original observations to inform its conclusions.

■ CONCLUSION

The unique aspects of internal identity conflicts require a mediator who can deal with the heated emotions of the disputants. There is nothing like threatening the "fatherland" or "motherland" to provoke strong sentiments. Mediators of identity-related conflicts must be prepared to deal with both negative and positive emotions in a constructive manner that does not delegitimize the feelings of one side at the expense of the other. The mediator must promote discourse and an exchange of ideas that works to both humanize and inform each disputant about the needs of the other while also recognizing that each party has certain requirements.

Besides mediation, bilateral negotiation has worked to resolve some internal identity conflicts. Arguably, it is not as effective as mediation. One reason bilateral negotiation might not be as helpful in settling internal identity conflicts is that a mediator can decisively help the parties change from a backward-looking to a forward-looking viewpoint. Forward-looking negotiations try "to establish a new political order to handle future outbreaks of conflict" (Zartman, 2005, p. 2). In many cases, forward-looking solutions come from a mediator who induces the parties to look inward and picture a more peaceful and just future. Forward-looking agreements are achieved in a step-by-step manner, and though there can be two steps forward and one step backward, inevitably "forward movement" arises from "forward-looking negotiations" (ibid., p. 301). To resolve an identity-based conflict, the parties must move beyond their perspectives and feelings of the other based on past actions, myths, and histories.

It takes time to change perspectives. Perhaps the mediator should strive, during the mediation process and in the initial stages of postconflict societal reconstruction, to divide rather than unite. Since both communities will most likely feel aggrieved and wronged, it might be necessary in the short term to separate first so that, in the long term, integration can occur. In Northern Ireland, while a unity government exists today, different school systems are in place for each sectarian community, and high walls divide sectarian neighborhoods from one another. This separation allows each group to exist within its identity community while allowing a location for the other identity community too. In the Treaty of Lausanne of 1923, Article 142 approved the reciprocal exchange and restitution of Greek and Turkish internal citizens to their respective nations representing their ethnic and religious heritage (i.e., Greece or Turkey). If communal partition or separation happens, it is also paramount to construct avenues of trade and finance that promote and lead to greater prosperity for all concerned groups. Joint business arrangements, tax-free economic zones, and government grants that support coexisting business endeavors can achieve this. However, when it comes to identity conflicts of a communal type, "partition may be the most humane lasting solution" (Muller, 2008, p. 34).

Finally, it should be noted that for the successful resolution of identity-based conflicts, time is a double-edged sword. If the conflict persists and future generations are raised with a mindset of hatred, then a solution is further and further postponed. But if the generations of today can reach some sort of accommodation that respects the needs and identities of both sides, the potential for a solution that endures the inevitable spoilers of today and tomorrow is achievable. If the past is negotiated properly in an adequate and respectful manner for all concerned parties, then the potential exists to improve future relations.

Mediators must realize that the suppression of identity will only prolong conflict. Correspondingly, to deny identity does not make it disappear. With identity-related conflicts, the tangible is always bound up in the intangible; the land is part of one's identity in the same way that one's identity is part of the land. These elements cannot be separated, and must be engaged and recognized for what they are: crucial hurdles that need to be addressed and overcome to foster an enduring settlement to a seemingly tenacious issue: identity conflict.

Notes

1. I would like to thank I. William Zartman for his guidance and advice throughout this research. Rudolf Avenhaus and Thomas Krieger provided valuable assistance and direction with the game theory section of this research. I am deeply indebted to the Steering Committee members of the Processes of International Negotiation program at the International Institute for Applied Systems Analysis (IIASA), currently located at the Clingendael Institute in the Netherlands. I would like to thank the IIASA Young Scientists Summer Program and a fellowship from the National Academy of Sciences as part of

National Science Foundation grant OISE-0533957 for providing the resources to make this work possible.

2. The views expressed in this chapter, which he wrote before joining the International Crisis Group, are the author's.

3. One way to test the logic of the assumption about the salience of tangible or intangible aspects to the mediation of internal identity conflicts is through the use of game theory, although only empirical research can test its reality. In the Appendix, the Southern Sudan-Khartoum conflict is examined from this perspective.

References

Abbas, M. (1997). *Through Secret Channels: The Road to Oslo: Senior PLO Leader Abu Mazen's Revealing Story of the Negotiations with Israel. Reading*, U.K.: Garnet Publishing.

Allport, G. W. (1954). *The nature of prejudice*. New York: Doubleday.

Anstey, M. (1993). *Practical peacemaking: A mediator's handbook*. Cape Town, South Africa: Juta and Company.

Arnson, C. J., & Zartman, I. W. (Eds.). (2005). *Rethinking the economics of war: The intersection of need, creed and greed*. Washington, DC: Woodrow Wilson Center Press; Baltimore: Johns Hopkins University Press.

Avenhaus, R. & Zartman, I.W. (Eds) (2007). *Diplomacy Games: Formal Models and International Negotiations*. New York: Springer.

Bercovitch, J., & Derouen, K., Jr. (2004). Mediation in internationalized ethnic conflicts: Assessing the determinants of a successful process. *Armed Forces and Society*, 30(2), 147–170.

Bercovitch, J., & Elgstrom, O. (2001). Culture and international mediation: Exploring theoretical and empirical linkages. *International Negotiation*, 6(1), 3–23.

Bercovitch, J., & Gartner, S. S. (2006). Is there method in the madness of mediation? Some lessons for mediators from quantitative studies of mediation. *International Interactions*, 32(4), 319–328.

Bercovitch, J., & Houston, A. (2000). Why do they do it like this? An analysis of the factors influencing mediation behavior in international conflicts. *Journal of Conflict Resolution*, 34(2), 170–202.

Bercovitch, J., & Jackson, R. (2001). Negotiation or mediation? An exploration of factors affecting the choice of conflict management in international conflict. *Negotiation Journal*, 17(1), 59–78.

Bercovitch, J., & Schneider, G. (2000). Who mediates? The political economy of international conflict management. *Journal of Peace Research*, 37(2), 145–165.

Bercovitch, J. & Houston, A. (1996). The Study of International Mediation: Theoretical Issues and Empirical Evidence. In J. Bercovitch (Ed.), *Resolving International Conflicts: The Theory and Practice of Mediation*. Boulder, Colorado: Lynn Rienner.

Brewer, M. B., & Gardner, W. (1996). Who is this "we"? Levels of collective identity and self representations. *Journal of Personality and Social Psychology*, 71, 83–93.

Brown, M. E. (1993). Causes and implications of ethnic conflict. In M. E. Brown (Ed.), *Ethnic conflict and international security*. Chichester, UK: Princeton University Press Books.

Bush, R. B., & Folger, J. (1994). *The promise of mediation*. San Francisco: Jossey-Bass.

Capelos, T., & Smilovitz, J. L. (2008). As a matter of feeling: Emotions and the choice of mediator. *The Hague Journal of Diplomacy*, 3(1), 63–85.

Caporael, L. R., & Brewer, M. B. (1995). Hierarchical evolutionary theory: There is an alternative, and it's not creationism. *Psychological Inquiry*, 6, 31–80.

Carnevale, P. J., & Arad, S. (1995). Bias and impartiality in international mediation. In J. Bercovitch (Ed.), *Resolving international conflicts: The theory and practice of mediation* (pp. 39–53). Boulder, CO: Lynne Rienner.

Carnevale, P. J., Lim, R. G., & McLaughlin, M. E. (1989). Contingent mediator behavior and its effectiveness. In K. Kressel, D. G. Pruit, et al. (Eds.), *Mediation research: The process and effectiveness of third-party intervention* (pp. 166–189). San Francisco: Jossey-Bass.

Carnevale, P. J., & Arad. S. (1996). Bias and Impartiality in International Mediation. In J. Bercovitch (Ed.), *Resolving International Conflicts: The Theory and Practice of Mediation* (pp. 39–53). Colorado: Lynne Rienner.

Celik, A. B., & Rumelili, B. (2006). Necessary but not sufficient: The role of the EU in resolving Turkey's Kurdish question and the Greek–Turkish conflicts. *European Foreign Affairs Review, 11*, 203–222.

Clancy, M. A., & Nagle, J. (2010). *Shared society or benign apartheid? Understanding peacebuilding in divided societies*. Basingstoke, UK, and New York: Palgrave-Macmillan.

Cobb, S., & Rifkin, J. (1991). Practice and paradox: Deconstructing neutrality in mediation. *Law and Social Inquiry, 16*(1), 35–62.

Crawford, N. C. (2000). The passion of world politics: Propositions of emotion and emotional relationships. *International Security, 24*(4), 116–156.

Crocker, C. A., Hampson, F. O., & Aall, P. (2007). *Leashing the dogs of war*. Washington, DC: United States Institute of Peace Press.

Diehl, P. F. (1992). What are they fighting for? The importance of issues in international conflict research. *Journal of Peace Research, 29*(3), 333–344.

Druckman, D. (2001). Negotiation and identity: implications for negotiation theory." International Negotiation, 6(2), 281–291.

Faure, G. & Rubin J. Z. (1993). *Culture and negotiation: the resolution of water disputes*. Thousand Oaks, California: Sage Publications.

Fearon, J. D. (1995). Rationalist explanations for war. *International Organization, 49*(3), 379–414.

Fisher, R. & Shapiro, D. (2005). *Beyond Reason: Using Emotions as You Negotiate*. New York: Viking.

Fogg, R. W. (1985). Dealing with conflict: A repertoire of creative, peaceful approaches. *The Journal of Conflict Resolution, 29*(2), 330–358.

Gartner, S. S., & Bercovitch, J. (2006). Overcoming obstacles to peace: The contribution of mediation to short-lived conflict settlements. *International Studies Quarterly, 50*, 819–840.

Goertz, G., & Diehl, P. F. (1992). *Territorial changes and international conflict*. London: Routledge.

Gopin, M. (2001). What do I need to know about religion and conflict? In J. P. Lederach & J. M. Jenner (Eds.), *The handbook of international peacebuilding: Into the eye of the storm* (pp. 107–114). San Francisco: Jossey-Bass.

Hopf, T. (1998). The promise of constructivism in international relations theory. *International Security, 23*(1), 171–200.

Irwin, C. (2002). *The people's peace process in Northern Ireland*. United Kingdom: Palgrave.

Jesse, N. G., & Williams, K. P. (2005). *Identity and institutions: Conflict resolution in divided societies*. Albany: State University of New York Press.

Jones, D. L. (2000). Mediation, conflict resolution and critical theory. *Review of International Studies, 26*, 647–662.

Keashly, L., & Fisher, R. (1996). A contingency perspective on conflict interventions: Theoretical and practical considerations. In J. Bercovitch (Ed.), *Resolving international conflicts: The theory and practice of mediation* (pp. 235–261). Boulder, CO: Lynne Rienner.

Leach, C. W., & Williams, W. R. (1999). Group identity and conflicting expectations of the future in Northern Ireland. *Political Psychology, 20*(4), 875–896.

Maundi, M. O., Zartman, I. W., Khadiagala, G., & Nuamah, K. (2006). *Getting in: Mediators' entry into the settlement of African conflicts.* Washington, DC: United States Institute of Peace Press.

Muller, J. Z. (2008). Us and them: The enduring power of ethnic nationalism. *Foreign Affairs,* March/April. 18–35.

Nicholson, M. 1 (1991). Negotiation, agreement, and conflict resolution: The role of rational approaches and their criticism. In R. Vayrynen (Ed.), *New directions on conflict theory: Conflict resolution and conflict transformation* (pp. 57–78). Newbury Park, California: Sage.

Norlen, T. C. (2003). *Sacred stones and religious nuts: Negotiating ethnic disputes over absolute space.* Interim Report IR-03–007. Laxenburg: Austria. International Institute of Applied Systems Analysis.

Posthuma, R. A., Dworkin, J. B., & Stella, M. (2002). Swift mediator tactics and sources of conflict. *Industrial Relations, 31*(1), 94–109.

Posthuma, R. A., Dworkin, J. B. & Swift, M. S. (2002). Mediator Tactics and Sources of Conflict: Facilitating and Inhibiting Effects. *Industrial Relations, 41,* 94–109.

Rosoux, V. (2008). Reconciliation as a Peace-Building Process: Scope and Limits. In J. Bercovitch, V. Kremenyuk & W. Zartman (Eds.), *Handbook of Conflict Resolution* (pp. 543–563). London: Sage Publications.

Rothman, J. (1997). *Resolving identity-based conflict in nations, organizations and communities.* San Francisco: Jossey-Bass.

Rothman, J., & Olson, M. L. (2001). From interests to identities: Towards a new emphasis in interactive conflict resolution. *Journal of Peace Research, 38*(3), 289–305.

Rubinstein, A. (1982). Perfect Equilibrium in a Bargaining Model. *Econometrica, 50*(1), 97–110.

Salacuse, J. (2004). The Top Ten Ways That Culture Can Affect Your Negotiation. *Ivey Business Journal,* 1–6.

Saunders, H. (2003). Sustained dialogue in managing intractable conflict. *Negotiation Journal,* (19), 85–95.

Savir, U. (1999). *The Process: 1,100 Days that Changed the Middle East.* London, U.K.: Vintage.

Stahl, I. (1972). *Bargaining Theory.* Stockholm, Sweden: Stockholm School of Economics.

Touval, S., & Zartman, I. W. (2007). International mediation in the post cold war era. In. C. A. Crocker, F. O. Hampson, & P. Aall (Eds.), *Leashing the dogs of war* (pp. 261–278). Washington, DC: United States Institute of Peace Press.

Touval, S., & Zartman, I.W. (Eds.), (1985). *International Mediation in Theory and Practice.* Boulder, Colorado and London, U.K.: Westview Press.

Touval, S., & Zartman. I. W. (2001). International Mediation in the Post Cold War Era. In C. A. Crocker, F. O. Hampson and P. Aall (Ed.), *Turbulent Peace: The Challenges of Managing International Conflict* (pp. 427–443), Washington D.C.: United States Institute of Peace Press.

Treaty of Lausanne, July 24, 1923. Retrieved April 13, 2008, from http://www.untreaty.un.org

Treverton, G. F., Gregg, H. S., Gibran, D., & Yost, C. W. (Eds.) (1985). *International mediation in theory and practice.* Boulder, CO, and London: Westview Press.

Treverton, G. F., Gregg, H. S., Gibran, D., & Yost, C. W. (2005). *Exploring religious conflict.* Conference proceedings. Santa Monica, CA: National Security Research Division, RAND Corporation.

Vasquez, J. (1983). The tangibility of issues and global conflict: A test of Rosenau's Issue Area typology. *Journal of Peace Research*, *20*(2), 179–192.

Vasquez, J. A. (1995). Why Do Neighbors Fight? Proximity, Interaction, or Territoriality. *Journal of Peace Research*, *32*(3), 277–293.

Wehr, P., & Lederach, J. P. (1991). Mediating conflict in Central America. *Journal of Peace Research*, *28*(1), 85–98.

Weiss-Wik, S. (1983). Enhancing negotiators' successfulness: Self-help books and related empirical research. *The Journal of Conflict Resolution*, *27*(4), 706–739.

Welsh, D. (1993). Domestic politics and ethnic conflict. In M. E. Brown (Ed.), *Ethnic conflict and international security* (pp. 43–60). Chichester, UK: Princeton University Press Books.

Wendt, A. (1994). Collective identity formation and the international state. *The American Political Science Review*, *88*(2), 384–396.

Zartman, I. W. (2005). *Cowardly lions: Missed opportunities to prevent deadly conflict and state collapse*. Boulder, CO: Lynne Rienner.

Zartman, I. W. (2003). Ripeness. In G. Burgess & H. Burgess (Eds.). *Beyond Intractability Conflict Research Consortium*. University of Colorado, Boulder, Colorado. http://www.beyondintractability.org/essay/ripeness/.(accessed 4/15/2008)

Zartman, I. W. & de Soto, A. (2010). Timing Mediation Initiatives. United States Institute of Peace Peacemaker's Toolkit series. www.usip.org/files/resources/Timing%20Mediation%20Initiatives.pdf (accessed 10/28/2010).

Zartman. I.W. (Ed.) (2007). *Peacemaking In International Conflict: Methods And Techniques*. Washington, D.C.: United States Institute of Peace Press.

Zartman, I. W. & Rubin, J. Z. (2003). *Power and Negotiation*. USA: The University of Michigan Press.

Zartman, I. W. (2006). Negotiating internal, ethnic and identity conflicts in a globalized world. *International Negotiation*, *11*(2), 253–272.

Zubek, J. M., Pruitt, D. G., Pierce, R. S., Mcgillicuddy, N. B., & Syna, H. (1992). Disputant and mediator behaviors affecting short-term success in mediation. *The Journal of Conflict Resolution*, *36*(3), 546–572.

■ APPENDIX

Game theory is one of the primary theoretical means for analyzing negotiations. This is because negotiations are based on a circumstance in which an individual's choice or action depends on the decisions or actions of another individual. Ideally, game theory allows parties to a negotiation to recognize strategies, either pure or mixed, that can be used to achieve favorable results and attain particular objectives (Avenhaus & Zartman, 2007). However, since "models are logical simplifications of reality . . . they need to test the logic in the relationships they posit" (Avenhaus & Zartman, 2007, p. 7). A model should replicate reality, and should be understandable and not too complex. This is particularly true for identity conflicts that involve a mix of tangible and intangible aspects and a situation in which the decisions taken by one party influence the other party.

An example of a mediated identity conflict involving both tangible and intangible features is the conflict between Northern Sudan, also known as Khartoum, which is dominated by Arabs and Muslims, and Southern Sudan, also called the South, populated mainly by black Africans of Animist or Christian belief, and who controls the local oil resources. The efforts to model this conflict were not successful because it was too complicated and the negotiation process displayed too many different options and possibilities. The mix of tangible (oil) and intangible (ethnic and religious homeland) issues makes the Sudan an ideal example for illustrating the difficulty of modeling identity-related conflicts.

To begin the modeling efforts, a normal game with four clear possible choices for each disputant was used. The strategic choices focused on two sets of issues: who controls the oil and whether the South will have autonomy, independence, or neither. Based on this, the four choices for each disputant were: Khartoum controls the oil and there is no autonomy for the South, the South controls the oil and there is no autonomy for the South, Khartoum controls the oil and there is autonomy for the South, and finally, the South controls the oil and there is independence for the South (future researchers can also investigate strategic choices that include sharing oil resources). The model demonstrated strategic combinations that were highly unrealistic under real- world conditions. For instance, imagine the combination of strategies where Khartoum offers the South control of oil and independence, and the South counters by offering not to control the oil and stating no desire for autonomy. An equilibrium in which such a strategy combination is selected, even with a small probability, is not at all acceptable for both parties.

Given this observation, a sequential model following the lines of Stahl (1972) and Rubinstein (1982), where payoffs are discounted over time, was attempted. The hope was that this model would better explain the dynamics in play because it could describe, step by step, the offer and counteroffer dealings of the parties to the negotiation effort. When this descriptive model was used, it was apparent that adequate information was not available, resulting in numerous technical difficulties. Essentially, because there were so many possibilities with a dearth of data, the information used to sequentially demonstrate the cooperation/coordination between Khartoum and the South became highly unrealistic. However, it is still contended that the types of offers modeled, that is, oil and autonomy or independence, and the way they were modeled parallel to one other was a satisfactory way to represent this negotiation effort. But the model could not be filled in with particular offers or counteroffers based on realistic data. In passing, it needs to be mentioned that the equilibrium of Stahl and Rubinstein's sequential bargaining model implies that both parties agree after the first round of offers, which means that it does not describe an iterated negotiation process lasting for several rounds of offers and counteroffers.

Presumably, sequential modeling is the right approach to improving our understanding of the interaction between tangible and intangible factors within an identity conflict. However, if the model cannot be filled in with genuine details, then it does not sufficiently explain the problem as a whole. Mediators must deal with both tangible and intangible features. Modeling can help elucidate connections, linkages, and relationships between these two sets of issues. For identity conflict, there is a necessary interaction between tangible and intangible characteristics, so there is much modeling left to be done.

11 The Challenge of Partnerism

■ MOTY CRISTAL

Prevention, containment, management, or resolution of intractable conflicts, within which negotiations on identity conflicts are conducted, have become more challenging, and their complexity is manifested on four main fronts: multiple agents and multiple issues noted as characteristics of international negotiations (Zartman, 2003) and more recent elements of information overflow and unstable evolution.

Multiple Agents

While in the past international negotiations were conducted through a limited number of agents, such as government officials, rebels' representatives, terrorist organizations, and national and international nongovernmental organizations (NGOs; Mawlawi, 1993), the range of participants has expanded to include nontraditional agents such as interested networks (mainly criminal and terror; Starkey, Boyer, & Wilkenfeld 1999), communities of knowledge (Agha, Feldman, Khalidi, & Schiff, 2003),[1] ideological supporters, unorganized diasporas (such as the role of Armenian communities in shaping Europe's policy toward Turkey), and even powerful individuals who hold no official and accountable position.[2]

Multiple Issues

Beyond the traditional claims for independence, power or power sharing, and access to natural resources, the prevention, containment, management, and resolution of intractable conflicts face the need to address issues such as justice[3] and identity, which are unquantifiable and dynamic in nature,[4] making the analysis and structure of the international negotiation process more challenging than ever (Khalidi, 1997, chap. 8; Zartman & Kremenyuk, 2005).

Information Overflow

While in the past information relevant to the management or resolution of deep-rooted conflicts was in the possession of a few knowledgeable actors, who could use it and manipulate the underprivileged ones, in today's conflicts the majority of relevant actors have sufficient information to process in conducting their belligerent or reconciliatory actions. Moreover, technology today allows even the underprivileged to collect and disseminate information—manipulated or accurate—through mass media channels including satellite networks, emails, and blogs, and to mobilize their publics without exerting actual control over a certain territory and without monitoring the consequences. Mobilizing constituencies using "rumorization" of political moves during negotiations becomes a common tactic in moving the process in a certain direction.

Unstable Evolution

The theory of ripeness posits a certain moment at which the parties face a mutually hurting stalemate, see a way out, and manage to identify a valid spokesperson (Zartman, 2006).[5] Since one of the most apparent characteristics of intractable conflicts today is their dynamic nature (Coleman, Bui-Wrzosinski, Vallacher, & Novack 2006),[6] a "moment of ripeness"[7] could exist for only a few days or weeks. A moment of ripeness becomes a window of opportunity, and unless the negotiation designer—be it one of the parties or, more likely, the mediators—plans, prepares, and is operationally ready to capture it, the dynamic of the conflict will change or escalate in a way that will require a new set of actors to redesign the next ripe moment.

Beginning with a definition of *negotiation* as "a process of identifying an appropriate partner and constructing a joint pact" often involves the actual creation of that partner, the subject that will be the focus of this chapter. A systemic view of the negotiation process defines the *negosystem*[8] and differentiates among various levels of participating actors. Following the initial distinction between side and party, the definition of a *side* as "the spectrum of actors, collective and individual, who are implicated in the rebel and government elements of the conflict" can be expanded to view the sides as the general groups that range themselves along the conflict lines, whereas the *parties* are the subgroups, political parties, ideological movements, or agencies within each side. In the Israeli–Palestinian conflict, the important sides are Israel, the United States, the Arab countries, and the Palestinians, and the parties are those such as Fatah, Hamas, the Central Intelligence Agency, and the Israeli right-wing movements. The challenge is to identify and create the right negotiation partners who can negotiate an agreement in a given context.

These negotiation *partners*, as well as their parties and even the sides, are the subjects of external intervention, advocacy efforts, coercive strategies, or any other type of engagement. Therefore, in today's reality of intractable conflicts—be it in early stages, before atrocities begin, or following the atrocities, when a torn society seeks both revenge and reconstruction—the primary challenge of the external intervener, usually a capable mediator, is twofold: to clearly identify the dynamics within each side and party, and to engage with or be able to create the conditions for the emergence of a relevant negotiation partner. For the purposes of addressing the second dimension, the concept of partnerism is offered. It will be presented in its general terms and from a wide view, with occasional use of conflict examples to allow the external intervener to use a general framework that is applicable broadly to identity-based conflict.

■ THE CONCEPT OF PARTNERISM

While the term *partnership* assumes a certain set of (usually agreed-upon) values and relationships between two or more participants in the negotiations (Mohr & Spekman, 2006), *partnerism* in negotiations is defined as the notion of clarity about who are the relevant negotiation partners for a given negotiation process. While partnerism as an emerging economic theory calls for an economic system that supports optimal human development (Bagwell & Staiger 1999), partnerism in negotiation theory calls for negotiation in a setting set with the relevant actors and supports to enable the establishment of a sustainable negotiation process leading to an agreement, pact, or series of understandings.

The concept of partnerism takes further the idea of *set-up* as the "third dimension" in the Lax and Sebenius (2006) three-dimensional (3-D) negotiations concept. According to Lax and Sebenius, the setup happens away from the table before negotiation begins and consists of the scope, sequence, and process of the negotiation, similar to the conceptualization of prenegotiation (Stein, Janice, ed (1989)). To set up the scope or the "who and what" of a negotiation, the 3-D negotiator develops an "all-party map," consisting of a full set of the parties involved in the negotiation, both potential and actual. The map should also include the interests of the parties and their relationship with each other. Partnerism develops the setup dimension and calls the parties, and especially the mediators, to take an active role in influencing this map. Lax and Sebenius summarize the third dimension as "acting to ensure that the right parties have been involved, in the right sequence, to deal with the right issues, that engage the right set of interests, at the right table or tables, at the right time, under the right expectations, facing the right consequences of walking away if there is no deal" (p. 12). Partnerism offers a conceptual framework and an operational tool for international interveners in intractable conflicts to implement that challenge regarding the first issue: ensuring that the right parties have been involved. It has five elements, the required characteristics of any negotiation partner indicating the necessary policy directions toward creating the relevant negotiation partner: representation, legitimacy, responsibility, capability, and accountability.

Representation

Negotiations in internal conflicts exist in certain political, military, and economic systems; hence, the negotiating partner has to be a true and genuine representative of his own party, people, side, or group. True representation varies from conflict to culture and cannot be predetermined by the external intervening party, the international community, or the other negotiating partner. Representation depends on the political, organizational, and institutional structure of the party itself. Whether a democratically elected government, a rebels' group, or a terrorist cell, the party has its own internal processes, dynamics, and modes of selecting representatives. For some parties, it will be the leader himself; for others, his son. The party could also consist of a group decision or a natural evolution of the cruelest terrorist. For some parties, it will be the senior member of all prisoners or a tribal committee;

each of them, depending on the parties' political structure, will be considered a true representative.

A key dimension of this requirement for any external intervener is to identify, acknowledge, and respect the party's internal selection processes rather than force, intervene, impose, or prefer a certain representation. Intractable conflicts face reality where a well-established government or an international organization, which is the "other side," or the external intervener, determines with whom they should negotiate in order to end hostilities. Often external interveners from the international community will be reluctant to negotiate with the true representative of one of the parties for several reasons: The true representative does not accept the mediator or the external preconditions to talk (like immediate cessation of violence), or party A is unwilling to negotiate with that true representative of party B.

Failure to negotiate with the true representative causes setbacks in the negotiation process and flaws in the desirable outcome. The genuine and authentic interests and needs of the people will not be met, as they were misrepresented by the wrong negotiating partner; therefore, failure to negotiate with a true representative will cause delays in reaching a sustainable agreement as it stirs internal conflicting dynamics within the side that was misrepresented (Lax & Sebenius, 2006). In this case, the negotiated outcome carries the risk of not including all issues that matter to the misrepresented parties, and even if an agreement is reached, the exclusion of the true representative introduces structural incentives for breaching that agreement in order to reach a better, fairer deal in the eyes of those who feel misrepresented or not represented at all.

Moreover, true representation should reflect an accurate balance of power within the party that the negotiation partner is sent to represent. External intervention can produce a "democratically" elected group or a certain "approved" individual to become the negotiation partner, even though they have no political power and cannot be considered a genuine representative of their people's interests. An external intervention that will force such a false representation will have to confront the second challenge when examining whether this representative is their relevant negotiation partner: the challenge of legitimacy.

Legitimacy

Legitimacy is the most fundamental dimension of partnerism and therefore the most sensitive for being undermined by external interventions. A legitimate partner is a partner who enjoys its party's public approval. This is a descriptive rather than a normative requirement and has to be judged in every specific political context, be it a democracy, an NGO, an organization—governmental or non-governmental, or a democracy, militarily or otherwise forcefully or a diaspora. Its imperative derives from the difference between being an official representative, usually determined and capable of being measured by objective parameters, and being a legitimate representative, which is far less objective, more subjective, and perceptual. In negotiating the 2001 Taba round with Yasir Arafat, Ehud Barak, despite being prime minister of Israel and therefore its official representative, had no public legitimacy to negotiate due to the fact that he negotiated a month before elections he knew he was going to lose. An effective negotiation process that will lead to a sustainable agreement has to be established only between legitimate negotiating partners. A negotiating party who is not, or is not considered to be, a legitimate representative should not be perceived by the other party or by the external intervener as a relevant negotiating partner. The legitimacy dimension of partnerism depends solely on the internal dynamics and structures of each of the rivalries. When Eduard Said, the late Palestinian-American scholar, published a statement during the 2000 Camp David summit that Arafat has no legitimacy to compromise on *his* right of return as a Palestinian refugee, he enjoyed overriding support from the Palestinian diaspora.

Acceptance by the other side is not required to establish a party's legitimacy. Actually, reality might prove the opposite: When a party has the acceptance of the other side, it may lose its legitimacy to represent its people's interest, as noted in the introductory chapter by Anstey and Zartman. When a certain political party or a certain fraction of a rebels' group decides, either independently or in response to external pressure, to move from violence to negotiation, it will face an internal dynamic that might undermine its legitimacy as the messenger of its people. It will then be the role of the mediator to seek avenues to hold this party to its decision to negotiate while making an effort to preserve its legitimacy. This is probably one of the most challenging tasks of an external intervener, and it should be done through back channels and public statements, based on a deep understanding of the conflict's dynamics.

A different approach to meet this challenge can be sought in the world of crisis negotiation. A hostage negotiator does not "accept" the hostage taker. He negotiates with him because he is the one who holds the hostages and he is the relevant partner. No approval is required, just adherence to the "rules of the game" agreed to by the two negotiators across the street. The same is true in international conflict: The mediator need not accept the rebels' leader, but rather should negotiate with him according to the rules of the game and maintain his legitimacy as leader throughout the entire negotiation process.

As with official representation, a negotiating party who lacks legitimacy carries the risk of derailing the whole negotiation process, and encouraging spoilers and extremists to take violent action in order to make its lack of legitimacy clear and visible. Thus, once the external interveners have identified the legitimate representative party, they still need to examine the three following criteria—responsibility, capability, and accountability—in order to be convinced that they are dealing with the relevant negotiation partner.

Responsibility

Responsibility as a required characteristic of a relevant negotiating partner reflects the party's will. As the result of either an individual or a collective decision, the partner needs to carry out its role as a legitimate representative and to engage in a negotiation process. Unlike representation and legitimacy, which are two external characteristics that operate within the conflict system, responsibility is—like the two following elements of partnerism—an internal element in the sense that the party itself, rather than the system, develops it. A party to a conflict, which is and perceives itself as a legitimate representative, takes responsibility to lead its people, group, or side toward ending the violence through negotiations and a political process. This responsibility is usually developed gradually: internal discussions within the legitimate representative entity, minor signaling to the mediators or to the other side, agreeing to send a confidential emissary to conduct prenegotiation talks, and public statements or actions—such as unilateral cessation of violence— that are publicly perceived as willingness to negotiate (Berton, Kimura, & Zartman, 1999).

It is, however, imperative to differentiate between a party's willingness to negotiate and its willingness to agree to a certain outcome. Responsibility and the concept of partnerism refer solely to the former: the partner's genuine engagement in a negotiation process without any precondition concerning its outcome. Hamas' stated willingness to negotiate a long cease-fire with Israel should not be seen as indicative of anything other than its willingness to take responsibility and engage in a negotiation process. Negotiation processes have their own dynamics; therefore, a capable intervener will be able to design a political process that will transform conflicting parties into negotiating partners without predetermining the political outcome of these negotiations. The work done by Senator George Mitchell in the Northern Ireland conflict emphasizes this process of turning conflicting parties into negotiation partners without predetermining the negotiation outcome (Curran & Sebenius, 2003).

Ability to Deliver

The ability to deliver is another internal characteristic of partnerism. In current intractable conflicts, where public opinion is shaped more by actions on the ground and their amplified effect in the media sphere than by statements and declarations, even the most legitimate and responsible representative has to prove its capability in order to gain—or maintain—the status of a relevant negotiation partner (Wolfsfeld, 1997). *Ability to deliver* refers to two fundamentals of the negotiation process: the Zone of Possible Agreement (ZOPA; Fisher & Ury, 1983) and the implementation of an agreed-upon outcome.

A conceptual debate exists when trying to link the negotiation parties with the negotiation outcome. Understanding the negotiation process as a dynamic system, the concept of partnerism argues that a legitimate representative who is willing to engage in a negotiation process becomes a relevant partner if it can deliver any type of outcome that will be agreed upon. According to the concept, the question "Who is the relevant negotiation partner?" is examined when entering the negotiation room, takes into consideration the dynamic changes throughout the process, and therefore does not limit or designate a specific outcome to a specific partner.[9] Understanding the dynamic nature of conflicts, and in particular that of negotiation systems, rules out the notion that a certain negotiation party will agree only to a certain negotiation outcome, and if this outcome is not achieved, that party will withdraw from the negotiation process. A negotiation partner is determined in the early phases of the negosystem. Changes in the negosystem that occur throughout the process affect the negotiation partners, the ZOPA, and system itself (Watkins & Passow, 1996).[10] That is to say, a party could become a relevant partner while having in mind a specific outcome, but as a result of the negotiation dynamics it could find itself agreeing to a different outcome, since the ZOPA, as well as that party itself, change over time.

The second dimension of capability, and probably the most significant in the eyes of the other party to the negotiations, is the ability of a party to exercise authority over other fractions, organizations, political parties, or armed groups within its own people. Negotiation theories recognize the importance of implementation[11] to the process of conflict resolution (Curry, 1998; Gordon & Ertel, 2007). In current and future conflicts, where the participation of fractions and splinter groups becomes common, the partners' ability to deal with spoilers becomes a precondition for successful implementation of what was agreed upon (Baker, 2009; Ramsbotham, Woodhouse, & Miall, 2005).

One of the most common failures in recent conflict resolution attempts is the failure to sustain cease-fire agreements, usually the first step toward a more comprehensive agreement. This failure is caused mainly by the inability of the negotiation partner to enforce the cease-fire agreement and to impose it on its own party, from the Islamic Jihad firing Kassam rockets opposing the Hamas-led cease-fire with Israel to the Provisional IRA's attempts to undermine Sinn Fein's efforts to stabilize Northern Ireland. Therefore, one of the most challenging tasks of the external intervener in internal conflicts will be to strengthen the delivery capacity of a potential partner. If one of the stakeholders emerges, or has the potential to emerge, as a relevant negotiation partner, the mediator or the international intervener, as well as the other side, should seek actions to strengthen its ability to deliver. On the other hand, if the mediator negotiates with one of the fractions that evidently has no ability to deliver or cannot enforce any agreement, despite being a legitimate representative of its people, it becomes clear that this fraction is *not* the relevant negotiation partner, and the mediator has to seek a partner that is able to back up, militarily or forcefully, this legitimate representative.

Accountability

Accountability is the last requirement for turning a legitimate representative who shows responsibility and is able to deliver into a relevant negotiation partner. *Accountability* is the extent to which a negotiation partner can be held to account for actions committed by its people, including all fractions, military groups, and political parties. It is essential for the sustainability of any agreement, and it should be examined during negotiations, not after an agreement is signed. Any agreed-upon outcome to terminate internal conflicts will face opposition from groups that will try, through terror, outbidding, violence, or the threat of using violence, to undermine the agreement. A relevant negotiation partner is expected to find the right methods—according to its culture, norms, and value system—to confront those who will try to derail the process and return to violence (Miall, Ramsbotham, & Woodhouse, 1999).

A negotiation partner who refuses to be held accountable, and who consistently and constantly fails to confront its internal opposition (usually due to political or military weakness or unwillingness to intensify domestic bloodshed), should not be considered a relevant negotiation partner. This decision should not be perceived as a punishment but rather as an instrumental requirement that can be used by the mediator as an incentive to encourage that party to make an effort to confront its internal opposition in order to regain the status of a negotiating partner (Kramer, Pommerenke, & Newton, 1993; Ward, Diston, Brenner, & Ross 2008).

■ IMPLEMENTING PARTNERISM

The concept of partnerism identifies the required characteristics of a negotiation partner. However, the translation of this normative concept into prescriptive advice for mediators faces two challenges: the failure to set the right table, as indicated in this book's introductory chapter, and the consequences of losing a negotiation partner during the process. These challenges are two critical moments in the evolution of the negosystem (Druckman, 2001). While mediators face the first challenge of identifying the relevant partner in the early stages of the process, the second might appear at any point, and has the potential to delay or derail any process that is already underway.

"Why are we unable to find the right partner?" is an operational question whose answers should be sought in the worlds of social psychology and international politics as well as international mediation. Probably the most comprehensive and thus operational answer is provided by the works on the linkages between partner selection and outcomes and bounded awareness (Bazerman, Church, Moore, & Valley, 2000; Church & Bazerman, 2004, Patton (1999), Mohr & Spekman (2006)). The mediator is a political actor and the mediator's choices are political choices, a mixture of power, values, and political preferences. Although conducted in laboratory quantitative environment, the conclusion about partner selection is applicable to the world of international mediation, as it states that "when relationships are not allowed to influence the matching process, there are more economically optimal agreements, a larger market surplus, and more search activity."

When setting the right negotiation table, the invitation list should not be made up of the mediator's preferred parties but rather of the relevant negotiation partners: representative, legitimate, responsible, capable, and accountable for their actions. Once a negotiation table is set with "no relationships allowed," it guarantees a more challenging, and probably longer, negotiation process, though one that is more likely to produce "economically optimal agreements," which—in the world of intractable conflicts—translates to an implementable and sustainable agreement. Choosing the wrong negotiation party as a result of a wrong political choice is likely to delay or derail the search for an agreement, but a more likely mediation failure can occur when the mediator negotiates with an irrelevant party as a result of ignoring signs and signals from the people. Engaging Palestinian president Abu Mazen and abandoning the attempts to build Hamas as a relevant negotiation partner is only one of the recent examples of such a mediation failure.

Bounded awareness is the phenomenon by which individuals do not "see" and use certain accessible, perceivable information during the decision-making process while seeing and using other equally accessible and perceivable information. Thus, useful information remains out of focus for the decision maker. A *focusing failure* results from a misalignment between the information needed for a good decision and the information included in the decision-making process (Saaty, 2008). Once the all-parties' map has been completed, the mediator should determine which information remains out of focus and which early signs and signals have been ignored. Here as well, setting the wrong negotiation table, trying to reach an agreement with irrelevant parties, is unlikely to produce an implementable and sustainable agreement. It even carries the risk of escalating violence and intensifying despair.

Losing the Partner

Rooted in system thinking, the negotiation partner also has a dynamic, and sometimes even unstable, status. The characteristics of a negotiation partner are all subject to the dynamics of the conflict; a party who was weak and irrelevant in the early stages of the negotiation process may gain power, representation (mainly if the conflict resolution process involves elections), legitimacy, and even the ability to deliver an agreement as the conflict and negotiations proceed. The reverse is equally true; a negotiation partner who was relevant in the early stages can lose relevance—for example, due to constant failure to exercise authority in a certain territory.

Once the negotiation partner is identified and engaged, a skilled mediator has to use all of his professional wisdom and political powers to take measures that will strengthen the negotiation partner, balancing the conflicting demands from party A and even from political or military fractions within party B that are trying to undermine the negotiation partner. Coleman and Bartoli (2003) identify key strategies that can be used by the mediator in dealing with extremists. Indeed, by defining those who object to the negotiation partner as "extremist," the mediator falls into a systemic trap that will weaken the negotiation partner, but can be sprung by one of the strategies—rarely used—of intragroup work within polarized groups in intergroup conflicts. According to Coleman and Bartoli, and as developed in the chapter by Rothman, this approach will encourage and facilitate intragroup dialogue and problem solving in an attempt to actively address the concerns of more extreme members and reduce the incidence of splinter groups and spoilers.

■ CONCLUSION

One of the most challenging tasks faced by any international mediator who intervenes in intractable conflict is whom to bring to the table. This chapter provides a conceptual framework to answer that question. The concept of partnerism is a framework that identifies and analyzes five necessary characteristics—representation, legitimacy, responsibility, capability, and accountability—required to turn a party into a relevant negotiation partner. All five are cumulative, and practice shows that without all of them, no sustainable agreement can be reached. Partnerism is rooted in the approach that sees conflict as a dynamic system. Hence, it has to be applied in a systemic manner by skilled mediators. Once he decides to intervene, at the early stages of the negosystem, the main challenge of the mediator will be to identify the appropriate party who is qualified to be a relevant negotiation partner and to work within the conflict system to strengthen that party. However, if the conflict dynamics undermine the status of the negotiation partner, a skilled mediator has to be ready to work with a new emerging negotiation partner.

This means that working with a negotiation partner who is unacceptable to other stakeholders and the international community will still be the right thing to do if the mediator manages to agree to and guarantee certain adherence to nonbelligerent behavior. That is the minimal requirement not only to gain the status of a partner but also to convince the mediator that this partner is willing to move from violence to negotiation.

Notes

1. *Community of knowledge* is a term adopted from the worlds of technology and innovation, where *community of knowledge* or *community of practice* became a platform to enhance profitability. (http://www.entovation.com/innovation/cokp.htm). The stable participation of scholars in Israeli–Arab track II diplomacy should be seen as a result of the sizable community of knowledge that has been created in this field, where its participants seek to apply their academic knowledge to the real-life negotiations. For more on the participation of academics in Israeli-Arab track II diplomacy see Agha, Feldman, Khalidi, and Schiff (2003).

2. For the role of nonofficial agents, see Patton (1999).

3. For a comprehensive analysis of the Justice dimension, see Zartman and Kremenyuk (2005).

4. For the dynamic changes in the religious-secular identity of the Palestinian society, see, for example, Khalidi (1997, chap. 8).

5. A summary of the comprehensive ripeness work can be found in Zartman (2006).

6. For a summary of the comprehensive work done about the dynamic nature of conflict see Coleman, Bui-Wrzosinska, Vallacher, and Nowack (2006).

7. Zartman (2000).

8. The Negosystem™ model was developed by the author in his doctoral thesis for the Department of International Relations at the London School of Economics and Political Science. A *negosystem* is a particular case of a complex evolving system and captures a negotiation reality throughout a definite timeline. *Negosystem* is comprised of five groups of distinctive elements: *actors/agents, negotiation patterns, off-the-table developments, concepts* (such as power, justice, and fairness), and the *linkages* among these four groups.

9. In this, the idea of partnerism differs from the characteristics of negotiation as pacting laid out in the introductory chapter by Anstey and Zartman.

10. For the effect that other negotiations and alternatives have on the ZOPA see Watkins and Passow (1996).

11. For the role of implementation in negotiation processes and relationships management, see Gordon & Ertel (2007) as well as Curry (1998).

References

Agha, H., Feldman, S., Khalidi., A., & Schiff, Z. (2003). *Track II diplomacy–Lessons from the Middle East*. Cambridge, MA: MIT Press.

Bagwell, K., & Staiger, R. W. (1999). An economic theory of GATT. *The Economic Review, 89*(1), 215–248.

Baker, D. 2 (2009, March 9). Update from Northern Ireland: Staring into the abyss? Dissident Republicans carry out fatal attacks. *Mission Connections* Retrieved April 15, 2009, from http://gamc.pcusa.org/ministries/missionconnections/baker-doug-and-elaine-20090310/

Bartoli, A., & Coleman, P. T. (2003, September). Dealing with extremists. *Beyond Intractability.* Retrieved April 1, 2009, from http://www.beyondintractability.org/essay/dealing_extremists/

Bazerman, M., Church, J. R., Moore, D. A., & Valley, K. I, (2000). Negotiation. *Annual Review of Psychology, 45*(4), 519–544.

Berton, P., Kimura, H., & Zartman, I. W. (Eds.). (1999). *International negotiation, actors, structure/process, values*. Palgrave-Macmillian.

Church, D., & Bazerman, M. (2004). *Bounded awareness: What you fail to see can hurt you*. Cambridge, MA: Harvard Business School, Division of Research.

Coleman, P.T., Bui-Wrzosinska, L., Vallacher, R. R., & Nowack, A O. (2006). Protracted conflicts as dynamical systems. In A. K. Schneider & C. Honeyman (Eds.), *The negotiator's fieldbook* (pp. 61–74), Washington, DC: American Bar Association, Section on Dispute Resolution.

Curran, D., & Sebenius, J. K. (2003). The mediator as coalition-builder: George Mitchell in Northern Ireland. *Journal of International Negotiation, 8*(1), 111–147.

Curry, J. E. (1998). *International negotiating,* Planning and Conducting International Commercial Negotiations, World Trade Press.

Druckman, D. (2001). Turning points in international negotiation, a comparative analysis. *The Journal of Conflict Resolution, 45*(4), 519–544.

Gordon, M., & Ertel, D. (2007). *The point of a deal: How to negotiate when yes is not enough*. Boston: Harvard Bussiness School Press.

Khalidi, R. (1997). *Palestinian Identity: The construction of modern national consciousness*. New York: Columbia University Press.

Kramer, R. M., Pommerenke, N., & Newton, E. (1993). The social context of negotiation effects of social identity and interpersonal accountability on negotiation decision making. *The Journal of Conflict Resolution, 37*(4), 633–654.

Lax, D., & Sebenius, J. (2006). *3D negotiation: Powerful tools to change the game in your most important deals,* (p. 12). Boston: Harvard Business School Press.

Mawlawi, F. (1993). New conflicts, new challenges: The evolving role for non-governmental actors. *Journal of International Affairs, 46*(2).

Miall, H., Ramsbotham, O., & Woodhouse, T. (1999). *Contemporary conflict resolution: The prevention, management and transformation of deadly conflicts*. Malden, MA: Polity Press.

Mohr, J., & Spekman, R, (2006). Characteristics of partnership success: Partnership attributes, communication behavior, and conflict resolution techniques. *Strategic Management Journal, 15*(2), 135–152.

Patton, B. (1999). Commentary: The role of agents in international negotiation. In R. Mnookin & L. Susskind (Eds.), *Negotiating on behalf of others: Advice to lawyers, business executives, sports agents, diplomats, politicians and everybody else*. Thousand Oaks, CA: Sage.

Ramsbotham, O., Woodhouse, T., & Miall, H. (2005). *Contemporary conflict resolution: The prevention, management and transformation of deadly conflicts*. Malden, MA: Polity Press.

Saaty, T. L. (2008). Decision making with the analytic hierarchy process. *International Journal of Services Sciences*, 1(1), 83–98.

Starkey, B., Boyer, M., & Wilkenfeld, J. (1999). *Negotiating a complex world: An introduction to international negotiation*. Lanham, MD: Rowman & Littlefield.

Ward, A., Disston, L. G., Brenner, L., & Ross, L. (2008). Acknowledging the other side in negotiation. *Negotiation Journal*, 24(3), 269–285.

Watkins, M., & Passow, S. (1996). Analyzing linked systems of negotiations. *Negotiation Journal*, 12(4), 325–340.

Wolfsfeld, G. (1997). *Media and political conflict: News from the Middle East*. Cambridge: Cambridge University Press.

Zartman, I. W. (2000). Ripeness: The hurting stalemate and beyond. In P. Stern & D. Druckman (Eds.), *International conflict resolution after the cold war* (pp. 225–250). Washington, DC: National Academy Press.

Zartman, I. W. (2003). Managing Complexity, *International Negotiation*, 8(1), 179–186.

Zartman, I. W. (2006). Timing and ripeness. In A. K. Schneider & C. Honeyman (Eds.), *The negotiator's fieldbook* (pp. 143–152). Washington, DC: American Bar Association, Section on Dispute Resolution).

Zartman, I. W., & Kremenyuk, V. (Eds.). (2005). *Peace vs justice: Negotiating forward and backward looking outcomes*. Lanham, MD: Rowman & Littlefield.

12 Conditions for Internal Conflict Resolution through External Intervention

■ FRANK R. PFETSCH

Identity conflicts are among the most difficult to deal with because they touch upon emotional values dear to every collectivity. It is the self-identification of a group through language, culture, religion, customs, and so on that is called into question. Internal conflicts between such groups can lead to civil wars. Weak states suffer from such quarrels especially when groups are supported by external powers. Cases that come immediately to mind are the struggles between the Moslem groups in Iraq, the Moslem–Hindu rivalry in Kashmir, the Greek–Turkish quarrel in Cyprus, the ethnic-religious struggles in Bosnia and Kosovo, and the Tamil–Hindu quarrels in Sri Lanka, the Kurds in Iran, Turkey and Iraq, and, more recently, the independence movements in Abkhazia and South Ossetia. In all of these cases, the various groups are being supported by external powers that, in most cases, aggravate the fight between these groups. It is a situation comparable to the enmity between the two families of Montague and Capulet in Shakespeare's play *Romeo and Juliet*. Since the families do not get along, their children cannot enjoy their love. Is it possible in such cases to find a solution at all, a solution brought about by negotiations or mediation?

The project "Reducing Identity Conflicts and Preventing Genocide" consists of three different fields of research: first, identity and identity conflicts leading toward genocide; second, intervention by external powers; and third, conflict prevention and termination by negotiation and mediation.

Following these three aspects, the structure of this chapter has three parts. The first concentrates on identity and identity conflicts, the second on the global political framework within which external interventions in internal conflicts occur, and the third on the necessary conditions to resolve conflicts by negotiation. Methodologically, two approaches are employed. One type uses quantitative data over a wide range of such external–internal relationships. The other uses qualitative studies of particular cases that can be analyzed in a comparative manner. This chapter will use both approaches as it focuses on two aspects of third-party intervention in handling identity conflicts: how and where ethnic conflicts are located on a conflict-instrument cycle for management, especially mediation efforts, and the necessary and sufficient conditions for a durable solution of conflicts.

■ MANAGEMENT OF IDENTITY CONFLICTS

Political conflict is the clashing of overlapping interests (positional differences) around national values and issues (independence, self-determination, borders and territory, access to or distribution of domestic or international power). The conflict has to be of some duration and magnitude between at least two parties (states, groups of states, organizations, or organized groups) that are determined to pursue their interests and win their case. Identity conflicts have to do with the self-determination of a group that is discriminated within a larger nation. Identity is the object as well as the political goal of a population or a group within it. It is, according to Carl von Clausewitz, the political goal that characterizes a conflict and determines war.

Identity conflicts refer to conflicts involving a group having in common identifiable characteristics in culture, religion, language, race, and so on distinctly different from those of other groups. The politization of such groups increases the in-group feeling (we-feeling) and can be used for political power (instrumentalization). Conflict arises when political (or military) entrepreneurs make use of identity feelings to pursue their own power ambitions. Ethnic identity can be based either on birth or on construction. Whereas identities by birth are fixed and consequently nonnegotiable, ethnic identities, in the constructivist view, are flexible social constructions and hence are more open to negotiations. Ethnic conflicts, according to Kaufmann (1996), are on the whole "almost completely rigid," whereas ideological conflicts are "quite fluid." Hence, identity conflicts are value loaded and hard to deal with, especially on the basis of negotiation and mediation, since they are ingrained in the heart and soul.

Since identity conflicts are by nature value loaded, the difference between political and economic issues is of the utmost importance since *soft-power* instruments and *hard-power* means are being used. Empirical research proves that value-related issues, such as territorial integrity or sovereignty (borders, territorial affiliation, population, government), are more difficult to bargain over than disputes over economic goods (Pfetsch & Rohloff, 2000, p. 129). As a result, value-loaded issues related to components of national identity (frontiers/territory, population, government) are more difficult to deal with than economic issues.

Management deals with the attempts to control and regulate a certain social, political, or military development. It is commonly understood that the intention of an external conflict manager is not to aggravate the situation for the affected groups, that is, intensify the use of force, but to redirect, to reorient, and to transform the conflict into a setting that allows for peaceful and consensual resolution by all participating parties. Possible management instruments used in the course of a conflict are negotiations, authoritative decisions, threat, pressure, passive or active withdrawals, and physical violence and war (Pfetsch & Rohloff, 2000).

Conflict management can take various forms. It can be conducted by the affected parties themselves. This self-management of conflicts requires a large degree of political autonomy by the responsible parties. In many nonviolent conflicts, the issues are being negotiated in bilateral meetings of delegates. In nonviolent internal conflicts, round tables are an effective form for negotiating the issues in dispute with all affected parties. International regime building is another effective form of handling potential sources of conflict, especially those that transcend national regulation capacities, such as environmental issues. The term *global governance* best describes the global political handling of issue-oriented regimes and networks in an interdependent global communication society.

Conflict management is understood as deescalating action by the parties to settle the conflict either by themselves or with the help of intervening, mediating third parties. This management is a process over time that eventually will lead to a certain outcome, result, settlement, or resolution of the conflict. In general, four outcomes are conceivable: negotiated consensual agreements, undecided arrangements, resolutions by threat, and termination by force.

■ INTERVENTION THROUGH MEDIATION

The international system has evolved from a Westphalian state system to a post-Westphalian system, that is, from prohibition to intervene in internal state affairs to permission to intervene under certain conditions. The Westphalian system insisted on the sovereignty of states, on nonintervention and territorial integrity. The post-Westphalian system emphasizes interdependence, common or collective security, and the obligation to intervene under specific circumstances, such as acute human rights violations or ethnic cleansing. Thus, the sacred concept of sovereignty and noninterference in internal state affairs has become permeable.

Throughout history, most wars among peoples and states began with some kind of formal announcement, and they ended with an agreement on truce or peace. Wars were regarded as a natural and inevitable part of human history, and the formal opening and ending of wars legitimated one's actions. War as a legitimate means of politics was not outlawed before the first half of the twentieth century. The universal ban on war, except for self-defense, evidently led to the disappearance of formal declarations of war (while in reality, the number of wars worldwide kept growing throughout the twentieth century). The function of peace treaties has changed accordingly. Peace treaties in modern undeclared wars implicitly acknowledge the existence of a war, and they express the will of the parties to end it, however illegal and illegitimate the war is considered. Modern peace treaties often have the character of a compromise solution, since the concepts of absolute victors and losers no longer apply. Spoils have become illegal, and guilt is regarded as an inadequate concept for cooperation. Today annexation, occupation, colonization, slavery, or subjugation of conquered territories and peoples are outdated concepts that, so far, have not been replaced by equally accepted codes of conduct or norms concerning the legality of the beginnings of war, the endings of war, and the beginnings of peace. Peace treaties have more and more the function of reconciling hostile parties and opening new ways of coexistence and cooperation for the future. They try to bridge the normative gap[1] between the high aspirations in the United Nations (UN) Charter, which outlaws war and refers to war in the narrow and traditional context of "aggressors" and "self-defense," on the one hand and, on the other hand, the grim reality of 375 violent crises and wars between 1945 and 1995 that, by and large, were neither caused by genuine aggressors nor conducted as self-defense measures. When analyzing peace treaties and other forms of formal endings of violent and nonviolent conflicts, empirical conflict researchers must be aware of these additional functions that the documents have had since 1945.

External intervention can take various forms according to the issues at stake, the addressees, and the political system (government, opposition, ethnic groups, nongovernmental organizations [NGOs]) and operate through different means:

military troops, arms supply, financial and diplomatic support, mediation/negotia-
tion, brief, instruments ranging from soft (Article VI) to hard (Article VII) according to the UN Charter. Interventions can be made in favor of a suppressed group or
in favor of a government. Interventions can be made by neighboring states or/and
by the great powers or—during the era of the Cold War—by the superpowers. But
external intervention has been confronted by an inviolable and overriding principle
of international law, namely, that of national sovereignty. During the 1990s, certain
precedents were created to override this sacred principle in order to prevent ethnic
cleansing or genocide, arrest war criminals, restore democracy, or provide disaster
relief when national governments were unable or unwilling to do so. The George H.
W. Bush administration intervened in Somalia to prevent famine and to aid the
Kurds in Northern Iraq, the Clinton administration returned an elected leader to
power in Haiti, the North Atlantic Treaty Organization (NATO) ended the war in
Bosnia and stopped Slobodon Milosevic's terror in Kosovo; the British halted a civil
war in Sierra Leone; and the UN authorized lifesaving missions in East Timor and
elsewhere. George W. Bush's intervention in Afghanistan was covered by the UN as
a self-defense measure after 9/11. But his military intervention in Iraq generated a
negative reaction and has weakened the support for cross-border intervention. The
recent Myanmar experience showed how a military junta regime can prevent international help even in cases of human disasters. It can be argued—as the former U.S.
Secretary of State, Madeleine Albright, did—that the concept of humanitarian
intervention has lost momentum (*Herald Tribune*, June 12, 2008).

Internal Conflicts and the Reactions of Neighboring States

Out of a multitude of behavioral relations, six categories of possible relations
between neighboring states and directly involved parties in an identity conflict can
be discerned. Figure 12.1 shows possible relations among direct and external conflict parties.

1. No intervention in internal conflicts by external neighboring governments
2. Conflicts between two states (K, L) without intervention by another state
3. Conflicts between internal groups (x, y) without external intervention by
   another state
4. Conflicts between internal groups (x, y) with external intervention by
   another state (M)
5. Conflicts between two states (K, L) with external intervention by another
   state (M)
6. Conflicts between two states (K, L) supporting each other's opposing groups
   (y, z; x, w)

Empirical findings for the period 1945 to 1995 show that in about half of the 661
conflicts counted, there was no intervention recorded (Pfetsch & Rohloff, 2000,
p. 182). Most often (181 cases) neighboring states remained passive (1), followed
by 117 cases of political nonviolent conflicts between two governments without
external interference (3). External interventions mostly (88 cases) occurred in situations where internal groups (x, y) of one state were being supported by another
government (L) by subversion or intervention (4, 6). External political interference

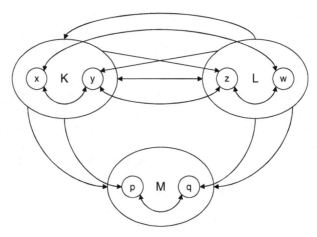

Figure 12.1 Relations among direct and external parties to a conflict.

by neighboring states only occurred in fewer cases. This, of course, has to be seen on a case-by-case basis and in a regional environment. The Great Lakes region in Africa has certainly more spillover effects of internal conflicts to neighboring states.

Based on a selection of 29 ethno-political conflicts from 1980 to 2000 in Africa, Asia, and Central America, a recent analysis (Khosla, 2004) presents some generalizations that contradict our findings, such as: military assistance is the most common form of intervention; neighbors are the most frequent interveners; and when foreign states intervene competitively in domestic ethnic conflicts, escalation is not the expected result. These generalizations are not confirmed by our data. The different data sets of the conflict cases may be an explanation.

Negotiation as a nonviolent instrument to interfere in an internal quarrel most often is directed toward some kind of power sharing or federation model. The success of this strategy is not very promising. Power sharing, involving joint exercise of governmental power, proportional distribution of governmental funds and jobs, autonomy on ethnic issues, minority veto power, and so on, did not work in places such as Lebanon, Cyprus, and Sri Lanka, and hardly worked in Spain (the Basque territory) or the United Kingdom (Northern Ireland). On a rational choice basis, the fighting parties must realize that further fighting will bring them more costs than profit, as Cunningham discusses in a later chapter. Outside interference can help to restore a more equal relationship by arming the weaker side or blockading the stronger one, creating a hurting stalemate (Zartman, 2000). Since such efforts are difficult to achieve, some authors see separation as the only promising way of ending civil wars (Kaufmann, 1996). In contrast, Nicholas Sambanis (2000), who examined 125 civil wars, which produced 21 partitions, found that partition did not help prevent the recurrence of ethnic war.

The Role of Great Powers and Superpowers

The involvement or engagement of superpowers and dominant states or their non-involvement in a conflict can greatly influence the course of a dispute. Superpowers and great powers can interfere in the conflicts of smaller powers and their internal identity groups in a variety of ways, which are grouped into five categories, as shown in Figure 12.2. For the 1945–1995 period, we consider the United States and the Soviet Union as superpowers and the People's Republic of China (between 1971 and 1986), France, and Great Britain (between 1945 and 1956) as great powers, grouped together as external powers.

1. Great powers (A, B) remain neural or inactive
2. Great powers (A, B) support smaller power (K) against their internal rebel groups (x, y)
3. Conflict between a great power (A) and a smaller power (K)
4. Conflict between a state (K) and its internal rebel group (x) supported by a great power (A)
5. Great power(s) (A, B) mediate(s) between conflicting parties (L, K; x, y; x, w).

Our empirical findings suggest that here too, the great powers remained neutral or inactive. In half of the 661 cases listed, no activity could be observed. In case of intervention, a great power (A) supported a smaller state (K) against an internal nongovernmental group (x, or y) (71). But quarrels between a great power (A) and a smaller power (K) also occurred frequently (49). A great power (A) supported an internal nongovernmental group (x) against another state (K) (33). Mediation efforts by great powers or superpowers could be observed in 60 conflicts cases. No dictated settlement could be observed (Pfetsch & Rohloff, 2000, p. 183). In the period of the Cold War, the United States intervened 104 times in ongoing conflicts, 92 of which were nonmilitary interventions; the Soviet

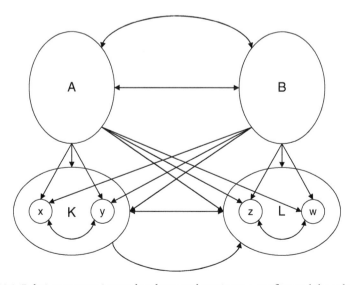

Figure 12.2 Relations among internal and external parties to a conflict and the role of great powers and superpowers.

Union intervened 82 times, 77 of which were nonmilitary (Pfetsch & Rohloff, 2000, pp. 167–168).

Mediation as Means to Intervene

The analysis of third-party interventions and mediation in crises has matured in the past ten years, and the body of literature is rapidly growing. In particular, the end of the Cold War and the euphoric desire for a new world order nourished the belief that proper instruments of negotiation and a humanitarian and rational approach free of ideological chains would be steps toward world peace. The debacles in Somalia and Yugoslavia have shown that these high hopes, which focused especially on the UN, were misplaced. Instead, new types of conflict, namely, identity-based conflicts in unstable, weak, or corrupt Third World states, top the agenda. Mediation and negotiation theory has developed a set of premises, criteria, and scenarios for the management and deescalation of these types of conflict. For the time being, it seems that professional mediation is one of the few effective, noncoercive instruments to handle escalated conflicts.

When, where, and why does mediation occur? KOSIMO cannot answer the "why" question on the basis of its data, but it can offer a comparatively detailed profile of conflicts with and without mediation. This profile allows for some general conclusions about global trends in mediation. Table 12.1 lists eight types of conflict separated into mediated and nonmediated forms.

Mediation has only recently become an object of systematic empirical research. Few researchers have counted and categorized mediation efforts in conflicts. Haas (1983) has observed mediation in 75% of 108 conflicts from 1945 to 1965. Butterworth (1976) found mediators in 77% of his cases; Bercovitch (1986) and Bercovitch and Rubin (1992) analyzed 79 international conflicts since 1945 and counted 44 conflicts with a total of 257 mediation efforts. The Hamburg-based "working unit on the causes of war" (AKUF[2] 1995) reports 131 mediated endings of wars from 1945 to 1992. KOSIMO[3] has found in 55% of its 661 conflicts attempts at mediation by one or more parties (Table 12.1). This number is the lowest result when compared with the findings of other data banks, because our sample includes not only wars or violent conflicts, but also nonviolent conflicts. Yet it confirms the trend that, depending on the data set, more than 50% and up to 75% of all conflicts are mediated at one point in their development.

For the 286 nonviolent conflicts, the frequency of mediated conflicts is slightly lower, at 50%. This finding can be interpreted in two ways. On the one hand, it is plausible to assume that in nonviolent conflicts, the parties are still autonomous and capable of developing rational approaches and constructive resolutions to their conflict. Both parties feel solely responsible for their conflict and capable of solving it without external interference. Therefore, the need for a mediator is low. On the other hand, it can be argued that all violent conflicts developed from nonviolent phases after constructive communication broke down. Therefore, negotiations should be monitored or accompanied by mediators at the earliest stage possible. In this respect, the 50% frequency of nonmediated, nonviolent conflicts is too low.

TABLE 12.1. *Mediated and Nonmediated Conflicts (Violent/ Nonviolent, Internal/External)*

Type	Frequency	%
Total conflicts	**661**	**100%**
Nonmediated conflicts	297	45%
Mediated conflicts	364	55%
Nonviolent conflicts	**286**	**100%**
Nonviolent nonmediated conflicts	142	50%
Nonviolent mediated conflicts	144	50%
Violent conflicts	**375**	**100%**
Violent nonmediated conflicts	155	41%
Violent mediated conflicts	220	59%
International conflicts	**398**	**100%**
International nonmediated conflicts	138	35%
International mediated conflicts	260	65%
International nonviolent conflicts	**228**	**100%**
International nonviolent nonmediated conflicts	95	42%
International nonviolent mediated conflicts	133	58%
International violent conflicts	**170**	**100%**
International violent nonmediated conflicts	43	25%
International violent mediated conflicts	127	75%
Internal conflicts	**263**	**100%**
Internal nonmediated conflicts	159	60%
Internal mediated conflicts	104	40%
Internal nonviolent conflicts	**58**	**100%**
Internal nonviolent nonmediated conflicts	47	81%
Internal nonviolent mediated conflicts	11	19%
Internal violent conflicts	**205**	**100%**
Internal violent nonmediated conflicts	112	55%
Internal violent mediated conflicts	93	45%

Source: Pfetsch and Rohloff (2000, p. 190).

Of the 375 violent conflicts that were entered into the KOSIMO data bank, 59% were mediated. This finding supports the assumption that in violent conflicts, the parties lost some or all control over constructive conflict management forms and were in need of third-party intervention. On the other hand, 41% of all violent conflicts between 1945 and 1995 were carried out without third-party mediation. One reason for this result is that the most frequent type of violent conflict, internal conflict, is not subject to international law and the UN crisis mechanism. Similarly, regional organizations have a very limited right to intervene in the internal affairs of one of their member states without the member's consent. Although in 1992 former Secretary General Peres de Cuellar stated that the trend toward international enforcement of human rights within member states is irreversible, the realization of this goal is still in the distant future.

Of 263 internal conflicts, only 40% were mediated—45% of the violent internal conflicts and only 19% of the nonviolent internal conflicts. In contrast, two-thirds of the 398 international conflicts were mediated—75% of the total 170 international violent conflicts and 58% of the nonviolent international conflicts.

The general conclusion from Table 12.1 is that nonviolent and internal conflicts are mediated less frequently than international and violent conflicts. On the one hand, this can be explained by a shortage of internationally accepted instruments for the mediation of internal conflicts. On the other hand, international violent conflicts have a much greater potential to become a threat to world peace and international security than other types of conflict. The world's concern for this type of conflict is understandably higher—although violent international conflicts have been decreasing in number since the early 1970s and are exceptional today.

Are there regional differences in the frequency of mediated conflicts? The literature on cross-cultural negotiations assumes different styles and attitudes to concepts such as *mediation* and *compromise*. Whereas *compromise* as a Western concept is a positive term, it is rather mistrusted in the oriental style of negotiations. From our data, we cannot deduct cultural differences with regard to acceptance of mediation. However, the regional frequencies of documented mediation efforts can serve as a basis for inductive speculations. The overall trend shows that Europe, South America, and Asia/Oceania have rather low frequencies of mediated conflicts, whereas the Middle East/Maghreb, Central America, and sub-Saharan Africa have higher frequencies than the global average of 55%. North America, with two mediated conflicts out of three conflicts, cannot be accepted as a significant sample (Pfetsch & Rohloff, 2000, pp. 191–193).

The third aspect of a global analysis of mediation, after the analysis of types of conflict and regions of conflict, is the issues over which the conflicts have escalated, divided into seven issues and a residual eighth category. The focus is on the proportion of mediated conflicts within each issue subset, regardless of the size of the subset. There is multiple coding of up to three issues for each conflict (Table 12.2).

TABLE 12.2. *Issues in Mediated and Nonmediated Conflicts*

Items (*multiple choice)	Frequency	% of all items (n = 1059*)	Non-mediated conflicts	Row %	Mediated conflicts	Row %
Territory, borders, sea borders	224	21%	85	38%	139	62%
Internal power conflict	180	17%	81	45%	99	55%
Ideology, system conflict	150	14%	80	53%	70	47%
Ethnic, religious, or regional autonomy	121	11%	67	55%	54	45%
Decolonization, independence	116	11%	50	43%	66	57%
International power conflict	117	11%	34	29%	83	71%
Resources	103	10%	28	27%	75	73%
Other	48	5%	20	42%	28	58%
Total	1059*	100%				

Source: Pfetsch and Rohlof (2000, p. 193).

The seven issues can be grouped into international issues and internal issues. Conflicts over territory, land borders and sea borders, international power conflicts, and conflicts over resources are found in conflicts with an international dimension, where the highest frequencies for mediated conflicts are found for conflicts involving resources (73%), international power conflicts (71%), and conflicts over territory, land, and sea borders (62%). Conflicts over decolonization, national independence, ethnic, religious and regional autonomy or secession, ideological system conflicts, and internal power conflicts are typically found in internal conflicts. From the subset of typically internal issues of conflicts, the category "decolonization and national independence" shows the highest proportion of mediated conflicts (57%). The other internal issues—autonomy or secession, ideological system conflicts, and internal power conflicts—show frequencies around or below 50% of all conflicts over the respective issue. The number of non-violent negotiated resolutions is—as expected from the analysis of internal conflicts—low. Out of 121 conflicts over ethnic, religious, and regional autonomy, only 13 conflicts (or 11%) were resolved by negotiations. Half of these conflicts remained undecided, and 40% of them were resolved by the use of force. A similar trend can be observed for conflicts over decolonization and national independence.

In contrast to the internal issues, conflicts over territory and borders, as well as over access to and the distribution of resources, have a different profile. Only 16% of the territorial conflicts and 21% of the conflicts over resources were resolved by the use of force. Also, threats and pressure played a subordinate role in the resolution of these conflicts. On the other hand, nonviolent negotiated resolutions make up 37% of the territorial conflicts and 32% of the conflicts over resources. In the group of territorial conflicts, the percentage of undecided cases (41%) is rather high. It seems that territorial issues do not top the agenda of states when it comes to their actual resolution.

Taken together, these findings seem to allow a widening gap between global trends of conflicts and global trends of mediations. On the one hand, the frequency of internal conflicts over autonomist or secessionist issues and internal power positions is on the rise, while the number of violent international conflicts has been decreasing for decades and is negligible today. Yet, the conflicts that are most frequently approached by mediation are these international conflicts over material issues as compared with value and identity disputes in internal conflicts.

■ CONDITIONS TO RESOLVE

Two considerations could enlighten our thinking about resolving interstate and intrastate conflicts. One concerns the adequate instruments to be used in accordance with the severity of the conflict. The other is empirically and/or intuitively tested conditions that must be present if a durable resolution is to be achieved.

Balance of Means and Ends

The first focal point concerns an acceptable position on opposing interests by the use of appropriate means to achieve a successful outcome. Recent events, such as the wars in Somalia, Bosnia, Kosovo, and Afghanistan, have demonstrated the shortcomings of negotiations, which have contributed to an unfavorable picture of international organizations, especially the UN. An awareness of the causes of negotiation failures can contribute to a more realistic appreciation of such organizations. According to the intensity of a conflict, successful management depends on the fairly symmetrical use of instruments of conflict management. Low-intensity conflicts require the use of soft diplomatic skills; high-intensity conflicts require hard methods. An appropriate relationship between means and ends should prevail.

The negotiation process can be divided into different *phases*, similar to the process of conflict development. Conflict can also be separated into phases (initiation, development, resolution) with different intensities (latent and manifest conflicts, crises, severe crises, and wars), and the process of negotiation can be divided into the prenegotiation, main, and postnegotiation phases. These classifications are obviously analytical in nature; in real life, a clear distinction is rarely possible. The relations between the conflict phases and the negotiation phases are *complex* and require clarification. However, it is possible to relate the phases of a conflict to particular courses of action, given that the appropriate course of action is partly determined by the intensity of conflict: A latent conflict requires a course of action such as prevention or early warning, as presented in the introductory chapter by Anstey and Zartman. The appropriate course of action for a predominantly nonviolent conflict is conflict management according to Chapter VI of the UN Charter, which states that the parties should "seek solutions by negotiation, enquiry, mediation, conciliation, arbitration, judicial settlement, resort to regional agencies or arrangements or other peaceful means of their choice." A violent conflict must be countered by war prevention, and the termination of war demands the peace enforcement measures mentioned in Chapter VII of the UN Charter. Finally, the postwar period requires peace consolidation measures, which means the building up of stable, preferably democratic, institutions, the organization of elections and their observation, and the creation of facilities for economic reconstruction. As mentioned above, all the phases of conflict development can be accompanied by negotiations but with varying degrees of success (Figure 12.3).

The developments arising from different stages in the escalation process can be thought of in terms of a cycle. It has frequently been observed that conflicts can break out over and over again but can also remain dormant for a while (Collier, 2003). This fluctuation is evident in the contexts of the Northern Irish, Tamil, Basque, and Kurdish conflicts. The cyclical model permits the location of the different instruments of conflict management, as mentioned by Boutros Boutros Ghali (1992) in his "Agenda for Peace," and, in particular, the determination of the phase in which conflict negotiation has the best chance of success. Early-warning measures may therefore prevent a latent conflict from escalating into a crisis. Management techniques may prevent a crisis from escalating into a severe crisis. Deterrence may hinder parties from going to war. Peace enforcement may lead to an armistice agreement and peacekeeping to an effective state of peace. The conflict cycle ends with peace-consolidating measures and the building of a legitimate government.

With respect to international conflicts, the formal conclusion can take the form of a peace agreement or treaty, a cease-fire agreement, a declaration of independence, a communiqué, the decision of an arbitration court, or simple proclamations. As far as internal national conflicts are concerned, new or revised constitutions, armistices, peace agreements, rearrangements of government, decisions of an arbitration court, and proclamations or referenda are common. Some conflicts are left without a written document of conclusion, which means that demands are abandoned or resolved by silent withdrawal from the conflict. All these forms of outcomes require negotiations, which eventually lead to an acceptable solution.

The appropriateness of the instruments forms the basis for a second limitation to negotiation. The use of soft measures, such as diplomacy, as mentioned in Article VI of the UN Charter, is inadequate for the termination of a war. Only hard methods or the threat of such methods can prevent or stop aggressive militant behavior. One important lesson that both the politicians of Western Europe and those of international organizations have had to learn is that in situations of war, and confronted with aggressive nationalistic power policy, only actors with symmetric instruments of power can hinder an aggressor. If one side is employing coercive means, the other side must do the same to prevent further damage. These limitations to negotiations also apply to democracies. If, however, conflicts remain latent or are on the brink of becoming manifest, negotiations may prevent further escalation (preventive diplomacy). It is always better to talk than to shoot, but the effectiveness of talking depends, among other things, very much on the nature of the conflict and the issues involved and, above all, on the actors.

Thus, negotiation and mediation probably have a chance to succeed only in very specific conflict situations, that is, before the conflict reaches high intensity. Within the conflict cycle, preventive diplomacy and other tools of conflict management like mediation may have a chance to succeed. In other conflict situations where military means are employed, negotiation can only serve as an accompanied tool or help to arrange a truce.

The main interest in the analysis of formal endings of conflicts is to find out which factors contribute to stable and lasting conflict resolutions. From negotiation and mediation theory, we know that in order to be effective in the future, agreements must have a win-win character; they must be based on mutual compromises and on mutual confidence. Formal treaties may be an instrument to document this change in attitudes and behavior among former enemies. However, we cannot conclude that formal treaties are necessary to end wars and to begin peace.

Since, in the foreseeable future, the dominant type of conflict seems to be internal disputes over ethnic and minority issues, international peace treaties will remain relevant in internal conflicts only when external mediators or guarantors become part of the peace accord. Constitutional changes; revisions; treaties about religious, regional, or cultural autonomy; and regime changes have become increasingly important instruments to end periods of violence and to make a new start.

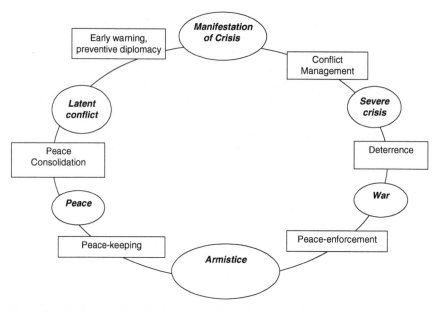

Figure 12.3 Cycle of conflict development with conflict management instruments.

■ SIX CONDITIONS FOR DURABLE PEACE

The second focal point is that conflict termination can—as seen—take various forms, from written or verbal agreements to militarily forced new situations. However, certain conditions are required in order to lead to a durable peace. Treaties considered fair and just must be based on mutual trust and must fulfill six conditions: *First* of all, peace negotiations must include all the conflicting and affected parties; *second,* treaties should be negotiated freely and be based on consent; *third,* all the relevant issues of the conflict have to be included in the negotiations, and all the controversial issues should be removed; *fourth,* consensus has to be reached without any secret reservation; *fifth,* an agreement should reflect the power relations among the negotiating parties; and, *finally,* it should take into consideration the prevailing historical circumstances (see Pfetsch, 2007). If—and only if—all parties involved in, or affected by the conflict agree of their own free will on all the issues to be negotiated, then—and only then—can the result of the negotiations be called a *solution,* meaning a just and fair outcome. The stability of an agreement—as the argument goes—depends, on the one hand, on the external conditions and the modalities fundamental to it and, on the other hand, on the nature of the relationship (symmetrical or asymmetrical) between the negotiating partners. In other words, the life expectancy of a negotiated agreement depends on how and under which circumstances it was reached, and this depends to a large extent on the structural relations that pervade the whole negotiation process. Symmetry and asymmetry are important background variables to the negotiation process and its outcomes. It goes without saying that these conditions are ideally conceived and, in reality, are rarely fulfilled. Yet, as guiding principles, they may be helpful. What are the empirical findings for unsuccessful and successful cases?

Unsuccessful Cases

Because the six conditions mentioned above have existed only in rare cases, peace treaties were either not concluded at all or such peace treaties did not last long, were revised, or triggered further conflicts. Statistics illustrate this point: 79 out of the 104 violent conflicts counted by us between 1945 and 1995 later led to further conflicts; 65 of them were wars (Pfetsch & Rohloff, 2000, p. 108). In most cases, wars of independence were followed by struggles over matters related to nation-building and state-making, and sometimes one ethnic war led to another one. The unfinished—because unrecognized—Algiers Agreement of 1975 between Iran and Iraq did not prevent Saddam Hussein's aggression toward Kuwait in 1991, and the 1995 and 2000 agreements of Dayton and Paris did not impede Milosevic from perpetrating ethnic cleansing in Kosovo. War was over, yet the conflict continued.

Kaufmann (1996), studying 27 ethnic civil wars from 1944 to 1994, found that 12 ended with a complete victory of one side, 5 ended with partition, and 2 were suppressed by military occupation by third parties. Only eight identity-based conflicts were ended by an agreement that did not partition the country and ended in a full or partial status of autonomy. These "success stories" of negotiated agreements are relevant to my topic. The cases show that in most of the eight ethnic civil wars (Nagas vs. India, Basques vs. Spain, Palestinians vs. Israel, Moros vs. the Philippines, Abkhazians vs. Georgia) the agreements did not result in a durable peace situation: Today the Palestinians are still striving for independence, the Tipuras secession movement is still at the level of a crisis, the Basques in Spain with Euzkadi ta Azkatasuna (ETA) are still seeking secession with sporadic violent actions, the Nagas in India are still seeking secession with occasional attacks, and on the Chittagong hill in Bangladesh regional predominance strife is still at the level of a crisis, as is the Abkhazian secession movement (HIIC: *Conflict Barometer*, 2007). Hence, it is important to define what a durable solution is.

Success Stories

Although in a large number of conflicts (especially in military warfare) negotiation/mediation failed to achieve any deescalating results (see above), there are many cases in which negotiation and/or mediation succeeded. As evidence for the theory—that is, agreements reached by consent and according to the six above-mentioned criteria—several empirical cases of some duration (at least ten years) can be listed. In 1956 the resolution of the Saar question between France and Germany through the integration of the Saar region into the Federal Republic (on January 1, 1957) after a referendum can be considered a durable solution. It was reached by bilateral negotiations without third-party intervention. Other examples are the border corrections between the Netherlands and Germany of April 8, 1960, and, last but not least, the resolution of German reunification after the conclusion of the 2+4 negotiations on October 3, 1990, which was a masterpiece of multilevel diplomatic negotiation; third parties were involved. These agreements demonstrate that coerced situations can be revised by consensus. The Camp David Agreement of March 26, 1979, which was reached between Israel and Egypt with the help of U.S. mediation and which stipulated the return of some of the territories conquered by the Israelis, was implemented and has remained stable up to now. It was, however, only a partial agreement between two countries and did not touch upon all the complexities of the Middle East conflict constellation. Another example is the agreement on the Beagle Channel between Chile and Argentina of 1977 mediated by the Vatican. Equally stable are the 13 decisions made prior to 1995 by the International Court of Justice (e.g., over the affiliation of islands [for instance, Minquiers and Ecrehos], borders [cf. Honduras–Nicaragua], or fishing rights [Great Britain–Norway]), which were accepted by the disputing parties and have remained durable to this day. Even the revision of inequitable peace treaties can be brought about by consensus and without coercion—in changed contexts.

Other outcomes reached by means of negotiation are not of the same nature, either because not all parties affected by the conflict were involved or because not all the disputed issues were negotiated or accepted without reservation. In terms of the conferences on climate change, another empirical case, one (still) cannot talk of a final agreement. The framework of agreement has led to further (partial) agreements (the Kyoto Protocol with quantified emission reduction rates) that were subject to consultations at the subsequent conferences in Buenos Aires, Bonn, and The Hague. However, some states that were parties to the agreement have so far failed to agree on its binding guidelines. Negotiators were under pressure from the of victims of pollution, and that prompted, among other things, the U.S. negotiators to withhold their signature and thus invalidated the agreement. The controversial issues were negotiated, but concrete targets for the respective pollutants were missing. A lack of consent over the convention and the most important partner's final refusal to sign reduced the effectiveness of the agreement. The framework conditions have, after all, probably changed. One would expect that awareness of the threat posed by environmental damage will increase and compel the United States to make concessions as well. In short, the agreement reached at the conference corresponds only in part to the six conditions of a durable solution and, consequently, remains subject to change and further deliberation.

In sum, negotiation results are just if they take into account the six conditions for durable solutions, that is, if they take into consideration given power relations and historical circumstances, and are accepted by all affected parties voluntarily, without force and without reservation. Agreements forced upon parties can initiate new conflicts or even wars. Peace agreements that are deserving of their name do bring about peace. If the twentieth century had respected these facts, it would have been spared many of the wars that took place, most of them on ethnic and/or national cleavages.

■ CONCLUSION

This chapter has dealt with the three aspects involved in the title of this book: identity and identity conflicts, the external way to approach these internal conflicts, and the mediation efforts to deal with these conflicts. At the end, we have to ask, what chance do external mediation efforts have to resolve internal ethnic conflicts? The answer is: not very much. By nature, ethnic conflicts are by far the most difficult ones to resolve from outside because of their value-loaded nature and because of the restrictions on intervening in the internal affairs of countries. The international community has institutionalized mechanisms to punish those who violate peaceful means of dealing with conflicts, but it did not manage to prevent and cool down ethnic thrives. If violence is used by the conflicting parties, the appropriate symmetric means is not negotiation or mediation but the threat or use of force. Very rare are internal ethnic conflicts that have been resolved by external mediation.

It is just as important to consider the termination of a conflict as its beginning since the modalities of a conflict's termination determine its future development. It would be fair to say that the conclusions of the so-called peace treaties in the first half of the twentieth century laid the foundations for the various wars in the second half of the century. Bad peace treaties became the source of wars. All five Parisian treaties after World War I led to further wars thereafter.

Notes

1. The idea of the United Nations peacekeeping is a similar pragmatic reaction to the existing gap between the principle of collective self-defense and widespread violence without clearly identifiable aggressors.

2. AKUF (Arbeitsgemeinschaft für Konflikt- und Friedensforschung) is a project of Hamburg University; see Gantzel/Schwinghammer (1995).

3. KOSIMO stands for Konflikt-Simulations-Modell, a project of Heidelberg University; see: Pfetsch and Rohloff (2000).

References

Bercovitch, J. (1986). International mediation. In *Cooperation and Conflict, 21*, 155–168.

Bercovitch, J., & Rubin, J. Z. (1992). *Mediation in international relations.* Houndmilles, UK: Macmillan.

Boutros Boutros-Ghali (1992). An Agenda for Peace: Preventive diplomacy, peacemaking, peace-keeping. UN report.

Butterworth, R. L. (1976). *Managing interstate conflicts, 1945–1974.* Pittsburgh: Pittsburgh University Press.

Collier, P. (2003). The market for civil war, *Foreign Policy, 136*, 38–45.

Gantzel, K. J., & Schwinghammer, T. (1995). *Die Kriege nach dem Zweiten Weltkrieg.* Münster: Litt.

Haas, E. B. (1983). Regime decay: Conflict management and international organizations 1945–1981. *International Organization, 37*(2), 189–256.

HIIC (Heidelberg Institute for International Conflict Research). *Conflict Barometer,* 1992–2007 ff.

Kaufmann, C. (1996). Possible and impossible solutions to ethnic wars. *International Security, 20*(4), 136–175.

Khosla, D. (2004). *Third party intervention in ethnic conflicts.* Doctoral dissertation, University of Maryland.

Pfetsch, F. R. (2007). *Negotiating political conflicts.* London: Macmillan.

Pfetsch, F. R., & Rohloff, C. (2000). *National and international conflicts, 1945–1995.* London and New York: Routledge.

Sambanis, N. (2000). Partition as a solution to ethnic war. *World Politics, 52*(3), 437–483.

13 Who Gets What in Peace Agreements?

■ DAVID E. CUNNINGHAM

When negotiations in internal identity conflicts succeed and lead to an agreement implemented by all sides, they can fundamentally change societies. Mozambique emerged from years of war with the signing of the Rome Accords on October 4, 1992. That process ended fourteen years of civil war and led to the integration of the military, the transformation of the former rebels into a political party, and eventually to multiparty democratic elections. Twenty years later, Mozambique's economy has expanded rapidly, millions of people have been lifted out of poverty, and the country is frequently held up as a model for post-conflict recovery and development.

When negotiations fail, by contrast, they can have disastrous consequences. The Rwandan government and the Rwandan Patriotic Front (RPF) signed a peace agreement in Arusha, Tanzania, in July 1993, just nine months after the Rome Accords ended the war in Mozambique. The Arusha agreement also called for political power sharing, military integration, and a timetable for multiparty elections. Less than nine months later, however, the Arusha Accords broke down in the Rwandan genocide, the worst example of mass slaughter since World War II.

The dramatic difference between the consequences of successful and failed negotiations has led many scholars to analyze the determinants of negotiation success in internal conflicts. In general, this literature has focused on two separate, but related, topics. The first set of studies examines the conditions that make combatants more or less likely to negotiate in civil war.[1] Scholars such as Zartman (1989), Walter (2002), and Stedman (1997) have analyzed the factors that lead combatants to initiate negotiations, sign agreements, and actually carry through and implement those agreements. The second set of studies (such as Hartzell & Hoddie, 2007, and Nilsson, 2008) focuses directly on peace agreements, and looks at the types of agreements that survive and those that break down. These scholars have analyzed whether agreements are more likely to successfully end war and build peace when they include power-sharing provisions, military integration, peacekeeping, and so on.

These approaches have contributed to our understanding of peace processes; however, they have not addressed an important aspect of the negotiation process. Peace agreements do not just transform society by taking power out of the hands of the government and spreading it out among a variety of groups. They also specify which groups get what share of the power in the new postconflict order. Sharing arrangements do not just specify that power will be shared, but also indicate how many seats and cabinet positions each participant in the power-sharing government will get. The Arusha Accords, for example, gave the RPF and the government each one-third of the seats in a transitional government, with the other one-third going to other political parties that were seen as more moderate and represented both Rwandan Hutu and Tutsi. A provision for power-integration agreements, likewise, specifies the size of the postconflict military and the percentage of that force that will be made up of each combatant. The Rome Accords, for example, established that the army in Mozambique would have 30,000 soldiers, half of whom would come from the former government and half from the rebels. Negotiated settlements are designed to have a large impact on the balance of power in a postconflict setting.

The distribution of power specified by an agreement can have dramatic consequences, including those concerning the likelihood that an agreement will actually stick. The breakdown of the Arusha Accords in Rwanda illustrates the importance of the distribution of power. There is a substantial debate among scholars over whether the Arusha Accords was a workable agreement or was doomed from the start. For those who think the agreement was fundamentally unworkable, the main argument is that the agreement gave too much to the rebels. Essentially, the RPF and the Rwandan government received equal shares of the postconflict military and the power-sharing government. The Rwandan government, however, was led by the Hutu, one of two main Rwandan ethnic groups that made up about 85% of the population. The Tutsi, who dominated the RPF, made up at most 15% of the population. Lemarchand (1994) states the case against the Accords most clearly by arguing that the government could never have accepted an agreement that gave the Tutsi half of the power in the country.

For others (e.g., Jones 2001; Walter 2002), however, the distribution of power specified in the Arusha Accords was justified because, by late 1992, the RPF was winning the war. Its advantageous position on the battlefield led the RPF to demand significant concessions in the Arusha peace process. In the absence of an agreement that gave it substantial power, the RPF would have had little incentive to sign a deal that required it to stop fighting.

This debate, then, revolves around a fundamental disagreement about what should determine who gets what in a negotiated settlement. For those like Lemarchand, the suggestion is that societal divisions, such as the ethnic balance, should determine the distribution of power. For those like Jones, however, the implication is that the distribution of power in a negotiated settlement should be driven by the military balance. This debate suggests that a theoretical and empirical exploration of the determinants of the content of peace agreements is needed.

This chapter begins to address this gap by examining the determinants of who gets what in peace agreements. Current theoretical literature on conflict bargaining leads to clear predictions about what types of groups are likely to do well in negotiations—namely, combatants that have the greatest chance of winning the conflict militarily and the lowest costs associated with fighting. This chapter argues, however, that mediators can actually have a profound effect on the content of peace agreements and that normative views of what a peace agreement "should" look like affect the content of the final agreement. Empirical tests of this argument that examine the content of all peace agreements signed in civil wars since 1989 show that the presence of mediators that are biased toward the rebels has a significant effect on what peace agreements look like, but that the military capabilities of groups do not appear to have an effect.

■ **WHAT DETERMINES THE CONTENT OF PEACE AGREEMENTS?**

Violent conflicts create winners and losers. This is clearly true if one side prevails militarily, as happened in Nigeria when the "Republic of Biafra" was defeated by the Nigerian military or in Ethiopia when the rebel alliance Ethiopian People's Revolutionary Democratic Front overthrew the government of President Mengistu Haile Meriam. In both of these cases, the losing side was completely stripped of political and military power in the aftermath of the conflict. Negotiated settlements, however, also create winners and losers as, generally, one or more actors get more of what they want than the others do. The long peace process in the Democratic Republic of the Congo (DRC), for example, created a transitional government in which two of the rebel groups, the Rally for Congolese Democracy (RCD) and the Congolese Liberation Movement (MLC), each received 94 seats but the Kisangani-based faction of the RCD only received 15 seats. What determines success in a negotiated settlement? That is, what determines which combatants get more of what they want?

The question of who gets what in negotiated settlements has not been directly addressed. However, the dominant theoretical framework for examining conflict bargaining leads to clear implications for who should do well in negotiations. Specifically, this framework suggests that those combatants that are most likely to do well militarily should also get more in negotiated settlements.

The Battlefield and the Negotiating Table

The determinants of military success in civil war appear quite obvious, as the side with greater military might is more likely to prevail militarily. In general, then, the stronger side should get more of what it wants when the conflict is decided by military victory. Winning on the battlefield and at the negotiating table would appear to require substantially different skills. However, a significant body of literature suggests that the determinants of military victory and negotiation success may be the same.

One of the main theoretical advances in the study of war has been the recognition that bargaining and fighting are not contradictory, but are often in fact different strategies armed groups use to try to achieve their demands. Much like the conception of warfare as "politics by other means," the so-called *bargaining and war* approach conceptualizes combatants in conflict as using both negotiation and fighting as separate strategies to obtain what they want. Combatants fight, then, not only in an attempt to win but also to improve their bargaining position at the negotiating table. For these models, those groups with the greatest chance of winning the conflict through military victory also are most likely to win at the negotiating table by getting more of what they want (Fearon, 1995; Reiter, 2003; Wagner, 2000).

In this conception, violent conflict breaks out because one or more groups are dissatisfied with the state of affairs in the country. This dissatisfaction can arise because aggrieved groups want specific policies changed, feel excluded from power, want a greater share of power, wish to obtain greater monetary resources (potentially through conflict profiteering), want to break away from the state entirely, or any other of a set of goals that groups have. Dissatisfaction alone is not enough to motivate conflict, however; potential combatants must also anticipate that they can do better by fighting than by not fighting.

The expectation of doing better through fighting can arise for two reasons. First, a group may think it has a realistic chance of winning the conflict and being able to implement its desired agenda unilaterally. Groups would prefer to get all of what they want, and if they think that they can prevail militarily, their incentive to fight can be quite high. At the same time, however, groups may be willing to fight even if they have little expectation of military success if they find themselves having no other option. Potential combatants may choose violence, then, if they see no nonviolent means to try to achieve their goals. In that case, the relative attractiveness of violence may increase even if the likelihood of achieving success through violence is low in absolute terms. The combination of dissatisfaction with the status quo and the expectation of a possibility of changing that status quo through violence leads actors to begin civil war.

Prior to the outbreak of conflict, then, potential combatants evaluate how well they are doing versus how well they anticipate doing if they begin a civil war. The decision about whether to use violence to pursue their goals does not stop once fighting begins; combatants also decide whether to continue or stop fighting based on their anticipated likelihood of winning and the relative costs of fighting. If rebel organizations have a low probability of military victory and high costs of fighting, they may exit the conflict without achieving any of their objectives. There are cases in identity-based conflict where rebels essentially stop fighting without being defeated militarily or given what they want through a negotiated settlement. Several of the low-intensity conflicts in Burma and India, for example, essentially ended without any decisive termination when the rebel groups largely stopped fighting.

When negotiations begin, combatants have an additional option beyond just continuing to fight to win or ceasing the conflict: They can sign and implement a settlement that gives them some, but not all, of their demands. In the negotiation phase, then, combatants evaluate the relative utility of signing and implementing a settlement versus continuing to fight in the hope of winning the conflict outright.

The logic of talking and fighting being separate strategies to achieve the same objectives leads to several implications about when negotiations are likely to succeed. First, negotiations are more feasible when conflict is more costly for the parties involved, because high costs reduce the expected benefit of continuing to fight. The importance of costs is central to the logic that negotiations are most likely to succeed in the case of a "mutually hurting stalemate" (Zartman, 1989) because combatants anticipate having to pay high costs to have a chance of eventually winning the conflict militarily. Conversely, so-called *lootable resource* approaches have argued that conflicts are hard to resolve when there is positive utility from fighting, because actors profiting from war have little incentive to negotiate and give up the benefits of fighting. Collier (2000), for example, argues that civil war can often be a "quasi-criminal" activity in which combatants operate more like criminal racketeers than revolutionary groups.

Second, negotiations become more likely when combatants are realistic about their chances of winning the conflict. A significant literature has examined the role of *information* in conflict bargaining (e.g., Filson & Werner, 2002; Slantchev, 2003; Smith & Stam, 2004). Essentially the argument is that bargaining becomes hard, if not impossible, if combatants are overly optimistic about the likelihood that they will prevail militarily, because this overoptimism makes them overestimate the benefit that they will gain from continuing to fight. Negotiation is easier, then, when information asymmetries do not represent a barrier to bargaining.

A similar logic can be used to generate predictions about who gets what in negotiations between identity groups. The costs of continued fighting and the like-lihood that they will prevail not only affect whether combatants will negotiate, they also determine the extent of concessions that they require in order to find an agreement acceptable. Actors evaluate the expected utility of fighting versus nego-tiating, and the better they anticipate doing from fighting, the higher the benefit they need to perceive from negotiating to prefer that strategy.

How well an armed group anticipates doing by continuing to fight is affected by three factors—the probability that it will actually win the war, the value that it attaches to military victory, and the anticipated costs of fighting to the end. The expected utility that the group attaches to a negotiated settlement, meanwhile, is affected primarily by two factors—the extent of concessions that it receives in the settlement and the value that it attaches to those concessions. In general, we assume that combatants would prefer to win the conflict outright, because they can then impose a new political order and not have to compromise on any of their demands, but that military victory itself has no intrinsic value. If we assume that combatants are indifferent as to whether they obtain what they want through negotiating or through fighting, then, the value they attach to concessions obtained through negotiation versus the value they attach to being able to impose their demands unilaterally through military victory should wash out. That is to say, an armed group would accept a negotiated settlement that gave it everything it wanted even if it was virtually assured of military victory, as in Rhodesia in 1979, for example.

This leaves, then, three factors that affect combatants' calculations: their antici-pated probability of victory (their BATNA or security point), the costs of fighting, and the extent of concessions included in the settlement. Armed groups compare, in essence, the extent of concessions to their probability of victory and the costs they anticipate paying if they continue to fight. As a combatant's probability of vic-tory increases, the extent of concessions that it requires to find a negotiated settle-ment acceptable also increases. Likewise, as a combatant anticipates having to pay greater costs to achieve military victory, the extent of concessions that it requires decreases because continuing to fight is a less attractive option.

The effect of the probability of victory and the costs of conflict are slightly different. The probability of military victory in identity conflicts may be a zero-sum game. As one combatant becomes more likely to win the conflict militarily, the other combatants become less likely to do so. We would expect that combatants with a higher likelihood of victory should get more of what they want in an agreement than those with a lower probability of victory.[2]

The costs of fighting are not, however, necessarily zero-sum. Some civil wars are more costly for all parties involved than others, and greater costs overall should make negotiation easier. Even so, the relative costliness of conflict should affect concessions. Those combatants who find conflict least costly can most clearly threaten to continue the war, and so can demand greater concessions in a negotiated settlement.

Thinking about how groups evaluate the relative costs and benefits of fighting versus negotiating, then, leads to two clear predictions about which combatants will do well in negotiations:

Hypothesis 1: In internal identity conflicts, combatants that have the highest probability of military victory will get the most of what they want in negotiated settlements.

Hypothesis 2: In internal identity conflicts, combatants that bear the lowest costs of fighting, relative to the other parties, will get the most of what they want in negotiated settlements.

The External Dimension of Conflict Negotiations

The above discussion of the bargaining process in internal conflicts is very combatant-centric. Combatants evaluate the prospect of military success, and the costs they anticipate paying to achieve it, and compare that to what they would get out of an agreement and decide whether to continue fighting. Indeed, the theoretical literature on conflict bargaining tends to focus exclusively on the costs and benefits to combatants in understanding when bargaining is possible.

To the extent that outside actors are included in these theoretical approaches, they often serve to facilitate the bargaining already taking place between the parties. Mediators can, for example, provide information to the combatants about the capabilities and resolve of the other side that decreases uncertainty and increases the ability of the parties to negotiate efficient agreements. The international community can help parties to overcome commitment problems that come up during bargaining by offering to deploy peacekeepers to observe whether parties are abiding by the agreements they signed.

An examination of recent negotiation processes reveals that international actors often play a more substantial role in determining the shape of negotiation processes than that depicted above. Mediators and facilitators, in particular, often impact two crucial elements of the negotiation. First, they can determine which actors are invited to, or even allowed to participate in, negotiations. In the Burundian negotiations in Arusha from 1998 to 2000, for example, Julius Nyerere opened up the process to many unarmed political parties and would not allow two of the main insurgent groups, the Forces for the Defense of Democracy (CNDD-FDD) and the National Liberation Forces (Palipehutu-FNL), to participate (Bentley & Southall, 2005). These decisions created an environment for 19-party talks that excluded two of the main combatants. In Somalia, the 2002–2003 peace talks in Eldoret, Kenya, were opened to a huge number of armed factions and clan groups. However, the International Crisis Group (*Negotiating a Blueprint for Peace 2003*, p. 2) reported that "criteria for participation in the reconciliation committees and the peace process as a whole appeared to be entirely arbitrary," and many Somali groups walked out due to dissatisfaction with the composition of the negotiations.

Mediators can also have a profound effect on the agenda under negotiation. In the 1992–1995 war in Bosnia-Herzegovina, the international community facilitated several rounds of negotiations among the warring factions. The early rounds of talks primarily involved the facilitators presenting different plans (such as the Lisbon Proposal, the Vance-Owen Plan, and the Owen-Stoltenberg Plan) for a political division of Bosnia and allowing the combatants to negotiate about the details of these plans (Woodward, 1995). In the Dayton process of November 1995, the combatants were given greater freedom to negotiate a wider range of issues; however, they could only negotiate the political future of a single Bosnian state, not the division of Bosnia.

The role that mediators can play in determining who is at the table and what is under negotiation can have profound effects on the shape of agreements reached. A peace process that involves the combatants, as well as many other political parties and representatives of civil society, and addresses a broad set of socially relevant issues is likely to lead to a much different peace agreement than one that only involves the main combatants and focuses the agenda on the core issues in the conflict.

Once negotiations begin, with the composition of participants and the agenda set, mediators can continue to have a significant influence on how the negotiations play out. Two primary factors give mediators this role. First, there is often a significant range of acceptable agreements, and mediators can influence where within this range the actual settlement lies. Second, the international community can alter the costs and benefits of fighting for combatants and therefore affect their openness to negotiation and the extent of concessions they are willing to accept.

The discussion in the previous section focused on how each combatant's probability of victory and the relative costliness of fighting affected the minimal concessions that group was willing to accept. Civil war negotiations, however, generally contain some room for negotiation between the minimal concessions for each group. If the conflict is sufficiently costly, then there should be a significant set of agreements that all combatants would prefer to continued conflict. This is referred to as the "bargaining range" (Ikle & Leites, 1962) or as the "Zone of Possible Agreement" (Sebenius, 2002). In essence, the concessions the government would be willing to offer may be greater than those that the rebels require to stop fighting.

Mediators can have a significant influence on where within this zone the specific agreement lies by putting pressure on groups to sign agreements with certain provisions. That is, mediators can significantly influence whether an agreement favors the rebels or the government. In the Yugoslavia negotiations, for example, the mediators would not allow the partition of Bosnia to be on the agenda and required the combatants to negotiate within the framework of an existing plan.

In this way, groups such as the Bosnian Serbs, who were in favor of partition, were prevented from negotiating for that concession.

Additionally, mediators/facilitators can impact the shape of agreements directly by affecting the incentives each side has to negotiate, acting as a "mediator as manipulator" (Touval & Zartman, 1985). If groups base the extent of concessions they are willing to accept at least partly on the costliness of fighting, the international community can expand the bargaining range by raising these costs. In recent years, for example, there has been increasing focus on limiting the sale of "blood diamonds" and other conflict resources that are seen as providing groups with an incentive to continue fighting.[3] By removing this economic incentive, the international community hopes to make conflicts more amenable to resolution.

All of this discussion suggests that while theoretical models of conflict bargaining often treat negotiations as driven primarily by the combatants, the content of peace agreements can be highly affected by outside influence. International mediators can shape who is at the negotiating table and what is on the agenda, pressure combatants to negotiate specific provisions, and affect the incentives that combatants have to abandon negotiations and return to the battlefield. If mediators have specific preferences about what peace agreements should look like, then these preferences can have profound effects on the settlement that results. In particular, if mediators think that the content of agreements should be based on something other than the probability of military victory and the costs of fighting for each side, then settlements should look substantially different than the predictions derived above. There are at least two reasons that mediators may have specific preferences for agreements that shape their content.

First, mediators may go into peace processes with a conception of what types of peace agreements are likely to be most stable. (See Zartman, 2010, on Martti Ahistaari's approach to mediation.) This conception, in particular, can be driven by the distinction made often in the conflict resolution literature between positive and negative peace. *Negative peace* is defined as the absence of violence, while *positive peace* includes the presence of social equity and other factors that are seen to create the conditions for a stable and lasting peace.

Basing the distribution of power in a peace agreement solely on the distribution of military power during the conflict can be seen as a negative conception of peace. That is, it removes the main cause of continued violence by eliminating the incentives that groups have to keep fighting. Much of the literature on conflict resolution, however, argues that peace is more likely to last if a positive conception is used. Mediators, based on this kind of thinking, often use peace processes as an opportunity to bring together a wide range of voices within the country and to address a large set of conflictual issues in society. Additionally, the concept of positive peace may encourage mediators to push combatants to create agreements that distribute power in a way that mirrors the divisions in society, in an effort to give each group an equal voice and decrease the feeling of exclusion. Using peace processes to create agreements that have a fair distribution of power representing the various groups in society can move them away from a distribution of power based on the military attributes of combatants.

Second, mediators may be biased in favor of one side. Accusations of bias are common in civil war negotiations. The government of Serbia saw the United States as biased in favor of the Bosnian Muslims and the Kosovar Albanians in those two conflicts, and the government of Sudan frequently accuses the international community of bias in discussions over how to resolve the conflict in Darfur. These claims are often inaccurate, and combatants are likely to see themselves as treated unfairly regardless of the intentions of the mediator. There are plenty of cases, however, where bias may in fact motivate actions of the international community. There is frequently a sense among international actors that one side or the other in a conflict is more legitimate. Many observers, for example, see the rebels in Colombia as simply narco-traffickers, rather than as a group fighting for some legitimate agenda. Likewise, the conflict in Sierra Leone was often viewed as involving a money-hungry organization, the RUF, that had little interest in political change. While the conception of mediation is that mediators are unbiased facilitators of negotiation, often international actors perceive one side as the aggressor, or as unfairly intransigent, and work to strengthen the other side.

There is a significant theoretical literature, in fact, that suggests that biased mediation may be more effective in building peace.[4] This literature focuses primarily on the role of bias in overcoming information and commitment problems rather than on the actual content of peace agreements. It does suggest, however, that there are theoretical reasons that mediators may see bias as a way to more effectively promote negotiation success. In either case, the presence of a biased mediator should clearly affect the outcome of a peace process.

Both the motivation to create a more permanent and just peace and bias on the part of mediators can shape peace agreements in addition to the impact of group costs and benefits of fighting. This analysis suggests, then, that understanding the content of peace agreements requires looking beyond the attributes of combatants and at the motivation of mediators. This discussion leads to two predictions about the effect of mediators on what agreements look like.

Hypothesis 3: The preference of mediators affects the distribution of power in peace agreements.

Note that this hypothesis is very general and does not make any specific predictions about how mediation will affect the distribution of power (that is, who will do better when there is mediation). The exact impact of mediation is likely to differ greatly on the dynamics of the conflict, that is, whether the government or the rebels are seen as more intransigent or as deserving greater concessions, as well as on the specific preferences of the mediator. One aspect of mediator preferences that is likely to affect the distribution of power is bias toward one side or the other, leading to the next prediction:

Hypothesis 4: When there are mediators that are biased toward one party, that party will receive more in a peace agreement.

This prediction suggests that, in addition to playing a role in alleviating information and commitment problems, biased mediators can also directly affect the substance of peace agreements.

■ EMPIRICAL ANALYSIS

This section tests the four hypotheses arising from the two different conceptions of what affects the content of peace agreements by examining the distribution of concessions in all peace agreements in civil war since 1989. While this is a book about identity conflicts, all civil wars over the last twenty years are included for two reasons. First, the theoretical argument here should apply to civil wars of all types, not just those fought over identity issues. Second, coding which of these conflicts are identity conflicts and which are not, and then limiting the sample to the former cases, has the potential to introduce a high degree of subjectivity into the analysis. However, as described below, a measure of whether the conflict was an ethnic conflict is included to give an indication of whether violent conflicts over identity are different than other civil wars.

To identify peace agreements, the dataset from Harbom et al. (2006) is used. Their data include information on agreements signed in all civil wars in the Uppsala Conflict Data Project/Peace Research Institute Oslo Armed Conflict Dataset (ACD) from the period 1989–2005.[5] They find 144 agreements in the 121 armed conflicts active during that period.[6]

The unit of analysis in this study is the civil war dyad. A *dyad* is defined as a relationship between the government and a rebel group. The analysis here, then, examines how attributes of the rebel groups and the presence of mediation affect the distribution of benefits between a government and a rebel group that are both signatories to a peace agreement. In the case of peace agreements with multiple signatories, the agreement is divided into a series of government–rebel group dyads.

Peace processes in civil war often result in a series of agreements. Harbom et al. (2006), for example, identify 16 agreements between the Guatemalan government and the Guatemalan National Revolutionary Union. Some of these settlements are actually "peace process agreements" addressing the agenda for comprehensive talks that would come later. In some conflicts, however, the combatants split the various issues and negotiate separate agreements over areas such as military/security issues, political power sharing, economic issues, and territorial administration. In this analysis, I am interested in the concessions received by rebels in the overall peace process, so I have coded a composite measure of the concessions in all of the agreements signed in the dyad.

All of the hypotheses in this chapter are predictions about which groups in conflict will get more of what they want. Evaluating this question through a statistical analysis presents some difficulties, because doing so requires a way to compare the concessions that groups receive across cases. On a theoretical level, it makes sense to think about civil war as a contest between a government, which would like to retain the status quo, and rebels, who would like to change it in some fashion. One way to measure who "wins" in a negotiated settlement, then, would be to examine whether the new status quo created by the agreement is closer to that desired by the rebels or the government.

Measuring the new status quo in a way conducive to statistical analysis is nearly impossible, because the specific preferences of rebels and governments are difficult to ascertain. However, we can assume that rebels, in general, would rather gain more political and military power and/or greater control over territory in a peace agreement and that governments, in general, would rather give up less power and territory. Getting more political and military power and territorial control does not necessarily address rebels' dissatisfaction with the status quo, but it does give them an opportunity to change that status quo by having a greater role in the postconflict government and the military and greater freedom to manage affairs in their own region.

The dependent variable in this study, then, is a measure of the number of concessions given to rebel groups in terms of their participation in military and political power in the postconflict setting. Harbom et al. (2006) code a number of components of peace agreements, divided primarily into three areas—military components, such as military integration, demobilization, and a cease-fire; political components, such as allowing the rebels to form a political party, holding elections, and power sharing; and territorial components, such as granting the region of the country under dispute autonomy or independence. Some, although not all, of these components can be seen as concessions to rebels because they take power away from the central government and give it to the rebels. I include 10 potential concessions: integration into the military, the right to transform into a political party, integration into the government/civil service, integration into an interim government created by the agreement, power sharing in the new government, territorial autonomy, territorial federalism, local government, independence of the disputed region, and a referendum on the status of the region.[7] The dependent variable is a count of the number of concessions that rebels receive, so the assumption is that when a peace agreement includes more of these types of concessions, the rebel group has done better.

The measure of rebel concessions has a potential range from 0 to 10, and in the dataset here a range from 0 to 7. The most concessions were given to the Sudanese People's Liberation Movement (SPLM) in the conflict between northern and southern Sudan, as the SPLM was integrated into the military, the civil service, and the interim government, a power-sharing government was created, southern Sudan received autonomy, a federal state was created, and southern Sudan was granted a future referendum on the status of the region. There were nine conflicts in which the rebels received none of these concessions, with the peace process merely establishing a cease-fire or calling for future elections, but not granting political or military power directly to the rebels.

The question behind the analysis here, then, is why some rebels get more concessions from their governments than others do. The hypotheses to be tested refer to four main factors—the probability of military victory, the costs of fighting to groups, and the presence and bias of mediation. I describe how I measure each of these factors.

■ THE PROBABILITY OF MILITARY VICTORY

As described earlier, the probability of military victory in civil war is a zero-sum game—as one side becomes more likely to win militarily, the other side becomes less likely to do so. An indicator of the likelihood of victory in a state–rebel group dyad, then, is best measured as a relative concept. Cunningham et al. (2009) present data on the military strength of rebel groups relative to the government. This measure of strength is a composite indicator based on the ability of rebel groups to fight, mobilize troops, and procure arms relative to the government. Rebels are coded as being "weaker," "at parity," or "stronger" than the government. This strength variable is divided into three dichotomous variables indicating whether groups are weaker, at parity, or stronger than the government and uses them as a measure of the likelihood that groups will win the war. The assumption here is that weaker rebels are less likely to win the conflict than rebels at parity with the government, who are less likely to win than stronger rebels. If hypothesis 1 is correct, rebels that are more likely to win the conflict should get greater concessions from the government.

■ THE COSTS OF FIGHTING

Measuring the costs of fighting, to test hypothesis 2, is difficult. A variety of different factors can affect the costliness of conflict to the decision makers involved, and it is difficult to have cross-conflict indicators of these costs.[8] It becomes more complicated in this case because the hypothesis refers to the relative costs of conflict between the rebel group and the government.

In this analysis, two proxy measures are used. The first is a dichotomous measure of whether the rebel group controls territory in the periphery of the country (from Cunningham et al., 2009). Territorial control can give rebels a base from which they can operate outside of the coercive reach of the state, and so can lessen the ability of the government to impose costs on them. In those cases, conflict should be less costly for the rebels, and they should receive greater concessions.

The second measure of the costliness of conflict to rebels is a dichotomous measure indicating whether they receive support from an external state (from Cunningham et al., 2009). In many so-called "internal conflicts" there is actually a high degree of external involvement. External states can provide many different types of support to rebels by allowing them to establish a base on their territory, helping them obtain weapons, providing military assistance, and giving money directly (see Salehyan, 2009, for a discussion of the various types of external support that states can provide). Each of these activities can lower the costs of fighting to rebels and therefore increase the incentives that the group has to fight. When rebels have external support, therefore, they should receive greater concessions.

■ MEASURING MEDIATION

The third and fourth hypotheses both refer to the effect of mediation on peace agreements. Hypothesis 3 cannot be tested here because it is too general, and there is no good measure of the preference of mediators for specific conflicts included in the dataset. However, the impact of mediation generally is gauged by including a measure of whether a mediator was present in the peace process at all.

That variable comes from Svensson (2007), and in his data mediation is coded as "efforts to help to regulate the incompatibility."

In addition to indicating whether a mediator was present, Svensson (2007) includes a list of the external actors mediating the conflict and indicates whether those mediators are biased in favor of the rebels, the government, or neither. To test hypothesis 4, dichotomous variables are used indicating whether the peace process had a mediator who was biased in favor of the government or the rebels. These variables are not mutually exclusive; a peace process can have both mediators that are biased in favor of the rebels and the government at the same time, or neither.

Because of the importance of these variables to testing the theoretical argument here, it is useful to elaborate on how they were coded. Svensson (2007) builds on Kydd's (2003) conceptual definition of bias as indicating that the mediator has preferences over the outcome of the conflict that are closer to one of the parties.[9] Carnevale and Arad (1996) differentiate between two types of bias—"source bias," or the expectation of bias because the mediator has supported one side in the past, and "content bias," which is bias indicated by the settlement the mediator proposes. In his dataset, however, Svensson only focuses on source bias, and codes mediator bias based on whether the mediator has provided support to the government or the rebels previously.

■ ADDITIONAL VARIABLES

In addition to these variables that test hypotheses 1–4, measures of three other factors that could affect the shape of peace agreements are included. The first two are measures of the type of conflict. A measure of whether the conflict is over government or territory is also included (the "incompatibility" measure from the ACD). The measure of concessions used here includes two types of political concessions: those such as power sharing and integration into the government and civil society that bring the rebels into the government and those over political decentralization in which power is dissolved to local areas. It is possible, however, that rebels in different conflicts may not care about all of these concessions. In particular, in nonterritorial conflicts, rebels may not be seeking a federal solution or autonomy, and so the overall pool of concessions sought may be less, meaning that a smaller number of concessions could still give the rebels all of what they want.

Second, a dichotomous variable is used indicating whether the conflict is an ethnic conflict or a conflict over other factors, such as ideology. Many scholars believe that ethnic or identity-based conflicts have fundamentally different dynamics than nonethnic wars and that, in particular, negotiations over ethnicity may have fundamentally different dynamics. This variable will allow for an examination of whether rebel groups gain greater concessions in ethnic or nonethnic wars (based on a division of conflicts into "ethnic" and "revolutionary"; State Failure Task Force, 2008).[10]

Third, a measure of whether there are other state–rebel group dyads in the same conflict is also included. The analysis here looks at relationships between a government and one rebel group, but many conflicts and negotiations contain multiple different combatants. The number of combatants could affect the number of concessions given to rebel groups, since multiparty negotiations work fundamentally differently than two-actor processes (Cunningham, 2006), a topic also explored in Jannie Lilye's chapter on outbidding.

■ ANALYSIS

An ordinary least squares regression (OLS) with the number of concessions as the dependent variable is used to test the effect of the probability of victory, the costs of conflict, and the presence of mediation on the concessions that rebels receive. Table 13.1 presents three models. The first includes only the measures testing hypotheses 1 and 2, as well as the control variables. The second model tests the effect of mediation (hypotheses 3 and 4) without including the measures of probability of victory and costs of fighting. Model 3 includes all of the variables.

The analysis in Table 13.1 shows several interesting results. First, hypothesis 1 receives no support. In neither of the models in which it is included does the measure of weaker rebels have a statistically significant effect on the extent of concessions that rebels receive.[11] In fact, the sign on the coefficient is positive in both cases, suggesting that weaker rebels are associated with greater concessions, although the large standard error does not allow us to say this with any confidence.

In regards to hypothesis 2, the measure of territorial control is insignificant, but in Model 1 the variable measuring external rebel support is significant and positive, suggesting that rebels that have support from an external state gain greater

TABLE 13.1. *OLS Regression of Concessions to Rebels*

	Model 1	Model 2	Model 3
Weak rebels	0.138		0.431
	(0.426)		(0.421)
Territorial control	−0.035		0.216
	(0.376)		(0.407)
External support to rebels	0.729*		0.029
	(0.356)		(0.432)
Mediation		0.406	0.343
		(0.456)	(0.513)
Rebel bias		0.964**	1.087**
		(0.402)	(0.516)
Government bias		0.071	0.148
		(0.396)	(0.435)
Governmental conflict	1.795***	1.223***	1.562***
	(0.443)	(0.393)	(0.434)
Ethnic conflict	1.195***	1.007***	1.017**
	(0.397)	(0.388)	(0.395)
Other dyads	−0.381	−0.014	−0.281
	(0.399)	(0.353)	(0.391)
Constant	−1.833*	−1.18	−2.102**
	(0.99)	(0.806)	(0.995)
Observations	66	69	65
Adjusted R-squared	0.208	0.262	0.274

Reported are coefficients with standard errors in parentheses.
*$p < .1$; **$p < .05$; ***$p < .01$, two-tailed tests.

concessions. In Model 3, however, when the measures of mediation are included, the finding on external rebel support falls away. Rather, that model shows that rebels are likely to get significantly more concessions when there is a mediator who is biased in their favor, and the effect of external rebel support is no longer significant. This suggests that external support to rebels may not have a direct effect on peace processes by lowering the costs of fighting, but rather that in conflicts where rebels receive external support there is also likely to be a mediator that is biased toward the rebels (potentially the supporting state) and that it is that presence that leads rebels to gain greater concessions.

This finding, along with those in Model 2, provides support for the argument that mediation can have a greater effect than the fighting capacity of groups. In neither model was the "mediation" variable significant, although this is not completely surprising since hypothesis 3 suggests only that the preferences of the mediator will affect the content of peace agreements, not whether mediation in general will cause rebels or the government to do better. The dependent variable as it is measured here is not well set up to measure the effect of mediation generally (I examine this in more detail below). The prediction of hypothesis 4 about mediator bias, however, is supported in the case of rebel bias. The presence of a mediator that is biased in favor of the rebels increases the average number of concessions that rebels receive by about one, a substantial number since the range of that variable is from 0 to 7. Government-biased mediators do not have a significant effect.

Of the additional variables, both indicators of the type of conflict (governmental/territorial and ethnic/nonethnic) are statistically significant. Rebels in conflict over control of the government get substantially more concessions, on average, than those in territorially based conflicts. This finding could suggest that rebels in territorial conflicts generally only get territorial concessions (such as autonomy or local government) and that rebels in governmental conflicts are more likely to get both political and military concessions such as integration into the military, government, and civil service.

Rebels in ethnic wars, meanwhile, get greater concessions than those in nonethnic wars. This is an interesting finding, and it is difficult to interpret on this general level. It may be an indication that governments are more disposed to grant concessions to groups representing ethnic minorities than to groups fighting over ideological differences. It could also indicate that mediators generally look more favorably on ethnically organized parties. The relationship between ethnicity and concessions is one that requires further examination and could benefit especially from qualitative analysis. In particular, case studies comparing the effect of mediation in ethnic and nonethnic wars could examine whether mediators push for more favorable settlements for ethnically organized rebels.

These results suggest, then, that the external dimension of civil war negotiations—the presence of mediation—has a larger and more consistent effect on the outcome of those negotiations than either the military strength or the costs of fighting to the combatants. The analysis, based on new and detailed data on the specific content of peace agreements, allows for an examination of exactly what rebels get in peace agreements. However, the analysis in Table 13.1 does have several potential problems that could inhibit our ability to fully examine the hypotheses.

The main potential problem in Table 13.1 is with the assumptions in OLS regression. Using OLS assumes that the distance between all points in the dependent variable is the same—in this case, the assumption is that rebels value all 10 of these concessions equally. A measure of 2 on the dependent variable is treated the same way even if, in one case, that means that rebels were allowed to create a political party and federalism was introduced, and in the other case it means that rebels were integrated into the military and into an interim government. To address this problem partly, I have rerun these analyses using ordered logit, a statistical model that does not assume that the values on the dependent variable are equally distant, but simply that they are ordered (4 is greater than 2, but not necessarily twice as great). That analysis produced generally similar results.[12]

Three logit analyses to determine how these variables affect specific concessions are used in Table 13.2 to test this relationship further, examining the determinants of whether rebels are integrated into the military (Model 1), whether they receive any political concessions (Model 2), or whether they receive any territorial concessions (Model 3). This analysis, then, does not test which rebels get more concessions, but rather how the probability of victory, costs of fighting, and presence of mediation affect the likelihood that rebels will get any of these concessions. The assumption here is less restrictive than in Table 13.1; it is merely that all rebels would like military integration and some political or territorial concessions.

The analyses in Table 13.2 reveal some interesting patterns. First, although not statistically significant, the results on the weak rebels variable are interesting.

TABLE 13.2. *Logit Analyses of Specific Concessions*

	Model 1 Military integration	Model 2 Any political concessions	Model 3 Any territorial concessions
Weak rebels	1.507	−1.757	0.053
	(1.026)	(1.161)	(1.059)
Territorial control	−1.687*	−1.191	1.623*
	(0.966)	(0.915)	(0.933)
External support to rebels	0.996	1.639*	0.124
	(0.978)	(0.923)	(0.99)
Mediation	2.559**	0.05	−0.268
	(1.2)	(0.928)	(1.391)
Rebel bias	2.441*	−0.3	1.114
	(1.32)	(1.044)	(1.166)
Government bias	−1.577	1.271	−0.238
	(1.087)	(0.922)	(1.04)
Governmental conflict	3.356***	2.777***	−2.205***
	(1.109)	(0.952)	(0.988)
Ethnic conflict	1.296	1.152	0.136
	(0.932)	(0.879)	(1.164)
Other dyads	0.517	−0.482	−1.041
	(0.852)	(0.816)	(0.881)
Constant	−9.77***	−3.281	1.282
	(2.871)	(2.114)	(2.307)
Observations	65	65	65
Log likelihood	−23.628***	−27.961***	−20.943***

Reported are coefficients with standard errors in parentheses.
$*p < .1; **p < .05; ***p < .01$, two-tailed tests.

Weak rebels are more likely to get military integration but less likely to get political concessions (there is little effect on territorial concessions). In both cases the coefficient is quite large, suggesting a substantial effect. Because of the high standard errors, it is difficult to discuss these results with much confidence, but the finding that rebel strength has opposite effects on military integration and political concessions suggests that further thought is needed about these concessions. The analysis here assumes that rebels care equally about military integration and political concessions, but that may not be true, and if rebels have a stronger preference for political integration, these results could partially support hypothesis 1 (that weaker rebels get less of what they want). Additionally, the analysis here examines whether there is any military integration, but an implication of hypothesis 1 would be that stronger rebels should get a larger share of the military. Further analysis could examine how large a stake in the postconflict military rebel groups get.

Table 13.2 shows that rebels that control territory are less likely to be integrated into the military but more likely to get territorial concessions, even when controlling for whether the conflict is over government or territory. This suggests that governments are more likely to grant peripheral rebels official control over territory they already in practice control, but not to bring them into the military or integrate them into the central government. The findings on the governmental conflict variable confirm the expectation that rebels fighting over territory are more likely to get territorial concessions but less likely to be integrated into the military or the central government. Externally supported rebels, meanwhile, are more likely to get political concessions, but there is no statistically significant effect on military integration or territorial concessions.

These analyses also show that meditation can have different effects on different types of concessions. When there is any mediation in the conflict, rebels are more likely to be integrated into the military, but are not necessarily more likely to receive political or territorial concessions. These results suggest that mediators may have specific preferences about certain types of concessions, that is, they may see military integration as an important component of peacebuilding, regardless of the attributes of the combatants. There are plenty of reasons that mediators may favor military integration. In particular, much of the literature on conflict resolution stresses the danger of rebels feeling excluded from military power, and this conception could drive mediators to prefer agreements that contain this component.[13]

The presence of a mediator with a bias toward the rebels increases the likelihood of military integration even more, suggesting that these mediators have a strong preference for integrating rebels into the military through civil war settlements. The presence of a government-biased mediator, meanwhile, makes military integration less likely but increases the chances of some political concessions (these results are almost, but not quite, statistically significant).[14]

These results suggest that mediators can have different interests, and that these interests affect the shape of peace agreements reached. Both the total number of concessions that the rebels receive and the types of concessions they get are affected by the presence and type of mediator present in the conflict. This analysis illustrates a role for mediation much greater than that indicated by the general literature.

■ DISCUSSION AND CONCLUSION

Much of the theoretical literature on conflict bargaining focuses solely on the impact that the attributes of combatants have on negotiations and the settlements that result. This literature examines the conditions under which negotiations are more likely to succeed, and focuses on the incentives that combatants have to negotiate agreements rather than to continue to fight. The dominant theoretical approach has direct implications for the content of peace agreements as well, namely, that groups should get more concessions in a settlement when they can anticipate getting more benefit from continuing to fight, although these implications have not previously been directly spelled out theoretically or tested empirically.

The analysis in this chapter, however, suggests that the relationship between the military strength and costs of fighting to combatants and the resulting negotiated settlements is not as clear. Instead, it is the presence and characteristics of mediators that can have a profound effect on what concessions different groups receive in these settlements. This is an important finding because the general conception is that mediators simply facilitate bargaining between the parties by helping them to, for example, overcome informational and commitment problems. This result, however, suggests that understanding who gets what in negotiated settlements requires an understanding of the interests and preferences of the mediators, not just a focus on the attributes of combatants.

This study is focused specifically on the content of negotiated settlements, but the argument has implications for the stability of peace in the aftermath of an agreement as well. Combatants do not stop evaluating the costs and benefits of fighting versus not fighting when conflict stops. In fact, the period after the signing of a peace agreement can be very treacherous, and agreements often break down after a period of partial implementation. In Angola, the Lusaka Protocol of November 1994 broke down in 1998 when the rebel group UNITA returned to warfare. In Sierra Leone, the Lomé Accords of July 1999 broke down quickly and war resumed later that year.

A major factor that determines whether combatants abide by peace agreements is whether they believe that doing so makes them better off than returning to the battlefield. If a peace process forces one side to grant the other side greater concessions than are warranted by the distribution of military power, then the aggrieved party is likely to have a greater incentive to abandon peace and return to the battlefield. In those cases, then, when the presence and type of mediation have had a profound effect on the content of peace agreements, peace is likely to be less stable.

The effect of the content of the agreements on the duration of peace should fade as the negotiated settlement recedes into the past. Settlements often establish temporary political arrangements and pave the way for elections or other processes that then replace them. Additionally, efforts at reconciliation or other processes of conflict resolution can transform societies in ways such that the original axis of conflict no longer exists. In fact, we know that peace agreements are more likely to break down in the early months after their signing and become more stable as they last longer. In this dangerous early phase, however, agreements with a mismatch between military and political power may be particularly prone to breakdown.

As during the negotiation process, international actors can affect the incentives that former combatants have to stick to peace in this volatile period after agreement. Substantial peacekeeping or peace enforcement missions, for example, can monitor implementation of the agreement but also raise the costs to groups of potential defection. Understanding the incentives of the former combatants to abide by peace, however, suggests that when mediators have a greater role in determining the content of peace agreements, the international community will also need to take a greater role in enforcing peace in the years following the signing of the settlement.

The results presented in this study, then, have significant implications beyond the question of who gets what in peace agreements. There are several unanswered questions, however, that remain after this analysis and that warrant further study. First, this analysis looks generally at concessions in a variety of categories, but does not link that analysis specifically to what combatants actually want. The analyses in Table 13.2 suggest that mediators may have specific preferences, such as for military integration, regardless of the preferences of rebels. Rebels will also have different preferences in different conflicts, and it would be fruitful to examine whether biased mediation helps rebels get more of what they want, or if there are certain concessions that are more likely to be granted generally when there is a biased mediator.

Second, further theoretical and empirical examination of the effect of the type of mediation is needed. Here, I have argued that the preferences of mediators affect peace agreements, and I specifically examined the impact of biased mediation. However, if normative views of what a peace agreement should look like affect the shape of those agreements, then different mediators or mediation in different conflicts should lead to different agreements. Further exploration of the effect of the type of mediation on settlements is needed.

This chapter examined an important and largely ignored question—who gets what in peace agreements? It showed that the general literature on conflict bargaining has implicit assumptions about the answer to this question but that this conventional wisdom is not supported. Rather, the international community has a major impact on the content of peace agreements, which has profound effects on the ability to successfully resolve identity conflicts.

Notes

1. While this is a book about identity conflicts, the literature I am referencing here looks at civil war more broadly. However, none of these authors suggests that their arguments should work differently in civil wars that are fought over identity issues than in others.

2. This excludes win-win outcomes and the possibility of sharing or reframing, an integrative strategy, as in the Franco-German, South African, or Mozambican conflicts; see Walton and McKersie (1965) and Zartman & Berman (1982).

3. The United Nations Security Council, for example, imposed sanctions on the sale of "blood diamonds" from the rebel group UNITA in Angola and established an expert panel

to monitor the exploitation of resources by the external participants in the conflict in the Democratic Republic of the Congo.

4. See, for example, Kydd (2003, 2006).

5. For a discussion of the ACD, see Gleditsch et al. (2002) and Harbom et al. (2008).

6. Note that these peace agreements do not have to have been implemented to be included in this dataset; rather, it includes all agreements signed since 1989.

7. The concessions I am not including are whether there was a cease-fire, a provision for disarmament, demobilization, and reintegration, the withdrawal of foreign forces, the establishment of national talks, an agreement for regional development, cultural freedoms including the freedom of language use in schools, and border demarcation. It was difficult to determine whether these concessions were systematically more advantageous to the rebels or the government.

8. In the quantitative literature on civil war this problem has been profound, because it has meant that distant proxies like gross domestic product are used to measure this concept. The effects of these proxies can be difficult to interpret.

9. Kydd (2003, p. 601) writes, "Mediator bias is defined in terms of the preferences of the mediator. If the mediator's preferences are aligned with one party or the other, she is said to be biased in favor of that party."

10. This variable is coded based on the State Failure Task Force's division of conflicts into "ethnic" and "revolutionary" wars. The State Failure project data are available at http://globalpolicy.gmu.edu/pitf/.(retrieved September 9, 2008).

11. Here, for convenience, I have only included the dichotomous measure of weak rebels. In unreported tests, I also included the measures of rebels at parity in Models 1 and 3. That variable was not close to significance, and the results on the weak rebels variable did not change.

12. In the ordered logit analyses, in Model 1 the external rebel support, governmental conflict, and ethnic conflict variables were statistically significant, and in Model 2 the rebel bias, governmental conflict, and ethnic conflict variables were significant, the same as in the OLS results reported in Table 13.1. The main difference in these analyses was that in Model 3 the rebel bias variable was not statistically significant (p-value of .15 in a two-tailed test). All of the signs on the significant variables were the same.

13. Walter (2002), for example, argues that the disarmament and demobilization period in the aftermath of the signing of an agreement is when the peace process is most likely to break down and rebels are likely to return to war.

14. The p-values for the government–biased mediator variable are .15 in Model 1 and .17 in Model 2, two-tailed tests.

References

Bentley, K. A., & Southall, R. (2005). *An African peace process: Mandela, South Africa, and Burundi*. Cape Town, South Africa: Human Sciences Research Council.

Carnevale, P. J., & Arad, S. (1996). Bias and impartiality in international mediation. In J. Bercovitch (Ed.), *Resolving international conflicts: The theory and practice of mediation* (pp. 39–53). Boulder, CO: Lynne Rienner.

Collier, P. (2000). Rebellion as quasi-criminal activity. *Journal of Conflict Resolution*, 44(6), 839–853.

Cunningham, D. E. (2006). Veto players and civil war duration. *American Journal of Political Science*, 50(4), 875–892.

Cuningham, D. E., Gleditsch, K. S., & Salehyan, I. (2009). It takes two: A dyadic approach to civil war duration and outcome. *Journal of Conflict Resolution*, 53(4), 570–597.

268 ■ The Slippery Slope to Genocide

Fearon, J. D. (1995). Rationalist explanations for war. *International Organization*, 49(3), 379–414.

Filson, D., & Werner, S. 2 (2002). A bargaining model of war and peace: Anticipating the onset, duration, and outcome of war. *American Journal of Political Science*, 46(4), 819–838.

Gleditsch, N. P., Wallensteen, P., Eriksson, M., Sollenberg, M., & Strand, H. (2002). Armed conflict 1946–2001: A new dataset. *Journal of Peace Research*, 39(5), 615–637.

Harbom, L., Hogbladh, S., & Wallensteen, P. (2006). Armed conflict and peace agreements. *Journal of Peace Research*, 43(5), 617–631.

Harbom, L., Melander, E., & Wallensteen, P. (2008). Dyadic dimensions of armed conflict, 1946–2007. *Journal of Peace Research*, 35(5), 697–710.

Hartzell, C. A., & Hoddie, M. (2007). *Crafting Peace: Power-Sharing Institutions and the Negotiated Settlement of Civil Wars*. University Park, Pennsylvania: The Pennsylvania State University Press.

Jones, B. D. (2001). *Peacemaking in Rwanda: The dynamics of failure*. Boulder, CO: Lynne Rienner.

Kydd, A. H. (2003). Which side are you on? Bias, credibility, and mediation. *American Journal of Political Science*, 47(4), 597–611.

Kydd, A. H. (2006). When can mediators build trust? *American Political Science Review*, 100(3), 449–462.

Leites, N., & Ikle, F. C. (1962). Political negotiation as a process for modifying utilities. *Journal of Conflict Resolution*, 6(1), 19–28.

Lemarchand, R. (1994). Managing transition anarchies: Rwanda, Burundi, and South Africa in comparative perspective. *Journal of Modern African Studies*, 32(4), 581–604.

Negotiating a Blueprint for Peace in Somalia. (2003, March 6). International Crisis Group Africa Report No. 59. Mogadishu/Brussels:

Nilsson, D. (2008). Partial peace: Rebels inside and outside of peace. *Journal of Peace Research*, 45(4), 479–495.

Reiter, D. (2003). Exploring the bargaining model of war. *Perspectives on Politics*, 1, 27–43.

Salehyan, I. (2009). *Rebels without borders: Transnational insurgencies in world politics*. Ithaca, NY: Cornell University Press.

Sebenius, J. (2002). Negotiation analysis. In V. Kremenyuk (Ed.), *International negotiation: Analysis, approaches, issues* (pp. 229–254). San Francisco: Jossey-Bass.

Slantchev, B. (2003). The principle of convergence in wartime negotiations. *American Political Science Review*, 47(4), 621–632.

Smith, A., & Stam, A. (2004). Bargaining and the nature of war. *Journal of Conflict Resolution*, 48(6), 783–813.

Stedman, S. J. (1997). Spoiler problems in peace processes. *International Security*, 20(2), 5–53.

Svensson, I. (2007). Bargaining, bias and peace brokers: How rebels commit to peace. *Journal of Peace Research*, 44(2), 177–194.

Touval, S., & Zartman, I. W. 1 (1985). Introduction: Mediation in theory. In S. Touval & I. W. Zartman (Eds.), *International mediation in theory and practice* (pp. 7–17). Boulder, CO: Westview Press.

Wagner, R. H. (2000). Bargaining and war. *American Journal of Political Science*, 46(3), 469–484.

Walter, B. F. (2002). *Committing to peace: The successful settlement of civil wars*. Princeton, NJ: Princeton University Press.

Walton, R., & McKersie, R. (1965). *A behavioral theory of labor negotiations*. New York: McGraw-Hill.

Woodward, S. L. (1995). *Balkan tragedy: Chaos and dissolution after the cold war*. Washington, DC: The Brookings Institution.

Zartman, I. W. & Berman, M. (1982). *The practical negotiator*. New Haven: Yale University Press.

Zartman, I. W. (1989). *Ripe for resolution: Conflict and intervention in Africa*. Oxford: Oxford University Press.

Zartman, I. W. (2010). *Preventing identity conflicts leading to genocide and mass killings*. New York: International Peace Institute.

14 Evolving International Law of Intervention and Prevention

■ FRANZ CEDE

Any study of the most violent expressions of identity conflicts, such as genocide, mass killing, and ethnic cleansing, will at some point have to address the legal aspects of these atrocities. To a large degree, the response of the international community to these criminal acts is determined by the rules of international law (IL).

This chapter focuses on the legal aspects of the issues concerned. Two key concepts (*genocide, humanitarian intervention*) have been selected that occupy a central place in any legal debate about international crimes and their punishment, to paraphrase Dostoyevski. The chapter attempts (1) to give an overview of the development and scope of the concept of humanitarian intervention—the legal arguments put forward to justify the use of force in carrying out a mission under the title of humanitarian intervention will receive particular attention in this context—and (2) to clarify the crimes of genocide and mass killing within the meaning of the Genocide Convention and the Rome Statute of the International Criminal Court (ICC).

■ DEFINING HUMANITARIAN INTERVENTION

The following presentation will concentrate on the notion of humanitarian intervention (HI) that occupies a central place in the present debate. In the legal literature, one finds different and often contradictory definitions of the concept. As a working proposition, in the present context, HI will be confined to military interventions of one or more states to deal with humanitarian disasters in a third country. The humanitarian disaster may be caused by humans (e.g., gross and systematic violations of human rights such as genocide or ethnic cleansing, as in Rwanda in 1994) or by nature (e.g., catastrophes such as the cyclone in Myanmar in 2008). The HI may be carried out with or without the consent of the concerned state or the United Nations Security Council (UNSC). Interventions based on consent of the concerned state or those based on an enabling resolution of the UNSC do not pose major legal problems. The legal controversy starts if an HI is decided on and carried out against the will of the state in question and without an enabling resolution of the UNSC (e.g., North Atlantic Treaty Organization [NATO] operations against the former Yugoslavia in 1999). It is worth noting that the development of the HI concept owes much to the activities of the French nongovernmental organization (NGO) Doctors without Borders (Médecins sans frontières) under its former chairman, Bernard Kouchener, who became French Foreign Minister under President Nicolas Sarkozy.

At the end of the nineteenth century and well into the twentieth, sovereign nation-states were considered the primary subjects of international law or of the *law of nations*, as it was called in the past. According to the international system that prevailed in much of the developed world before World War I, the sovereign state exercised supreme authority over all individuals under its jurisdiction. The treatment of all persons in the territory of the sovereign nation state fell essentially within the purview of its domestic jurisdiction. The way a state treated its subjects was none of the business of IL. The view that a state had the right to exert supreme power over all persons under its jurisdiction was supported by the fact that the sovereign represented the state at the international level. Foreign affairs were usually seen as typical matters over which the head of state had uncontested rights (*domaine réservé*). In this environment, foreign policy was conducted outside the public domain. Diplomacy was considered as a typical occupation of the ruling class in the society. In the arcane world of traditional diplomacy, the destiny of individuals was as irrelevant as the plight of soldiers who lost their life for the fatherland in wars. In most regimes in power before World War I, the role of parliaments or other entities such as NGOs, which have now asserted themselves as powerful factors in the international system, was negligible. They had little or no influence on shaping or implementing foreign policy decisions by the executive power. It is worth noting that the achievements of the French Revolution (the Declaration of Human Rights and Civil Liberties, 1789) or the American War of Independence (Virginia Bill of Rights, 1776) did not immediately change the parameters of IL with regard to the status of individuals or the concept of state sovereignty.

In spite of this legal situation, at the end of the nineteenth century, a newspaper campaign began to arouse public opinion in Britain with horrendous reports on the brutal treatment of the indigenous population in the Congo by the colonial regime of King Leopold of Belgium, who ruled over this vast African country as the master of a private property. In many respects, King Leopold personified the extremes of the sovereign state at its worst in a colonial context. Had British newspapers not continuously reported on what is now known as the "Congo horrors," world public opinion would have done nothing to protest against the scandalous maltreatment of the black population in the Congo. However, this protest movement proved to be the exception rather than the rule. It did not alter the system of state sovereignty at all.

To sum up, within the old system, the scope of sovereignty was almost unlimited. It left little or no room for outside intervention on humanitarian grounds. The very idea of human rights allowing individuals to lodge complaints against their own state was alien to the traditional concept of IL. International obligations of states vis-à-vis their own citizens were generally considered incompatible with the prerogatives of the nation-state.

A second factor explaining the weakness of humanitarian ideas in the traditional system of IL was the lack of international institutions of global reach before World War I. The international community was not yet organized within the framework of organizations such as the League of Nations before World War I or the UN after World War II. There is no doubt that the establishment of an international institutional framework served as a powerful stimulus to the development of an international human rights regime that provided legitimacy to interventions in the humanitarian interest. In the absence of an efficient multilateral mechanism that could be activated in cases of gross and systematic human rights violations, the concept of absolute state sovereignty prevailed.

In 1945, the adoption of the UN Charter revolutionized IL in many respects. For the first time in human history, an organization of global reach and authority was created. The UN Charter provided a system of collective security and outlawed the use of force in international relations (Article 2, paragraph 4). The Charter allows one exception only, namely, the individual or collective right to self-defense in the case of an armed attack (Article 51). The second major innovation of the UN Charter is the mandate given to the UN General Assembly (UNGA) to promote cooperation in the field of human rights (Article 13, paragraph 1b). In keeping with this mandate, in 1948 the GA adopted the Universal Declaration of Human Rights, which became the point of departure for the further evolution of the UN human rights system. It can be said without exaggeration that the development of the international body of human rights law gradually eroded the concept of absolute state sovereignty prevailing prior to the foundation of the UN.

The erosion of the concept of absolute state sovereignty took place irrespective of the fact that, for a long time, a number of influential UN member states continued to adhere to a broad interpretation of this concept. The former socialist states come to mind in this context. The former Soviet Union, its satellites, and such powerful states as China, but also a large number of developing countries, clubbed together in the UN in the G-77 group, opposing the view that effective implementation of human rights obligations was a matter of international concern that could be brought before international instances. Rather, they asserted that raising concerns about human rights abuses committed in their sphere of jurisdiction was tantamount to interfering in the domestic affairs of their state, which, they said, was forbidden under the UN Charter.

■ THE EMERGING CONCEPT OF HI

The often controversial debate on the legitimacy of the concept of HI usually centers on the following principles and rules of IL: the nonuse of force, the notion of sovereignty, and the role of the UNSC.

The prohibition of the use of military force in international relations enshrined in the UN Charter constitutes one of the cornerstones of the entire UN system. One of the key questions at issue is the exact scope of this rule in extreme cases of gross and systematic violations of human rights obligations by states with regard to their own nationals or other populations, such as ethnic cleansing, mass killing, and genocide. The debate often rages between those who hold the principle of nonuse of force as sacrosanct and those who make a value judgment and argue for intervention, if necessary even by military means, in response to situations of particular humanitarian concern.

The notion of state sovereignty and the human rights regime is covered in Article 2, paragraph 7, of the UN Charter, which stipulates that, in principle, the

UN is not authorized to intervene in matters "which are essentially within the domestic jurisdiction of any state." The claim that the relationship between the government of a sovereign state and the persons under its jurisdiction falls exclusively under the category of "domestic jurisdiction" is used to prohibit states or international organizations from raising human rights concerns with regard to the treatment of people by a particular state. However, with the progressive development of the international human rights system, this claim can no longer be maintained. In the Vienna Declaration adopted by consensus at the World Conference on Human Rights in 1993, the effective protection of human rights was recognized as a legitimate concern of the international community of states. The Vienna Declaration also reaffirmed the principles of universality and indivisibility of human rights. Against this background, it is no longer possible to object to the validity of international action for humanitarian reasons by pointing to the inviolability of state sovereignty. In the current state of IL, such an argument would have to be dismissed.

The role of the UNSC is the third controversial question raised when HI problems are discussed by international lawyers. Under the system of collective security established by the UN Charter, it is for the UNSC to decide whether there is a threat to international peace and security and, accordingly, to take appropriate action if it determines that such a threat exists. Article 24 of the UN Charter explicitly confers on the SC primary responsibility for the maintenance of international peace and security. Gross violations of human rights endangering entire ethnic groups or populations may undoubtedly destabilize international peace and security and, therefore, call for the activation of the system of collective security of the UN. Unfortunately, divisions between the permanent members of the SC over political controversies on the issues at stake and their often opposite views on the very concept of state sovereignty have prevented the involvement of the UNSC in resolving human rights dramas.

Recent practice of the UN with regard to the problem of intervention in humanitarian "emergencies" presents a very diverse picture. When the United States defended its military intervention in Nicaragua in the mid-1980s with the argument that it had acted to protect human rights in that country, the International Court of Justice (ICJ) rejected that argument (Military and Paramilitary Activities Case, *International Law Reports*, 1986). The court held that in this case the use of force by the United States was not justified under IL. However, in all fairness, it must be said that in the mid-1980s, the whole concept of HI did not exist in its present form.

The idea developed only a decade later, when new situations involving gross and systematic violations of human rights arose.

The term *humanitarian intervention* was first used in the context of the Allied operation Provide Comfort in Northern Iraq in the wake of the 1991 Gulf war when U.S. and British forces moved into Northern Iraq to enable humanitarian relief missions to reach the predominantly Kurdish population there. This action was at least partially covered by UNSC resolutions. Operation Provide Comfort also saw the first use of the now familiar concept of civil–military cooperation (CIMIC). In the following years, a series of decisions by the UNSC authorized the use of force by states for humanitarian reasons. In view of the human tragedy caused by the internal conflict and unrest in Somalia, UNSC Resolution 794 (1992) allowed member states to intervene militarily in order to enable humanitarian relief efforts to reach the suffering civilian populations, as in the U.S.-led Unified Task Force, deployed in 1992–1993 between the UN's own operations UNOSOM I and UNOSOM II. In the same spirit, the UNSC allowed foreign interventions on humanitarian grounds in Haiti by the U.S.-led Multinational Force (SC-Res. 842[1993]), in Rwanda by the French Operation Turquoise (SC-Res 929[1994]), and in Albania by the Italian-led Operation Alba (SC-Res. 1101[1997]).

The use of HI without UNSC authorization constitutes the most sensitive part of assessing the admissibility of HI. The air war of NATO against Yugoslavia during the Kosovo crisis in 1999 provides a textbook case for the study of this issue and deserves discussion in greater detail.

The Kosovo crisis put the principle of nonuse of force as one of the main tenets of IL to a severe test during NATO's Operation Allied Force against the former Yugoslavia (then consisting of Serbia and Montenegro) from March to June 1999 (not the ensuing peacekeeping force (KFOR), which was also organized by NATO but under a UNSC mandate). The acerbic debates in the legal community on the IL aspects of the NATO operation reiterated the well-known arguments of the defenders of military force and of the arguments against it. They again raised the problems linked to the deficiencies of the UN system of collective security, which became particularly evident in the debates on the Yugoslav crisis when, due to the political divisions between the permanent members of the UNSC, the UN was paralyzed. The UN security system proved unable to react, in any credible manner by military means, to the outrageous developments in the Balkans characterized by gross and systematic violations of human rights perpetrated by the Serbian forces against the ethnic Albanian population in Kosovo, at that time a province within the Yugoslav federation. From a classical point of view the NATO operation, decided on and carried out without an enabling resolution of the SC, was a clear breach of one of the most fundamental principles of IL: the prohibition against the use of military force except in the case of self-defense against an armed attack (Article 2, paragraph 4, and Article 51 of the UN Charter). The proponents of the traditional position asserted that even humanitarian motivations could not justify the breach of the nonuse-of-force rule. For them the NATO operation in 1999 undermined the very foundation of the international system based on respect for the principles enshrined in the UN Charter.

Those who found that the use of force was ultimately justified in Kosovo presented the following arguments: (1) The UNSC was paralyzed and did not assume its responsibility to take resolute action in order to stop the genocide and ethnic cleansing being committed by the Serbian forces against the ethnic Albanian population in Kosovo. In this situation, the responsibility to take action had to be assumed by NATO, whose member states were willing and able to take remedial action in this urgent and dramatic situation. (2) Like a state, an ethnic group had the right to defend itself when it became a victim of the oppression of its own government, which was the case in the former Yugoslavia under the Milosevich regime, in consequence of the right to self-defense in the case of an armed attack enshrined in Article 51 of the UN Charter. (3) Three of the permanent members of the SC (the United States, the United Kingdom, and France) took part in the NATO decision to intervene militarily. The opposite views taken on the legal aspects of the Kosovo issue show that the international legal community was deeply divided in assessing the NATO operation as a HI.

■ LATEST DEVELOPMENTS IN SHAPING THE CONCEPT OF HI

The malaise among international lawyers that followed the NATO air strikes against Belgrade led to a flurry of academic studies and diplomatic initiatives designed to draw the lessons from the Kosovo experience. These activities attempted to redefine the legal parameters of HI and to sharpen the notion of responsibility of states vis-à-vis the persons under their jurisdiction. The first effort led to the elaboration of legal criteria for HI, while the second contributed to the development of the new concept of the "responsibility of states to protect."

New criteria for HI were worked out in 2000 by a group of Dutch experts as a possible basis for future decisions. Known as the *Scheveningen criteria*, they seek to promote formal processes to overcome the dilemma between human rights considerations and the concept of state sovereignty. These criteria include:

- The threat or occurrence of grave large-scale violations of human rights
- The presence of clear and objective evidence of such a threat or occurrence
- The unwillingness or inability of the state to take remedial action
- The presence of clear urgency
- The use of force as the last resort
- The clear explanation of purpose to publics and the international community
- The limitation of the purpose to stopping the human rights abuses
- The support by those for whom the action is intended
- The support of regional states
- The high probability of success
- The existence of a mapped-out transition to postconflict peacebuilding
- The use of force proportionate to achieving these goals
- The observance of IL on the conduct of war during the action

These criteria do not mention the role of the UNSC in the decision-making process, since their purpose is to provide objective elements permitting robust missions of HI precisely in those situations in which the UNSC is unable to assume its responsibility to take remedial action.

It is too early to assess if and how these criteria will determine state practice with regard to cases in which decisions have to be taken on HI in the absence of an enabling resolution of the SC. What can be said with certainty is that this effort has already significantly influenced the international discussion on this important topic. For many international lawyers, the Scheveningen criteria are considered a valuable point of reference for the further development of the emerging concept of international HI.

The responsibility to protect is an important and daring new development in IL The UN World Summit in 2005 for the first time recognized the responsibility to protect as a common responsibility of the international community to prevent, and if necessary to stop genocide, crimes against humanity, and the most serious war crimes. In keeping with this responsibility, each state has the obligation to protect its own population against these crimes, and the international community is called upon to provide support to states in achieving these goals. In case of failure of the preventive measures the international community, through a decision of the UNSC, has the responsibility to react, if need be, even by military means.

The concept of the responsibility to protect draws its inspiration from some work done on Africa in a project led by Francis Deng, former Sudanese foreign minister. The work found its way into the 1991 *Kampala Document* fostered by Sudanese President Olusegun Obasanjo, which contained the declaration that "domestic conditions constituting a threat to personal and collective security and gross violations of human rights lie beyond the protection of sovereignty."[1] At the Brookings Institution, the Africa project sponsored a collective work, *Sovereignty as Responsibility: Conflict Management in Africa*, that viewed sovereignty as a responsibility, which was to be exercised by the state and shared by other states if the primary state did not exercise its own responsibility for the welfare of its people, than as a protection of the state.[2] Intervention was justified by failed or repressive states' loss of legitimacy and by the existence of the "higher authority . . . of [the] international system . . . to ensure that states conform to accepted norms or face the consequences."[3]

The direct predecessor of the World Summit resolution was a report submitted in 2001 by the International Commission on Intervention and State Sovereignty (ICISS) and taken up by former UN Secretary General Kofi Annan in the debate on the reform of the UN in 2004. In a remarkable development, the principal ideas of the responsibility to protect principle as elaborated by the ICISS were enshrined in the final document of the UN Summit 2005 held at UN headquarters to mark the 50th anniversary of the UN. In what can be considered aa landmark decision, the final document of the Summit, adopted by consensus, strengthens the legal justification for limited forms of unilateral and regional action—including military action—if the UN fails to act to protect populations from genocide and other atrocities. The outcome of the Summit sets limits on national sovereignty by affirming a state's responsibility to protect its own citizens and establishes clear responsibilities for the international community when a country fails to assume its own responsibility. If in such cases the UN fails to act and to fulfill the duty to protect, possible actors have a strong argument on their side to justify the unilateral action they might eventually be willing to take in order to stop genocide and mass killings in a concrete situation.

It should be noted that, like its predecessor, the notion of sovereignty as responsibility to protect is ambiguous and potentially dangerous. The previous notion of sovereignty, set up in the Peaces of Westphalia of 1648, protected small states from interference by large states in their internal affairs but was dangerous to their populations, which had no recourse for protection. The new doctrine, still to be elaborated beyond the Scheveningen criteria, reverses the danger: It protects the populations but is dangerous to their states, since it is particularly larger states that are likely to intervene on behalf of small-state populations. Perfection is hard to find, even in IL, but the world wll continue to work to find, in theory and in practice, an appropriate balance.

■ GENOCIDE AND MASS KILLINGS: CRIMES UNDER IL

In the wake of World War II and the Holocaust, conditions were ripe to push for an international legal instrument that would outlaw genocide as a crime under international law. In December 1948, only three years after the founding of the UN, the GA adopted the Convention on the Prevention and Punishment of the Crime of Genocide (CPPCG) by Resolution 260(III). The CPPCG entered into force in January 1951 after it was ratified by more than 80 states that had passed legislation incorporating the provisions of the CPPCG into their municipal law. In Article 2 the Convention gives the following definition of genocide:

> In the Convention, genocide means any of the following acts committed with intent to destroy, in whole or in part, a national, ethnical, racial or religious group, as such:
>
> (a) Killing members of the group;
> (b) Causing serious bodily or mental harm to members of the group;
> (c) Deliberately inflicting on the group conditions of life calculated to bring about its physical destruction in whole or in part;
> (d) Imposing measures intended to prevent births within the group;
> (e) Forcefully transferring children of the group to another group.

This definition of genocide is silent about the crime of mass killings. However, one may derive some elements of this crime from the legal definition of genocide. For instance, "killing members of the group" implies that mass killings are also covered by the crime of genocide, especially if they were committed with the intention to destroy a national, ethnic, racial, or religious group within the meaning of the CPPCG. If the above elements do not fit in a particular situation, the description of the "crime against humanity" over which the ICC has jurisdiction allows subsuming of mass killings in most cases.

Although the CPPCG constitutes a binding instrument of IL and states have consistently underlined their commitment to the obligations deriving from their ratification, the instrument had little effect for decades. As long as there was no international judicial body in place that could pass judgments on the crime of genocide, the international crime of genocide went unpunished in most cases. For more than 40 years, the establishment of an international criminal court was put on the back burner of the international agenda. Two notable precedents, the Nuremberg and Tokyo War Crimes Tribunals established immediately after World War II to bring German and Japanese war criminals to justice, remained episodes without any direct follow-up. Repeated efforts undertaken within the framework of the UNGA and the International Law Commission of the UN designed to establish an international criminal tribunal related to the CPPCG did not bear fruit.

It took another series of atrocities at the end of the twentiethth century to give a decisive impetus to the creation of two special international tribunals in the field of criminal justice—the International Criminal Tribunal for the Former Yugoslavia (ICTY) and the International Criminal Tribunal for Rwanda (ICTR). Both institutions were set up by resolutions of the SC, thereby shortcutting the GA, which had been conspicuously unsuccessful in promoting the project of a world criminal court with general jurisdiction over international crimes and their perpetrators. No doubt the activities of the ICTY and the ICTR considerably established the climate that, at last, led to the international conference held in Rome in 1989, which was given the mandate to finalize a statute for an International Criminal Court (ICC). The conference culminated with the adoption of such a statute. In the provisions of the Rome Statute of the ICC, a number of crimes falling under the jurisdiction of the ICC were listed. Among them are notably the crime of genocide, war crimes, crimes against humanity, and the crime of aggression (still to be defined). With the entry into force of the ICC Statute on July 1, 2002, the international community created, at last, an institution that, under certain conditions, has the competence to bring to justice persons who are responsible for crimes as such as genocide, war crimes, and crimes against humanity.

It is true that the weaknesses of the ICC cannot be overlooked. For instance, it suffers from the handicap that important states (e.g., the United States) have not ratified the ICC Statute. Another difficulty lies in the fact that a number of states have made reservations to their acceptance of the Statute, significantly limiting the competence of the Court in their respect. These deficits weaken the functioning of the ICC and run counter to the very concept of a universal system of criminal justice. In all fairness, though, it has to be noted that the system of international criminal jurisdiction is still in its infancy. It will take perhaps another few decades before the ICC develops the "teeth" enabling it to carry out its important functions without undue limitations.

■ CONCLUDING OBSERVATION

A whole array of legal and diplomatic instruments is available to third parties in order to resolve internal identity conflicts. Article 33 of the UN Charter lists some of them: negotiation, mediation, conciliation, inquiry, arbitration, and judicial settlement. The parties to a conflict are free to resort to any of these means in order to settle the disputes dividing them. This chapter has focused mainly on the most extreme cases, in which such conflicts degenerate into violent hostilities accompanied by atrocities such as genocide, mass killing, and other crimes against humanity. In these cases, third-party intervention usually is carried out in a repressive manner. Third parties are prepared to intervene for humanitarian purposes by using their armed forces to stop the atrocities only if the human rights abuses present a systematic pattern or if they have reached a significant dimension. The punitive action is often followed by the attempt to bring the persons guilty of severe crimes (e.g., genocide, war crimes, crimes against humanity, mass killing) to justice through an international criminal tribunal. In recent times, this has been the case with regard to the genocide in Rwanda and the atrocities committed in the former Yugoslavia. On the other hand, unfortunately, the international community has not been very successful in preventing internal identity conflicts through legal means and avoiding their escalation.

Notes

1. Olesegun Obasanjo (1991). *The Kampala Document*. New York: Africa Leadership Forum; Francis Deng and I. W. Zartman (2002). *A Strategic Vision for Africa*. Washington, DC: The Brookings Institution, p. 165.

2. Francis Deng et al. (1996). *Sovereignty as Responsibility: Conflict Management in Africa*. Washington, DC: The Brookings Institution.

3. Ibid., pp. 32–33.

15 The International Community Response

■ PETER WALLENSTEEN, ERIK MELANDER,
AND FRIDA MÖLLER

The most shocking genocide since the end of the Cold War is the one in Rwanda of 1994. In a very short time, more than 800,000 people were slaughtered, often by their neighbors, encouraged by hate media, political leaders, and armed actors. The feeble international reactions have continued to haunt international organizations, political leaders, and scholars. The literature on the failure is now vast: Scholarly work, special reports, and international commissions have dealt with the lessons. In their work on the success and failure of peacebuilding, Doyle and Sambanis point to a host of factors that accounted for this failure: the mandates and resources restricting the international peacekeepers; the confusion between the United Nations (UN) headquarters and the UN staff on the scene; the contrasting evaluations by the head of the UN operation and the special rapporteur for the conflict; the internal deliberations in New York, notably the Secretariat and its relations to the Security Council; the uninformed and late actions by the Council; and the reluctance of the United States to get involved. Thus, the picture is complex, and the authors conclude that the tragedy was one of "many hands" (Doyle & Sambanis, 2006, pp. 294–302). This case contrasts the authors' general findings that UN peacebuilding missions actually succeed in post–civil war transitions, and that they do so if they have greater capacity in situations where the local capacity is weak (p. 131).

In this chapter, we discuss the ability of international action to prevent genocide and learning from events before and after Rwanda. We focus on international capacity with a specific idea: There are a number of measures at the disposal of the international community to react early on in conflict situations to prevent genocides from taking place. A peacekeeping mission is one of these, sometimes enlarged into multidimensional peacebuilding operations. There are also other types of actions: Preventive diplomacy has been the hallmark of many UN Secretary Generals (particularly Dag Hammarskjöld and Kofi Annan), including the creation of special envoys or representatives for these issues (Special Representatives of the Secretary General, SRSGs; a post was specifically created for the prevention of genocide on the 10th anniversary of the start of the genocide in Rwanda), and the use of sanctions, such as arms embargoes and individually targeted sanctions.

Thus, we will present the arsenal available to the international community and relate it to situations that constitute genocides or possible genocides. The thesis is that if all the tools are used for the same goal, the international community is equipped to deal with threats of genocide. It requires a conscious strategy and, in the case of the UN, consensus in the Security Council. Furthermore, with the development of a doctrine of a responsibility to protect populations from genocide and mass violence, there is a normative commitment. In fact, before the responsibility to protect comes the responsibility to prevent wars, mass violence, and genocide (Hampson, 2008). With the available instruments, the political will, a normative agreement, and a focus on the early stages of armed conflict, there should be enough information to find ways to prevent future genocides.

This chapter is divided into six general parts building on the result of ruoont global data collections and one case study. First, we establish the link between genocide and civil war. Then the three instruments of peacekeeping, preventive actions, and sanctions are studied one by one, based on global perspective, in the second, third, and fourth sections, respectively. The interaction between these instruments is studied in the fifth section. The case is Côte d'Ivoire is followed closely for the ten-year period 1999–2008. The situation in the country is evaluated in terms of its application of these international instruments to end an internal armed conflict and prevent genocide. The events following the Presidential elections in November 2010 and the armed conflict in April 2011 are also analyzed. In the sixth section, some general conclusions and implications are suggested.

▪ GENOCIDE AND CIVIL WAR

The genocides that have attracted most attention, the Holocaust and Rwanda 1994, took place in the midst of wars. Thus, there are reasons to explore the connection between genocide and war. Most research on such connections has focused on the period following the Second World War. The genocide that created the term, the one targeting Armenians during the First World War, would point to such a war connection, although this was an interstate war situation. Similarly, the origins of the Holocaust can be related to a particular interpretation of the outcome of the First World War. It was carried out during the Second World War. Major wars, in other words, provide covers as well as instruments for genocides. Since 1945 there have been continued experiences of genocide, but obviously no world wars. Civil wars provide parallel conditions, however. This we will explore by largely building on the widely used information on mass murder, genocides, and politicides compiled by the Political Instability Task Force (formerly the State Failure Task Force), prominently presented by its principal investigator, Barbara Harff (2003). The dataset now covers 1955–2004 and includes "massacres, unrestrained bombing and shelling of civilian-inhabited areas, declaration of free-fire zones, starvation by prolonged interdiction of food supplies, forced expulsion ('ethnic cleansing') accompanied by extreme privation and killings" (Marshall et al., 2001, p. 15). In civil conflicts, mass killings by either the government or the rebel side are recorded, and only unarmed civilian victims are counted, not combatants. According to these data, most mass killings of civilians are perpetrated by governments, and in times of ongoing civil conflict.

The Political Instability Task Force records 6 onsets of genocide in civil conflicts in the post–Cold War period (Angola, Bosnia-Herzegovina, Burundi, Indonesia,

Rwanda, and Yugoslavia [Kosovo]) and 30 onsets during civil conflicts in the period 1955–1989 (e.g., Guatemala, Nigeria, Burundi, Somalia, Sudan, Iraq, Afghanistan, Pakistan, Sri Lanka, Cambodia, and Indonesia). It also maps repetitions. Burundi experienced five different onsets of mass murder since 1955, two other countries suffered four events (Indonesia and Iraq), and six countries had two episodes (Angola, the People's Republic of China, the Democratic Republic of the Congo, Iran, Rwanda, and Sudan). These numbers are not only tragic in themselves, but are also important for our understanding of which situations are the most dangerous in terms of the risk of genocide. Harff (2003) reports that a history of mass killings increases the present risk that a new episode will commence. Significant for this chapter is the observation that most of the countries with two or more episodes of genocide also saw peacekeeping missions.

From these data and other similar compilations, we can conclude that the most important cause of mass murder identified in previous research is major societal upheaval or state failure, particularly in the form of civil war (Davenport, 1995, 1999; Gurr 1986, 1988; Krain, 2005; Poe & Tate, 1994). Indeed, the overwhelming majority of campaigns of systematic massacres of civilians begin in times of armed conflict. For example, a recent study by one of the authors of this chapter found that 36 out of 46 episodes of genocide/politicide in the period 1955–2004 were initiated during ongoing intrastate conflict. This study also shows that the intensity of intrastate armed conflict is a very important determinant of genocide. Although few if any episodes of genocide begin outside of a context of intrastate armed conflict, the relative risk is much higher when the intensity of fighting has reached the level of full-scale civil war, that is, with more than 1,000 battle-related deaths in a year (Melander, 2009).

The observation that genocide since the Second World War is closely associated with intrastate armed conflict, and with full-scale civil war in particular, presents both opportunities and challenges concerning the prevention of genocide. The opportunities consist of the clear early warning signals that an armed conflict sends and the generally higher level of engagement by the international community when problems in a country have manifested themselves in open fighting. At the same time, the challenge is to deal with the difficulties and risks that come with third-party engagement in situations of heavy or escalating warfare.

Compared to many other potential signs of early warning of genocide, intrastate armed conflict is easy to define and detect in a systematic manner. Thus, it would be simple to demarcate a set of situations where the risk of genocide is heightened. Ongoing armed conflicts are typically considered to be so serious that the international community—and intergovernmental organizations (IGOs) in particular—is likely to focus on them and review options for action. As civil war is both devastating and difficult to curb, the international community will be aware and concerned. At the same time, the inherent dangers and volatility of the situation may deter action and will almost certainly make any attempted third-party engagement more difficult. This means that when IGOs step into the breach, they may be find themselves in the most challenging crises, where the chances of success are the slimmest. This selection effect needs to be taken into account when discussing the relative effectiveness of IGO engagement. We will return to this phenomenon of selection bias repeatedly in this chapter, as it does affect the choices open to international organizations.

The issue of which situations generally attract IGO engagement is, we submit, central when the possibilities for effective third-party action are discussed. In the next section, we will review research that incorporates the possibility that IGOs systematically tend to insert themselves in the most difficult—or the easiest—cases. This research concerns one of the most important forms of IGO engagement, namely, peacekeeping.

■ PEACEKEEPING AND THE PREVENTION OF GENOCIDE

Dispatching peacekeeping missions is one of the most visible and direct ways in which the international community may act to prevent genocide. Especially in the last two decades, various forms of peacekeeping missions have more frequently been deployed to countries in civil conflict to promote peace or to assist and protect civilians. The primary tasks of most peacekeeping missions are to prevent the escalation of armed conflict and contribute to a lasting peace, and the prevention of genocide may not be an expressed purpose. Yet, since armed conflict in general and full-scale civil war in particular are conducive to mass killings of civilians, any reasonably successful peacekeeping mission is likely to have a benign indirect effect on the risk of genocide. Moreover, as will be briefly discussed below, it is likely that even small and weak peacekeeping missions may directly influence the decision calculus of potential genocide perpetrators among warring parties.

At first glance, the track record of peacekeeping missions in the prevention of genocide may appear to be poor. Yet, a recent study shows that the benign effect of peacekeeping is underappreciated, and that peacekeeping indeed contributes to lowering the risk that civilians will be massacred in times of intrastate armed conflict (Melander, 2009). That first glance may be deceiving if peacekeepers tend to be sent to the most serious conflicts, where the risk of genocide is deemed to be highest. In statistical analyses, the standard approach to this complication is to control for the seriousness of the conflict. That means comparing the outcomes of equally serious conflicts when peacekeepers are present and when they are not. For example, we may take into account that conflicts in countries with a history of prior genocide are more at risk.

If we find that, even after the introduction of such controls, there are still unmeasured factors that simultaneously influence both the dispatch of peacekeepers and the risk of mass killings, this approach is inadequate. This unmeasured selection will produce biased findings, so that we may, for example, fail to pick up a preventive effect. The solution in recent research has been to explicitly take into account the unmeasured seriousness of the conflict, and to model how this may be a factor in the decision to deploy peacekeeping missions as well as part of what drives the onset of genocide. The statistical technique employed—seemingly unrelated probit regression—simultaneously predicts peacekeeping and the onset of mass killings of civilians, taking into account the correlation between the disturbances of the equations (Greene, 2003, p. 717).

When using this procedure, it can be demonstrated that peacekeeping does significantly reduce the risk of mass killings when one takes into account that peacekeeping missions may be more likely to be established in the most difficult conflicts (Melander, 2009). It was also found that mass killings are more likely to commence the higher the number of previous such episodes a country has suffered. Semidemocracies and countries with political institutions in transition or collapse were found to be more at risk, as were countries in full-scale civil war. Peacekeeping missions, in turn, are more likely to be sent to countries with previous episodes of mass killings. Such missions tend to go to semidemocracies near the middle of the democracy scale and when the political institutions are in transition or collapse. Not unexpectedly, they are more common in the post–Cold War period, in countries with smaller populations, and in Europe, including the former Soviet Union. Even after these controls were taken into account, there remained a tendency that peacekeeping missions were sent to the most threatening places in terms of the risk of genocide.

The key result regarding the benign preventive effect of peacekeeping only emerged after the application of this advanced statistical technique, which takes into account that there may be unobserved omitted factors that simultaneously increase the probability that peacekeepers will be deployed and the risk that the conflicting parties will resort to mass killings. The theoretical rationale underlying the use of this joint model was that some of the factors that drive the deployment of peacekeeping missions are also likely to be related to the risk that civilians will be massacred, but that much of what jointly drives mass killing and peacekeeping is very difficult to observe systematically. Most importantly, decision makers have access to analyses from intelligence agencies, media, nongovernmental organizations, and actors with special information on the intentions and capacities of the warring parties. It is reasonable to assume that this type of intangible information should, on average, be more right than wrong about the risk of mass killing (Melander, 2009). The results as well as the theoretical rationale means that, all else equal, decision makers indeed do tend to send peacekeepers to places where civilians are most at risk.

Although dealing with slightly different research questions, several other studies have concluded that when selection is taken into account, third parties tend to become involved in the most difficult conflicts. For example, Svensson (2006) finds that mediators tend to be active in conflicts where the prospects of successful mediation are the least promising, and that mediation does increase the chance that intrastate conflicts will end in negotiated agreements. DeRouen (2003) examined the effectiveness of UN involvement in interstate disputes, and concludes that the UN tends to insert itself in the most difficult disputes and that the effects of UN involvement are benign. Fortna (2008) finds that peacekeepers are sent to places where the most fragile peace exists and that they increase the chances that the peace will last.

Given that peacekeeping missions tend to be deployed in the most difficult situations, it becomes all the more important to ask how such missions can influence warring parties not to resort to the massacre of civilians. This is important, as their forces typically are small numerically and are equipped with weak mandates and light weapons. Prominent analyses of genocides and mass killing hold that powerful military interventions that directly confront perpetrators are most likely to succeed in halting or curbing the slaughter (e.g., Krain, 2005; Power, 2002; Valentino, 2004). It is important, however, to distinguish between the ability of peacekeeping missions to prevent potential mass murderers from actually resorting to genocide, on the one hand, and the capacity of peacekeepers to stop already ongoing massacres, on the other. In the latter case, the perpetrators have already committed an enormous atrocity and must, reasonably, be extremely determined or desperate. In particular, those perpetrators who persist in killing huge numbers of civilians are by then likely to have largely dismissed potential or actual countermeasures by third parties (Melander, 2009; cf. Harff, 1986, p. 168). When thinking about the potential for prevention of genocide, we would thus risk being misled by a biased selection of observations if we were to base our inferences only on the study of the most extreme cases, where the perpetrators may seem not to care about international reactions to the killing (e.g., Rwanda, Sudan). This, then, is another form of selection problem that may bias our analyses when we as analysts focus too much on the most dramatic cases (Melander, 2009).

Keeping in mind, then, that preventing the onset of mass killing may be quite different from stopping already ongoing genocide, a study by Krain (2005) nevertheless offers several mechanisms through which peacekeepers could conceivably influence potential mass killers in a situation of armed conflict. Krain examines third-party military interventions in already ongoing state-sponsored mass murder, and is thus concerned with the conditions under which ongoing mass killings can be halted or minimized. Krain finds that interventions that directly challenge the perpetrator or aid the victims are the only effective types of military responses. But given the differences between prevention by peacekeepers and forceful military intervention in already ongoing mass killings, the other mechanisms identified by Krain could well be just as relevant for a discussion of the possibility of using IGOs to prevent genocide (Melander, 2009).

The first mechanism noted by Krain is the Challenging Intervention Model, according to which the third party directly challenges the perpetrators and forces them to reassess the costs and benefits of massacring civilians. Krain contrasts the Challenging Intervention Model to the Impartial Intervention Model. According to this alternative logic, the type of intervention that is most likely to succeed is impartial and nonthreatening: "If the intervening force can make it clear that stopping the killing, rather than victory for either side in the conflict, is the primary concern, then the assumption is that an impartial intervention should reduce the severity of state-sponsored mass murder" (Krain, 2005, p. 367). A third relevant model is the Witness Model, according to which the mere fact of intervention in the conflict situation with personnel on the ground might signal "at the very least an interest in the situation by the international community, and an unwillingness to be complicit by remaining passively on the sidelines" (Krain, 2005, p. 368). In this connection, Krain also stresses that the intervening third parties become potential eyewitnesses to the killings. While most peacekeeping missions are unlikely to exert much influence through the Challenging Intervention Model (because of limited numbers, equipment, and mandates), both the Impartial and Witness Models would seem to be widely applicable (Melander, 2009).

These are some examples of how IGOs, through peacekeeping, may influence warring parties so that the risk of genocide is reduced. The most important conclusions to emerge out of this research so far (Melander, 2009) is that peace-keepers, on average, seem to be sent to the most murderous conflicts, and that when this selection is taken into account, peacekeeping has a benign preventive effect on the risk of genocide. This finding, in turn, underscores the importance of keeping potential selection effects in mind when discussing the ability of IGOs to contribute to preventing genocide. Also, whereas the most resolute perpetrators may be more or less immune to all forms of influence except force, many conflict actors thinking about resorting to mass killings may be dissuaded by impartial interventions or the presence of international witnesses.

■ PREVENTIVE DIPLOMACY, WAR, AND GENOCIDE

Peacekeeping thus can be an effective way of preventing an armed conflict from sliding into war and genocide. Let us now turn to other forms of preventive actions, drawn from the diplomatic field. This is a field with surprisingly little systematic investigation. Often genocides may appear too overpowering for diplomacy and negotiations to be of relevance. These instruments may appear too weak. There is still no basis for making a general judgment. Using a dataset of measures to manage internal armed conflict in their early stages throws some light on the question and may stimulate further work along this line. The Managing Intrastate Low-Intensity Conflict (MILC) dataset covers third-party measures to prevent the escalation and spread of intrastate low-intensity conflicts for the period 1993–2004. A total of 3,018 third-party activities are registered in the dataset. This shows that the inter-national community indeed is taking action in potentially serious situations and also that some of the third parties include major powers and IGOs (Melander et al., 2009a). In fact, IGOs were responsible for close to one-third of all measures taken by the international community. This demonstrates that IGOs are significant preventive actors and that their efforts warrant a closer look. This is, thus our focus in this section.

The UN and the European Union (EU) are among the three most active inter-mediaries, surpassed only by one major power, the United States. Among the 10 most active actors we also find the (Organization of African Unity, OAU/African Union, AU). Figure 15.1 displays the regional distribution of the preventive mea-sures taken by IGOs in low-intensity conflicts. It shows that IGOs are particularly active in Europe and Africa but also in the Middle East. They are less engaged in the Americas and Asia even though Asia has almost constantly experienced the highest number of conflicts—and in recent times also the most intense ones.

However, using the Uppsala Conflict Data Program (UCDP) One-sided Violence Dataset (version 1.3) for 1989–2006 to locate genocide situations in con-flict settings (genocide situations are defined as attacks by the government of a state or by a formally organized group on civilians that result in a large number of fatalities), only one such situation was found to occur in Asia: Afghanistan in 1998,

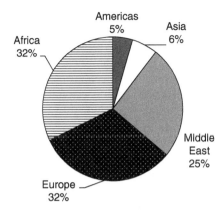

Figure 15.1 Regional distribution of IGO measures, 1993–2004.

the perpetrator being the Taliban government. At the same time, the conventional war between the Taliban government and the Northern Alliance had intensified. These data also show that there were no genocide situations in the Americas in this period.

Of all the genocide situations recorded by UCDP from 1989 to 2006, all but a few occurred in Africa. Africa has experienced several violent attacks on civilians in recent time. Citizens of the Democratic Republic of the Congo, Sudan, Angola, Burundi, and Rwanda have all been victims of attacks by their own governments or by rebel groups operating in the country. The data also confirm the picture presented in the previous section: All countries experienced conventional armed conflict, most of them at devastating levels of intensity, at the same time with one-sided violence. Thus, we ask, does the pattern observed for peacekeeping also apply to preventive actions: that they are undertaken in situations with the greatest risk of large civilian fatalities and in genocide-prone situations?

This pattern can be observed in Table 15.1, which shows the conflicts with the most IGO preventive initiatives. Three of the listed conflicts have experienced genocide situations since the 1990s: Bosnia-Herzegovina, the Democratic Republic of the Congo, and Burundi; four have not. We can legitimately ask if the special attention from IGOs did in fact prevent escalation to mass violence in the Israeli–Palestinian conflict as well as in Croatia, Côte d'Ivoire, and Macedonia. International attention to some of these conflicts may very well have averted further deterioration and possible genocidal acts. For instance, Macedonia is often recorded as a successful case of conflict prevention (Broughton & Fraenkel, 2002; Lund, 2002, p. 100; Väyrynen, 2003, p. 50). In a later section, we will look more carefully at the case of Côte d'Ivoire. There are methodological difficulties, of course, in estimating whether certain developments have been prevented, but comparisons and statistical methods give some insights (Wallensteen & Möller, 2003). For instance, third parties are more likely to make verbal threats to the parties in ethnic disputes that actually escalate to wars than to the parties in ethnic disputes that do not escalate further. These threats may in fact reflect the underlying seriousness of the conflict rather than being a direct impact of third-party action. Also, this shows that verbal engagement alone may not be sufficient in preventing escalation. If coupled with additional measures, such as humanitarian assistance, verbal engagement seems to have a more deescalating effect (Öberg et al., 2009).

Table 15.1 gives rise to a number of reflections on the preventive diplomacy of international organizations. Let us look more carefully at the seven conflicts most attended to by IGOs in this period, representing the three regions receiving most attention, as seen in Figure 15.1.

Table 15.1 points to the heavy international interest in the Balkan conflicts, with three conflicts among the seven receiving most attention. The MILC dataset has 1993 as its starting point, and thus we have no systematic data on IGO activity in the early phases of some of the post-Yugoslavia conflicts. Note that Table 15.1 includes those conflicts that had a lower level of intensity. It is possible to argue that there was some degree of success in preventing escalation in some dyads in the whole web of conflicts. A Bosniak-Croatian federation was formed in 1994, which ended the war between Bosnian Croats and Muslims relatively quickly. Similarly, the Croatian–Serbian conflict in Croatia was high on the international agenda. The EU and UN were leading organizations in many of the peace moves in the region, often in close cooperation. In both of these cases, however, they failed to prevent continued ethnic cleansing.

A more clear-cut case of successful preventive diplomacy is Macedonia, as already mentioned. In 2001, there were fears that Macedonia could turn into another brutal Balkan war, as the polarization was increasing between Macedonians and Albanians following the war in Kosovo. Consequently, direct talks began in 2001 with the Macedonian government, involving both the EU and the North Atlantic Treaty Organization (NATO). It is likely that these intense diplomatic efforts averted escalation and instead directed the conflict into peacemaking, in which the Macedonian parties themselves gradually took the lead, after the conclusion of the Ohrid peace agreement in August 2001. In a way, the international efforts can be seen to have created space for the parties to work out their differences directly among themselves.

Perhaps not unexpectedly, the Israeli–Palestinian conflict received more attention than any other low-intensity conflict in this period. Even though there are no genocide situations registered in this conflict, there were many terrorist deeds

TABLE 15.1. *Low-Intensity Conflicts with the Most IGO Preventive Action, 1993–2004.*

Name of conflict	# of events
Israel (Palestine)	164
Croatia (Serb)	84
Bosnia (Croat)	80
Democratic Republic of the Congo	68
Côte d'Ivoire	50
Burundi	37
Macedonia	36

directed at civilians in events that may well have led to quick escalation in other conflict situations around the world. Thus, the fact that many third-party actors have been active in this conflict may have been significant in preventing further deterioration. The primary IGO third party is the EU, which has been more active than the UN. In addition, the United States has played a major role, and sometimes there was also Russian involvement. These four actors formed the Quartet pushing not only for conflict prevention but also for conflict resolution. There have been continued flare-ups in this conflict, most recently in Gaza in 2008–2009, making the international efforts appear futile. Also, attempts to direct negotiations between the parties have so far achieved little. On the other hand, we have to keep in mind that the Israeli–Palestinian conflict may be typical of how the international community becomes involved in the most difficult conflicts. It is, furthermore, possible that many worse atrocities could have been committed in this conflict if international engagement had been weaker.

Of the three African conflicts, according to the UCDP One-sided Violence Dataset (version 1.3) for 1989–2006, the Democratic Republic of the Congo and Burundi have been identified as genocide situations but not Côte d'Ivoire. There has been considerable activity in all three conflicts, often by the same organizations (e.g., AU/OAU with different representatives and the UN). The UN, followed by the Southern African Development Community (SADC), were particularly engaged in the Congo. The Economic Community of West African States (ECOWAS) and France were early in acting in Côte d'Ivoire. It is interesting to ask how the efforts and initiatives in the latter case differ from those in the other two cases. Looking more closely at the international efforts in Burundi (where mainly the UN and the OAU/AU were active), it is found that only a few activities took place before the genocide situations of 1995 and 1996. The international community became engaged *after* the events, and even then, its activities were more sporadic and spread out over a long period. A similar pattern is found in the Democratic Republic of the Congo, where a genocide situation was recorded in 1997, 1998, and 2003. Diplomatic efforts continued in 1998 and 1999, but again largely after the events, as was the case in 2003. It seems that the actions taken in Côte d'Ivoire took place earlier and were more consistent than in the other cases. This may reflect stronger concerns that the conflict in Côte d'Ivoire could have become entangled with the civil wars in neighboring Liberia, Sierra Leone, and Guinea. Neither Burundi nor the Democratic Republic of the Congo may at the time have been seen in a similar light.

Perhaps the most infamous genocide situation in Africa is that of Sudan. Since its independence in 1956, Sudan has been marred by mass killings of civilians in all years except the ten-year period 1973–1982. After a bout of slightly lower levels of battle intensity in 1993–1994, the Sudan conflict escalated again to full-scale civil war in 1995. Most of the third-party activities aiming to help bring the conflict with Southern Sudan to an end are thus not included in the MILC dataset since the conflict had by then already escalated. In this sense, third-party peacemaking came too late in Sudan.

Preventive diplomacy, as recorded here, is a frequent activity. We also see that it attends to the most difficult conflicts. The record in curtailing genocide is limited, however. We find two cases where a plausible argument can be made for a prevention achievement in the period studied: Macedonia and Côte d'Ivoire. This suggests that the conflicts that international organizations choose to enter with preventive actions are more complicated than other conflicts. Also, it appears that IGOs often act only *after* the onset of large-scale massacres. The two divergent cases warrant more analysis, and we have chosen to focus on Côte d'Ivoire. However, before taking up this case, we need to look at the third tool available to the international community: targeted sanctions.

■ TARGETED SANCTIONS AND THE PREVENTION OF GENOCIDE

Sanctions and genocide have a particular history not paralleled by the other international instruments discussed in the chapter. The comprehensive sanctions of the past have meant that entire economies have been sealed off, thus, creating considerable harm for the civilian population. This is the way sanctions were used during World War I, and the hardship suffered by the German population was a factor in that country's capitulation. This made sanctions popular with the victors. Sanctions were introduced as the prime measure in the League of Nations to be used against aggressors. Indeed, the ferocity of their impact was even seen as a preventive measure: The threat of being exposed to sanctions, it was thought, would deter a would-be aggressor from committing aggression. However, it did not deter Italy from attacking Ethiopia in 1935, and since then, sanctions have had a more limited role in international affairs. It remains, however, a legitimate tool for the UN, the EU, and individual countries.

In the 1990s, a new debate arose with respect to the sanctions on Iraq. It was claimed that the sanctions created such hardship that they amounted to genocide of the Iraqi population (Halliday, 2000). This critique of the sanctions led to the creation of a major UN effort, the Food for Oil program, based in the UN headquarters, to alleviate their impact. It also resulted in the development of new tools, *smart sanctions*, that would avoid the dramatic effects of comprehensive sanctions (Lopez, 2000). These new sanctions would include measures such as arms embargoes and measures targeted to particular individuals, their financial holdings and travel opportunities, and to commodities that could sustain their noncompliance with international requests (e.g., diamonds, timber). In this form, sanctions may become more helpful in the prevention of genocide. These are the types of sanctions that are most important in our context. This conclusion is reinforced by evaluations of the Iraq sanctions experience. For instance, it has been asked whether or not the arms embargo may have been the most important component in preventing Iraq from acquiring weapons of mass destruction (Wallensteen et al., 2004, p. 21).

Thus, here, we are concerned primarily with targeted sanctions (particularly arms embargoes) in genocide prevention. There are no studies specifically addressing this issue, although some attention has been given to it (Lopez, 2000; Lopez & Stuhldreher, 2007). Thus, we have to resort to studies that consider the more general questions of arms embargoes and their effect on conflicts. A number of recently published reports have shed light on the efficacy of arms embargoes, and they constitute the basic material for the following reflections on sanctions as a tool in genocide situations.

In recent articles, Morgan, Bapat, and Krustev point out that there may be a selection effect in sanctions study and policy debates. The focus tends to be on the most difficult and protracted conflicts. Presenting a new dataset of 888 cases of economic sanctions imposed in 1971–2000, the authors find that sanctions are normally shorter in duration than was previously thought and also more successful: 30% of those with known final outcomes ended with partial or total concessions from the target and another 25% ended with negotiations. The authors have succeeded in compiling a more comprehensive dataset than was previously available for systematic sanctions study. Some common notions may have to be revised. One is that multilateral sanctions, in fact, are more successful than unilateral ones, as earlier studies seemed to imply. Again, this may be a result of a bias in the collection of data: There has been a tendency to include only high-profile cases rather than more limited and less well known cases (Bapat & Morgan, 2009; Morgan et al., 2009).

This makes it interesting to study international organizations and sanctions. There is recent work of relevance to the question of genocide. In 2007 a study of 27 UN arms embargoes for the period 1990–2006 was published in Sweden. It was the result of a joint effort of the sanctions research program at Uppsala University (The Special Program on the Implementation of Targeted Sanctions, SPITS) and the arms transfer project at Stockholm International Peace Research Institute, (SIPRI) (Fruchart et al., 2007). The following year, Brzoska published a study of 74 arms embargoes for the period 1990–2005, including not only UN sanctions but also those of the EU and the United States (Brzoska, 2008). These studies deal directly with the sanctions and are highly relevant for our arguments.

Interestingly, although not particularly focused on sanctions, Regan and Aydin (2006) included this measure as part of their study of interventions. Their work covers 1945–1999, and they report that sanctions are not related to whether conflicts are terminated earlier or later. The duration of conflict is their measure of whether interventions succeed or not. Thus, in their analysis, sanctions do not stand out as a measure of consequence. Instead, they find diplomacy to be the central factor. They also give more credit to economic inducements—the reverse of sanctions, so to speak—in shortening conflicts. These findings are challenging to sanctions studies. Obviously, sanctions also deal with issues other than active conflicts, and thus their results are only partially relevant for the sanctions discussion. However, their main point—that joint effects of economic interventions and diplomacy are more effective—is of great value in our further deliberations. Sanctions may often have been used as an alternative to diplomacy rather than as a tool integrated in diplomacy. Regan and Aydin statistically support the latter approach.

An innovative study by Della Vigna and La Ferrara (2008) comes to the conclusion that embargoes actually do have an impact, at least in constraining the arms trade. The authors arrive at this conclusion through a study of eight UN arms embargoes and stock market changes in more than 150 companies engaged in the arms trade. They find that companies from low-corruption countries are affected by increasing conflict in the targeted countries, implying that their sales are likely to suffer due to continued restrictions on legal trade (pp. 4, 13, 22–23, 28). Their interpretation is that these companies may risk incurring reputational costs if they violate the embargoes, and thus that the stock market is waiting for opportunities for legal trade. Companies from high-corruption countries are not affected the same way. This actually suggests ways in which the arms trade can be monitored. The constraints on the arms trade are, of course, a first element if sanctions are also to have an impact on the target's behavior—for instance, preventing the target from initiating a genocide.

However, this makes the SPITS/SIPRI (Fruchart et al., 2007) and Brzoska (2008) studies the only systematic ones that deal with the impact of sanctions both on arms flows and on target behavior. They are, consequently, most relevant for our topic.

The SPITS/SIPRI study divides UN sanctions into three categories with respect to the goals they want to achieve: (1) Conflict Management, notably the ending of a war or of hostilities; (2) Government Authority, aiming at affecting regimes, sometimes trying to change authoritarian regimes, sometimes aiming at maintaining particular governments; and (3) Global Security, which includes the goals of preventing proliferation of weapons of mass destruction and terrorism. (Fruchart et al., 2007, p. 3). All three goals have a preventive purpose, although in slightly different ways.

The Conflict Management sanctions aim at stopping an ongoing interstate or intrastate war means that one prevents it from escalating or spreading regionally. These are the situations in which an arms embargo intuitively makes sense. It is a way to curtail the flow of arms to the fighting actors. If all sides are equally exposed to the sanctions, it also means that a conflict will freeze more or less at the situation that prevails at the time the sanctions are imposed. This may sometimes benefit an already well-armed actor more than others, whether intended or not. In most recent civil wars, however, this may not have been the most typical effect.

Government Authority sanctions include cases of the restoration of a previous democratic order. The Global Security sanctions are explicitly preventive: to maintain the nonproliferation treaty as well as to prevent new terrorist activities, which, by definition, are actions directed at civilians. Thus, the preventive ambition is present in most UN uses of sanctions, although not necessarily strongly spelled out in the mandating documents. In some cases, this also relates to the possibility of preventing genocide.

In this context, the focus is on the Conflict Management category, which is also the largest group of sanctions in the SPITS/SIPRI (Fruchart et al., 2007) study, with 16 cases. There are significant aspects of genocidal risks in all of these cases, and in some of them, specific actions were taken to reduce or eliminate such dangers.

An example is the Iraq sanctions following the Gulf War in 1991. A general uprising took place against Saddam Hussain's regime. His offensive against the Kurdish population resulted in a mass exodus of Kurds from large areas of Iraq and left refugees in difficult conditions in the mountains. The sanctions on Iraq were extended, but a military measure was also instituted: a no-fly zone in Northern Iraq. At the same time, humanitarian efforts were authorized by the UN Security Council (UNSCR 688). This provided for the safe return of the refugees and possibly prevented another genocide of the Kurdish population. However, international attention to the situation of the Shi'ites in Southern Iraq was limited.

The conflicts in Yugoslavia similarly had genocidal aspects, as previously mentioned (the 1992–1995 as well as the 1998–1999 conflicts), and sanctions were used to reduce the capacities of, in particular, the Serb actors to pursue war and ethnic cleansing. Sanctions on Rwanda, however, were not instituted until the end of the genocide and armed conflict in 1994. The measures were directed at the forces of the previous regime, thus preventing it from returning to power.

Even the interstate war between Ethiopia and Eritrea had aspects of ethnic cleansing: Inhabitants defined as belonging to the other side were forced to leave. The situations in Somalia, Liberia, Angola, Sierra Leone, the Democratic Republic of the Congo, Darfur (Sudan), Liberia, and Côte d'Ivoire all have similar aspects, but in varying degrees. In many there have been mass violence and cruelty against exposed groups, only sometimes being officially defined as genocide by some actors (e.g., in Darfur). Many of these situations, if unchecked, may, however, have moved far beyond ethnic cleansing.

The question thus is whether conflict management through an arms embargo had an impact. The statistical result of the SPITS/SIPRI study (Fruchart et al., 2007) shows this to be the case when annual data on sanctions and conflict development are analyzed. There are more than 100 such observations. Overall, arms embargoes had an impact in 25% of the observations. In Government Authority and Conflict Management cases the percentage increases to 29%; when there is some restraint on the borders, the figure becomes 36%; and when UN peacekeepers are present, it becomes 47% (Fruchart et al., 2007, pp. 33–35). There is an important outcome here: The sanctions may work in conjunction with other measures, notably peacekeeping, to reduce the dangers of escalation, diffusion, or possibly prolongation of the conflict. If, at the same time, neighbors contribute by strengthening border controls, the arms embargo is more likely to have an impact on the behavior of the parties.

These are indeed strong results, and they go beyond those reported by Brzoska (2008). He finds that effectiveness in term of policy change is only 8% for all arms embargoes, although those that ended prior to 2005 were effective in 14%. The methodology is different from that of the SPITS/SIPRI report (Fruchart et al., 2007), which focused only on armed conflict and dealt with annual shifts and events, not whole cases. Also, the definition of effect differs, as Brzoska reports much lower numbers than SIPRI/SPITS for the impact on the target's action. When the UN sanctions are separated out, effectiveness increases, as it does when studying all cases where the sanctions aim at ending civil wars. Unfortunately, Brzoska (2008) does not report specifically on UN sanctions aimed at ending civil wars. The strongest effect, however, is achieved in cases where the arms embargo is an "element in targeted sanctions package" (p. 15) and this is also the chief conclusion: Arms embargoes are "most effective when utilized as a consistent element of larger policy packages" (p. 24). Furthermore, multilateral sanctions are more effective than others, particularly in conjunction with accompanying measures and when aimed at stopping civil wars. Thus, this study supports the notion that arms embargoes actually may have an impact on the escalation of conflicts. If an ongoing armed conflict can be stopped, it is also likely that the moves toward genocide can be curtailed.

All of these studies report on economic measures taken once a conflict has broken out. Sometimes this can be late in developments leading toward genocide. Thus, earlier threats of action become relevant. The new data by Morgan et al. (2009) will allow for more studies of this situation in the future. For the time being, only the SPITS/SIPRI study (Fruchart et al., 2007) deals with threats of sanctions, estimating their impact, and its conclusions are not encouraging. For instance, of the 15 Conflict Management cases with threats of sanctions, the threat was deemed credible in only 3 instances. In all the other cases, there were disagreements among permanent members of the Security Council on the sanctions policy. It is interesting, however, that the threat issued in 2005 against Ethiopia and Eritrea is associated with changes in behavior. None of the parties acted to restart the war or challenge the UN (Fruchart et al., 2007, p. 19). However, they have not moved to a final settlement of their disagreement. Still, the study underlines a significant aspect: the importance of consensus among, in particular, the permanent members of the Security Council. In too many cases, sanctions have been instituted as the least common denominator among these major powers, rather than as part of a coherent strategy aiming at changing the behavior of a particular targeted actor.

Thus, a successful sanctions policy to prevent genocide requires the cooperation of the leading powers, accompanying international measures, support from neighboring countries in controlling borders and other forms of access to the warring parties, and explicit monitoring of the sanctions— for instance, in the form of professional peacekeeping. This means that sanctions may help to reduce the likelihood of genocide if they are part of an international genocide prevention strategy. We now turn to the case of Côte d'Ivoire to see how this might work.

■ SUCCESS IN GENOCIDE PREVENTION? THE CASE OF CÔTE D'IVOIRE[1]

The international community, as we have seen, is equipped with a set of tools that can be used to prevent armed conflicts from escalating or spreading: peacekeeping, preventive diplomacy, and targeted sanctions. Each of these can have an impact separately, but the present state of research suggests that when they are used in a coherent way, the chance of success in achieving prevention is enhanced. Let us now investigate if this is also a way of preventing a disaster such as genocide from happening by looking at a pertinent recent case.

This has to be a case where there is agreement among observers at the time that there is a serious threat of genocide. It has to be pertinent in that it corresponds to a common understanding of genocide, that is, that political violence follows ethnic lines of division. It has to be recent, as the tools have to be available to the international community and the lessons from Rwanda integrated into the political consciousness of leading decision makers. The case fitting these criteria is Côte d'Ivoire during the period 1999–2008. We have already seen that this case figures strongly in prevention activity (Table 15.1), and we argue that it is highly relevant in a discussion on the prevention of genocide. A first test of whether the case is an example of successful prevention was in the 2010 presidential elections. It was successfully conducted, but the second test, the adherence to the outcome was not. The aftermath turned violent, resulting in a short armed conflict in April 2011, before the winner of the election could take office.

Genocide Danger in Côte d'Ivoire

The armed conflict was most intense in 2002 but lingered on in the following years, as Table 15.2 demonstrates. The outlines of the armed conflict can be understood from the following statistics, drawn from the conflict database of the UCDP.

Table 15.2 summarizes the strict coding of battle-related deaths for the four years 2002–2005 in Côte d'Ivoire. The categories are defined so that they do not overlap and thus can be added. The total number of deaths directly connected with political violence during this period is 1,800. This is, no doubt, a conservative esti- mate. If we add data on refugees, the human toll of the conflict will become more evident. The United Nations High Commissioner for Refugees, (UNHCR) esti- mated that there were over 700,000 internally displaced person, but most joined family members or host families. The UN Secretary General estimated that by July 2009, close to 80,000 of the 120,000 persons who had no host families had returned to their original areas (UN Security Council, S/2009/344:8).

Table 15.2 also shows that the armed conflict itself was responsible for less than half of the 1,800 fatalities (737 to be exact). The armed conflict was contained fairly quickly, but nonstate violence continued, as did one-sided violence. In 2002, with close to 1,000 people killed in organized conflict, 60% per cent of the deaths occurred in the armed conflict; in 2003 the share was 18% and in 2004 16%; by 2005 no armed conflict was active. Other types of political violence continued, albeit at a lower level. By 2006 there was no further record of organized violence along the political divides, according to UCDP. Thus, the conflict shifted for a while to other forms of violent action. However, at no point was the number of battle-related deaths so large as to be defined as war, and there was no genocide in this case. This makes it very interesting to analyze. How can this development be explained?

TABLE 15.2. *Battle-Related Deaths, Côte d'Ivoire, 2002–2005*

	Armed conflict	Nonstate conflict	One-sided violence	Total
2002	594	53	331	978
2003	88	207	190	485
2004	55	240	42	337
2005	0	141	28	169

Source: http://www.pcr.uu.se/gpdatabase/ (retrieved September 2, 2009), using the best estimates and adding different dyads for the different conflicts.

Surprisingly, the writings on the armed conflict in Côte d'Ivoire from the point of view of a possible genocide are fairly limited, as is the academic treatment of the crisis in general. Collier (2009) has a chapter on the "Meltdown in Côte d'Ivoire," pointing to economic explanations and political manipulations as the origin of the conflict. Other works include short articles (Badmus, 2009; Daddieh, 2001; Kirwin, 2006; Toungara 2001), a book chapter (Miran, 2006), and graduate theses (Boyer, 2006; Rametsi, 2006), as well as International Crisis Group reports (since 2003), apart from the works of Francis Akindès (e.g., 2004). The developments are largely unknown to readers outside the immediate vicinity of the conflict. There is a need for a short recapitulation of the events.

The central concern in the conflict, and thus in the attempts to solve it, was the issue of identity: Who was actually a citizen of the country? This is an element in the many attempts to define what constitutes the beginning of a process toward genocide. Stanton (1998) calls this the "stage of classification." In the case of Côte d'Ivoire it was an important issue, deciding, for instance, who was entitled to run for public office, own land, or have a job in the public sector. Strict laws on this issue began to emerge in the mid-1990s. In late 1994 an electoral code was passed for the presidential elections in 1995, stating that only candidates whose parents were Ivorian were eligible to run. This code was—according to most observers— instituted to bar a strong candidate from the North of the country, the previous prime minister, Allasane Dramana Outtara (Badmus, 2009, p. 51; Boyer, 2006, p. 5; Daddieh, 2001, p. 17), whose nationality was questioned and this remained an issue (Akindès, 2004, pp. 36–40). Following this, laws were instituted restricting land-ownership and eligibility for public office in a similar way. This led to a form of ethnic cleansing in the South of the country (Badmus, 2009, p. 52). The coup of 1999 upset the institutional stability of the country and opened the way to the 2000 changes in the constitution, again barring the same candidate from running for office (Badmus, 2009, p. 53; Boyer, 2006, pp. 5–6; Daddieh, 2001, p. 18). Following the elections, which led to Laurent Gbagbo's victory, immigrants in the south were harassed and began to leave the country (Daddieh, 2001, p. 18).

The ideology of *ivorité* was underpinning these developments (Akindès, 2004, pp. 26–33; Badmus, 2009, pp. 50ff; Daddieh, 2001, pp. 17ff; Kirwin, 2006; Rametsi, 2006, pp. 18ff). The southerners were seen as the carriers of the state; they had access to education and controlled most of the resources. Through this ideology, which analysts say began to spread more strongly in the mid-1990s, it was possible to exclude a large fraction of the population from power as well as from employ-ment, income, and wealth. There was also, some writers point out, a religious dimension to this: the South was more Christian, the North more Moslem (Boyer, 2006, pp. 2–3), but no religious group constituted a majority. Interestingly, early violence included attempts at polarization along religious lines, but this process was countered, primarily by Moslem leaders who took a conciliatory approach (Miran, 2006). Thus, the use of identity criteria to exclude potential competitors from power positions was not only a matter of intraelite rivalry but had an impact on the entire nation. The regulations also affected legal immigrants who had worked for a long time on the plantations in the South, whether they came from the North of the country or from neighboring countries (Badmus, 2009, p. 49).

To document one's ancestry was an added problem. It is not difficult to link the introduction of identity criteria to a decrease in export prices on, in particular, cocoa and coffee. Competition for jobs intensified, and politically identity became an expedient card to play as an explanation for the troubled economy (Collier, 2009, pp. 157–158).

The classifications had real significance for the fortunes of many of the 18 million inhabitants of Côte d'Ivoire. In fact, by 2002, an additional stage on Stanton's (1998) ladder had been passed. The Northern population was not only excluded from access to the highest levels of power, as it consisted of populations that also were related to those of the neighboring countries (Burkina Faso, Mali). The Northerners also began to be identified with a "foreign power" that was instigating unrest and attempting to undermine the country (Daddieh, 2001, p. 18). This is what Stanton describes as the second stage, "symbolization," which can easily turn into a third stage, "dehumanization." Reports make it clear that in 2002, militia groups defining themselves as "patriotic" emerged; in response, defense militias appeared on the other side. Violence was increasing, initially related to mobs, later turning into militias with criminal connections (Boyer, 2006, p. 6, Collier, 2009, p. 165). This constitutes the fourth stage on Stanton's scale: "organization." Genocide Watch defined the situation at this time as even further along toward genocide (Boyer, 2006, p. 10).

In September 2002, a military coup was attempted but failed. However, enough troops supported the attempt for a civil armed conflict to begin. In a short time, the country was divided into two parts with their respective armies. In fact, the divisions widened very quickly and additional rebel groups emerge in the West of the country, no doubt with outside support. By late 2002, a cease-fire was reached between the government and some rebel groups, thus, cementing the division of the country into two parts. A year later, the rebel groups united into Forces Nouvelles (FN), led by Guillaume Soro.

The International Response

The international response to the unfolding crisis consisted of three parallel measures: peacekeeping missions, economic and military sanctions, and preventive diplomacy. The measures reinforced each other.

Peacekeeping

By late 2002, international reactions began to generate momentum. The region had already seen wars in Liberia and Sierra Leone. Guinea-Bissau was unstable, and a low-level conflict was going on in Senegal. One more West African country on the brink of war would threaten to bring further instability to the entire region. However, the triggering factor for international action seems to have been a threat to French nationals in late 2002. French and U.S. troops were sent in to help the evacuation (Rametsi, 2006, p. 25). By January 2003, France had approximately 4,000 troops in the country (Boyer, 2006, p. 17) helping to keep the cease-fire in place. Similarly, ECOWAS sent in some 1,500 troops by January 2003. Negotiations between the opposing sides were initiated in Paris, and a peace agreement was concluded in 2003. The UN was asked to assist in its implementation. In 2004 the UN contingent was further increased and the ECOWAS forces were integrated into this operation, called United Nations Operation in Côte d'Ivoire, (UNOCI). By 2006 the UN strength amounted to 7,000 troops, 700 police, and more than 400 civilians (Boyer, 2006, pp. 17–2).

The deployment of these troops was associated with a reduction in violence, as can be seen in Table 15.2. The armed conflict was winding down. The parties had already agreed to a cease-fire, and the international presence made violations more difficult. In 2004, the government tried an offensive, attacking the French forces, which retaliated by destroying the government's helicopters. Since the arrival of the UN operation, armed action has almost entirely ceased between the warring actors.

As Table 15.2 makes clear, there were also other violent activities, at some points seemingly taking over the dynamics. The arrival of international police may have had something to do with the gradual waning of these types of acts.

Sanctions

The Security Council decided on an arms embargo in November 2004. This action paralleled France's attack on the government's air force, thus preventing its reconstruction. SIPRI's Arms Transfers Database records that these helicopters had been bought from Belarus, Bulgaria, and Romania (Fruchart et al., 2007, p.30, fn. 103). Further deliveries were made more difficult with the UN action. The Security Council also threatened to impose sanctions on individuals creating obstacles to the peace process. In February 2006 three persons were put on the UN sanctions list (Wallensteen et al., 2006, p. 8).

In a detailed analysis of the military developments in Côte d'Ivoire and their relationship to the sanctions measures, Strandow (2006, p. 36) finds that implemented arms embargoes actually had an effect independent of the military stalemate in increasing the parties' interest in conflict resolution. It is likely to be a measure that was important in the case of Côte d'Ivoire. It was followed up in several ways. In February 2005, the Security Council gave the peacekeeping operation a mandate to monitor the arms embargo. Together with the Security Council's independent panels of experts and measures instituted by neighboring countries, the embargo served to make the parties uncertain about future deliveries, thus making a resumption of hostilities unpredictable. In fact, in the peace agreement of 2007, the FN and the government agreed to demand the lifting of the arms embargo on light weapons immediately and on all deliveries three months after the presidential elections. They also asked for the removal of the targeted sanctions (ICG, 2007, p. 18). Clearly, these sanctions frustrated both sides. The Security Council has maintained the measures and, in fact, threatened in July 2009 to sharpen them.

Preventive Diplomacy

As can be seen in Table 15.1, this conflict led to considerable international preventive action. France and Senegal were among the first to react, but a contact group including Ghana, Mali, Nigeria, Niger, Togo, and Guinea-Bissau was also important. South Africa was a key mediator for a period. The ECOWAS, the AU, and the UN appointed special representatives for different aspects of the conflict. A series of peace agreements was concluded under international auspices. However, none of them was implemented.

Remarkably, in late 2006, President Gbagbo announced his own peace plan, outside of the UN and regional frameworks, and initiated direct negotiations with the central FN leader, Guillaume Soro. Even more remarkable, President Blaise Compaoré, of Burkina Faso (chairman of ECOWAS), served as the facilitator, although he and his country had previously been accused of interference. To Gbagbo, Burkina Faso was too close to FN, but in this situation, such a bias might have been seen to serve a purpose (Svensson, 2006). The negotiations resulted in an overall agreement, the Ouagadougou Political Agreement of March 2007. It was followed by a series of additional agreements between the parties. The direct involvement of the UN, France, and other actors was limited, although they provided basic security for the country and for the peace process.

This notwithstanding, the combined use of peacekeeping, sanctions, and preventive diplomacy may have helped to make the warring parties change their goals. Instead of victory (as the rebels intended in 2002 and the government sought with its offensive in 2004), a settlement emerged as a different and not necessarily negative route.

Côte d'Ivoire: The Route Away from Genocide?

The Ouagadougou Political Agreements included a settlement on the identity issue through an open identification and registration process using mobile courts and with considerably relaxed requirements for documentation. The process was completed by September 2009, in time for the scheduled presidential elections on November 29. Also, some of the stipulated efforts for the reunification of the country were made by the parties. Disarmament of former combatants and dismantling of militias was continuing (UN Security Council, 2009). The country appeared to be on track for regaining coherence and legitimate governance. Repeatedly, the Security Council extended the mandate for the UN peacekeeping missions untilthe electoral process, was completed.

As we have seen, Côte d'Ivoire had many of the elements of a possible genocide. The outbreak of the war in 2002 made this a distinct possibility: The state was weak and semidemocratic, the economy was depressed, and the region was in disarray. What stopped the process? Militarily, there was a stalemate, but the parties may well have seen this as a temporary situation. Indeed, we have seen that the government acquired new military equipment and actually tried to restart the armed conflict. An important difference from genocides is that Côte d'Ivoire lacked an internal precedent. Propagandists tried to compare the situation directly to that of Rwanda (Wallensteen et al., 2006, cites an example), but they could not point to Ivorian experience along such lines. This may have helped to reduce the drift toward escalation.

However, one has to conclude that the international reactions played a decisive role, unparalleled in other African cases. Clearly, the rapid deployment of peacekeeping operations (first by France, then by ECOWAS, and later by the UN) had an impact on the parties and resulted in an early cease-fire agreement. All the elements of peacekeeping approaches seem to have come into play. With France the forces actually could strike back, as implied by the Challenging Intervention Model. However, most of the time, the peacekeepers assumed a traditional role following the Impartial Intervention Model. Gradually, however, the UN forces received additional tasks, in line with the Witness Model: They monitored the arms embargo but also the Ivorian media, and in particular, they tried to counter hate messages through a special UN broadcasting station. By providing more impartial, credible information to the general public, they reinforced the impartial role, but in fact, they brought in new information and thus gave witness to what was actually happening.

The immediate start of peace negotiations (first by France and neighbors, later on by AU) may also have played an important role. The story of the many failed, resurrected, and modified peace agreements is illustrative. At least the parties must have asked themselves questions such as: What is acceptable to the other party? What are my own minimum requirements? What do I have support for on my side? When the actors began their own direct negotiations, some ground had already been established through the previous processes.

The use of sanctions, in particular the arms embargo (by the UN), also helped to avert the immediate danger of genocide. Even if genocides have been carried out without arms, the perpetrators need protection by their own forces against retaliation from the other side. Also, they may need more arms to achieve their war aims, and thus the sanctions may work as a deterrent against war and genocide at the same time. Without a continuous flow of arms, military forces cannot operate. In this case, arms imports were a necessity, as storage of weapons and munitions was limited, and vehicles needed spare parts not produced in the country. The mandate to the peacekeepers to monitor arms flows demonstrates the significance of the presence of outside forces.

The internationally mediated peace process did not reach agreements that the parties actually were willing to implement. Direct negotiations between the parties themselves turned out to be more fruitful. It should be noted that this initiative came four years after the cease-fire and after a great many peace efforts. All this activity may well have contributed to the realization that this conflict could only be solved between the parties themselves in direct conversations. The international actors clearly favored peace rather than war, which may have served to limit their options. The arms embargo was not going to be lifted, and it appeared that the consensus favoring peace was maintained, both in the region, in Africa as a whole, and in the Security Council. Unlike many other situations, the international consensus was maintained, restricting the possibilities for the parties to maneuver among dissenting major powers. The consensus may effectively have blocked other options for the parties. They had to find their own way of ending the impasse. There are obvious and strong benefits of such direct agreements. Based on this, the presidential elections were finally held in November 2010. Outtara, whose ivorité had been questioned, could run and came out as a clear winner with more than 54 % of the votes in the second round. That was the first test of political recovery.

However, incumbent Gbagbo refused to accept the result and hang on to power. The peacekeeping operation was reinforced, sanctions were expanded and diplomacy focused on finding ways to get Gbagbo out of office (Edgren-Schori & Schori 2011). After a short war in April 2011, Gbagbo was captured and Outtara could be in stalled in the presidential offices. The extent of the violence needs to be analyzed. Reconstruction, rehabilitation and reconciliation are urgent issues on the agenda of the new president. However, the international coalition behind the UN operation was kept intact throughout this process.

■ INTERNATIONAL COHERENCE AND GENOCIDE PREVENTION

Nobody can doubt that the recent and ongoing campaigns of mass murder of civilians are among the most pressing humanitarian crises facing the international community. Sadly, the question of what IGOs can do to prevent genocide undoubtedly remains a burning issue. Third-party efforts are often tragically ineffective, which may cast doubt on the whole premise that third parties can contribute meaningfully to preventing genocide. Considering all the cruelty and violence in the world, it is perhaps easy to be overcome with despair.

Yet, we find that the world has in recent decades become a less violent place in terms of organized conflict and genocide (Melander et al., 2009b), although all trends have their fluctuations. This provides reasons to think about how new tragedies can be averted. In this chapter, we have demonstrated that genocides since World War II have been connected to civil strife. As long as an armed conflict is not too entrenched or turned into a war (i.e., with more than 1,000 battle-related deaths in the armed conflict), the chances of preventing escalation and genocide are high. The later the reaction, the more difficult it is to intervene and the harder it is to protect innocent civilians from eviction, mass violence, and genocide.

In particular, we have pointed to the importance of a coherent international approach. Peacekeeping operations, preventive diplomacy, and sanctions need to work together. Then the preventive effect is likely to be the strongest, even if an armed conflict has started and has begun to gain momentum. We have illustrated this combined effect with the case of Côte d'Ivoire. In this case, we also found that a peacekeeping operation may be able to step outside the traditional role of providing impartial intervention. If it has a component that can act rapidly in response to provocation, this strengthens its capacity to maintain a stalemate. In this case France had that role, but in other circumstance there could be a rapid deployment force within the UN operation, such as in United Nations Mission in Liberia (UNMIL). In addition to this, the peacekeeping operation would benefit from acting as a witness: monitoring the media and embargoes and possibly also collecting information on war crimes committed by the parties for later prosecution.

To this we should add that persistent efforts are necessary for peacemaking: Keeping a peace process going is central. It becomes, at a minimum, a learning process for the parties and possibly also a way of showing them innovative ways to solve the incompatibility problems they are facing. We also note that recent research demonstrates that sanctions can be effective, particularly an arms embargo, if done in a multilateral setting, with support of regional actor—for instance, in controlling borders with permanent international monitoring and as part of a political strategy.

The experience of Côte d'Ivoire suggests that such concerted international action may push the parties in the direction of peace. Other alternatives are closed off; thus, they have to work out their differences among themselves. Côte d'Ivoire is now in a fragile situation where this is brought to a test. We have also pointed to Macedonia, which was also under international pressure to solve its problem. Following a peace agreement in 2001, the Macedonian sides continued the peace process on their own. This is the most reasonable way to build peace for the future.

The most important message derived from this research is that there are ways to deal with violence in preventing genocide. We suggest that international activism may be much more important in curbing civil war and genocide than is commonly believed. In this chapter, we have also reviewed recent research showing that peacekeeping missions tend to be sent into the most difficult situations. The same seems to be true for international preventive action and for multilateral sanctions. Such selection effects have to be taken into account when assessing the effectiveness of IGOs in the prevention of genocide.

A factor that may be central in preventing war and genocide is the shared determination of major outside actors not to allow a situation to get out of hand. The UN Security Council must continue to maintain a peacekeeping mission, even in difficult places, foster the support of neighboring countries for the prevention effort, and undertake actions that reduce the options of the actors and ultimately force them to deal constructively with each other. This seems to be the story of both Macedonia and Côte d'Ivoire: The peace is built by the parties themselves, giving them ownership of the process, but with unified support from the region and the major powers. In this way, peace may come to the most difficult conflicts.

Note

1. The support of Mr. Stephen Oola for research on the case of Côte d'Ivoire is gratefully acknowledged.

References

Akindès, F. (2004). *The roots of the military-politcal crisis in Côte d'Ivoire*. Uppsala: Nordiska Afrikainstitutet, Research Report 128.

Andersson, A. (2000). Democracies and UN peacekeeping operations, 1990–1996. *International Peacekeeping, 7*(2), 1–22.

Badmus, I. A. (2009). Even the stones are burning: Explaining the ethnic dimensions of the civil war in Côte d'Ivoire. *Journal of Social Science, 18*(1), 45–57.

Bapat, N. A., & Morgan, T. C. (2009). Multilateral versus unilateral sanctions reconsidered: A test using new data. *International Studies Quarterly, 53*, 1075–1094.

Boyer, T. E. (2006, April). *Ivory Coast: A case study in internvention and the prevention of genocide*. Maxwell Air Force Base, Alabama: Air Command and Staff College, Air University.

Broughton, S., & Fraenkel, E. (2002). Macedonia: Extreme challenges for the "model" of multiculturalism. In P. van Tongeren, H. van de Veen, &, J. Verhoeven (Eds.), *Searching for peace in Europe and Eurasia: An overview of conflict prevention and peacebuilding activities* (pp. 264–279). Boulder, CO: Lynne Rienner.

Brzoska, M. (2008). Measuring the effectiveness of arms embargoes. *Peace Economics, Peace Science and Public Policy, 14*(2), Art 2.

Collier, P. (2009). *Wars, guns and votes: Democracy in dangerous places.* New York: HarperCollins.

Daddieh, C. E. (2001). Elections and ethnic violence in Côte d'Ivoire: The unfinished business of succession and democratic transition. *African Issues, 24*(1/2), 14–19.

Davenport, C. (1995). Multi-dimensional threat perception and state repression: An inquiry into why states apply negative sanctions. *American Journal of Political Science, 39*(3), 683–713.

Davenport, C. (1999). Human rights and the democratic proposition. *Journal of Conflict Resolution, 43*(1), 92–116.

Della Vigna, S., & La Ferrara, E. (2008, March 18). *Detecting illegal arms trade.* University of California, Berkeley: NBER Working Paper.

DeRouen, K., Jr. (2003). The role of the UN in international crisis termination, 1945–1994. *Defence and Peace Economics, 14,* 251–260.

Doyle, M. W., & Sambanis, N. (2006). *Making war and building peace: United Nations peace operations.* Princeton, NJ: Princeton University Press.

Edgren-Schori, M & P. Schori. (2011). *Elfenbenskusten. En utmaning för FN och Afrika* (Côte d'Ivoire. A Challenge to the UN and to Africa). Stockholm, Sweden: Leopard.

Fortna, V. P. (2008). *Does peacekeeping Work? Shaping belligerents' choices after civil war.* Princeton, NJ: Princeton University Press.

Fruchart, D., Holtom, P., Wezeman, S. T., Strandow, D., & Wallensteen, P. (2007). *United Nations arms embargoes: Their impact on arms flows and target behaviour.* SIPRI and Uppsala University: SPITS, Department of Peace and Conflict Research. Retrieved from http://www.smartsanctions.se

Greene, W. H. (2003). *Econometric analysis* (5th ed.). Upper Saddle River, NJ: Prentice Hall.

Gurr, T. R. (1986). The political origins of state violence and terror: A theoretical analysis. In M. Stohl & G. A. Lopez (Eds.), *Government violence and repression: An agenda for research* (pp. 45–72). New York: Greenwood Press.

Gurr, T. R. (1988). War, revolution, and the growth of the coercive state. *Comparative Political Studies, 21,* 45–65.

Halliday, D. J. (2000). The deadly and illegal consequences of economic sanctions on the people of Iraq. *The Brown Journal of World Affairs, 7*(1), 229–233.

Hampson, F. O. (2008). The United Nations and the responsibility to prevent. In A. Mellbourn & P. Wallensteen (Eds.), *Third parties and conflict prevention* (pp. 21–40). Hedemora, Sweden: Gidlunds.

Harff, B. (1986). Genocide as state terrorism. In M. Stohl & G. Lopez (Eds.), *Government, violence and repression: An agenda for research* (pp. 165–88). New York: Greenwood Press.

Harff, B. (2003). No lessons learned from the Holocaust? Assessing risks of genocide and political mass murder since 1955. *American Political Science Review, 97*(1), 57–73.

ICG (International Crisis Group). (2007, June 27). *Côte d'Ivoire: Can the Ouagadougou Agreement bring peace?* Africa Report No. 127.

Kirwin, M. (2006). The security dilemma and conflict in Côte d'Ivoire. *Nordic Journal of African Studies, 16,* 42–52.

Krain, M. (2005). International intervention and the severity of genocides and politicides. *International Studies Quarterly, 49*(2), 363–387.

Lopez, G. (2000). Economic sanctions and genocide: Too little, too late and sometimes too much. In N. Riemer (Ed.), *Protection against genocide: Mission Impossible?* (pp. 67–84). Westport, CT: Praeger.

Lopez, G. A., & Stuhldreher, K. (2007). Sanctions as counter-genocide instruments. In S. Totten (Ed.), *The prevention and intervention of genocide* Vol. 6 of *Genocide: A critical bibliographic review*, vol. 6, (pp. 131–144). New Brunswick, NJ: Transaction Books.

Lund, M. (2002). Preventing violent intrastate conflicts: Learning lessons from experience. In P. van Tongeren, H. van de Veen, & J. Verhoeven (Eds.), *Searching for peace in Europe and Eurasia: An overview of conflict prevention and peacebuilding activities* (pp. 99–119). Boulder, CO: Lynne Rienner.

Marshall, M. G., & Ted R. Gurr. (2001). *Political instability (state failure) problem set: Internal wars and failures of governance, 1955–2004*. Political Instability Task Force. Retrieved from http://globalpolicy.gmu.edu/pitf/PITF%20Problem%20Set%20Codebook%20v2001.doc

Melander, E. (2009). Selected to go where murderers lurk? The preventive effect of peacekeeping on mass killings of civilians. *Conflict Management and Peace Sciences, 26*(4), 389–406.

Melander, E., Möller, F., & Öberg, M. (2009a). Managing intrastate low-intensity armed conflict 1993–2004: A new dataset. *International Interactions, 35*, 1–28.

Melander, E., Öberg, M., & Hall, J. (2009b). Are "new wars" more atrocious? Battle intensity, civilians killed and forced migration before and after the end of the Cold War. *European Journal of International Relations, 15*(3), 505–36.

MILC (Mangaging Intrastate Low-Intensity Conflict). Dataset. Uppsala Conflict Data Program. Retrieved July 2009, from http://www.ucdp.uu.se

Miran, M. (2006). The political economy of Islam in Côte d'Ivoire. In H. Weiss & M. Bröening (Eds.), *Islamic democracy? Political Islam in Western Africa*. Berlin: Lit Verlag. Retrieved September 5, 2009, from http://ceaf.ehess.fr/docannexe.php?id=536

Morgan, C. T., Bapat, N., & Krutsev, V. (2009). The threat and imposition of economic sanctions, 1971–2000. *Conflict Management and Peace Science, 21*(1), 92–110.

Öberg, M., Möller, F., & Wallensteen, P. (2009). Early conflict prevention in ethnic crises, 1990–98: A new dataset. *Conflict Management and Peace Science, 26*(1), 67–91.

Poe, S. C., & Tate, C. N. (1994). Repression of human rights to personal integrity in the 1980s: A global analysis. *American Political Science Review, 88*(4), 853–872.

Power, S. (2002). *A problem from hell*. New York: Basic Books.

Rametsi, S. (2006). *South Africa's diplomatic involvement as a peace-broker in West Africa: The case of Côte d'Ivoire*. Master's thesis, University of Witswatersrand, Johannesburg, Department of International Relations.

Regan, P. M., & Aydin, A. (2006). Diplomacy and other forms of intervention in civil wars. *Journal of Conflict Resolution, 50*(5), 736–756.

Stanton, G. H. (1998). *The 8 stages of genocide*. Working Paper, Yale Program in Genocide Studies. New Haven, CT: Yale University.

Strandow, D. (2006). *Sanctions and civil war: Targeted measures for conflict resolution*. Uppsala: Uppsala University, Department of Peace and Conflict Research (SPITS).

Svensson, I. (2006). *Elusive peacemakers: A bargaining perspective on mediation in internal armed conflict*. Uppsala: Uppsala University, Department of Peace and Conflict Research.

Toungara, J. M. (2001). Ethnicity and political crisis in Côte d'Ivoire. *Journal of Democracy, 12*(1), 63–72.

UCDP (Uppsala Conflict Data Program). Dataset on one-sided violence. Retrieved from http://www.ucdp.uu.se Retrieved September 2, 2009.

UCDP (Uppsala Conflict Data Program). Database Retrieved in September 2, 2009 from http://www.ucdp.uu.se/database.

UNHCR. Retrieved from http://www.unhcr.org/refworld/docid/49a8f198b9.html

UN Security Council. (2009, July 7). *Twenty-first progress report of the Secretary-General on the United Nations Operation in Côte d'Ivoire* (S/2009/344). New York: United Nations.

UN Security Council Resolutions. Retrieved from http://www.un.org/sc

Valentino, B. A. (2004). *Final solutions: Mass killing and genocide in the 20th century* Ithaca, NY: Cornell University Press.

Väyrynen, R. (2003). Challenges to preventive action: The cases of Kosovo and Macedonia. In D. Carment & A. Schnabel (Eds.), *Conflict prevention: Path to peace or grand illusion?* (pp. 47–70). Tokyo: United Nations University Press.

Wallensteen, P. (2011). *Peace Research: Theory and Practice*. London: Routledge.

Wallensteen, P., Eriksson, M., & Strandow, D. (2006). *Sanctions for conflict prevention and peace building: Lessons learned from Côte d'Ivoire and Liberia*. Uppsala: Uppsala University, Department of Peace and Conflict Research (SPITS). Updated in Wallensteen, P. 2011. Peace Research: Theory and Practice, London: Routledge, 206–228.

Wallensteen, P., & Möller, F. (2003). *Conflict prevention: Methodology for knowing the unknown*. Uppsala: Uppsala University, Uppsala Peace Research Paper No. 7. Updated in Wallensteen, P. 2011. Peace Research: Theory and Practice, London: Routledge, pp 125–142.

Wallensteen, P., Staibano, C., & Eriksson, M. (2004). *The 2004 roundtable on UN sanctions on Iraq: Lessons learned*. Uppsala: Uppsala University: Department of Peace and Conflict Research. Retrieved from http://www.smartsanctions.se

16 Between Mediation and Negotiation

HCNM Interventions in Identity Conflicts

■ FEDOR MEERTS AND TASSOS COULALOGLOU

The High Commissioner on National Minorities (HCNM) of the Organization for Security and Cooperation in Europe (OSCE) is an extraordinary actor in the arena of conflict resolution and negotiation with a unique mandate to autonomously "identify and seek early resolution of ethnic tensions that might endanger peace, stability, or friendly relations between participating states of the OSCE" (Van der Stoel, 1999, p. 68). The position of HCNM was negotiated in late 1992 by the participating states of the (then) Conference on Security and Cooperation in Europe (CSCE) in response to the ethnic violence in the early 1990s throughout Central and Eastern Europe, in general, and the former Yugoslavia, in particular. While previously the CSCE had been an important forum for dialogue between East and West on (mainly) politico-military and human security issues, the creation of the HCNM and the "upgrading" of the CSCE to the OSCE marked a new focus on conflict prevention and democratization in post–Cold War Europe.[1]

Under the guidance of the first High Commissioner, Max van der Stoel, the HCNM quickly developed into the main instrument of interethnic conflict prevention in Europe. The HCNM played a key role in influencing minority politics, especially in Central and Eastern European countries (CEECs), an observation that stands in clear opposition to Samuel P. Huntington's (1996) bleak prospects for neutral third party intervention in identity conflicts. The HCNM's largely successful experience is invaluable in providing preliminary answers to some of the prying questions posed in that chapter: How has the HCNM been instrumental in overcoming identity conflicts, and how did he prevent and mediate S^5 (soft, stable, self-serving stalemate) situations? What pressures and techniques did he apply? Why has the HCNM been particularly well suited for intervention in internal identity conflicts?

This chapter provides an analysis of the HCNM's behavior as an external promoter of negotiation in identity conflicts.[2] It draws on existing literature to identify the HCNM as a unique insider third party who practices quiet diplomacy to defuse identity conflicts. However, the chapter transcends conventional scholarly work by arguing that the HCNM is a mediator with a very flexible modus operandi who, while maintaining his position of mediator within the relational set, travels between activities traditionally described as *mediation* and *negotiation*

(Chigas et al., 1996; Kemp, 2001). This behavior is analyzed in case studies on the HCNM's work in Estonia, Romania, and Ukraine.[3]

Three High Commissioners have been active since the post's inception: Max van der Stoel (1993–2001; the Netherlands), Rolf Ekeus (2001–2007; Sweden), and Knut Vollebaek[4] (2007–present; Norway). While all three men come from countries with strong traditions in the fields of international law and conflict management, they have proven to be three different characters, working in three different political eras: the period of post-Communist transition in the last decade of the twentieth century, the rebalancing of Europe at the beginning of the new millennium, and the so-called "new balance of power" in Europe at the end of the first decade of the twenty-first century. The analysis provided in this chapter focuses heavily on Max van der Stoel, who pioneered the HCNM's modus operandi. While there is an abundance of scholarly research on Van der Stoel's activities as HCNM, limited information is available on his successors. To compensate for this gap in the literature, the authors conducted interviews with the three High Commissioners and officials of the Office of the High Commissioner on National Minorities, and the Dutch Ministry of Foreign Affairs.

The first section of this chapter sets the background against which the mandate of the HCNM was negotiated in the CSCE and describes the negotiations on the establishment of the HCNM. The second section argues that the HCNM is a unique mediator who is free to move between traditional mediation and a more competitive stance that is perhaps better described by the term *negotiation*. This section additionally outlines the HCNM's modus operandi, to lay the groundwork for a more in-depth analysis of his activities, and reveals differences between the three HCNMs to date. The third section analyzes the HCNM's behavior in three case studies, paying particular attention to his mediation (and negotiation) activities, his mode of conflict management,[5] and his subsequent use of negotiating tactics. Finally, the conclusion draws inferences from the case studies, attempting to distill in which situations the HCNM was primarily involved in more traditional mediation and in which cases his interventions looked more like negotiations with one (or more) of the parties in the conflict.

■ NEGOTIATING THE POSITION OF THE HIGH COMMISSIONER ON NATIONAL MINORITIES

To properly understand the mandate and activities of the HCNM, it is imperative to closely examine the context in which the position was negotiated. The OSCE began life as the institutionally weak CSCE, a forum for dialogue between East and West initiated in 1973 and birthed by the Helsinki Final Act in 1975. An informal structure and Cold War constraints on the depth of discussions ensured that it would remain a "non-bureaucratic, flexible and pragmatic process, consisting of a series of ad hoc meetings" (Zaagman, 1993). Roughly fifteen years later, with the fall of the Iron Curtain, optimism brimmed that a new post–Cold War world order based on democracy, the rule of law, and human rights would allow for peaceful transitions in Central and Eastern Europe. In December 1990, the second Summit of the CSCE produced the Charter of Paris for a New Europe, which not only focused heavily on the human dimension of security, but also prepared the way for a transformation from the dialogue-based CSCE to the more operational OSCE. "The CSCE was beginning to shift the emphasis of its work from broad-ranging diplomatic negotiations to fairly specific conflict prevention" (Kemp 2001, p. 8). This focus on conflict prevention proved indispensable. Throughout Central and Eastern Europe new identities, often hidden or suppressed by the Soviet empire, began to (re)emerge within and between states, clashing with existing or newly forming identities. The old paradigms of "us" and "them" based on communist versus capitalist ideology gave way to national identities predicated on ethnicity, requiring histories to be rewritten, myths reinterpreted. The resurgence of ethnic nationalism created obvious tensions, and Europe was at its most unpredictable since the end of World War II. Although largely nonviolent, interethnic relations were especially tense in Estonia and Latvia (which had sizable Russian-speaking minorities), Romania (whose Hungarian minority in Transylvania demanded autonomy), and Ukraine (where Crimean authorities demanded independence/ autonomy). In rather quick succession, fighting erupted in the Caucasus and Moldova, but it was the escalating conflict in the former Yugoslavia that provided the major catalyst for the creation of the HCNM.

It was in this context that the position of HCNM was negotiated in the CSCE. An idea for an independent observer had already been floated by the Swedish delegation during the Copenhagen Meeting in June 1990, but it was not seriously pursued at the time (Brenninkmeijer, 2005). In April 1992, at the Fourth Follow-Up Meeting in Helsinki, the Netherlands presented a concrete proposal to create the position of "high commissioner *for* national minorities" after careful preliminary consultations with various member states. The Dutch proposed a mechanism for flexible and efficient conflict prevention that revolved around "building a capacity for 'early warning' and 'early action' focused on the priority problem issue of minorities" (Brenninkmeijer, 2005, p. 28).

The French, while less vocal than their American and British counterparts, questioned whether a high commissioner for national minorities was necessary, as French law allowed for no distinctions based on ethnicity. At the same time, the United States argued that the high commissioner should focus not only on national minorities, but on a much broader range of human dimension issues. The Dutch resisted for fear that the high commissioner would become bogged down by myriad individual human rights cases (lawyer), jeopardizing his role as a conflict preventer focused on security (diplomat). Dutch Ambassador Bert Veenendaal argued that "the High Commissioner should not be seen as an addition to the CSCE human dimension mechanisms, but as the earliest stage of the conflict prevention capacity . . . related to national minority issues" (Brenninkmeijer, 2005, p. 60). Eventually, in order not to be seen as disregarding the serious problems caused by ethnic strife in Central and Eastern Europe, the United States (along with other countries) accepted the national minority focus of the Dutch proposal, but with reservations.

The participating states could agree there was a need for a high commissioner, but there was pushback on a number of sensitive issues regarding his mandate, most prominently the independence of the new position and the sanctity of national sovereignty. The United Kingdom, along with other countries such as Spain, Turkey, and the United States, was worried that the high commissioner, given carte blanche powers of inquiry, would overstep his intended mandate and focus attention in their countries. Moreover, the HCNM would be speaking with sub-state entities and nongovernmental organizations (NGOs), which some countries feared could legitimize certain secessionist causes or spark conflict by providing a forum to air grievances. As Arie Bloed (2008) noted,

> at the end of the day it was the United Kingdom that pushed the hardest against such a broad mandate. While the United Kingdom delegation at the negotiations was supportive and accepted, the United Kingdom Home Office was blocking it. They were really stuck on the issue of Northern Ireland and the worry that the HCNM would interfere in the problems in Northern Ireland.

In July 1992, at the third summit of the CSCE in Helsinki, a compromise was reached in the final proposal to address these concerns. First, the title of the position was changed to High Commissioner *on,* rather than *for,* National Minorities, a more neutral formulation to accurately describe a role as an advisor rather than as an advocate, securing the focus on national minorities (instead of the broader theme of human rights). Second, the HCNM could not become involved where terrorism or violence had occurred or was condoned by minority representatives,[6] a necessary compromise to garner the support of states that had suffered from secessionist violence or terrorism. Third, to allay fears that the HCNM would be institutionally unaccountable, the OSCE Chairperson-in-Office (CiO) would be consulted, confidentially, on all country visits.

While the mandate was not as strong as some proponents had hoped, for the first time a non-state actor could intervene in a state's internal affairs without explicit consent from the host government. The mandate specified that the HCNM "will work in confidence and will act independently" through the use of "democratic means and international instruments" to provide "early warning and early action at the earliest possible stage in regard to tensions involving national minority issues."[7] After consulting the CiO and notifying the state concerned before a visit, the HCNM will collect information from minority representatives as well as official sources, NGOs, and other nonstate actors, and where "appropriate promote dialogue, confidence and co-operation between them."[8] After the visit, the HCNM "will provide strictly confidential reports to the Chairman-in-Office on the findings and progress of [his] involvement in a particular question."[9] If the HCNM concludes that there is "*prima facie* risk of potential conflict . . . he/she may issue an early warning."[10] Without legal mechanisms for coercion, the HCNM had to rely on persuasion, backed by normative leverage, as well as institutional leverage gained through OSCE participating states and other international organizations.[11] The HCNM, as an "eminent international personality with long-standing relevant experience," was expected to use the tools and tactics of the diplomatic arts to prevent conflict, provide solutions, and negotiate compromises.[12]

■ QUIET DIPLOMACY: BETWEEN MEDIATION AND NEGOTIATION

The position of High Commissioner on National Minorities thus created by the participating states of the CSCE is exceptional in the world of conflict prevention. It is difficult to categorize the HCNM, who "fulfills several functions simultaneously: adviser, negotiator, and intermediary"—free to act as any one of these, as he deems necessary, to prevent interethnic conflict (Kemp, 2001, p. 24). The dual capacity of negotiator and mediator is of particular interest.

Armed with little more than general operational parameters, Van der Stoel traversed unknown territory with little in the way of precedent to guide him. However, the rather vague mandate gave him substantial freedom of action to flesh out his own modus operandi (Van der Stoel 2008). He developed an approach of "quiet diplomacy" characterized by "independence, co-operation, impartiality, incrementalism, persistence, confidentiality, trust and credibility" (Kemp, 2001, p. 21). His tactics were consequently designed to maximize trust so as to facilitate collaboration with all relevant parties, which, as discussed below, has been his preferred "mode of conflict management" (Thomas & Kilmann, 1977).[13]

Starting from the assumption that issuing an "early warning" denotes prime facie evidence of failed conflict prevention, Van der Stoel took the second part of his mandate, "early action," to heart and engaged proactively with OSCE states (Chigas et al., 1996, p. 51). He judged that "[t]he sooner third party conflict prevention is initiated, the greater the chance that the dispute will not reach a high level of tension and that the parties may still be willing (and politically able) to find compromises and accommodate each other's demands" (Van der Stoel, 1999, p. 70). In practice, this took the form of visits to OSCE participating states, followed by a confidential letter to the respective country's minister of foreign affairs, which restated the discussed recommendations for the improvement of interethnic relations.[14] These diplomatically phrased and nonbinding recommendations aim to lubricate the process," providing both sides of the conflict with the opportunity to benefit from an independent assessment by the HCNM (Cohen, 1999, p. 66). Yet, as the case studies below detail, these recommendations were often more than mere advice, and became the basis of persistent attempts by the HCNM to make governments reform their minority policies.

Van der Stoel's successors, Ekeus and Vollebaek, have largely followed the quiet diplomatic approach, but have displayed different styles in their interventions. While Van der Stoel was a quiet diplomat, he did not refrain from making public statements when he deemed them necessary. The Staff of the Office of the HCNM (2008) pointed out that Ekeus was more "quiet" than Van der Stoel, opting for maintaining dialogue and avoiding confrontation (and publicity). The current High Commissioner, Vollebaek, appears to be much more open and externally oriented than either of his predecessors.

Taking Kenneth Thomas and Ralph Kilmann's (1977) well-known "modes of conflict management" as a template, the default mode of conflict management for all three High Commissioners can be called *collaboration*, which is unsurprising given the HCNM's mandate to work with OSCE states. Yet, when collaboration with uncooperative governments proved ineffective, the High Commissioners seem to have opted for different modes of conflict management. Especially when backed by international organizations such as the European Union (EU) or by important OSCE member states, Van der Stoel did not shy away from adopting a *competitive* position when he believed this would break the government's opposition—as can be seen in the case study on Estonia below. Ekeus, in contrast, attached more intrinsic value to dialogue and the process of interethnic conflict resolution, and was therefore more likely to avoid confrontation and "accommodate" where necessary (HCNM Staff, 2008). Often seen as "softer" than Van der Stoel, Ekeus (2008) himself argued that taking a "hard" stance was in certain cases unwarranted (and perhaps also counterproductive): For instance, in Estonia and Latvia, he deemed it more appropriate to remain collaborative on language rights for the Russian-speaking minority, even when faced with less than genuine government participation.[15] Although Vollebaek's appointment has been recent, it seems that he is more willing to take a harder stance than Ekeus; for instance, like Van der Stoel, Vollebaek makes use of the EU where possible, speaking to Commissioner for Enlargement Olli Rehn and letting his dialogue partners know that he has spoken to him (HCNM Staff, 2008).

Chigas et al. (1996, p. 50) have aptly characterized the HCNM as an "insider third party" who "combines some of the basic characteristics of traditional mediation by international organizations with those of an 'insider' to the conflict" with extensive knowledge of the conflict as well as close (and good) contacts with the major parties" (p. 49). In his capacity as an "insider third party," the HCNM

> acts as a trusted adviser and partner-in-dialogue, rather than a detached mediator. . . . In this role, the third party seeks not to resolve the conflict but to improve all parties' policies and actions regarding the ongoing relationship among them. The process serves to empower moderate parties inside the conflict itself and to resolve the conflict by strengthening the voices of moderation on all sides and creating and preserving a space within which they can sustain a dialogue and jointly develop and carry out policies without being undercut by extremist elements on their flanks. (Chigas et al., 1996, p. 50)

As an insider third party, the Commissioner's role is largely consistent with the description of a mediator, who is "part of the interaction but not [a party] to the conflict or the solution" who "transforms the bargaining structure from a dyad to a triangle, even if [his point on the triangle] is in a different position in regard to the interaction than the other two" (Zartman, 2002, p. 79). The case studies below show that the HCNM has been highly effective as a mediator when parties could not extricate themselves from an acute crisis situation that was also a mutually hurting stalemate.

Yet, while the HCNM is an impartial actor without "vested interests in the substantive issues at stake," he is not a mediator as understood in the traditional sense, mandated to *prevent* conflicts rather than *settle* them (Chigas et al., 1996, p. 49; Kemp, 2001, p. 24). As such, the HCNM is not only an "insider third party" but also an "interested third party," whose main interest—conflict prevention—may well differ from the (immediate) interests of the actual parties to the conflict (Kemp, 2001, p. 24). As will be discussed in more detail below, the HCNM has become very active as a promoter of particular solutions, some of which were not conceived by majority/minority representatives but rather by the HCNM himself—putting pressure on governments to implement recommended policies. Chigas et al. (1996, p. 54) have dubbed this rather competitive advisory role of the HCNM "mediating with one party" (this phrase is better suited to describe his role as a *negotiator*). Even though it would go too far to describe the HCNM as a party to the *conflict*, in such situations his role to resolve the conflict transcends that of an advisor or deal broker interested in a solution.

In these cases, his advocacy of particular solutions backed by international norms and leverage brings to mind qualities of a negotiator, albeit within the mediation role. This advocacy generally involves persuasion on the basis of international norms as espoused by international organizations such as the OSCE or the EU but sometimes also involves quite direct pressure.[16] For example, the High Commissioner's "review" of the interethnic situation for international actors, such as the EU, has in the past given him substantial leverage over governments. For the issue of minorities, prospective member states often considered him an agent of the European Commission—whose job it was to review whether international standards were adhered to by the country.[17]

The positioning, and concurrent strategies and tactics, of the HCNM are very flexible and highly context dependent. As the discussion of the HCNM's activities in Estonia, Romania, and Ukraine below demonstrates, he adopts different roles depending on the demands of the situation, sometimes mediating (whether as communicator, formulator, or manipulator) between minority and majority representatives and at other times mediating or negotiating with the government about taking certain actions to improve interethnic relations. For instance, when faced with an S^5 situation in which the conflict was not yet ripe for resolution, the HCNM has either monitored the situation and waited for an opportune moment to step in as a mediator (i.e., wait for the S^5 situation to become a mutually hurting stalemate) or pushed one of the two parties (in most cases the government) to change its position and policies. Quite often, however, the HCNM faced a situation in which the minority side of the conflict was too weak or divided—compared to the government—to press for its demands. In such a situation, there can be no true negotiation between majority and minority representatives, discounting two-party mediation as a solution. Therefore, the HCNM has had to adapt his strategies accordingly and has often found himself mediating with one party in the conflict or even negotiating with the government.

■ **CASE I: THE HCNM IN ESTONIA**

Following its incorporation into the Soviet Union, Estonia's ethnic composition changed drastically. When Estonia reasserted its full sovereignty in 1991, it had a large, mainly Russian-speaking, minority population (40% in 1993 compared to 8% during the interwar independence period; Zaagman, 1999, p. 31). In February 1992, the Estonian Supreme Council effectively disenfranchised most members of this minority and excluded them from early privatization arrangements when it reenacted the 1938 Law on Citizenship, stipulating that "citizens of the inter-war

Republic of Estonia, as well as their descendants in the paternal [and, later added, maternal] line were to be considered as Estonian citizens" (Sarv, 2002, p. 21). This restrictive citizenship legislation was fueled not only by a "restoration ideology," but also by doubts over the loyalty and intentions of the Russian speakers (Galbreath, 2005, pp. 81, 160). It was designed to encourage emigration of ethnic non-Estonians, which was "considered by the authorities a key issue for Estonia's future security" (Lahelma, 1999, p. 21).

The insecurity and intransigence of the Estonian political elite were heightened by the presence of Russian Federation troops in the country and pervasive fears about renewed Russian suzerainty. Among these heightened tensions, "Estonia [became] the first country to volunteer for [the] presence" of an CSCE Mission in December 1992—not only to show its Westward orientation and benefit from the Mission's expertise, but also to shield itself from Russian allegations of serious and systematic human rights violations (Galbreath, 2005, p. 79; Pettai, 2001, p. 267).[18] In January 1993, the HCNM visited Estonia. His subsequent letter to the government acknowledged the "political and psychological background of many of the [minority] questions," underlined that successful integration also depended on noncitizens' efforts to learn the titular language, and emphasized that his recommendations were intended to provide assistance in reducing interethnic tensions.[19] His recommendations stressed that broadening opportunities for the acquisition of citizenship would help ensure loyalty to Estonia, a stable interethnic situation, and positive Estonia–Russia relations.[20] This balanced assessment facilitated his insider third party position, establishing "a reputation of impartiality" (Zaagman, 1999, p. 33). The following sections focus on key representative events regarding, first, immigration and citizenship policy and, later, language policy in Estonia.[21]

After the HCNM's initial recommendations, his first major involvement in Estonia was during the so-called *aliens crisis*, which was most immediately caused by the brewing tensions around the draft law on citizenship in the summer of 1993. The law stipulated that all noncitizens who held only Soviet passports had to apply within one year for new five-year residency permits. Understandably, this roused fears of deportation among the Russian-speaking minority, which were further aggravated by the vague formulation of terms. During the drafting phase, the government's response to concerns of minority representatives and international organizations (including the HCNM) was largely unsympathetic and unbending (Galbreath, 2005, p. 162). Consequently, minority organizations called for civil disobedience, and the town councils of the largely Russian-speaking cities of Narva and Sillamae planned referenda on local autonomy. The Law on Aliens was passed on June 21, 1993, but President Lennart Meri, in line with advice from the HCNM, refused to promulgate the law and sent it to the Council of Europe (CoE) and the CSCE for an "unbiased professional" assessment (Kemp, 2001, p. 143). Despite changes in the law, the town councils decided to go ahead with the autonomy referenda, creating a potentially explosive situation. In an attempt to diffuse the crisis, the HCNM (and the CSCE Mission)—recognizing that lack of communication and misperceptions were creating exaggerated fears on both sides— engaged in "shuttle diplomacy" between minority representatives and the Estonian government, acting as a conduit and advisor for both parties (Birckenbach, 2000,

p. 42). These mediative efforts were facilitated first of all by the CSCE instruments' access to—and reputation as trustworthy and impartial interlocutors among— both sides of the conflict. Of equal importance, both sides wanted to find a way out of this mutually hurting stalemate, in general, and to avoid violent confrontations, in particular (Smith, 2002, p. 88). The HCNM's mediation "between government officials, the representatives of Narva and Sillamae city councils and the Russian Representative Assembly . . . resulted in compromises on both sides" (Sarv, 2002, p. 45). As Walter Kemp records, on July 12, 1993, the HCNM "took the unusual step of issuing a public statement in which he listed the assurances he had received" (2001, p. 144). The publication of these declarations was a tactical move designed not only to bring "clarity to the situation and put to rest some of the anxieties" but also to lock in deescalatory measures (Sarv, 2002, p. 45). The town councils, on their part, pledged to respect the territorial integrity of Estonia and accept the upcoming ruling on the legality of the referenda. The government promised not to use force to prevent the referenda, restated that its policy was not aimed at expulsion or permanent exclusion of noncitizens, and pledged to make the procedures for issuing residence permits and aliens' passports simple and smooth.

While the HCNM's mediation was crucial in deescalating the aliens crisis, concrete implementation of recommendations regarding integration of the Russian-speaking community, Estonian citizenship tests, and automatic citizenship for the elderly, disabled persons, and children born in Estonia to stateless parents was partial at best, and the underlying conflict remained unresolved. Still, after the aliens crisis, "ethnic tensions have not [risen] to threatening levels in Estonia" (Sarv, 2002, pp. 26, 57).[22] This outcome "owed much to socio-economic, cultural and political divisions within the 'Russian-speaking population'" that were reflected in the formation of two contrasting bodies: the moderate Russian Assembly and the radical Russian community (Sarv, 2002, p. 26; Smith, 2002, p. 76). The absence of clearly established institutional bases for national-based mobilization was compounded by an apparent lack of interest in politics. In the face of this relative weakness of minority representatives compared to the Estonian government, the HCNM's subsequent role in the internal identity conflict in Estonia is perhaps best described as *mediating with one party* or as *negotiating*, with the actual negotiation a drawn-out and potentially never-ending process covering a multiplicity of issues.

From 1993 to 1996, the HCNM had to rely mainly on persuasion in his mediation with the Estonian government. Where there was stiff domestic opposition to his recommendations, he had little leverage to make the Estonian government change minority policies. He tried to explain that integration and the protection of the minority identity would not pose a threat to the identity of Estonians or the integrity of the Estonian state, and followed international standards and good governance practices that Estonia had endorsed and was in the best security interests of the country" (Kemp, 2001, p. 146). While maintaining confidentiality, Van der Stoel used a relatively tough and competitive approach in his efforts to persuade the Estonian government. His persistence, frequent visits, and recommendations in trying to mediate with the Estonian government quickly led to a perception of stigmatization and "Van der Stoel fatigue," while talk of "Estonia bashing" became ever more audible.

The minority situation in Estonia improved little until 1997 when Estonia began the accession negotiation process in the EU Agenda 2000 (Kelley, 2002, p. 106). Van der Stoel (2008) stressed that Estonia's EU candidacy provided important leverage, especially in light of the HCNM's close cooperation and good relationship with the Commission, of which the Estonian polity was well aware. In his words, it was not difficult to get the Commission to "write a nasty telegram" to reinforce his persistent efforts to ensure implementation of his recommendations. Moreover, Estonian officials knew that the EU effectively used the High Commissioner's recommendations as benchmarks, which gave the HCNM immense bargaining power in his dealings with the Estonian government (Sarv, 2002, p. 100). Indeed, recommendations that had previously been ignored were quickly implemented when the HCNM could show that they were necessary for EU accession. While the HCNM's 1993 and 1997 recommendations on stateless children were ignored, the EU's 1997 opinion that "[t]he Estonian authorities should consider means to enable stateless children born in Estonia to be naturalised more easily" elicited a swift response by the government (Agenda 2000: Commission Opinion on Estonia's Application for Membership of the European Union, 1997, p. 19). In the face of strong opposition in parliament, the government proposed an amendment to the Law on Citizenship, which was eventually passed in December 1998 (Kelley, 2002, p. 106). The new law gave stateless children under the age of fifteen, born to stateless parents after February 1992 and resident in Estonia for at least five years, the right to automatic citizenship, provided that their parents applied on their behalf. However, in late 1998 and early 1999 rightist politicians responded to this liberalization by seeking to tightening language requirements for candidates in parliamentary and local elections as well as for employment in the public and private sectors (Sarv, 2002, p. 90). The HCNM's and OSCE Head of Mission's criticisms of these laws were not well received, but in cooperation with the EU, the HCNM managed to secure an almost complete reversal from the 1999 changes after "the European Commission suddenly warned Estonia that progress toward accession would be affected" (Jurado, 2003, p. 259).

After these changes the HCNM's involvement has been low-key, even though integration and stability are still threatened by the large number of stateless persons, impediments to political participation, and the socioeconomic impact of restrictive language and citizenship policies (Van Elsuwege, 2004, p. 55). Priorities have shifted away from the Baltics, but in relation to his involvement in new EU member states such as Estonia, Vollebaek mentioned that it is a big challenge to apply the same pressure after EU accession (Vollebaek, 2008; HCNM Staff, 2008). The HCNM has had to adapt his strategies and tactics accordingly, again focusing on collaboration and dialogue, and helping to formulate solutions to practical problems while reminding the country of its international obligations such as the CoE conventions, which it still has to live up to.

▪ CASE II: THE HCNM IN ROMANIA

The end of Communist rule in Romania came violently and without much warning, with several hundred deaths in December 1989 (Gallagher, 2001, p. 383).

Despite positive signs that the newly empowered, moderate but unreformed, former Communists of the National Salvation Front (FSN; later renamed the Party of Social Democrats of Romania, PDSR) and their leader, Ion Iliescu, were willing to accommodate the country's minorities, "nationalism [quickly] became the dominant discourse" (Horváth, 2002, p. 25). Interethnic tensions were furthermore fuelled by demands (and protests) for Hungarian language education by the Democratic Alliance of Hungarians in Romania (UDMR), a well-organized political party generally accepted as the representative of the country's large Hungarian minority.[23] In March 1990, the Transylvanian city of Tirgu Mureş became "the first place in post-communist Eastern Europe where interethnic conflict spilled over into fatal violence" (Gallagher, 2005, p. 84). There were no further clashes, but the Hungarian minority was largely isolated in domestic politics until 1996, despite the fact that the UMDR took roughly 7% of the vote in the 1990 and 1992 elections (Horváth, 2002, p. 30).

The perception of a Hungarian "threat" was strengthened by the poor bilateral relationship between Hungary and Romania and by Hungary's vocal support of autonomy and collective minority rights for Hungarian minorities abroad (Sardemann, 1997, p. 63). In light of these tensions, the HCNM visited Bucharest and Transylvania in June and August 1993. Although his involvement was not always welcomed, "nearly all Romanian mainstream actors [saw the HCNM] as an institution of arbitration with the legitimate authority to assess whether a certain course of action [met] international minority standards"—greatly enhancing his position as an insider third party mediator (Horváth, 2002, p. 63). The following will address the HCNM's successful mediation regarding Hungarian language education, which comes close to the ideal typical insider third party position described by Chigas et al. (1996).

In September 1993, the HCNM sent his first letter to Romanian Foreign Minister Teodor Meleşcanu, summing up observations from his visits and making several recommendations.[24] Perhaps the most crucial recommendation stressed that a new law on education was needed, since Hungarian-language education was "the main and most urgent inter-ethnic problem in Romania" (Horváth, 2002, p. 90). However, the 1995 draft law only increased tensions because it stipulated that Romanian history and geography as well as vocational classes were to be taught in Romanian. Tertiary education in minority languages was permitted "only for pedagogical profiles and in existing institutions," and for all levels of education most admission and graduation exams were to be taken in Romanian (Horváth, 2002, pp. 90, 94). While the High Commissioner managed "to dissuade the UDMR from mounting a civil disobedience campaign in opposition to the proposed law on education," the amendments he proposed to the government were disregarded and the law was adopted in June 1995 (Kemp, 2001, p. 237). Van der Stoel subsequently issued a public statement during his visit in September, in which he emphasized the need for "considerable flexibility in [the law's] implementation" but also called for a revision of the law in two years.[25] Importantly, he also "made public a number of clarifications and explanations which he had received from the Government" (Kemp, 2001, p. 238). The statement was a smart tactical move, not only effective in reassuring the UDMR, but also successful in locking in the assurances he had received from the moderate part of the government, bypassing the extremists and delaying implementation of a law that would have sharply increased tensions (Horváth, 2002, pp. 98, 101).

The HCNM had also urged Romania and Hungary to conclude a Treaty on Friendship and Cooperation, since better bilateral relations would go a long way toward reducing the fear of Transylvanian separatism and consequently interethnic tensions. Through the Stability Pact, the EU had made it clear that bilateral treaties were prerequisites for membership, and members of the North Atlantic Treaty Organization (NATO; especially the United States) put pressure on the Hungarian and Romanian governments to come to a compromise over the most contentious issue: collective rights and local autonomy for national minorities, as espoused by Recommendation 1201 of the CoE (Gallagher, 2001, p. 390; Kelley, 2002, pp. 154–155). The situation became tense in July 1996 when the Hungarian government signed a Joint Declaration that advocated autonomy for Hungarians living abroad. The HCNM subsequently engaged in shuttle diplomacy between Budapest and Bucharest, and his mediation and assistance in clarifying and interpreting Recommendation 1201 and other international minority standards were instrumental in managing the crisis (Horváth, 2002, p. 44). In September 1996, both countries signed a bilateral treaty, which included Recommendation 1201, but interpreted it as not referring to collective rights and not granting the right to autonomy (Sardemann, 1997, p. 66). The Romanian Foreign Minister later "stated that the activities of the High Commissioner had the effect of a 'catalyst'" (Kemp, 2001, p. 239).

The defeat of the PDSR in the November 1996 elections, and the subsequent inclusion of the UDMR in the new government, signified a major change in Romanian domestic politics and a key turning point in interethnic relations (Horváth, 2002, p. 54; Sasse, 2005, p. 17; Vachudova, 2001, p. 5). The new government got off to a promising start on July 10, 1997, when it issued an emergency ordinance on the Law on Education allowing instruction in minorities' mother tongue at all levels of education (Kelley, 2002, p. 152). However, the ordinance was poorly implemented and the government faced major difficulties in parliament. The situation was further complicated by UDMR demands for a Hungarian-language university. The HCNM, recognizing that UDMR withdrawal from the government would seriously set back interethnic relations, became actively involved. Horváth (2002, p. 101) argues that his mediation was effective in helping to keep the UDMR in the governing coalition. A compromise Law on Education, removing legal limitations on minority-language education at all levels, was finally passed while Van der Stoel visited the country in June 1999. The law retained the provision regarding tuition in Romanian about Romanian history and geography, but the other changes were closely in line with the HCNM's 1993, 1995, and 1996 recommendations.

On the whole, ethnic tensions between the Romanian majority and the Hungarian minority decreased significantly after de facto UDMR participation in all post-1996 governments and the implementation of progressive minority legislation. As McMahon (2005, p. 22) argues, ethnic relations in Romania have become more cooperative than conflictual. Subsequently, the HCNM's involvement in the interethnic relations between the Hungarian minority and the Romanian majority has been relatively low key—although he still monitors the situation.

■ CASE III: THE HCNM IN UKRAINE

After the population voted overwhelmingly in favor of independence from the Soviet Union in December 1991, the newly established state of Ukraine had to accommodate various ethnic (and linguistic) minorities and deal with separatist elements in Crimea. According to the 2001 census, ethnic Russians constituted 17.3% of the Ukrainian population, making up significant minorities in eastern and southern Ukraine and a majority on the peninsula of Crimea (58.3%).[26] While early in 1991 Crimea's special status had been confirmed when it was granted formal autonomy, in April 1992 the Ukrainian parliament unilaterally reduced Crimea's constitutional position (Sasse, 2007b, p. 145). In response, Crimean authorities adopted an act on state independence and a constitution on May 5 and 6, 1992, respectively, which—pending a referendum on the act—would have given Crimea a status between autonomy and independence. The Ukrainian parliament declared the former illegal and the latter invalid, heralding a period of unsuccessful bargaining between central and Crimean authorities during which pro-independence sentiment was steadily increasing (Kulyk, 2002, p. 33). The situation was further aggravated by the mass return of Crimean Tatars, whom Stalin had deported to Central Asia and Siberia in 1944. Their share in the population of Crimea increased from close to naught in 1980 to 12% (243,400 persons) in 2001.[27] Needless to say, Crimea was unprepared to handle such a large and rapid influx, which created problems on access to employment, resources, and social services (Graumann, 2007, p. 4).

The state of affairs was complicated by the role of Russia, with which Ukraine was negotiating over the division of the Black Sea Fleet and the status of Sevastopol. After the Russian Duma passed an antagonizing resolution on Sevastopol, Ukrainian Foreign Minister Anatoly Zlenko sent an open letter to all CSCE participating states in July 1993, triggering the involvement of the HCNM. Following his visits in February and May 1994, Van der Stoel sent a letter to Zlenko with recommendations regarding, among others, the two main issues with a significant minority dimension: Crimean autonomy and the integration of Crimean Tatars.[28]

Early in 1994, the situation in Crimea began to escalate when the overtly separatist politician Yuriy Meshkov was elected to the newly created post of Crimean president (Kulyk, 2002, p. 34). During the next year, a veritable war of laws ensued between Kyiv and the Crimean capitol, Simferopol, despite the HCNM's appeals for restraint. Van der Stoel monitored the situation and maintained contact with Kyiv and moderate forces in Simferopol, choosing not to interfere directly with Crimean politics (Sasse, 2007b, p. 239). He visited Ukraine often and built up good interpersonal relations with the two parties involved in the conflict: the Ukrainian government and the Crimean government (Kulyk, 2002, p. 42).[29] In the absence of any leverage to bring about or maintain a compromise, he considered quiet diplomacy as best suited to deal with the situation (Kulyk, 2002, 43). Kulyk persuasively argues that this, on the whole, "reactive intervention" can be explained by a lack of EU or NATO weight to back up the HCNM's suggestions (ibid., p. 127).

When on April 25, 1995, the Crimean parliament took the controversial decision to hold a referendum on support for reinstatement of the May 6, 1992, constitution, tensions flared, while negotiations were gridlocked. At this point the conflict became ripe for third party mediation. The Ukrainian government had been ready to accept the HCNM as a mediator as early as spring 1994 in order to stop escalation of the conflict and prevent Russia from intervening on behalf of the separatists (Kulyk, 2002, p. 127). The Crimean government, however, was not ready to accept third party mediation until early 1995 when, after minimal progress during years of bilateral negotiations, it viewed external mediation as the only solution.[30] The Crimean parliament therefore requested mediation by the HCNM. From May 11 to 14, 1995, the HCNM, in cooperation with the OSCE Mission in Ukraine, organized a roundtable in Locarno, Switzerland for high-level Ukrainian and Crimean officials and parliamentarians. The roundtable was helpful in bringing the participants' views closer together and reducing immediate tensions – both the Crimean referendum and proposals by the central government to dissolve the Crimean parliament were called off - but little progress was made toward a substantive solution (Kulyk, 2002, p. 44).[31] In particular, the HCNM's tactics were successful in preparing the ground for genuine and open dialogue: a confidential setting; private consultations between parties, as well as between parties and the mediator; proactive agenda setting; and summations of positions.

However, by the beginning of 1996, the cooperative atmosphere was dissipating once more, as neither party was willing to implement the HCNM's recommendations before the other. Tensions rose again, especially when the Ukrainian parliament started discussing a draft Ukrainian constitution that would have demoted Crimea from an "autonomous republic" to an "autonomy" (Kulyk, 2002, p. 54). From March 14 to 17, 1996, the HCNM and the Mission organized another roundtable in the Netherlands, which "had a moderating effect and helped recover some of the mood for compromise" (Sasse, 2007b, p. 242). In line with the roundtable discussions, the HCNM recommended that the Ukrainian parliament pass a Crimean constitution "with the exception of those articles which [were] still in dispute" and would be reconsidered by the Crimean parliament.[32] Unlike in 1995, this was done, but it took until December 1998, after new elections to the Crimean parliament, for the entire constitution to be approved by both sides. Although the Autonomous Republic of Crimea has been described as "weakly empowered" and its status as "constitutionally ambiguous and weakly implemented," the process of elite bargaining itself has helped to significantly reduce the potential for conflict (Sasse, 2002, p. 2; Sasse 2007a, p. 2; Sasse, 2007b, p. 256). Given the relatively stable relations between the Crimea and the central government, the HCNM's subsequent involvement regarding this issue has been largely limited to monitoring.

The HCNM's involvement in the conflict between the Crimean Tatars and the Crimean and Ukrainian authorities has taken a form quite different from his involvement in the Crimean autonomy negotiations. Quite problematically, this conflict showed few signs of ripeness. Kulyk (2002, p. 127) points out that the HCNM's effectiveness was severely compromised by the negative attitude regarding OSCE involvement in this issue of both the Ukrainian government (which preferred to keep the role of mediator to itself and limit OSCE involvement to fund-raising) and the Crimean authorities (who viewed the HCNM as biased toward the Crimean Tatars).[33] It is unsurprising that, without external leverage (for instance, the desire for EU/NATO membership), the HCNM's involvement here has been largely reactive and ultimately not very successful.[34] While the HCNM was not accepted as a mediator, he was also not in an ideal second- or third party position to bargain with the Ukrainian authorities, as he had little to bargain with. He had to adjust his strategy and tactics accordingly: Unlike in Estonia, the HCNM could not afford to be highly vocal and competitive (since this would most likely have sidelined him) but rather, as in the Crimean autonomy negotiations, he had to "go with the flow," collaborate with the Ukrainian authorities, and, where possible, push his recommendations. The HCNM truly found himself mediating with one side of the conflict, the Ukrainian and Crimean authorities, to advocate measures to improve the socioeconomic and political situations of the other side, the Crimean Tatars (Chigas et al., 1996, p. 54).

Along with his efforts to raise international, as well as national, awareness of and funding for the Crimean Tatar plight, the HCNM focused on institutionalization of political participation and facilitation of citizenship acquisition. In his 1994 letter, the HCNM recommended the institutionalization of the (then one-time) quota system for political representation of Crimean Tatars in the Crimean parliament.[35] Despite frequent consultations on the issue with the HCNM, the Ukrainian government proved unwilling to institutionalize the quota or take other measures to ensure roughly proportionate representation. When the 1998 elections under a majoritarian system produced just one Crimean Tatar representative, radicalization among Crimean Tatar youth became extremely worrisome and "[d]emonstrations turned increasingly violent" (Kemp, 2001, pp. 226–227). Although unable to convince the Ukrainian authorities of the need for Crimean Tatar representation, the HCNM helped contain the immediate crisis through regular contact with all parties and requests for restraint to all sides, in particular to the Mejlis (the representative body of the Kurultay, the "national" assembly of all Crimean Tatars; Kulyk, 2002, p. 132). Immediate tensions were reduced by a presidential decree in May 1999 legalizing the Mejlis by granting it advisory status to the President, largely in line with the HCNM suggestion in his October 12, 1995, letter.[36]

The HCNM's letters of October 12, 1995, and February 14, 1997, to Foreign Minister Hennadiy Udovenko dealt with the crucial issue of citizenship, emphasizing that statelessness should be avoided and recommending former deportees be granted Ukrainian citizenship, on the condition that they apply and (when applicable) renounce their prior citizenship. The HCNM considered the issue of citizenship a major concern, since in the mid-1990s about 82,000 Crimean Tatars were citizens of other successor states (primarily Uzbekistan) and about 23,000 were stateless (Kulyk, 2002, p. 91). While the recommendation regarding statelessness was taken to heart in the April 1997 revision of the Law on Citizenship, which granted stateless inhabitants the possibility of citizenship through a simple procedure, there was little movement regarding the recommendation on citizenship for former deportees (Kulyk, 2002, p. 131). As a result, in January 1998 the HCNM had to change his targets, instead joining the United Nations High Commissioner for Refugees (UNHCR) in pushing for a more realistic agreement between Ukraine and Uzbekistan on simplified renunciation of citizenship. The Ukrainian-Uzbek agreement was sealed in August 1998, providing former deportees with the opportunity to renounce their Uzbek citizenship (for free) while simultaneously applying for Ukrainian citizenship (avoiding a period of statelessness as well as double citizenship). Subsequently, the HCNM stayed very much involved in the Crimean Tatar issue, raising international and national awareness of the situation of the returnees, since the causes of interethnic tensions have not been removed and there is still great conflict potential, as both Crimean Tatar and Russian radicalism are on the rise (Graumann, 2007, p. 4).

■ CONCLUSIONS

This chapter has analyzed the unique role of the HCNM as an external intervener in internal identity conflicts, pointing to his mediation and negotiation activities and functions. Provided with a rather general mandate, Van der Stoel developed a flexible approach of quiet diplomacy that has been effective in mediating and negotiating solutions to identity conflicts in the three countries covered by the case studies—Estonia, Romania, and Ukraine. The case studies showed in which situations the HCNM's activities come closer to traditional two-party mediation and in which situations his activities take the form of mediation/negotiation with one party in the conflict (Table 16.1).

In the three case studies, the HCNM's activities can be described as mediation between majority and minority representatives primarily when he was faced with (1) an immediate crisis involving (2) two relatively clearly defined and strong parties that were (3) facing a mutually hurting stalemate. During the aliens crisis in Estonia, the HCNM functioned as a conduit and provided suggestions that offered a nonviolent way out of the stalemate between the Estonian government and minority representatives (in particular, the city councils of Narva and Sillamae). During the protracted negotiations on Hungarian language education, the HCNM was particularly active as a mediator at key moments of heated ethnic tensions, helping to deescalate the dispute after the adoption of the 1995 Law on Education and convincing the UDMR to stay in the governing coalition after 1996. In the conflict between the Ukrainian and Crimean authorities on Crimean autonomy, the HCNM waited for an opportune moment to intervene (i.e., for both parties to be ready to accept his mediation) and organized two roundtables that seem to have contributed to breaking the stalemate the parties found themselves in. The case studies detail how the HCNM's success as a mediator has been facilitated by his perceived neutrality/impartiality, as well as the trust he managed to engender through his insider knowledge and balanced assessments. Moreover, they show the HCNM's effective use of tactics such as public announcements (to clarify positions and lock in commitments) and the provision of confidential or private consultations (to draw out parties' real positions away from the limelight).

In the countries under examination, the HCNM's mediation role was characterized more by competitive or collaborative negotiation when a minority was perceived by the government to be either too diffuse or too weak to be allowed a genuine seat at the table. As the potential for conflict was nonetheless considered

TABLE 16.1. *Summary of Case Studies*

Country	Issue(s)	Second Party[1]	MHS[2]	HCNM role[3]	Outcomes
Estonia	Aliens crisis (immediate crisis)	Clear/ strong	Yes	Mediation	Escalation prevented; improved interethnic dialogue
Estonia	Stateless children, language requirements (protracted)	Unclear/ weak	No	Negotiation (competitive)	Positive legal changes; relatively stable interethnic relations
Romania	Hungarian language education (protracted but with crises)	Clear/ strong	Yes	Mediation	Escalation prevented; minority partaking in government; relatively stable interethnic relations
Romania	Romanian-Hungarian treaty (immediate crisis)	Clear/ strong	Yes	Mediation	Escalation prevented; treaty signed
Ukraine	Crimean autonomy (protracted but with crises)	Clear/ strong	Yes	Mediation	Escalation prevented; workable compromise solution
Ukraine	Crimean Tatar integration (protracted but with crises)	Clear/ weak	No	Negotiation (collaborative)	Escalation prevented (so far); unstable interethnic relations

[1] The second party is the representation of the country's minority in all cases but the Romanian-Hungarian treaty (where it was the Hungarian government). The first party has generally been the host government. *Clear/unclear* refers to the presence/absence of clear, well-organized representation, while *strong/weak* refers to the bargaining power of the second party.
[2] Denotes whether or not the parties found themselves in a situation that can be described as a mutually hurting stalemate.
[3] Denotes whether the activities of the HCNM mostly involved mediation between two (or more) parties, or whether he was negotiating predominantly with the government.

high, the HCNM mediated with the government to persuade it to accommodate its minorities in accordance with (and sometimes even beyond) international standards. The HCNM seems to have been more successful in changing minority policies in Estonia, where he could make use of leverage provided by the EU enlargement process, than in Ukraine concerning Crimean Tatar integration, where he had little external leverage. External leverage allowed the HCNM to be much more vocal and competitive in Estonia relative to his approach in Ukraine. Yet, the adoption of a hard stance or a aggressive position is not only a function of the context (such as the country the HCNM is operating in or the amount of leverage the HCNM has over a party), but also a function of the HCNM's character: To a certain extent, the Estonian experience shows that Van der Stoel and Vollebaek were much more willing to play tough than was Ekeus.

The case studies showed that majorities and minorities settle for extremely different outcomes, depending largely on the bargaining position of both parties, which changes in time and per issue. However, the case studies also demonstrate that the HCNM, as a third party intervening in internal identity conflicts, is able to have a definite influence on the substance of the outcomes: In most cases, the HCNM's persistently advocated recommendations have been implemented to a surprising extent.

What can we expect from the HCNM in the future? As a result of his unique independence, his "top-heavy" mandate, and his flexible modus operandi, the HCNM's office is one of the few OSCE institutions that seems largely unaffected by the political—and perhaps even existential—crisis in the OSCE (Vollebaek, 2008). Yet, the case studies on Estonia and Ukraine show that (EU) leverage is important for the HCNM in overcoming domestic opposition regarding contentious issues. Van der Stoel (2008) could not "emphasize enough that eagerness to join the European Union was of great help." Problematically for the HCNM's office, with the exception of the Western Balkan states, the majority of OSCE participating states with severe interethnic problems, primarily Russia and several Caucasian and Central Asian states, are not only the countries least willing to accept OSCE involvement in their domestic politics, but also the countries where the EU (and other organizations, such as NATO) exerts the least push and pull (HCNM Staff, 2008). It will be interesting to see how Vollebaek and his successors adjust to this changed context. After the EU's absorption of the Western Balkans, the heyday of the High Commissioner might well be over—partly as a result of his great successes in helping to improve interethnic relations in the new EU member states and partly as a result of the brick wall he will be hitting in many uncooperative countries without an EU perspective. However, as argued by Van der Stoel (2008), if you can get through and convince authorities that you are not there to "blow up the regime . . . you can do more than often is expected."

Notes

1. Where both the CSCE and OSCE processes are concerned, the acronym OSCE will be used.

2. According to Anstey and Zartman, negotiation in internal identity conflicts can often be defined as "a process of identifying an appropriate partner and constructing a joint pact," the latter being defined as "an agreement to cooperate in the establishment of future relations and the handling (management or resolution) of the conflict" (this volume, p. 221). While such a definition is warranted for many internal identity conflicts, in particular ones that have escalated into violence, the HCNM's experience in Central and Eastern Europe points to the prime importance of the—diffuse and protracted—negotiations on (substantive) settlement of the conflict instead of party identification and pact making. As conflicts had not yet escalated, one can discern in most cases a (tacit) agreement (or at least an understanding) that the conflict cannot be resolved by unilateral action. Indeed, the conflict is not one between "rebels" and the government, but between an "underprivileged" national minority and a—often nationalizing—majority (that generally controls the government; Brubaker, 1996).

3. These case studies, and minor parts of other sections, are based on Fedor Meerts' MSc dissertation for the University of Oxford. The three countries have been selected

because they provide a good cross section of HCNM activity in CEECs (where the HCNM has been most active).

4. The authors would like to thank Ms. Höglund for this valuable contribution.

5. In this regard, the chapter uses Kenneth Thomas and Ralph Kilmann's (1977) time-honored model, featuring five modes of conflict management: competing (high assertiveness/low cooperativeness), avoiding (low assertiveness/low cooperativeness), compromising (moderate assertiveness/moderate cooperativeness), collaborating (high assertiveness/high cooperativeness), and accommodating (low assertiveness/high coopera-tiveness).

6. CSCE Helsinki Document 1992 "The Challenges of Change."

7. Ibid.

8. Ibid.

9. Ibid.

10. Ibid.

11. The HCNM's activities are also greatly facilitated by the OSCE Missions, which are the on-the-ground presence of the OSCE. They have been described as the "the eyes and ears of the High Commissioner," providing up-to-date information and following up upon HCNM recommendations (Ugglas, 1994, p. 26).

12. CSCE Helsinki Document "The Challenges of Change" (1992).

13. Zartman and Berman (1982) list several ways in which negotiators enhance trust—many of which have been vital to the HCNM's "quiet diplomacy" (pp. 32–37). Firstly, the HCNM aims to understand all angles of the conflict and the problems of all sides in the conflict. Secondly, given his mandate, he is able to demonstrate to all parties that he has "a genuine interest in trying to help the other side[s] reach [their] objective while retaining his own objective and making the two appear compatible" (p. 33). Thirdly, the HCNM has been very careful not to make any promises, or issue any threats, that he cannot make good on. Fourthly, the HCNM realizes that in many cases step-by-step (pragmatic and minor) agreements will help increase trust and pave the way for a long-term settlement. Finally, the HCNM has made a point of making both governments and minorities aware that, from a security perspective, in the long term neither side will benefit from poor interethnic relations—thereby showing that compromise is indeed in both sides' interest.

14. Upon first arriving, van der Stoel often found not only a complete lack of dialogue between parties, but also a multiplicity of parties and a conflict constellation in which sides were not clearly constituted. Therefore, his first task was to "identify and crystallize viable partners while clarifying issues" (Anstey and Zartman, this volume). Subsequently—once he had identified his key partners—his goal was to promote (institutionalized) dialogue and participation. In an interview with the authors on May 29, 2008, Bloed poignantly pointed out that "when he first arrived in Estonia he found that no one talked; their only communication with the other side was essentially shouting matches through the media." This institution building to foster dialogue was accomplished by establishing forums, roundtables, and meetings between the government and minority leaders. Van der Stoel himself pointed out in an interview with the authors on April 1, 2008, that real dialogue meant not only talking about the future, but also dealing with the past and the difficult questions related to national identity.

15. Interview by Kristine Höglund on behalf of the authors with Ekeus, August 26, 2008. The authors would like to thank Ms. Höglund for this valuable contribution.

16. The HCNM often made use of the push and pull of the European Union (and NATO) enlargement process to leverage target states. In such cases, negotiations can be argued to involve bargaining between the target state (which can agree to implement the HCNM's

suggestions) and the HCNM (who can, in return, provide a more positive review of the domestic minority situation toward actors such as the European Commission).

17. Authors' interview with van der Stoel, April 1, 2008.

18. Since "restoration" effectively legalized the disenfranchisement of Russian speakers, the Mission and other international observers did not find evidence of gross human rights violations.

19. Letter of April 6, 1993, to Velliste.

20. Ibid.

21. Other major developments concerned interethnic dialogue, education, and the creation of an ombudsman.

22. His practical recommendations to increase transparency and uniformity in (implementation of) legislation, to provide stateless residents with aliens' passports, and to count the residence requirement from March 30, 1990, were largely heeded. Although several changes were made to the citizenship and language tests, their overall difficulty level remained prohibitive. Only some disabled and elderly persons were exempted from parts of the language test, despite the HCNM's calls for full exemption.

23. The Hungarian minority, heavily concentrated in Transylvania, made up roughly 7% of the country's population in 1992 and has remained fairly stable since (Horváth, 2002, p. 14). The current case study focuses on minority politics concerning the Hungarian minority, since this has been the main area of HCNM involvement in Romania (although the situation of the Roma has also been given apt attention by the HCNM).

24. Letter to Meleşcanu, September 9, 1993.

25. HCNM statement during his visit to Romania, September 1, 1995.

26. Population Census 2001 <http://2001.ukrcensus.gov.ua/eng/>. Accessed 15 June, 2008.

27. Ibid.

28. Letter to Zlenko, May 15, 1994. A third recommendation concerned the linguistic rights of the Russian minority, which has not been addressed in great detail by the HCNM and Ukrainian authorities.

29. These actors were far from unitary. Most notably, the Crimean Tatar representatives in the Crimean parliament (who felt threatened by the Russian majority and found a natural, though not fully appreciative, ally in Ukrainian politicians) were fervent opponents of an independent Crimea. However, the Ukrainian and Crimean governments were widely seen as the main parties in negotiations on a settlement (by each other as well as by the HCNM).

30. It had also become clear that Russia was unwilling to follow up on its earlier rhetoric in support of the separatists.

31. The HCNM's substantive recommendations, on the demarcation of powers and the creation of an interim conciliatory body, were not implemented.

32. Letter to Udovenko, March 19, 1996.

33. Kulyk forcefully argues that the above-mentioned settlement on Crimean autonomy "was achieved at the cost of the Crimean Tatars, whose demands, and respective recommendations of the High Commissioner, have largely been ignored" (2002, p. 69).

34. Most importantly, the causes of interethnic tensions have not been removed and there is still great conflict potential, as both Crimean Tatar and Russian radicalism are on the rise (Graumann, 2007, pp. 4–5).

35. This provided Crimean Tatars with 14 (out of 100) seats in 1994.

36. Ultimately, in 2004, domestic political struggles resulted in a change of the regional electoral system to proportional representation; the 2006 elections yielded eight Crimean Tatar representatives.

References

Birkenbach, H. (2000). *Half full or half empty? The OSCE Mission to Estonia and its balance sheet 1993–1999*. ECMI Working Paper 6. Flensburg: European Centre for Minority Issues.

Bloed, A. (2008, May 29). Interview with the authors.

Brenninkmeijer, O. (2005). *The OSCE High Commissioner on National Minorities: Negotiating the 1992 conflict prevention mandate*. PSIO Occasional Paper 5. Geneva: Graduate Institute of International Studies.

Brubaker, R. (1996). *Nationalism reframed: Nationhood and the national question in the new Europe*. Cambridge: Cambridge University Press.

Chigas, D., McClintock, E., & Kamp, C. (1996). Preventive diplomacy and the Organization for Security and Cooperation in Europe: Creating incentives for dialogue and cooperation. In A. Chayes & A. Chayes (Eds.), *Preventing conflict in the post-communist world: Mobilizing international and regional organizations* (pp. 25–97). Washington, DC: The Brookings Institution.

Cohen, J. (1999). *Conflict prevention in the OSCE: An assessment of capacities*. The Hague: The Netherlands Institute of International Relations Clingendael.

The Challenges of Change, CSCE Helsinki Document 1992 (1992). Paper presented at Conference for Security and Co-operation in Europe.

Ekeus, R. (2008, August 26). Interview by Kristine Höglund on behalf of the authors.

Elsuwege, P. van. (2004). *Russian-speaking minorities in Estonia and Latvia: Problems of integration at the threshold of the European Union*. ECMI Working Paper 8. Flensburg: European Centre for Minority Issues.

Galbreath, D. (2005). *Nation-building and minority politics in post-socialist states: Interests, influences and identities in Estonia and Latvia*. Stuttgart: Ibidem.

Gallagher, T. (2001). Building democracy in Romania: International shortcomings and external neglect. In J. Zielonka & A. Pravda (Eds.), *Democratic consolidation in Eastern Europe* (vol. 2, *International and transnational factors*, pp. 383–413). Oxford: Oxford University Press.

Gallagher, T. (2005). *Theft of a nation: Romania since Communism*. London: Hurst & Co.

Graumann, S. (2007). Crimea: From conflict prevention to development. *Development and Transition*, 6, 4–6.

Horváth, I. (2002). *Facilitating conflict transformation: Implementation of the recommendations of the OSCE High Commissioner on National Minorities to Romania, 1993–2001*. CORE Working Paper 8. Hamburg: Institute for Peace Research and Security Policy.

Huntingon, S. (1996). *The clash of civilizations and the remaking of the world order*. New York: Simon & Schuster.

Jurado, E. (2002). *Complying with European standards of minority protection: Estonia's relations with the European Union, OSCE and Council of Europe*. D.Phil. Thesis, Oxford University.

Kelley, J. (2002). *Ethnic politics in Europe: The power of norms and incentives*. Princeton, NJ: Princeton University Press.

Kemp, W. (2001). *Quiet diplomacy in action: The OSCE High Commissioner on National Minorities*. The Hague: Kluwer Law International.

Kulyk, V. (2002). *Revisiting a success story: Implementation of the recommendations of the OSCE High Commissioner on National Minorities to Ukraine, 1994–2001*. CORE Working Paper 6. Hamburg: Institute for Peace Research and Security Policy.

Lahelma, T. (1999). The OSCE's role in conflict prevention: The case of Estonia. *Helsinki Monitor, 10*(2), 19–38.

McMahon, P. (2005). Managing ethnicity: The OSCE and trans-national networks in Romania. *Problems of Post-Communism, 52*(1), 15–27.

Pettai, V. (2001). Estonia and Latvia: International influences on citizenship and minority integrations. In J. Zielonka & A. Pravda (Eds.), *Democratic consolidation in Eastern Europe* (vol. 2, *International and transnational factors*, pp. 257–280). Oxford: Oxford University Press.

Sardemann, R. (1997). The Hungarian approach to minority rights for national minorities in neighbouring countries. *Helsinki Monitor, 8*(4), 59–73.

Sarv, M. (2002). *Integration by reframing legislation: Implementation of the recommendations of the OSCE High Commissioner on National Minorities to Estonia, 1993–2001.* CORE Working Paper 7. Hamburg: Institute for Peace Research and Security Policy.

Sasse, G. (2002). Conflict prevention in a transition state: The Crimean issue in post-Soviet Ukraine. *Nationalism and Ethnic Politics, 8*(2), 1–26.

Sasse, G. (2005). *EU conditionality and minority rights: Translating the Copenhagen Criterion into policy.* European University Institute Working Paper 16. Florence: European University Institute.

Sasse, G. (2007a). Crimea: conflict prevention through institution-making. *Development and Transition, 6*, 2–4.

Sasse, G. (2007b). *The Crimea question: Identity, transition, and conflict.* Cambridge, MA: Harvard University Press.

Smith, D. (2002). Old wine in new bottles: The politics of independence. In D. Smith, A. Pabriks, A. Purs, & T. Lane (Eds.), *The Baltic states: Estonia, Latvia and Lithuania* (pp. 65–112). London: Routledge.

Thomas, K., & Kilmann, R. (1977). Developing a forced-choice measure of conflict handling behaviour: The mode instrument. *Educational and Psychological Measurement, 37*, 309–325.

Ugglas, M. (1994). Conditions for successful preventive diplomacy. In S. Carlsson (Ed.), *The challenge of preventive diplomacy: The experience of the CSCE* (pp. 11–32). Stockholm: Ministry of Foreign Affairs.

Vachudova, M. (2001). *The leverage of international institutions on democratizing states: Eastern Europe and the European Union.* European University Institute Working Paper 33. Florence: European University Institute.

Van der Stoel, M. (1999). The role of the OSCE High Commissioner in conflict prevention. In C. Crocker, F. Hampson, & P. Aall (Eds.), *Herding cats: Multiparty mediation in a complex world* (pp. 65–84). Washington, DC: United States Institute of Peace Press.

Van der Stoel, M. HCNM Staff (2008, 8 April). Interview with the authors.

Vollebaek, K. HCNM Staff (2008, 15 March), Interview with the authors.

Zaagman, R. (1993). Helsinki-II and the human dimension: Institutional aspects. *Helsinki Monitor, 3*(4), 52–64.

Zaagman, R. (1999). Conflict prevention in the Baltic area: The OSCE High Commissioner on National Minorities in Estonia, 1993–1999. *Helsinki Monitor, 10*(3), 30–44.

Zartman, I.W. (2002). The structure of negotiation. In V. Kremenyuk (Ed.), *International negotiation: Analysis, approaches, issues* (pp. 71–84). San Fransisco: Jossey-Bass.

Zartman, I. W., & Berman, M. (1982). *The practical negotiator.* New Haven, CT: Yale University Press.

17 Negotiating Out of Conflict

External Interventions in Africa

■ MARK ANSTEY

Because genocide requires organization, there is usually warning and opportunity to prevent it or at least bring mass killings quickly to an end. This places special onus on external actors to intervene, but it does not make intervention easy. Military intervention may prevent violent conflict from escalating, and negotiation may enable conflict management to ease tensions. But long-term peace requires attention to development and the complexities of justice and reconciliation in deeply cleaved societies. Effective intervention is therefore a systemic, multidimensional process.

Violent conflicts in Africa continually confront the international community with dilemmas of intervention, generating almost a third of the world's refugees and "persons of concern,"[1] and accounting for 80% of the United Nations (UN) peacekeepers and 60% of the time of the UN Security Council (Abedajo, 2006). Conditions are not helpful. Over half of the continent's 800 million people live in absolute poverty at less than $1 a day; 34 of its 48 states are ranked among the poorest on earth; and only 12 are ranked as "free" by Freedom House. A hemorrhage of capital and skills has left many states too weak to resuscitate themselves. Even in collapse, however, some, such as Zimbabwe (like Myanmar in Asia), have been obdurately resistant to humanitarian assistance from nations critical of their regimes, let alone intervention carrying the risk of behavioral or political change. Rogue governments resist external intervention or assistance threatening control, but more principled ones are also cautious about such actions.

Dilemmas of intervention arise as a consequence of resistance by individual states under scrutiny, but also as a result of the politics, commitment, and capacity of those who would intervene. Internal conflicts are both the cause and consequence of divisions in the international community. Inevitably, the interests of secondary actors enter the decision-making process, influencing not only in-principle decisions about intervention (whether to) but also implementation strategies (how to) in terms of the supply and resource allocations of peacekeeping troops, the appointment of mediators, and the terms of reference for their work. Problems of consensus, credibility, commitment, and capacity plague the ranks of external agents.

■ CONDITIONS AND COMPLEXITIES OF IDENTITY CONFLICTS

An understanding of identity has already been presented in the opening chapter of this book. This short section reviews some of the debate surrounding this elusive concept. Africa is home to a large diversity of ethnic groups. Boundaries drafted to meet European interests in 1884 often resonate poorly with the interests, political systems, or social systems of indigenous peoples today. A cluster of conflicts grumbles continuously along the Afro-Islamic identity fault line across the southern Sahara, a religious overlay to other dimensions of regional diversity.

Africa's conflicts are usually intra- rather than interstate, but they do straddle boundaries. The roiling conflicts in the Great Lakes region and the Horn of Africa are not wars over national boundaries in the tradition of Europe. Adversaries play out localized conflicts over land, water, and power almost without regard to definitions of statehood. In the context of collapsed and failed states in which many governments can neither collect revenues nor deliver political goods to citizens much beyond their capitals, this is perhaps not surprising. Boundaries do, however, have tactical usefulness for adversaries with militias in the Great Lakes region, for instance, using neighboring states to build forces and for purposes of retreat.

Within nations, as groups jockey for support and access to resources, conflicts interlock in unexpected ways. For instance, Autesserre (2008, p. 101) suggests a conflict-perpetuating symbiosis between local leaders in the Democratic Republic of the Congo (DRC), who learn to frame their conflicts within the dynamics driving the national discourse (ideology, ethnicity, religion, class) to enlist support from players at this level, and national leaders who, in turn, use local leaders to access the resources they need to pursue their own ends in contests with each other.

By tradition, conflict analysts separate communal (ethnic) from class conflicts—the former being about social cleavage, the latter about social stratification. This distinction has validity, but in many instances (as in white–black tensions in apartheid South Africa; Shona–Ndebele tensions in Robert Mugabe's Zimbabwe; Kikuyu–Luo tensions in Mwai Kibaki's Kenya; and Tutsi–Hutu tensions in Rwanda) they are conflated. Those who mobilize under class banners are as committed to their cause as those as who do so under ethnic ones; each reflects a form of the identity game in which in- and out-groups are defined for mobilization purposes. In poorly developed societies, it is easier to mobilize around cultural markers than class ones, but such mobilization is still usually about access to and control of opportunities and resources.

Cultural primordialists see ethnic differences as profound and immutable, making for intractable conflicts and zero-sum outcomes. Class theorists argue that conflicts are the product of poverty and dualism, seeing ethnic divides as a "false consciousness," useful for power holders in power retention strategies. The communal/class debate runs unresolved through many conflicts. When South Africans turned on foreigners in the context of rising unemployment and social hardship toward the end of the first decade of the 2000s, some pointed to xenophobia, others to scarce resources (the unemployment rate is 40–60% in many South African townships) as the root cause of the conflict. In Kenya, some explained the violence following the 2008 presidential election crisis as tribal, others as the consequence of selective poverty. An unresolved debate rages over recognizing ethnicity as an issue in Rwanda, some arguing that tensions will not be resolved until ethnic differences are openly attended to (van Eck, 2007), others that they should be denied as generating and perpetuating conflicts that might be better dealt with through other approaches (Kagame, 2008; Sezibera, 2007). Whichever view is correct, ethnicity remains a major factor in hostilities; "once a group consciousness has emerged, it is a political reality. It cannot be ignored, nor will it simply disappear because others think it 'false'" (Hanf, 1989, p. 110).

Identity groups may seldom attack each other simply over issues of cultural difference (Laitin, 2006), but in many societies they cluster rather than integrate, and in struggles over scarce resources or for reasons of protection, participation, power, privilege, or purpose, they mobilize around ethnic markers. In poorly developed economies, communal rather than class identity becomes a central factor in contests over boundaries, economic opportunity, the distribution of wealth, and electoral systems. Group identities may be difficult to work with, but they can be molded, their sense of threat reduced, and their expression redirected. People make social and political choices about their identity and, in so doing, about the identity of others. Identities are both assumed and ascribed. Some identity groups may not have a choice—other groups, for instance, may ascribe them a "threatening" identity to mobilize internal unity. Not all participants in identity conflicts are necessarily willing ones; they have reactive rather than proactive identities.

From a systems perspective, social and political systems evolve through periods of order and disorder. Periods of system stability occur when actors are sufficiently satisfied with their lot within it, or power realities oblige some to accept an unhappy situation. Conflict is regulated within accepted rules, procedures, and institutions of the existing system or through oppression and compliance. But the designs of systems often lose their fit with new environmental conditions; the goals and power relativities of social actors change, new actors emerge, and conflict management systems lose effectiveness. Conflict emerges over the shape of the system itself. Unable to accommodate change, rigid or weak systems may fall apart. History is replete with collapsed empires and states, violent struggles against repressive regimes, and genocidal drives to eliminate "problem groups." Resilient systems (those that survive internal conflicts and external threats) are adaptive rather than simply stable. Their actors are responsive to signals of change, continuously redesigning systems within which they operate through negotiation and joint problem solving. They recognize that system preservation is best achieved through system adaptation based on a continual search to ensure that it meets as wide a range of needs and interests as possible. Democracies may not guarantee economic growth or equity, wise government, or minority protections, but they offer the best prospect of adaptability and system resilience because they offer a voice to diversity. Dissatisfaction with current arrangements and alerts to changing conditions are raised early and can be responded to.

Periods of disorder in systems may be necessary for system revitalization and survival, but they also carry the potential for massive destruction (Anstey, 2006; Nathan, 1996; Wheatley, 1994). It is the management of conflict that renders its forces constructive and positive. Societal groups are not static, their relative power fluctuates in the context of changing environmental conditions, they change in their form and belief systems over time, diverge where once they were allies, find their needs and interests incompatible as social arrangements change. To the extent that they ignore their differences, and avoid pushing their own interests or blocking the interests of others, conflict remains latent or unexpressed, sometimes at a low level of consciousness even to the parties themselves and invisible to external observers. It is when it becomes overt that conflict is most readily identified, when parties recognize their perceived incompatibilities, mobilize around their differences, and use their power to pursue or protect their interests by trying to eliminate, defeat, neutralize, assimilate, accommodate, or control the needs and interests of others. Conflict is about change; how it is managed determines its cost. Poorly managed conflicts in the previous century saw over 187 million lives lost in wars and their consequences (Hobsbawm, 1994) as empires ended, nation-states took shape, and authoritarian governments gave way to democracies. The post–World War II stability of Western nations has a long and bloody history (Gress, 1998; Zakaria, 2004). "It took Europe a millennium and a half to resolve its post-Roman crisis of social and political identity; nearly a thousand years to settle on the nation-state form of political organization, and nearly five hundred years more to determine which nations were entitled to be states. Whether civilization would survive the raids and conflicts of rival warrior bands; whether church or state, pope or emperor, would rule; whether catholic or protestant would prevail in Christendom; whether dynastic empire, national state, or city-state would demand fealty . . . were issues painfully worked out through ages of searching and strife, during which the losers . . . were often annihilated" (Fromkin, 2001, p. 565). It is a never-ending journey. Changing conditions—migration, changing demographics, the consequences of globalization, perceptions of external threat—inevitably see new periods of disorder and conflict within and between nations. Africa's conflicts too reflect an evolutionary character (Kaarsholm, 2006).

The questions now are whether change must necessarily follow a repetitive bloody passage and whether the conditions generating violent conflict can be identified. If group consciousness or identity cannot be ignored as a factor in many conflicts, defining its utility becomes important to those involved, but also more generally identifying the mix of conditions in which identity assumes prominence. Answers to these questions might inform the shape of external interventions to prevent, contain, and manage identity conflicts.

It appears that identity groups seldom attack one another simply over their difference, or indeed, even where there is fragmentation or deep enmity between groups (Laitin, 2006). The potential for mobilization under ethnic markers and violent conflict is raised, however, under conditions of scarcity, especially if competition is limited to a few rather than many identity groups. Social stability is improved in situations of homogeneity and extreme heterogeneity (Collier, 1998). Laitin, (2006) suggests the major problem to be weak states that are unable to deliver services or offer basic protections to citizens There political goods are unevenly distributed, and systems of clientelism often limit privilege and power to particular ethnic groups, fueling perceptions of relative deprivation, out-group mobilization along ethnic lines, and blocking social integration. The weakness of states does not imply imminent collapse; as Zimbabwe has demonstrated, these states may be strong enough to crush opposition and toy with the international community for a period. Tensions over scarcity are aggravated where there are perceptions of relative deprivation or unfair discrimination in which identity groups perceive inequality in their rights (to worship, to express their beliefs, to access courts, to freedom of movement or assembly, or to compete for political power) or in cases where land or food distribution is restricted to certain groups for political purposes (as in Zimbabwe; Arnson & Zartman, 2005).

High-threat–high-frustration scenarios carry fear and a particularly high potential for violent conflict. In Kenya and Zimbabwe, tight electoral contests evoked violence in situations in which the aspirations of dominated groups were blocked after a period of progress ("almost there but cheated") and dominant groups faced a real threat of loss of power and privilege.

Group perceptions are key to understanding identity conflicts. Groups develop narratives and a memory of the conditions and events that shaped their particular identities. Previous interactions shape their understanding of issues; the desirability and possibility of negotiated outcomes; the intentions, trustworthiness, and relative power of other parties involved; potential outcomes of a conflict; and the feasibility of alternative approaches in achieving these outcomes.

Leadership choices are critical in shaping perceptions. Groups perceiving themselves as under threat are vulnerable to manipulation by leaders promising protection from or dominance over other groups. The influence of these leaders is heightened during periods of national despair and social disintegration. Hitler, Mussolini, and Lenin, for instance, offered people new meaning and identity in mass movements through which they could meet needs for protection, participation, power, privilege, and purpose. Ethnic entrepreneurs mobilize around ethnic markers when they are seen to offer an advantage in retaining or accessing power or privilege. Leaders of privileged groups (referred to as *big men* in Africa) mobilize lower ranks (the most threatened in their ranks if systems of patronage should disappear); leaders of upwardly aspirant groups mobilize around frustration and the inequity of the existing system. In cases where dominant groups have held power for long periods of time through repression, there may also be fears that loss of power will expose corruption and that they will be held to account for previous atrocities. In short, identity has utility for mobilizing groups offensively or defensively. In Rwanda, Hutus and Tutsis had been mobilizing for some time before the 1994 genocide. The genocide itself was triggered by the shooting down of the presidential plane en route home after a peace deal and the invasion of the country by the Tutsi Rwandan Patriotic Front (RPF) at a moment when Hutus felt under direct threat. The culture of impunity that had developed as a result of the lack of consequence after previous mass killings probably reduced the sense of risk among the genocidaires (Ngoga, 2008; Schabas, 2008). The Rwandan case also reflects the terrible consequences of slow response times on the part of the international community. In Sudan it has taken the UN years to commit resources to the Darfur problem, where its intentions are still considerably ahead of its delivery and at a time when mass killing effectively trailed off, its purpose having been accomplished.

External interventionists, then, need to give attention to the conditions under which people have made identity choices, what sorts of choices they made, and why. They need to have an idea of the range of possible outcomes of their intervention, and of what has potential under what circumstances. How the parties to the conflict define themselves, and how leaders within the mix place themselves and mobilize within and across groups, are critically important.

Identities appear to have a hard core with malleable outer layers. Under threat, or to mobilize strength for offensive purposes, ethnic groups retreat to the "trusted core" of those with a shared language, culture, and/or religion. The boundaries between "us" and "them" are more narrowly and sharply drawn (and it only takes one group in a mix to draw them; as soon as others want to redraw them, conflict emerges over who can hold the pen). Although many leaders mobilize around a core group identity (it's easier),[2] the Mandelas, Ghandis, and Titos have shown it possible to mobilize within the softer, more malleable layers of identity, locating overlaps across groups to create larger inclusive identities. Leadership choices and capacity, then, are key to how groups are mobilized in identity conflicts and in determining which options for resolution have potential—assimilation, accommodation, or partition to avert destructive alternatives. Deadly consequences may follow when dominant groups refuse space to other identity groups, which in turn refuse subjugation or compliance; when groups refuse assimilation but a dominant group makes it the sole option; and when mutual accommodation is not seen as feasible in the context of power relativities and animosities created through time.

The fact that some conflicts appear intractable, however, does not mean that they will always be so, or that moments may not occur in which unique opportunities for peaceful change through negotiation might become not only viable but attractive. The relatively peaceful South African transition from a repressive racial corporatism to a tolerant constitutional democracy is a case in point.

■ OPTIONS FOR MANAGING IDENTITY CONFLICTS

There may be large variance in the detail of how identity conflicts might be managed at a political level, but using Hanf's (1989) basic typology they fall into several major categories and a few main subcategories. Identity groups mobilize around ethnic markers to eliminate other groups or convince them of proposals for subjection, accommodation, assimilation, or separation.[3]

- *Elimination of the other (genocide)*
- *Subjection*
  - Domination by one group (either a majority or minority) of others, with repression gauged to the degree of resistance to the dominant group
- *Cooperation within a state*
  - Accommodation of ethnic differences in a system of tolerance in which all groups are given room to express themselves (South Africa)
  - Assimilation of minorities into a national identity under an espoused values system of equality for all (Jacobinism) and requiring the elimination of all but national symbols of identity (France)
- *Separation*
  - Partition by agreement (Europe; India/Pakistan; Cyprus; Singapore/ Malaysia; Sweden/Norway; Belgium/Netherlands) or
  - Separation by imposition (as in the Kosovo secession) in order that the groups do not have to work within the same system together

Accommodation strategies seek a "unity in diversity" in which identity groups can give expression to their diverse cultures and religions under the ambit of a larger national identity. South Africa's constitution offers protections to all ethnic and religious groupings—a syncretistic (fruit salad) rather than a Jacobin (fruit blend) approach. Such approaches depend on intergroup tolerance and perceptions of equity in political and economic dispensations. Multicultural societies are threatened when some identity groups use the social space offered to try to close down the space of others or to attack the larger society.

Assimilation might achieve social stability in cases where multiple identity groups commit to a new national identity (the United States), where a ruling minority disguises minority rule by a tolerant government ruling over a large, dominated, but compliant majority (Rwanda, South Africa), or where a large ruling majority (which can rule on its own) governs small, dominated minorities afraid or without incentive to mobilize (France). Such balances are easily disturbed. A majority may lose interest in assimilating a minority group or scapegoat it as the cause of social problems, pushing it to submit, leave the society, or mobilize in response. Mobilization will likely be within the identity frame defined by the dominant group, reinforcing the stereotype. Large, confident minorities may mobilize for secession or to reshape the system in which they find themselves. Threats of secession, civil war, or a flight of capital or skills may require a search for new ways of accommodation.

Although Africa has chosen largely to live within the boundaries imposed by Europe in 1884, *partition* or *ethnic separation* also offers options for conflict reduction. Groups might cluster separately within nations adhering to accommodationist policies at a national level (as in South Africa) or seek separate national identities (as in Sudan). Muller (2008, p. 31) argues that where the United States found stability through assimilation, Europeans have done so through ethnic *separatism*. "Europe has been so harmonious since World War II not because of the failure of ethnic nationalism but because of its success, which removed some of the greatest sources of conflict both within and between countries." As empires disintegrated, people mobilized along communal lines to demand regional independence, self-governance, control of public services and commerce, and removal of "foreigners" from positions of power—a push for self-determination by identity groups (Muller, 2008, p. 23). As communal groups were configured across and between empires rather than within regions, the situation quickly devolved into violent communal conflicts over dominance of a state and boundaries (ethnic turf), the repression of minorities, mass migrations, and deportations. After World War II, there was a massive shakedown of populations into the ethnic clusters reflecting modern Europe's nation-states, the last stage being the violent breakup of Yugoslavia (Muller, 2008, p. 29). Ethno-nationalist disaggregation extended into decolonization with huge ethnic migrations in the creation of India, Pakistan, and Bangladesh, in the creation of the Israeli state, and in the development of independent African states.

Ethnic separatism has costs—in terms of insularity, hardened "us-them" boundaries, inward thinking, and less diverse cultures. Many new states struggle to achieve economic viability. However, ethnic separatism reduces conflicts between identity groups within nations, and has in-group benefits of unity, cohesion, conformity, and a stronger sense of belonging and security. It has served to bond nations under siege, reduced boundary disputes, and in Europe seen a period of territorial and political stability. Muller (2008) argues that this has enabled Europeans to seek new ways of mutual accommodation and cooperation at a regional level through the European Union. While costly to implement, Muller advocates partition as "the most humane lasting solution to intense communal conflicts" (p. 34), transforming internal conflicts over accommodation within states into less difficult problems of interface between states.

These conceptual categorizations are expressed in mixed forms in practice. Simple domination and assimilation are easily blurred when the dominant group is a majority. Using a hybrid assimilation/accommodation approach, many nations expect people of other nations who become citizens to indicate primary allegiance to national symbols and those who take up residence to operate according to national norms and laws. They regulate expression of other cultures and religious beliefs within the bounds of national law and culture. This is more flexible than strict assimilation, more bounded than open accommodation.

Problems arise over preferred means of dealing with difference. Minorities feeling that they will never have self-governance may mobilize for independence/secession, regardless of the space provided by the majority but especially if there is a history of repression. Jacobinists resist any cultural expression outside defined boundaries, their rigidity generating resistance and conflict. Ethnic mobilization/extremism by one group herds others into groupings. Privileged groups need markers to retain superiority; aspirants need them to mobilize against privileged groups. Democratic societies are marked by accommodation and tolerance in which group differences are muted (Goodin, 1995). Accommodation arrangements are hard to sustain if any groups assume more aggressive positions of identity that others experience as denial or discrimination.

External interventionists enter conflicts already shaped by the choice mixes of the parties directly involved. Discarding elimination and domination as a solution, internal identity conflicts may be resolved through the design of systems of assimilation, accommodation, or separation. If negotiated outcomes are to be achieved in identity conflicts, the various parties' range of feasible options must find resonance (often a core task of mediators). Groups have identity by virtue of self-perception and the perception of others. *Assimilation* can only work if a minority group is willing to see itself "reidentified" as part of the majority and the majority is willing to absorb it as "equal and the same." Jacobinism requires willingness to forgo certain ethnic symbols for a new identity. *Accommodation* is only viable if all participants commit to tolerance and agree that each should enjoy space for cultural or religious expression. Effective external intervention, then, works first with the identity definitions of the parties in a conflict. It seeks to understand their relational boundaries and the reasons for them; looks to design systems enabling nonviolent coexistence either within or across states; and searches for ways to reconcile groups that have inflicted damage on one another.

■ EXTERNAL INTERVENTION: OPTIONS AND DILEMMAS

External interventions in internal identity conflicts are complex processes requiring answers to several interrelated questions: Who can intervene, under whose authority, under what circumstances, using what methods, for what purposes? Any form of external intervention in internal conflicts presents dilemmas. Interventions in identity conflicts are difficult because they suggest external influence not only on issues of contention between parties, but also on the core character of the parties themselves. Issues and identity become conflated. Changing a position or accommodating the expression of beliefs and values of an "other" may imply softening beliefs, values, and rules core to a group's own identity. Negotiation, with its implications of compromise, accommodation, and consensus, may threaten group identities more than sustained conflict, which preserves in-group cohesion, loyalty, and conformity even as it sharpens their divides (Anstey, 2006b; Coser, 1956). These are questions to which the remainder of this chapter is devoted.

Who Can Intervene, Under Whose Authority?

Interventions have greatest legitimacy when conducted by a person or agency invited by the parties involved—as in the case of Masire's facilitation of the DRC conflict. Legitimacy may not, however, translate into empowerment. Quett Masire was the 12th name on a list, and in the face of obstructionism from Laurent Kabila struggled for years to even bring the parties together. Progress was made only after the assassination of Laurent Kabila. Regimes such as those of Laurent Kabila and Robert Mugabe toy with mediation processes, using them tactically within larger strategies of power preservation to buy time, pull others into rounds of nonproductive negotiation, and achieve a veneer of respectability. Third parties become witting or unwitting accomplices to perpetuating rogue regimes. Quiet diplomacy in the contexts of Kenya in 2000 and later in Zimbabwe has been criticized as lacking influence and providing a soft way out for a regime and international actors more interested in "not rocking the boat" than in changing situations (Anstey, 2007).

Legitimacy and, theoretically, greatest power are provided at the next level by the authority of the international community through the United Nations. But such authority is not easily achieved. The UN Charter reflects a primary concern with conflicts endangering international peace and security. Africa's conflicts are largely intrastate rather than interstate in character, but in many instances they threaten regional stability, as in the case of the crises in the DRC, Zimbabwe, and Sudan. Because their own interests are almost always affected, the UN Security Council and the wider General Assembly are beset with dilemmas in every case in which the question of intervention arises. For example, China has resisted intervention in Darfur and offered legitimacy to the Mugabe regime. Smaller nations resist UN intervention in internal conflicts invoking the principle of sovereignty. In 1998 UN Secretary-General Kofi Annan failed to persuade the Security Council to intervene in Kosovo to avoid a repeat of the 1994 response paralysis to genocide in Rwanda. He argued that the UN Charter was intended to protect the sovereignty of peoples rather than offer protection for leaders who murdered or trampled the rights of their citizens. Third World nations opposed the North Atlantic Treaty Organization (NATO) bombing campaign that brought the Serbian government to heel as a violation of sovereignty. In a policy leap in 2005, the UN did, however, adopt the principle of "responsibility to protect," accepting a duty to intervene for humanitarian reasons, but it still faces constraints of capacity and commitment (Traub, 2006, p. 93).

Traub's (2006, p. 341) observation on the slow and controversial start to the UN's mission in the DRC has resonance for external intervention in many African conflicts: "The Congo's capacity to generate chaos seemed vastly greater than the UN's capacity to contain it." The ongoing crisis of undercapacity is due partly to the size of UN resources and partly to the competing interests of its constituents; the factor that gives it legitimacy also erodes its capacity and slows its responses. The credibility of the UN has been tarnished by the criminal behavior of some of its peacekeeping forces and, in recent years, by its largest funder, the United States, which has treated it with contempt, acting unilaterally when it chooses and refusing to subject itself to many of the UN's international standards, resolutions, or systems of international justice. This is a pattern of behavior mirrored in the tactics of rogue regimes in Zimbabwe and Sudan, which recognize and exploit the limits of UN capacity and commitment.

The dilemmas of the UN are reflected in the politics of the Darfur mission. Arguably, the Sudanese government accepted an African Union (AU) peacekeeping force only because it was insufficiently resourced to protect itself, to stem attacks in the region, or to exert any meaningful influence over the government. Increasing the UN presence had to overcome Sudanese government resistance, as well as divisions within the Security Council and the wider international community. Finding a multinational force or a country willing to lead such a mission was a problem. The AU, unable to deliver on its mandate, also refused to be sidelined. The Sudanese government framed any Western incursion as an attack on Islam. Movement on the Darfur issue was further mired in the politics of the UN itself—the controversial reform of the Security Council, the behavior of the United States within it, and Kofi Annan's "lame-duck" period in the context of the "oil for food" scandal involving his son. These factors all seem very far away from the basic human needs of those caught in the crossfire on the ground. Thereafter, the International Criminal Court (ICC) issued warrants for Sudan's President Bashir for war crimes. The AU (with the voluble exception of Botswana) refused to implement them, arguing that their timing was not helpful to prospects for a negotiated peace and claiming that targeting Africans while ignoring transgressions by leaders of developed nations showed inequity in an international war crimes system.

Africa's rogue regimes recognize the incapacity of the UN to do much about their activities in the context of an increasingly complex international relations environment characterized by a rapid rise in the number of member states (from 69 in 1920 to 192 in 2008), many unable to sustain economic viability (Ferguson, 2004). The Zimbabwean government refused Western groups permission to monitor elections, warning of neo-colonialism and painting opposition groups as puppets of British imperialist ambition. Ignoring UN pleas and pressures for changes in behavior, it ejected humanitarian organizations accused of distributing aid with "a political agenda."

Huntington (1998) has argued that in "macro-identity" disputes, neutral and impartial third parties are virtually impossible to find, the usual pattern of settlement being one in which powerful secondary parties use their influence to pressure internal protagonists into a deal. Nathan (1999, pp. 23–25) counters that power brokerage of this sort, however, aggravates rather than ameliorates tensions and has called instead for low-power approaches directed at confidence building between protagonists and the use of neutrals. Masire's facilitation of the DRC process demonstrates how difficult such a process can be. With plenty of encouragement from the international community but few resources, and in the face of an obstructionist regime, he made slow progress. Tenacity coupled with the removal of Laurent Kabila in the DRC eventually produced results, but facilitation was made difficult by the very parties who had agreed to it. Of course, there are various strategic reasons for agreeing to a cease-fire and then stretching out the search for a facilitator or mediator, initiating the process, and coming to grips with the issues. However, within such strategic plays, further lives are lost and economies fall deeper into crisis.

In March 2011 the UN Security Council invoked its 'responsibility to protect' in response to the civilian uprising in Libya. The Qaddafi regime's fight back against rebels created a surge of refugees, and under pressure mostly from Britain and France, the UN quickly passed Resolution 1973 enabling all necessary measures to protect civilians under threat of attack. It soon became evident however that there were differences in interpretation of this with some such as the USA, UK and France openly calling for the termination of the Qaddafi regime, and offering recognition and support to rebel groups. Others, such as NATO (which eventually assumed responsibility for coordinating the campaign) took a narrower view–simply that the job was to protect civilians under threat. Countries such as Russia and South Africa voiced disquiet over the more expansive approach of pushing for regime change. Of course it could be argued that rebels would only really be protected in the long term by ending the regime, but this is simply one dimension of a complex situation. One did not have to pretend that the Qadaffi regime had legitimacy in order to recognize dilemmas in the situation. Who is a civilian in such a context? If the regime and rebel forces both have civilian supporters are some to receive more protection than others? When civilians take up arms in a rebellion are they still civilians or militia? If international forces protect and support such civilians/militia/rebels in a scenario in which they would otherwise have little prospect, has the battle not become one between a regime and external forces? Whose interests are really being served in such interventions–citizens or those of the interventionists? What are the determining factors in deciding on intervention in a Libyan scenario and non-intervention in a Syrian one? Is there inevitable 'mission creep' in such interventions with external agents finding themselves sucked progressively into deeper more direct engagement with domestic politics? The UN then still has much to do in clarifying the boundaries of protective action. The Libyan experience may well see the UN move back into a period of gridlock in the Security Council if it cannot achieve a consensus on guidelines for action in exercising the 'responsibility to protect' (Anstey 2011).

Using What Methods, for What Purposes?

Linked to the issue of agent legitimacy then are questions concerning the purpose and method of interventions. The purpose of external interventions may range from protecting civilians, to separating warring factions, to creating conditions that oblige adversaries to negotiate, to assisting them once such processes are underway, to helping to ensure that peace deals are given sustainable life, and where there has been violence, to creating conditions for interpersonal and communal relations that facilitate reconciliation. The Libyan case reveals the complexity of such interventions.

The UN offers three basic forms of intervention: peacekeeping (separating warring parties), peacemaking (brokering political deals), and peacebuilding (creating environmental and attitudinal conditions for a sustainable peace), some of which are discussed in Wallensteen's chapter. These have resonance with the phases of democratic transitions proposed by O'Donnell et al. (1986): liberalization, pacting, elections, and democratic consolidation. In tandem they reflect the shape of a conflict transformation process, in which parties shift their use of power from seeking to destroy one another, to negotiating deals to end hostilities, to working jointly together for nation-building purposes (Anstey, 2006a). From this perspective, external interventions must be seen not as discrete processes, but as attending to dimensions of a larger systemic change process at various times.

Diplomacy interventions may run along various tracks of influence—a track one form at a formal foreign policy level; a track two form at a less formal level involving influential citizens; and a hybrid "one and a half track" form in which high-level influential individuals facilitate discussions between official government representatives (Mapondera, 2006, pp. 66–81). The recently established "Group of Elders" comprising Jimmy Carter, Bill Clinton, Bishop Tutu, Kofi Annan, and others have the experience and capacity to conduct such interventions and proved influential in the Kenyan dispute. Quett Masire was appointed by the parties to the DRC conflict to facilitate a peacemaking process; Thabo Mbeki was appointed by the Southern African Development Community (SADC) to mediate tensions in Zimbabwe following several previous rounds of quiet diplomacy and by the Economic Community of West African States (ECOWAS) and the AU to mediate in Ivory Coast; UN peacekeepers in the DRC were eventually given a mandate to, in effect, create a context for a political solution. While appropriate for humanitarian bodies such as the International Red Cross, quiet diplomacy has been criticized in the Kenyan, Zimbabwean, and Darfur situations as a form of collusion between external agents (under pressure "to do something") and internal power holders (under pressure to respond to negotiate with struggle groups), each more interested in preserving its own interests than in effecting meaningful change (Anstey, 2007). The postelection crisis in Kenya in 2008, whether by design or coincidence, reflected a form of mediator flooding. The crisis area was immediately "visited" by the president of the AU (Kufuor) and by Archbishop Desmond

Tutu (of the Group of Elders), offering both formal and informal tracks of assistance to the protagonists. Neither of these lasted long, but their presence and statements signaled both international concern and a willingness to assist. A little later, a team led by Kofi Annan settled in for a longer haul, eventually assisting the parties to achieve a power-sharing deal. As they became partners in the process, Mwai Kibaki's coercion was tempered and Raila Odinga's mobilization against the regime redirected. A similar formula was used in Zimbabwe, though Mugabe again appears to have hijacked the process.

External parties may employ violent (military intervention) and nonviolent forms of intervention (sanctions, suspension of diplomatic relations, deployment of peacekeeping forces) to push parties into negotiation or create a context in which negotiation becomes the preferred option for managing change. A mix of external pressures and coordinated external intervention by the international community brought the Rhodesian civil war to an end in 1979. The AU too has intervened militarily to protect legitimate governments from coups. In 1998 South Africa, Botswana, and Zimbabwe entered Lesotho to suppress a military coup. In 1999 Zimbabwe, Angola, Chad, and Sudan invaded the DRC to prop up the regime of Laurent Kabila, who had toppled Mobutu, when it was threatened by Rwanda and Uganda. This led eventually to a cease-fire and initiation of the peace process leading to the 2006 elections. In April 2008 an AU force drove a self-proclaimed leader off a Comores island. Such actions are not always ethically clear. In 2008 France deployed troops to support Chad's President Idriss Deby, who himself had achieved power through a coup, from a rebel militia. Laurent Kabila's accession to power was hardly democratic, and nations that engaged in the DRC war certainly sought to secure their own political and economic interests as much as those of the indigenous people.

External interventions into the affairs of other nations are an ongoing international relations reality. A large range of purposes and methods exist for such actions, dependent on the nature of the conflict, external interests and capacity, objectives for the process, and power realities.

■ A SYSTEMIC APPROACH TO EXTERNAL INTERVENTIONS

External interventions may be of a short-term, limited-scope nature to end bloodshed and separate warring parties or conducted with long-term systemic thinking. Short-term peacemaking interventions may be used simply to assist parties negotiate a deal over an issue of dispute, but effective interventions recognize the need for longer-term support sometimes to facilitate nation-building processes. To bring parties to the negotiation table, external powers may apply coordinated pressure through economic sanctions, support for opposition groups, offers of mediation, or even direct force. To bring about an end to immediate hostilities, peacekeeping forces may be deployed. To create a context for negotiations and political solution searches, the role of peacekeepers may be expanded. To assist political deal making, various tracks of diplomacy may be utilized concurrently by different externals. To assist with nation building, a wide range of assistance may be offered to stabilize a nation and consolidate a new democracy. In the DRC, for instance, UN peacekeepers remained, assisting the newly elected government to deal with spoiler militias in the eastern regions and to broker a peace with them. Attention also needs to be given to the difficult issues of reconciliation in communities deeply scarred by violent conflict. Reconciliation is prevention.

Democratic Transitions as Conflict Transformation Projects

Many of Africa's conflicts are centrally concerned with issues of democratization and state building. Quick "in-out" peacekeeping operations or deployment of a mediation team to broker a political deal are often unlikely to produce sustainable results. Many African nations' means to implement peace agreements or create conditions for sustainable development are limited. Poverty constrains effective governance and delivery of social services and generates the very dynamics these nations seek to move beyond.

Democratization is a conflict transformation project. Transitions to democracy generally move through phases—from authoritarian rule and violence through liberalization (in which there is an expansion of civil society freedoms); pacting at political, military, and social levels to stabilize the society, limiting the risks of coups and revolutions; and then free and fair elections that bring popular leadership to power. An election opens the door to democracy but does not make it sustainable. From a conflict transformation perspective, external interventions shift from separating warring parties (peacekeeping), to getting them to a negotiation table, assisting them to negotiate viable peace agreements (peacemaking), and then to facilitating the creation of conditions and attitude change required to ensure a sustainable peace (peacebuilding). These are facets of the same conflict transformation, nation-building process. Each phase of a democratic transition project requires the design and implementation of effective conflict management systems. The real measure of their effectiveness has less to do with their technical sophistication and more to do with the extent to which they facilitate a change in mindset among the protagonists. Successful change requires parties to shift from seeking each other's destruction to recognizing each other's legitimacy, and searching for ways to coordinate their use of power to satisfy mutual needs and interests (Anstey, 2006a). They begin to see stakes in positive rather than zero-sum terms, accommodative attitudes supplant confrontational ones, and tendencies to violence are diminished in the context of viable conflict management alternatives (Zartman, 2001, pp. 7–16).

Peacekeeping: Creating Conditions for Negotiation

The traditional role of the international peacekeeping forces has been to separate warring parties, protect vulnerable groups, and suspend violence. Longer-term cessation of violence, however, requires attention to the causes of a conflict. The larger purpose of peacekeeping must be to create a context within which protagonists might be brought to the negotiation table to deal with issues dividing them through substantive deals (constitutions, electoral systems, transitional governments, partitions), but also for relationship building (mutual understanding, trust, confidence). In the case of the DRC, following a disastrous start, the mandate of the peacekeeping force of the UN Organization Mission in the Democratic Republic of the Congo (MONUC) was expanded to forcible implementation of the Lusaka cease-fire agreement, monitoring and reporting violations, disarmament, demobilization, repatriation, resettlement, reintegration, and facilitating the transition to credible elections. This redefined their role from passive peacekeeping to active creation of a context within which other dimensions of peacemaking could be attended to and then supporting these processes as they unfolded. In short, peacekeeping had coherence as part of a larger systemic, conflict transformation intervention. Despite this, Autesserre (2008) argues that the intervention fell short, failing to address local conflicts driving national tensions.

In the context of international pressure and support, South Africans chose to manage their transition to democracy internally. This included peacekeeping activities. Political negotiations were founded on changes already well advanced at a civil society level. The churches, businesses, and organized labor brokered a National Peace Accord that extended nationally through a system of peace committees across the country to stabilize relations on a daily basis. These committees comprised civil society leaders who met to negotiate the peaceful management of marches and protests, temper police actions, and mediate police–community disputes and wider community conflicts across racial and other lines. The committees had mixed fortunes across the country but served to reduce violence and manage some dangerous big-march situations. Despite their ideological diversity, business, labor, and the churches worked strongly together at this level following a decade of labor reform in which leaders had learned to negotiate with each other, saw new integrity in one another, and developed trust relations. White business leaders began to take positions against the detention of union leaders, supported political change, sponsored *indabas*, (conferences of decision-makers), participated in peace committees, and met black leaders in and out of the country. Black workers had acquired a decade of experience of democracy and negotiation following labor reforms in 1979. For many, the first vote they cast was for union rather than political leadership; the labor court was their first experience of a court of protection rather than repression; a trade union offered their first experience of a constitution, an accountable leadership, and negotiation. People across identity lines "humanized" one another, and found sufficient common ground and trust to take the process to a higher level. The UN offered support without trying to take over.

Peacekeeping may assume various forms and be integrated into later peacemaking and early peacebuilding initiatives. External intervention may be direct or in the form of sponsorship and support of processes such as South Africa's Peace Accord. One of the benefits of the South African approach was that peacekeeping became also a peacebuilding process as diverse interest groups coordinated their efforts to deliver a peaceful change process.

Peacemaking: Pacting the Redesign of Social Systems

In pacting processes discussed in the introductory chapter, parties redirect adversarial power to negotiation, to solution searches shifting relations from destruct to design mode, and from violent confrontational conflict to regulated competition or coordination. To have prospect in identity conflicts, pacting must resonate with the needs of the various parties for protection, participation, power, privilege, and purpose.

South African pacting centered on the design of systems of political and economic participation. The South African deal was one in which a white minority ceded power in a manner that would see it permanently politically sidelined (as a racially defined grouping); and the black majority demonstrated willingness to extend rights, freedoms, and protections to those who had oppressed them. Power was ceded in a manner that would see a quick transfer of political power, but a far slower one of privilege in terms of land redistribution, and laws intended to phase in black economic empowerment in a manner that would attract new investment and retain existing capital and skills. The objective was to create a rapid growth economy in which there would be opportunity for all. The success of the political transition process has to date been only partially matched in the social and economic spheres (Anstey, 2005). The racial demography of the legislature and the civil service is now representative of the population as a whole, but there is black frustration with the slow pace of economic transformation in the private sector (measured through black ownership of enterprises and the demography of workforces at every level), as well as at universities, within the judiciary, and in sports teams. At the same time, many whites (despite retention of senior positions) feel threatened and alienated in the evolving change process.

Robust debate surrounds the meaning of *nonracialism* in South Africa, particularly whether it is a color-blind or color-bound concept, based on racial proportionalism using the identity categories of an apartheid past. Some argue that while ideally it should be the former, moral redress and political stability require that it be achieved through a period in which policies are driven by the latter. Others counter that this simply lays foundations for entrenching power and privilege on the basis of ascriptive criteria. Many whites (based on generations of privileged access to wealth and education and faced with the reality of their minority status) would now prefer a competency-based nonracialism; many blacks (driven by past racial injustices, new opportunities, and a sense of justice based on racial majoritarianism) prefer a route of racial proportionalism. In short, identity has utility depending on where one is located in a system, who has the power to define membership of which groups, and which groups matter. South Africa, as a consequence, faces many dilemmas in its ongoing change process, even though few pine for the apartheid past. A rapidly demographically transformed civil service is struggling with social delivery to an electorate that feels shortchanged by the pace of delivery of quality housing, water, electrification, education, and health and welfare services (despite huge improvements in spending in these areas). New political conflicts are arising in this context. The implications of retaining or denying ethnic categories for reconciliation are further explored later in this chapter.

On a political level, several dimensions of pacting are critical. In the first instance, repressive regimes must find the courage to liberate political prisoners and permit free political activity, removing restrictions on free association, assembly, movement, and the media. This requires a massive leap of faith, and can only really be taken if victims of repression promise not to reciprocate once in power. In short, consent to relinquish power is contingent. If the parties can move into this zone of exchange, they can focus on creating a transitional or interim government. The design of a new political system is important for purposes of stabilizing relations into the future. If this can be achieved, then the parties can turn their energies to the design of a future government and the form of electoral system appropriate to accommodate the needs and interests of its various identity groups. The design of an electoral system is critical to future peace. Identity groups must feel that their interests are equitably represented in the new system.

Lesotho's first-past-the-post system aggravated conflicts between parties, and it has struggled to design a system to manage internal differences (Matlose and Sello, 2005). Protections under South Africa's interim constitution, and its list system of proportional representation, gave political actors sufficient confidence to institute democracy in 1994. The design of political/electoral systems is key to managing identity conflicts. Successful political outcomes rest on whether the design of a system offers the variety of identity groups sufficient confidence of protection, participation, and representation in the future. Power-sharing deals in Kenya and Zimbabwe may not have made Raila Odingwa or Morgan Tsvangirai feel less cheated of electoral victory, but opportunities to create internal influence clearly outweighed the prospect of constantly fighting from without.

In the DRC, Masire stuck doggedly to creating a multiparty process involving large and small parties, regardless of their use of violence. He recognized the complexities created but felt participation to be critical to the credibility of the process, to holding the process together, keeping communications open, understanding the range of needs and interests in play, and designing a viable intervention strategy. Multiparty participation, of course, does not mean shared commitment to either the use of the negotiation process or its outcomes. Some may be there to push through a deal, others simply to monitor the actions of others, or to spoil the process or delay an outcome—pacting is often a multimotive reality (Anstey, 2006a, pp. 47–48). As evidenced in the Rhodesian settlement in 1979, external parties often play a vital role in pressuring internal negotiators to remain involved in the process (Anstey, 2007; Zartman, 1985).

Inclusiveness may be difficult to achieve. About 250 actors were involved in the Darfur talks in Abuja and over 1,000 in the Somalia talks (Adebajo, 2006)! As talks progress, existing groups may split (as in the case of the Sudan Liberation Army), initial alliances may break down (as in the case of rebel militias in the DRC), and new alliances may emerge. Complexity increases with the number of international observer missions and nongovernmental organizations seeking participation (sometimes competitively). Complexities arise if external agencies "assist" by brokering side deals between some of the parties, especially when these are at the expense of others at the table, as happened in the DRC process (Masire, 2006). Competition to be the mediator or key peace institution reflects more on the agendas of agencies offering assistance than on the needs of the parties directly involved. Single agencies or facilitators may lack the influence, capacity, information, or contacts to conduct complex multitrack processes alone. This means that partnerships, allegiances, and collaboration with regional bodies and secondary parties with influence and interests becomes critical; the challenge is how best to manage their inputs in the interests of the parties involved. Effective pacting, then, may require coordination of external interventionists over and above those of the protagonists in a conflict.

It is important to give structure to process. Masire structured talks on the DRC through five commissions—defense and security, political and constitutional, economic and finance, social and cultural, peace and reconciliation. Progress was uneven. Although good progress was achieved in the latter three, with 36 clear joint resolutions, the process stalled in the first two commissions. Preserving his role as facilitator, Masire asked President Mbeki to make proposals on participation by interest groups in an interim government, later assisted by a special envoy appointed by Kofi Annan. Kabila remained head of state of an interim government and commander-in-chief of the army, assisted by four vice presidents from the main opposition groups (armed and nonarmed); a formula was agreed to on the distribution of ministerial posts as well as the distribution of seats in an interim legislature. An independent electoral commission, human rights observer body, media authority, truth and reconciliation commission, and anticorruption commission were established. The number of provinces in the country was increased from 11 to 25, more accurately reflecting its ethnic diversity. This was a very complex design process indeed (Anstey, 2006a).

Military pacting requires that militias and armed forces cease hostilities. Then guarantees are needed from government forces and militias that they will not resort to violence to force change and that each has the necessary degree of internal control to ensure that spoiler elements will not sabotage peace deals at critical moments. Government forces long used as agents of repression may face the prospect of being held to account for human rights abuses or crimes against humanity; incentives for laying down arms in the form of conditional amnesties may be needed to convince them not to pursue war. The supervision of armed forces by external forces such as UN peacekeepers, or by internal bodies of civilians, may be considered. In the DRC, UN peacekeepers remained after election of the new government, giving assistance to efforts to bring to heel militias operating in the east of the country.

Finally, pacting is required at social and economic levels (Anstey 2004). Sustainable democracies are premised on development and economic growth. This requires that parties participate in the design of policies that will attract investment, retain and develop skills in the workforce, offer the prospect of decent work and returns on labor, and ensure that foreign aid will not be corrupted. This is a tricky area in developing economies where international investors are often seeking low-cost, high-return business environments and voters are pushing their governments for increased returns on their labor and protections. In South Africa, business, government, the shadow government, and organized labor initiated a National Economic Forum (NEF) to consult on economic policy in the lead-up to 1994 in an effort to stabilize the economy, offer hope to one another, and limit disruptive protest actions. One of the first acts of the new government after 1994 was to create the National Economic Development and Labor Council (NEDLAC), through which the parties are meant to consult on all social and economic policy and labor laws. This preserved a high level of social dialogue and civil society participation in South Africa's democratic dispensation in its early years.

A large range of interventive opportunities arises within such pacting processes—assisting with electoral design, facilitating the establishment of interim governments, assisting the development of effective police and military forces focused on national rather than party interests, and offering advice and resources to stabilize and grow national economies.

Elections

Elections regulate political contests within a state. They are the gateway to democracy. They are also high-risk events for those in power and those seeking it. Violent conflict is more likely when dominant groups are at risk of losing power and aspirant groups are close to attaining it (Zimbabwe from 2000 with the rise of the Movement for Democratic Change (MDC); Kenya in 2008). With this in mind, the new wave of conflicts across Africa may reflect a strengthening of democracy, with more resilient opposition groups and more strongly contested elections. Dominant groups are tempted to rig narrowly lost elections because the fear of losing them is high and because only a small fiddle is required to change a result. Opposition is repressed because of its strength rather than its weakness. In Zimbabwe's 2008 elections, Mugabe accepted MDC victory in the lower house, but the government-controlled electoral commission refused to release the results of the presidential poll. Armed police blocked opposition lawyers seeking an interdict for their publication from entering the court to do so, and "war veterans" mobilized in support of Mugabe. Eventually, following a recount, a result was released showing Tsvangirai had won—though not with a clear majority, thus requiring a run-off. The MDC claimed the theft of an election it had clearly won and stated that an opportunity had been provided for Mugabe to manipulate the final outcome. It eventually stopped campaigning in the context of rising violence and made a power-sharing deal with Mugabe.

External interventions traditionally take the form of observer and monitoring missions to facilitate free and fair elections, reduce the potential for rigging, and confirm the legitimacy of governments. Such missions may carry international or national status or come from civil society bodies. In extreme situations, external armed forces may assume the role of protecting voters in high-conflict scenarios (as in Iraq). Other forms of intervention include information sharing, education, and training on electoral administration and conflict management, as offered by bodies such the Electoral Institute of Southern Africa (EISA). The Mugabe regime refused accreditation to any observer missions or media coverage it considered hostile to its cause.

Election monitoring and support can be an extraordinarily complex logistical process. In the DRC, over 9,700 candidates stood for parliamentary elections across 11 provincial centers, 64 liaison offices, and 50,000 voting stations, involving over 200,000 electoral staff and 45,000 police. A total of 15,500 UN peacekeepers, 520 UN military observers, 324 civilian police, and 2,493 civilian support staff facilitated the elections. Many voting stations were located in remote areas devoid of road systems. Despite some unrest in the lead-up to elections it was an amazingly peaceful process, with a short skirmish between supporters of Kabila and Bemba quickly terminated (Anstey, 2006a, pp. 52–54). However, Autesserre (2008) argues that all was not what it seemed. The election itself may have been peaceful but electioneering fueled ethnic hatreds, and the process failed to offer some groups the security they needed to accept the outcomes, giving rise to a continuation of conflicts in the east of the country.

Consolidating Democracies: Building Sustainable Economies

Getting to democracy is one thing; institutionalizing it is another (Bova 1997; Diamond 1996; Schmitter and Lynn 1991; Huntington 1991; van de Walle 2001). Effective earlier pacts should diminish the potential for contest, but, of course, losers may immediately question the design of the system and demand its redesign. If elections have been free and fair, the legitimacy of the government is not in question even though a redesign exercise may be embarked on for future rounds.

Strong states are characterized by full control of their territory, the capacity to deliver high-quality political goods to all their citizens, competent legislatures and law enforcement systems, and efficient revenue collection to enable these outcomes. They perform well on human development and freedom indicators. Failed states, on the other hand, are unable to protect their citizens from violence, or guarantee rights at a domestic or international level, or maintain viable democratic institutions. They are often guilty of attacks on their own citizens as a dominant identity group secures control of state goods for its own interests and seeks exclusion of others (Chomsky, 2006; Herbst, 2000; Rotberg, 2002). State building, according to Fukuyama (2004, p. 2), is the major challenge in modern politics. Effective states direct their energies toward ends regarded as legitimate by all their citizens, are accountable, govern constitutionally, collect revenues effectively, and deliver protection and services to all citizens.

In weak and failed states, this capacity is missing. Once a government can only deliver protection and other services to a privileged elite, cannot protect its citizens from one another, and represses groups of its own citizens, it is in crisis. Opposition groups mobilize against the government, and often seek or are offered support by external governments or forces in destabilizing the regime further. Such groups may lack the capacity to govern, but they can make a nation ungovernable.

An election may briefly accredit the legitimacy of a government, but if it cannot effectively broadcast power, collect revenues, or deliver political goods, it is soon in trouble. African governments face a crisis of capacity, making it difficult to build a sense of national identity, a culture of constitutionalism, or a rule of law. Mobilization under identity markers can be expected if particular regions, tribes, or religious groups feel themselves discriminated against. In cleaved societies with scarce resources, a government may seek to protect itself first by providing opportunities to identity groups that support it—reinforcing ethnic, religious, or class divides.

External intervention at this stage, then, is about nation building and democratic consolidation. For all the investment of resources in the DRC's elections, its conflicts continue. Over 2 million have died since the signing of the 2003 peace accord, largely from malnutrition and disease in the context of postwar economic and infrastructural collapse. Investment of resources in deals at the national and provincial levels has not been matched by attention to contests between ethnic groups over land and power at local levels as root causes of the ongoing problem. The electoral process, Autesserre argues, "fueled ethnic hatred and marginalized ethnic minorities, making the emergence of armed movements all the more likely" (2008, p. 95). Autesserre suggests a conflict-generating symbiosis to have been generated, with local leaders enlisting support from national leaders by framing their conflicts within the dynamics driving the national discourse (ideology, ethnicity, religion, class) and national leaders pandering to local leaders for resources they need to pursue their own ends (p. 101). She states that the electoral process was marred by intimidation and hate speech, fueling ethnic tensions and leaving Tutsi exiles without representation. Fears of ethnic cleansing promoted General Laurent Nkunda's popularity and renewed fighting in the eastern Congo. With the government unable to extend the rule of law to the region to offer protection to citizens, militias have filled the vacuum. Lacking coherent leadership and structure, these militias fight among themselves. In short, Autesserre (2008) argues that the failure of the UN process to attend to conflicts such as land issues through institution building at a local level (such as courts) has served to perpetuate ethnic tensions.

If governments are unable to effectively broadcast power, local militias fill the space. Weak governments may seek to defeat them, or to secure their allegiance through reward systems, as the DRC and Sudanese regimes have done. But it is a high-risk game, with some militias moving beyond government control and perpetuating rather than diminishing conflicts. In the DRC, militias drive local conflicts even as national deals are done, feeding off the fear of local groups of ethnic cleansing and the space afforded by the inability of the government to broadcast power in the area.

Reconciliation

Peacekeeping, facilitating political system design, assisting elections, and brokering pacts to sustain peaceful change are complex activities, but they may be insufficient to prevent further violence. Some conflicts seem perpetual. History becomes the future. Reconciliation between warring groups, and between perpetrators of violence and their victims, becomes key to breaking cycles of violence. But there remains uncertainty about how best to achieve this, who should do it, how to frame the issues, and whether it is a matter for negotiation or counseling. This level of exchange often involves deep personal and community pain. What is required is less the expertise of political or judicial design and more the capacity to facilitate personal and group healing at the level of communities.

South Africans tried to deal with this dimension of the transformation process through a Truth and Reconciliation Commission (TRC). Offering a middle road between criminal trials for apartheid atrocities and total amnesty, it diluted resistance to change by the armed forces. Amnesty was offered for politically motivated acts, provided that perpetrators "came clean" in public hearings. The TRC offered victims catharsis and perpetrators the opportunity to confess and atone. The hope was that truth would emerge and that the forums would create a climate of forgiveness and reconciliation. In often emotionally wracking processes over 20,000 people testified, including 8,000 perpetrators. The results were mixed. Leaders of the apartheid government were experienced variously—as openly hostile (P. W. Botha), as offering a technical truth without genuine remorse (F. W. de Klerk), or as honest and penitent (Leon Wessels). The African National Congress (ANC) resisted airing of its own human rights abuses in camps of exiles. Leaders sought to exonerate themselves by pleading ignorance of the actions of foot soldiers, foot soldiers by pleading that they were following orders. The TRC struggled with identity and jurisdictional issues (Slabbert, 2000), and at least one analyst felt that by 2001, the process had "degenerated into a game of racial name-calling" rather than one of reconciliation (Mangcu, 2003).

The work of the TRC was an extraordinary process, but there was perhaps some naiveté about the nature of reconciliation. As a transformative process, reconciliation requires deep emotional and cognitive changes (Mayer, 2000). There is no doubt that the TRC revealed truths about apartheid atrocities and provided an opportunity for public expression of the pain it caused. There is doubt over the extent to which it produced reconciliation in the sense of deep changes in relations. Boraine (2000), who cochaired the hearings, concluded that reconciliation was less about achieving perfect harmony between peoples and more about restorating relations to a point where they could move on in peace while accepting each other's dignity in a climate of trust. Reconciliation in South Africa will be a long-term process requiring far more than one-time confessions of actions in the past, moments of forgiveness, or reparation payments. The TRC is perhaps best understood as having facilitated the political change process, regulated conflict at a critical period, and initiated rather than concluded a social transformation process. South Africans still struggle to find one another across racial divides. The ANC in government has retained the racial classifications of apartheid in legislation intended to bring about redress (on employment equity, affirmative action, and black economic empowerment). A very live debate concerns whether this strategy entrenches categories of the past in a new era of ascriptive entitlement trapping the population in the very racial conflicts it is trying to move away from. Is the "unity in diversity" dream feasible?

Rwandans have made different decisions about reconciliation. Their dilemmas of justice and reconciliation are captured in Clark and Kaufman's (2008) book *After Genocide*. The widespread involvement of the population complicated the design and implementation of a system to bring perpetrators of the 1994 genocide to justice. In the belief that accountability would destabilize the building of an inclusive democracy, successive Rwandan governments from 1959 granted amnesty to those involved in pogroms, creating a culture of impunity (Ngoga, 2008; Schabas, 2008). The Kagame regime was adamant after the 1994 genocide that perpetrators be held to account.

Having failed to respond to the genocide in process, in November 1994 the UN passed Resolution 955 setting up an International Criminal Tribunal for Rwanda

(ICTR). The Rwandan government was unhappy over its location outside the country, the involvement of some suspected of supporting genocidaires, and the fact that it would not pass capital sentences. It has been successful in confirming the genocide (negating denialists and revisionists), in the trials of some key leaders, and in establishing principles of leadership accountability, but its location outside Rwanda removed justice from the community in which the crimes were committed, negating reconciliation, and its processes have been slow, expensive, and blighted by corruption and by confused administration and jurisdiction (Ngoga, 2008).

In 1996 Kagame's government passed the Organic Law to deal with the tens of thousands of persons accused of committing genocide. It provided four categories according to severity of crimes, separating out those who planned and organized, incited, or supervised genocidal acts from those who carried out such acts, killed unintentionally, or caused damage to property. A plea bargaining system was introduced to induce confessions in exchange for lesser sentences. After the first trials in the genocidal courts 22 persons were publicly executed, but no further death sentences were carried out, and in 2007 capital punishment was abolished. By 1997, 120,000 accused persons were awaiting trial in Rwanda's prisons (Steward, 2008), but by 2006 only 10,000 had been tried. It was estimated that the process might take 80–200 years. Changing its approach, the government passed the gacaca law in January 2001, assigning judicial powers to communally elected judges and involving communities in hearings. The intention was to expedite hearings and promote reconciliation. Schabas (2008) notes, however, that an unexpected outcome of the process was that it became clear that the number involved in the genocide might be closer to 1 million than the 100,000 first estimated (up to a third of the adult population). In 2003 the government passed a law making it a serious criminal offense to negate the fact that genocide occurred or to attempt to minimize it. Unlike the South African approach, it has also outlawed reference to ethnicity (the crime of divisionism). A divide exists between those who think that ethnic tensions should be brought to the surface and dealt with openly and those who believe that this simply reinforces cleavages that led to the genocide, and possibly to another one (Buckley-Zistel, 2008; Hintjens, 2008; Lemarchand, 2008; Sezibera, 2008; van Eck, 2008).

Designing a system of justice and reconciliation in a context in which up to a third of the adult population might stand accused of genocidal acts was always going to be difficult. The creativity and reconciliatory promise of the gacaca system, some argue, is threatened by the policy of ethnic denialism. It conceals a system in which Tutsi have assumed control of all key positions in government and a drift to authoritarianism. It is also argued that it seals a picture of the genocide as one in which Hutus were perpetrators and Tutsi victims, closing down memory of several hundreds of thousands of Hutus as victims during the genocide and its aftermath in the DRC (French, 2005; Hintjens, 2008).

In light of the very active identity-based mobilization that led to the genocide and the understanding that the victims of "race killing" were Tutsi, Hintjens (2008) asks how new forms of political identity that facilitate reconciliation might be created. There are concerns that the gacaca courts will be unable to facilitate reconciliation in light of the government's policy of denying ethnicity, which in effect denies Hutus identity as survivors and casualties, leaving them simply grouped as perpetrators or genocidaires (Buckley-Zistel, 2008; Hintjens, 2008; Lemarchand, 2008). Ethnic denialism purports to create a new, unified Rwandan identity beyond ethnic groups, but it has been introduced and enforced in a particular context and with particular effects. Far from ending a culture of impunity, Hintjens (2008) suggests that the Kagame regime has in effect given itself amnesty from atrocities by the RPA in 1994 and beyond. Because the Hutus have not been officially counted as either victims or survivors, their pain is not openly expressed. Race terms are banned in public discourse. People are increasingly categorized by their presumed rather than actual roles in the genocide. Their concern is that, within this context, the minority Tutsi have taken control of the government and, through sleight of hand, have created a system in which the Hutu, as a group, are now denied expression. Power is retained in the hands of a particular ethnic group under different nomenclature, as victims of the other now excluded group. Under the banner of closing down divisionalism, an authoritarian state has emerged with Tutsi now in control of government—disguised by the fact that it may not be named. Lemarchand (2008, p. 66) raises other concerns, arguing that Rwandan policy allows the government to ban organized opposition and legislate ethnic identity out of existence.

So, is reconciliation between identity groups best managed through open discourse or denialism? Will outlawing reference to ethnicity facilitate reconciliation and produce a new common political identity? Outlawing reference to ethnic identity does not end it—as Soviet leaders discovered during 70 years of repressive effort to eliminate ethnic, religious, and regional identities. Its reality is too embedded in the lives of citizens. Ethnic differences remain. In gacaca courts the accused are largely Hutu, the accusers Tutsi. Ethnicity might not be named, but if transformation of government is perceived to take the form of Tutsis replacing Hutus, perceptions of ethnic discrimination will form regardless of legal proscription. Buckley-Zistel (2008) argues that different groups have different memories of a long past of ethnic violence and pogroms. Tutsi casualties are openly commemorated (although now not ethnically identified), but the Hutu feel denied, wanting all suffering expressed. There is a chosen amnesia about past conflicts in a memory of a harmonious past (despite previous pogroms). People "pretend peace" for purposes of social equilibrium and pragmatism.

However, at the gacaca courts, survivors of the genocide fear elimination as witnesses; Hutus fear unjust processes and outcomes. Processes can also be used for ulterior motives. Identifying someone as a perpetrator "has become a convenient way of getting rid of personal enemies and competitors" (Buckley-Zistel, 2008, p. 137). Rwandans across ethnic groups live together and must find ways to manage the issues of anger, trust, resentment, and fear in the aftermath of the genocide. Ethnic cleavages and intergroup resentments of the past remain current despite the law, and unexpressed and unresolved tensions could become violent again. Denial of identity does not create room for groups to negotiate or work through their sense of difference, or their associated fears or anger. People carry memories and organize information to explain their past. As Buckley-Zistel (2008) points out, narratives are useful to establish collective identities of those who share an interpretation of the past. People are created by, and create, their past by the way they refer to it. In this way, memory shapes the future.

Reconciliation requires that the past be confronted, not denied; that diverse groups wrestle with issues of accommodation, mutual tolerance, and national identity while retaining their ethnic identity. Because the politics of memory is a social product and subject to distortion, its management is critical to reconciliation. The past is experienced through different ethnic lenses with different constructions of the same reality. Tutsis were overwhelmingly victims in the genocide of 1994, but carried out atrocities and mass killings of their own in the aftermath. Hutus were perpetrators of the genocide, and were victims of its aftermath in Rwanda and the eastern Congo during 1996 and 1997. It is important that each group's memories find expression in exchanges across groups to enable distortions to be remedied, deeper intergroup understanding developed, and the evolution of critical memory based on accounts from across the board. Competition exists within memories over the extent of the killing, the degree to which it was planned, how it was triggered, and the identity of killers and victims. Lemarchand (2008) argues that the memory of the work of moderate Hutus and those who risked their lives or died trying to save Tutsis, or because they were married to Tutsis, is thwarted in denial. He also suggests some selective memory on the part of Kagame, who, he suggests, played a major part not only in stopping the genocide but also in triggering it through the possible shooting down of President Habyirimana's plane following the Tanzania peace deal and his invasion of the country. Kagame (2008) rejects his views.

Reconciliation is facilitated if diverse ethnic groups commit to larger goals of nation building, creating a common unifying national identity, and developing systems of accommodation based on mutual respect for each other's cultures. The question raised by analysts is whether such a commitment can emerge if the memories of one group are denied; whether the identity of victim has been "captured" by one group (the Tutsis) while denying this to the other (Hutus). If history is written simply with Tutsis as victims and Hutu as perpetrators, the identity of Hutu as victims is erased from history. It is an echo of Slabbert's *The Other Side of History* (*2006*), where he suggests that the contribution of whites in South Africa's transition to democracy is being progressively erased from history—and from memory. If particular identity groups usurp control of memories by obliging "official" accounts of genocide, by excluding the memories of their own atrocities, or by erasing the contributions of moderates and heroes among those from other groups, a dangerous situation arises. Open exchange of memories between ethnic groups is closed down, and one group's memories prevail at the expense of others' for purposes of political domination. By law, the genocide may not be negated or minimized. It should, of course, not be negated or minimized, but it should be accurately and fully identified, named, and understood. Its temporal history and context require unraveling. The misery, fears, loss, and mourning of all Rwandans should find expression. In short, some analysts fear that the Rwandan genocide has been "hijacked," that its memory is already being distorted, and that Rwandan society as a whole is being denied expression.

A victim identity offers ethnic groups political space and leverage. Once a history (the official memory) is entrenched in a particular form, it shapes the future of internal social systems and the perceptions and behavior of external actors. If one group dominates the shaping of this history, it is given space to exclude its own atrocities from memory, to exonerate itself as it assigns all guilt to others, and to pass laws that close down political and civil liberties (such as declaring an ethnic identity) or political opposition while declaring these actions necessary as part of a larger commitment "that genocide must never be allowed to happen again." The genocide of Tutsis is not denied by allowing Hutus expression as victims in their own right; the memories of the horror do not belong only to Tutsis. Hutus need identity not only as genocidaires but also as victims, moderates, and heroes; the atrocities of the RPA should not be expurgated from history; the role of its leaders in provoking as well as stopping the genocide should be recorded; laws against denialism, revisionism, and divisionism should not be used to close down political opposition, freedom of expression, or the identity of ethnic groups. The argument of Lemarchand (2008) and others is that what is needed is neither a rekindling of ethnic hatreds nor a denial of ethnicity in the mix of the horror, but a more complex identification of the systems and conditions that generated them and then a sharing of suffering, blame, and victimhood. Reconciliation, Lemarchand argues, cannot come through imposed memory purged of ethnic references and dislocated from reality while setting in concrete the good guys and bad guys of history, nor through a compulsive rehashing of one's own memories that is subject to distortion and carries the risk of entrenching ethnic hatreds. A process of memory sharing allows for reframing, new insight, empathy, and integration in a process he terms "critical memory."

So, there remain unresolved questions concerning how to achieve common truth and reconciliation among actors in deep identity-based conflicts, and especially so in genocides. The challenges of mediating memories toward reconciliation rather than entrenched hatreds are huge. Peace perhaps can only be pretended to exist for so long. Problems exist with all approaches, but policies that seek to deny ethnic identity close down rather than facilitate reconciliation.

■ CONCLUSIONS

Identity conflicts are notoriously difficult to resolve. Identity through cause, culture, ethnicity, race, or religion serves core human needs for protection, participation, privilege, power, and purpose. In itself, difference may generate neither ethnic hatred nor violent conflict. It can become dangerous in particular contexts—in conditions of scarcity generally, but particularly when a few identity groups are in contest over scarce resources, or where groups perceive injustice in the distribution of power and privilege based on their identity. Leaders mobilizing mass movements find conditions helpful in periods of national economic and political crisis, in the context of weak states and a sense of national despair. Polarization is facilitated if there is a particular identity group that can be blamed for the crisis or identified as threatening the existence of other groups (Tutsi "cockroaches," white "neocolonial" farmers, foreigners "stealing our jobs"). Identity under ethnic or religious markers, once assumed, is a powerful force producing self-reinforcing pressures for belonging, conformity, and certain leadership styles. It has utility in offering individuals collective power as a means of meeting core human needs and interests. There is unresolved debate as to whether conflict is highest where identity groups are poorly integrated and live separately, or whether close proximity serves to aggravate differences and tensions.

Many identity conflicts are expressed in and may be managed in other terms—economic, territorial, political design. These indeed offer a route to attenuating or resolving conflicts between groups feeling threatened by others. To be effective, however, external interventions must find processes and outcomes that have resonance with the needs and interests of parties that inform the conflict and drive mobilization under ethnic or other identity markers. A range of options is available to parties in a conflict expressed in identity terms—subjection, cooperation, or separation and their subforms. These are interactive in character; groups make choices in relation to one another in the context of their situations and their perceptions of what represents the best alternative to protect or preserve their interests. Where such choices are not congruent, conflict occurs.

External interventions to facilitate negotiations may take a variety of forms, and may be conducted by a range of parties individually or in concert with each other. Most credibility lies with external agents invited by protagonists to assist them, but this is no guarantee of easy progress in mixed-motive scenarios. Interventions by bodies such as the UN have legitimacy but are often slow as they struggle to deal with problems of consensus, capacity, and commitment. If interventions are to be meaningful beyond quick "in and out" peacekeeping or mediations, what is needed is a more holistic approach in the transformation process in which not only is violence ended and deals brokered but a profound shift in attitudes and behavior takes place. The use of power to destroy must be redirected into projects of joint system and reconciliation. Such interventions are often long-term, complex, and expensive, as reflected in the UN's continued presence in the DRC after elections and the detailed implementation schedule of the South Sudan Comprehensive Peace Agreement through 2011 (Adebajo, 2006).

Effective mediation in identity conflicts requires timing (in terms of ripeness) and credible third parties (either invited or imposed), and brings an end not only to immediate violence but also to the situations in which it is rooted (conditions and attitudes). It requires sensitivity to the needs, fears, and interests of the parties involved and their reasons for mobilizing under identity markers. At one level the intervention is one of design, assisting parties to design immediate systems of peacekeeping and sustainable conflict management systems for the longer term; then assisting them to use their energies in the design of workable forms of interim government, constitutions, electoral systems, and systems of restorative justice that all parties are prepared to live with; then elections are often required. If new systems are to be sustainable in the long term, support is usually required—the presence of peacekeepers, external experts to assist with integration of warring militia, the development of an economic policy likely to attract investors and ensure growth and redistribution, the development of a culture of constitutionalism and a rule of law, and facilitation of reconciliation at the grassroots level. In short, identity conflicts require well-coordinated multitrack interventions if they are to succeed. Identity is an important feature of many internal conflicts but seldom the only one. As conflicts endure and escalate through time, causes become confused with expression—groups mobilize, create identities, splinter, forget origins of disputes but fight over last week's attacks, become more motivated by the desire to punish or avenge recent activities by the other, and weave current differences into the myths of more long-standing ones. The new becomes the old; the old is renewed.

Peace agreements often fail in implementation. They require sound action plans, responsibilities, resourcing, and deadlines, accountability by parties to the process to delivering on agreements, and the capacity to do so. Implementation issues are part of the peacemaking agenda. Processes can be abused by actors to reestablish themselves, stall progress, or undermine arrangements, as in Darfur, where the government was arguably happy to accept an inadequate AU presence that gave it legitimacy but applied few behavioral brakes.

External interventions to facilitate political peacemaking may assume many forms: mediation between conflicting parties, peacekeeping support, pressure on parties to make peace, sharing of expertise, or consolidation support. A policy seminar conducted under UN auspices in Cape Town aimed at informing the establishment of Mediation Support Units internationally proposed 10 recommendations for UN decision makers, the AU, and other players involved in African conflicts, including strengthening capacity through training, improved gender representivity, mediation support units, improved coordination, development of cadres of mediation support persons with regional expertise, and strengthening of transitional justice systems (Adebajo, 2006). A long-term vision and support are required for external interventions if they are to have nation-building value. In implementation, they need to be well structured, resourced, and coordinated across the many dimensions of a conflict, as discussed further in the concluding chapter of this volume.

Achieving peace agreements is difficult, but it is easier than implementing them. Adebajo (2006) proposes that they contain detailed implementation plans, mechanisms, and schedules enabling a seamless rollout from the negotiation table. They should be detailed and inclusive, address root causes of conflicts, ensure that parties are representative and trustworthy, have a win-win element to optimize the prospects of success, build in continuous dispute resolution systems to overcome problems of implementation, and be scheduled with deadlines and accountability for delivery. Beyond this, it is critical that issues of reconciliation are properly addressed; political solutions are always at risk if they are disconnected from the shape of relations at the level of civil society.

Notes

1. The UNCHR estimates that there are 10 million refugees and 33 million "persons of concern" globally.

2. Leaders of the ilk of Lenin, Hitler, and Mussolini used moments of national despair to mobilize "new identity" groups, conferring on certain groups identities other than those traditionally adhered to. To belong to other identity groups or to provoke internal dissent

was dangerous. Equally, however, also in the context of deeply cleaved societies, the likes of Nelson Mandela, Mahatma Ghandi, and Tito, in concert with leaders of other groups at particular points in time, managed to move internal identity groups to larger national identity groupings and develop a sense of unity for causes beyond immediate differences. Such larger identities appear fragile once such leaders depart from positions of power, however, with lesser (or perhaps self-interested) persons retreating into the easier leadership role of mobilizing sections of societies against others or favoring some above others.

3. Rothchild (1986) presents nine categories short of genocide, similarly arrayed: subjection, isolation, assimilation, avoidance, displacement, buffering, protection, redistribution, and sharing.

References

Abedajo, A. (Ed.). (2006). *United Nations mediation experience in Africa*. Cape Town: Centre for Conflict Resolution.

Anstey, M. (2004). African renaissance—Implications for labour relations in Africa. *South African Journal of Labour Relations, 28*(1), 34–82.

Anstey, M. (2005). *Social Transformation in South Africa: Workplace Tensions and Interventions*. Paper presented at the 13th International Conference on Conflict Resolution, St Petersburg, Russia.

Anstey, M. (2006a). Can a fledgling democracy take flight in the Democratic Republic of the Congo? *African Journal of Conflict Resolution, 6*(2), 35–68.

Anstey, M. (2006b). *Managing change, negotiating conflict*. Cape Town, South Africa, Juta.

Anstey, M. (2007). Zimbabwe in ruins: Prospects of mediation in a conflict not yet ripe for resolution. *International Negotiation, 12*(3), 415–442.

Anstey, M. (2011). Change in the Middle East: mixed, muted and muddled. *PINpoints, 36*, 27–32.

Arnson, C. & Zartman, I. W. (Ed.). (2005). *Rethinking the Economics of War: The Intersection of Need, Creed and Greed*. Baltimore: Johns Hopkins University Press.

Autesserre, S. (2008, May/June). The trouble with Congo: How local disputes fuel regional conflict. *Foreign Affairs*, 94–100.

Boraine, A. (2000). The language of potential. In W. James & L. van der Vijver (Eds.), *After the TRC: Reflections on truth and reconciliation in South Africa* (pp. 73–81). Cape Town: David Philip Publishers.

Bova, R. (1997). Democracy and liberty: The cultural connection. *Journal of Democracy, 8*(1), 112–126.

Buckley-Zistel, S. (2008). We are pretending peace: Local memory and the absence of social transformation and reconciliation in Rwanda. In P. Clark & Z. D. Kaufman (Eds.), *After genocide* (pp. 125–144). London: Hurst & Co.

Chomsky, N. (2006). *Failed states*. Crows Nest, New South Wales, Australia: Allen & Unwin.

Clark, P., & Kaufman, Z. D. (Eds.). (2008). *After genocide*. London: Hurst & Co.

Collier, P. (1998). *Some fundamental relationships in ethnic conflict*. Prepared for South African consultation on the "Nexus between Economic Management and the Restoration of Social Capital in Southern Africa" cosponsored by the World Bank's Post-Conflict Unit and the Centre for Conflict Resolution (SA) with funding from the Swiss Agency for Development and Cooperation.

Coser, L. (1956). *The functions of social conflict*. New York: Free Press.

Diamond, L. (1996). Is the third wave over? *Journal of Democracy, 7*(3), 20–37.

Ferguson, N. (2004). *Colossus: The price of America's empire*. New York: Free Press.

French, H. W. (2005). *A continent for the taking: The tragedy and hope of Africa*. New York: Vintage Books.

Fromkin, D. (2001). *A peace to end all peace*. New York: Owl Books.

Fukuyama, F. (2004). *State building: Governance and world order in the twenty-first century*. London: Profile Books.

Goodin, R. E. (1995). Politics. In R. E. Goodin & P. Pettit (Eds.), *A companion to contemporary political philosophy* (pp. 157–182). London: Basil Blackwell.

Gress, D. (1998). *From Plato to NATO.: the idea of the West and its opponents*. New York: Free Press.

Hanf, T. (1989). The prospects of accommodation in communal conflicts. In H. Giliomee & L. Schlemmer (Eds.), *Negotiating South Africa's future* (pp. 89–113). Johannesburg: Southern Book Publishers.

Herbst, J. (2000). *States and power in Africa*. Princeton, NJ: Princeton University Press.

Hintjens, H. (2008). Reconstructing political identities in Rwanda. In P. Clark & Z. D. Kaufman (Eds.), *After genocide* (pp. 77–99). London: Hurst & Co.

Hobsbawm, E. (1994). *Age of Extremes: The Short Twentieth Century History 1914–1991*. London: Abacus.

Huntington, S. P. (1991). *The third wave: Democratization in the late twentieth century*. Norman: University of Oklahoma Press.

Huntington, S. P. (1996). Democracy for the long haul. *Journal of Democracy, 7*(2), 3–13.

Huntington, S. P. (1998). *The clash of civilizations and the remaking of world order*. London: Touchstone books.

Kaarsholm, P. (Ed.). (2006). *Violence, political culture and development in Africa*. Scottsville, AZ: Pietermaritzburg, University of Kwazulu-Natal Press.

Kagame, P. (2008). Preface. In Clark P. & Kaufman Z. D. (eds). After Genocide. London: Hurst and Co.

Laitin, D. D. (2006). *Nations, states and violence*. Oxford: Oxford University Press.

Lemarchand, R. (2008). The politics of memory in post-genocide Rwanda. In P. Clark & Z. D. Kaufman (Eds.), *After genocide* (pp. 65–76). London: Hurst & Co.

Mangcu, X. (2003). The state of race relations in post-apartheid South Africa. In J. Daniel, A. Habib, & R. Southall (Eds.), *State of the nation: South Africa 2003–2004* (pp. 105–117). Cape Town: HSRC Press.

Mapondera, J. (2006). Track one and half diplomacy and the complementarity of tracks. *Culture of Peace Online Journal, 2*(1), 66–81.

Masire, Q. K. J. (2006). *Very brave or very foolish? Memoirs of an African democrat*. Gaborone: Macmillan.

Matlosa, K. and Sello, C. (2005). 'Political Parties and Democratisation in Lesotho', EISA Research Report No. 23, Johannesburg, SA.

Mayer, B. (2000). *The dynamics of conflict resolution*. San Francisco: Jossey Bass.

Muller, J. (2008). Us and them: The enduring power of ethnic nationalism. *Foreign Affairs, 87*(2), 18–35.

Nathan, L. (1996, September). Analyse, empower, accommodate. *Track Two*, 4–6.

Nathan, L. (1999, November). When push comes to a shove: The failure of international mediation in African civil wars. *Track Two*, 1–25.

Ngoga, M. (2008). The institutionalization of impunity: A judicial perspective of the Rwanda genocide. In P. Clark & Z. D. Kaufman (Eds.), *After genocide* (pp. 321–332). London: Hurst & Co.

O'Donnell G, Schmitter P and Whitehead L. (1986). *Transitions from authoritarian rule: Comparative Perspectives*. Baltimore: Johns Hopkins Press.

Rotberg, R. I. (2002). The new nature of nation-state failure. *Washington Quarterly, 25*(3), 85–96.

Rothchild, D. (1986). State and ethnicity in Africa: A policy perspective. In N. Nevitte & C. Kennedy (Eds.), *Ethnic preference and public policy in developing states* (pp. 15–61). Boulder, CO: Lynne Rienner.

Schabas, W. A. (2008). Post-genocide justice in Rwanda: A spectrum of options. In P. Clark & Z. D. Kaufman (Eds.), *After genocide* (pp. 207–228). London: Hurst & Co.

Schmitter, P. C., & Lynn, T. L. (1991). What democracy is . . . and what it is not. *Journal of Democracy, 2*(3), 75–88.

Sezibera, R. (2007, December 2). The problem isn't ethnic. *Sunday Times SA.*

Slabbert, F. van Zyl. Truth without reconciliation, reconciliation without truth. In W. James & L. van der Vijver (Eds.), *After the TRC: Reflections on truth and reconciliation in South Africa* (pp. 73–81). Cape Town: David Philip Publisher.

Slabbert, F van Zyl. (2006). *The Other Side of History.* Cape Town: Jonathon Ball.

Steward, J. (2008). Only healing heals: concepts and methods of psycho-social healing in post-genocide Rwanda. In P. Clark & Z. D. Kaufman (Eds.), *After genocide* (pp. 171–190). London: Hurst & Co.

Traub, J. (2006). *The best of intentions: Kofi Annan and the UN in the era of American power.* London: Bloomsbury.

Van de Walle, N. (2001). *African Economies and the Politics of Permanent Crisis.* Cambridge: Cambridge University Press.

Van Eck, J. (2007, November 18). Ignoring the ethnic cancer in the Congo precludes true peace. *Sunday Times SA.*

Versi, A. (2008). The Lisbon EU-Africa summit: Africa stands firm. *African Business,* Issue 338, 12–18.

Warah, R. (2008, January 11–17). Not ethnic cleansing but class war. *Mail and Guardian,* 12.

Wheatley, M. J. (1994). *Leadership and the new science: Learning about organization from an orderly universe.* San Francisco: Berret-Koehler.

Zakaria, F. (2004). *The future of freedom.* New York: W. W. Norton.

Zartman, I. W. (Ed.). (2001). *Preventive negotiation: Avoiding conflict escalation.* Lanham, MD: Rowman & Littlefield.

Zartman, W. (1985). *Ripe for Resolution; Conflict and Intervention in Africa.* Oxford: Oxford University Press.

PART FOUR

Conclusions

18 Lessons for Theory

■ I. WILLIAM ZARTMAN AND MARK ANSTEY

One doesn't negotiate identity! There are subjects conventionally agreed to be outside the scope of negotiation, and identity is one of them. Identity is what one believes one is, and it is generally not up for bargaining. Furthermore, identity is not inherently conflictual. I am what I am and you are what you are, and the two do not necessarily overlap. Of course, a person's identity may—and often does—contain important internal conflicts: What one part of my identity tells me to do may well conflict with instructions or implications from another part of my identity, and that conflict may well be the subject of intense intrapersonal negotiations, as in Dostoevsky's *Crime and Punishment* (Kremenyuk, 2003). However, one does negotiate the expression of identity—how to recognize, respect, and accommodate identities within social systems. In this process, groups' sense of identity may be changed and that of individuals within them modified.

Thus, as seen in the preceding chapters, identity can be a potent source of conflict under certain conditions, and most of the intrastate conflicts in the world can be seen to be identity-driven. Indeed, even more strikingly, while interstate conflicts may initially be less fundamentally identity-driven, states are under pressure to define them in identity terms in order to motivate their populations and distinguish the combatants. Identity becomes dangerously conflictual when two identities are felt to be negatively interdependent in a zero-sum or threatening relationship. It becomes a factor in situations of competition when parties perceive their identity to be under threat and fear for their selves, or when they see the fulfillment of their needs and interests as best pursued through mobilization under identity markers and the elimination of the other as necessary. When my being Me depends on your not being You, or when your being You threatens my being Me, there is an identity conflict. And when there is identity conflict, the road has been taken that can lead to mass killings and genocide.

The historical record abounds in cases. Begin with recognized genocide. Hitler's Aryan Nazis' identity depended on the elimination of the Jewish people, whom they feared as a threat to their self-identified Aryan civilization. The Hutu organized by the *akuzu* clique and the Coalition for the Defense of the Republic (CDR) feared the Tutsi's coming to power to destroy them, and their identity depended on the suppression and elimination of the Tutsi and their moderate (false-conscious) Hutu allies as well. In Sudan, initially in the North–South conflict, the self-defined identity of the Northern Muslims depended on their domination and conversion of the Southerners, referred to as *abid* (slaves), and the successive Northern regimes feared both the pan-Sudan revolutionary and the Southern Sudan secessionist doctrines as threatening to their identity as God-given rulers of their country. Since the Fur and other Darfur groups are also Muslim, the religious element did not come into play, but rather their economic ways of life as farmers and their place in the electoral geography on which the North depended for its maintenance in power to define what it meant to be Sudanese.

In other salient cases of identity conflicts, the logic is the same. Zionists see Palestinians as interlopers in God-given Eretz Israel and a threat to the Zionist dream that is part of their identity, whereas Palestinians see Israelis as interlopers in their land and a threat to their national existence; both dream of a one-state solution with themselves in charge as a tangible expression of their identity. To South African Whites in the apartheid era, their dominance over the Black majority of noncitizens was a religion-supported element of their identity, and their position and way of life were threatened by a potential democratic polity; to the Blacks, their identity was demeaned and denied by the apartheid vision, and they were continually under threat in the system (not least because they were denied protection, participation, power, and privilege in the land of their birth). In the Kampuchea, the self-image of the Khmer Rouge was safe only as long as the deviants and dangerous classes were wiped out, lest they eliminate the Khmer Rouge and their worldview, whereas the individual and group identities in the Cambodian population were directly threatened by the Khmer Rouge, both ideologically and physically. When multiparty democracy came to Congo Brazzaville in the 1990s, each of the new parties ran to its home constituency and became a tribal spokesman, so that any of them coming to power meant exclusion and domination of the others; a normal situation of competition became an existential conflict in which the identity of each group depended on exclusion of the others and incumbency in power for one group was a threat to the others. In all of these conflicts, identity and existence were bound together, and competition for power became an existential conflict; being oneself required putting down the Other, or "otherization," as Romero-Trillo indicates in his chapter. In addition, in many of these conflicts, identity became "territorialized," to use the term of Vasquez (1993), often by the will of a god, so encroachment by the other on the sacred territory was diminution of the self. The identitarian assertion creates its own basis for fear. "Ethnic conflicts are caused by fear of the future, lived through the past" (Pesic, 2002).

■ EXPLAINING GENOCIDAIRES' BEHAVIOR

How does one explain the actions of members of an identity group who attempt to annihilate another group? These are not the actions of psychologically disturbed individuals (such as serial killers) or those of small groups of social deviants who may have drifted into, and then become trapped in, violent exchanges with other groups and the wider society (gangs). Nor are they otherwise law-abiding people who have become trapped in escalating conflict situations and kill limited numbers of others whom they perceive as having attacked them or betrayed them within a dynamic beyond their control (see the case below).

No, in the case of genocidaires there is direct participation in a strategy to eliminate another identity group. It may take its perpetrators into moments of terrible personal crisis under conditions beyond their control, but for the most part, it seems relatively calmly planned and carried out. Parties in conflict mobilize by demonizing each other, escalating tensions, deepening polarization, and closing down communications, reducing relations to "with us or against us" status and outcomes to zero-sum games. But the behavior of people on the business end of the killing when it starts is different. Records do not indicate passionate mobilization, with people simply attacking others in a frenzy of hatred and anger. On the contrary, a sort of "ordinariness" is reflected in their actions. The agents of death appear dispassionate, somehow immune from the horror of their acts. To perform their tasks, they must deindividuate and dehumanize their victims, a denial of their humanity releasing them to do their dreadful work. They go about their business of killing as if it were simply daily work, requiring discipline, order, and a commitment to the task.

Studies by social psychologists of such dynamics have a long history, as Ervin Staub discusses in his chapter. Asch (1955) demonstrated how easily individuals could be swayed to change their views even on objective data to comply with those expressed by others in a group. Milgram (1963) showed that individuals have a strong tendency to obedience or conformity when instructed to perform painful acts on others even if this breaches personal moral codes, especially if they feel that they are ordered to act by a legitimate authority. Unwillingness to conform carries the risk of social rejection, and in genocide scenarios it may be especially great. Betrayal often carries risks not simply of rejection but of death or threat to loved ones.

Darley and Latané (1968) explored the phenomenon of bystander apathy, in which people in group situations delay or fail to act in the face of emergency situations, clearly showing that individual responses are inhibited in the context of a group; people wait for a signal from others to decide what is appropriate behavior in the situation (social influence), and everyone waits for everyone else in a group to act (responsibility diffusion) or for directions from those with social status. Thus, if leaders in political systems, organized religions, and the judiciary either call for action against a defined group or remain silent, they allow space for atrocities to occur: As Edmund Burke is supposed to have said "all that is necessary for the triumph of evil is that good men do nothing." There are, of course, hierarchies within leadership groups as well, and once the drift of a top leadership group's leanings has been ascertained, difference can become dangerous. Three levels of social influence have been identified—compliance, in which there is behavioral conformity while individuals maintain their private beliefs; *identification*, in which there is conformity to the desires of a respected individual; and *internalization*, in which individuals both conform behaviorally and change their belief systems (Kelman, 1958). In ambiguous situations, people tend to turn to leaders for guidance or to their group.

Coser (1956) laid out the early fundamentals of the effects of conflict group dynamics. Conflict serves to unify groups, building cohesion and bonding within groups and strengthening them against external threat. In short, conflict can have the important function of group preservation, externalizing tensions while enhancing internal unity. Identity conflict serves to remove dissidents and thus lends itself to outbidding, as Jannie Lilja shows in her chapter. The risk, of course, is that as relations polarize into the "with us or against us" shape, moderates or those questioning the group's direction become identified as "against"; they are removed from positions of power and sometimes from the group itself if their voices threaten internal unity. In this way, hawkish leaders are quickly able to displace doves. Internal dissidence tends to be experienced as a greater threat to the group than the external other, and alternative voices are seen as those of traitors. Individuals see themselves as acting on behalf of the group rather than themselves, conformity is rewarded by the group, and all group members become somehow inextricably bound in an inward-looking system that is immune to external calls for moderation or negotiation. Many of these findings have been elaborated on in the chapter by Staub.

▪ VIOLENCE IN ESCALATED CONFLICT

Research on group dynamics within escalated conflicts work informed the testimony of Anstey (2006) in the mitigation trial of 18 railway workers who had been found guilty of the murder of 4 strikebreakers following a six-week strike on South African railways at the peak of apartheid in 1986. How was it that these men, with no track record of violence or disciplinary problems, suddenly undertook to stab to death four fellow workers? The strike was triggered by the dismissal of one driver who had committed a relatively minor disciplinary offense. What started as a small work stoppage involving a few hundred workers escalated into an action involving tens of thousands, massive damage to property, and the dismissal of 22,000 workers. The context of relations further aggravated matters: The individual dismissal and the initial stoppage occurred shortly after security police had warned railways management of possible mobilization by Communist elements. It was understood by workers as the possible start of a mass dismissal of Black workers, which they suspected management undertook every year to avoid paying Black workers bonuses. The law prohibited management from engaging with those mobilizing Black workers. Good-faith attempts to negotiate a deal were scuppered through miscommunication, clumsy timing, and poor mutual understanding.

Problems were exacerbated by the absence of mutually legitimated negotiation forums, refusals by the employer to submit the matter to independent mediation or arbitration, and lack of access to a court system for workers. Worker demands proliferated, both parties accused each other of reneging on deals and negotiating in bad faith, attacks on property increased, and wider forces were mobilized. In the context of mobilization against an unjust system, with no access to legitimated systems of dispute resolution, strikers found themselves isolated from mainstream society. The workers' union struggled with internal coordination as it experienced rapid growth. Failure to resolve tensions gave rise to increasing frustration and anger, and to a change in internal dynamics within the struggle group. Hardliners displaced more moderate elements and powerful conformity pressures emerged—"if you are not with us, you're against us." Without access to independent dispute resolution systems and alienated from the wider social system, workers began to implement justice systems of their own. Just as deserters receive military trials, the group tried and punished those whom it saw as betraying the cause.

The killing of the four strikebreakers took place in a context of escalated conflict—a scenario of social breakdown reflecting heightened perceptions of injustice, rising demands, breakdowns in communication, increasing use of violent tactics, an absence of legitimate dispute resolution forums and processes, and, within the groups (management and labor), a shift to hard-line positions. Within the striker group powerful conformity pressures emerged, with punishment for those seen as betraying the cause. Even those within the group who had been trying to keep negotiation prospects alive became afraid of opposing internal disciplinary processes. In effect, as internal demands for obedience rise, the space for negotiation is reduced, with moderates running the risk of being seen as "sellouts." Behavior that previously might have been inconceivable may come to be seen as necessary, and then normative, in the context of a group perceiving itself as under mortal threat.

The annihilation of Tutsis and those Hutus who sought to assist them, or even distance themselves from the killing in Rwanda in 1994, was conducted by their Hutu neighbors, friends, relatives, and teammates on sports teams. The tales, quite dispassionately recounted, of those who participated in these killings are captured in Hatzfeld's (2005) book *A Time for Machetes*. Hutu men were called to action and obeyed. The collection of stories of those who murdered their friends and neighbors reflects the deindividuation of those they killed. Here was a society in which men rose every day to go to work—the killing of Tutsis—and came home every night to their families. They quibbled over workloads, demanded discipline among their ranks, punished shirkers, demanded that reluctant members demonstrate commitment, and worked out means of dealing with ethical problems such as how to deal with spouses in intergroup marriages. There were a few who took pleasure in the torture and suffering of their victims, but it seems that for the most part, men simply got up in the morning and went about their business of hunting and "cutting" those identified for elimination. They tried as far as possible to do their work dispassionately and efficiently.

These were not the actions of men in a frantic moment of life-threatening combat. The men acted within the context of a long stream of interethnic pogroms and violence, and there was a sense of danger with the shooting down of the president's plane and the invasion of Kagame's forces, but no sense of imminent threat is conveyed in their stories. They were not engaging in slaughter in the process of evacuating their loved ones. They were hunting rather than being hunted. Of course, it might be argued that they hunted out of fear, to prevent a reversal of fortunes, but the overriding impression is one of simple obedience and conformity—"they did what they had to do." Killing members of another identity group became normative, with participation key to group membership and protection. Participation was rewarded, reluctance punished; the process was led by those with social status; there were tangible rewards from looting; there was a sense of impunity owing to lack of consequences for those who had participated in previous pogroms; there was a sense of purpose in preserving one's own group while eliminating those identified by leaders as threatening its existence. In the words of Jacques Semelin (2008, p. 15), "The individual is not a monster as such but he becomes one when he engages in the mechanism of mass crime. It is through the group that the individual changes into a killer."

Hatzfeld (2005), interviewing these killers six years after the event, was struck by their placidity, the lack of depression or psychic disturbance they evidenced, their apparent fatalism, and their view that it was perhaps regrettable but now long past, and they had merely followed orders. They were more focused on their own place in the unfolding of events, and their own current circumstances, than on their killing of others and the consequences of this action—a sort of exaggerated egocentrism. In noting the absence of regret among these killers, Hatzfeld comments:

> The absolute character of their project was what allowed them to carry it out with a certain equanimity, and today this same absoluteness allows them to avoid fully understanding and agonizing over what they did. The monstrous nature of the extermination haunts the survivors and even tortures them with guilt, whereas it exculpates and reassures the killers, perhaps protecting them from madness. (2005, p. 227)

One of Hatzfeld's subjects argued that there were those who claimed that they were unable to talk properly about the period because they had changed into "wild animals" during the killings and "buried our civilizations." He commented (p. 229):

> That is a trick to sidetrack the truth. I can say this: outside the marshes, our lives seemed quite ordinary. We sang on the paths, we downed Primus or urwagwa, we had our choice amid abundance. We chatted about our good fortune, we soaped off our bloodstains in the basin, and our noses enjoyed the aromas of full cooking pots. We rejoiced in the new life to begin by feasting on a leg of veal. We were hot at night atop our wives, and we scolded our rowdy children. Although no longer willing to feel pity, we were still greedy for good feelings. The days all seemed much alike, as I told you. We put on our field clothes. We swopped gossip at the cabaret, we made bets on our victims, spoke mockingly of cut girls, squabbled foolishly over looted grain. We sharpened our tools on whetting stones. We trade stories about desperate Tutsi tricks, we made fun of every "Mercy!" cried by someone who'd been hunted down, we counted up and stashed away our goods. We went about our business without a care in the world—provided we concentrated on killing during the day naturally. At the end of that season in the marshes we were so disappointed we had failed. We were disheartened by what we going to lose, and truly frightened by the misfortune and vengeance reaching out for us. But deep down, we were not tired of anything.

■ NEGOTIATING FEAR AND THREAT

This understanding deals with the mass hysteria that animates the group in the ultimate act of genocide, who in the final mechanical wave are beyond negotiation. But it does not explain the organizers, the political entrepreneurs who both fuel and manipulate the element of fear, turning it into otherization, conflict, and violence. How can negotiation be possible with such existentially threatened groups, and how is it to be done? The answer, as discussed from various angles in the preceding chapters, is in the question itself. What is needed is a process that removes the feelings of zero-sum threat and fear, and that process has to come from positive interaction between the parties, that is, from negotiation.

The blockage of such interaction is what makes the conflict, a procedural problem that will be discussed below, but first, the substantive problem needs clarification. The nature of the blockage or conflict imposes its requirements on the substance of the negotiations, and removal of the blockage means the resolution of the conflict. Two types of contributions to a solution are available—structural and attitudinal, with continual interrelations between the two. Attitudinal changes are necessary to embark on structural solution searches; effective structural solutions give confidence to parties that there are systems in place to protect identities and make structures stick—they are symbiotic.

Parties need to develop a new narrative with regard to their relations in which the perception of "evil" of the Other, and the sense of threat, are reduced. In their dualistic theory on the nature of hate, Sternberg and Sternberg (2008) propose that it is a condition characterized by a negation of intimacy (disgust), passion (anger and fear), and a form of commitment in which the Other is devalued and diminished (contempt). When all three elements are in place in conjunction with a narrative of the Other as posing a serious threat, hate can become lethal in its expression. Hatred is instigated through propaganda, indoctrination of youth, and pressures for group conformity associated with authoritarian cults. The authors make several proposals for managing hate, giving emphasis to the fundamental importance of changing the propaganda. The problem, however, is a chicken-and-egg one: To change the propaganda, one must change those who are driving messages of hate through a propaganda machine and threatening those who do not conform. Processes of attitudinal change and reorienting group thinking, of reconciliation and forgiveness, are very difficult in a system in the grip of a leadership mobilizing on hatred. Leadership then is critical in the change mix.

Structures of identity conflict can be deliberately created or historically evolved. Structural solutions begin with confidence-building measures and end in institutionalized cooperation and competition (Ignatieff, 2003; Maoz, 2004; Rosoux, 2009). The aim is to gradually create institutionalized situations whereby neither party can threaten or dominate the other. Pfetsch's and Cunningham's chapters show the importance of distributing benefits to both sides in order to achieve a stable and resolving agreement, so that both feel they have gained something from the peace agreement and are better off with the agreement than without it. This is possible through the establishment of either a higher neutral authority to guarantee the nonthreatening functioning of relations or a system of interlocking interdependence on the part of the parties to ensure that each side's welfare depends on its cooperation with the other. The first removes supreme authority from the grasp and threat of either of the conflicting identities, whereas the second reverses the stalemate so that each party's welfare depends on the goodwill of the other. Structural solutions make it impossible to harm the other without harming oneself.

For instance, at the time of South Africa's political transition, it was important to reframe the expression of diverse identities in non-zero-sum terms. The minority White group came to see that its survival as an identity group might not depend on the repression of other racial identity groups. The architects of apartheid did not want to live as international outcasts or go down in history as domestic oppressors, but neither did they want to lose privilege, participation, protection, power, or purpose (Zartman, 1995). They did, of course, face loss of political power as a racial identity group, but not loss of participation in the economic and political systems. Political power was ceded in exchange for constitutional provisions that afforded protection of individual and cultural rights, retention of privilege, the right to participate at all levels of society, and a new common nation-building purpose with other identity groups. South Africa instituted a structural mechanism of interlocking interdependence in the power-sharing arrangement following the 1994 elections, the deliberate attempt to fall short of the 66% limit for constitutional revision, and, more broadly, the tacit agreement to leave the economic system for the time being in White hands (slow transformation) and the political system in the hands of the Black majority (quicker transformation).

In short, identity was not negotiated per se; what was negotiated was ways of expressing identity in a manner that did not preclude expression of the identity of other groups. Pacing change in this manner provides, on the one hand, stability, limiting prospects of economic collapse with implications for all parties, but, on the other, opening up ongoing tensions in a new regime concerning whether change has really happened or has gone far enough. Black South Africans are frustrated with slow progress; White South Africans point out how very different the country is since 1994. For the latter, the change has been profound; for the former, especially the poor, little has happened. Admittedly, structural change without attitudinal change may actually exacerbate conflictual feelings, but attitudinal change is difficult to obtain—albeit slowly—without changes in the structural base.

A similar structural solution through the 1979 Lancaster House Agreement in Zimbabwe worked for a while but then fell prey to the rapacious efforts of Robert Mugabe to turn the settler landholdings into a sacrificial cow. Structural efforts to overcome the identity conflict in Israel–Palestine through the 1993 Oslo Agreements, in Rwanda through the 1993 Arusha Agreement, or in the Congo through the 1999 Lusaka Agreement showed their flaws in a much shorter period of time. Third-party guarantees, including stationing of UN or even foreign (American) troops on a Palestinian–Israeli border, may be the structural price of conflict management; conflict resolution is generations away (and at the mercy of generational outbidding). Structural solutions in identity conflicts pose the chicken-and-egg question of requiring attitudinal solutions first. A crucial structural change with attitudinal repercussions is the installation of joint projects. On the international level, in the Franco–German dispute, the attitudinal change accompanying the construction of Europe is a fine case of attitude change and structural change moving hand in hand (Rosoux 2001; Zartman & Kremenyuk, 2005).

The triangular situation created by mediation is itself a structural measure, the strategies of which are well reviewed in the chapters by Peter Wallensteen, Erik Melander and Frida Möller, by Fedor Meerts and Tassos Coulaloglou, and by Slimovitz, the first two chapters focusing on the role of international organizations. Intrusive interventions, whether challenging, impartial, or witnessing, change the structure of the conflict, in various ways separating the parties and in some way even seeking to soften their relations. Short of direct intervention, sanctions are a third party's way of pressing the antagonists to rethink their policies, as in many other cases a structural situation that is designed to change conflicts by increasing the cost of their continuance. The "softest" intervention is exemplified by the Organization for Security and Cooperation in Europe's (OSCE) High Commissioner on National Minorities, specifically instituted to deal with impending identity conflicts. The High Commissioner concentrates various forms of persuasion on parties in the early stages of escalating conflict to mediate (as a third party) or even negotiate (as a direct manipulator of pressure). Attitudinal change in these situations is only an incidental accompaniment of the effect of the temporary triangular structure, but the policy changes sought stand somewhere between structure and attitude even if they do not indicate a deep change of heart.

Attitudes are marvelously manipulable and obstinately entrenched. Attitudinal solutions are a slow phased process but are by nature less concrete, less formalizable, and less deliberate than structural change (Abu Nimer, 2001; ben-Tal & Bennink, 2004; Kriesberg, 1998; Lipschutz, 1998). Changing people's attitudes often depends on changes in structured relations, yet, as seen, structural changes do not hold unless accompanied by attitudinal change. In Black–White relations in the United States, the impact of *Brown v. Board of Education* in 1953, a structural change, was complex and multidirectional, and even the election of an African American president over half a century later does not complete the story of structural and attitudinal changes. It was preceded by such seemingly insignificant measures as biracial rooming arrangements in college dormitories and the realization that a Black neighbor does not mean a Black neighborhood, which wore away the zero-sum or fear-inducing view of racial relations. In South Africa this would raise the question of why it should not be a Black neighborhood and what would be the problem if it was. The demographic mix shapes identity demands and expectations in many ways, and the game is played differently according to whether one is in a minority or a majority group.

As in the case of restructuring reforms, attitudinal change, the removal of the sense of fear and threat, comes either from a neutral authority or social interactions, as through civil society. A problem in South Africa fifteen years after the shift in power is that bitter contests over the racial composition of many institutions remain. The country in many senses remains color bound rather than color blind, with every form of organization subject to scrutiny over its racial composition— sports teams, private businesses, the public sector, universities. In the judiciary, too, appointments are intensely contested, with race an important factor in the mix. Behind this are concerns that ethnic entrepreneurs may increasingly play for power through the "neutral authority" of the courts, with even some of the very competent Black judges seen as too conservative in transformation processes.

Political parties have an active interest in attitudinal change. Just as identity conflicts are spurred, if not started, by political entrepreneurs who play on the latest public fears, often in times of difficulty, as Staub points out in his chapter, positive entrepreneurs are needed to reverse the feeling, to show that there is nothing to fear in the other party or that maintaining one's identity does not depend on demeaning that of the other group. National culture festivals, affirmative action, and doctrinal revisions are ways of changing people's attitudes toward each other, instituted by higher authority or by the civil society.

Donohue, in his chapter, emphasizes the Identity Trap that drives even straightforward or normative bargaining over tangibles into a crisis mode involving identity. A constant concern for "face restoration" and the avoidance of a focus on the person rather than the object is important in order to move away from the intrusion of identity issues and demonizing escalation (Faure, 2008). Romero-Trillo's chapter also focuses on the dangers of otherizing and the need to consciously make efforts to prevent language from becoming the object rather than the vehicle of negotiation. But changing attitudes is a long, slow process; the slightest backsliding restores fears and impedes open communication and cooperation.

■ MEDIATING IDENTITY EXPRESSIONS

Direct negotiation between the parties in identity conflicts is unlikely to take place without a mediator's help due to the very reasons for the conflict. The parties are unable to communicate credibly and confidently with each other; they are unable to think creatively of solutions; they are unable to provide adequate terms of trade to make an agreement worthwhile. And they are unable to conceive of anything less than efforts to defeat the opponent and protect themselves, unable to perceive the creative potential of the stalemate they are in, and unable to recognize the pain caused by that stalemate—in a word, unable to see and seize a ripe situation. All these inabilities call for third-party efforts to help overcome the various sources of blockage, above all on the attitudinal front. As has been often noted, mediators have a particularly difficult time achieving entry into internal conflicts, since the rebels' commitment and the state's sovereignty leave little room for an external third party (Crocker, Hampson, & Aall, 1999; Maundi, Zartman, Khadiagala & Nuameh 2006; Zartman, 1995). Huntington (1998) argued powerfully that it is simply not possible to locate mutually acceptable mediators in "civilizational" conflicts. Rather, their resolution depends on their fit within a game of secondary party relations and brokerage, subject to the interests and power exchanges of external actors with interests.

One can distinguish between conflicts that arise as a consequence of cultural differences creating tensions in communication (misunderstandings, confusion, misinterpretations) and those in which cultural differences themselves are the issue of conflict (everyone understands, but they fundamentally disagree on an issue). Brokering positive outcomes in the former has good prospects, less so in the latter. If adherence to the letter of holy teachings is understood to involve punishments of beheadings, stonings, and amputation of hands, change is going to be more difficult than for those who might use such measures simply to "teach people a lesson." If female circumcision or honor killings are seen as fundamental to group identity, they will continue in the face of laws seen to lack authority.

Two classic functions of the mediator have already been established in the literature, having to do with the "what" and the "when" of conflict management. One function is to help the parties find an agreeable solution somewhere between or including their positions. Negotiation literature identifies the three ways of finding agreement: concessions, compensations, and constructions. Through *concessions*, the parties edge toward each other, each giving in a bit on its demand on the basic item of conflict, to meet somewhere in the middle, each party getting somewhat less than it originally wanted. This works best with tangible, divisible issues of conflict. At Oslo in 1993, the Palestinians got some, but not all, of the autonomous territory they wanted; at Camp David II in 2000, they got between 92% and 96% of the West Bank. At the South African Multiparty Talks in 1992, the enabling majority for constitutional revision was set at 66%, not 50% or 75%, as the contending parties had demanded. The Aceh 2005 Memorandum of Understanding granted the autonomous province an "independent and impartial court system including a court of appeals" and without appeal to the Indonesian supreme court, but "within the judicial system of the Republic of Indonesia" (MoU, 2005).

Through *compensation*, the parties add additional elements to the terms of trade to pay for items that the other might find of prime importance. At Oslo, Israel and the Palestine Liberation Organization (PLO) exchanged recognition (as a state and as a legitimate spokesman, respectively); at Helsinki in 2005, the GAM (Free Aceh Movement) won a number of points to give substance to its "self-government," such as passport powers, inclusion of local political parties, and an independent judiciary, among others, in exchange for other elements, such as the continued presence of the Indonesian National Military (TNI) and human rights provisions delayed in deference to confidence-building measures.

Through *construction*, the parties redefine the stakes at conflict so that the new concept of the situation fits the interests of both sides. This type of agreement is often what is required for a change in attitudes, as parties no longer define themselves in terms of the other. A newly discovered common enemy often defines the new situation. At Oslo, the parties made a pact to cooperate to exclude Hamas, although each then thought it saw more gains in working alone against the pact (a Stag Hunt Game in game-theoretic terms); at Helsinki in 2005, the recent tsunami demanded cooperation between former enemies to overcome its effects. But the new concept can also be positive: The New South Africa arose in people's minds when both sides realized that they could not accomplish their goals without the help of the other side, and this necessary cooperation began, ever so slowly, to diminish fears. In fact, all agreements involve some sort of constructive formula and joint pact to achieve the parties' goals, using means other than violence. This is standard negotiation conceptualization, and it becomes material for mediation when a third party is brought in to help the conflicting parties do what they cannot do by themselves.

That help also comes in three forms, depending on the obstacle to bilateral negotiation, according to established literature (Bercovitch, 2009; Touval & Zartman, 2007). If the parties simply cannot communicate with each other, due to lack of trust, status differences, language differences, or other reasons, they need a mediator as a communicator, sometimes called a *facilitator*. The mediator is needed to carry messages and ensure their credibility. Establishing trust and communication are the basic functions of the mediator; this is particularly important when the characteristics of identity conflict—fear and zero-sum identity—are salient. But if the conflict keeps the parties from even conceiving of a solution, they need a mediator as a *formulator*. The formulator is not just a neutral telephone wire, as is the communicator, but becomes actively engaged in the substance of the search for a solution, putting forth ideas, suggesting formulas, and offering paths to solutions (always making the parties feel that it was they who thought of them, of course). This function is particularly important, as will be seen, when it comes to the element of ripeness that is termed the *Way Out*, the sense that a solution is possible and that the other party believes this too. The communicator and the formulator are particularly important in dealing with attitudinal conflict. But if the payoffs of a possible solution are simply not big enough to be attractive to the parties, and to draw them to an agreement, then they need a mediator as a *manipulator* to address structural problems. Manipulators are fully engaged in the search for a solution, to the point where they add new elements, sweeten the pot, enlarge the pie, keep the parties in the game, and guarantee the results. The degree of engagement makes this third role a dangerous one for the mediator but often a necessary one if a solution is to be achieved.

The second classic function established in the literature on mediation has to do with the "when" of conflict resolution (Zartman, 1989, 2000, 2010). Conflicting parties are unable to find a resolution to their conflict at just any time. They are ready to do so only when the conflict is ripe, that is, when they recognize that their efforts to prevail are stalemated and that the stalemate is painful to them, more painful than the fears that caused the conflict, and also when they feel that the other party is willing and able to search with them for a conceivable solution. Again, as in the substantive search for a solution, the parties locked in an identity conflict are not likely to arrive at a sense of ripeness by themselves; the stakes involved in the assertion and defense of their identity are too high for them to admit stalemate, to feel pain, or to see the other party as capable of joining in a constructive pact. In this they need the help of the mediator, who plays a major role in ripening the conflict for efforts to resolve it.

Ripening involves major efforts of persuasion to get the parties to see the mutually hurting stalemate in which they are caught, first to realize the impasse and then, most importantly, to acknowledge that it is more costly and painful to them than their fears of the Other. These efforts not only help the parties recognize their situation but also impel them to turn to someone for help, and the mediator is already involved in the ripening process, just ready to be of further assistance. The paradox in constructing that ripening, of course, is that the feared parties must at least tacitly cooperate to show that the Other's fears are groundless.

The important contribution of this work, however, is to bring to light a third major function of the mediator, pertaining to the "who" of conflict resolution (Zartman 2009). Mediators need to be active in developing an appropriate choice of partner for the state in preventing and/or managing the identity-based conflict. As the introduction and the chapters by Moti Cristal and Jannie Lilja in this volume indicate, before the substance of the agreement can be considered, the key to an effective negotiation is the identification of appropriate parties to the deal. The qualities of an appropriate partner, among the range of potential representatives of the confronting identity group, are clear in the abstract: legitimacy as a recognized spokesman for the identity interests, location in the middle and not just at the friendly edge of the spectrum, representative of a sizable portion of the opposing group, deliverability to carry out the agreement, and possibly some other virtues.

If the challenge to the mediator is great in regard to the first two functions—suggesting an outcome ("what") and encouraging a perception of ripeness ("when")—the problem of finding an appropriate partner from among the opposing group ("who") is enormous. Conflicting parties dislike being told whom to negotiate with even more than they dislike being led to an outcome or told that they are in a hurting stalemate. The usual tendency is to try to make a deal with the party on the other side who is closest to the first party: the state. The hope is that it will be necessary to concede less to the neighboring party, which in turn reduces the legitimacy of the interlocutor for not having been demanding enough. Furthermore, bypassing the moderates in the search for a representative closer to the more radical side of the spectrum punishes rather than rewards the moderates for their moderation. Better, it can be argued, to make a deal with the moderates in an effort to quell fear and repressiveness, and then let the others into the tent of the partnership as they themselves moderate their attitudes. Moti Cristal calls for a recognition of parties that emerge from the conflict as legitimate representatives of their side; the selection of the parties determines the durability of the solution. Jannie Lilja discusses the strategies for involving various factions of the rebel leadership through mediation as they become caught in outbidding among themselves. It may become important for some key parties to begin a dialogue to gain momentum in a process, building this momentum in a manner that is not exclusive and that allows other parties to join as they begin to see the prospect of participation rather than boycotts. The outbidding process makes participation risky, so it must be very carefully managed. Much of the answer depends on how legitimate, well located, majoritarian, and deliverable the moderates are, and how difficult it would be to handle extremists who will act as spoilers, as Marie-Joëlle Zahar analyzes. Polarization tends to remove and delegitimize the moderates, so negotiation and engagement must enable them to show something for their moderation in terms of group goals. Paradoxically, mediation must enable them to outbid the radicals. All these questions and answers are judgment calls, with little to go on in the conceptual realm to help make the decision.

Yet, experience shows how important they are to the range from success to failure. In Macedonia in 2001, the North Atlantic Treaty Organization (NATO) mediator secretly helped the radical National Liberation Army and the other, moderate Albania parties meet at Prizren to craft a common platform and form a moderate negotiating partner for the government. In Sudan after 2000, in a reverse selection problem, the African and American mediators helped the Sudanese Peoples Liberation Movement/Army (SPLM/A) develop negotiations that led to the Comprehensive Peace Agreement (CPA) with the Islamist/military National Congress Party (NCP) rather then with the established (and doubtless majoritarian) opposition parties. In Darfur in 2006, U.S. and African mediators achieved an agreement with one of the Darfuri rebel groups, the Sudanese Liberation Movement of Minni Arkoi Minawi (SLM-M), which then fell apart under the weight of the excluded groups, all turned spoilers. In Rwanda in 1993, the mediators pushed for inclusion of the Hutu *akazu* in the Arusha negotiations but were rebuffed by the Tutsi Rwandan Patriotic Front; the *akazu* had their revenge. In Palestine after 2006, as already noted, the Western mediators joined Israel in refusing to talk with

Hamas, in or out of a Palestinian coalition government, but they did not give enough concessions to the moderate Fatah movement. In all of these notable cases, the importance of the mediator was key in performing the third function.

■ **CONCLUSION**

The management of fear and repression and the selection of appropriate partners are two crucial elements in reducing identity conflict, either in prevention or as a path to resolution. To identify these elements—which have been too little studied as part of the path to genocide—is merely to open the door to more research on both topics. Measures to bring attitudinal change encompass a huge subject, yet to be fully focused on identity problems relating to fear and repression. Measures to bring structural change seem to be more specifically identifiable, yet greater development of social engineering techniques is still wanting. The whole topic of selecting partners in making a negotiated deal has been ignored, as negotiation studies make strides on the "what" and lately the "when" questions. The doors opened in this work have large rooms behind them to explore.

References

Abu-Nimer, M. (Ed.), (2001). *Reconciliation, justice, and coexistence: theory and practice.* Lanham, MD: Lexington Books.

Anstey, M. (2006). *Managing Change, Negotiating Conflict.* Cape Town: Juta.

Asch, S. E. (1955). Opinions and social pressure. *Scientific American, 193,* 31–35.

Bar-Simon-Tov, Y, (Ed.). (2004). *From conflict resolution to reconciliation.* Oxford: Oxford University Press.

Bar-Tal, D., & Bennink, G. (2004). Dialectics between stable peace and reconciliation. In Y. Bar-Simon-Tov (Eds.), *From conflict resolution to reconciliation* (pp. 64–75). Oxford: Oxford University Press.

Bercovitch, J. (2009). Mediation and Conflict Resolution. In J. Bercovitch V. Kremenyuk & I. W. Zartman (Eds.), *The SAGE Handbook if Conflict Resolution*: London: Sage.

Coser, L. (1956). *The functions of social conflict.* New York: Free Press.

Crocker, C. A, Hampson, F O and Aall, P., (Eds.). (1999). *Herding Cats: Multiparty mediation in a changing world.* Washington: USIP.

Darley, J. M., & Latané, B. (1968). Bystander intervention in emergencies: Diffusion of responsibility. *Journal of Personality and Social Psychology, 8,* 377–383.

Faure, G. O. (2007) [sic]. Demonizing and Negotiation. *PINPoints, 28,* 7–10 Laxenburg: IIASA.

Hatzfeld, J. (2005). *A time for machetes. The Rwandan genocide: The killers speak.* London: Serpents Tail.

Huntingon, S. P. (1998). *The Clash of Civilizations and the Remaking of the World Order.* London: Touchstone Books.

Ignatieff, M. (2003). Recollections on coexistence. In A. Chayes & M. Minoiw (Eds.), *Imagine coexistence: Restoring humanity after violent conflict.* San Francisco: Jossey-Bass.

Kelman, H. (1958). Compliance, identification and internalization: Three processes of attitude change. *Journal of Conflict Resolution, 1,* 51–60.

Kremenyuk, V. (2003). Negotiating with oneself. In Guy Olivier Faure (Ed.), *How people negotiate*. Dordrecht: Kluwer.

Latané, B., & Darley, J. M. (1969). Bystander apathy. *American Scientist, 57*, 244–268.

Lederach, J. P. (1997). *Building peace: Sustainable reconciliation in divided societies*. Washington: USIP.

Lipschutz, R. D. (1998). Beyond the neoliberal peace: From conflict resolution to social reconciliation. *Social Justice, 25*(4), 5–19.

Maoz, I. (2004). Social-cognitive mechanisms in reconciliation. In Y. Bar-Simon-Tov (Ed.), *From conflict resolution to reconciliation*. Oxford: Oxford University Press.

Maundi, M, Zartman, I. W., Khadiagala, G, and Nuameh, K. (2001). *Getting In*. Washington: USIP.

Milgram, S. (1963). Behavioral study of obedience. *Journal of Abnormal and Social Psychology, 67*(4), 371–378.

MoU (2005, August 15). Memorandum of understanding between the government of the Republic of Indonesia and the Free Aceh Movement.

Pesic, V. (2002, October–December). Quoted in M. Singh, Ethnic conflict and international security. *World Affairs, 6*(4). Retrieved from.

Rosoux, V. (2001). *Les usages de la mémoire dans les relations internationales*. Brussels: Bruylant.

Rosoux, V. (2009). Reconciliation as a peace-building process: Scope and limits. In J. Bercovitch, V. Kremenyuk, & I. W. Zartman (Eds.), *SAGE handbook of conflict resolution* (pp. 543–563). London: Sage.

Semelin, J. (2008). Comprendre notre barbarie. *Justice et Démocratie*, 23.

Sternberg & Sternberg. (2008). *The Nature of Hate*. Cambridge: Cambridge University Press.

Tanaka, M. (2010). Limitations in maximilist definitions of reconciliation. *SAIS Toolkit*. Retrieved from http://www.sais-jhu.edu/dev-cmtoolkit/index.htm

Touval, S. & Zartman, I. W. (2007). International mediation. In Crocker, C. A., Hamson, F. O., & Aall, P. (Eds.) *Leashing the dogs of war* (pp. 437–454). Washington: USIP.

Vasquez, John (1993). *The War Puzzle*. New York: Cambridge University Press.

Zartman, I. W. (1995). Negotiating the South African conflict. In I. W. Zartman (Ed.), *Elusive Peace: negotiating an end to civil war* (pp. 147–174). Washington: Brookings.

Zartman, I. W. (1989). *Ripe for Resolution*. New York: Oxford University Press.

Zartman, I. W. (2000). Ripeness: The hurting stalemate and beyond. In Paul Stern and Danilee Druckman (Eds.), *International conflict resolution after the cold war* (pp. 225–250). Washington: National Academy Press.

Zartman, I. W. (2009). Choosing negotiating partners. *PINPoints, 33*, 13–16. (Clingendael: The Hague, Netherlands).

Zartman, I. W. (2010). *Timing mediation initiatives*. Washington: USIP.

Zartman, I. W., & Kremenyuk, V, (Eds.). (2005). *Peace vs. justice: Negotiating forward-vs. backward-looking outcomes*. Lanham, MD: Rowman & Littlefield.

19 Lessons for Practice

■ MARK ANSTEY AND PAUL MEERTS

Identity might seldom be the direct subject of negotiation processes, but negotiation, at the level of both issues and processes, is often infused with identity concerns. Identity groups seldom enter negotiations to change their identities as much as to make demands around them for territory or power or rights. Dealing with issues of boundaries, the design of political systems, representation and the distribution of power, economic opportunity, or human rights is often implicitly about issues of identity. Processes of social programming create and reinforce identities. People cluster in identity groups to meet needs for protection, participation, power, privilege, and purpose. They interpret the world through perceptual screens developed by such social programming. Perception determines reality. Negotiators are negotiating over their perceived needs and those of others, their differing interpretations of history, their different understandings of fairness and justice. The subjective reality of identity groups in conflict is the objective reality of negotiation, and is why third parties need to listen so carefully to the parties in any intervention to develop strategies that have a fit for the conflicts at hand. There is plenty of learning to be drawn from the way various conflicts have been handled through time, but there is no template. The first task of any third party is to achieve understanding. Yet, this is an elusive commodity. Third parties bring their own needs and interests into conflict situations, they perceive some outcomes as more desirable than others, and they must make choices about their use of power even as they try to facilitate understanding and more effective problem solving among protagonists.

■ THE ELUSIVE GOAL OF MUTUAL UNDERSTANDING

Many of the authors in this book argue that it is critical for the parties involved in conflict (antagonists and third parties) to achieve understanding of each other, of each other's fundamental needs, of the interests behind positions, of the cultural programming and historical experiences that create perceptual screens through which they interpret each other's behavior, and of communication processes that trap people in conflict spirals. It is helpful if parties have empathy for one another's concerns and insight into the needs and interests that inform their positions and the arguments used to defend or motivate these concerns. Empathy requires first an understanding of self, then a step beyond in which, without loss of self, understanding at both a cognitive and an emotional level of the other. Understanding of self facilitates understanding of the other in relations of interdependence. Escalated conflicts typically give rise to closed or selective communications, demonization of the other, "with us or against us" sentiments, and dehumanization of the other—in short, a drive to reduce interdependence. Genocide is an extreme form of this process. It is an effort by one group to eliminate another because it has reduced the other to a point at which no interdependence is recognized or the continued existence of the other is a threat to one's own. In cases where there are long-established working relations in which conflicts have been successfully managed through negotiation and problem solving, empathic mutual understanding develops and is continuously reinforced. In high-conflict conditions it is not only absent but, owing to the level of threat, very hard to develop. In short, it may simply be beyond the grasp of the parties at precisely the moment they need it most—in situations with a high potential for mass killings and genocide.

Negotiations in the European Union (EU) stretch over years, being performed by negotiators who often know each other for a long time. There are controversies, of course, but they are often of a rather technical nature. At one point in a Working Group negotiation, the diplomats decided to change hats. They seriously negotiated progress on the subject at hand by representing the countries of their colleagues: The Dutch diplomat got to represent the United Kingdom, the British one took France, the Frenchman fought for the Swedish interests, and so on. It went very well. They perfectly understood the positions and motivations of the other parties and had no problem using the most effective arguments needed. By contrast, on a different occasion, diplomats from Azerbaijan and Georgia were attending a training session in Baku when the trainer proposed to analyze the Nagorno–Karabagh problem by asking the Azeri to look at it through the eyes of the Armenians and the Georgians to do the same through the eyes of the Azerbaijanis; the proposal failed. The Azeri said that they could not do this exercise "because they were not from Armenia." Unlike the EU delegates from member states, they lacked empathy for each other's needs and interests.

The dictum "understand yourself, understand your enemy" (not least because it often in your interest to do so) is difficult to implement in a situation of identity conflicts. This is especially the case when traumatic events of the past bedevil the parties involved. First of all, each party may not want to achieve some understanding of the other party that killed so many of their kin. It may even be seen as a kind of betrayal. Over time this unwillingness might be softened, but in some cases it freezes and become even more problematic. The "goodness of self" and "evil of the other" becomes a mythical thing, and myths are notoriously difficult to negotiate. Myths are part of national history and are easily violated. While the process of negotiation and cooperation might seem to be the obvious way out of such circumstances, actors will often refuse to start the process and thereby miss the opportunity to go from peace to justice to a common project for the future. As an example of an exception we could look at the EU, overcoming the trauma of World War II by taking the bilateral relationship between Germany and France to the supranational level. But it took catastrophe to awaken recognition of mutuality; it took World War II as a mutually hurting disaster for Europeans to see the need for inter-European cooperation. The crisis in itself could not do the job. An outside threat was needed in order to give European integration a chance to flourish. Paul Henri Spaak once said that there should be a statue of Stalin in Brussels, as without the threat of the Soviet Union, the EU would not have pursued its integration. It should be noted that a third unavoidable factor had to be in play: the readiness of the Germans to acknowledge the damage they had done. They did acknowledge it and, in doing so, made the trauma of destroyed identities far more manageable.

Identity at individual and group levels is a multilayered phenomenon. It is difficult to become tolerant of other identities if one is not secure in one's own. Complexities arise because identities are both assumed and ascribed, and not always with synchronicity. Commonly, identity groups define themselves by identifying who they are not—difference from others is key to internal coherence. This does not mean that in-group definitions of identity have commonality with ascribed identities. Groups struggle both to maintain difference but also to establish the nature of the identities they are given and assume. Thus, people may feel that they know what makes up their identity—their history, rituals, language, behavioral norms, food, housing styles, and so on—but how this knowledge intertwines and interfaces with other cultures, and what it really means for the group and others, is not always clear. Turkish, Greek, Serbian, and Bulgarian coffees are—according to their producers and users—completely different, but they are all the same in reality. While certain songs and dances are typical of a certain region, they can be found in other regions as well. While Serbian and Croatian are—according to Serbs and Croats—different languages, an outsider can hardly hear the difference. Identity is a vital ingredient for survival, but the exact makeup of one's own identity is often difficult to explain. It is sometimes more difficult to understand one's own identity and culture than those of the another. It has been argued for instance that the best books on Dutch history and culture, have been written by British authors and the best books on American political sociology have been written by French and British authors.

Things are even more complicated if negotiators are in doubt about their own identity, as a person and as a nation, and project these internal identity problems on the other side. By artificially creating differences from an opponent, a party can strengthen own identity. Identity, after all, is about difference from others. It might be hypothesized that countries with a "glorious past" have fewer internal identity conflicts than countries where the population is insecure about its identity. At an international level, countries with a strong internal identity seem to negotiate in a more assertive way, showing more dominant behavior. By contrast, instability could be the fruit of insecurity about one's own identity. Take the example of the Austrians, who, after the fall of the Austro-Hungarian Empire, became insecure about their destiny and identity. Were they Austrian Germans or Austrians proper? In other words, should they be part of Germany or should they create a country of their own? Two civil wars (in 1934 and 1938) were at least partially the consequence of this insecurity about their identity. Some authors see the rise of Hitler as a consequence of identity doubts in Germany after its collapse in 1918.

It took Belarus and the Central Asian countries a long time after their sudden independence to develop a sense of identity. Identity was deliberately created in countries like Kazakhstan, for example, by introducing Kazakh as the national language even though many felt more at ease with Russian. After all, that was the language they had learned in school. Kemal Atatürk created a new Turkish identity, which led to ethnic conflicts with the Kurds as a consequence. Identity is both a regulator and a source of conflict: Even as new identities are shaped through wider inclusiveness, for instance, they exclude certain groups, or some within the old circle lose allegiance and break away, mobilizing under new identity banners. People with a strong identity feel less threatened by others if they are convinced of their own inner orientation. But this strong sense of identity, in turn, might create friction with others in addition to the divergence between their interests. Identity is not simply a cognitive reality; it is the vehicle through which deep emotions are infused into the negotiation process. It can help to create a better understanding between the negotiating parties, or it can create intractability. In order to deal with this problem, the intervention of a third party can be of help. The chapters in this book give us some practical insights into the questions of when and how third parties should approach internal identity conflicts and what needs to be done by whom.

■ EARLY INTERVENTION TO PREVENT MASS KILLINGS AND GENOCIDE

Prevention of genocide and violent conflicts between identity groups requires first an understanding of the general conditions that foster such choices and then the dynamics of identity conflicts in particular situations. Two forms of early intervention can be identified: rapid responses to group violence once it has started (e.g., peacekeeping forces), and the identification of situations in which there is a high risk of genocide and steps are needed to change conditions to reduce that risk (requiring much earlier analysis and commitment of resources). An episode of mass killings preceded the Armenian genocide by a decade. Rwanda had a long history of pogroms and identity-based purges before 1994. The international community in this case might be accused not only of responding late once violence broke out in the 1994 crisis, but also of failing to respond much earlier with offers of assistance in a situation that clearly carried a high risk of genocide. As noted in the first chapter, "genocide does not break out unannounced"!

If early intervention is key, under what conditions should alarm bells start ringing? At a general level, research suggests that identity differences alone seldom lead to violent conflict or genocide. People who share an identity tend to cluster to meet needs for protection, participation, power, privilege, and purpose. Under certain extreme conditions, this can lead to violent conflict between groups and genocide in which one group seeks to eliminate another. Dangerous conditions include conditions of scarcity, particularly in situations of limited heterogeneity (as opposed to homogeneous or very heterogeneous societies); scenarios in which there is a strong perception of relative deprivation and inequality based on ascriptive factors; conditions of high threat and frustration; cases where leaders mobilize in-group unity among members of groups in stress around hatred for other identity groups; and situations where a culture of impunity has developed over time, with no consequences for perpetrators of violence, as laid out by Mark Anstey. Ervin Staub, in his chapter, argues that genocide is the product of a complex mix of cultural, political, and social circumstances. He concludes that, if genocides are to be prevented, it is of the utmost importance to improve the overall life conditions of people; to enhance education as a means of developing understanding of and respect for other cultures; to reduce power differences; to manage traumas from the past instead of covering them up; to make people feel responsible for their deeds and for the security of their society and those of their neighbors; and to take steps to "humanize the other," reduce negative stereotyping, and change values and norms that foster hatred and fear of others. In the short term, he advises early intervention, training of those directly involved in problem situations, intensifying contacts between stakeholders, introducing constructive ideologies, giving positive examples, and showing peaceful alternatives like best practices in the development of democratic societies based on tolerance.

■ THIRD-PARTY OPTIONS FOR INTERVENTION

External interventions may take many forms, depending on the nature and stage of a conflict, the identity of the parties involved, and the identity and power of third parties seeking to intervene. As already indicated, meaningful early intervention should be understood as starting well before the actual breakout of violence. This suggests a mix of focused development projects to reduce poverty and nation-building assistance to strengthen democracies and develop the government's capacity to collect revenues and deliver political goods. It also suggests the need for programs of education, human rights, and reconciliation in high-risk situations to give life to Staub's recommendations for social change at attitudinal levels. Postconflict reconciliation should be understood as a form of long-term conflict prevention.

If violence appears imminent or once it has broken out, separation, often by the rapid deployment of peacekeeping forces, is required. Anstey suggests that such forces need a broad mandate if they are to contribute to a larger peacebuilding project rather than simply keep the warring parties apart. Wallensteen, Melander, and Möller, along with Staub and Anstey, argue that international coherence is a prerequisite for the use of sanctions and peacekeeping operations as means to prevent internal identity conflicts from escalating into genocide. This concerto should align preventive diplomacy, peacekeeping operations, and economic sanctions in the same direction. Without international activism genocides may not be prevented, but uncoordinated action might not only create ineffectiveness but make things worse. It is important to transfer the final responsibility for the durable restoration of peace to the parties themselves in concurrence with the international interveners. For some time the international and regional communities will have to remain involved, but sustainable peace is a daydream if the directly involved stakeholders do not take their future into their own hands.

Once one moves past peacekeeping, a wide variety of third-party roles and points of intervention are available—facilitation, mediation, various tracks of diplomacy, expert advice, pressure groups, training, and work with both sides to facilitate in-group coherence in preparation for intergroup negotiations. The authors in this book offer a wide range of proposals and examples in this regard.

Fedor Meerts and Tassos Coulaloglou analyze the role of the Organization for Security and Cooperation in Europe's (OSCE) High Commissioner on National Minorities (HCNM) as a legitimate facilitator in his own right. Because of his institutionalized and broad overarching mandate, the HCNM can act not only as a facilitator, but as a mediator and a negotiator as well, depending on the circumstances, as he sees fit. However, his effectiveness very much depends on the overall political context in which he works. An important lesson from the experience of the HCNM is that his preemptive actions can facilitate an effective peaceful solution to internal identity conflict only if there are external drivers helping him to put pressure on the parties involved. Context change is the most important force in this process—for example, a country's wish to become a member of the EU or of any other important international organization. This suggests the importance of coordinated international responses to bring about effective change.

Two sides of the mediating process are presented by Joshua Smilovitz and Moti Cristal. First, an acceptable mediator has to be identified. Then the conflict at hand has to be recognized and explored, sides and appropriate parties identified, and strategies and tactics developed while implementation and verification measures are secured. For the mediator, good time management and the respect of the identity groups involved are of the utmost importance. At the same time, mediation effectiveness requires that the contending parties be transformed into partners in the process of finding effective and just solutions. Cristal proposes the concept of *partnerism*, in which the mediator identifies the potential partners and makes them visible, especially to their counterparts. These partners require legitimacy in the eyes of those involved in the process. Furthermore, the partners have to be representative of their constituencies; otherwise, implementation of agreements will be sabotaged by those who have an interest in a failed mediation and negotiation process. Partners must be made responsible and accountable for their deeds and their ability to deliver. And finally, partners have to be—and remain—engaged in the process if the mediator is to be able to help them reach an inclusive, acceptable, and workable settlement.

Some important lessons can be drawn from the choices of third parties in the case of the Democratic Republic of the Congo (DRC) peace agreement recounted by Anstey. Quett Masire as a mutually agreed-upon facilitator was not daunted by being low on the initial list of third parties of choice, or by the prolonged game playing of Laurent Kabila to prevent him from gaining traction in his work. In the face of major obstacles he stuck doggedly to his task and to his role as facilitator. He displayed the courage to resist a quick-fix solution engineered by a superpower that would have seen a less inclusive deal emerge, and the wisdom to bring in Thabo Mbeki to make substantive proposals on power sharing in an interim government when he thought that undertaking this himself might compromise his role as an impartial facilitator. In short, personal qualities of humility, tenacity, courage, and good judgment matter. In low-power interventions, these are important lessons for third parties. When the United Nations (UN) did commit to the DRC project, it did so fully with a full-fledged peacekeeping operation and electoral support system. Yes, it was flawed but perhaps less so than in many other instances where it has arrived late or with weak capacity.

Different kinds of conceptual puzzles are presented by David Cunningham's findings that mediators play a more important role than is generally assumed, and that their interests and preferences have a profound effect on what concessions different groups receive in negotiated settlements. More particularly, and a little problematically, he concludes that rebels get more than states in civil war scenarios, particularly when a conflict is mediated by a third party with bias. Here perhaps lie some gaps between theoretically based research and practice. There is a risk in understanding trade-offs as simple linear processes in zero-sum conditions. Governments, of course, do want to retain power and rebels to achieve it. The fact that rebels achieve such things as more political and military power in postconflict arrangements, however, does not necessarily mean that they win more concessions. Such measures, based simply on status quo versus movement hypotheses, inevitably reflect greater wins for rebels. To sustain a simple status quo would require merely the crushing of rebel forces in the manner of Sri Lankan forces over the Tamil Tigers—and even here, the situation remains quite fluid despite the defeat of the rebel military forces. Where negotiations occur, deals tend to be more complex and layered than this. Thus, a government may appear to concede far more than rebel forces simply because the latter have little to concede other than the continued use of violence; they cannot concede formal political or military power because they have none within the framework of current arrangements. Governments offering participation in political arrangements and integration into military forces may see these as concessions, but, more importantly, as concessions that offer control over rebels through incorporation. In short, they seek to retain power by sharing it. Accommodation and integration may offer more palatable options, along with a reduction in violence, than either the status quo or revolution. Governments giving concessions do not always simply do so in the way that rebels want.

Another area of debate arising from Cunningham's conclusions concerns the nature of bias. Cunningham indicates that "support bias" by mediators influences the outcomes for rebels. Again, life is more complex than this. The United States, for instance, is known to have supported many sides concurrently in internal conflicts before deciding which one to back in its own interests—in the Congo in the 1960s or 1990s, for instance. External powers may support rebels but continue to trade with governments in power in their own interests; whom are they supporting? The support of the United States and other Western governments for Saddam Hussein's regime changed in the 1980s and 1990s. British support for Robert Mugabe's government shifted. Western support for internal rebel forces changed in Afghanistan through time. What Cunningham really alerts us to is the changing nature of allegiances in complex political scenarios, as well as some of the problems in drawing conclusions and lessons in international dispute resolution. None of this detracts from the message that it is essential that a mediator have a good understanding of the most effective distribution of the spoils in a postconflict situation in order to keep parties from restarting a civil war due to disappointed expectations.

While separation of parties in violent conflict may not require a deep understanding of the causes of their conflict, the design of social systems (electoral processes, constitutions, dispute-resolving mechanisms) and wider reconciliation certainly do. So, once there is a shift from peacekeeping to peacemaking, there is an immediate imperative to come to grips on an in-depth basis with the meaning of the conflict to the parties themselves.

Effective external intervention in identity conflicts requires knowledge and use of a wide range of techniques to prevent violence, to limit it quickly and effectively once started, to design social and political systems that meet needs for participation and power, and to achieve a degree of reconciliation sufficient for a new history and culture of peaceful exchange to take root.

Drawing on the range of contributions in this book, several conclusions can be drawn about external interventions to prevent genocide. They should be as inclusive as possible, but at least involve appropriate parties for constructing pacts that might move a peace process forward. Agendas, interventions, and agreements should be comprehensive rather than piecemeal in character—a systemic multidimensional approach. Time and energy should be spent in setting the scene before negotiations; in intragroup prenegotiations, this includes preparation to limit the risk of breakdowns, to manage outbidding processes, and to prepare strategies to deal with spoilers. Interventions should fit the shape and stage of a conflict, be timely, and be properly planned and project managed. Third parties should be credible, act coherently, be committed, and have capacity, whether they are individuals, diplomats, international organisators or civil society factors. They should understand the dynamics, history, parties, perceptions, and issues of the particular conflict, as well as the language of the parties that traps them in conflict spirals. They should be able to use such understanding to end hurting stalemates, which might commit parties to negotiation, and be able to reframe disputes as problem-solving exchanges. Agreements should carry no hidden agendas, be comprehensive and realistic, and reflect the power realities between parties.

Several key lessons deserve more focused consideration and can carry forward this work.

Build Coherence within Sides

Several chapters in this book refer to the importance of managing intragroup negotiations before and during negotiations between sides. Jannie Lilja considers the problem of outbidding—the process in which the most violent factions on the nonstate side are likely to prevail in intragroup contests over whether to negotiate. Outbidding among parties within a side can see a hardening of positions, sharpen identity boundaries, heighten fears among parties, reduce communication and understanding, and give rise to an escalation of violent conflict. Outbidding within sides occurs at horizontal (to eliminate competitors) and vertical levels (to secure constituents). Internal competition can radicalize the process, with peace being lost less on the basis of between-group differences than within-group competition for power. It is therefore important for third parties to identify such processes early and to take steps to assist parties within and across sides to manage them in a way that does not jeopardize exchanges. Communication and information infrastructures are needed to facilitate internal and external transparency. In other words, external interveners should try to diminish uncertainty and insecurity in order to prepare the ground for a successful negotiation process in which the need for outbidding is reduced.

It is partly for this reason that Jay Rothman argues that parties should not be brought together until there is a degree of certainty that agreement is feasible. In short, the risks of failure in peace negotiations might be reduced through extensive pre-work between the parties within a side in which they seek to discover internal commonalities and differences among themselves and, through this process, achieve a better understanding of the needs, values, interests, and attributional tendencies of their opponents. Rothman proposes that much might be gained through intragroup prenegotiation in which parties seek internal consensus before attempting intergroup resolution. On the basis of such work, the parties might, with the assistance of a third party, prepare an agenda with a better prospect of success and approach negotiations with a reduced risk of deadlock based on attributional error. Rothman also emphasizes the importance of a forward-looking rather than a backward-looking dialogue, with constant checking of assumptions, perceptions, and expectations during the process to keep negotiations on track. In addition, he reminds us that effective management of emotional issues is often critical to dealing with substantive matters. The trick is to turn identity-based problems into objective-based discussions and a resource-based solution.

In a similar vein, Marie-Joëlle Zahar tackles the problems of getting spoilers to the table and keeping them there in a constructive mode. The challenge is how to make nonparticipation in a peace process more rewarding than obstructing it. This can be very difficult when dealing with parties that have little popular backing, that adhere to a hard line on identity boundaries for outbidding purposes, and whose power lies in the capacity for violence. With little to win in a democratic process, such actors are dangerous to peace processes. The use of violent tactics at key moments can seriously undermine trust among mainstream parties at a negotiation table. Tactics of threat or reward may be utilized, but it is essentially the task of the mainstream side in which they fall to bring them into the process and/ or to punish actions that threaten deals in the larger public interest. The shift in positions required is evident in the Northern Ireland situation, where recalcitrant extremist cells using violent tactics have been condemned by the Irish Republican Army and Sinn Fein. Effective third-party assistance, then, requires first a deep understanding of the conflict dynamic, and the priorities of the parties involved, and then the development of a reserve of "carrots and sticks" to keep the process as inclusive as possible.

A paradox is evident in the internal coherence debate. Internal division may be an obstacle to intergroup negotiations and problem solving, but internal unity along sharply defined identity lines may also facilitate mass killing and genocide. The chapter by Zartman and Anstey on lessons for theory explored the dynamics of social conformity, the tendency to obedience, and bystander apathy, especially in contexts in which respected leaders and valued membership groups give legitimacy to actions. Escalated conflicts see tighter in-group bonding, stronger pressures for conformity, polarization, and reduced tolerance of difference within groups. Those calling for caution, or for peaceful resolution of differences through negotiation, or for understanding of the other group are easily portrayed as threats to the integrity of the group and are sidelined or punished. As hawks replace doves in leadership positions, deviant views become increasingly rejected.

When the call comes to eliminate another identity group, compliance prevails over the tendency to feel compassion. Killers are somehow able to dehumanize and deindividuate their victims, to rationalize their acts as necessary in the larger picture, and to reduce the taking of many lives to the ordinary business of the day. The horror of mass murder is made ordinary through the challenge of devising effective and efficient operating procedures, of meeting group expectations and conforming to the requirements of respected leaders.

So, there is indeed a need to work within groups to limit internal division, that is, to deal with the dynamics of outbidders and spoilers. Those who would intervene must recognize, however, that they are dealing with very powerful, almost primal, forces and that as groups acquire greater internal coherence they may also become more dangerous. Strategies for intervention might include seeking ways to reduce perceived threat among identity groups; promoting intergroup understanding and common projects; reducing the influence and capacity of extremists calling for elimination of or violence against members of other groups; empowering moderates advocating negotiation and the use of nonviolent methods of engagement across identity lines; clarifying individual accountability for violence and reducing any sense of protection from the consequences of participation in mass violence; controlling media messages promoting attacks on other identity groups; and, in extreme situations once violence has started, moving quickly to establish protected safe zones where at-risk groups can assemble. Because it is usually those groups with state power that embark on projects of genocide, it is the international community that must undertake projects of protection for at-risk groups. Such interventions are inevitably complex and riddled with dilemmas of right, capacity, and coordination (as noted in the chapters by Anstey and Cede), but ways must nevertheless be found for rapid action where the responsibility to protect is salient.

Improving Communications between Identity Groups

Negotiation is centrally about the use of persuasive communication. Donohue's contribution in this book unravels what he terms the Identity Trap and offers ways to change communications to reduce tensions that might lead to violence. Identity conflicts commonly involve parties in exchanges of a high-power/low-affiliation nature in which there is low trust and a backward orientation with an emphasis on past injustices. Constructive peace talks, by contrast, tend to have a forward-looking orientation and to be characterized by messages of trust and affiliation. The character of communications is an important indicator of the state of relations in identity conflicts, and has relevance for understanding and action whether one is involved in preventing genocide or attempting reconciliation after its occurrence. Individuals face challenges of inclusion, control, and integration for identity within social groups. When individuals face problems in these areas, negotiation strategies are more crisis than normative in style, reflecting relational tensions.

Referring to Relational Order Theory, Donohue reminds us that all negotiations have material and relational dimensions, with the latter assuming salience when identity is denied. When there are problems of affiliation and interdependence, trust is reduced and parties seek separation or make demands to rectify perceived injustices. In short, relations become more hard-edged, suspicious, strategic, and demanding. *Collaboration* (involved, relaxed, task-focused relations) is reflected in the use of high-affiliation/high-interdependence communications; *coexistence* (no fighting but isolationist and not moving forward) in the use of low-affiliation/low-interdependence communications; and *cooperation* (parties retain role autonomy but send signals of affirmation to one another) in the use of low-interdependence/high-affiliation communications. The real problem area is that of *competition*, in which parties communicate through signals of disapproval and rejection and/or make demands on one another to reassert rights and resist obligations. This is the shape of communications in which a group feels that its identity is under threat. A competitive paradox arises trapping the parties in communications in which they must increase their interdependence in order to intensify their aggression to defeat a rival while also sending signals of rejection or disaffiliation. Fighting back strengthens identity. Donohue suggests that the means to manage this paradox is for parties to send signals that are "affiliative but cautious." They consciously pursue a route of strategic ambiguity in which they manage a delicate dance of communicating acceptance of the other but avoid immediate hard or detailed positioning on material issues. In this way, competition is transformed into coexistence based on removal of the need to define identity by fighting back. Identity crises are avoided by communication styles that do not threaten interpersonal needs. Over time, this allows more collaborative exchanges to emerge.

Negotiations carry multiple paradoxes at any given moment, with third parties continually searching for ways to transform exchanges from crisis into normative bargaining. The core lessons are to avoid challenging the interpersonal needs for inclusion and control that compromise affiliation. Mediators therefore manage the discourse between identity groups by using less inflammatory language (such as reframing, dropping, or muting attack language in conveying messages) and by understanding the contests and sticking points over autonomy and interdependence that emerge between parties in their use of language.

To break through such traps requires active listening on the part of mediators, responsiveness to signals sent by parties, and then building an interactional code in which all those involved shift to more positive interactional styles. If mediators are to have an agenda, it is one of creating more constructive dialogue, enabling problem solving, and helping parties develop principles of fairness in their relations in order to shift exchanges to alternative modes away from destructive competition. They can assist parties by developing their awareness of being trapped, showing empathy to the other party, shying away from blaming and shaming, reframing interaction by focusing on nonsensitive issues, and by showing understanding and respect for the feelings of the opponent. A rhetorical early warning system will have to be created in order to detect the language stirring people up against each other. To mitigate the problems and manage the paradoxes involved, the comfort zone of the parties will have to be enlarged—for example, through economic aid and development.

Managing Media Communications

Another dimension of communication is dealt with in the chapter by Romero-Trillo, who considers the role of the media in identity conflict situations. The media can have both an escalating and a deescalating impact. A case in point is the Hutu government's use of the radio to call on members of their identity group to murder Tutsis—to "kill the cockroaches." A practical step might be to monitor the media in high-risk scenarios to evaluate shifts to language that might provoke genocide. This might provide useful lead time in planning interventions if it becomes clear that certain identity groups are at risk. Dilemmas arise in action beyond monitoring, of course. External intervention might involve the use of technology to jam national media systems evaluated to be contributing to mass violence. A further step might be to use this capacity to send alternative signals in which hate messages are replaced with messages of caution and the responsibility to avert violent escalation of tensions; warning of the consequences of participating in violent acts against identity groups, the imminent arrival of peacekeepers, and the location of safe zones; and indicating who might be called on to mediate for purposes of tension reduction. Jamming national media systems is inevitably riddled with ethical dilemmas; in addition, it is likely to have only short-term usefulness in an era where so many groups have easy access to communication systems. Ethical dilemmas need perhaps to be subsumed under the "duty to protect debate" in which external agents must inevitably engage before acting; if they decide to act, this would be one interim step to slow the spread of violence before peacekeeping forces can be deployed. It is usually states that carry out genocide, and such states are likely to own and control the media. Interference with media systems is therefore part of a much larger strategy for intervention.

Commitment and Coherence among External Agents

Finally, attention must be given to the nature of external agents of intervention. Several of the contributors to this book allude to the importance of coordinating the efforts of external actors in internal identity conflicts. Wallensteen, Melander, and Möller argue that international coherence is essential if sanctions and peacekeeping operations are to be effective in preventing the escalation of identity conflicts to genocidal actions.

A salient lesson from the Rwandan genocide is the importance of a rapid international response. As Anstey points out, however, this is often a major problem; the international community, for many reasons, is seldom ad idem in relation to interventions in conflicts within nation-states. Not unusually, nations find their own interests directly or indirectly affected by internal conflicts, see an opportunity to block the regional interests of others, or see interventions as potentially costly and irrelevant to their own national interests. It has been very helpful that the UN has adopted a "principle to protect" that might override resistance to intervention on grounds of national sovereignty, and Franz Cede's guidelines provide a useful point of reference in any such planning, but this change does not in itself overcome problems of capacity, commitment, or tactical coordination. Cede calls on the interveners to balance the necessity, the legitimacy, and the probability of success of the intended external action. Failure might be one risk of not taking action, but it can be worse. An intervention might instigate more internal violence and even genocide and prove counterproductive. Abstention is sometimes more advisable than intervention. There are no easy choices in such scenarios.

In his contribution on the Philippines conflict, Ariel Macaspac Penetrante highlights the importance of nongovernmental organizations (NGOs) in assuming responsibility for preventing escalations of conflict in identity conflicts. When parties in conflict do cluster around a negotiating table, however, there must be room for them, and they should not be hijacked by external interests in a hurry to produce particular preferred settlements. Adebajo (2009) has pointed out the complexities of negotiation that occur when multiple parties must be accommodated at a negotiating table along with multiple external agents. In his facilitation of the Congo peace process, Masire faced the problem of an external power trying to push the process forward with a subgroup of key players. Some important insights emerge from the African experience, including the need to strengthen the capacity for mediation through training and early involvement of mediators; improved gender representativeness and resourcing in mediation initiatives; developing mediation support units (MSUs) to serve as expert advice centers for international mediators; coordinating UN agency information in conflict areas to inform mediation interventions; developing a cadre of mediation support officers with regional expertise who are available at short notice to assist UN envoys in the field; strengthening African NGOs to bolster civil society participation; providing adequate financial and human resources to operationalize mediation support; establishing and resourcing transitional justice systems (truth and reconciliation commissions, war crimes tribunals); tightening links with the International Criminal Court (ICC) to synchronize efforts to manage the administration of justice with peacemaking efforts; and more systematic debriefing and documentation of mediation efforts, possibly through research partnerships.

Multiparty negotiations involving numerous external third parties raise complex management questions. The key is not to lose the parties whose perspectives are central to the process. Coordination of external parties may often be necessary to bring an end to violent conflict, set up negotiation tables, and ensure that the right people participate and continue to do so when the going gets tough. Then, if a systemic approach is to be followed, the process needs to be structured in a manner that enables the parties to deal with the many aspects of the conflict: cease-fires; border demarcations; demobilization, disarmament, and reintegration of militias; power and wealth sharing; security sector reform; constitutional and electoral processes; governance issues (human rights, rule of law, gender issues); and transitional justice issues and reconciliation. Procedural arrangements require careful planning and then great flexibility in terms of managing and having the capacity to manage joint and separate meetings, bilaterals, and coordinating secondary influences. All parties need a sense of who is mediating what, coordination, and the use of technical committees and specialist task teams. Media relations require planning and capacity.

Peace Deals as Points of Departure for Peacebuilding Rather Than Points of Arrival

Macaspac Penetrante and Anstey demonstrate clearly that a negotiation process does not end with the signing of a peace agreement—that such an agreement is rather the beginning of the peace process itself. Ensuring that peace agreements are properly implemented is important for confidence building among parties. Systems of transitional justice and reconciliation need to be thought through and adequately resourced to prevent recurrences of violence in deeply damaged societies. It is therefore important that external interveners offer focused and sustained support for peacebuilding processes and that internal interveners—foremost the civil society—help to stabilize the situation through involvement in the process as a whole and in administrative processes in particular. Both external and internal interveners must be conscious of the danger of being drawn into the conflict itself and thereby becoming one of the contending parties, losing their ability to facilitate a settlement. Negative internal dynamics within the collaborating parties and other sources of future mass violence will have to be dealt with at an early stage, as they might emerge to threaten the sustainability of the new developments.

■ CONCLUSIONS

The regulation or resolution of identity conflicts is not about eliminating identities. It is about developing nonviolent ways to express identities and designing social and political systems to accommodate identity groups that are felt to meet needs for protection, participation, power, privilege, and purpose. External interventions may assume political or military form for purposes of peacekeeping or peacemaking, but there are many other types of intervention that may be brought to bear, involving civil society or credible individuals to facilitate rapport between groups and foster reconciliation. A rich array of ideas and proposals emerges from the various contributions in this volume. A tough challenge faces the international community in responding to such conflicts—that of coordination of effort. Internal identity conflicts divide external nations along lines of ideology, vested interests, capacity, and differences over legitimacy of action in individual cases. Delays are counted in lives. Once decisions have been made to intervene, they have to become operational and require coordination and commitment, introducing further tensions.

Identity groups do not have to lose their identities but rather seek new ways of expressing them in a way that accommodates the identity needs of others and does not threaten them. It is not a matter of resolving identity differences in themselves as much as designing social and political systems that reduce perceptions of threat or injustice and, over time, transform relations from destructive competition to more collaborative forms. This requires that all identity groups achieve a sense of legitimacy and respect, becoming partners in a new order of mutual accommodation.

■ INDEX